ROUTLEDGE LIBRARY EDITIONS: ISLAM

ISLAMIC LAW IN AFRICA

ISLAMIC LAW IN AFRICA

J. N. D. ANDERSON

Volume 12

Routledge
Taylor & Francis Group
LONDON AND NEW YORK

First published in 1955

This edition first published in 2008 by
Routledge
2 Park Square, Milton Park, Abingdon, Oxon, OX14 4RN

Simultaneously published in the USA and Canada
by Routledge
270 Madison Avenue, New York, NY 10016

Routledge is an imprint of the Taylor & Francis Group, an informa business

Transferred to Digital Printing 2008

British Library Cataloguing in Publication Data
A catalogue record for this book is available from the British Library

Library of Congress Cataloging in Publication Data
A catalog record for this book has been requested

ISBN 10: 0-415-42600-6 (Set)
ISBN 10: 0-415-44288-5 (Volume 12)

ISBN 13: 978-0-415-42600-8 (Set)
ISBN 13: 978-0-415-44288-6 (Volume 12)

Publisher's Note

The publisher has gone to great lengths to ensure the quality
of this reprint but points out that some imperfections in the
original copies may be apparent.

ISLAMIC LAW IN AFRICA

J. N. D. ANDERSON

WITH A NEW PREFACE
BY THE AUTHOR

FRANK CASS

Published in Great Britain by
FRANK CASS AND COMPANY LIMITED
Gainsborough House, Gainsborough Road,
London, E11 1RS, England

and in the United States of America by
FRANK CASS AND COMPANY LIMITED
c/o Biblio Distribution Centre
81 Adams Drive, P.O. Box 327, Totowa, N.J. 07511

Reprinted by permission of the
Controller of Her Majesty's Stationery Office

First published as
Colonial Research Publication No. 16, 1964, by
H.M.S.O. January, 1955

Fieldwork in East and West Africa for this book
and its publication in 1955 were financed from
Colonial Development and Welfare funds

First edition	1955
New impression, with preface	1970
Second impression, with preface	1978

ISBN 0 7146 1905 1

Printed in Great Britain by offset lithography by
Billing & Sons Limited, Guildford, London and Worcester

PREFACE TO THE 1970 EDITION

This book has been out of print since comparatively soon after its publication in 1955, and many requests have been made for a reprint or a new edition. For some years, indeed, I have intended to prepare a new edition as soon as circumstances might permit; but it would scarcely be possible to do this in any adequate way without another visit to all the countries concerned and a detailed study of any changes that have occurred, whether in the form of new legislation, administrative arrangements or decisions of the courts. And this is, I fear, impossible at present, or even in the foreseeable future.

The only alternatives are a partial and inadequate second edition or a reprint of the book in its existing form. On balance, the second of these seems preferable, and is certainly less exacting. It is true that the situation has changed radically in Northern Nigeria following the recommendations of a Panel of Jurists on which I myself had the honour to serve. As a result the Islamic criminal law has been replaced by new codes, both substantive and procedural; the court system has been somewhat modified; and the Islamic law (although sometimes applied as the law under which a contract was concluded or as the law of tort or land tenure locally in force) is chiefly applicable today—in Northern Nigeria as in most other Muslim countries—only as the family law of Muslim litigants.

Other major changes which should be noted concern Tanzania and Somalia. In the former, Zanzibar has, of course, been united—nominally, at least—with Tanganyika; the jurisdiction of the *Ibāḍī qāḍī* has, I understand, been terminated; and the Government in Dar es Salaam has not only concerned itself with the codification of customary law but has recently published the first four chapters of "Statements of Islamic Law" under Section 2(i) of the Islamic Law (Restatement) Act, 1964. In the latter, moreover, the former British Somaliland has now become an integral part of the Republic of Somalia.

No major changes have, I think, occurred in any of the other territories, but minor developments in the law are, no doubt, comparatively widespread.

J. N. D. ANDERSON

8th August 1967

CONTENTS

FOREWORD

I have recently had occasion to compare the extent of the studies made by French and British scholars respectively regarding the position occupied by the large Muslim communities in Africa south of the Sahara. It is true that the Muslims of this part of Africa cannot claim, as the Muslims in India have claimed, that they should be accorded a political status which will distinguish them from the rest of the population, nor indeed is there any such analogy between their circumstances and those of the Muslims in India as would justify this claim. But there are nevertheless some circumstances which give these Muslim communities a character of their own. They have their own system of law, which is an integral part of their religion. They are capable of developing on occasion a distinctive sentiment of Muslim solidarity. The more educated among them are constantly made conscious that they form part of a larger Muslim world outside Africa. Though Muslims may constitute only a small part of the population in some of the territories south of the Sahara, there are others in which they form either the majority or a very noticeable proportion of the whole. That is pre-eminently the fact in the colonies constituting the Federation of French West Africa. Muslims comprise 95 per cent. of the population in Mauretania, 90 per cent. in the Niger, from 80 to 85 per cent. in Senegal and some 60 per cent. in the French Sudan. They are less conspicuous in the colonies comprising French Equatorial Africa, but in British West Africa they comprise 84 per cent. of the population of the Gambia and roughly 41 per cent. of that of Nigeria, the most populous of the British African territories. They are not so numerous in Central and East Africa, but Zanzibar is in point of constitution a "protected" state in which Arabs, though they form only about 16 per cent. of the population, have the most prominent and most influential position in the administration.

It was natural that the French approach to the administrative problems created by the large Muslim communities in West Africa should at the outset have been coloured by conceptions drawn from their experiences in Algeria. But the problems of West Africa were in fact of a somewhat different order from those of Algeria, where the major preoccupation of the French authorities was created by the influx of European traders and colonists into a country of which the African inhabitants were almost entirely Muslim. Today, it will be recalled, there are in Algeria about one million European to nearly eight million African inhabitants. In French West Africa, on the other hand, there was never the same conflict of interests between European colonists and African population, or, if it existed at all, it was on a relatively minor scale.

At the outset the French Administration in West Africa saw itself as waging a crusade to liberate indigenous Africa from the grasp of a militant Islam, and the colonial literature of the period was full of references to "le peril de l'Islam". If this attitude had in truth some of the elements of a crusade, it was met in the same spirit by the more active among the Muslims of this region. M. Robert Delavignette quotes in his interesting *Service Africain* the translation made by Gilbert Vieillard of the Fulani poems of the Muslims of the Fouta-Djallon in French Guinea. They abound with phrases such as—"From the rage of the Unbelievers, O Lord, deliver us", or again "The Mahdi, whose hour we await, will come and bring succour to our religion".

This period soon passed as the French authorities gained experience of the true character of the Muslim population of the region. But the feeling behind it survived in some measure when they adopted a policy which M. Jules Brevié (afterwards one of the best known of the Governors General at Dakar) described in 1911 as the attempt to achieve " l'équilibre de notre domination en opposant à l'Islamisme le contrepoids du fétichisme organisé ". An effort was to be made to stay the growing disruption of indigenous institutions; regard was to be paid to the traditional authority exercised by the Chiefs; the customary law of the principal tribes was to be codified; and the sons of the Chiefs were to receive at school an instruction in their own customary law on the same lines as the instruction in the law of Islam given in the Madrasas to young Muhammadans. But this change of policy did not prove to be fruitful of any permanent result. This was partly because it was in the nature of things impossible to treat the amorphous and ill co-ordinated institutions of the " animistes " as a system which could compete against the spiritual and temporal organisation of the Muslims. But it was also due to the fact that the majority of the officers of the Administration showed themselves impatient of indigenous institutions which appeared to be ill adapted to make their contribution to the type of civilisation which it was the mission of France to introduce to her African colonies. The Administration soon ceased to interest itself in the completion of the studies of the Bambara, the Malinkes or the Mossi which were to form the basis of the instruction in indigenous institutions designed to be given to tribal schoolboys. The attitude to Islam itself ceased to be one of conscious opposition. There were indeed many who saw in its spiritual discipline a more fruitful avenue of approach to the introduction of a European type of civilisation than was to be found in the more primitive mentality of the " fétichistes ". If there has been any hesitation in making a more open avowal of an interest in Islam, it has been due to an apprehension lest a revival of Pan-Islamism in other parts of the world might create forces in the African Colonies which would prove an embarrassment to the Union Française.

In the British African dependencies the influences which have determined the attitude to be observed towards Islam have taken a different course. Islam has not been seen as presenting a problem to be dealt with on any question of general principle. If groups of Muslims were at an early period conspicuous in opposing the introduction of a régime of order in Nyasaland or Uganda, the fact that weighed most with the British authorities of the time was that the main interest of one of these groups was in slave raiding, and that the other constituted one of the militant factions fighting to gain control in Buganda. Their religion was not the chief consideration. In Northern Nigeria most of the opposition to the measures which preceded the establishment of the Protectorate came, it is true, from the Muslim Emirates, but when once the Emirates had been brought under Protectorate rule, they were speedily recognised as forming the most suitable agencies for the use of the system which exercised local rule through Native Authorities. Their sense of order, their readiness to co-operate with the Administration in works of social and economic progress, their maintenance of a judiciary detached from the executive, all of these features appealed strongly to the officers who initiated the new Administration.

The studies of Islam which have been made by French and British scholars respectively tend to reflect the difference in the attitude of their governments towards the political problems to which Islam has given rise. It is by no means the case that French scholars have neglected the study either of the character of Islamic institutions or of the principles and practice of Islamic law. On the contrary, the French Government maintains at Paris the Centre de Hautes Etudes d'Administration Musulmane, which has a special section concerned with Islam in West Africa. Its members, besides undertaking research in Islamic subjects, provide lectures to Colonial cadets and others who may be concerned with affairs in West Africa. French authors have given us works of great interest describing the social and political aspects of "la politique Musulmane", of which the recent work of M. Alphonse Gouilly, "l'Islam dans l'Afrique Occidentale Française", may serve as an example. But they have paid less attention to a subject which is of peculiar concern to the British, namely, the interaction of Islamic law on the indigenous custom of Africa and of indigenous custom on Islamic law and institutions.

That is a subject which, apart from any academic interest it may possess, owes its practical significance mainly to the existence of the current British system of Native Administration. To those familiar with that system as practised in most of the British African dependencies the reason for this special concern will be obvious. In predominantly Muslim areas justice is administered in the first instance through the agency of Muslim Courts, which must accordingly deal on occasion with issues affecting both Muslims and non-Muslims. On the other hand, in areas where Muslims are in the minority, the Native Courts administering the customary law may have to pay regard to Islamic law when dealing with issues affecting the personal law of Muslims. There is, therefore, in the first place a wide field for the conflict of law. In the second place, the procedure followed by Muslim Courts differs widely from that followed in most of the indigenous Native Courts, and experience shows that to the more primitive peoples the procedure followed by a trial Court may be of more importance than the law it administers. But there is more than this. Though Islamic law (the Sharī'a) as expounded in the handbooks of the recognised schools of law (as for instance that of the Mālikīs in West Africa and the Shāfi'īs in East Africa) cannot in theory be modified by contact with indigenous law, yet in practice the decisions of the Muslim Courts may represent a fusion of Islamic law and local customary law varying according to the relative orthodoxy of the Court concerned. On the other hand there are equally a number of areas where justice is administered by Native Courts, but where the indigenous law has in varying degrees assimilated parts of Islamic law.

The problems which arise from these interacting influences are of very considerable consequence in the administration both of civil and criminal justice. In East Africa, the range taken by the application of Islamic law is in practice limited to matters of "family" law, such as marriage, succession or divorce; but even though the application of Islamic law may be limited to these issues, very difficult questions sometimes arise, as for instance whether it is the customary or the Islamic law of succession which is applicable to members of a matrilineal tribe, or again, whether the Islamic or the customary law of inheritance applies when a family is divided in religion. In Nigeria the range taken by the application of Islamic law is wider, for the long years of Muslim rule have made a marked impression on the indigenous customary law. Moreover, the acknowledged efficiency and prestige of the Muslim Courts has led to their being accorded enhanced powers by the Administration, particularly in criminal matters. In Northern Nigeria, for instance, some sixteen of the Courts have powers to try homicide cases under Islamic law, and twelve regularly do so. This means that non-Muslims may frequently be tried by a procedure prescribed by the Islamic law, which attaches (in strict theory at all events) a different value to the evidence of Muslims and non-Muslims. The application of the land law by Muslim judges creates particular difficulty, for the land law is only superficially Islamised. Furthermore, in proportion as the country develops, there is inevitably a growth of civil litigation between Muslims and non-Muslims, and Muslim Courts may find themselves administering a "law merchant" for which Islamic law makes no adequate provision.

A Conference of the Judicial Advisers of different British dependencies in Africa, which met in Uganda in February 1953, discussed the problems arising from the application of Islamic law and analysed some of the difficulties which had been encountered in the administration of justice by Muslim Courts in areas which contained large groups of non-Muslims. But it was clear that the subject was of a scale which could only be dealt with after a detailed and comprehensive survey of the whole position, and all authorities concerned will now welcome the expert treatment given to it by Professor J. N. D. Anderson in his present work. This is particularly valuable in its comparison of the position occupied by Islamic law in the legislation and judicial practice of different British dependencies in Africa. The Administrations concerned have not hitherto dealt with the question of jurisdiction on any uniform principle, and Professor Anderson's Survey should now make it possible to readjust current legislation on some comprehensive basis. The issues involved, and particularly the issues arising in the field of personal and "family" law, are of vital concern to African society.

HAILEY.

ISLAMIC LAW IN AFRICA

(Being a Survey of the application of Islamic law in the British Colonial Territories in Africa and in the Colony and Protectorate of Aden)

INTRODUCTION

THIS Survey covers the work of six months in Africa, three of them spent on a rapid tour of Tanganyika, Nyasaland, Zanzibar, Kenya, Uganda, British Somaliland and the Colony and Protectorate of Aden, and the other three on similar visits to Nigeria, the Gold Coast, the Gambia and Sierra Leone. The time spent in each of these territories differed considerably, but was always extremely brief, and the number of centres visited varied accordingly. A primary emphasis was placed on conversations with Qāḍīs, Liwalis, Alkalai and other local authorities on both the substance and application of Islamic law, most of whom happily spoke Arabic; but valuable information was also obtained from talks with British administrative and legal officers, with tribal chiefs and with members of native tribunals, etc. Much time was also spent studying administrative files, law reports, records of cases and similar material. The vastness of the area to be covered, both geographically and juridically, in the course of a strictly limited and pre-arranged programme, necessarily precluded the study of certain aspects of the problem in more than general terms: but it is hoped, none the less, that this Survey will provide a reasonably accurate and comprehensive account of the application of Islamic law throughout the territories concerned and will at least furnish a framework into which detailed studies of more limited aspects of a vast subject may conveniently be fitted.

It would be impracticable to express my gratitude individually to all who generously gave of their time and knowledge, and invidious to single out a few names for special mention.[1] Suffice it to say, therefore, that my path was everywhere made easy: and I gained the impression that such a Survey was warmly welcomed in most territories and cheerfully tolerated, at least, elsewhere. It was something which had, apparently, never been attempted before;[2] it concerned a subject which many regarded as almost a closed book; and its connection with everyday life and administrative problems was obvious. Nor was this co-operation limited to British officers, for I found the Muslim Qāḍīs and other jurists, even in those places reputed to be most fanatical, willingly prepared—once they found the questioner to be a serious student of Sharī'a law—to submit to what must often have appeared almost a cross-examination; for the constant difficulty was not to extract a reply but to persuade them to answer in terms of actual practice rather than text-book orthodoxy. In almost every case, moreover, those

[1] I must, however, make a single exception in regard to Sir John Gray, the Chief Justice of Zanzibar, to whose learning, counsel and help I am particularly indebted.

[2] Except for a valuable visit to Northern Nigeria in 1950 by Dr. J. Schacht.

questioned seemed gratified and even flattered by the interest evinced rather than suspicious of the motive which might prompt it. As a result, the tour was uniformly happy.

II

A question which immediately confronts the lawyer who undertakes a Survey of this kind is the juristic basis on which Islamic law is, or may be, applied throughout these regions of Africa, both to indigenous Muslims and to immigrant Muslim communities. This poses a problem of considerable perplexity, for the utmost diversity prevails in this matter from territory to territory. Thus in the Colony of Aden, in the Somaliland Protectorate, and (in so far as the British, as distinct from the Sultan's, courts are concerned) in Zanzibar, authority for the application of Islamic law in matters of personal status and the family law of Muslim litigants may be found in Bombay Regulation 4 of 1827, section 26, which provided that the Bombay courts should apply, in the absence of specific enactments, both the "usage of the country" and the "law of the defendant" and which has always been interpreted as including the Islamic personal law according to its local variations; for this Regulation has been inherited by the British courts in Aden, Somaliland and Zanzibar respectively.[1] In the Sultan's courts in Zanzibar and in parts of the Aden Protectorate, on the other hand, Islamic law has been declared to be the fundamental law, although largely displaced in the former by specific enactments—and this is also true in general terms of the Protectorate of Kenya. Again, in much of the Aden Protectorate Islamic law may be regarded as at once distinct from, and yet in part identified with, local customary law; while it is everywhere extensively applied by indigenous courts[2] with virtually no interference from the Protecting Power in the East and by its direct encouragement in the West. Yet again, in the coastal and certain inland[3] areas of Tanganyika Territory, Islamic law is judicially applied, to a varying degree, in all matters of family law among Muslim litigants: and this may, of course, be explained by the fact that it was so applied under German rule before the territory was occupied[4]; but it seems preferable to hold that this law is really applied in these areas, in a modified form, as a variety of "native law and custom" —and the same may, perhaps, be true of Somaliland also.[5] In the Protectorates of Uganda and Nyasaland and the Colony of Kenya, indeed, it is on this basis alone that Islamic law is ever applied—if it is applied at all—by the native courts:[6] for it seems eminently arguable that the phrase "native law" in the relevant Orders in Council, etc., should be construed, at least in the absence of any other provision, to include Islamic law in so far as this has in fact been locally adopted by the people. In addition, of course, Ordinances exist in the Colony of Aden, in Somaliland, Zanzibar, Kenya, Tanganyika and Uganda expressly authorising the application of the Sharī'a among indigenous Muslims within specified limits: in all matters of family law, etc., before the ordinary British courts in Aden[7] and before the Qāḍīs' courts in Somaliland[8]; in regard

[1] For authority for this statement see the relevant sections of this Survey. In addition, of course, there are local enactments in all three territories which both authorise and regulate the application of certain specific sections of Islamic law—while Bombay Regulation 4 was formerly applicable in the East Africa Protectorate also.

[2] For this no statutory authority, on the part of the Protecting Power, either exists or is needed.

[3] e.g., centres on the main trade routes (especially those of the quondam slave-trade).

[4] On the grounds that the laws of a conquered or ceded territory remain in force until they are altered. cp., *Campbell v. Hall* (1774) 1 Cowp. 204.

[5] But see above regarding Bombay Regulation 4 of 1827.

[6] Except, that is, in the two Qāḍīs' courts which have been set up in the Colony of Kenya and which are empowered to hear cases of personal status among specified Muslim litigants (see pp. 84, 88-9 and 119 ff.).

[7] cp. the Interpretation and General Clauses Ordinance, 1937, sect. 41.

[8] cp. the Subordinate Courts Ordinance, 1944, sect. 10(2).

to the distribution of the estate of a deceased Muslim before any court in Zanzibar[1]; in questions of Muhammadan marriage, divorce and inheritance before either Qāḍīs' courts or the Supreme Court in Kenya[2]; in regard to the estates of certain deceased natives before the appropriate court in Tanganyika[3]: and in matters of Muhammadan marriage and divorce before the High Court in Uganda.[4]

When we turn to West Africa, on the other hand, we find that it is unequivocally and exclusively as " native law[5] and custom " that Islamic law is more extensively followed and enforced in Northern Nigeria than anywhere else in the world outside Arabia.[6] It is, moreover, exclusively on this basis that it is applied, where and in so far as it is applied at all, throughout the rest of Nigeria and the whole of the Gold Coast and Sierra Leone, except, in the Gold Coast, in so far as concerns the infinitesimal number of persons whose marriages have been registered under the Marriage of Muhammadans Ordinance and, in Sierra Leone, within the scope of the Muhammadan Marriage Ordinance (which is in any case applicable only in the Colony). It is in the Gambia alone that statutory provisions exist for the Qāḍīs' courts of the Colony to exercise jurisdiction, under Muhammadan law, " in all causes and matters, contentious or uncontentious, between or exclusively affecting Muhammadan natives, relating to civil status, marriage, succession, donations, testaments and guardianship "[7] and for the ordinary native tribunals of the Protectorate to apply " the Muhammadan law relating to civil status, marriage, succession, divorce, dowry, the rights and authorities of parents and guardianship whenever the parties are Muhammadans "[8]—in the latter case, of course, alongside their ordinary jurisdiction under " native law and custom " on the one hand and local Orders, etc., on the other.

III

This inevitably raises, therefore, the basic question of whether, and how far, Islamic law may correctly be identified with, or enforced as, the native law and custom of an African territory or people; and we are at once confronted by the well-known dictum of the Court of Appeal for Eastern Africa that the law of Islam cannot be described as " native law " for the purpose of article 7 of the Kenya Colony Order in Council " merely because it is the law applicable to many or even all of the natives of the Kenya Protectorate."[9] It seems probable, however, that this dictum should be interpreted as meaning that it cannot be so regarded merely because a Muslim ruler such as the Sultan of Zanzibar may have sought to impose it on his subjects, rather than as implying that Islamic law can never be so embraced and assimilated by the people themselves as to mould or partially replace their own indigenous customs[10]: for however objectionable it may be to the purist to regard a system of law worked out centuries ago in lands of very different circumstances and culture as the " native law and custom " of certain East African peoples today, yet the fact remains that in some localities Islamic law has become as inextricably combined with indigenous

[1] cp. the Succession Decree, 1917, sect. 7.
[2] cp. the Muhammadan Marriage, Divorce and Succession Ordinance, 1920.
[3] cp. the Administration (Small Estates) (Amendment) Ordinance, 1947, and (by implication) the Muhammadan Estates (Benevolent Payments) Ordinance, 1918.
[4] cp. the Marriage and Divorce of Muhammadans Ordinance, 1906.
[5] From the British, rather than the indigenous, point of view (see below).
[6] Except, perhaps, Afghanistan.
[7] cp. the Muhammadan Law Recognition Ordinance, 1905, sect. 6 (with sects. 3, 7, and 9).
[8] cp. the Native Tribunals Ordinance, 1933, sect. 11.
[9] *Khamis* v. *Ahmed* (1934), 1 E.A.C.A. 130, p. 133.
[10] Particularly since Arabs, Somalis, etc., were formerly regarded as " natives " in the Kenya Protectorate.

law as has Arabic with the indigenous language in Kiswahili.[1] It has already been noted, moreover, that it is precisely as "native law and custom" that Islamic law is extensively enforced throughout large areas of West Africa, particularly Northern Nigeria; while the West African Court of Appeal has construed the phrase in a deceased African's will "Muhammadan Law or Custom" as "Muhammadan customary law" or "Muhammadan lawful custom" and observed "We think that these expressions mean the same thing and designate the lawful custom or customary law of the particular locality."[2] For practical purposes, therefore, the test of what constitutes "native law and custom" would seem to be not whether the law concerned is truly indigenous to the locality concerned but whether it has in fact been adopted as established usage by any considerable section of the population. And the stamp of the highest judicial authority has been given to this thesis by the remarks of their Lordships of the Privy Council in *Eshugbayi* v. *Nigerian Government*[3]: "Their Lordships entertain no doubt that the more barbarous customs of earlier days may under the influence of civilization become milder without losing their essential character of custom. It would, however, appear to be necessary to show that in their milder form they are still recognised in the native community as custom, so as in that form to regulate the relations of the native community *inter se*. In other words, the Court cannot itself transform a barbarous custom into a milder one. . . . It is the assent of the native community that gives a custom its validity, and, therefore, barbarous or mild, it must be shown to be recognised by the native community whose conduct it is supposed to regulate."

This last sentence, moreover, seems to provide the key to the difficult problem of when a change of custom should be recognised and enforced by the courts. In an early Gold Coast case[4] the English rule of "immemorial custom" was solemnly applied; while in a later case[5] the view seems to have been taken that the relevant date was that of the Supreme Court Ordinance, 1876. It is noteworthy, however, that the Gold Coast Native Courts (Colony) Ordinance, 1944, in effect follows the Privy Council in defining native customary law as simply established "native usage"[6]; while for Lord Lugard it appears that the only test was that it "must be admitted as being such by the community and its competent spokesmen."

It is, however, vital to remember that the attitude of indigenous Muslims to the basis on which Islamic law is applied may, and often does, differ considerably from that of British lawyers or administrators. Where the latter enforce it, or permit its enforcement, merely as native law and custom, the former will regard it as binding on their consciences by Divine command, however much they may restrict or evade its application in practice, and also, in parts, as imposed by the political command of some Muslim Sultan or Emir. This, of course, explains the anomaly of, e.g., an Alkali in Northern Nigeria enforcing the precise prescriptions of the classical Arabic compendiums of Mālikī law under an Ordinance which only authorises the application of native law and custom. Yet the British view, alien though it is to Muslim thought, has, in practice, much to support and commend it, for the Mālikī law has to a great extent become fused with the customary law of many of the inhabitants of these Emirates, and it as such,

[1] cp. also, in this context, the provision in the Kenya Native Courts Regulations, 1897, art. 57, that the High Court, in hearing appeals from Qāḍīs' courts, might take whatever steps it deemed right to satisfy itself as to the "Muhammadan laws and customs applicable to the case."

[2] *Sulia Ayoola and others* v. *Muritale Folawiya and others*, 8 W.A.C.A. 39.

[3] 1931. A.C. 662: cp. also in this context *Marko Kajubi* v. *Kulanima Kabali* (1944), 11 E.A.C.A. 34.

[4] *Welbeck* v. *Brown* (1882) F.C.L. 185, at p. 188.

[5] *Mensah* v. *Wiaboe* (1925) D. Ct. 1921-25, 170, at p. 172.

[6] Sect. 2.

rather than as originally prescribed or as divinely authoritative, that the Protecting Power provides for its enforcement; while this nomenclature has the double advantage of providing, on the one hand, equal authority for the application of Islamic law where this has been accepted and embraced and of pagan customary law where this still prevails, and, on the other, the clearest justification for those variations of the pure Sharī'a in favour of local practice which are noticeable, in greater or less degree, even in the most solidly Muslim areas.

Nor is it only as the customary law of some particular locality that Islamic law is applied. The Courts Ordinance in the Gold Coast, for instance, provides for the application of "any native law or custom existing in the Gold Coast";[1] and while the various Native Courts Ordinances in that territory expressly define the customary law which these courts are to enforce as that prevailing within their jurisdiction, yet they, too, commonly enforce in practice not only the local customary law but also that of any alien litigants. To an African native court, moreover, there can be little that is strange in admitting Islamic law as arbiter in, e.g., the family relations of those who profess that religion, for the basic concept of such litigation is arbitration, and the criterion by which a decision is reached is that of custom, whether local, tribal, or confined to any particular family or group. It is chiefly when such religious law, ardently embraced by individual converts, cuts right across the customary law of a compact and homogenous group, or when individual members of one family follow different religions, that cases of "conflict" occur. And even in such cases the issue varies greatly from territory to territory. In some localities, for instance, the conversion of a tribesman to Islam will in no sense be regarded as exempting him from the scope of the customary law of his tribe[2] or locality; while in others the native court will be prepared to apply the law of Islam, as expounded by a "Muslim member" or some local learned man, to the matrimonial causes and intestate succession of the most recent convert.[3]

It is clear, however, that this whole subject has been obscured by a good deal of muddled thinking, as will appear, e.g., from the Tanganyika section of this Survey. Logically, it seems, the application of Islamic law in African territories should properly be classified under at least three categories, somewhat as follows:—

A. Where it has been declared to be the *fundamental* law, as in Zanzibar,[4] parts of the Aden Protectorate and—substantially—in the Kenya Protectorate; or where its application *per se*[5] in, e.g., all matters of personal status between suitable litigants has been expressly decreed, as in the Colony of Aden, the Protectorate of Somaliland, and the Colony and Protectorate of the Gambia. In these cases the British and indigenous views largely coincide, for Islamic law is enforced as authoritive both theologically and administratively—with the British, of course, putting the main emphasis on the latter, and local Muslims on the former. Here, too, Islamic law should never be termed native law and custom, however much the two may have become assimilated in practice, for it is never as the latter that the former is applied: on the contrary, the latter is only properly enforceable, where the Sharī'a has been declared the fundamental law, as an exception authorised either by express enactment or by Islamic law itself (whether expressly, tacitly, or by means of some casuistical device), or, in those territories where the Sharī'a has been limited to matters of personal status, etc., in matters outside its scope.

---

[1] Provided, of course, it is not repugnant to natural justice, nor incompatible with any Ordinance, etc. See sect. 74(1).

[2] e.g., among some of the Digo of the Kenya Protectorate.

[3] e.g., among the Jarawa of the Bauchi Emirate of Northern Nigeria.

[4] However much it has been ousted, in practice, by statute law.

[5] i.e., as the law of Islam, rather than as defined and prescribed by the terms of some specific Ordinance or Ordinances.

B. Where Islamic law may be regarded as the *dominant* law, within a wider or more restricted range of subjects, as in Northern Nigeria and parts of Tanganyika Territory. In these cases the British and indigenous views sharply diverge, since the latter considers Islamic law as such to be theologically, and sometimes also politically, binding, while the former merely identifies it with native law and custom—with which, in practice, it has largely become fused. In such circumstances local customs still at variance with pure Islamic law should always, of course, in the British view, prevail: while in the view of local Muslims the pure Sharī'a is theoretically supreme, and sometimes—but by no means always—actually enforceable at the expense of local variants.

C. Where Islamic law must be regarded as a *particular* law, attaching, to greater or less extent, to some group, tribe, family or individual, as in the Gold Coast, Sierra Leone, Uganda, Nyasaland, and the rest[1] of Nigeria, Kenya and Tanganyika. In these cases the British and indigenous views again approximately coincide, except that the latter tends to give a somewhat wider and more flexible content than the former to the term " native law and custom." Here, too, the local customary law should be dominant and Islamic law enforced, if at all, as a sort of equitable exception.

It is noteworthy in this context that the comparative lawyer may find a suggestive parallel to some of the above phenomena in Roman-Dutch Law. In his *Introduction* to this subject[2] Professor R. W. Lee writes: " Derived from two sources, Germanic Custom and Roman Law, the Roman-Dutch law may be said to have been anticipated so soon as the former of these incorporated elements derived from the latter. Undoubtedly such a process was at work from early times. Long before the Corpus Juris of Justinian had been 'received' in Germany, the Codex Theodosianus had left its mark upon the customary laws of the country . . . Later, the Frankish Monarchy, the Church through the medium of its Canon Law, the Universities and the Courts of Law forged fresh links between Rome and Germany. The general reception of the Roman Law in Germany and Holland in the fifteenth and sixteenth centuries completed a process which in various ways and through various channels had been at work for upwards of a thousand years." In this gradual process of infiltration by a " foreign " and written law and the partial assimilation of German custom thereto, on the one hand, and also in the official, although in reality incomplete, " reception " of that law on the other, appear apt illustrations of the dual phenomenon now presented in Africa of the infiltration of Islamic law, through somewhat similar channels, and the partial assimilation of African custom thereto, in some territories, and the acceptance of Islamic law as the " fundamental " law, but in a truncated form, elsewhere.

IV

When we turn to litigation among immigrant Muslims in the different territories, a similar distinction may be observed. Litigation regarding matters of family law between members of non-native communities are decided by the British courts in the Colony of Aden and the Protectorate of Zanzibar as a matter of course,[3] on the Indian model, according to the school of the litigants[4];

[1] i.e., other than those parts classified under A or B above.

[2] *Introduction to Roman-Dutch Law*, 4th Ed. pp. 3 f.

[3] Again, basically, under Bombay Regulation 4 of 1827, sect. 26. But in practice such cases seldom come to court in any of these territories, since they are almost always settled within the community concerned.

[4] For details see the Zanzibar section of this Survey, p. 68.

while the Sultan's courts in the latter would equally as a matter of course[1] try such cases, between litigants not subject to the jurisdiction of the British courts, according to the school of the Qāḍī concerned. In the Protectorates of Aden and Somaliland, again, Indian and other immigrant Muslims generally litigate in such matters, if at all, before the ordinary Sharī'a courts, but could, presumably, apply to the British courts[2] if they wished. In Kenya, Uganda, Tanganyika and Nyasaland, on the other hand, it has been thought necessary to introduce Ordinances expressly affirming the validity of Islamic marriages and divorces among Asiatic Muslims[3]—or Muslims in general—and in most cases authorising the Supreme or High Courts to hear matrimonial causes and questions of inheritance between such litigants under Islamic law.[4] In West Africa nothing corresponding to Bombay Regulation 4 has ever existed: but no provision has been made for any court to apply the personal law of any immigrant Muslims except within the terms of the Marriage of Muhammadans Ordinance in the Gold Coast, the Muhammadan Marriage Ordinance in Sierra Leone (Colony only), and the Muhammadan Marriage and Divorce Ordinance in the Gambia (again Colony only). Brief notes on the more important immigrant Muslim communities found in East, and to a much less extent West, Africa will be found in Appendix B.

V

The dominant school of Islamic law throughout East Africa is that of the Shāfi'īs, while in the West that of the Mālikīs almost everywhere prevails. The only serious rival to the Shāfi'īs in the East is the heterodox Ibāḍī school,[5] which has a considerable following in Zanzibar (and a much smaller one on the mainland) among those of 'Umānī extraction and the few Africans who have become converts thereto. Virtually the only other minority element among the indigenous peoples of Africa is provided by the small Aḥmadī following found on both sides of the continent. This sect has officially broken with all the orthodox schools and follows, in some legal matters, a largely eclectic doctrine of its own, while adhering to Ḥanafī law in all else: but its African converts tend to follow their original schools and customs, in matters of law as distinct from theology. Among the immigrant communities, however, almost all the schools and sects of Islam are represented. On the East there are Indian (and Baluchi) Ḥanafīs, Ithnā 'Asharīs, and Ismā'īlīs of both the Khoja (Nizārī) and Bohora (Musta'lī) factions, besides Shāfi'īs from Arabia, Madagascar, the Comoro Islands and

[1] As applying the local "fundamental" law, at least in the case of Muslim litigants.

[2] In Aden these exist only in the Colony; while in both these territories such jurisdiction would, of course, again be based on Bombay Regulation 4 of 1827.

[3] Or "non-Christian Asiatics" in the case of Tanganyika and Nyasaland. It is only in Uganda and Kenya that these Ordinances apply to indigenous Muslims as well.

[4] It is, however, remarkable how widely such legislation differs as between territory and territory. True, in Nyasaland and Tanganyika the Asiatics (Marriage, Divorce and Succession) Ordinance, 1929, and the Marriage, Divorce and Succession (Non-Christian Asiatics) Ordinance, 1923, were closely similar, as originally drafted: but the subsequent amendment of the latter has empowered the courts in Tanganyika to grant dissolution of marriage under Islamic law, while in Nyasaland the courts may only recognise a divorce validly pronounced or agreed by the parties. But in Kenya the Muhammadan Marriage, Divorce and Succession Ordinance includes all Muslims in its scope and differs from the above Ordinances in other respects also; while in Uganda the Marriage and Divorce of Muhammadans Ordinance, 1906, makes no reference to succession.

[5] The only survivors of the early Khārijīs. The Sultans of Muscat and Zanzibar follow this rite, as does also the Imām who rules in the interior of 'Umān—while large pockets of Ibāḍīs still survive also in Algeria and Tripolitania. But the differences between the Ibāḍīs and the orthodox schools in matters of law are in reality no greater than those between the orthodox schools themselves.

elsewhere, Ithnā 'Asharīs from Persia and Baḥrain, and Zaydīs from the Yemen; while in the West there are chiefly Syrians and Lebanese who follow either the Ḥanafī or Ithnā 'Asharī schools, together with a few Indians of heterogeneous allegiance.

VI.

Further differences concern the courts which apply this law and the rules of evidence and procedure which they follow. The British courts everywhere, of course, hear such cases under the ordinary rules of evidence locally applied and according to their normal methods of procedure. The Qāḍīs' courts in the Protectorates of Aden, Somaliland, Zanzibar and Kenya, on the other hand, all in reality follow the Islamic rules of evidence with varying degrees of rigidity, although this is perfectly in order in the first two territories but directly contrary to the Evidence Decree and the (applied) Indian Evidence Act in the last two respectively. As for the Liwalis' courts in Tanganyika and the various courts in the Aden Protectorate which are not specifically "Sharī'a" in character, these follow a form of procedure and rules of evidence which are loosely Islamic; while the native courts elsewhere apply rules of evidence and procedure which are frankly "customary." Such is the general position: but it must be emphasised that in the case of Qāḍīs and Liwalis in particular minor differences occur not only between locality and locality but individual and individual, some adhering more strictly to the ancient texts and others making more concessions to indigenous custom, to British concepts, or to common-sense principles of fair play. In West Africa, again, any cases under Islamic law tried by British courts are heard under the ordinary rules of procedure and evidence therein applied; cases tried by the Alkālai of Northern Nigeria or the Qāḍīs of Bathurst are conducted according to the Islamic rules, more or less strictly enforced—and the same is also true to a varying degree of the Emirs' courts of Northern Nigeria; while in all other native courts throughout West Africa ordinary customary rules of evidence and procedure are followed, except, e.g., in the more strictly Muslim districts of the Gambia, where Islamic doctrines exercise a considerable influence.

When we turn to the question of appeals and revision, we find that in the Protectorate of Aden the jurisdiction of the Qāḍīs is virtually independent of any British control, while in Somaliland they have their own Court of Appeal but are subject to the revisory powers of British magistrates in matters of fact or miscarriage of justice (although not in any question of the "interpretation of the Sharī'a law").[1] In Zanzibar and the Protectorate of Kenya, on the other hand, the Qāḍīs' courts form part of the regular judicial hierarchy and are subject to the ordinary system of appeals;[2] in Tanganyika the Liwalis' courts are part of the "local" (i.e., native) court system and appeals therefrom go first to other local courts and then to administrative officers; while the native courts of Nyasaland and Uganda occupy a medial position between those two arrangements. In West Africa, again, we find in Northern Nigeria a system of appeals from native courts which is very complex and extends, in some cases, to the British courts, but not in "any matter relating to marriage, family status, guardianship of children, inheritance, testamentary disposition or the administration of an estate;"[3] while administrative officers have an unfettered right of revision. The same is true of appeals from, and revision of proceedings in, the

[1] See Subordinate Courts Ordinance, 1944, sect. 30.

[2] Except that in Kenya the Chief Qāḍī always sits with the Supreme Court as an assessor in such cases.

[3] Except in so far as the Governor may direct to the contrary—(see Native Courts Ordinance, sect. 30). But the powers of revision accorded to administrative officers are applicable even in these cases, and British courts may try them if transferred thereunder.

native courts of the Gold Coast, but without this important exception[1]; and much the same prevails also in Sierra Leone, except that every sentence of more than fourteen days' imprisonment passed by a native court must be reported to the District Commissioner by a method which virtually operates as an appeal. Finally, appeals from the Qāḍīs' courts in Bathurst lie to the Supreme Court, and from the native tribunals in the Gambia Protectorate to a Protectorate Court; while in the latter case administrative officers also have the right to review their proceedings.

VII

Again, it is to some extent the dual question of the juristic basis on which Islamic law is applied and the type of court which exercises this jurisdiction which governs the extent of its application in different territories; although this is, of course, primarily determined by specific enactments. Thus in parts of the Aden Protectorate Islamic law is still applied in cases of homicide and certain crimes, with only minor modifications, by courts which are usually not specifically "Sharī'a" in character[2]; while the Qāḍīs, on their part, enforce much of the Islamic law of contract and tort, in addition to matters of family law. Again, in the Protectorates of Zanzibar and Kenya the Islamic law of tort and odd remnants of the law of contract are still applied in the Qāḍīs' courts, in addition to family law, waqf, etc.; and the same is also true of the Liwalis' courts of Tanganyika Territory. In Somaliland, on the other hand, the application of Islamic law is virtually limited[3] to a comprehensive jurisdiction over matters of personal status and family law (together with the computation of blood-wit) by the local Qāḍīs; in the Colony of Kenya and the Protectorate of Uganda it is largely confined to the application by the Supreme and High Courts of the Muhammadan Marriage, Divorce and Succession Ordinance and the Marriage and Divorce of Muhammadans Ordinance respectively; while in Nyasaland it is scarcely applied at all[4].

Similarly, in West Africa, Islamic law is applied by native courts throughout much of Northern Nigeria not only in matters of personal status but even in contract, tort, homicide and parts of the criminal law, while even non-Muslims are sometimes included in its scope; in the Gambia it is applied in matters of personal status between Muslim litigants, somewhat strictly by the Qāḍīs' courts of the Colony and much more laxly by most of the native tribunals of the Protectorate; while in the Gold Coast, Sierra Leone and the rest of Nigeria it is applied, if at all, as a sort of equitable exception to the prevalent customary law—except, of course, under the terms of the relevant marriage Ordinances.[5] In addition it is also applied to immigrant Muslims, chiefly but not exclusively in East Africa, by those courts and within those limits described above.

VIII

It seems best to arrange this Survey of the application of Islamic law in the different Colonies and Protectorates territory by territory, making each section

[1] Although land cases are treated quite differently from all other cases, in the Colony and Ashanti.

[2] e.g., those of the Ḥākim 'Urfī in the W.A.P., of the Nā'ib and Qā'im in the E.A.P., together with the Tribal courts, the Commercial Court and the Supreme Court of Mukallā, etc. But in the Sultanate of Mukallā homicide cases go to the Qāḍīs of the Supreme Court.

[3] Except, that is, for any Islamic law applied by the subordinate (and other) courts as "native custom."

[4] Except, again—in all these cases—if and when applied as "native law," whether by British courts or native tribunals.

[5] See above.

complete in itself, even at the expense of a certain repetition. Unhappily, legislation regarding Islamic law, and the courts and procedure by which it is applied, not only differs widely in substance from territory to territory, but the spelling of such terms as Qāḍī, Sharī'a, waqf and even Muhammadan is equally diverse. After much hesitation, therefore, I have decided to adopt a uniform spelling throughout this Survey, even to the extent of altering the spelling of the relevant Ordinances and other quotations. To such a policy there are, of course, grave objections, but the chaos and even misconceptions to which any other procedure might give rise seem even more objectionable. Footnotes have, moreover, usually been inserted in the different sections to mark the first occasion when this liberty has been taken in regard to each particular term. In general, diacritical points have been used in the transliteration of Arabic terms, except in regard to those which (like sultan, sheikh, emir, etc.) have become thoroughly anglicised. Appendices provide, *inter alia,* certain notes on immigrant communities, a summary (for comparative purposes) of the position in the Anglo-Egyptian Sudan, a glossary of technical terms, and an exposition of certain points of law, while a table of legislation gives the references of Ordinances and Decrees in the latest Revised Editions of the Laws. For the rest, however, no attempt has been made in this Survey to give any account of the origin, development or nature of Islamic law—according to its various schools—or of its detailed provisions, since these are subjects which can more satisfactorily be treated in a Handbook which I have been asked to write. Books and other authorities consulted have been mentioned as fully as possible in the footnotes; but no Bibliography has been attempted, on account partly of the vastness of the subject and partly of the essentially personal character of the present Survey.

It must be emphasised that the field-work on which this Survey is based was completed during the summer of 1950 in East Africa and the beginning of 1951 in West Africa. Certain more recent developments have, indeed, been included; but no claim can be made to any full information of any changes subsequent to these dates.

Part I. Aden and East Africa

ADEN

It is in the Aden Protectorate that Sharī'a law finds its widest application in the whole region of East Africa,[1] for there—in some localities—it holds almost undisputed sway. Yet it is only recently, and under the pax Britannica, that Sharī'a courts have been established in any organised form, except in isolated instances: for previously the only authority within each tribal unit was its sheikh and within each confederacy the sultan[2] or some local *manṣab,*[3] and the law they applied was that of ancient custom. Virtual anarchy was only averted by a system of tribal sanctions between tribe and tribe, tribe and sultan and confederation and confederation; while any litigation was referred to tribal judges or arbitrators. These normally made no attempt to execute their judgments in the modern sense, for it was the contending parties who sought their aid and deposited hostages or pledges as guarantees of good faith: all they did was to hear their pleas and then declare that it was for this party or that to produce so many witnesses, to swear such and such oaths, or undergo this or that ordeal, whereupon the other party must do so and so; while if, on the other hand, the first party could not produce the necessary witnesses or sustain the ordeal, then the other, in his turn, must take certain oaths, etc. There was even a recognised scale of fines, at least in some localities, for different offences.[4] For the rest, blood feuds and self-help held the field. The impact of Sharī'a law was felt chiefly through two channels: the general influence of such Islamic teaching concerning marriage, divorce, etc., as had percolated through to the people as a whole and succeeded in amending or even replacing pre-Islamic customs inconsistent therewith—and this would naturally be felt chiefly in the towns; and the "judgments" and arbitration awards of local holy men, whether *sayyids*[5] from the Ḥaḍramaut or *'ulamā'* from the Yemen.

Sharī'a law appears in South Arabia largely as the tool of the centralised Government, whether indigenous or foreign. It is a moot point, however, how far British initiative in the extension of its sway, popular though this no doubt is with the *'ulamā'*, can be regarded as an unmixed blessing to the country as a whole. It is too little realised how often local customs have persisted, even in family law, among communities which were thoroughly Muslim, while in the field of criminal law and commercial practice the pure Sharī'a has never been exclusively applied. To the Protecting Power there is, of course, a natural

---

[1] Regarding Aden as part of East Africa in the sense that appeals therefrom now go to the Court of Appeal for Eastern Africa, etc.

[2] Or emir, etc. The powers of a sultan or emir are usually defined, in South Arabia, in a document made by agreement amongst the tribes. See the 'Awdhalī Code—published by Dr. R. B. Serjeant in "Western Arabia and the Red Sea."

[3] The *manṣab,* in South Arabia, is the ruler of one of the sacred enclaves known as a *ḥawṭa.* These serve as neutral territory for the tribes for both trade and the settlement of disputes—whence the influence of the *manṣab,* whose office may be elective or hereditary.

[4] See the 'Awdhalī Code. Also a most interesting MSS. in the possession of Dr. Serjeant entitled "Kitāb al-Ādāb wa'l-Lawāzim fī Aḥkām al-Man'a" concerning the differences between South Arabian tribal sanctions and Sharī'a law.

[5] See Glossary. Not, of course, that most *sayyids* have any real knowledge of the Sharī'a.

tendency to champion the Sharī'a, for it is "tidier" than the vagaries of local custom from the administrative point of view and provides better political propaganda.[1] But there is often little to commend the policy from the social angle, unless local customs are themselves objectionable: and it is by no means certain that it is even wise politically on a long-term basis. In the Eastern Protectorate, of course, Ḥaḍramaut has always been famous as a centre of learning, in both theology and law, and the Sharī'a needed no championship there: but even in Ḥaḍramaut it is not many years since anarchy and blood feuds largely prevailed, and it is only with the improvement of security that the Sharī'a has come into its own.

No Order in Council or Aden Ordinance covers the application of Islamic law in the two Protectorates. On the contrary, although in most cases it is only under the pax Britannica, and sometimes under direct British influence, that Sharī'a courts have been organised, the law these courts administer is regarded as excluded from the "advice" which some (but not all) local rulers have bound themselves by treaty to accept. In some cases this exclusion is explicit, as in the treaty with His Highness the Sultan of Shiḥr and Mukallā, where article I provides that the Sultan shall accept the advice of his Resident Adviser "in all matters except those concerning Muhammadan religion and custom"; while in others it is regarded as implicit, as in the treaty with Baiḥān, where article II provides that the Regent will "accept the advice of the Governor of Aden in all matters connected with the welfare and development of the territory of Baiḥān and its Dependencies."

The population of the Protectorate is almost solidly Muslim. The only important exception used to be certain Jewish colonies in the Western districts, which have now practically disappeared as a result of the modern exodus to Israel; while in the East no non-Muslims were, until recently, allowed in the interior at all. With but isolated exceptions, moreover, all follow the Shāfi'ī rite, to the tenets of which many cling with fanatical devotion. The dominant group in religion and learning are the numerous *sayyids* of Ḥaḍramaut, who trace their origin to a certain Aḥmad b. 'Īsā al-Muhājir, a descendant of al-Ḥusayn, who is said to have come as an emigrant (or refugee) from Baṣra in the fourth century A.H. It is, however, a matter of local dispute whether this Aḥmad was a Sunnī when he came, or whether the *sayyids* of Ḥaḍramaut subsequently adopted Sunnī views the more successfully to combat the Ibāḍīs who were then predominant in the country, and chose the Shāfi'ī[2] rite as closer to their former Shī'ī tenets than were the other Sunnī schools. Some traces of allegedly Shī'ī tendencies[3] can, moreover, be found in certain Ḥaḍrami writers till this day, largely, perhaps, because of their staunch championship of the house of 'Alī.

The Qu'ayṭī Sultanate of Shiḥr and Mukallā.

This Sultanate is certainly the most progressive in the Protectorate and its Sultan is himself a man of considerable learning in the Islamic sciences.[4] Nominally, at least, the Sharī'a is the fundamental law of the state in every particular, and articles 9 and 10 of Decree No. 5 of 1940 read: "The law of Islam is, and is hereby confirmed to be, the fundamental law of Our Dominions. In the application of Our Decrees Our Courts shall also be guided by and have

[1] As enabling the Administration to pose as in some degree the champion of Islam, in partial imitation of the Governments of the Yemen and of Sa'udi Arabia.

[2] The first important *sayyid* of Ḥaḍramaut seems to have been al-Faqīh al-Muqaddam (of 653 A.H.), and his name is presumably indicative of his preoccupation with legal studies.

[3] Or, alternatively, tendencies closely related thereto.

[4] He gave me several of his own publications.

regard to the general principles of the law of Islam, and to any tribal laws, customs or usages not repugnant to Islam, justice, equity and morality." [1] Qāḍīs' courts, consisting of a single *'ālim,* are established in a number of centres, and have exclusive jurisdiction over questions of personal status, waqf and matters of contract and tort (*ḥuqūq*). But Decrees have also provided for the establishment of Provincial and District courts, courts of the "Ḥākim al-Sūq," Tribal courts, and for the Mukallā Commercial Court.

The Provincial courts are presided over by the Nā'ibs (Arab Provincial Commissioners) and, in Mukallā itself, by the State Secretary; have jurisdiction in all criminal cases other than those of homicide; and may pass sentence up to 12 years' imprisonment or Rs. 5,000 fine[2] (or, where authorised, corporal punishment not exceeding 24 lashes).[3] Until recently, however, they had no Penal Code and largely followed their unfettered discretion in regard to procedure, substantive law and suitable sentence[4]—nominally, of course, "in the light of Sharī'a principles": but in February, 1950, a Code was introduced to which further reference must be made. This also applies to the District courts, which are presided over by the Qā'ims (Arab District Commissioners), exercise more restricted criminal jurisdiction and may not impose penalties exceeding one year's imprisonment or a fine of Rs. 300.[5] The Ḥākim al-Suq[6] is a town magistrate, with petty jurisdiction in cases of vagrancy, breaches of the peace, petty larcency, minor municipal and minor "religious" offences: and the maximum penalty he may impose is 14 days' imprisonment or Rs. 25 fine.[7] All these courts may be said, in general, to conform to good Islamic precedents, for criminal law has usually been enforced as part of the comprehensive judicial powers of the Sovereign, which he delegated largely to administrative or police officers rather than the official Qāḍī, to be exercised in accordance with such instructions as he or his local representative might issue.[8] This was reluctantly accepted, in most cases, even by the most conservative opinion, for Islamic criminal law usually concerns itself in detail only with the few offences[9] for which the *ḥadd* punishments are specifically prescribed in the divine texts, but under such stringent conditions that they can seldom in fact be imposed. For the rest, the prevention and punishment of wrongdoing is left to the discretion of the Ruler, only general principles, at most, being discussed in the texts.

The Mukallā Commercial Court[10] in theory has unlimited jurisdiction in commercial matters arising outside or inside Mukallā, and is composed of a magistrate sitting with assessors drawn from a panel of merchants: but outside

[1] It is clear that the Sultan is here preserving the usual fiction that the Ruler's administrative Decrees, on the one hand, and local customs, on the other, do not in any real sense conflict with the divine law.

[2] Decree No. 5 of 1940, art. 12.

[3] Ibid. art. 19.

[4] This, at least, is what the supporters of the new Code allege. But even here custom must have exercised a powerful influence.

[5] Decree No. 5 of 1940, art. 13.

[6] This appointment inevitably recalls that of the *muḥtasib,* but is much more restricted.

[7] Decree No. 2 of 1940, arts. 2 and 3.

[8] cp. remarks in a (unpublished) Paper by Dr. J. Schacht on Northern Nigeria.

[9] e.g., illicit sexual intercourse, for which the punishment is stoning or flogging for both offenders, according to whether or not they have ever enjoyed a valid marriage; stealing (with a technical definition), for which the punishment is mutilation; brigandage, for which the punishment varies, but may even include "crucifixion"; slander of a chaste person's continence, and taking alcohol—for both of which the punishment is flogging. Apostasy, for which the punishment is death, is also sometimes termed a "*ḥadd*" offence. See Glossary for *ḥadd*: also *'ālim* and *ḥuquq* above.

[10] This, again, conforms to good Islamic precedents, for unofficial commercial tribunals have frequently existed alongside the official jurisdiction of the Qāḍī.

Mukallā disputes between traders are often referred to the Qādis' courts,[1] who may or may not call in merchants as assessors. In Shibām, for instance, there is a commercial committee of nine members whose help is frequently invoked by both Nā'ib and Qāḍī: but the latter alone actually give judgment.

Again, the tribal courts include both " Chief's courts " and " Beduins' courts," the former consisting of " Manṣabs, Muqaddams, Sheikhs and others ruling in settled towns and villages not under our direct rule,"[2] and the latter of one tribal sheikh (or three, if both parties so demand), well versed in tribal procedure and customs, chosen from a panel of tribal judges.[3] The Chiefs' courts may pass " any judgment, finding, sentence, decree, award or order in conformity with the law of Islam, tribal or local custom, or usage not repugnant to justice, equity or morality,[4] while Beduin courts enjoy a similar freedom " in conformity with the customs and usages of their tribe " provided they do not transgress " justice, equity and morality,"[5] except that cases concerning immovable property and others which the Nā'ib considers should be referred to the state courts are excluded from their competence.[6] It is further prescribed that these tribal courts are to have jurisdiction in all cases in which the Nā'ib is of opinion that the parties " by ancient custom follow tribal procedure."[7] If the case concerns members of nomadic and settled tribes it must be referred to the appropriate Beduin or Chief's court if both parties agree, or else to the District court with the Qā'im sitting with an appropriate tribal judge and with the appropriate chief[8]; while if the case concerns members of different settled tribes it must go to the appropriate Chief's court if both parties agree, or else to the District court with the Qā'im sitting with the two appropriate chiefs.[9] Copies of the judgments of tribal courts must always be forwarded to the Nā'ib of the Province,[10] who may refer the matter back for the completion of any deficiencies or even pass the matter to the Provincial Beduin Court of Appeal[11] (see below).

It must, of course, be realised that customary law still largely prevails in the tribal districts and has considerable influence even in the towns. But in the latter local customs have usually been islamicised, superficially at least, for in most cases jurists have either found an argument on which to support their validity or a device by which they can be followed without transgressing the letter of the divine law.[12] This, however, is a wide and detailed study in itself into which I could not enter in the time available.

No appeals are allowed from judgments of the Ḥakim al-Sūq, but "the general powers of review and supervision conferred on the Judge by the State Courts Decree "[13]—but now exercised presumably by the Qāḍīs—include his court in their scope. Appeals from the District courts lie to the Provincial

[1] Art. 27 of Decree No. 5 of 1940 provides for this only if both parties agree. Even so, however, these courts are not really suitable for commercial cases, since they must of necessity attempt—or at least pretend—to follow the pure Sharī'a, which has never been elastic enough for commercial practice. If, on the other hand, they frankly act as arbitrators in such cases, the duty could probably be performed better by others.

[2] Decree No. 1 of 1940, art. 3.

[3] Ibid. art. 6.

[4] Ibid. art. 7.

[5] Ibid. art. 11.

[6] Ibid. art. 9.

[7] Ibid. art. 12.

[8] Ibid. art. 12(1).

[9] Ibid. art. 12(2).

[10] Ibid. art. 14.

[11] Ibid. art. 15.

[12] See below, p. 34 note (5).

[13] Decree No. 2 of 1940, art 5. But see below.

courts, and appeals from the latter (whether in first instance or second appeal) to the Supreme Court,[1] while "non-appealable findings, sentences or orders" of all such courts were formerly subject to revision by the Judge (except that no such findings were to be set aside on the ground of any error, omission or irregularity in practice or procedure unless the Judge were of opinion that it had occasioned a failure of justice[2]). Appeals from the Mukallā Commercial Court (provided the sum involved exceeds Rs. 500 or leave to appeal is specially granted[3]) and from Qāḍīs' courts also lie to the Supreme Court,[4] formerly to the Judge's and Qāḍīs' divisions respectively: for article 4 of the "Courts Decree" provided that the Supreme Court should sit at Mukallā and consist of "the Judge and two Qāḍīs appointed by Us"; that it should sit in two divisions, the Judge's division and the Qāḍīs' division; and that the former should exercise jurisdiction "in all criminal and commercial cases and in other cases not decided by the Sharī'a," and the latter in "all civil cases decided by the Sharī'a," including questions of homicide (the latter, alone, in first instance).

In tribal cases an appeal lies from a Chiefs' court to the Provincial court (in Sharī'a cases with the Qāḍī sitting with the Nā'ib),[5] and thence to the Supreme Court—formerly to the Qāḍīs' division, if the case had been decided according to the Sharī'a, and to the Judge sitting with two sheikhs where tribal custom had been followed.[6] Appeals from Beduin courts lie to the Provincial Beduin Courts of Appeal, each of which consists of the Nā'ib as President, the Officer Commanding the Ḥaḍramī Beduin Legion, and a suitable tribal sheikh; may refer cases to other tribal sheikhs as assessors[7]; and has the power to increase or decrease the penalty, quash or vary the judgment, or return the case for retrial.[8] A further appeal lay to the Supreme Court "with the Judge sitting with two sheikhs well versed in tribal law."[9]

It is also expressly declared that "the Supreme Judicial Authority is, and remains, vested in Our Royal Person as part of the Sovereign prerogatives which we enjoy by inheritance from our predecessors . . . and shall be exercised by Ourselves in Council,"[10] and that "it shall be lawful for any person to apply to Ourselves in Council for permission to appeal against a decision of the Supreme Court."[11] This Council consists of the Sultan himself, the Resident Adviser, the Heir Apparent, the Assistant to the Resident Adviser, and the State Secretary (or persons authorised to act in their place) as *ex officio* members, together with two nominated members.[12]

All this looks clear and impressive enough on paper, but unfortunately much of it has never really been put into effect. For a time an Indian judge was, indeed, appointed to the Supreme Court; but he experienced continual opposition from the Qāḍīs, who resented any limitation of their own jurisdiction or the bare suggestion that there were any cases "not decided by the Sharī'a": everything, they held, should be subject to the divine law, in detailed letter in cases

[1] Formerly, to the Judge's division. But see below.

[2] State Courts Decree No. 5 of 1940, arts. 16, 17.

[3] Ibid. art. 28.

[4] Ibid. art. 24. This transgresses the pure Sharī'a in two respects, for the latter knows only revision of judgments which are bad in law, not appeal and re-hearing, and does not recognise a bench of judges. But the pure Sharī'a has almost everywhere been abandoned in both these respects, in the public interests.

[5] Decree No. 1 of 1940, art. 8.

[6] Ibid. art. 20.

[7] Ibid. arts. 16, 17.

[8] Ibid. art. 18.

[9] Decree No. 1 of 1940, art. 20.

[10] Decree No. 5 of 1940, art. 2. This conforms to good Islamic precedents.

[11] Decree No. 4 of 1940, art. 7.

[12] Ibid. art. 3.

of personal status or civil rights, and at least in spirit in criminal or commercial cases.[1] In the event the judge in due course returned to India and no successor has yet been appointed. Instead, the judge's functions are exercised either by the Qāḍīs of the Supreme Court or by the Sultan in Council.[2] Unhappily, too, the Qāḍīs' courts do not enjoy a very high repute locally, and instances have occurred of a Qāḍī being left in one District far too long.

There have been three comparatively recent developments of outstanding juristic interest in the Sultanate, each of which demands comparatively detailed notice.

A. In the first place, a Decree of 92 articles was issued by the Sultan in 1942 defining the law his courts were to apply in various matters of sale, option, *'uhda* (a local form of mortgage or redeemable sale),[3] surety, release, interdiction, settlement, acknowledgment, partnership, lease, waqf, inheritance, marriage (including *'idda*), maintenance, dissolution of marriage, custody of infants, procedure, testimony, etc. Many of these articles, moreover, either represent a variant view in the Shāfi'ī school, which was thereby preferred to the opinion of Ibn Ḥajar previously regarded as authoritative,[4] or even the view of some non-Shāfi'ī jurist. This was a landmark in the path of progress, for it meant the adoption, in however mild a form, of the principle on which the far more extensive reforms recently introduced in Egypt, the Sudan, Lebanon, Syria, etc., have all been based—namely that the Sovereign has the right to command his judges which of the variant opinions held by the classical jurists, regardless of school, they are to apply in given circumstances. For this principle, moreover, there is good Shāfi'ī authority, for Ibn Ḥajar is quoted as saying that a " weaker " opinion in that school, or from another recognised Sunnī school, is so strengthened by the Sultan's command, based on the public interests, as to become dominant and obligatory on the courts. True, most of the reforms introduced by this Decree were not outstandingly controversial, but several are of considerable importance, e.g.: —

(1). The invalidity of an " acknowledgment " in favour of an heir, made in death sickness, where the circumstances show that the purpose was to deprive others (Art. 40). This has Mālikī (and some Shāfi'ī) authority.

(2). The legality of selling waqf land, in certain urgent circumstances (Arts. 48, 49). This is of Ḥanbalī origin.

(3). The (temporary) continuance of the rights of inheritance of a wife, divorced by her husband in his death sickness, when it is known that his motive was to deprive her thereof (Art. 51). This has both Ḥanafī and Mālikī authority.

(4). The disregard, in suitable cases, of the rules regarding " equality " (*kafā'a*) in marriage (Art. 54). This is of Mālikī inspiration.

(5). The validity and enforcement of a stipulation by a husband that he would not make his wife leave her parents' house or go to another town against her will (Art. 60). This is Ḥanbalī in origin.

(6). The right of a wife to refuse to travel with her husband more than forty-eight miles, and yet to remain entitled to support, if she can produce circumstantial evidence that he means to injure her by the demand (Art. 64). This represents one Ḥanafī opinion.

---

[1] i.e., the fiction that in these, too, the Sharī'a is followed must be preserved.

[2] Chiefly the former, it seems.

[3] See article by Dr. R. B. Serjeant in the Bulletin of the S.O.A.S., xiii, 1950, pp. 591, ff.

[4] Officially—although some of these articles probably represent, in reality, the authorisation of existing local practice.

(7). The obligation on a husband intending to take a long journey to pronounce a suspended divorce, to appoint a representative to supply his wife with maintenance on demand during his absence, or to leave her adequate provision, etc. (Art. 65). This is attributed to the *Tuḥfa* of Ibn Ḥajar.

(8). The right of a wife, who cannot obtain maintenance, to a judicial dissolution of marriage, where the appropriate conditions are fulfilled, even though the husband owns property which she cannot utilize or obtain (Art. 67). This follows a Shāfi'ī work much esteemed in the Protectorate entitled *Fatāwā Mashhūr* or *Bughyat al-Mustarshidīn.*

(9). The right of a mother to take her infant child on a journey not exceeding forty-eight miles from the father's place of domicile (Art. 68). This is based on the view that a journey of less than this distance is equivalent to not travelling at all.

(10). The adoption of certain periods of limitation (Art. 73). This rests on the principle that the Ruler may forbid his judges to hear certain suits.

(11). The disregard of certain tricks often used to evade the right of pre-emption (Art. 77). This comes from the opinions of Ibn al-Qayyim, the Ḥanbalī reformer of the fourteenth century.

(12). The right of the Qāḍī to put a witness on oath in case of doubt (Art. 83). This, too, is attributed locally to Ibn al-Qayyim, but can also find support from the very early jurist Ibn Abī Layla, and many others.

(13). The acceptance as evidence, under certain conditions, of documents, etc., signed by Qāḍīs (Art. 87). This is said to be Mālikī in origin.

(14). The acceptance of the deceased's written bequest, in the absence of witnesses, if signed and not known to have been revoked (Art. 88). This represents a Ḥanbalī opinion.

(15). The acceptance of certain other documentary evidence (Art. 89). This is attributed to both Abū Ḥanīfa and Mālik.

(16). Measures to prevent the recovery of excessive interest on an *'uhda* mortgage[1] (Arts. 14, 15).

(17). The calculation of a wife's maintenance by exclusive reference to her needs (Art. 63).

(18). The non-enforcement of a vow[2] (*nadhr*) by a parent in favour of some of his or her children to the exclusion of others, unless some reason exists to justify such discrimination (Art. 78). These three all represent variant Shāfi'ī opinions.

B. In the second place, a Decree of four articles, this time concerning homicide, was similarly promulgated in 1945. The only points of particular interest here are that this Decree allows the execution of a murderer at the request of the adult and sane " heirs of blood " without awaiting the majority or recovery of any minor or insane heirs, unless the contrary appears to be in the public interest; and that it also provides that no execution is to be carried out except by authority of the Sultan or State Secretary. The first of these provisions is attributed to Mālik among others; the proviso retains the ordinary Shāfi'ī rule, where no

[1] This must not exceed the " ordinary " rent for leased property, etc.—fixed by Proclamation at a maximum of ten per cent.

[2] Such a vow is often so phrased as to come into operation three days before its author's death, as a device to evade the rules of intestate succession.

change seems warranted; and the last provision means that executions will now normally be carried out by a police firing squad—i.e., the Shāfi'ī principle that the heirs of blood may themselves kill the culprit, generally in the very way in which he killed his victim, has been abandoned.

C. In the third place, a Decree entitled "Sharī'a Criminal Laws" was promulgated in February, 1950. It consists of 66 articles, and covers certain points of procedure and evidence, of the prevention of crime, and of the maximum punishments for a number of different offences, etc. It was drawn up by the most learned jurist of the coastal area, Sayyid Muḥsin of Ghail, and then revised by a committee; and is said to be based on principles all of which find support among the dicta of some reputable jurist. Its main purpose was to provide an "indigenous" code as an alternative to the unfettered discretion (or alleged caprice[1]) of Nā'ibs and Qā'ims on the one hand or a "foreign" system such as the Indian or Sudan Penal Code on the other. But it has met with criticism and opposition from many quarters. Purists object that it represents another example of what they term "*talfīq*,"[2] or the combination in a single whole of precepts drawn from a number of different schools and jurists; liberals stress that it gives certain despotic powers to the Nā'ibs, who may even imprison a bad character for life without proof of guilt,[3] and seems "designed for asses, from the prevalence of beating in the punishments prescribed"; jurists point out that it is woefully inadequate and incomplete, as the absence of any reference to embezzlement, fraudulent conversion, breach of trust, etc., sufficiently shows, and is also in parts inconsistent with other enactments; Nā'ibs and Qā'ims say that some of its articles are unsuitable and impracticable; while to the criticisms of the Ḥaḍramīs of the interior reference will be made later. In practice such officials as were questioned freely admitted that they only applied it as and when they thought fit. It must be remembered that the principle of *ta'zīr*, or punishment for any form of wrong-doing at the discretion of Ruler or Court, is an exceedingly elastic principle in Sharī'a law which can be made to cover most, at least, of the requirements of a modern penal code.[4]

In addition to the formal courts, moreover, a "Religious Court" was recently set up in Mukallā to deal with offences against the religious law such as eating during the Ramaḍān fast, neglecting prayer, and a variety of other matters. For a time it showed considerable activity; although it had, happily, been little in evidence just before my visit. Feeling against it was strong in some quarters, on the grounds that it was both reactionary and despotic; that it did not confine itself to proper processes of law; and that its members did not command adequate confidence.

---

[1] Or, indeed, local custom.

[2] See Glossary.

[3] cp. art. 25. Sayyid Muḥsin himself maintains that the apparently despotic powers granted to Nā'ibs in certain articles are based on and justified by the wider discretion allowed by jurists to administrative and police officers—in contradistinction to Qāḍīs—in dealing with suspected cases of crime *before* proof thereof. These wider powers include the hearing of evidence as to whether the accused is "of the people of" the offence of which he is suspect: if he is, the suspicion is "strengthened," the process of investigation may be more stringent, and the accused may even be subjected to a beating without proof of guilt (but there are special rules concerning a confession obtained thereby). Again, a suspect may be imprisoned without proof as a precautionary measure in the public interests—even for life, in the case of an habitual offender. Oaths by the triple divorce, etc., may also be imposed, and "repentance" induced even by a threat of execution which cannot lawfully be put into effect (in which case the threat is not to be regarded as a lie, but as a permissible form of punishment!)

[4] There can, of course, be no doubt that a "ready-made" Code, proved by experience, would be much more efficient than anything locally produced—and there could be no valid objection on purely Islamic grounds to the vast majority of its provisions. But it would inevitably be regarded as foreign and un-Islamic by the conservative, and highly orthodox, local opinion.

Sayyid Muḥsin struck me as easily the most learned of the jurists of the coast, although the Chief Qāḍī is also well-informed. I found that the basic principle of reform—that the Sultan might command the adoption of the view of any recognised Imām in any matter of controversy—had not only been used in the Decrees discussed above but had found general acceptance among local jurists, although it had not as yet been applied in any extreme form. The Chief Qāḍī, however, opined that even a Shī'ī view might be accepted if its juristic support were adequate.

In cases of homicide the responsibility for prosecution rests with the heirs of the deceased, although the Public Prosecutor will assist them: only if there are no heirs, or the heir is a minor or insane, will the Public Prosecutor assume full responsibility. After conviction, again, it is for the heirs to decide whether to insist on talion, where applicable, accept blood-wit, or even let the culprit go scot-free: although in the last case the Government would almost certainly impose a term of imprisonment as a discretionary punishment to safeguard public security. All this conforms to Shāfi'ī principles, as do also the rules that the remission of talion by a single heir is sufficient to exclude its infliction and that, except as provided by the Sultan's Decree of 1945, the culprit may not be executed until every entitled heir has been able to make his decision. But talion, where demanded, is now executed by a firing squad (since no expert headsman is available) provided by the Government[1]—although the Chief Qāḍī opined that if the heirs of blood were bedouin accustomed to shooting they might be allowed the privilege of doing it themselves. Yet as recently as 1945 the whole population is said to have turned out to watch a man slit the throat of a woman who had chosen that means to murder her mother-in-law: she was stretched on the ground beside her open grave, where her executioner three times knelt down to despatch her, before one of the heirs finally yielded to the pleas of mercy proffered by bystanders; by which time the culprit was, not surprisingly, "dazed." It was this incident, indeed, that provided the occasion for the issue of the Decree of 1945 outlined above.[2]

In any homicide in which there are grounds for suspicion but no adequate proof, compurgation (*qasāma*), applied according to normal Shāfi'ī principles, is still practised; but talion is excluded in all such cases, and the heirs of blood must be content with blood-wit.[3] Talion in cases of wounding (an eye for an eye, and a limb for a limb, etc.), on the other hand, has apparently not been enforced for years, and suitable compensation, together with criminal punishment where applicable, is alone exacted in all such cases.

Qāḍīs were usually evasive when questioned about the *ḥadd* punishments prescribed by Sharī'a law (e.g., stoning for "adultery" on the part of one who has enjoyed a valid marriage; mutilation for theft; etc.). Most contented themselves with emphasising that these punishments can never be inflicted on a culprit who receives proper advice from his lawyer: for not only are either four or two competent male witnesses required, respectively,[4] to the very act—unless the culprit not only confesses his guilt but maintains his confession to the bitter end—but any claim of right or supposed right, however specious, is regarded as giving rise to sufficient "doubt" to avert the punishment. Some, however, admitted that these punishments would never now be inflicted, as a matter of public policy. Accusations by husbands that adultery has been committed with their wives, common as they are elsewhere, here never come to court—both

[1] This, as noted above, represents a modification of normal Shāfi'ī principles in two directions, since these not only allow the heirs of blood themselves to kill the culprit, but to kill him (within certain limits) in the same way as he killed his victim.

[2] pp. 17 and 18.

[3] This is quite regular, following al-Shāfi'ī's later opinion.

[4] i.e., in regard to illicit sex relations and theft respectively.

because of the punishment for slander to which such an accusation, unless adequately supported, would properly expose the plaintiff and also because of the public ridicule it would evoke: but cases of theft, whether fulfilling the technical definition of *sariqa* or not, were previously punished at the discretion of the Nā'ib and are now dealt with, nominally at least, under the new Criminal Code. A sentence of eighty lashes for slander of a chaste person's continence (*qadhf*) had, however, fairly recently been passed, but was subsequently remitted by the injured party.

The usual Shāfi'ī rules of procedure, evidence, etc., are followed in general in all Sharī'a courts, including the "screening" (*tazkiya* or *ta'dīl*) and discrediting (*tajrīḥ or ṭa'n*)[1] of witnesses. It seems, however, that the discrediting of witnesses by finding some flaw in their general piety (a favourite device to secure the miscarriage of justice in ultra-conservative circles) is not taken too seriously—unless, one suspects, the Qāḍī is induced to be extra-orthodox on this point. The swearing of witnesses at the discretion of the court and the acceptance of documentary evidence have both been noted above as innovations authorised by the Sultan's Decree of 1942.

In questions of marriage, ordinary Shāfi'ī principles are followed regarding the father's or grandfather's right compulsorily to marry a virgin girl of any age to any socially-eligible suitor for an appropriate dower, even if he be blind or decrepit[2]; but it is apparently rare for an immature girl to be sent to her husband's house.[3] The dower (*mahr, ṣadāq*) named at the actual contract of marriage is always small[4] and its payment is not, it seems, normally demanded, except among certain arms-bearing tribes and urban artisans, either then or even at divorce or the death of one of the parties, unless bad blood has developed between them or their heirs. But a considerably larger sum, usually termed *daf'* but identified by some jurists with the bride's *jihāz*,[5] is also provided by the bridegroom—part, at least, normally in advance. It is this payment which represents the bride-wealth of pre-Islamic Arabia and elsewhere, and part may be recovered if the bride runs away from her husband early in married life; while the *mahr* represents the specifically Islamic payment which goes by that name.[6]

Where a wife deserts her husband he can get a judgment of "obedience" (restitution of conjugal rights) and she may even be imprisoned if she ignores this: but it is seldom, if ever, executed by the police dragging her back to her husband's house. Conditions inserted in marriage contracts in favour of the wife—e.g., that her husband will not marry a co-wife, or beat her, etc.—are regarded as void (except under article 60 of the Decree of 1942[7]): but stipulations in her favour are occasionally made the basis for a suspended divorce or an obligation assumed by means of a vow (*nadhr*), when they can no longer be disregarded. In marital disputes the Qur'anic prescription of two arbitrators is not, in practice, followed by the courts, and a wife can in no circumstances

[1] For these technical terms, see Glossary.

[2] Only a few Qāḍīs showed any inclination to follow the "weaker" Shāfi'ī opinion that a match which "injures" the bride in this way is invalid—although all recognised the exception where there was manifest hostility between guardian and ward. See Appendix C.

[3] But not unknown, if the husband "promises" to delay consummation.

[4] It varies, but seldom exceeds twenty shillings, it seems.

[5] The bride's outfit, furniture, jewellery, etc. The supply of this, once it has been promised and the marriage consummated, can now be enforced. (Art. 56 of Decree of 1942).

[6] In this connection see a very interesting law case described by Dr. R. B. Serjeant in the *Journal of the Royal Asiatic Society,* 1951, p. 156 ("Two Tribal Law Cases . . . The Dispute over the Runaway Wife").

[7] See p. 16 above.

get judicial divorce or dissolution of marriage for either cruelty or physical desertion. If she can prove a cruel beating she is regarded as justified in running away for a day or two, but the Chief Qāḍī maintained that her right to maintenance would lapse thereafter unless she returned to her husband or applied to the court.[1] In case of repeated cruelty, however, he admitted that she might be entitled to refuse to leave her own people to accompany him to his tribe. But much difference of opinion prevails among Qāḍīs on both these last two points.

Annulment of marriage on the grounds of the disease of either party is allowed according to ordinary Shāfi'ī principles. Similarly, a wife can get her marriage annulled if her husband, present or absent, is proved to be impecunious and unable to support her; but if the husband has property elsewhere he will be given a suitable time in which to obtain it,[2] while an absent husband will be contacted if possible (and then treated as though he were present): only if his whereabouts are unknown will she obtain her release without this preliminary. Nor will the Qāḍī seize and sell the property of an absent husband in execution of a maintenance order until an attempt, at least, has been made to contact him, etc.[3] These points are all matters of dispute in the Shāfi'ī school. Marriage contracts, in the towns, are almost invariably concluded before the Qāḍī, so irregular marriages are rare. Divorce by imprecation (*li'ān*)[4] is extremely rare, and by vow of continence (*īlā'*)[4] unknown, as is also delegation of the right of divorce to the wife: but suspended divorce, whether used as a threat or otherwise, is common, as is also divorce for a consideration.. The latter, however, must always be by the parties' consent (of the husband to the divorce, and of the wife to the consideration)[5]: it might, in suitable cases, be urged by the court, but never decreed or compelled.[6]

Questions of testate and intestate succession, acknowledgments, waqf, majority and the custody of infants (*ḥaḍāna*) are all alleged to follow normal Shāfi'ī principles in the towns, except for the points covered by the Sultan's Decree of 1942. The bedouin tend to limit the divorced mother's custody of infants to two years or some other period less than the Shāfi'ī seven, and in some cases to exclude females from rights of inheritance: but I was assured that orthodox Shāfi'ī law would be followed in any case which reached the regular Sharī'a courts. Land cases were also alleged to follow normal Shāfi'ī principles, but here local custom plays a big part: and all admitted that the popular *'uhda* contract (as a device to evade the prohibition of usury)[7] was contrary to the "dominant Shāfi'ī opinion"[8] so rigidly observed in most other respects, although strongly supported by most Ḥaḍramī jurists. The same largely applies to matters of purchase and sale, etc., where the pure Shāfi'ī principles are considerably modified in practice by local customs. This can be clearly seen in some of the articles of the Decree of 1942. Thus articles 1-7 provide that *mu'āṭāt* (purchase and sale by action, without words) is to be accepted as valid wherever it is

[1] The soundness of this view, however, is distinctly doubtful.

[2] This is contrary to the normal Shāfi'ī rule, which only allows three days in such circumstances (if it is more than 48 miles away).

[3] But it is alleged that even the immovable property of an absent husband will be sold to provide support for his wife where perishable articles, movables not likely to increase in value, and other chattels (in that order) are not available, or are no longer available, for this purpose.

[4] For these technical terms, see Glossary.

[5] Unless this is provided by a third party, which is regarded as valid.

[6] Although considerable pressure is probably sometimes applied. Here local practice follows the dominant Shāfi'ī view.

[7] See p. 16.

[8] See *al-Tuḥfa* vii, p. 38 (Bulaq edition).

customary; that adequate " delivery " may be given of a house or boat by allowing the donee (etc.) to exercise the rights of ownership, without removal of the donor's belongings; and that the sale of an article which has not been seen but accurately described is valid, although the purchaser has an option of rescission. It is also apparent in the statutory limitation of rates of interest on the *'uhda* contract, or on any other device which is regarded as not inconsistent with the prohibition of usury, to not more than ten per cent.[1] Slavery, on the other hand, is alleged no longer to exist, except where persons are seized and carried outside the Protectorate: but this probably means no more than that anyone in the position of a slave can gain his or her freedom by application to the authorities. In any case, past slavery would certainly be recognised by the courts in such cases as a claim to inheritance by right of patronage (*walā'*), or on the part of a child born to the deceased in concubinage with a woman who would have been his slave but for the abolition of that status.

The Kathīrī Sultanate.

The Wādī Ḥaḍramaut is divided between the Qu'ayṭī and the Kathīrī Sultanates. Thus Shibām, for instance, is Qu'ayṭī, and most of what has been said about the coastal regions applies there too; while Tarīm and Say'ūn are Kathīrī. There can, of course, be no doubt that the influence of the jurists of these two famous centres of learning is more felt in Shibām than in more distant Mukallā: but the fact that Shibām is far more devoted to trade than learning has tended to minimise this.

In general terms the jurists of the Kathīrī Sultanate may be said to be more learned, more conservative, and far more strongly 'Alawī[2] than those of Mukallā. But in the matter of conservatism there is one outstanding exception, for Sayyid 'Abd al-Raḥmān b. 'Ubaydillāh of Say'ūn, indubitably the most learned jurist whom I met in South Arabia and often called the Muftī of Ḥaḍramaut, is progressive to a degree. While, however, his learning seems everywhere to be acknowledged, many of his bolder opinions receive little support.

The Mukallā Decree of 1942 is not, of course, applied in the Kathīrī domains. It seems, indeed, that in only two instances has the Sultan here given any general instructions that the authoritative Shāfi'ī view[3] should be abandoned—namely, regarding the acceptance by the courts of officially authenticated documents of sale, agency, etc., from foreign countries (a virtual necessity in Ḥaḍramaut, whence so many have emigrated to South East Asia) and regarding the change of currency from Maria Theresa dollars to rupees introduced in 1943. Yet the principle seems to be admitted by most that he may properly issue such general instructions where circumstances demand this, or alternatively may give *ad hoc* directions to a Qāḍī to follow the view of some other recognised jurist in any specific case of hardship or complexity. It is also noteworthy that the papers of appointment of some (but not all) Qāḍīs expressly authorise them to give judgment, in suitable cases, in accordance with their own knowledge.[4]

As for the new Qu'ayṭī Criminal Code, the chief Qāḍī of Mukallā had visited Ḥaḍramaut just before my own arrival to win support for its provisions. Some

[1] Edict No. 1367 of 11 July, 1940. But c.p. also arts. 14 and 15 of the Decree of 1942 (p.17 above).

[2] i.e., champions of the rights and dignity of the family of the Prophet.

[3] The usual rule for ascertaining which of any variant views is "authoritative" is to follow the " Two Sheikhs "—al-Nawawī and al-Rāfi'ī; while, if they differ, al-Nawawī is to be preferred. In more detail, however, the Shāfi'īs of S. Arabia, Somaliland, etc., follow Ibn Ḥajar; while those of Egypt, Palestine, etc., follow al-Ramlī. But the matter of *'uhda* is an exception.

[4] i.e., as distinct from the testimony of witnesses. But Ibn Ḥajar can here be quoted in support of the right of all Qāḍīs to do so.

of the jurists of Tarīm had opposed it *in toto,* on the broad ground that the Sultan of Mukallā had no right to command his Qāḍīs to forsake the authoritative view of their school. They admitted, of course, the principle enunciated in the books of *fiqh* that a "weak" view[1] may be so strengthened by the command of a Sultan as to become the authoritative opinion and obligatory on the courts; but they argued that this only applies to a Sultan who has unrestricted power and not one whose power is as limited as that of the Quʻayṭī (or Kathīrī) Sultanate.

This argument shows the weakness of their juristic position. The history of Islam has been full of Sultans whose power was far from absolute, and all that seems relevant in this context is whether the Sultan concerned has the authority to give this particular command and the power to remove from office a Qāḍī who disobeys it: and the treaties between the two Sultanates and the Protecting Power leave no room for doubt on either of these points. It is difficult to be sure, moreover, whether the jurists concerned were really conscientiously unable to agree to *any* departure from the authoritative Shāfiʻī opinion[2] or whether the basis of their opposition was not their fear that, once the principle of the Sultan's right to issue such orders was admitted at all, it might be more difficult to resist the possible application of that principle to the vexed question of "equality in marriage."[3] To the ʻAlawīs of Ḥaḍramaut this is a burning question, for they regard the marriage of an ʻAlawī girl to a non-ʻAlawī as an insult to every descendant of the Prophet: and they go right beyond the generality of jurists in holding that such a match may be annulled even where both the girl and her guardian have consented thereto, on the grounds that all other ʻAlawīs also have the right to object.[4] This principle of equality in marriage is, of course, thoroughly undemocratic and may cause much unhappiness in individual circumstances: but it seems most unfortunate that the Quʻayṭīs included this matter among their earliest reforms, aware as they must have been of the bitterness of ʻAlawī feeling on the subject.

But the Chief Qāḍī of Mukallā found a much less frigid reception for the new Criminal Code among the other Ḥaḍramī jurists. He was, indeed, rebuked for the precipitancy of its composition and promulgation; for the fact that the jurists of the Wādī had not previously been consulted, particularly in view of their greater repute for learning; and for certain of its detailed provisions. Provided these were amended, however, Ibn ʻUbaydillāh and others were, apparently, willing to give the Law their blessing and support. Thus the future of the Code, in this Sultanate at least, now hangs on the willingness of the Quʻayṭīs to introduce the required amendments and the ability of its Kathīrī supporters to induce their Sultan to introduce it in his dominions, in defiance of a certain amount of opposition.[5]

---

[1] i.e., that supported by some Shāfiʻīs, but not by Ibn Ḥajar, etc.; or that accepted by some other recognised school.

[2] After stating categorically that for a Qāḍī to forsake the authoritative view in any particular, whatever the Sultan commanded, would be to disobey the Creator in order to obey a creature, Sayyid ʻAbdillāh admitted that there were exceptions to the rule about the "authoritative opinion" on the grounds of necessity (e.g., putting witnesses on oath).

[3] cp. the Mukallā Decree of 1942, art. 54 (p.16).

[4] This view has been upheld in a number of S. Arabian treatises. The five particulars in which local Shāfiʻī jurists usually insist on such "equality" are (*a*) freedom from such illnesses or defects as would give rise to a right to dissolution of marriage, (*b*) good character, (*c*) trade or profession, (*d*) blood and (*e*) freedom. Under blood, moreover, descendants of the Prophet rank first, then those of the family of Hāshim, then other members of the tribe of Quraysh, then arms-bearing tribes of pure Arab descent, tribes whose forebears were learned, etc.—all taking precedence over tribes of "unknown" origin or mixed descent. This is of great importance in Ḥaḍramaut.

[5] When I visited Ḥaḍramaut its adoption seemed probable.

The court system is much the same as in the Qu'ayṭī Sultanate. Sharī'a law is regarded as supreme, but Nā'ibs, Qā'ims and (in minor cases) the Ḥākim al-Sūq "[1] try criminal cases, largely following the light of nature[2] regarding the offences they punish and the sentences they impose. Commercial cases are said normally to be tried by the Nā'ibs sitting with two merchants; but the plaintiff may choose, or the defendant demand, that the case should go to the Sharī'a court, where the Qāḍī may or may not call in merchants to assist him.[3] Tribal cases go to the Nā'ib, assisted by tribal sheikhs—for in the tribal districts customary law, here as elsewhere, largely prevails. I was told that the repute of local Qāḍīs had until recently been low, but that there had not been any official complaints of bribery for the last two or three years.

In matters of procedure, the Kathīrīs keep more rigidly to orthodox Shāfi'ī principles than do the Qu'ayṭīs. Documentary evidence is not acceptable, except official documents from abroad, and a written bequest is not admissible *per se* unless two witnesses will testify to having heard an oral statement of its provisions: but their testimony to an "acknowledgment" by the testator that this document represents his last will and testament will have the same effect, even if they have no knowledge of its contents; while a wife is held justified in acting on a letter of divorcement. There are no official periods of limitation, although a Qāḍī would presumably draw appropriate conclusions[4] from a plaintiff's persistent failure, without excuse, to bring his case to court. Some Qāḍīs, as we have seen, are officially authorised to give judgment according to their personal knowledge, but this does not include mere conviction, and still less conjecture: no Qāḍī, however, should give a judgment which is contrary to his knowledge of the facts. Witnesses are screened and can be impugned; but only, apparently, regarding their habits of truthfulness and falsehood, and not their general piety.[5] And evidence of an alibi may always be brought by the defendant, as this is regarded as testimony to an affirmation rather than a negation.

In cases of murder, the culprit may not be executed until minor, insane or absent heirs of blood have all attained majority, regained sanity or returned home and decided either to demand or remit talion:[6] but execution is by a Government firing squad, and not by the method employed by the murderer.[5] There can be no talion where guilt is only established by compurgation.[6] If the heirs of blood choose blood-money, there is no further punishment for the culprit: but should they forgo even this he would probably be imprisoned by the State. No instances of talion for wounding could be remembered: instead, culprits are punished, where suitable, by the Nā'ib and ordered to pay compensation fixed by the Qāḍī.

Regarding the *ḥadd* punishments, I was told that amputation of a thief's hand had taken place only twice in recent years, the last occasion being some six years ago. This was usually attributed to the fact that this punishment could so easily be averted: but it was also admitted that other punishments were now considered more suitable and that the Sultan would probably never again allow

---

[1] It is noteworthy, however, that towns in Ḥaḍramaut are divided into quarters, where the tribal type of organisation prevails: and each quarter, to some extent, deals with its own market disputes, etc.

[2] Or in many cases ancient custom, no doubt.

[3] The disadvantages of this procedure have been noted above (p. 14).

[4] e.g., as to the trustworthiness of the witnesses produced in support; for this is the only point on which he may—officially—exercise his discretion.

[5] This represents a tendency which is clearly beneficial.

[6] This is pure Shāfi'ī law: see above, pp. 17, 18 and 19 respectively. It is also noteworthy that a *sayyid* accused of murder recently "acknowledged" the victim as his son, to exclude the possibility of talion; since no school except the Mālikīs ever allows an ascendant to suffer talion for the killing of a descendant.

mutilation. No cases of persons being sentenced for *zinā* (illicit sexual intercourse) could be remembered,[1] but this was not surprising owing to the virtual impossibility of a conviction for this offence under Shāfi'ī law. There had been no convictions for brigandage in the last seven years; but this would in any case today be punished by imprisonment. The only recent instance of a conviction for *shurb* (wine-drinking) concerned a Somali driver of a locust officer, and since the officer was in a hurry the Sultan had ordered a fine and the offender's expulsion from the territory: but indigenous cases, should they occur, would probably again be punished by imprisonment. An accusation of the *ḥadd* offence of *qadhf* (slander) could in theory still be brought, but such cases were usually settled out of court, or at most punished by fines or imprisonment by what amounts to a customary form of *ta'zīr*.[2]

In regard to marriage, I was informed that girls were often married at eleven or twelve in Shibām, but not till rather later among the better-class Kathīrīs: almost always, moreover, they had reached puberty. Polygamy is not, apparently, very common among *sayyids,* except where a man has a " secret " wife in addition to his regular establishment, or one wife in one town and another in another. Divorce, too, was said to be rare among the *sayyids,* except in the case of " secret " marriages: but it seems to be common enough among others.

There is some difference of opinion regarding the father's and grandfather's right to marry a girl by compulsion. Even Sayyid 'Abdillāh, for all his championship of the authoritative Shāfi'ī opinion, was emphatic that such marriages must be " beneficial," as Ibn Ziyād (the famous Yemenī contemporary of Ibn Ḥajar) had maintained in a special treatise. Such marriages were invalid in any case, he affirmed, if for less than the suitable dower, if open hostility existed between the bride and her guardian, or if open or secret hostility existed between the bride and her groom,[3] unless she nevertheless permitted consummation. Conditions inserted in marriage contracts in favour of wives are always considered void,[4] while those in favour of husbands are regarded as valid in some cases and void in others.[5] The Qur'anic prescription regarding the appointment of two arbitrators in cases of marital dispute is never used by the Kathīrī courts, nor can a wife ever get a divorce for cruelty. If a husband were to beat his wife cruelly and she ran away to her parents and stayed there until he demanded her return, Ibn 'Ubaydillāh considered her right to maintenance would not be forfeit, for it was the husband who had offended and who must assert that she could again trust herself to him: if this had happened more than once, moreover, she could successfully resist a claim to travel to his tribe with him. But the difficulty in all such cases would be to prove the beating by Muslim standards of evidence.[6]

It seems that dissolution of marriage because of a husband's failure to maintain his wife is very rare in Tarīm, where such dissolution is most unpopular (presumably because of the frequency of emigration). Instead, I was told, certain precautions are taken before a man emigrates: for he is virtually compelled either to leave property, to appoint a representative or to utter a suspended divorce

[1] Although I understand that *zinā* is, in fact, far from rare,

[2] A discretionary punishment: see above, p. 18.

[3] It is disputed, however, whether this is a condition of *iqdām* or of *ṣiḥḥa*. The former means that it is a sin for a man to proceed with the contract in such circumstances; the latter that the contract, if so made, is invalid *per se*. See Appendix C and Glossary.

[4] But such conditions could be reinforced by a suspended divorce or a vow in certain circumstances.

[5] e.g., a condition of the bride's virginity would be valid, but of her beauty void. This is normal Shāfi'ī doctrine.

[6] For even evidence to the wife being well and happy just before her husband's return home, and bruised and bleeding soon after, would not constitute any acceptable proof (in theory, at least) that he had beaten her.

which would become operative if maintenance failed.[1] The "three-day rule" advocated by many Shāfi'ī writers, according to which a wife is almost invariably[2] entitled to dissolution of marriage if she is unable to obtain maintenance for three consecutive days, is never applied, unless the husband is present and the wife can actually prove his destitution—a most difficult task, as it virtually amounts to proving a negative. If the husband claims to have property elsewhere he will be granted a suitable respite (at least unless it is more than forty-eight miles distant)[3], and the marriage of an absent husband is never dissolved without correspondence and delay.[4]

On this subject, however, Sayyid 'Abd al-Raḥmān bin 'Ubaydillāh holds highly independent views. He upholds the principle that a wife is entitled to dissolution of marriage in all cases where she cannot obtain maintenance, and has frequently given *fatwās* that a wife who cannot prove her husband's destitution—or whose circumstances are such that the Qāḍī, bound as he is to follow the authoritative Shāfi'ī opinion, cannot help her—should herself pronounce the dissolution of her marriage before witnesses, preferably after stating that she was deliberately following the opinion of those Imāms who grant relief in her particular circumstances. He even gives such *fatwās* where the wife's complaint is not failure of maintenance but protracted sexual desertion. In the case of inability to prove destitution, he quoted an opinion of Ibn Ziyād that the right of a wife herself to pronounce dissolution of marriage in such circumstances was the "authoritative" view; while for the right of dissolution for physical desertion he could quote only such authors as al-Samhūdī and 'Abd al-Qādir al-Jīlānī among the Shāfi'īs. He also quoted Aḥmad Mu'adhdhin bā Jamāl in support of the opinion that a weaker view in the Shāfi'ī school would become authoritative if it coincided with the dominant view in other schools—e.g., the Mālikī and Ḥanbalī opinions concerning the matter of physical desertion.

Other jurists, however, are most opposed to these *fatwās*, greatly though they respect Ibn 'Ubaydillāh's learning. They point out that to give wives the right themselves to pronounce the dissolution of their marriages without recourse to, or in defiance of, the courts would produce social chaos: only if she had been remarried by her guardian, after observing the *'idda* period following such dissolution, would the courts accord the latter any judicial recognition. As for the argument about the dominant views of other schools, the sufficient answer was that the local Qāḍīs had no adequate knowledge of such matters.[5]

Waqf property can never be sold in the Kathīrī Sultanate: but in case of need the lease of such property for, e.g., two hundred years may be "sold" and other waqf property bought with the price. *'Uhda* contracts are exceedingly common; and although the chief champion of the "authoritative Shāfi'ī opinion" admitted that their validity had originally been a "weak" view, he claimed that it had been "chosen" by Mas'ūd bin 'Alī al-'Ansī the Yemenī, whom he alleged to be a *mujtahid* of the "*bi'l-fatwā*" class.[6] Other devices to avoid the restrictive rules concerning usury are also frequently used, e.g., to sell a future date crop at much less than its normal price; to undertake to pay the lender a monthly sum, not specifically stated to be interest, by an obligation made binding by vow (*nadhr*); to acknowledge a debt in excess of the sum actually borrowed, etc. If, in the last case, the borrower were subsequently to claim that part of the

---

[1] cp. art. 65 of the Qu'ayṭī Decree of 1942 (p. 17). This rule is based on the *Tuḥfa*.
[2] i.e., except when the husband is present and able to support her.
[3] This is the official view: but he would probably in reality be granted respite in all cases.
[4] At the very least. For the sale of the property of an absent husband to provide maintenance for an indigent wife, see p. 21 note (3) above.
[5] And even Ibn 'Ubaydillāh admitted this answer to be convincing.
[6] Others, however, do not rate al-'Ansī so highly. For these technical terms, see Glossary.

sum acknowledged represented interest and was therefore illegal, the lender would be put on oath to the contrary; but the borrower would not be allowed to produce evidence to rebut his acknowledgment. Of slavery few legal traces were admitted to survive. There had been a comparatively recent case of inheritance successfully claimed by the descendants of the liberator of a slave whose descendant had died without heirs: and jurists admitted that the paternity of one who claimed to be the son of his father by a concubine slave would still be admitted if the woman acknowledged that such was her position. This shows that the status of slavery is still recognised by local opinion, although none can be forced to retain that status.

In questions of land, sale, lease and other contracts the Sharī'a is nominally applied, but local customs abound, whether brought into superficial agreement with the Sharī'a or not. But time did not permit detailed study of this interesting but complex point.[1]

Visits to the other " states " of the Eastern Protectorate—the Wāḥidī Sultanates of Balḥāf and Bīr 'Alī, the Mahrī Sultanate of Qishn and Socotra, and Sheikhdoms such as that of 'Irqa—could not be fitted in. The first two have concluded " adviser " treaties with Her Majesty's Government and conditions have improved greatly of late, and in the island of Socotra the authority of the Mahrī Sultan is undisputed; while elsewhere conditions are far from settled. But in none of these princedoms has the administration of justice and the organisation of the courts reached any standard comparable with that of the Qu'ayṭī and Kathīrī Sultanates.

The Western Protectorate.

Such work as I was able to do in the Western Aden Protectorate was limited to two long talks with the Qāḍīs of Zinjibār, Dathīna, Aḥwar, Ḥuṣn and Jibuti (a native of the Protectorate, home on leave); shorter talks with the Nā'ib (and virtual ruler) of the Fadhlī State, and with the " Ḥākim 'Urfī " of Zinjibār and of a neighbouring centre; with the Judicial Adviser, the President of the Court and several other leading jurists of Laḥej: and with a few Political Officers. In the broadest terms, the position seems to be as follows.

Outside Laḥej, all organised courts are of very recent institution. They have taken the place of the rough tribal justice administered by sheikhs, sultans and *manṣabs* in accordance with ancient law and customs, and the occasional judgments and awards of local *sayyids*, etc., in accordance with their real or assumed knowledge of the Sharī'a. Now, however, Qāḍīs' courts have been set up, in a considerable number of centres, to administer the Sharī'a in all questions of family law, contract, tort, etc. (and especially in land cases). But they have no criminal jurisdiction, with the exception of matters of blood-wit and compensation in cases of homicide and wounding; for criminal jurisdiction belongs to the Ḥākim 'Urfī (judge of customary law), who also deals with the punishment of persons accused, e.g., of assault, only passing the assessment of compensation to the Qāḍī.[2] In some localities, however, the Ḥākim 'Urfī's powers are strictly limited, and more serious cases have to be referred to a special committee. There is a general right of " appeal " in non-Sharī'a cases by petition to the " executive " (Sultan, Sheikh, Nā'ib, etc.). Small commercial cases go to the Ḥākim 'Urfī; while more important ones, if any, may be dealt with by a special committee.

[1] In this connexion reference might profitably be made to a work noted by Dr. R. B. Serjeant in his " Materials for South Arabian History " (B.S.O.A.S., xiii, 1950, p. 593) entitled " Jumal min al-Muhimmāt al-Dīnīya fī Ba'd al-Murtakab min al-Manāhī'l-Rabbānīya " by 'Alī b. Aḥmad b. Sa'īd Bā Ṣabrayn, which describes un-Islamic practices current in Ḥaḍramaut in 1877.

[2] In the court of the Ḥākim 'Urfī ancient custom still reigns supreme, as his name implies.

Tribal cases are dealt with by the Nā'ib or Sultan, assisted by tribal chiefs, chosen *ad hoc*. I was told that the distinction between Sharī'a cases and 'Urf cases was quite plain, and that no dispute between the courts commonly arose: it seems, however, that all cases go first to the Ḥākim 'Urfī—at least in some localities—and that it is his duty to pass on Sharī'a cases to the Qāḍī; while complaints that the former has usurped jurisdiction do in fact occur.

Cases of homicide are almost invariably settled by blood-wit, partly because the people are so poor as not lightly to forgo the rich compensation entailed, and partly for lack of central authority: so talion is almost unknown. All homicide cases go direct to the Nā'ib or Sultan himself. The *ḥadd* punishments are never imposed: so cases of theft, slander, etc., are all dealt with according to " custom " or the Ḥākim 'Urfī's discretion, unless the Sultan has either limited his jurisdiction or prescribed maximum penalties in the *qānūn asāsī* or " fundamental law."

Turning to the Sharī'a courts, it is noteworthy that the Qāḍīs with whom I talked were all either *sayyids* or Yemenīs, for such learning as exists in the Western Protectorate almost all emanates from the Yemen or Ḥaḍramaut. These courts profess to follow strict Shāfi'ī rules of procedure. Witnesses are nominally " screened," but in practice it seems that the court leaves it to the other party to impugn their eligibility if he can. It is just here, of course, that a major problem may arise in such conservative circles. Suppose the "plaintiff" produces as witnesses two respectable local merchants, with the truthfulness of whose testimony the Qāḍī is in fact satisfied, but the " defendant " can bring evidence to show that one or other of them is slack in prayer or fasting: is the Qāḍī in such a case to follow those ancient texts which utterly exclude the testimony of such witnesses and give judgment against his convictions, or is he to disregard their lack of piety and accept their testimony? The attitude adopted in the Eastern Protectorate has already been noted; but the Western Protectorate Qāḍīs whom I questioned at first professed that they could never accept the evidence of such witnesses, whatever their feelings regarding the truthfulness of their evidence in the particular case in issue: when pressed, however, only the Qāḍī of Dathīna maintained this attitude, the rest subscribing to the well-known rule that in degenerate days a Qāḍī must be content with the best witnesses available. The Qāḍī of Jibuti advocated the expedient, when a defendant attacked the plaintiff's witnesses on grounds of impiety, of allowing evidence of the defendant's own religious omissions: where this were forthcoming, he said, he should not be allowed to discredit witnesses whose impiety was no greater than his own. All, moreover, agreed that witnesses should be questioned one by one,[1] and most that they might be put on oath in case of doubt. It is obvious, however, that this question of the eligibility of witnesses gives enormous scope for judicial corruption.

Documentary evidence is in theory unacceptable, although all in fact accept documents which bear the handwriting of a well known Qāḍī, or papers bearing an official stamp. Most of the Qāḍīs said that they would also in practice accept a written bequest where two witnesses could testify to the testator's statement that it was his, although they had heard no oral statement of its terms: but all considered this against the " authoritative " view of their school, and obviously had no idea of the difference between such testimony to the creation of the will on the one hand and to subsequent acknowledgment of it on the other. A Qāḍī, they all agreed, might certainly give judgment according to his personal knowledge, but not according to his conviction or discretion: yet there can, of course, be no doubt that it is according to his discretion that he does in fact frequently decide, in the Western Aden Protectorate as elsewhere; the only question is what form this discretion takes and how it is justified.

[1] This is the normal Shāfi'ī rule, and virtually amounts to cross-examination by the court.

Contracts of marriage, in the towns, are normally concluded before the Qāḍī and duly registered, while divorces are also supposed to be registered, and do not seem very frequent; but both marriage and divorce are valid, of course, whether registered or not. Bride-price (*daf'*) is paid to the father, who frequently spends it all, or even more, on the *jihāz* (trousseau, furniture, etc.): but this differs widely according to the locality and individual concerned, since it is not legally obligatory on a father to provide *jihāz* at all and he may instead put all the *daf'* in his own pocket. This payment, while plainly originating in the ancient bride-wealth, is now sometimes likened to the "prompt dower" (*mahr mu'ajjal*) of the Sharī'a, and some Qāḍīs professed[1] that they would give judgment that it belonged to the bride if she were, most improbably, to claim it. The payment actually fixed as "*mahr*" (dower) is never claimed until divorce or the death of one of the parties, so it is often termed "deferred dower." Other customary payments are the "*ṣubḥīya*" from husband to wife on the morning after the consummation of marriage, and the "*raḍwa*" given by a husband to his first wife at the time when he marries another. Such gifts can apparently be enforced, where customary, even if never delivered nor even specifically promised.[2] The normal Shāfi'ī rules about the giving of daughters or granddaughters compulsorily in marriage are applied, and no claim by the girl of hardship or damage would be entertained by the courts unless she alleged "inequality," insufficient dower, or the "hostility" of her guardian.[3]

Divorce by *li'ān, īlā'*[4] or powers delegated to the wife herself are apparently unknown. One case of *ẓihār* was mentioned, where expiation had been ordered; while *mubāra'a* is regarded as virtually synonymous with *khul'*,[4] and suspended divorce is very common, whether used as a threat or safeguard to the wife. Dissolution of marriage for cruelty is never allowed, nor for physical desertion: and while the system of arbitration is apparently sometimes used in cases of marital dispute, the recommendations of the arbitrators are never enforced by the courts. It seems that no petitions for dissolution of marriage for failure of support where the husband is present ever reach the courts: but, if they did, the Qāḍīs professed that they would dissolve the marriage after a suitable interval (some said three days, others longer) if the husband was destitute. Where a husband was absent they affirmed that they would seize his property without delay to supply his wife's necessary maintenance (after the usual proof and oath, etc.), but that they would never dissolve the marriage without an attempt to contact him by correspondence, ascertain his condition, and act accordingly. Where the husband was of wholly unknown whereabouts and therefore could not be contacted, however, most opined that they would give some two months' respite before dissolving the marriage; but the Qāḍī of Dathīna maintained that he would wait only three days. All were bitterly opposed to Sayyid bin 'Ubaydillāh's *fatwās* about a wife presuming herself to dissolve her marriage; and they said that they would in no case recognise such action, even if she had meanwhile been remarried. The procedures of *taḥkīm* and *tawlīya*[5] in marriage are apparently unknown.

[1] This, however, should be taken with reserve. The treatment of the *daf'* in the W.A.P. provides a good illustration of the superficial islamicisation of something earlier than, and really contrary to, the Sharī'a.

[2] This is now also true in Mukallā, under arts. 57 and 58 of the Decree of 1942, which presumably means that the practice in fact prevailed there previously.

[3] See above, p. 25.

[4] For all these technical terms, see Glossary.

[5] *Taḥkīm* is the term used when a man and woman who wish to marry in the absence both of her guardian and of any regular Qāḍī agree to empower someone with adequate knowledge of the law to act for the latter in marrying them; while *tawlīya* is the term used when a woman who wishes to marry in the absence of both her guardian and any regular Qāḍī authorises anyone eligible as a witness to act in the place of the former (i.e., her guardian).

The normal Shāfi'ī rules about *'idda*[1] are said to be strictly observed. Those concerning custody of infants (*ḥaḍāna*) are also, it seems, strictly applied by the courts, including the rule that a divorced mother may not take the child away from the locality where the father lives, but that a father may take his child, however young, if he is travelling in order to settle permanently elsewhere: but some tribes have a custom that the father may claim his child well before the age of seven, and this may be enforced locally. Bequests are said to be fairly common in the towns and to be governed by the usual Shāfi'ī rules: most, however, admitted that they would disregard an acknowledgment made in death sickness in favour of one heir where the circumstances showed that the motive was to defraud others (the Qāḍī of Dathīna alone dissenting).[2] In inheritance many tribes formerly ignored the rights of females, and this persists in parts: but the Qāḍīs, I was assured, would themselves always give judgment according to the books, and the influence of the Sharī'a was spreading.[3] Questions of majority, etc., go by ordinary Shāfi'ī rules. There are few waqfs, and the Qāḍīs admitted that they had little knowledge of the details of this branch of the law. Regarding slavery they gave the usual answers: no cases of claims of inheritance by patronage had come to their courts, but such would be valid if brought; and so would a claim of paternity by concubinage, if the concubine acknowledged that such was her status.

The contract of *'uhda* is very common. Other devices to evade the laws of usury are a misuse of the contract of *salam* (i.e., sale of future crops), the double-sale, the acknowledgment of the debt of a sum really representing capital and interest, etc. The vow (*nadhr*) is here used as a form of gift rather than a means of assuming an obligation, and is not commonly phrased to come into operation, e.g., " three days before my death," as a device to evade the Qur'anic rules of inheritance.

Most Qāḍīs are apparently expressly instructed, either orally or in their letters of appointment, to follow the view of Ibn Ḥajar (or the *Tuḥfa*) in all matters of dispute. They thus have no liberty to take a broader view and apply some other opinion even where the public interests seem to require this—although certain minor exceptions in practice have already been noted. While in general very conservative, they freely admitted that certain variations would be beneficial; but they were apprehensive that such would be quashed on appeal. All accepted the principle that the Sultan or other ruler may command the adoption of a variant view in specific circumstances, and they felt that the issue of such instructions would be most helpful, in the interests both of uniformity and the introduction of reforms: but such instructions, they maintained, should be applied in the Colony as well as the Protectorate, because it was in the Colony that appeals were heard.

At present appeals from Sharī'a courts are forwarded by Political Officers to the Headquarters of the Western Aden Protectorate and are thence referred to some eminent jurist at the discretion of the Resident Adviser. This method is used partly because there is no link between the different Sultanates, etc., except the Protecting Power, and partly because the uncertainty as to which jurist will hear the appeal lessens any danger of corruption. Such appeals take the form of " revision " rather than a rehearing of the case.

The Ḥākim 'Urfī seems to follow Islamic rules of procedure in broad outline—e.g., concerning the burden of proof, the putting of oaths, etc.—but is not bound thereby. The evidence of fellow-tribesmen is often, moreover, regarded as wholly unacceptable in his court. " Slander " is actionable in the 'Urfī courts, if at all, for cases of " *ḥasham* " (insult) are within their exclusive competence.

[1] The period during which a widowed or divorced woman may not remarry.
[2] cp. art. 40 of the Mukallā Decree (p. 16): but elsewhere no such authority exists.
[3] Largely, of course, through British influence.

Dr. R. B. Serjeant has collected some most interesting legal documents in connection with South Arabian customary law which throw much light on the relevant procedure. Court records, apparently, normally comprise the *sās* (ordering of procedure) the *da'wā* (suit or accusation), the *taqwā* (defence or counterclaim) and the *ḥukm* (judgment). Cases are, of course, often settled out of court, or by mutual consent with the "judge" acting as arbitrator: but not infrequently the tribal judge or judges give an actual award (*qaḍā'*), after much heated argument between the individuals or tribal representatives concerned. Hostages and guarantees of good faith (e.g., the parties' daggers) are commonly handed over either to the judge or to some third party.[1]

Laḥej

The Sultanate of Laḥej is chiefly remarkable, in regard to its judicial organisation, for the fact that its Sharī'a courts have been in existence considerably longer than those of any other part of the Western Protectorate and enjoy a very extensive jurisdiction, shared only with the Ḥākim al-Sūq, a sort of agricultural customary court, and the *ad hoc* treatment of tribal cases.[2]

Talion for "deliberate" homicide is extremely rare, owing partly to the difficulty in producing adequate proof and partly to the common preference for blood-wit. The usual Shāfi'ī rules are followed regarding minor, insane or absent heirs of blood: but on the rare occasions when talion has been inflicted the actual execution has been by a firing-squad provided by the police,[3] while where blood-money is chosen by the heirs the Government may also sometimes impose a term of imprisonment in the interests of public security.[4] Talion in cases of wounding has apparently not been enforced within living memory, and it seems most unlikely that it would ever now be allowed.

Of the *ḥadd* punishments, mutilation for theft was last inflicted, it seems, in 1924, since when the Sultan has given unofficial instructions that this is not to happen again. No case of stoning or beating for illicit sex relations (*zinā*) could be remembered: but in principle the punishment of stoning would not now be inflicted, while that of beating would. A beating for wine-drinking (*shurb*) was inflicted some two years ago, but there are very few such cases, since testimony to a man smelling of drink, etc., is not considered sufficient and nothing less than a sustained confession or adequate testimony to the very act of drinking is required.[5] No case of the *ḥadd* punishment for slander (*qadhf*) could be remembered, but a discretionary punishment is sometimes imposed for insults. Such punishments in Laḥej, it seems, almost always mean imprisonment, and there is a rough system of maximum and minimum penalties for different offences.

The Qāḍīs professedly follow Islamic procedure in all particulars, but the Chief of Police takes certain extra-judicial "precautions" regarding suspects, etc.[6] No special procedure is followed in commercial cases, and local customs contrary to Sharī'a law are allegedly never applied as such (except, presumably, in agricultural matters and minor affairs of the market): instead, recourse is had to one of the various devices by which such customs can receive a colour of orthodoxy. The *'uhda* device is not, apparently, officially recognised,[7] but

[1] See article on "Two Tribal Cases" by Dr. R. B. Serjeant in J.R.A.S., 1951, pp. 33 ff.

[2] Either by the Ḥakim al-Sūq, a specially appointed representative of the Sultan or the Sultan himself.

[3] As in the Qu'ayṭī and the Kathīrī Sultanates.

[4] This, as noted above, is perfectly correct in Sharī'a law.

[5] This, again, is pure Shafi'ī doctrine.

[6] p. 18. This is perfectly normal Islamic practice.

[7] Which seems very strange, and perhaps of dubious validity, since the contract is widespread in Laḥej—as elsewhere in the Protectorate.

acknowledgments and vows, double sales, etc., are all used to evade the rules prohibiting "usury." Witnesses are "screened," may be impugned, are sometimes interviewed and questioned alone and may *not* be put on oath: but on the vexed question of the discrediting of witnesses for slackness in their religious duties, some of the jurists questioned admitted that the Qāḍī would in fact use his discretion, to a considerable extent, as to what testimony was admissible and what was not. Only "official" documents are accepted without oral testimony, and written bequests would not be recognised unless witnesses could speak to their detailed contents; while even testimony to the acknowledgment of a written bequest would not be admitted unless the document remained thereafter in the safe keeping of the witnesses or the court. Testimony to a denial is not allowed except in the case of failure of maintenance or the existence of an alibi, where the testimony is in fact regarded as supporting an affirmation (i.e., the debt of maintenance or the fact of being elsewhere at the time). Even so, however, the President of the Court was doubtful of their admissibility.

In questions of marriage the local opinion regarding *jabr* (compulsory marriage) is much as elsewhere, except that the absence of hostility between the bride and her groom is regarded as a condition of "*iqdām*" rather than "*ṣiḥḥa*"[1]: that is, it is considered wrong for a guardian to conclude the contract in such cases, but that the contract, if concluded, cannot be annulled. The system of appointing two arbitrators in cases of marital dispute is not used, nor can a wife in any circumstances get a judicial dissolution of marriage for cruelty. If a wife could prove that she had been cruelly beaten she would be held justified in running away, and until the husband demanded her return she would remain entitled to maintenance (on the grounds that she had not refused him his rights); while in cases of repeated ill-treatment she would be regarded as justified in refusing to travel with him. But proof of such ill-treatment would be very hard to produce, as even the marks of blows and strong circumstantial evidence would not suffice.

In cases of failure of maintenance, however, the Laḥej courts seem rather more favourable to wives. If a husband is present and able to support his wife he is, as elsewhere, forced to do so; while, if he cannot, she is granted dissolution of marriage (allegedly) after three days, and repute[2] of destitution is accepted as adequate proof. Nor is he, apparently, allowed any longer period for the production of property from a distance. Where an absent husband has property in Laḥej this would be seized in execution without delay, whether movable or immovable, but the marriage would not be dissolved until he had been contacted: only if he had no property in Laḥej and was of wholly unknown whereabouts would the marriage be dissolved (again allegedly after three days). These answers were given with considerable confidence and apparent conviction.

The most controversial legal question in Laḥej concerns a Code for the organisation of the courts and their procedure which was introduced in 1949. This was largely based on the Egyptian Code of 1931 (but in an enormously truncated and modified form) and had been drawn up by the Judicial Adviser, who had recently returned from some twelve years at the Azhar. It provides for courts of limited and general jurisdiction, for a system of appeals and revision, and for the detailed work of the courts. But the points of greatest controversy in the Sultanate are the provisions that courts of general jurisdiction should consist of a bench of Qāḍīs giving judgment by agreement or a majority view;[3] that a summons to a defendant to appear must include, in all major cases, a statement of the points at issue seriatim, together with other relevant

---

[1] See above, p. 25.

[2] i.e., *shuhra.*

[3] Art. 6.

details;[1] that a plea should not be invalidated by the plaintiff's failure to use particular phrases or expressions;[2] that the Qāḍī should question him about any omission, and that such questioning should not be considered "prompting" unless it actually increased his knowledge;[2] that even if the plaintiff failed to correct his plea the court might question the defendant and act on his confession, if any;[3] that the defendant must answer each point of the charge or plea separately;[4] that third parties might be allowed to intervene in an action, under certain conditions;[5] that the failure of a party to answer a question put to him by the other, or to appear for questioning when required to do so, might be taken into account by the court in its findings;[6] that judgment must be given according to the articles of this Code and "the most authoritative Shāfi'ī opinion" in the absence of any other law laying down special rules for the case, but that any rules so prescribed must be obeyed;[7] that if it seemed necessary, in the interests of justice or the public welfare, to abandon the most authoritative Shāfi'ī opinion in any matter and substitute some weaker Shāfi'ī opinion or that of some other school, the Sultan should command the formation of a committee to decide what view should be adopted and should embody the same in a Decree, to be added to existing Decrees of the same sort;[8] that no Qāḍī might issue a *fatwā* in any claim due to be heard (or which had been heard) by any court of law, any *fatwā* issued contrary to this rule should be entirely disregarded, and no court should regard itself as in any way bound by a *fatwā* issued before litigation began: [9] that Qāḍīs must not entertain cases in which the plaintiff had failed, without excuse, to bring his action for fifteen years (or, in regard to inheritance and waqf, thirty-three years), provided the right claimed were denied throughout this period;[10] and that ex parte judgments might be given without further warning or judicial appointment of a representative, when the defendant had failed either to appear or to send a representative after proper summons.[11]

Several of these points are of great interest, particularly articles 98 and 99—to which further reference will be made throughout this Survey.

The Colony.

The position with regard to Sharī'a law in the Colony of Aden is entirely different from that in the Protectorate—or, indeed, in any of the East African Colonies or Protectorates. Its application is limited to the family law of Muslims together with their gifts, waqfs and right of "pre-emption,"[12] and it is administered by the same judge, magistrates and courts as apply all other matters of civil and criminal law. This system is, of course, a direct heritage of Aden's historical connection with Bombay. Statutory authority for the application of Sharī'a law in these matters is provided by section 41 of the Interpretation and General Clauses Ordinance, 1937, which reads:—"Subject to the provisions of any Statute . . . and of any enactment . . . Courts in the Colony shall exercise their jurisdiction in conformity with usage . . . ", and continues "nothing in this section shall prevent the continued[13] application of rules or customs of any community in matters of marriage, dower, divorce, woman's property, minority, guardianship, maintenance, legitimacy, succession, inheritance, coparceners and coparcenary property, wills, gifts, religious and charitable endowments, waqfs, debts, pre-emption, partition, and any other matters in any case in which prior to the commencement of this Ordinance such rules or customs would have been

[1] Art. 46. [2] Art. 75.
[3] Art. 76. [4] Art. 80.
[5] Art. 86. [6] Art. 92.
[7] Art. 98. [8] Art. 99.
[9] Art. 100. [10] Art. 102.
[11] Art. 106. [12] i.e., *shuf'a*.
[13] Such application was originally based on Bombay Regulation 4 of 1827. See below, in the Somaliland and Zanzibar sections of this Survey, pp. 40 and 60.

applied, unless such rules or customs have been expressly superseded by legislation coming into operation subsequent to the commencement of this Ordinance."

Examples of such subsequent legislation are, however, not wanting. Thus the Majority Ordinance and the Guardians and Wards Ordinance, both of 1937, virtually reproduce the relevant Indian Acts. Similarly the Oaths Ordinance, 1938, corresponds with parallel legislation in India, Uganda, Zanzibar, etc., and does something to bridge the gulf between Muslim and English principles of procedure.[1] The Succession Ordinance, 1938, which expressly excepts Muslims from those provisions which run counter to Sharī'a law in any major respect, is again a virtual replica of the Indian Succession Act: and the Cutchi Memons Ordinance, 1939, also follows an Indian model. Of more questionable drafting is the Muhammadan[2] Waqf Ordinance, 1939, which combines the equivalent of the Indian Mussalman Wakf Validating Act, 1913, with provisions for the better management of waqf property, the proper maintenance and publication of waqf accounts, and other details. Here the point at issue is that the Aden Ordinance allows a Shāfi'ī[3] Muslim, as well as a Ḥanafī, to make a waqf in which the first charge is his own maintenance and support or the payment of his own debts:[4] for while justification for this can be found in the Ḥanafī school in the dicta of Abū Yūsuf, no authority whatever appears to exist among Shāfi'ī jurists for this proposition as such. I was unable, however, to ascertain whether this innovation was intended as a deliberate extension to Shāfi'īs of a facility enjoyed by Ḥanafīs, regardless of their traditional denial of its validity; whether the reference to Shafi'īs was included merely because the majority of the inhabitants of Aden—unlike India—follow that school, and the conflict of opinion between the schools on this point was not appreciated; or whether its authors had realised that Shāfi'īs can in fact attain this same result by the device of not naming themselves as such as beneficiaries but by means of some circumlocution or mode of description,[5] and were determined to call a spade a spade. But in any case those Arabs whom I questioned were quite unaware of this provision; and I heard of no instance of a Shāfi'ī having availed himself of its terms. It is noteworthy in this context that the Zanzibar Waqf Validating Decree states that such waqfs are valid for Ḥanafīs and Ibāḍīs (only), although there, too, the Shāfi'īs are in a majority. In addition, the objections relevant to the Indian Act are of course equally applicable to this Ordinance, e.g., that while it was presumably designed to reintroduce " pure " Sharī'a law it has scarcely accomplished that purpose, in at least three respects: —

(*a*) because it seems doubtful whether the courts would regard a waqf to a third party and his children in perpetuity as valid, even where the ultimate beneficiary is some permanent charity;[6]

(*b*) because it seems probable that the courts in Aden would follow the restricted view of the meaning of an " implied " reservation for some permanent charity, etc., adopted by the courts in India;[7]

(*c*) because it is highly questionable whether section 5 (" Nothing in this part shall affect any custom or usage whether local or prevalent among Muhammadans

[1] cp. the Evidence Ordinance, 1939. Again, see below (under Zanzibar), p. 61.

[2] Here spelt " Mohammedan " and " Wakf " respectively: but see Introduction regarding the liberty taken in re-spelling Arabic words, to avoid confusion and possible misconception.

[3] Spelt " Shafei."

[4] Sect. 3.

[5] e.g., where the income is reserved, during the life of the founder, for the Imām of such and such a mosque, or for " the eldest of my father's sons "—the Imām and eldest son concerned being in both cases the founder himself. This is an interesting example of a " trick " by which an evasion of the ordinary law is regarded as justified: cp. al-Shaybānī's *Kitāb al-Makhārij fi'l-Ḥiyal*, edited by Dr. J. Schacht.

[6] cp. sect. 3. See Tyabji's *Muhammadan Law* (3rd Ed.) p. 600.

[7] Sects. 2 and 3. See ibid, p. 600.

of any particular class or sect") would be held to preserve the validity of a Shāfi'ī waqf in which there was no ultimate reservation for a permanent charity at all.

Again, the Islamic law of marriage is in part transcended in the Colony by certain provisions of the Marriage (Christian) Ordinance, 1940, and the Indian Penal Code. The former would make it possible for a Muslim woman of more than twenty-one years of age—or less, if previously married[1]—to marry a Christian man, were it not for the express provision that "Nothing in this Ordinance shall be deemed to validate any marriage which the personal law applicable to either of the parties forbids"[2]; while it seems that a marriage between a Muslim man and a Christian woman, perfectly valid according to most schools of Islamic law, would be regarded as void in Aden unless solemnised according to the provisions of this Ordinance.[3] No marriage so solemnised, moreover, may be dissolved otherwise than by a judicial decree under the Divorce Ordinance, 1938; while the latter expressly provides that "It shall be no defence to a charge of adultery that the persons alleged to have committed it have contracted a polygamous marriage permitted by their personal law."[4] As for the Indian Penal Code, section 375 includes in its definition of rape the act of a man who consummates his marriage with a child wife before she reaches the age of thirteen; and this provision is both more stringent and more definite than the Sharī'a.[5]

Two more examples of recent legislation on matters of personal status which affect Muslims must also be noted. The Child Marriage Restraint Ordinance, 1939, makes no attempt to declare child marriages invalid *per se*, but prescribes penalties for the man who contracts a child marriage,[6] for any persons who perform or assist at such a marriage (unless they had reason to believe it was not such)[7] and for the guardian, whether *de jure* or *de facto*, who either promotes it or even negligently fails to prevent it:[8] and it defines a child marriage as one in which the groom has not reached the age of eighteen and the bride fourteen.[9] If the court has reason to believe that a child marriage is about to be solemnised it may issue an injunction against any persons concerned; and if they proceed with the marriage in disregard of this injunction they become liable to heavier penalties.[10] Again, the Qādī[11] Ordinance of 1943 provides for the appointment of a Qādī[12] to maintain registers of Muslim marriages and divorces,[13] but expressly states that "nothing contained herein shall be deemed to confer any judicial powers on the Qādī[14] . . ." In other words, the so-called Qādī is no more than a *ma'dhūn* or registrar of marriages.

This last point, it seems, is a cause of some dissatisfaction in the Colony. It is, of course, common practice in most East African Colonies for the British courts to hear cases of personal status between, e.g., Indian Muslims; although such cases are extremely rare, since the different Indian communities almost invariably settle all such cases among themselves: but books of reference are obtainable in English covering both the Hanafī and Ithnā 'Asharī law as applied in India, and much assistance can also be obtained from the Indian Reports. The case is very different regarding Arabs and others of the Shāfi'ī rite, since there

[1] Sect. 2.
[2] Sects. 11 and 13.
[3] Sect. 3.
[4] Sect. 5(4).
[5] See below, pp. 44 etc.
[6] Sects. 3, 4 and 7.
[7] Sect. 5.
[8] Sect. 6.
[9] Sect. 2. It is noteworthy in this connection that in India the Child Marriage Restraint Act was amended in 1949, the minimum age for the bride being raised to fifteen.
[10] Sect. 10.
[11] Spelt "Qadhi" in this Ordinance, but see Introduction for spelling of Arabic words.
[12] Sect. 3.
[13] Sects. 4-15.
[14] Sect. 16.

is a remarkable dearth of both text books and law reports to aid an English court in deciding points of Shāfi'ī law, while the local Muslims are accustomed in most African Colonies to have recourse to their own courts in such matters. In addition, it is felt that litigation before a local Qāḍī would be both cheaper and more expeditious. Whether it would be so satisfactory in other ways, however, is of course a moot point—for it is certain that as the law now stands he would make less concessions to humanitarian principles.

From conversations with the British Judge, a leading Indian Muslim lawyer, the Qāḍī, and two or three of the most learned local jurists, the following points emerged.

Procedure in the courts is, of course, entirely governed by the Evidence Ordinance, 1939, and other enactments. In cases where Islamic law is applicable expert evidence of its substance and application is admissible, presumably on the basis of expert evidence to "custom" rather than "foreign law." In "mixed cases" (i.e., conflict) the law of the defendant is usually applicable, and all schools of Islamic law are regarded as equally authoritative: but such cases are not, apparently, common. While, moreover, the court normally considers itself strictly bound by the rules of the school concerned, a certain tendency naturally exists to be influenced by British ideas of equity and justice. Thus in a case where a father married an adult but virgin daughter entirely contrary to her wishes the Supreme Court dissolved the marriage, partly on the basis of statements in the writings of modern Muslim jurists such as Amir Ali that such compulsion was foreign to Islam (statements, it may be remarked, which do more credit to these eminent writers' humanitarian principles than to their objective knowledge of the historical texts), and partly because there were circumstances in this particular case which were held to provide adequate evidence of such hostility between father and daughter as to destroy his right to marry her by compulsion even if that right originally existed.[1] It seems probable, moreover, that the compulsory marriage of an adult woman would now always be held voidable by the Aden court, even if the parties were Shāfi'īs. Again, the court would no doubt endeavour to regard the marriage by compulsion of a young daughter to a decrepit or blind old man as itself evidence of such hostility, but might not, in the event, feel free to do so.[2] As for cruelty after marriage, this is never held to entitle the wife to a judicial dissolution of marriage[3] but is regarded as an adequate defence to a petition for "restitution of conjugal rights": and this, coupled with the wife's continued right to maintenance in such circumstances, would normally induce her husband to divorce her. The arbitration procedure advocated in the Qur'ān is never used in such cases. With regard to deserted wives, applications for maintenance orders[4] go to the magistrates' courts and claims for recovery of past maintenance to the Supreme Court. No case has, apparently, recently occurred of a petition by a wife for dissolution of marriage on the grounds that her husband, though present and not impecunious, refused to maintain her, probably because a maintenance order would normally be adequate in such circumstances. Dissolution of marriage on the grounds of his inability to maintain her would, of course, depend on the school of the defendant. If the husband were absent but of known locality no dissolution would normally be granted, to either a Hanafī or Shāfi'ī wife, until evidence was forthcoming that he was destitute: and the procedure in such cases might be for the court to request the Qāḍī to write to the Qāḍī of the town where the

[1] It was argued for the father, however, that the circumstances were not such as to show that degree of hostility which alone should properly deprive him of his right.

[2] Where such a marriage is plainly injurious, however, it would almost certainly be held voidable by the Court.

[3] Only the Mālikīs allow this, and there are very few Mālikīs in Aden.

[4] i.e., litigation regarding current rather than past maintenance.

husband was residing, for the court to forward letters from the wife through official channels, or for the court itself to correspond with the local administrative authorities.[1] But where a husband is of unknown whereabouts (which seems to be the usual allegation in such cases) the court gives a decree *nisi* provided that the wife is still residing in her husband's house, that there is no evidence of her *nushūz* (marital disobedience) and that none of his relatives are prepared to support her: and this decree is made absolute three months later, if the position remains the same. This last practice represents, of course, a thoroughly British rather than Muslim approach to the subject, but differs little in result from the rule adopted in the Sharī'a courts of the Protectorate in such circumstances.[2] No equivalent exists in the Colony to the important reforms introduced in India by the Dissolution of Muslim Marriages Act, 1939—which seems regrettable.

Cases concerning the custody of children go by the strict rules of the school concerned, except for the usual tendency of British courts to try to make the welfare of the child the major consideration. Testate and intestate succession, again, follow the school of the deceased,[3] except in so far as the Succession Ordinance has varied the priority of certain debts, and made English machinery applicable in probate and administration. The position regarding waqfs is considered[4] to be somewhat unsatisfactory, as the advisory committee prescribed in the Ordinance seems never to be used. There has never in the Judge's experience been a sale of waqf property, but the income thereof is often used in ways authorised by the Ordinance[5] but disputed among the standard Muslim authorities. No case of pre-emption has apparently occurred in which the court has had to decide whether the purchaser, as well as the vendor and the pre-emptor, must be a Muslim,[6] but there would always be a tendency for the court to follow the decisions of the High Court of Bombay, for historical reasons. In any case it is clear that the right of pre-emption is regarded in Aden as a personal right rather than one " attaching to the land " or common to all the inhabitants. In a case between, e.g., a Ḥanafī and a Shāfi'ī, moreover, it seems that the more restricted Shāfi'ī right of pre-emption (i.e., by co-owners only) should in all cases be applied: on general principles, where the vendor is a Shāfi'ī, and on the principle of reciprocity, where the pre-emptor is one.

From a talk with one of the outstanding Indian lawyers I gathered that the Indian communities in Aden—Ḥanafīs, Ithnā 'Asharīs, Bohoras, Memons and Khojas of both the Ismā'īlī and Ithnā 'Asharī factions—normally settle questions of family law within their community by means of their Community Councils, etc.,[7] but that there is a tendency among some of the younger members to insist on taking cases to court. Divorce seems to be very rare among such communities —as, indeed, among most Indian Muslims. He seemed entirely ignorant of the Shāfi'ī rules concerning waqf and said that although he had drawn up waqf deeds for Ḥanafīs and Shī'īs he had never done so for a Shāfi'ī. He was equally vague about the complications of the law of pre-emption where the parties were of different schools; and, indeed, about the detailed provisions of Shāfi'ī law in general.

---

[1] e.g., the local D.C. of a British Colony.

[2] For which there is some authority in Shāfi'ī law, but none in the Ḥanafī system.

[3] Except that the return to the spouse relict would, apparently, always be allowed in the absence of any other heir—on Indian precedents.

[4] e.g., by the Judge.

[5] e.g., the Court may settle, cancel or alter a scheme for the administration of a waqf or may direct " the application, investment, or deposit of the funds of a waqf or any surplus thereof " in a particular manner or to a particular purpose—provided it is " not inconsistent with the objects and purposes of the waqf " (sect. 21(2)).

[6] See the conflict of decisions in India on this point. cp. Tyabji, pp. 663ff.

[7] For more details, see Appendix B.

The Qāḍī was emphatic that his position was really that of a *ma'dhūn*. Besides acting as registrar of marriages and divorces[1] he sometimes acts as an arbitrator, but with no coercive powers. In the past, he said, the court used sometimes to enforce the decisions of his predecessors, but this practice had fallen into disuse (which presumably means that cases used on occasions to be officially referred to the Qāḍīs for arbitration). He also maintained that unless marriages and divorces were properly registered in the Colony the courts would give no judicial relief;[2] that the courts gave maintenance orders in favour of wives without adequate enquiries as to whether they were "disobedient" and therefore not entitled thereto; and that while husbands were punished if they assaulted their wives no legal penalty was imposed on the wives for their recalcitrance: on the contrary, they could frequently even retain their right to maintenance, by claiming that their husbands had failed to provide a legal domicile, which was a matter of the greatest difficulty in Aden.[3] As a consequence the courts were accused by some of favouring wives at the expense of their husbands and of allowing the former to get out of hand.

Regarding the vexed question of a wife's right herself to dissolve her marriage, he agreed that there was good authority for this if the Qāḍī concerned had demanded payment for his services. A somewhat parallel case, he remarked, was presented by a wife who heard of her husband's death but could not prove it, for she was justified in herself deciding to observe the *'idda* of widowhood and getting her guardian to remarry her, although this would be regarded as null and void by the courts if her missing husband eventually turned up. But all such action could only lead to chaos. As for the Shāfi'ī provisions in the Wakf Ordinance, he had not so much as heard of them.

The best informed jurist whom I met in the Colony was the blind preacher Muḥammad bin Sālim al-Bayḥānī. He opined that Ibn 'Ubaydillāh was the most learned lawyer in South Arabia, but that his *fatwās* were often more subtle than sound. In principle he was himself utterly against being bound by the detailed rules of one particular school, although he so regarded himself, as the law now stood, when cases were referred to him on appeal; and sometimes he had even felt compelled to annul, as contrary to the authoritative Shāfi'ī opinion, decisions with which he privately agreed. When acting as an unofficial *muftī*, however, he felt so bound only when specifically consulted as to the Shāfi'ī view; if asked for a general opinion, he gave himself that freedom of choice only properly allowable, he said, to a *mujtahid* of the "*bi'l-fatwā*" class.[4] As a teacher, moreover, he always tried to summarise the variant views and train his pupils to make their own choice. He was much in favour of the issue of proper instructions about the views which were to be applied by the courts in all cases of doubt or need for reform: he had himself at one time put forward certain specific suggestions, but nothing had come of them. He thought that a committee of some seven jurists representing the Colony and the Eastern and Western Protectorates should be carefully chosen, from those who believed

[1] An interesting example of how pagan survivals can be intermingled even with the functions of such an official is provided by the certificate which the Aden Qāḍī regularly gives to the father of a girl born without the hymen if he is satisfied that she was born under *al-Nathra*—to be handed in due course to her bridegroom. Such a girl is called "*bint al-Nathra.*" I am indebted to Dr. R. B. Serjeant for this information.

[2] But in this at least he was under a misapprehension; although it does seem that the court will not dissolve a Muslim marriage contracted elsewhere, unless the parties have become domiciled in Aden.

[3] Where couples frequently marry and continue to live in the same house as the husband's parents, largely because no other accommodation is available. Should any dispute subsequently arise, the wife will often demand a legal marriage home and then, in default, decamp: and in all such circumstances the courts feel bound to maintain her right to maintenance.

[4] See Glossary.

in such action, to study the question of what detailed instructions of this sort were required—and the Qu'ayṭī experiments, the Laḥej Code, and his own suggestions would all give them something to work on. This would bring uniformity, progress and certainty to the Sharī'a courts.

He, again, had no knowledge of the provision in the Wakf Ordinance about Shāfi'ī founders: but as a member of a private waqf committee he sometimes sanctioned the repair of one public waqf out of the income of another, etc., although this was against the most authoritative Shāfi'ī opinion. He told me how the 'Alawī exaggeration of the principle of equality in marriage had led to much dispute between them and the "Irshādīs" even in Java. He also described some of the unorthodox methods—e.g., *bish'a*,[1] the employment of an astrologist, and the vision of a first-born child—used in parts of the Protectorate to detect criminals, but emphasised that he had himself frequently preached sermons against such superstitions and abuses. Of the variant Shāfi'ī view that the decision of the two arbitrators to be appointed in cases of marital dispute might be enforced by the courts he had never heard, but was delighted with the discovery: he fully agreed it might be a most beneficial principle in difficult cases. This view was also shared by other jurists questioned.

In general, it seems that in the Eastern Protectorate the policy of "hands off" in regard to the Sharī'a has been carried to somewhat unnecessary lengths—e.g., the mode of execution of murderers in Mukallā up till 1945, and the activities of the Religious Court more recently. True, all such matters may be claimed to concern the "Muhammadan religion" and thus to be outside the terms of the treaties with the Protecting Power: but they also plainly concern politics, order and good government, so a word of timely advice should neither be ignored nor resented. In the Western Protectorate, on the other hand, the tendency to exert British influence to secure the establishment of Sharī'a courts where none have previously existed seems to require further examination and reflexion; as also the suggestion that a committee of jurists should be called to recommend points on which uniformity or reform could conveniently be introduced, by the expedient of an authoritative pronouncement on which opinion of some reputable jurist—be he Shāfi'ī or otherwise—is most consonant with present-day conditions. This also applies to the Colony; but there, as an alternative, an Ordinance similar to the Indian Dissolution of Muslim Marriages Act[2] might be promulgated. It is also worthy of consideration whether the Shāfi'ī Qāḍī should not be allowed to try cases of personal status between Shāfi'ī litigants: and it would seem advisable, should any such decision be reached, to provide that he might follow Islamic rules of evidence and procedure, except that wherever the decision of a case turned on the ineligibility of a witness on grounds of religion, impiety or self-interest, his evidence must be recorded in full and the record passed to the High Court for review.[3]

[1] cp. A. Kennetts, *Bedouin Justice*, pp. 109 ff.
[2] See Appendix E.
[3] See fuller discussion of this subject in the Kenya section of this Survey, pp. 99-101.

SOMALILAND PROTECTORATE

In the Somaliland Protectorate, the Principal Order in Council, 1929, as usual provides that " In all cases, civil and criminal, to which natives are parties, every court (*a*) shall be guided by native law, so far as it is applicable and is not repugnant to justice and morality, or inconsistent with any Order in Council or Ordinance, or any regulation or rule made under any Order in Council or Ordinance; and (*b*) shall decide all such cases according to substantial justice, without excessive regard to technicalities of procedure and without undue delay."[1] Similarly, in making Ordinances, the Governor must " respect existing native laws and customs except so far as the same may be opposed to justice or morality."[2] The definition of " native " applicable to this Order in Council, moreover, is much wider than that adopted in some of the territories further south, for it includes any " indigenous inhabitant of Africa or Arabia."[3] While, therefore, the primary reference of these articles is clearly to local and tribal customary law, there can be little doubt that they may also be regarded as including such Islamic law as has in fact been adopted by the people.[4]

For the rest, the Principal Order in Council also decrees that " Subject to the other provisions of this Order . . . Her Majesty's criminal and civil jurisdiction in the Protectorate shall, so far as circumstances admit, be exercised on the principles of, and in conformity with, the enactments for the time being applicable as hereinafter mentioned of the Governor-General of India in Council, and of the Governor of Bombay in Council, and according to the course of procedure and practice observed by, and before, the courts in the Presidency of Bombay . . . and so far as such enactments, procedure and practice are inapplicable, shall be exercised under, and in accordance with, the Common and Statute Law of England.[5] Again, " Subject to the other provisions of this Order, the Code of Civil Procedure, 'The Bombay Civil Courts Act', 1869, and the other enactments relating to the administration of civil justice for the time being applicable to the Protectorate, shall have effect as if the Protectorate were the Presidency of Bombay."[6] These two articles are almost identical with articles 8 (a) and 21 respectively of the Zanzibar Order in Council, 1884: since, therefore, it has been judicially held[7] that in virtue of the latter[8] article Bombay Regulation 4 of 1827 was made applicable to the British Courts of Zanzibar, it follows that this Regulation is also applicable in Somaliland. And this, in turn, means that the Somaliland Order in Council, 1929, provides authority for the application of Islamic law, as the " law of the defendant ", in circumstances which are not covered either by some express enactment or some " usage of the country."[9] It is also noteworthy that the Indian Acts which have in fact been applied in Somaliland include the Indian Penal Code (1860), the Indian Succession Act (1865), the Indian Evidence Act (1872), the Indian Contract Act (1872), the

[1] Art. 12.
[2] Art. 15(iii).
[3] Art. 3.
[4] See discussion of this subject in the Introduction to this Survey.
[5] Art. 16(i).
[6] Art. 27.
[7] *Rana Ramji* v. *Radhabai* (1937), 5 Z.L.R. 91.
[8] While J. H. Vaughan has argued (*Dual Jurisdiction in Zanzibar*, p. 48) for its applicability in virtue of art. 8 (a). *Sed quaere.*
[9] Bombay Regulation 4, sect. 26: c.p. p. 60, note (6).

Indian Oaths Act (1873), the Indian Majority Act (1875), the Transfer of Property Act (1882), the Indian Limitation Act (1908), and the Code of Civil Procedure (1908).

It seems, therefore, that the application of Islamic law may be justified in Somaliland, in the absence of any express enactment covering the question in issue, (*a*) in regard to the indigenous inhabitants of Africa or Arabia, either as their " native law and custom " where it has in fact become such by adoption and assimilation, or as the " law of the defendant " where there is no local usage to the contrary; (*b*) in regard to immigrant Muslims from countries other than Africa and Arabia, as the " law of the defendant " (in suitable circumstances). For practical purposes, however, the application of this law in Somaliland is principally based on the Subordinate Courts Ordinance, 1944, which repealed (and largely incorporated) the Qāḍīs'[1] Courts Ordinance and Akils' Court Ordinance of 1937. This Ordinance empowers the Governor, by warrant under his hand, to establish within the Protectorate " such subordinate courts as he may think fit, which shall exercise over natives " (defined here as any member of the Somali race, or any person known as a Zeilawi or of Sudanese or Arab origin born or domiciled in the Protectorate)[2] " such jurisdiction and within such limits as may be defined by such warrant."[3] This may extend to " all causes and matters where, in civil suits, all parties are native, or where, in criminal suits, the accused is a native "[4] or (by express authority in its warrant) " over classes of persons who are not natives within the meaning of this Ordinance but who, having regard to their general mode of life, may, in the opinion of the Governor, nevertheless be made amenable to the jurisdiction of such court."[5] Equally, however, the Governor " may direct that any native or class of natives shall not be subject to the jurisdiction of subordinate courts except with the consent of such native or class of natives, as the case may be, or with the consent of the Governor."[6]

It appears, however, that the drafting of this Ordinance has been unnecessarily complicated by the attempt to include the Qāḍīs' courts under the general title of subordinate courts,[7] as it is not always apparent when the latter term is intended to include the former, and when not. Section 10 makes a clear distinction, for whereas sub-section 1 deals with subordinate courts (without further specification or limitation), sub-section 2 deals exclusively with Qāḍīs' courts. Thus sub-section 1 provides that " Subject to any express provision to the contrary, no subordinate court shall have jurisdiction in:—

(*a*) any criminal proceedings in which a person is charged with an offence in consequence of which death is alleged to have occurred;

(*b*) any proceedings concerning marriage or divorce except when the marriage was contracted solely under and in accordance with native law and custom[8] or when the claim arises only in regard to bride-price or adultery and is founded on native law and custom;[9]

(*c*) any proceedings affecting the title to or any interest in land other than those arising out of any question of gift, succession or wills under native law and custom.

---

[1] Spelt " Kadi " in Somaliland Ordinances: but see Introduction for policy adopted in this Survey regarding the spelling of Arabic words.

[2] Sect. 2.
[3] Sect. 3(i).
[4] Sect. 7(i).
[5] Sect. 7(ii).
[6] Sect. 8.
[7] See sect. 2.

[8] This phrase was primarily intended to exclude from the jurisdiction of subordinate courts any question of Christian or monogamous marriage and divorce. Marriage under the Sharī'a is provided for by sub-sect. 2 below. See p. 42.

[9] Which may, of course, be true of both " Christian " and " Muslim " marriage.

(*d*) any proceedings taken under any Ordinance or any English or Indian law . . . unless such court has been (so) authorised . . .;

(*e*) any proceedings excluded from the jurisdiction of such court by the terms of its warrant;

(*f*) any other class of proceedings which the Governor may . . . exclude from the jurisdiction of subordinate courts."

Sub-section 2, on the other hand, reads: —

"(*a*) a Qāḍī's Court shall have jurisdiction in—

(i) any question regarding marriage, including divorce and maintenance, guardianship of minors and family relationship, under the Sharī'a law;[1]

(ii) any question regarding waqf,[2] gift, succession or wills under the Sharī'a law;

(*b*) a Qāḍī's Court shall not have jurisdiction in—

(i) criminal proceedings;

(ii) any matter upon which jurisdiction is not expressly conferred upon it: Provided that the Governor may by Order expressly confer or exclude jurisdiction in any civil proceedings upon any or from any Qāḍī's Court. . . ."

Later sections in the Ordinance provide that a subordinate court shall administer and enforce only: —

"(*a*) the native law and custom prevailing within the limits or among the tribal community . . . that is subject to the jurisdiction of the court so far as it is applicable and is not repugnant to natural justice or morality or is not, in principle, in conflict with . . . any law in force in the Protectorate; and (*b*) the provisions of any Ordinance or other law which the court is authorised to administer or enforce."[3] In addition, a subordinate court "shall enquire into any question involving the interpretation of native law and custom referred to it by any other court and shall certify its opinion in writing to such other court on the question referred."[4] Here, moreover, it seems that the term "subordinate court" is intended to include a Qāḍī's court and that this section, therefore, covers the normal practice of referring to the Qāḍīs the assessment of the compensation payable for wounds under the Sharī'a (here termed "native law and custom") in all actions for assault, etc., brought in District or other courts—a function of the Qāḍīs' courts expressly covered in the previous Qāḍīs' Courts Ordinance.

In a criminal case a subordinate court may impose a fine, imprisonment with or without hard labour or (today in the case of juveniles only) corporal punishment—subject, of course, to any limitation imposed by its warrant or the provisions of any law.[5] Again, subject to any express prescription, the practice and procedure in subordinate courts is to be regulated in accordance with the law and custom applicable to such courts.[6] No advocate or legal practitioner may appear for any party, but the husband, wife, son, guardian or native employer or friend may be allowed to act for such party in suitable circumstances[7]: while, subject to the directions of the Governor, a District Officer may sit as adviser in any subordinate courts in his district.[8] Here section 14 (1) is obviously inapplicable to Qāḍīs' courts, which have no criminal jurisdiction; sections 19 and 21 are applicable; while in section 22 the term subordinate court is never interpreted as including the Qāḍīs' courts.

[1] Spelt "Sheriat" in Somaliland legislation: but see Introduction.

[2] Here spelt "wakf": but see above.

[3] Sect. 12.

[4] Sect. 13.

[5] Sect. 14(1).

[6] Sect. 19.

[7] Sect. 21.

[8] Sect. 22.

As regards appeals, it is laid down that " An appeal shall lie from the order of a subordinate court to such court of appeal (which expression includes any subordinate or District Court or the High Court) as may be prescribed in the warrant establishing such subordinate court "[1]—and such court of appeal has the widest powers of revision.[2] No non-Sharī'a native courts of appeal have yet been set up, and at present District Courts hear all appeals from such subordinate courts: but provision has been made for appeals from Qāḍīs' courts to go to a Sharī'a Court of Appeal. The warrant of establishment of this Court provides that:—

" 1. All Qāḍīs entitled to hold Qāḍīs' courts under the Ordinance shall be *ex-officio* judges.

2. The court shall be held by not less than *two* Qāḍīs nominated by a Judge of the Protectorate. . . .

3. No Qāḍī may hear an appeal from any decision or order made by himself." This court, moreover, has " full appellate jurisdiction and may exercise all or any of the powers conferred upon a court of appeal by the Ordinance," whenever an appeal has in fact been lodged from a decision or order of a Qāḍī's court and leave to appeal has been granted by the High Court.

It is also provided that " A magistrate shall at all times have access to any subordinate court within the local limits of his jurisdiction and may send for and examine the records of such subordinate court "; that he shall " have all the powers conferred upon a court of appeal by this Ordinance and the provisions . . . relating to appeals shall apply *mutatis mutandis* to proceedings in revision "; but that " nothing in this section contained shall be deemed to authorise a magistrate to decide a question involving the interpretation of the Sharī'a law."[3] Where, moreover, it appears that " in any original, revisional, or appellate proceedings under this Ordinance an error material to the merits of any case or involving a miscarriage of justice has occurred, the High Court may, either upon the application of any person concerned or of its own motion . . . exercise all or any of the powers of revision vested in a magistrate by this Ordinance."[4] But no such appeal or revision must vary or declare void any " summons, warrant, process, order or decree . . . solely by reason of any defect in procedure or want of form."[5]

Finally the Akils' Court Ordinance and the Qāḍīs' Courts Ordinance, 1937, were repealed, but it was provided that " any court established under either of the said repealed Ordinances, and existing at the commencement of this Ordinance, shall be deemed to be a subordinate court established under this Ordinance."[6] In the event, an Akils' court still exists at Hargeisa, since the establishment of a subordinate court of the new pattern has not yet proved possible in this locality because of local factions and disputes: but new subordinate courts are in action at Berbera, Las Anod, Borama and (since my visit) Burao and Erigavo. These consist, normally, of a President and two Assessors, while the old Akils' courts consist of a bench of tribal Akils, serving in rotation. Qāḍīs' courts, on the other hand, exist at Hargeisa, Berbera, Burao, Erigavo, Las Anod, Borama, Zeila and Mandera; and the Sharī'a Court of Appeal is usually composed of any two of the three Qāḍīs of Hargeisa, Berbera and Borama.

To sum up, then, Sharī'a law is applied in the Qāḍīs' courts in all matters of personal status (in its widest definition) and in the assessment of the compensation payable for wounds. In such matters Indian Muslims, as well as "natives ", normally submit to their jurisdiction, presumably under section 10 (2) which gives these courts jurisdiction in "any question " of this kind " under the Sharī'a law "—although I am not aware whether any mention of Indians has

[1] Sect. 29.
[2] Sect. 29(2).
[3] Sect. 30(1), (2), and (5).
[4] Sect. 31.
[5] Sect. 32.
[6] Sect. 35(1).

been made in their warrants, as section 7 (2) would appear to require (see p. 41 above). These Indians are mostly Ḥanafīs or (rarely) Ithnā ʻAsharīs, but they do not seem to mind submitting to the application of Shāfiʻī law in any case which they take to court.[1] Criminal proceedings, and any matter other than questions of personal status, such as questions concerning land, contract, tort, etc., are expressly excluded from the jurisdiction of the Qāḍīs.[2] They follow Islamic rules of procedure,[3] and have their own Court of Appeal, to which cases may be referred by permission of the High Court.[4] A magistrate may exercise his powers of revision, etc., over the judgments or orders of a Qāḍī's court regarding points of fact or any miscarriage of justice, but not concerning the interpretation of the Sharīʻa,[5] and the same applies to the High Court itself. At the same time the new subordinate courts and the old Akils' courts apply—according to their respective warrants—Somali law and custom, together with certain local legislation, in both criminal and civil matters; and this customary law may often coincide with, or at least approximate to, the Sharīʻa. Even the High Court and the District Courts, moreover, are to be " guided " by native law and custom (including, presumably, such parts of the Sharīʻa as have been effectively adopted) in suitable circumstances.[6] But it is noteworthy that, in Somaliland as elsewhere, the Marriage Ordinance, 1902, would provide a way in which a Muslim woman could validly marry a Christian man[7] in defiance of Islamic law, for such a case would be excluded from the jurisdiction of any subordinate court[8]; and any marriage so concluded, of course, would not be susceptible to dissolution on any grounds except by valid decree of divorce[9], would prevent either party thereto from marrying any other person while it subsisted,[10] and would have the effects with regard to intestate succession set out in section 39; while the Indian Penal Code as applied in Somaliland makes it a criminal offence for a husband prematurely to consummate his marriage with a child wife[11] or for any one to abduct or kidnap any woman " with intent that she may be compelled, or knowing it to be likely that she will be compelled, to marry any person against her will."[12] Again, the respective jurisdiction of the Qāḍīs and of other subordinate courts comes very close together in certain matrimonial causes, where, e.g., questions of dower on the one hand or of wifely " disobedience " on the other would go to the former, while questions of bride-price and adultery, respectively, fall within the competence of the latter. It may be added that the Somalis are democratic to the point of anarchy, and there are virtually no Chiefs in their own right who would naturally exercise jurisdiction (although there are a few so-called " Sultans ", etc.): the office of Akil is purely a Government appointment and any indigenous " government " there ever seems to have been (apart from that of Muḥammad ʻAbdullāh Ḥasan—the so-called " Mad Mulla ") was chiefly exercised at tribal *shirs* or meetings. Even the Government Qāḍīs, moreover, often find their authority challenged, in the tribal areas, by unofficial *wadāds,* or bush lawyers.

[1] If they go to the Qāḍīs' courts they can, of course, expect no other. But they could, presumably, litigate in the District Courts, where their own personal law, or rather the " law of the defendant," would be applicable. See p. 41 above.

[2] Sect. 10(2) (*b*).

[3] Sect. 19, by implication (presumably).

[4] See Warrant thereof.

[5] Sect. 30.

[6] Order in Council of 1927, art. 12.

[7] Sects. 11 and 20. (Provided she has the necessary consent if minor and unmarried.)

[8] Subordinate Courts Ordinance, 1944, sect. 10(1) (*b*).

[9] Sect. 27.

[10] Sects. 35, 43 and 50.

[11] Sect. 375. See above, p. 35, and below, p. 62, etc.

[12] Sect. 366. See p. 62, etc.

Some of this merits further expansion, for there is often a close and interesting connection in Somaliland between the scope of the Penal Code, of Somali custom and of Sharī'a law. A good illustration is provided by cases of homicide. If the Crown is in a position to prosecute the case is tried under the Penal Code, and if a sentence of death or imprisonment for life is imposed (or possibly any sentence of imprisonment exceeding, e.g., ten years) no blood-wit is awarded; while if for any reason a lesser sentence is passed, a portion of the usual blood-wit termed the *jiffo* (i.e., 33 camels, representing that one-third of the normal *diya*[1] which is locally regarded as the right of the immediate relatives of the deceased) may be awarded at the discretion of the court—and is, in fact, normally allowed. If, however, the accused is acquitted or the Crown decides that there is insufficient evidence to prosecute under the Code, the case may be heard again, or for the first time, as a "political case"—i.e., a civil suit under Somali custom. In such cases, moreover, the plaintiffs may bring their accusation not against an individual as the actual culprit but against a group or tribe, and may demand that fifty oaths be sworn by selected representatives[2] of the accused that they were not responsible. The latter then have the choice of paying *dīya*, of taking the required oaths, or of returning these to their accusers, who may thereupon enforce payment only if they themselves first swear fifty oaths to the truth of their accusation.[3] In all cases, moreover, the responsibility for paying blood-wit for homicides is shared in Somaliland between the members of the *dīya*-paying group concerned.

This again provides a splendid example of the similarity, but distinction, between Somali customary law and the Sharī'a, for the fifty oath procedure among the Somalis corresponds to the normal Shāfi'ī rules for *qasāma* except that in the latter there must first be some ground for suspicion (*lawth*) and the oaths should then be taken by the heirs of blood rather than the accused, while the payment of *dīya* again conforms to the Sharī'a except that the Somalis make no distinction between deliberate and accidental homicide but—unlike the Sharī'a—throw the burden on the group rather than the individual even in cases of "murder." It is interesting, moreover, to note that when a married woman is killed half the fifty camels payable as blood-wit are accorded in Somaliland to her husband and half to her tribe. Where, therefore, it was the husband himself who killed her only the twenty-five camels due to her tribe were formerly payable, but the Government now insists on the other twenty-five being paid also and put on deposit for the benefit of his tribe. Again, the intrusion of modern life is apparent in the fact that no blood-wit at all, it seems, is payable in any case of death caused by traffic accidents or in townships;[4] while the courts also normally reject claims in respect of homicides caused by children.

The case is somewhat similar in regard to assaults or accidents which result in injury rather than death. The former are sometimes treated as crimes under the Penal Code, and punished (where suitable) by both a term of imprisonment and a fine, which is commonly given to the injured man by way of compensation. In other cases a civil action for compensation may be brought under Somali custom, either in the District Courts or the subordinate courts, and the practice is for such court, after conviction, first to ask the Qāḍī to assess the proper compensation under Sharī'a law, and then to give judgment as it sees fit (i.e., it may well award somewhat less than the Qāḍī's assessment).

Another respect in which the interplay of customary and Sharī'a law may be

[1] i.e., blood-wit. This is 100 camels for a man and 50 for a woman. See Glossary.

[2] Sometimes one 'respected' man, or those believed to have special knowledge of the facts. A single oath, or even an expression of willingness to swear, is usually now regarded as adequate.

[3] In theory; but this return of oath is not, it seems, practised in Somaliland today.

[4] Presumably because both vehicles and townships are foreign to Somali tribal life.

clearly seen is in the payments and presents commonly made in respect of marriage.[1] Here the payment called *yarad* represents the bride-price payable to the father by tribal custom, Arab, Somali and African; the *gabbāti*[2] is the name given to an advance payment of part of this; the *ḍibād*[3] represents a bridal present from the bride's father to the couple (or more accurately to his daughter) and—like the *gabbāti*—commonly bears some relation to the size of the *yarad*; while *mahr*[4] is the term used for the specifically Islamic payment always called by that name (or sometimes *ṣadāq*): but it is virtually never paid, in Somali custom, except on divorce or the death of one of the parties.[5] If the girl refuses marriage after her father has betrothed her and received part of the *yarad*, this may be reclaimed in the subordinate courts. If, however, she runs away from her husband soon after marriage and refuses to return, the repayment of part of the *yarad* is considered a gentlemanly act, but cannot normally be enforced in the courts[6]: but if the wife dies soon after marriage it is usual to replace her by her younger sister without further *yarad*, while if the latter refuses to comply with this arrangement part of the *yarad* may be returned. But disputes on such points are normally settled out of court, and it seems doubtful how far the return of *yarad* can be judicially enforced in such cases under customary law (except perhaps among the 'Īse tribe). If the husband dies and the wife is taken over by his brother, etc., a small amount of extra *yarad* only is sometimes payable. In all cases, however, where a younger sister is supplied to take the place of an elder, or a widow is taken over in levirate marriage, a new contract and new *mahr* are essential under Sharī'a law. Some Qāḍīs maintain that if a wife were to bring an action for payment of *mahr* during the continuance of her marriage they would order this, in accordance with the Sharī'a: but most admit that they would not attempt to enforce a payment before divorce or death, in accordance with local custom, often adding that the Government has intimated that custom must not be flouted in this matter.[7] In practice, however, the issue never seems to arise.

It must, of course, be realised that the references above to a girl who refuses marriage after being betrothed by her father, to a girl who refuses to be given in marriage to replace a deceased elder sister, and (by implication) to a widowed wife who refuses levirate marriage, all represent, in the main, modern innovations, since in the past there would have been no option in the matter.[8] Now, however, all these cases are covered by the Natives' Betrothal and Marriage Ordinance, 1928 (as amended). Thus section 3 (1) provides that "Any unmarried woman betrothed by her father or guardian shall have the right to

[1] Commonly, now, from 1 to 5 camels around Hargeisa; but it used sometimes to go up to 50.

[2] Which may be a token payment of cloth, sheep, goats or camels, in amount roughly proportionate to the total *yarad*. It constitutes, however, the pledge of betrothal, and thereafter *ḥāl* may be claimed for any breach, etc. (see below).

[3] Commonly gold, jewelry, furniture, etc.

[4] ("*Meher*") This often amounts to some 30 sheep or goats, but may be as many as 150.

[5] Properly, in Islamic law, the *mahr* or *ṣadāq* is payable by husband to wife in advance, unless some is "deferred"—for a period of years, or until death or divorce—by mutual agreement.

[6] Unless the parent or guardian concerned supports her, when return of *yarad* is apparently regarded as automatic and even enforceable: but such cases are usually settled between the families.

[7] Officially, Government has left this point to the people themselves; but it seems quite probable that individual District Commissioners may have advised any over-orthodox Qāḍī against flying in the face of custom. Under the Principal Order in Council, moreover, this is perfectly correct, since Sharī'a law is applied in Somaliland either as "native law and custom" or under Bombay Regulation 4, which only provides for the application of the "law of the defendant" in the absence of some "usage of the country."

[8] Except perhaps in the case of the widow, if a money payment were offered in lieu.

register personally before (a District Commissioner) . . . her refusal of the betrothal, and in that event her betrothal shall forthwith be terminated." The District Commissioner shall then "cause enquiries to be made as to whether any *gabbāti* or *yarad* has been paid and its return demanded. Until all such *gabbāti* and *yarad* shall have been repaid or until the expiry of two months from the date of the registration of renunciation of engagement, whichever is the earlier, any man who goes through the ceremony of marriage with such woman shall be guilty of an offence." Similarly section 3 (2) provides that "Any widowed or divorced woman shall have the right to register personally before (a District Commissioner) . . . her intention to marry contrary to tribal custom." The District Commissioner shall then cause notice of such woman's declaration of intention to be served upon her legal guardian and late husband or his relatives; and "should any suit lie" with regard thereto it must be filed within two months, after which the woman shall be free to marry contrary to tribal custom. This section, however, does not apply to women who hold divorce certificates granted by any Qāḍī in the employment of the Somaliland Government, for such may re-marry as they please.[1] A marriage in defiance of this Ordinance would, of course, be regarded as perfectly valid by the Qāḍīs' courts if it fulfilled the ordinary conditions of validity; but "Any parent or legal guardian who assists at, or abets, the commission of an offence under this Ordinance . . . shall be liable on conviction to imprisonment which may extend to two years and to a fine."[2] The Ordinance equally provides, however, that "Any man who goes through the ceremony of marriage with any unmarried woman whom he knows or has reason to believe to have been betrothed to another man, or with any widow or divorced woman contrary to tribal custom, shall be guilty of an offence and shall be liable to imprisonment on conviction for a term not exceeding one year and shall also be liable to a fine, and if the unmarried woman or widow were an unwilling participant of the ceremony of marriage to a term not exceeding two years and to a fine"[3]—but this offence may, with permission of court, be compounded by the offended party.[4]

This raises, however, the whole conception of "*ḥāl*", or insult, in Somali customary law. Of such insult there are many examples, among them the act of a betrothed girl's father in giving her in marriage to another man and the act of that other man in marrying her if he was aware that she was already betrothed. But claims for compensation for *ḥāl* may also be brought against one who strikes a man with a "wife-whip" or a sandal; who addresses him in very insulting terms; or who commits adultery with his wife, his betrothed wife or his unmarried daughter. The compensation payable is assessed in each instance by the Akils' or new subordinate courts and differs according to the custom of the tribe concerned.

In marriage the indigenous Somali customs are exogamous, and cousins, etc., do not normally intermarry. But the Qāḍīs generally uphold the validity of such a marriage under the Sharī'a if it takes place, and the marriage of cousins is said to be becoming increasingly frequent. The normal Shāfi'ī rules regarding "equality" in marriage, are, however, ignored both by custom and the courts, for the Somalis are extremely democratic; and only members of one of the "outcast" (and possibly aboriginal) tribes, the Tumāl or Handad[5], the Midgān or Khādim[6] and the Yibir or Toshan[7]—together with the 'Abīd or Ḥabash[8]

[1] Provided someone acts as their guardian, etc., in accordance with the law.
[2] Sect. 5.
[3] Sect. 2. In the case of a betrothed woman such action is strongly deprecated by the Sharī'a, and the imposition by the Government of some penalty on one who does so is perfectly in order—as tending to prevent something which ought not to happen.
[4] Sect. 6.
[5] Almost all blacksmiths and metal workers, etc.
[6] Almost all sweepers, barbers, shoemakers, hunters, etc.
[7] Almost all sorcerers, magicians, etc. [8] Literally, Ethiopian.

(terms loosely used for all persons of slave status)[1] scattered among the tribes—are regarded as social inferiors and no fit spouse for a true Somali girl.[2]

In the matter of the custody of children, again, tribal custom frequently parts company with the Sharī'a. Here the custom of most tribes is that the divorced mother should only keep her infant children until weaning, or some two years old —and then only if she is not going too far away. This is said to be partly due to the poverty of the people and the difficulty involved in the payment and receipt of maintenance, and partly to the fact that a divorced wife usually returns to her own tribe, which might mean a protracted separation from the father and his tribe. Sometimes, indeed, it is agreed between the parties that the mother should keep them longer than this, but in such circumstances she would not normally be entitled to claim money for their support. In all cases, moreover, it seems that the child will be taken by the father's tribe at the end of this period of custody, with no option to the child. Most Qāḍīs, however, maintained that they would give judgment according to strict Shāfi'ī principles in any case which came to court—i.e., that the mother, unless she remarried outside the prohibited degrees,[3] was entitled to the custody of her children up to the age of discrimination (e.g., seven),[4] after which the choice between father and mother lay with the children themselves; but that during the period of custody the mother might never, without the father's consent, take them further from his locality than would enable him to visit them and return in a single day, while the father (or, if he were dead, their other guardian) might take them at any age if he were emigrating in order to settle elsewhere. There was considerable confusion, however, about some of these details (e.g., a well-informed *wadād* told me that the mother might take the infant any distance provided the roads were safe). Only in Odweina did Sheikh Aḥmad bin Sheikh Mūsā, M.B.E. (who combined the functions of a subordinate court judge with those of unofficial Qāḍī) admit that he would give judgment in accordance with custom and allot the child to the husband at, or even before, the age of two years, according to his physique, etc. No scope, apparently, exists for consideration of the welfare of the child in the particular circumstances of any case pressed to judgment; but very few such cases reach the courts. The basic consideration in most cases, of course, is the maintenance of tribal strength—a point of the utmost importance to all primitive tribal communities.

In matters of intestate succession, again, the old Somali customs ran counter to the Sharī'a in that women were totally excluded. Now, however, I was informed that mothers and widows[5] usually get their proper shares, or at least something; but that daughters frequently get nothing,[6] the aggregate children's

---

[1] It should be noted here, of course, that the Abolition of Slavery Ordinance, 1930, enacts " that slavery in any form whatever is unlawful and that the legal status of slavery does not exist." It is probable, however, that the Qāḍīs' courts in Somaliland would take the same view of claims to inherit by patronage, or as the son of concubinage with a woman who would have been the father's slave but for the abolition of slavery, taken by Muslim courts elsewhere (see pp. 22, 27, 30, 76, etc.).

[2] The Somalis strongly disapprove of any of their women marrying non-Somalis (except, perhaps, Arabs). During the war a few Somali women married French Senegalese Muslim troops, their guardians succumbing to the temptation of the large *yarad* offered. But the women were left behind when the troops left, and the children of these unions are said to have been exposed.

[3] Or disqualifies herself by her manner of life, etc.

[4] *Sed quaere.* But the fact that a mother is not allowed to take the child away probably prevents this issue ever being decided *per se.*

[5] And also fathers, where sons are the primary heirs. *Sed quaere.*

[6] Except where, e.g., a daughter is the only heir, when she is apparently allowed to keep her father's property unless or until she marries outside the blood-wit paying group—whereupon she must leave the camels, at least, behind: and these are normally all that really matters.

shares being divided among the sons only—especially in the case of camels, which represent a tribesman's primary wealth—while the daughters, of course, would be supported until marriage by their brothers. Where cases come to court it seems that the Qāḍīs follow the strict rules of Shāfi'ī law,[1] but most tribesmen do not bring such cases to court and would even ignore a judgment if given. It is alleged, however, that the influence of the Islamic rules of inheritance is growing. In the special circumstances of a father who dies between receiving *yarad* for his daughter and paying the appropriate *ḍibād,* and whose heirs are this daughter, her full brother and her brother by another mother, the girl's full brother will normally claim the whole *yarad*: and here even the strictest Qāḍī will usually support him in excluding this sum from the estate, since it will be his duty alone to pay the *ḍibād.*

Somali customs in matters of contract and commerce are outside the jurisdiction of the Qāḍīs' courts but are by no means uninfluenced by the Sharī'a. Customs regarding sale and purchase, of course, frequently run counter to the pure law, in Somaliland as elsewhere, while the local form of mortgage, termed *bay' al-iqāla*, is of very questionable orthodoxy.[2] Its normal incidents are as follows: a man in need of a loan will sell his house to another, but continue to occupy it for rent[3]; and a parallel contract will provide that if he repays the loan in so many years he will regain his house, while, if not, it will either become the property of his creditor or will be sold in repayment of his debt. Open usury is not allowed, but the usual devices such as the acknowledgment of a debt which really represents both capital and interest, double-sales, etc., are all practised. It seems, however, that claims concerning live stock (e.g., lost camels) are by far the most common preoccupation of the Akils' and subordinate courts.

It is sometimes thought that Somali customary law cannot, or does not, change. This, however, is by no means true in any absolute sense. No formal authority exists which has the power of legislation in this matter; but even customary law, conservative though it is, cannot remain static, and gradual developments and modifications are inevitable. Thus the growing influence of Sharī'a law and the gradual abandonment of customs inconsistent therewith has already been noticed in several contexts[4]; while the intrusion of "statute" law is bound to have repercussions on tribal custom. These and other changes may, moreover, from time to time be recognised at a tribal gathering.[5] An interesting illustration is provided by the treatment of theft. In the past agreements were sometimes concluded between different tribes that compensation for stolen camels, at any scale up to fourfold the number stolen, might be demanded; but since camel-theft became a crime punishable under the Penal Code only the return of the stolen camel, or its value, is now normally enforced, in addition to the appropriate punishment: and this was apparently recognised by a tribal meeting in the Berbera area somewhere around 1920. There seems to be a considerable demand for further changes, particularly among the younger and more urbanised elements, who strongly object, e.g., to the danger of being murdered by way of reprisal for a tribal homicide of which they may have never heard; while changes in the composition of blood-wit paying groups are, apparently, common. Again, statute law may sometimes directly reverse

---

[1] Following the principles of "*ahl al-tanzīl*" in the case of "Distant Kindred" (*dhawū'l-arḥām*—properly "blood kindred"). See Glossary.

[2] i.e., it is clearly as inconsistent with the strict Sharī'a as the Ḥaḍramī *'uhda,* but could, presumably, be defended on much the same basis: cp. also the *bay' al-khiyār* contract in Kenya and Zanzibar, etc. See Glossary.

[3] Which really represents, of course, interest on the money lent.

[4] e.g., inheritance rights of women, etc. See above.

[5] It seems that before the war it was quite common for the members of a tribe to decide to change some custom and to ask the District Commissioner to record the new "*herr*" in a book kept for this purpose at the District Office: and these *herrs* were often referred to in litigation.

customary law, as in several provisions of the Natives' Betrothal and Marriage Ordinance, 1928[1]: and this is likely to lead in the course of time to a change in the customs themselves.

The subordinate courts (other than the Qāḍīs' courts) seem to follow a procedure which differs according to the type of case concerned. In cases covered by customary law the procedure is also customary, which approximates, it seems, to a loose and simplified form of Islamic procedure. Thus the burden of proof lies on the plaintiff, who must normally bring two trustworthy witnesses or support the testimony of one such witness with his oath; and the eligibility of these witnesses may sometimes be impugned by the other party[2]; while in default of adequate proof, or a confession by the defendant, the latter is proffered an oath which he may either take or return to the plaintiff. But the system is much less rigid than that of the pure Sharī'a, for testimony may be heard from either party, the common sense of the court is the final arbiter, and the main aim is to dispel bad feeling between the litigants and their supporters. Where, on the other hand, a subordinate court is empowered to apply certain sections of the Penal Code and other "statute" law, it is supposed to follow the Indian Evidence Act (etc.), although any minor deviations therefrom would be covered by the provision that no decree of such a court must be varied or declared void on appeal or revision "solely by reason of any defect in procedure or want of form."[3] It may be added that the Hargeisa Akils' court—the only surviving court of the old pattern—has an educated clerk who keeps a summarised record of its proceedings in English, and that the Berbera subordinate court—perhaps the most experienced of all the courts of the new pattern established under the Ordinance—has recently had its jurisdiction increased to allow the imposition, in criminal cases, of up to six months' imprisonment, a fine of Shs. 750, or (in the case of juveniles) twelve strokes, and to include civil cases involving sums not exceeding Shs. 1,500.

In the Qāḍīs' courts the procedure followed is naturally more rigidly Islamic. Most of the Qāḍīs questioned claimed that witnesses are duly "screened" (*tazkīya* or *ta'dīl*),[4] although some said that this does not really take place. For the rest, the court leaves it to the other party to discredit them (*ṭa'n, tajrīḥ*)[4] if he can. But even this seems of no great practical importance since most Qāḍīs admitted, when pressed, that they would do their best to accept such testimony as they in fact believed to be true and to reject what they suspected to be false: and this could be done, in the first case, on the principle that a strict insistence on, e.g., the piety of witnesses would cripple the administration of justice in these degenerate days and, in the second, on the grounds that their testimony did not exactly correspond with that of another witness or the allegation of the party concerned. In any case of doubt most Qāḍīs will put the witness on oath (in accordance with the views of Ibn Abī Layla, certain Ḥanafīs and Ibn al-Qayyim the Ḥanbalī reformer, etc.[5]); but some do not feel at liberty to do this. Jurists who are not Qāḍīs commonly allege that they themselves would rigidly apply the rules of *fiqh*, but that the Government Qāḍīs regularly substitute an oath for screening.[6] All agree, moreover, that false testimony abounds. As for documentary evidence, this is not allowed in the classical Shāfi'ī view regarded as authoritative in Somaliland: but "official" documents, such as papers of divorce duly stamped by a Qāḍī, are accepted. Some Qāḍīs follow the letter of the law in rejecting a

[1] See above, pp. 46 and 47.

[2] But only, it seems, on the grounds of self-interest, notorious untruthfulness, etc.—not impiety of life. See above, pp. 20, 24, 28, etc.

[3] Subordinate Courts Ordinance, 1944, sect. 32. See above.

[4] See Glossary.

[5] They claim that certain later Shāfi'īs have also advocated this.

[6] The unofficial Qāḍī of Odweina frankly affirmed that he would never allow *tajrīḥ*, as it would at once degenerate into an inter-tribal contest.

written bequest unless two witnesses can testify to having heard an oral statement of its detailed contents; while others would accept it provided that witnesses can testify to the document and its signature. The common attitude regarding such questions as burden of proof, return of oath, etc., seems orthodox and somewhat rigid; but where the defendant can produce testimony to rebut that of the plaintiff most Qāḍīs will hear both sides, and then try to estimate their respective credibility, rather than keep to the strict rule of excluding all "negative" testimony.

It is noteworthy in this context that the then Legal Secretary, when questioned, seemed inclined to give the widest possible application to the phrase "nothing in this section shall be deemed to authorise a magistrate to decide a question involving the interpretation of the Sharī'a law."[1] He would thus, apparently, feel unable to exercise his powers of revision if a Qāḍī's court were to give judgment against a party solely because his witnesses, however trustworthy, were non-Muslims or were deemed to be interested parties.[2] Again, he would regard the Shāfi'ī rule that a child born within four years of its mother's widowhood or irrevocable divorce is to be reckoned her former husband's legitimate child[3] as a substantive rule of the Sharī'a rather than a mere presumption of fact.[4]

It seems that the common age for a first marriage is when a boy reaches eighteen to twenty and a girl seventeen to eighteen. Child marriages do occur, but are not common; and such are seldom consummated before puberty. Marriage contracts, moreover, normally conform to the Sharī'a, and "tribal marriages" in a form contrary thereto, which are so common elsewhere, do not seem to present any great problem in Somaliland.

The Shāfi'ī rules about the right of a father or grandfather compulsorily to marry his virgin daughters are known and accepted, but the Natives' Betrothal and Marriage Ordinance, as amended,[5] provides a way in which a girl who is sufficiently determined can avoid such a marriage—unless she is prevented from reaching the District Commissioner, is married without previous betrothal (which is contrary to custom) or is married in defiance of the terms of the Ordinance. In all these cases the Qāḍīs' courts would no doubt declare the marriage valid, unless the girl could prove that her husband was not her "equal" (which is of very limited application in Somaliland[6]); was afflicted with a grave disease such as insanity, leprosy, elephantiasis or some serious defect of the procreative organs; was unable to pay the proper dower; or that there was manifest enmity between her guardian and herself: a mere plea of hardship, on the grounds that her husband was blind or aged, would not normally be accepted, although some Qāḍīs would declare the marriage void in case of "enmity", secret or open, between the bride and her groom. As usual, however, there was some doubt and hesitation regarding these points.

A kindred and much more burning question, in Somaliland, is how, and under what circumstances, a young couple can marry in defiance, or the absence, of the bride's guardian. She may, of course, appeal direct to the Qāḍī who, if it appears that her father or other guardian has no valid reason to resist the marriage she desires (but is, e.g., only holding out for a larger *yarad*) has the right to give her in marriage on his behalf. Several Qāḍīs assured me that they had in fact often done this. Another method is for the would-be bridegroom

[1] Subordinate Courts Ordinance, sect. 30(5).

[2] This appears to be a dubious opinion, since the phrase about a miscarriage of justice in sect. 31 would sometimes, at least, seem clearly applicable to such cases—which in practice would probably be dealt with by the District Courts and never reach the High Court at all.

[3] Unless she had already been remarried for at least six months before his birth.

[4] But this, though contrary to the view taken elsewhere, is eminently arguable.

[5] See above, pp. 46 and 47.

[6] See above, pp. 47 and 48.

to elope with the girl, either willingly or by abduction[1] (a relic of the old custom of marriage by rape), and take her more than forty-eight miles from her guardian's residence. The position would then, on one view, be the same as if the guardian had himself gone away to a place similarly distant, and a Qāḍī might be requested to act on his behalf or, if no Qāḍī were available, both parties might empower one who knew the rules of "*taḥkīm*"[2] and marriage to marry them, or the woman might appoint anyone eligible as a witness to act as her guardian and marry her accordingly.[3] Some Shāfi'īs, indeed, following the tradition that the Prophet repeated three times "there can be no marriage without a guardian", differentiate between the case of a guardian who leaves his ward and a ward who elopes from her guardian—and it seems that the Aḥmadī[4] fraternity in Somaliland inclines to this view (although by no means rigidly)[5]: but the normal Shāfi'ī view is that when the guardian is more than forty-eight miles distant it makes no difference how this came about—and it appears that in Somaliland the Qādirī fraternity supports this opinion. As to whether the elopement was originally by consent or abduction, all agree that this makes no difference if the girl gives her consent to the marriage at the time of the contract; but most say that they would annul a contract concluded by, e.g., a *wadād* where there was never any real consent at all.[6]

It seems that a fairly common marriage problem in Somaliland is presented by a wife who runs away from her husband, pretends to be unmarried, and gets herself married to another man. If, some years later, her first husband should find and claim her she would still be his, but any children of the second marriage would belong to the second husband—unless he was aware of the fact that she was another's wife, in which case the first husband could claim all the children if he wished. This is normal Islamic law.

With regard to maintenance, al-Shāfi'ī's later view that a wife does not become entitled to maintenance by the mere contract of marriage, but only by "*tamkīn*" or putting her husband in a position to enjoy his marital rights, is followed by the Somaliland courts. In a judicial assessment of maintenance, moreover, the husband's financial standing is the sole criterion—which is the dominant view in the school.

Dissolution of marriage on the grounds of the serious disease of either party follows the usual Shāfi'ī rules. But a wife can in no circumstances get a judicial divorce or dissolution of marriage for cruelty, and the Qur'anic prescription that two arbitrators should be appointed in cases of marital dispute is scarcely ever applied by the courts, nor would their recommendations be enforced in any case.[7] If a wife were cruelly beaten she would be regarded as justified in running away: but if she were to stay with her parents until her husband demanded her return (i.e., without returning to him or appealing to the courts in the meantime) the local Qāḍīs differ as to whether she would be entitled to claim maintenance; and they also differ as to whether, in case of

[1] Which is quite often "staged" where, e.g., the groom has not the means to pay adequate *yarad*. Here the girl in fact connives at her abduction, although she would deny this; and her family usually accept the *fait accompli*, which saves everyone's face.

[2] Being asked to act judicially in marrying a couple. See Glossary.

[3] This is known as *tawlīya*. See Glossary.

[4] This is a Ṣūfī fraternity (see below)—not the heretical sect which also goes by this name.

[5] In more detail, the Aḥmadīs would apparently agree to marry them if in a town, for fear of immorality; but not in the desert, where there would be less danger. This alleged difference between the fraternities (for which, see below) is interesting.

[6] Which is still very common, it seems, even today in cases of real abduction; i.e., the consent, if any, is forced. A *wadād* is a "bush lawyer" (see above, p. 44).

[7] Although some Qāḍīs hold that this would be legitimate, since it finds some support in the school. But this seems doubtful, as things stand; as it is not regarded as the "dominant" opinion. See below.

repeated cruelty, she would be entitled to offer him " obedience " among her own people but refuse to travel with him to his tribe. In the latter case, however, it is apparently common for the courts to insist on her going, after putting him on his oath not to ill-treat her, or even making him produce guarantors. But in all these cases it is exceedingly difficult for the wife to prove the beating, or other cruel treatment, under the rules of evidence applicable in the Qāḍīs' courts: although it might be possible for a wife sometimes to obtain redress under the Penal Code in courts where less rigid canons of evidence obtain.

Regarding a wife's right to a dissolution of marriage if she cannot obtain maintenance, the position, in Somaliland as elsewhere, is both uncertain and unsatisfactory. Thus: —

(*a*) Where the husband is present and able to support her, no Shāfi'īs allow dissolution: instead, the Qāḍī will make a suitable maintenance order and the District Commissioner will endeavour to enforce this.[1]

(*b*) Where he is present but wholly unable to support her, she is technically entitled to the dissolution of her marriage after three days: but this is hardly ever decreed, since the provision of the barest necessities of life will defeat her petition.

(*c*) Where, again, the husband is himself present but his only assets are elsewhere, the rule laid down in the books (dissolution of marriage after three days) is not normally followed: instead, he is allowed a suitable respite to collect his property, which may even be extended on demand. But here some Qāḍīs claim to differ and to apply the stricter view.

More debateable is the position when the husband is himself absent. In all such cases the wife must first prove the marriage and take an oath that she has not, to her knowledge, been divorced, is not disobedient, and has not been left any maintenance. Thereafter: —

(*d*) If the husband has property within the jurisdiction of the court where his wife is living, there is much dispute as to whether this may be taken in execution of a maintenance order. The prevalent view seems to be that movables and debts may be so utilised without previous correspondence, but that real property may never be sold without the husband's consent. Others, however, favour correspondence, with a time limit, in all such cases: meanwhile, the wife should raise her " usual " maintenance on his credit. This is a point which is much disputed.

(*e*) Again, where the husband has no property within the jurisdiction of the court, the marriage will not be dissolved until after correspondence and enquiries. Some would insist that his inability to support her must be actually proved, others would fix a time limit, while yet others make a distinction between whether he is inside or outside the territory. In the meantime, the wife will perhaps be authorised to raise " minimum " maintenance on credit.

(*f*) Where, however, the husband's whereabouts are wholly unknown, and there is no property which can be taken in execution of a maintenance order, the marriage will be dissolved, but not until all possible enquiries about his movements, etc., have failed.[2]

(*g*) Finally, where the husband is lost (*mafqūd*) but has property out of which his wife can support herself, the marriage will in no circumstances be dissolved, nor will the missing man be declared judicially dead, until all his contemporaries have died—although a few Qāḍīs would apparently declare him

[1] Where, however, the husband fails to obey this order, the Shāfi'ī Qāḍī of Zanzibar will dissolve the marriage. (See p. 73.)

[2] Some Qāḍīs assimilated these circumstances to those of (*g*) below if any derivative of the root of " *mafqūd* " was mentioned! For the latter, see Glossary.

dead some ten, twelve or fifteen years after his disappearance.[1]

It must, however, be observed that the above summary of the attitude of local Qāḍīs is almost certainly more theoretical than practical, or at least limited in its application to the small minority of urban Somalis. Among the tribes a destitute wife must always go and live on her husband's stock, if he has any: and only if he has none such would any question of living on credit or of dissolution of marriage arise. Again, the distinction regarding real property in (*f*) above is largely foreign to Somali concepts, where camels represent the basic wealth; while outside the towns such real property as exists consists of houses, small farms, gardens and trees, rather than land itself.

Divorce is extremely common, perhaps as many as seven out of every ten marriages ending in this way. This is said to be partially explained by the custom of a father insisting on excessive *yarad* for his daughter, allowing the couple to marry before it is all paid, and then—if any contention arises between the families—insisting on the payment of the rest of the *yarad* or the return of the girl (as he is entitled to do in customary law[2] in such circumstances); and partly by husbands neglecting their wives until the latter get disgruntled and out of hand. *Īlā'*[3] seems to be quite unknown, and *li'ān* and *ẓihār*[3] only of the rarest occurrence (although isolated cases of each are remembered). Again, delegation of the right of divorce (*tafwīḍ*) seems to be virtually unknown, but suspended divorce exceedingly common: and there is much dispute as to the effect of a common formula " If you do not ask for maintenance, accommodation, dower, etc., you are divorced."[4] *Khul'* and *mubāra'a* are regarded as almost synonymous and are the commonest form of the dissolution of marriage, since husbands normally exert considerable pressure to this end[5]: they commonly take the form of the wife renouncing her right to dower, which is always a deferred payment in Somaliland, and only receiving a "*mut'a*" gift, at the discretion and according to the means of her husband. It should be added that a Somali woman can in most cases, it seems, virtually force a *khul'* by running away, refusing to return, and threatening to turn prostitute—when pressure is brought to bear upon her husband to secure her release.

With regard to gifts, questions of *hiba* and *ṣadaqa* very seldom come to court; and I heard of only one isolated instance of a vow (*nadhr*) being used to confer a gift. Waqf, again, is extremely rare, and almost limited to Berbera. It may be created in favour of the founder's family, or any third party, but not of himself; there need be no ultimate devotion to the poor or to some permanent " charity "; and should named beneficiaries fail the income would be given to the nearest relative of the founder.[6] No instance of the sale of waqf property could be remembered. Bequests are uncommon, and mostly limited to the urban population or to the " learned ": but where they exist they follow the ordinary rules. Inheritance has been discussed above.

Land cases are not very numerous, and do not follow Sharī'a law, even in Berbera; while any litigation on this subject goes to the British courts. Little " freehold " exists except in the major towns, and the vast majority of the land is regarded—or was previously regarded—as apportioned between the different tribes. The partial breakdown in this system has had regrettable results, in the destruction of thousands of trees for firewood, etc. If an individual cultivates a piece of land it is regarded as his; and even if he abandons it for years,

[1] For this there is, however, no justification in the Shāfi'ī texts.

[2] Which here differs sharply from the Sharī'a.

[3] For these and other technical terms, see Glossary.

[4] The better jurists regard this as null and void, since the *'iwaḍ* (consideration) is not properly defined, etc. But others regard it as valid—a sort of suspended *khul'*.

[5] By refusing to eat together, by supplying poor food and clothes, and by other forms of ill-treatment.

[6] All this is normal Shāfi'ī law.

or dies and his heirs apparently take no interest in it, there is often the greatest difficulty in inducing another Somali to work it—without the express permission of the individual or family concerned, which is frequently hard to obtain. In the towns the Government claims no title to land which was already in occupation before the township was proclaimed, but the remainder is now public land; and this is normally either let out in leasehold plots or granted to squatters for their huts on a two-year license. Chaos seems to have resulted in Berbera, however, from the assertion of a former District Commissioner that all privately occupied land in that town was freehold—a statement which has not yet been effectively lived down. Apart from formal litigation, District Commissioners have a considerable discretionary power with regard to "squatters on sufferance", whose continued occupancy largely depends on good husbandry, etc.[1] Inheritance in such holdings is normally left to the customary courts, which may follow either customary or Sharī'a law in this matter; but the discretionary power of the District Commissioner concerning what is not officially regarded as "property"[2] finds expression in administrative decisions.

The execution of the judgments of Qāḍīs' courts, where this involves any use of force, always rests with the District Commissioner. This, of course, is one reason why decrees of "obedience" (i.e., restitution of conjugal rights) are not executed in the Protectorate either by dragging the recalcitrant wife back to the marriage home or even by imprisoning her. All action to obtain maintenance for deserted wives, discussed at some length above, also falls on District Commissioners: the Qāḍīs merely pronounce the judgment of the divine law, or what adaptation thereof public opinion seems to demand, and leave the rest to the Administration. Because of this they are apt, sometimes, to complain that they themselves can do nothing to punish false testimony and other abuses; although they could, of course, always pass miscreants to the District Courts for punishment, in suitable cases, as is in fact occasionally done when a Qāḍī becomes sufficiently exasperated.

One or two Qāḍīs expressed doubt about the legality, according to the Sharī'a, of the appeal procedure. They agreed, of course, that the revision of judgments was allowable, but they stressed the fact that the complete re-hearing of a case which had already been tried was a very different matter, and also that no authority could be found in the classical texts for a bench of judges. Others, however, brushed aside these objections on the broad grounds of public interest: many of the Qāḍīs, they said, gave such insufficient detail in their judgments that bare revision, without a re-hearing of the case, would be impracticable; while it was obviously easier for a bench of judges to reverse a judgment than for a single judge to overrule a colleague. It would clearly be preferable in theory to have a bench of three rather than two, notwithstanding considerations of economy and the difficulty of communications: for should these two disagree under the present system the original judgment must stand by default, as it were, while a bench of three would ensure a clear decision[3].

On the whole the basic postulate of all modern reforms of the administration of Sharī'a law—that the Ruler may issue orders as to which of certain

[1] Under the Cultivation and Use of Land Ordinance, 1930, the District Commissioner has the right to demarcate areas in his district for agriculture (sect. 2), and "Where any person cultivating a garden within a demarcated area shall, either by lack of cultivation or by bad methods of cultivation, act in a manner . . . detrimental to the best interests of the tribe, the District Commissioner of the district may forbid such person to continue to use such garden" provided that twelve months' notice of intention of such prohibition first be given (sect. 4).

[2] i.e., the right in such land only amounts to a right of use.

[3] It seems, however, that the Sharī'a Court of Appeal usually contrives to concur in its judgments.

variant opinions should be applied by the courts—met very general acceptance, and sometimes enthusiastic support, among those whom I questioned. It was emphasised that in several points such instructions would clear up uncertainties and in others enable Qāḍīs conscientiously to follow the path of reform—and this was warmly welcomed by most. Many felt that the best method would be for all the Qāḍīs to be called into conference (and such a conference, similar to that commonly called among District Commissioners, would also be welcomed on other and general considerations), set to study certain points of law, and asked to decide what view would in each case most conduce to the public welfare; and the Governor might then issue instructions to all courts that these recommendations were to be followed. A few, however, expressed doubt as to the reaction of the *wadāds* and the public to such a development, and felt that the first step in the path of reform should be the appointment of a Chief Qāḍī whose learning and repute would be such that none dare challenge his pre-eminence. This would almost certainly be the best course if the right man could be found: but a conference of Qāḍīs seems a perfectly feasible alternative, provided they feel their way slowly and avoid any action which would arouse opposition, until public opinion becomes accustomed to the idea and the spread of education further undermines the influence of the *wadāds*.

These *wadāds* are still the chief trouble-makers in the country, for many of them are fanatical, ignorant, and extremely self-interested. They are apt to take the attitude that they alone are the champions of the pure Sharī'a, while the official Qāḍīs are mere civil servants, the puppets of an alien government. It seems, however, that their influence is waning considerably, while every advance in education accelerates this process by throwing their ignorance and retrogressive outlook into bolder relief. This, of course, is why they combat the progress of education. More than one Qāḍī, however, openly averred that he had no fear of their opposition, since he felt confident that, provided the course of progress was cautious and well-chosen, it would be easy enough to confound them. On the whole it seems clear that while the time has by no means come when it would be wise, or necessary, to challenge these *wadāds* in any open sense, yet no excessive fear of their machinations need, or should, retard the steady but cautious process of reform. A particularly encouraging feature is the real advance which has recently been made in education—a development which deserves the utmost support. It may also be observed in this context that there now seems little justification for the complete prohibition, for long considered essential in the interests of public security, of all Christian missionary work, although missionary activities would have to be suitably directed and controlled.

A passing reference should, perhaps, also be made here to the Ṣūfī fraternities. The Order first established in the Protectorate was the Qādirīya, and its influence is still widespread. The Aḥmadīya[1] is a far more recent Order, since its founder, Aḥmad bin Idrīs, only died in the nineteenth century; while the Ṣāliḥīya is a still more recent branch of the same Order, brought into great prominence by Muḥammad 'Abdullāh Ḥasan.[2] The Rifā'īya also has some adherents in the Protectorate. To the slight difference of opinion about marriage by abduction alleged to exist between those jurists who are Qādirīs and those who are Aḥmadīs reference has already been made. In the past a considerable dispute existed regarding the question of the *jum'a* prayer,[3] still a burning question among the Baganda of the Uganda Protectorate[4]: for the Qādirīya previously held rigidly to al-Shāfi'ī's "new" opinion that the prayer was

[1] Also called the Idrīsīya.

[2] The so-called " Mad Mulla."

[3] The Friday congregational prayer.

[4] See below, pp. 157-161.

invalid in all cases unless the congregation included at least forty adult males who were domiciled in the locality, etc., but the Aḥmadīya, while agreeing with this view in the more populous localities where it was practicable, considered al-Shāfi'ī's older opinion (which largely coincides with that of Abū Ḥanīfa) applicable elsewhere. Among the Qādirīya, moreover, there was a further dispute between those who omitted the *jum'a* prayer altogether where the conditions of validity were lacking, and those who performed it and then prayed the ordinary mid-day prayer in addition. Now, however, this dispute has apparently died down, and all are alleged to be agreed that the "forty-rule" should be observed where possible, but not regarded as essential elsewhere.

It is apparent, then, that the Somalis are zealous—and sometimes even fanatical—Muslims. True, a number of their ancient customs which are plainly at variance with the pure Sharī'a survive, as we have seen[1]; but for the most part the influence of the Sharī'a seems to be waxing rather than waning, even at the expense of ancient custom.[2] Some of these customs, it may be observed, correspond closely with those of pre-Islamic Arabia, while others betray interesting differences—a good example being provided by the Somali form of levirate marriage which, while it conforms to the Semitic pattern in its broad conception, includes the novel feature that the first husband's offspring are regarded as belonging to the second, rather than vice versa.

In conclusion, it may be noted that my chief sources of information were the Qāḍīs of Hargeisa, Mandera, Berbera, Sheikh and Burao; the unofficial Qāḍī of Odweina; the "Director of Religious Instruction" at Sheikh; an ex-Qāḍī, an Imām and a leading *wadād* at Burao; a number of Secretariat Officers and District Commissioners; and the then Legal Secretary. Cases involving Sharī'a law never, it seems, come before the High Court, although this might always happen if a foreign Muslim owning property in Somaliland died abroad[3]; and there are virtually no "mixed marriages" or other problems of that sort, for the population is almost entirely Muslim and solidly Shāfi'ī. It seems, however, that the British attitude to Sharī'a law has in the past been somewhat unnecessarily remote,[4] for I found the Qāḍīs and others whom I met (with the solitary exception of one *wadād*) friendly, co-operative and delighted to discuss both their law and its application: as elsewhere, the chief difficulty was to make them answer my questions in terms of actual practice rather than textbook orthodoxy.[5]

N.B. For certain very recent developments in Somaliland, see Appendix F.

---

[1] This in itself is no contradiction of their fanaticism or attachment to Islam: cp. remarks in a (unpublished) Paper by Dr. J. Schacht on Northern Nigeria.

[2] It is said that "the Sharī'a will always oust custom if the two are brought out into the open except in certain matters which are distasteful or where money is involved." But it is noteworthy that these provisos are extremely wide.

[3] For another possibility see pp. 41 and 44 (note 1).

[4] Although intended, of course, to convince the people that the Protecting Power has no design to exert pressure in anything so intimately connected with their religion.

[5] For general information about Islam in Somaliland see J. Spencer Trimingham's excellent study, ***Islam in Ethiopia.***

ZANZIBAR

The organisation of the courts in Zanzibar, their respective jurisdiction, and the law which each applies are of more than ordinary interest on account of the "dual jurisdiction" exercised by the British courts and the Zanzibar courts respectively. Since, however, admirable monographs[1] on this subject are easily available, it will be sufficient here to summarise the position as it now stands in its broadest outline, devoid of details or of historical explanation.

The "British Court" has jurisdiction in all cases in which any plaintiff or defendant, accused or complainant is a British subject, a British "Protected person", a subject (etc.) of any of the foreign powers who have agreed thereto,[2] a subject of any other Christian Power not represented by a Consul in Zanzibar, or a person in the regular service of any of the above.[3] In addition, the British Court alone has jurisdiction under certain Decrees—e.g., the Insolvency Decree, 1917, the Fugitive Offenders' Decree, 1923, and the Trade Marks Decree, 1930—concerning which the Sultan has made a complete surrender of jurisdiction. The "Zanzibar Court" of His Highness the Sultan, on the other hand, has jurisdiction in all other cases, i.e., in criminal cases where both all the accused and all the persons against whom an offence is alleged to have been committed are either subjects of His Highness or of some non-Christian Power, and in civil suits where all the plaintiffs and defendants fall into one of these two categories[4]—except, of course, where the Sultan has expressly surrendered his jurisdiction.

Both the organisation and personnel of the courts which exercise the jurisdiction belonging to Her Britannic Majesty and to His Highness the Sultan respectively have, however, been completely assimilated by the British Subordinate Courts Order, 1923, and the Zanzibar Courts Decree of the same date (as repeatedly amended). Her Britannic Majesty's court is termed the British Court[5] and the following courts subordinate thereto have been established:—

(*a*) First class subordinate courts. (Courts of Resident Magistrates, etc.)

(*b*) Second class subordinate courts. (Courts of persons specially appointed, etc.)

(*c*) Third class subordinate courts. (Courts of District Officers, etc.)

[1] e.g., *The Dual Jurisdiction in Zanzibar,* by J. H. Vaughan, 1935, and *The Conflict of Laws in Zanzibar,* by H. E. Kingdon, 1940, both printed by Government Printer, Zanzibar.

[2] These now include all the Powers which once exercised exterritorial jurisdiction in Zanzibar, although France did not surrender her rights of testamentary jurisdiction until a Franco-British Convention in 1937 (art. 22, with art. 18)

[3] Originally under art. 6 (1) of the Order in Council of 1906 and sect. 3 (1) of the Jurisdiction Decree, 1908, but now under the Jurisdiction Decree of 1934, sects. 3 and 4. For the British Court's jurisdiction over any Zanzibar subjects charged with criminal offences jointly with any person subject thereto, see the Zanzibar Courts Decree, 1923, sect. 30, the Jurisdiction Decree, 1934, sect. 4 (*c*) and the Order in Council of 1924, art. 5 (3) [which provides that its terms should extend to any Zanzibar subjects or foreigners in the cases and according to the provisions specified in any Decree of the Sultan].

[4] Persons domiciled in the Kenya Protectorate (as distinct from the Colony) are presumably subject to H.H.'s courts in Zanzibar as H.H.'s subjects, although they are also, of course, British "protected persons." This, however, apparently remains an open question. A still more difficult problem, perhaps, is posed by certain persons who alternate between 'Umān and Zanzibar.

[5] Sect. 2.

(*d*) Qāḍis'[1] courts.

(*e*) Mudirial courts.[2]

Criminal jurisdiction, within prescribed limits, is vested in all except the Qāḍis' courts[3]; while the civil jurisdiction of each subordinate court is similarly prescribed.[4] To the jurisdiction of the Qāḍis' courts further reference will be made below. Appeals are allowed from all subordinate courts to the British Court (provided that, in civil cases, the sum or value involved exceeds two hundred shillings or special leave is obtained).[5]

The reconstitution of the Sultan's courts established an exactly parallel system. At the head stands His Highness the Sultan's Court for Zanzibar, which is usually called the "Zanzibar Court." It consists of the same personnel and "corresponds functionally, in both criminal and civil matters, to the British Court." Courts subordinate thereto again correspond "in designation and extent of jurisdiction" to those subordinate to the British Court, and are presided over by the same officers. And "to complete this assimilation, appeals from the Zanzibar Court are allowed . . . to the Court of Appeal for Eastern Africa and thence to the Privy Council."[6] As a consequence of this assimilation, therefore, the same judge will sit sometimes as the British Court exercising the jurisdiction of Her Britannic Majesty and sometimes as the Zanzibar Court exercising the jurisdiction of His Highness the Sultan.[7]

What, then, is the difference in the law they administer? In effect, not very much; for an enormous proportion of the law they both administer, whether substantive or adjective, is covered by the Sultan's Decrees which, when countersigned by the British Resident, are equally binding on all courts, while any Order of Her Majesty in Council, and any Acts of the Parliament of the United Kingdom which apply to Zanzibar, are now automatically applicable in the Sultan's courts as well as the British courts;[8] with the solitary qualification that Imperial Enactments are not to be construed as applying to His Highness' subjects "where a contrary intention appears." Thus the Penal and other Decrees contain the whole of the criminal law now applicable in Zanzibar. Similarly the Criminal Procedure and Evidence Decrees almost entirely cover their respective subjects; and "on any point not specifically provided for, the High Court (which term means Her Britannic Majesty's High Court for Zanzibar and His Highness the Sultan's Court for Zanzibar)[9] exercises its criminal jurisdiction according to the course of procedure and practice observed by Her Majesty's High Court of Justice in England.[10] The subordinate courts naturally follow the example of the High Court wherever that example is applicable, and indeed the British subordinate courts are bound by article 24 of the Zanzibar Order in Council to follow, on points not dealt with by any legislation, the procedure and practice

[1] Spelt Kathis in Zanzibar Ordinances, etc.: but see Introduction regarding the liberty taken in maintaining a uniform spelling of Arabic words throughout this Survey, to avoid the confusion and misunderstanding which might otherwise result.

[2] Sect. 4 (1). [3] Sects. 10 and 11. [4] Sect. 7.

[5] Sect. 15, as amended in 1947 (Government Notice No. 149).

[6] This was provided by the Zanzibar Courts Decree, 1923, the Eastern African Court of Appeal Order in Council and the Eastern African (Appeal to Privy Council) Order in Council, both of 1923. These quotations are taken from an article by S. S. Abrahams in Vol. VI (Third Series) of the Journal of the Society of Comparative Legislation, 1924, pp. 293 ff.

[7] This must sometimes prove very confusing, but an effective safeguard for any error has been provided in the Jurisdiction Decree, 1934, sect. 5, which enacts (in effect) that should H.B.M.'s Courts through inadvertance exercise jurisdiction in a case which should have been taken by H.H.'s Courts, their judgment will not on that account be liable to appeal or revision.

[8] Imperial Enactments (Application) Decree, 1939.

[9] Interpretation and General Clauses Decree, 1917, sect. 2.

[10] c.p. Criminal Procedure Decree, sect. 3.

observed by the Courts of Justice and Justices of the Peace in England on 7th July, 1897. The Evidence Decree, section 2, expressly excludes the Muhammadan[1] law of evidence from any court in Zanzibar; and on the civil side the Rules of Court, the Civil Procedure Decree and Rules, together with the Evidence and Limitation Decrees, govern procedure in both sets of courts."[2] This is also true of the Oaths Decree.

It is only in the substantive law applicable to civil proceedings, therefore, that the distinction remains of any great practical importance.[3] Here, too, legislation now covers much of the field: but the difference remains that, for the rest, the corpus juris in the Sultan's courts consists of Sharī'a law,[4] as locally applied, while in the British courts it consists of the common law and doctrines of equity,[5] together with that application of Muhammadan, Hindu and Buddhist personal law (in respect of matrimonial matters and questions of inheritance) which the British courts in Zanzibar inherited from those of Bombay under Regulation 4 of 1827.[6] In matters of inheritance, moreover, this is now expressly reinforced by the Succession Decree, 1917, section 7 whereof provides that "Muhammadans, Hindus, Buddhists and exempted persons" shall be governed by their own personal law in this respect. It should also be observed that the British Court will apply Sharī'a law in any suit concerning land not covered by any special enactment, on the common law principle of the *lex loci rei sitae*—for, however many encroachments have been made by statute law since 1908, section 7 of the Courts Decree of 1923 still declares that "in civil matters the Law of Islam is and is hereby declared to be the fundamental law of the Protectorate."

[1] Spelt Mahommedan in most Zanzibar Ordinances, etc., and in the passage quoted, but see Introduction regarding the spelling of Arabic words in this Survey.

[2] The Conflict of Laws in Zanzibar, by H. E. Kingdon, pp. 12, 13.

[3] It may, however, be added that in so far as H.H.'s jurisdiction is concerned sect. 4 of the Zanzibar Courts Decree, 1923, provides that "the Supreme Judicial Authority is and remains vested in H.H. the Sultan as heretofore;" sect. 8(2) has a proviso that "where two or more of H.H.'s subjects apply to Him in writing requesting that He shall determine any such matters stated to be in issue between them as would constitute a good cause of action in a civil suit and H.H. elects to accede . . . and in writing communicates His decision . . . to the Zanzibar Court, a decree may be issued giving effect to such decision which shall be final . . ."; while sect. 5 (as amended in 1948) enacts that "His Highness the Sultan in the exercise of His Royal Prerogative of mercy may grant to any offender convicted in any of His Courts a pardon either free or subject to lawful conditions, or may remit or commute the whole or any part of the sentence passed on such offender, or may respite the execution of such sentence for such period as He shall think fit and may remit any fines, penalties or forfeitures to which such offender may be liable."

It should, however, be noted that H.H.'s courts have jurisdiction over certain non-Muslims (e.g., Chinese) and certain Muslims who are neither Ibāḍīs nor Shāfi'īs, and it is not altogether clear to what personal law such are subject. Sect. 12 of the Courts Decree, 1899, provided for the trial of non-Muslims by a special court, but this has not been re-enacted. Presumably, however, their own personal law should be applied, unless their actions had given rise to the inference that they had adopted the law of the people among whom they had settled (see *Abdulrahim* v. *Halimbhai* [1Z.L.R. 669]).

[5] Zanzibar Order in Council, 1924, art. 24.

[6] This provided that the Bombay courts, in the absence of specific enactments, should apply "the usage of the country, the law of the defendant . . . and justice, equity and good conscience"—and here the "law of the defendant" obviously covers Islamic personal law, while the "usage of the country" makes that law subject to local variations. In Zanzibar H.M.'s courts were bound, by the terms of art. 21 of the Order in Council of 1884, to apply the principles of this Regulation. And this has been held to have been successively preserved by art. 29 of the Order in Council of 1897, art. 56 of the Order in Council of 1906, the proviso to art. 63 of the Order in Council of 1914 and by art. 44 of the Order in Council of 1924. See *Rana Ramji* v. *Radhabai* (1937), 5 Z.L.R. 91.

[7] See *Sec. of State* v. *Charlesworth, Pilling & Co.*, 1 Z.L.R. 105;28.I.A.121.

All the same, this "fundamental law" has been ousted by the Decrees of the Sultan, as has been noted, to an enormous extent. Nothing whatever of the Islamic criminal law or law of evidence and procedure officially remains, except, perhaps, such of the latter as may be indirectly preserved under the Oaths Decree of 1917.[1] But this does not mean that the Qāḍīs, in Zanzibar as elsewhere, do not in fact follow the basic rules of evidence and procedure laid down in the Sharī'a; and in practice their judgments are only quashed or varied on this account on appeal where some miscarriage of justice or flagrant breach of the law seems to have occurred.[2] Again, the Contract Decree and the Transfer of Property Decree, both of 1917 and countersigned, largely cover matters of contract and commerce, but section 1(2) of the former provides that "nothing herein contained shall effect . . . any usage or custom of trade, nor any incident of any contract, not inconsistent with the provisions of this Decree," while sections 2 and 116 of the latter enact that nothing in Parts II and VII respectively of this Decree "shall be deemed to affect any rule of Hindu, Muhammadan or Buddhist law."[3] Even in theory, therefore, cases may still come before the courts regarding contracts made under the Sharī'a, although such cases, except those concerning gifts, seem to be increasingly rare and unimportant. In addition, moreover, cases properly covered by the above Decrees are sometimes decided without reference thereto.[4] But in general the application of "the law of Islam" seems largely limited today to actions in tort before His Highness' courts and questions of Muslim family law (including, of course, testate and intestate succession), gifts, waqfs and certain real property cases under the respective jurisdiction of both sets of courts.

Even in these matters, however, the provisions of certain Decrees have affected the law to be applied. Thus the Marriage (Solemnisation and Registration) Decree, 1915 (countersigned), would, like similar legislation elsewhere, provide a way in which a Muslim girl could validly marry a Christian man, regardless of the attitude of her guardian, provided she was over twenty-one years of age,[5] or with the written consent of her father, or (if he were dead, of unsound mind or absent from the Protectorate) of her mother, etc., if under that age. This

[1] e.g., sect. 7 provides that "If any party to any judicial proceedings offers to be bound by any . . . oath . . . if such oath . . . is made by the other party . . . the court may, if it thinks fit, ask such party . . . whether or not he will make the oath . . . ;" sect. 9 states that "the evidence so given shall, as against the person who offered to be bound as aforesaid, be conclusive proof of the matter stated"; and sect. 10 provides that "if the party . . . refuses . . . he shall not be compelled . . . but the court shall record, as part of the proceedings, the nature of the oath . . . and that he refused it, together with any reason which he may assign for his refusal." It is obvious that this puts the defendant who refuses the oath proferred, under Islamic law, at the instance of the plaintiff who cannot otherwise prove this case, on a precarious footing. In *Ismailji Mohamedali* v. *Hasan* (1936) (5 Z.L.R. 87), where the trial magistrate commented unfavourably upon the refusal of one of the parties to allow the case to be settled by oath in the mosque, Law C.J. held that this was "an expression of the magistrate's opinion of the appellant's demeanour more than anything else, which the magistrate was entitled to do." Sect. 114 (illustration (*h*) and counter-illustration (*h*)) of the Evidence Decree also appears relevant in this context.

[2] e.g., where a plaintiff has lost his case because his witnesses are "interested" or otherwise ineligible under Islamic rules, but where the circumstances are such that the High Court regards his case as adequately proved—or where a party is adjudged to have lost his case solely because he refused to take some oath proferred by the Qāḍī. This is perfectly in order, since sect. 75 of the Civil Procedure Decree enacts that no decree shall be reversed or substantially varied on account of any defect or irregularity in any proceedings in the suit not affecting the merits of the case or the jurisdiction of the court: and this section has, it seems, always been liberally interpreted in dealing with appeals from Qāḍīs.

[3] Part II concerns transfers of property by act of parties, and Part VII covers gifts.

[4] See below, p. 69.

[5] Or a widow: sects. 9 (*b*) and 16.

is, of course, contrary to the Sharī'a both in the fundamental fact that no marriage of a Muslim girl with a non-Muslim man is ever regarded as valid thereunder and also in the subsidiary particular that in Islamic law a girl's marriage guardian, in default of her father, is not her mother but her nearest agnate.[1] No one, however, may marry under this Decree if already married "by native law or custom" to any person other than the intended spouse;[2] while anyone married thereunder is "incapable during the subsistence of such marriage of contracting a valid marriage under any native law or custom"[3]—and in both these clauses the phrase "native law and custom" must, it seems, be regarded as including Islamic law, however incorrect this nomenclature may be in Zanzibar. No marriage concluded under this Decree, moreover, may be terminated except by judicial decree, while the conclusion of a contract of marriage—even Islamic—with any other person before such dissolution would be an offence under section 39(*j*). And all the above provisions hold good, of course, whether or not one or both of the parties has subsequently embraced—or apostatised from—Islam, quite regardless of the relevant doctrines of Islamic law.

The Islamic law of marriage is also somewhat affected by the Penal Decree (countersigned) of 1934, for section 133(2) makes it an offence for a man carnally to know or attempt the knowledge of a wife who has not attained both puberty and the age of thirteen (unless he had reasonable cause to believe she had),[4] while section 130 makes it a felony for anyone to take away, or detain against her will, a woman of any age "with intent to marry or carnally know" her, or, indeed, "to cause her to be married or carnally known by any other person."[5] Again, the Native Christian Divorce Decree (countersigned) of 1925 includes a clause by way of protection of a Christian wife whose husband, since the solemnisation of their marriage, "has changed his profession of Christianity for the profession of some other religion and gone through a form of marriage with another woman,"[6] for she may petition the court for the dissolution of her marriage in such cases. Similarly, the Marriage and Divorce (Muhammadan) Registration Decree of 1935 and 1936 (as amended in 1944) provides that all marriages, divorces and revocations of divorce lawfully affected in accordance with the provisions of Muhammadan law (other than those where the parties thereto are Indian members of the Bohora, Ismā'īlī, Ithnā 'Asharī, or Memon sects or communities,[7] or such other sects or communities as the British Resident may exclude) must be registered, under penalties for failure to do so to which the parties to the marriage, the guardian of the woman, and the witnesses present at the ceremony, all (in suitable circumstances) become liable.[8] Originally it was also laid down that the courts would not normally take cognisance or give effect to unregistered marriages,[9] but this provision was subsequently repealed in the amendment of 1944.

Again, the Succession Decree (countersigned) of 1917, while it excepts Muslims from most[10] of the provisions which run counter to Sharī'a law, provides (*inter alia*)

[1] On the priority between such agnates there are minor differences between the schools.

[2] Sects. 9 (*d*) and 39 (*i*).

[3] Sect. 31.

[4] A provision which is both more definite and more stringent than the normal rule of Islamic law that she must be "able to bear" this. To this Tanganyika, alone in East Africa, has a parallel, but by no means identical, provision. But see also Aden and Somaliland (see pp. 35, 44, 88, 129, etc.).

[5] This provision is common to all E. African Codes, and might well expose to punishment a Muslim father who could claim that according to the Sharī'a he was only exercising his right to give his daughter in or under a compulsory marriage. See pp. 44, 88, etc.

[6] Sect. 5(2). Whereas she would enjoy no such protection under the Sharī'a.

[7] Sect. 1(2).

[8] Sect. 21, etc.

[9] c.p. sect. 20 of the Decree of 1935 and 1936.

[10] c.p. p. 34.

that in any case in which the *Bayt al-Māl*[1] is entitled, in whole or in part, it shall be lawful for the court in its discretion to order a sum not exceeding Rs. 100 to be distributed in such proportions as it may think fit among persons who were dependent on the deceased, and a sum not exceeding Rs. 500 to the spouse relict.[2] Similarly, the Administrator-General's Decree (countersigned) of 1925 allows the Administrator-General to " pay or transfer property not exceeding Rs. 500 in value to the husband or wife or wives surviving the deceased " in any case in which the *Bayt al-Māl* is entitled to the whole or any portion of an estate.[3]

The Slavery Decree of 1909 lays down categorically in section 2 that "the courts . . . shall not in any case recognise the status of slavery in Zanzibar."[4] But section 4 provides that " all concubines lawfully held at the commencement of this Decree, although free, shall, together with their children, continue to be entitled to all the rights and privileges which they had previously enjoyed under the Muhammadan law, except that any concubine who shall leave her master without his consent shall sacrifice all such rights and privileges, including her right to the custody of her children by him."

The Juvenile Offenders Decree, 1935, confers upon a Juvenile court, in regard to children in need of care and protection (as defined in section 15), the same power of committing to the guardianship of a fit and proper person as is allowed in similar circumstances under the Children and Young Persons Act, 1933.[5] These provisions are, of course, intended only for children living in an undesirable environment; but they might, in certain circumstances, run counter to normal Muslim principles regarding the care and custody of minors. It is also noteworthy in this context, moreover, that the Juvenile court has been constituted in the same manner as an English Juvenile court; that Muslim women are included in the panel; and that the Shāfi'ī Qāḍī has expressed the opinion that they are qualified to sit as Qāḍīs in such circumstances. Again, the Majority Decree (countersigned) of 1917 fixes the age of majority of all persons at either 18 or 21, according to circumstances,[6] but does not affect their capacity before such age in matters of "marriage, dower, divorce or adoption";[7] while the Arab and African Guardianship Decree (countersigned) of 1927 provides that no Arab or African of under 25 years of age shall be capable of being a guardian[8] or of receiving any property in the care of his guardian,[9] and that any contract made or debt incurred by such person as against property in the care of his guardian shall be void.[10] Both these Decrees may be said, therefore, to vary the relevant principles of Islamic law.

As regards waqf, the Waqf[11] Property Decree (countersigned) of 1916—which superseded two previous Decrees of 1905 and 1907 respectively—established a Waqf Commission of eight members, [12] and gave this Commission a right of

---

[1] Here spelt " Bet-el-Mal ": but see Introduction regarding the spelling of Arabic words. Cp. Glossary.
[2] Sect. 327.
[3] Sect. 12(3). Under the Sharī'a the spouse relict is never entitled to more than his or her Qur'anic share, except in so far as certain jurists and/or countries allow him or her to profit by the doctrine of the " return " in the absence of any other heirs. These two provisions have the effect, therefore, of extending that doctrine—in part—to Zanzibar, at the discretion of the court or the Administrator-General.
[4] This is, of course, entirely contrary to the Sharī'a.
[5] Sect. 15.
[6] Sects. 3 and 4.
[7] Sect. 2(*a*).
[8] Sect. 3.
[9] Sect. 4.
[10] Sect. 5.
[11] Spelt " Wakf " in Zanzibar Decrees: but see Introduction.
[12] Sect. 3.

general oversight over all waqfs[1] and particular oversight over any such property which had no properly appointed trustee or of which the trustees appeared to be acting in an improper manner.[2] In such cases it must adminster the property " in strict accordance with the intentions of the dedicator thereof, whether such intentions be traditional or otherwise ascertained . . . , provided that the same be practicable and lawful according to the laws of Islam."[3] Where, however, these intentions are unlawful, impracticable or unascertainable—or where any surplus revenue remains after such intentions have been carried out—the Commission may " make such arrangement for the due administration of such property or surplus revenue, as the case may be, for such good, lawful and charitable uses for the benefit of the holders of the tenets of Islam as they may deem advisable ";[4] and where they are satisfied that the intentions of the founder cannot reasonably be carried into effect, they may, with the approval of the British Resident, " cause the said property to be sold " and apply the proceeds of the sale accordingly.[5] Again, the Waqf Validating Decree of 1946[6] in general follows the Indian model, but approximates rather more closely to pure Sharī'a law in that it expressly includes the " kindred " of founders as well as their " families, children and descendants " in its scope: [7] but it is noteworthy (*a*) that its primary terms apply only to " any Arab or African professing the Muhammadan faith,"[8] while it provides in section 5 that the Indian Mussalman Wakf Validating Act of 1913 " shall apply to every waqf created on or after 7th March, 1913[9] by any person professing the Muhammadan faith other than an Arab or African in the same manner as the said Act applies to waqfs in British India "; (*b*) that it proclaims Ibāḍī waqfs in which the first charge is for the founder's own support to be valid.[10] It seems, moreover, that both the Zanzibar High Court and the Waqf Commissioners treat as valid a Shāfi'ī waqf in which no ultimate gift to a permanent charity is provided for at all. This is perfectly correct Shāfi'ī practice, and is adequately covered by section 6 of the Decree which reads: " Nothing in this Decree shall be deemed to affect any other custom or usage whether local or prevalent among Muhammadans of any particular class or sect." It would be much more difficult, however, for a similar discretion to be exercised in favour of, e.g., a waqf made by an Indian Ḥanafī where such implied dedication to a permanent charity was limited to the use of the word waqf or its equivalents and the absence of any provisions inconsistent therewith,[11] for here the decisions of Indian courts that there must be some reasonable indication, express or implied, in the waqf document as to its ultimate disposition might be regarded as decisive.

The law of waqf is also affected by the Land Acquisition Decree (countersigned) of 1909, section 31 of which provides that where, e.g., waqf land must necessarily be acquired for the building of a road, etc., and sale thereof is refused, the District Commissioner may tender payment and if necessary deposit this in court, while section 32 enacts that where any money is so deposited and

[1] Sects. 9, 10, 11, 16 and 17.

[2] Sect. 12.

[3] Sect. 13.

[4] Sect. 13.

[5] Sect. 14. Both these provisions go well beyond the usual Shāfi'ī rules. But, for comment, see the Kenya section of this Survey (pp. 93 ff.).

[6] Also countersigned. But now cp. Waqf Validating (Amendment) Decree, 1951 (see p. 330).

[7] Sect. 3.

[8] Sect. 3.

[9] Apparently it was not realised that this had been made retroactive in 1930.

[10] Sect. 3. This is a matter on which the Ibāḍīs are themselves divided (See below). The validity of such waqfs among Ḥanafīs is not mentioned, but the Indian Act is made applicable to almost all such (See above).

[11] Which is the view of Abū Yūsuf and those who follow his opinion in this respect.

"it appears that the land . . . belonged to any person who had no power to alienate the same, the court shall order the money to be invested in the purchase of other lands to be held under the like title and conditions, or . . . in . . . approved securities."[1] Again, the Registration of Documents Decree (countersigned) of 1919 rules that "No document executed after 1st January, 1920, purporting or operating to create, declare, assign, limit, or extinguish any right, title or interest, whether vested in or contingent to, in, or over immovable property in Zanzibar, except such documents as are of a testamentary nature, shall affect any immovable property . . . or be received as evidence in any civil proceedings of any transaction affecting that property, unless it has been registered as . . . prescribed: Provided that an unregistered document affecting immovable property and required by this Decree or the Transfer of Property Decree to be registered may be received in evidence (*a*) of a contract in a suit for specific performance where such suit lies; or (*b*) of part performance of a contract relating to immovable property where such part performance would otherwise be receivable as evidence of the existence of the contract; or (*c*) of any collateral transaction not required to be effected by registered instrument.[2] It has, therefore, been held that, since it is essential to the validity of a waqf that the settler shall entirely divest himself of his proprietary right in the property concerned, a waqf *inter vivos* must be registered under the terms of this Decree (section 4), even where the founder constitutes himself the first administrator (*mutawalli*). Presumably, however, a suit would lie for an agreement to create a waqf, and also to enforce registration, if the waqf had been made for a consideration and the agreement could be proved *aliunde* rather than only by the waqf instrument itself.

These last Decrees, however, do not primarily concern waqfs but immovable property in general. Other legislation concerning realty includes the Public Land Decree (countersigned) of 1921, the Land Alienation Decree (countersigned) of 1939, and the Ground Rent Restriction Decree (countersigned) of 1940—as amended in 1943 and 1947. The first of these defines Public Land as any land in the Protectorate "which is vested in or which is subject to any rights of disposal by either His Highness . . . in virtue of His Sultanate[3] or in or by the Zanzibar Government and includes all waste and unoccupied land and all land occupied by natives as hereinafter defined in accordance with local or tribal custom"[4]—and the definition of "natives" in this Decree "means and includes all Wahadimu, Wapemba, and the members of any indigenous African tribes who may be settled in the Protectorate, but does not include Swahilis nor persons who are or derive their descent from immigrants from the Comoro Islands or Madagascar".[5] It further provides that the British Resident on behalf of His Highness . . . "may from time to time take possession of and grant, sell, lease or otherwise dispose of any public land on such terms and conditions as he may think fit, but subject . . . to the payment of full compensation for any trees, crops or buildings which may be thereon and for any native right of occupation which may exist in respect thereof"[6]: and that His Highness in Executive Council may "make Rules (*a*) prescribing the terms and conditions upon which such land may be occupied by non-natives; and (*b*) prescribing the

[1] Both these provisions are designed to cover the case of land needed for public purposes which otherwise might be unobtainable because it belonged to a waqf the administrator of which would not, or could not, alienate it.

[2] Sect. 4.

[3] See below, for the way in which such property was formerly regarded as the private property of the Sultan and as part of his estate.

[4] Which is thus clearly differentiated in Zanzibar from the Sharī'a (see sect. 2).

[5] Sect. 2.

[6] Sect. 4.

terms and conditions upon which such land may be granted, sold or leased . . ."[1] The Land Alienation Decree, 1939 (which repealed and replaced the Alienation of Land (Restriction and Evidence Decree), on the other hand, was designed to prevent Arab and African land falling into the hands of immigrant money-lenders. It accordingly precludes any permanent alienation, lease for more than two years, or mortgage of land by Arabs or Africans, without the consent of a Land Alienation Board, which may impose suitable conditions with respect to such alienation,[2] the only exception to this rule being in the case of gifts or waqfs in favour of near relations. Similarly the Land Protection (Debts Settlement) Decree (countersigned), 1938, empowered the Government to acquire by compulsory assignment all mortgages of land by Arabs or Africans and to arrange for repayment of such debts by instalments spread over a number of years (and the only mortgages not so acquired were those in which the title of the mortgagor was defective or unsatisfactory).[3]

The effect of this legislation has been that such mortgages as are now created are almost invariably in the usual English form and that Islamic forms of mortgage may be said no longer to exist in Zanzibar. Mortgages acquired by the Zanzibar Government under the Debts Settlement Decree are, of course, governed by the special provisions of that Decree. But until the passing of the now repealed Alienation of Land (Restriction and Evidence) Decree in 1934 Islamic forms of mortgage, although tending to become less common, were still far from rare. The typical "mortgages" of Islamic law are, of course, the orthodox pledge (*rahn*), the questionable usufructuary mortgage,[4] and the still more questionable mortgage by conditional sale (*bay' al-khiyār*).[5] The last named is normally in the form of two separate contracts, an ordinary deed of sale of certain property by A to B, together with a collateral agreement to the effect that the sale shall become absolute if the loan is not repaid by a specified date but void[6] if it is—followed, in most cases, by a lease of the property by B to A for a "rent" which really represents the interest on the loan, etc.: and much confusion has arisen as to whether evidence of this collateral agreement to show the true nature of the deed of sale is admissible under the Evidence Decree (section 92).[7] It was for this reason that the (now repealed) Alienation of Land Decree, 1934, included the express provision that "Notwithstanding the provisions of the Evidence Decree, where an Arab or an African, having been . . . a party as vendor to a conveyance of immovable property, has remained in occupation of the property conveyed after the execution of the conveyance and has made or agreed to make to the purchaser periodical payments in respect of such occupation, oral evidence may be admitted to prove the existence of an oral agreement that the transaction should amount to a mortgage and not to a conveyance of the property; and the court on being satisfied of the existence of

[1] Sect. 6. All land in Zanzibar and Pemba not otherwise owned is now Public Land.

[2] Sects. 4 ff. The Decree also imposes certain restrictions upon the attachment and sale of land in execution of court decrees for certain kinds of debts.

[3] Sects. 12 ff. Some of these provisions may, of course, be said partially to restrict the almost unfettered right of an adult, sane Muslim, under the Sharī'a, to alienate his property as he sees fit.

[4] But see sect. 58(4) of the Transfer of Property Decree.

[5] Which Muslim purists originally regarded as contrary to the law, but was later accepted by many on the grounds of necessity. See sect. 58(3) of the Transfer of Property Decree: also full discussion in *Sheikh Burhan* v. *Khalfan bin Salim* (1929) 4 Z.L.R. 90, where it was shown that Zanzibar Qāḍīs had upheld these contracts, while rejecting other contracts of "usury," for many years; that they were specifically covered by rules issued under the Registration of Documents Decree; and that they must be regarded as a "polite fiction to enable persons needing money to obtain credit without incurring the possible guilt of dealing in transactions by way of interest."

[6] Or, at least, that the property should be re-conveyed.

[7] See *Said* v. *Mahfuz* (1906) 1 Z.L.R. 189, *Brit. Res.* v. *Hafiz* (1917), 1 Z.L.R. 526, and *Raschid* v. *Salem* (1918), 1 Z.L.R. 614.

such agreement shall impound the conveyance and declare it to be of no effect ".[1]

Again, the Ground Rent Restriction Decree, 1940, provides that no landlord shall be entitled to " charge, or recover from, any tenant in respect of the land upon which the tenant's house stands, whether as rent or as damages for use and occupation or otherwise, any ground rent in excess of the standard ground rent "[2]; to require a tenant to remove his house, except upon the production of a certificate as provided;[3] or to increase the standard ground rent without the sanction of the Ground Rent Tribunal.[4] Section 13 (as amended in 1947), on the other hand, prohibits the erection by a tenant of any additional structure on the land without the landlord's written consent (etc.), except for the purpose of complying with building regulations: and in case of contravention of this section, the landlord may apply to the Tribunal either to sanction an increase of rent or to make an order for the removal of the structure. These provisions may be regarded as an interesting modification of the Islamic rules regarding *ghaṣb*. The Tribunal, moreover, must sanction any order for the removal of houses, which would only be allowed where the land is properly required for other purposes, or the land rent was more than twelve months in arrears, or on other reasonable grounds: and compensation for such removal must be assessed by the same authority.[5]

Finally, two further points deserve mention, which emerge from successive amendments to the Courts Decree of 1923 [up to and including the Courts (Amendment) Decree[6] and the District Administration and Rural Local Government Decree (countersigned), both of 1947]. Firstly, the jurisdiction of the Qāḍīs has been defined as "matters relating to the personal status, marriage, divorce and inheritance (where the claim . . . does not exceed 1,500 shillings) of Arabs and Muhammadan Africans " together with " suits and proceedings of a civil nature in which the subject matter can be estimated at a money value and does not exceed 800 shillings ".[7] Secondly, the Mudirial courts have now been given jurisdiction over all persons in the Protectorate, except that those subject to the Zanzibar Order in Council, 1924, have the right to apply for the case to be heard by another court and must be so informed at the commencement of the proceedings:[8] their jurisdiction, moreover, is both civil and criminal,[9] and they may (and in cases concerning " native land " and " native law " must) call in the aid of two or more assessors;[10] while simple rules of procedure for civil and criminal cases have been specially laid down. The law which these courts are to apply is, moreover, defined as " any custom which is recognised by any natives residing in the Protectorate as being binding upon themselves as having the force of law " and which is not repugnant to justice or morality or inconsistent with any other law.[11] Here again, then, we find mention of a customary law (*mila*) in Zanzibar as distinct from the Sharī'a, although it has in fact assimilated a good deal of Islamic law in the course of the centuries—mostly Shāfi'ī, but some slight traces of Shī'ī influence, evidently introduced by early settlers from the Persian gulf (traditionally Shirāz), persist.[12]

---

[1] Sect. 18.
[2] Sect. 3.
[3] Sect. 4.
[4] Sect. 7.
[5] Sect. 8.
[6] cp. also the British Subordinate Courts (Amendment) Order, 1947.
[7] The Courts (Amendment) Decree, sect. 2(*d*).
[8] The Mudirial Court Rules, 1947, sect. 9.
[9] Ibid, sect. 3.
[10] Ibid, sect. 7.
[11] Ibid, sect. 2(1).
[12] e.g., the Wahadimu still celebrate Nawroz, the Persian New Year's Day, etc. It is said that Sultan Barghash " to break the influence of the chiefs, placed the Wahadimu under ordinary Arab law, administered by Qāḍīs of the Sunnī sect " (*Zanzibar in Contemporary Times*, by R. N. Lyne, p. 239).

In such matters as marriage and inheritance Zanzibar *mila* appears to have become fused with the Sharī'a, except among pagan immigrants: but in questions of land tenure certain differences remain.[1]

The sects and schools of Islam represented in Zanzibar must be as varied and diverse as in any town on earth. The majority of the inhabitants are, of course, Shāfi'īs, for the Shāfi'ī school is predominant throughout East Africa. But the Sultan and many of the Arab inhabitants are Ibāḍīs from 'Umān (although Shāfi'ī Arabs from the Hijāz, Yemen, Aden, Ḥaḍramaut, Baḥrain, etc.—many of them British protected persons—are also found in Zanzibar). Somalis, Comorians and Madagascans are all Shāfi'īs, and so are most of the Africans:[2] but the Indian immigrants include Ḥanafīs, Ithnā 'Asharīs, Bohoras and Khojas (of both the Ismā'īlī and Ithnā 'Asharī factions) and Aḥmadīs. There are also numerous Baluchis, who are Ḥanafīs, and a few Persians, who are Ithnā 'Asharīs.[3]

The vast majority of the personal and family problems of the Indian communities, however, never come to court but are settled within the community concerned.[4] Any case which does come to court from these communities—or, indeed, from the Baluchis, Somalis, etc.—is within the exclusive jurisdiction of the British court and is decided according to the school of the parties concerned (and, where they differ, normally, but not invariably, that of the defendant),[5] and any custom at variance with the usual principles of their school which can be proved to have been adopted by any group or sub-section would similarly be recognised.[6] In the Sultan's courts, on the other hand, only the two "local" schools of the Shāfi'īs and Ibāḍīs are recognised, and Qāḍīs who administer both these rites are available; so here it is for the plaintiff to decide which of the two schools is to be applied by his choice of which Qāḍī he favours with his suit. This leads to the curious result that the same British judge must apply (*a*) the school of the litigants (or defendant, etc.) when sitting as the British Court—except in such questions of real property as are still governed by Islamic law, when he must apply the local law (whether Shāfi'ī or Ibāḍī according to equity, but usually Shāfi'ī); (*b*) the school of the Qāḍī who originally tried the case when hearing appeals in the Zanzibar Court (for here he is only concerned to ascertain that the Qāḍī properly followed the school which he was bound to apply); and (*c*) whichever of the two local schools both parties follow[7] or, where they differ, whichever seems in the particular circumstances more equitable—but probably with a slight prediliction for the Shāfi'ī rite as that of the majority—when sitting as the Zanzibar Court in first instance. It must, however, be observed that the Succession Decree, 1917, specifically lays down that Hindus, Muhammadans and Buddhists "shall be governed, in matters related to inheritance, by the personal law to which they are subject"[8]; and this means that the school of the deceased must in such cases always be applied.[9]

From conversations with the Chief Justice (who has made a deep study of

---

[1] For this information, as for much else, I am particularly indebted to Sir John Gray, the Chief Justice of Zanzibar.

[2] Although certain of the ex-slaves (and their descendants) of Ibāḍī masters are themselves Ibāḍīs.

[3] Not to mention a few Zaydīs from the Yemen, African Aḥmadīs, etc.

[4] See Appendix B to this Survey.

[5] In cases of succession, etc., that of the deceased (sect. 7 of the Succession Decree); in others, that of the defendant (under Bombay Regulation 4); etc.

[6] See Bombay Regulation 4, above.

[7] See *Shawana binti Seif* v. *Ali bin Said* (1923), 3 Z.L.R. 6.

[8] Sect. 7.

[9] Even by the Qāḍīs (where the claim does not exceed Shs. 1,500). But it seems certain that the Qāḍīs would in fact follow their own schools, in such cases as in all else; although they should properly apply for the transfer of the case to another court where this principle clashes with that of the Decree.

Islamic law as locally applied and is incomparably the best informed Englishman on this subject in the whole of East Africa) and the Shāfi'ī and Ibāḍī Qāḍīs, and from a study of the Zanzibar Law Reports (and those of the Court of Appeal for Eastern Africa), the following points of interest emerged.

1. ATTITUDE OF THE QĀḌĪS TO DECREES FLAGRANTLY INCONSISTENT WITH SHARĪ'A LAW

The incongruity of a Decree issued by a Muslim Sultan and starting with the orthodox formula " In the name of God . . ." which then proceeds to enact provisions flagrantly contrary to the divine law must be obvious to all, but especially to the Qāḍīs—although it must be emphasised that it is by no means a new phenomenon. It is not surprising, then, that instances have occurred of Qāḍīs refusing to recognise such man-made substitutes for the Sharī'a. When, moreover, a Qāḍī refused to enforce, as contrary to the Islamic prohibition of " usury," a covenant for interest expressly charged on property,[1] it was exhaustively argued in his support that since in civil matters the law of Islam was the fundamental law of the Protectorate[2] any legislation to the contrary must be *ultra vires*. This contention was, however, expressly rejected: and in a subsequent case[3] the position was summarised in these words: " No supposed conflict with the fundamental law can derogate in the slightest from the validity and enforceability of His Highness' Decrees, though the Decrees clearly ought not to be construed as affecting the Sharī'a in any way unless they do so in clear and unequivocal language."

In most cases, fortunately, the enforcement of Decrees is outside the Qāḍīs' jurisdiction. Where, however, such an enactment covers a case triable in their courts and conflicts with the principles of their school they still, in the main, follow their consciences (especially in regard to the prohibition of both " usury," although here they sometimes compromise by awarding compensation or " mesne profits " in lieu of " interest," and of the sale of future goods, although here again they seem to stretch the law considerably in regard to the sale of clove and coconut crops) and leave it to the High Court to overrule them on appeal. Sometimes, however, they virtually apply the relevant Decree under some polite fiction or other conscience-saving device.

2. THE EVIDENCE DECREE

It has already been observed that the Qāḍīs in Zanzibar, as elsewhere, still follow the Islamic rules of evidence in broad outline, in spite of section 2 of the Evidence Decree, 1917. Thus they still apply the usual rules about the relative duties of the plaintiff and defendant, the burden of proof, the imposition of oaths (including the right of the defendant to return the oath to the plaintiff) and the circumstances in which the defendant may call testimony to rebut that of his opponent. But witnesses are no longer screened (*tazkiya or ta'dīl*)[4] nor questioned as to their religion,[5] but merely put on oath; and documentary evidence is accepted. In view of the Oaths Decree, therefore, the major conflict which arises between the rules of procedure and evidence which the Qāḍīs actually follow and those which they are officially bound to apply consists in their utter rejection of the testimony of those who have any personal interest in the case or are less than the minimum number required by the Sharī'a. In

---

[1] See *Mohd* v. *Abdulla* (1938), 5 Z.L.R. 26.

[2] Courts Decree, sect. 7.

[3] *Mbwana* v. *District Commissioner, Pemba* (1938), 5 Z.L.R. 20.

[4] See Glossary.

[5] But where witnesses are challenged on this point the Qāḍīs will not, it seems, accept non-Muslim witnesses in cases in which both parties are Muslims, although they may stretch a point where one party is a non-Muslim.

such circumstances the Qāḍīs still repeatedly ignore the Evidence Decree, as is apparent from *Baraka Mjanakhiri* v. *Khamis Nahoda* (Civil Appeal No. 9 of 1945—unreported), where the judge remarked, " As this court is constantly saying in regard to cases in Qāḍīs' courts, Muhammadan rules of evidence no longer apply . . . Each case must be judged by an intelligent weighing of all the evidence."

Even so, however, considerable differences exist between the system of oaths sanctioned by the Oaths Decree and that of the pure Sharī'a. The Decree, as has been seen, provides that where one party offers to be bound by an oath taken by the other the court may ask that party if he will take it: if he accepts, the " evidence so given shall, as against the person who offered to be bound as aforesaid, be conclusive proof of the matter stated "; while, if he refuses, the court may take his refusal and its alleged reason into consideration (but may not automatically decide for his opponent, provided he in turn takes the oath). As a consequence, where a Qāḍī had ordered a defendant to take an oath in the absence of proof on the part of the plaintiff and had given judgment against him when he failed to do so, he was overruled,[1] as also when he insisted on a plaintiff taking the oath of " *istiẓhār* ":[2] but where a magistrate decided a case partly on the basis of the defendant's refusal of an oath suggested by the plaintiff he was upheld on appeal, on the grounds that this was part of the defendant-appellant's "demeanour," which he was entitled to take into consideration. Another interesting point concerns whether a father or mother may be allowed to give evidence in Zanzibar today bastardising a child (cf., *Russell* v. *Russell* (1924), A.C. 687[3]). The *li'ān*[4] procedure clearly indicates the attitude of the Sharī'a to this question; while the only possible bar in the Evidence Decree consists in section 151, which enacts that " the court may forbid any questions or inquiries which it regards as indecent or scandalous." The Chief Justice informs me, however, that he has held that the absence of any evidence of *li'ān* by a husband at the time of the birth to his wife of a child whose legitimacy was in dispute raised a strong presumption in favour of legitimacy.

But the further problem has naturally arisen of where the line is to be drawn between matters of substantive law and those of evidence. What, for instance, of the Islamic principle that a child born to a woman within two years (Ibāḍīs and Ḥanafīs) or four years (Shāfi'īs) of her widowhood or irrevocable divorce is the legitimate child of her former husband (unless, indeed, the child is born more than six months after her marriage to another man after duly observing her *'idda*)?[5] Here it has been held in Zanzibar that while the status of legitimacy is a matter of substantive law, as is also the rule that a legitimate child is one born, or presumed to be born, of a valid marriage, yet the rules governing the means by which that presumption is to be arrived at are not so. Such cases, therefore, are now covered in Zanzibar by sections 2, 112 and 114 of the Evidence Decree, and a child is conclusively proved legitimate if born within 280 days of the dissolution of its mother's marriage, provided she has not remarried, while the court " may presume the existence of any fact which it thinks likely to have happened, regard being had to the common

[1] *Aley* v. *Mohamed* (1929), 4 Z.L.R. 63. The Qāḍī was, of course, acting perfectly correctly under Islamic law, provided the rule regarding the return of the oath to the plaintiff was observed.

[2] This oath is incumbent, e.g., on a wife who claims a maintenance order against an absent husband, to the effect that she has received no maintenance, has not to her knowledge been divorced, and is not " disobedient."

[3] But this rule has now been abrogated by the Law Reform (Miscellaneous Provisions) Act, 1949, sect. 7.

[4] See Glossary. By this means the father may bastardise a child born to his wife; while she on her part may deny this allegation.

[5] See Glossary. The *'idda* is the period of waiting prescribed for a widow or divorced woman before remarriage.

course of natural events."[1]

3. THE CONTRACT OF MARRIAGE

Under this heading a number of correlated points must be considered, such as the priority and rights of marriage guardians, the principle of "equality" in marriage, conditions sometimes included in marriage contracts, certain reasons for which the contract may be judicially annulled, and questions concerning dower.

(*a*) *Marriage Guardians*

The Shāfi'ī rules about marriage guardians and the right of *jabr*,[2] or marriage by compulsion, are applied in Zanzibar as in other parts of East Africa and need not be discussed in detail here. It is, however, noteworthy that the Shāfi'ī Qāḍī of Zanzibar (who is much respected throughout Kenya and Tanganyika) considers that a girl compulsorily married to, e.g., a blind or very aged husband might successfully apply for the contract to be set aside on grounds of hardship and injury;[3] and that he agreed with the present Chief Justice when the latter declared valid a contract where the woman was given in marriage by the local *shehe* instead of her guardian,[4] on the basis of a statement in the *Fatāwā* of Ibn Ziyād that "all the affairs of the common people such as sales, marriages, etc., are lawful and binding according to the precepts of the law, should they be done in accordance with the school of any recognised Imām, and no learned man in the law can take objection with regard to them, although the Imāms of the four recognised schools differ in opinion. For if it be asked whether the ignorant belong to any school, then an answer in the negative will be true."

The Ibāḍī rules are, however, somewhat different. Thus, a woman's son is regarded as eligible to be her marriage guardian, and there is a dispute as to where he comes in the order of precedence, e.g., after father and grandfather. The right of *jabr*, moreover, is only exercisable over minor virgins, and even they may apparently in all cases[5] apply for the marriage to be set aside, when they reach puberty, on the grounds of injury, etc. It has been held by the courts, moreover, that the Ibāḍī law does not regard the consent and intervention of the guardian of an adult girl at her marriage as essential, but only as highly desirable[6]—but it seems very doubtful if this decision really represents the Ibāḍī view,[7] and both the Ibāḍī Qāḍī and others questioned emphasised that in their school a woman could in no case marry without the intervention either of a guardian or of the Sultan acting for an absent guardian.

[1] cp. judgment of Court of Appeal for Eastern Africa in *Seif bin Mahomed El-Mauli* v. *Administrator-General* (Civil Appeal No. 21 of 1947—unreported). The present Chief Justice of Zanzibar has always, it seems, "applied the English rule that the court leans strongly in favour of legitimacy and in the absence of strong and cogent evidence to show that the child was the offspring of *zinā* has been prepared to go at least as far as the medical evidence before the House of Lords went in *Gaskill* v. *Gaskill* (1921)."

[2] See Glossary.

[3] This view is regarded as "weak" by Ibn Ḥajar (in the *Tuḥfa*). See Appendix C.

[4] Civil Appeal No. 7 of 1948 (unreported), concerning the right to inherit on the grounds of such a marriage.

[5] i.e., even when given in marriage by father or grandfather, in contrast to the Ḥanafī view.

[6] *Mbwana* v. *D. C. Pemba* (1938), 5 Z.L.R. 20. The statement of Ibāḍī law relied on in this judgment was taken from the judgment of a past Liwali of Mombasa, Sālim bin Khalfān al-Busaidī, himself an Ibāḍī, in *Athman* v. *Ali* (1915), 6 E.A.L.R. 91. His remark may be regarded as *obiter*, but the Liwali was a member of the royal clan, and his opinion may indicate a divergence of opinion between E.A. and Algerian Ibāḍīs. The tendency for the Ibāḍīs in E.A. to rely implicitly on *al-Nīl* (a text-book written by a North African Ibāḍī) is said to be relatively recent.

[7] cf., *al-Nīl*, iii, pp. 61-62 (as quoted). But I could not consult this.

(*b*) *Equality in Marriage*

Again, the Shāfi'ī Qāḍī follows the Shāfi'ī rules on this subject, in Zanzibar as elsewhere in East Africa; but while the Ibāḍīs agree that no non-Arab is the equal of an Arab woman, they differ among themselves concerning the other constituent elements in marriage "equality" (*kafā'a*). It is, however, noteworthy that the Chief Justice has held that the rule which prohibits an Arab woman from ever marrying a non-Arab except with the agreement of her marriage guardian cannot be applied in every case in Zanzibar today. In support of this attitude, moreover, he quoted the modern Shāfi'ī publication *Bughyat al-Mustarshidīn* to the effect that "if the old and strict view of "equality" is insisted on, it would cause much inconvenience and harm to the woman."[1]

(*c*) *Conditions included in Marriage Contracts*

Here, once more, the Shāfi'ī attitude in Zanzibar is perfectly normal, namely, that conditions included in the contract in favour of the wife (e.g., that she should not be made to leave Zanzibar, or have a co-wife) are void and without effect, while ones in favour of a husband are either valid or invalid according to their nature.[2] After marriage, however, stipulations in favour of a wife can, of course, be given weight by being made the basis of a suspended divorce. Among the Ibāḍīs, on the other hand, conditions inserted in the marriage contract in favour of a wife are valid and respected, and she is entitled to a judicial dissolution of marriage, if she has stipulated for this, should her husband disregard the condition (e.g., by marrying another wife), while in other cases she would not become "disobedient" by refusing to act in contravention of her stipulation (e.g., refusing to leave Zanzibar). And it is noteworthy that in Zanzibar even a Shāfi'ī wife can take advantage of the Ibāḍī opinion in this matter by taking her suit to the Ibāḍī Qāḍī.

(*d*) *Reasons for which the contract may be set aside*

Some of these have already been noted under (*a*), (*b*) and (*c*) above. It should, however, be added that the Ibāḍīs, like the Shāfi'īs, allow the contract to be set aside at the instance of either party if the other proves to have been inflicted with madness, leprosy, elephantiasis or some disease which prevents intercourse, without the knowledge of the party not so afflicted, at the time of the contract. It is only in very minor details that the schools differ in this matter. It should, however, be noted that a major difference occurs later in married life, for the Shāfi'īs allow dissolution of marriage if either party becomes mad, leprous or afflicted with elephantiasis subsequent to marriage (provided that the other party does not agree to continue the relationship notwithstanding): but the Ibāḍīs never allow a judicial dissolution of marriage for madness, leprosy or elephantiasis which developes subsequently. Both schools, however, allow dissolution for a disease preventing intercourse only if this develops before the marriage has been consummated, not afterwards.

(*e*) *Dower*

Again, the usual Shāfi'ī rules are observed, but it is common practice in Zanzibar, among both schools, for the dower to be deferred, often for an indefinite period.[3] It is noteworthy, however, that judicial recognition[4] has been given to the Ibāḍī principle that if a wife apostatises, or commits adultery, or exercises witchcraft, or commits suicide, or kills her husband or others, or if

[1] Civil Appeal No. 8 of 1949 (unreported). This seems scarcely an exact quotation.
[2] e.g., a condition of the bride's virginity is valid, of her beauty void.
[3] i.e., it is commonly claimed only on divorce.
[4] *Mohammad bin Juma and four Others* v. *Sufiah binti Nassor* (Application to Appeal No. 4 of 1944—unreported).

she is killed for a crime, she forfeits her dower": [1] as also "if she becomes disobedient in her bed to her husband, or runs away."[2]

4. MARRIED LIFE

(*a*) *Restitution of conjugal rights*

Husbands whose wives run away or prove recalcitrant may, of course, bring suits for "obedience" (restitution of conjugal rights) before either the Shāfiʿī or Ibāḍī Qāḍī; and judgment will, where suitable, be given accordingly. No such judgments, however, are now forcibly executed in Zanzibar by dragging the wife back to the marriage home or reinforced by committing her to prison—although the latter was allowed until comparatively recently.

(*b*) *A wife's maintenance* is calculated in Zanzibar by exclusive reference to her husband's means, according to both schools.[3] Past maintenance may be claimed before the Shāfiʿī Qāḍī from the date when the husband failed to provide it, at a suitable rate, provided the wife was entitled thereto; but before the Ibāḍī Qāḍī only from the date of a judicial maintenance order or a (witnessed) agreement between the spouses regarding a definite scale of maintenance. But it is noteworthy that thereafter her right to past as distinct from present maintenance does not lapse by disobedience—in contrast to the Ḥanafī view.

(*c*) *Accusations of adultery* can be heard today only under the Penal Decree.[4] No traces of the Islamic criminal law remain either in this respect or that of the "slander of a chaste person's continence" (*qadhf*)—or, indeed, in any other particular whatever.[5]

5. THE DISSOLUTION OF MARRIAGE

(*a*) Wives who are cruelly treated by their husbands and desire dissolution of marriage are in a much better position in Zanzibar than anywhere else in East Africa.[6] This is because Ibāḍī law allows the court to dissolve a marriage provided genuine cruelty[7] can be proved (and in Zanzibar a Qāḍī's insistence on Muslim rules of evidence in this matter is always liable to cause his judgment to be overruled on appeal): so even a Shāfiʿī wife can obtain relief in such circumstances by the simple expedient of applying to the Ibāḍī Qāḍī. While, moreover, the British judges will not dissolve the marriage of a Ḥanafī or Shāfiʿī wife on these grounds, they will grant her a judicial separation, coupled with a maintenance order: and this will normally induce the husband himself to divorce her (or to fail to provide the ordered maintenance, when the court will dissolve the marriage).[8] The Shāfiʿī Qāḍī, moreover, considers this procedure correct according to the principles of his school provided the judicial separation is only temporary—on the grounds that the husband cannot be trusted with the person of his wife, after such treatment, until he "repents," etc.

(*b*) In cases of matrimonial discord and alleged cruelty the courts occasionally order the parties to live near some *amīn* (reliable person) whose duty it is to

---

[1] *Al-Nīl*, iii, pp. 278-279 (as quoted).

[2] See Muḥammad b. Yūsuf Aṭfayyish's commentary on *al-Nīl* (as quoted).

[3] This is, of course, a disputed point in the Shāfiʿī texts, although the dominant view.

[4] Art. 154 provides that "Whoever has carnal knowledge of a person who is and whom he knows or has reason to believe to be the wife of another man, without the consent or connivance of that man . . . is guilty of a misdemeanour. In such case the wife shall *not* be punishable as an abettor".

[5] See above, p. 59.

[6] See also under 3(*c*) above.

[7] i.e., as distinct from the husband's legal right of chastisement, etc.

[8] Rather than distrain upon any property for the amount. This is the practice of the Qāḍīs where a husband fails to pay punctually the prescribed maintenance, and would probably be followed by non-Muslim judges also. But it is not the orthodox rule.

watch over and report on their conduct,[1] but the system of appointing two arbitrators to attempt reconciliation is not practised. If it were, the Ibāḍī Qāḍī was emphatic that the court would never enforce a decision by the arbitrators that the marriage should be dissolved either by *khul'*[2] or simple repudiation unless they had been so empowered by the parties concerned; while the Shāfi'ī Qāḍī was somewhat hesitant on this matter, in view of the variant opinion in his school which concurs with the dominant Mālikī doctrine in enforcing such a decision regardless of the opinions of the parties.

(*c*) Neither school will grant a wife a dissolution of marriage for physical desertion even if her husband stays away from her for years, provided he leaves her adequate maintenance. Both Qāḍīs say that they would order the seizure of any of the husband's movable property which was available in execution of a maintenance order,[3] and the rents and profits of immovable property might be similarly utilised; while both say that the wife is entitled to a dissolution of marriage if her husband, being present, is unable to support her for three consecutive days (and, again, proof of destitution would not be so difficult in Zanzibar as is often the case elsewhere, or rather an insistence on the more exacting rules in this matter would make a judgment liable to be quashed). In the case of absent husbands Ibāḍī principles apparently leave more to the discretion of the Qāḍī than do the Shāfi'ī texts,[4] for he may either correspond with the absent husband (or the Qāḍī of his locality, etc.) or dissolve the marriage, and that after such period as he thinks fit.

(*d*) Divorce is exceedingly common.[5] The Shāfi'īs of Zanzibar follow the normal Shāfi'ī rules in this respect: but it is noteworthy that among the Ibāḍīs the triple divorce uttered in a single sentence is regarded as only single and revocable[6]—although the repetition of the formula at, e.g., five minute intervals would make it triple and irrevocable; a divorce pronounced at the wrong time[7] as sinful but valid (as among the Shāfi'īs); and a divorce pronounced when culpably drunk or when jesting as valid and binding.[8] *Īlā', ẓihār* and *li'ān* are all known in theory but not found in practice among either school,[9] and delegated divorce is rare; but suspended divorce is apparently common, whether used as a threat or otherwise. Divorce for a consideration is exceedingly common, and *mubāra'a* considered one variety of *khul'*[10] (as in the Shāfi'ī texts). Marriages would also be dissolved in Zanzibar on the grounds of the " apostasy " of either party.

---

[1] cp. *Ali bin Amor* v. *Mwana Nziga* (1919), 2 Z.L.R. 2, and *Soud* v. *Jokha* (1936), 5 Z.L.R. 16.

[2] See Glossary: *khul'* is dissolution of marriage for a financial consideration provided by the wife.

[3] In practice, the provisions of the Civil Procedure Decree and Rules would, of course, apply to suits for maintenance against an absent husband. Where service could be effected upon him, it would be made in one of the manners prescribed by the Rules; if his whereabouts were unknown, one of the authorised modes of substituted service would be followed; while attachment of movable or immovable property would be granted in the manner prescribed by the same Rules. As a general rule the Qāḍīs would only allow the income of immovable property to be attached; but if the property did not produce any income or was only of small value they should order it to be sold.

[4] See Appendix C.

[5] The Shāfi'ī Qāḍī estimated that only about 20 per cent. of marriages did not end in this way.

[6] According to a *fatwā* given by a Zanzibar *mujtahid* (see Glossary), who died some years ago, Sayf bin Nāṣir al-Kharūsī by name (I am informed).

[7] e.g., during the wife's *ḥayḍ*, etc.

[8] Again, like the Shāfi'īs.

[9] The Ibāḍīs only allow *li'ān* in the presence of their " Imām "—i.e., only now in the interior of 'Umān, where the *ḥadd* punishments for *zinā* and *qadhf* are also applied. For all these terms, see Glossary.

[10] See Glossary.

6. THE CARE AND CUSTODY OF CHILDREN (*ḥaḍāna*)

The Shafi'ī rules on this matter have been set out fully above and need not be repeated. The Ibāḍīs, however, limit the mother's custody of a boy to two years, while for a girl they agree with the Shāfi'ī rule of seven years (after which she has an option).[1] But this is one of the points on which British judges, whether sitting as the British or Zanzibar Court, feel most justified in departing from the strict rules of the Sharī'a if the interests of the child so require.[2]. Of this a single example must suffice. A husband went abroad leaving his wife pregnant, subsequently divorced her, and for thirteen years took no interest in and provided no support for the daughter to whom she gave birth, leaving the girl, after her mother had remarried and subsequently died, to be brought up by one who was no relation. Ultimately, however, he returned and claimed the custody and guardianship of his daughter; and the Qāḍī felt bound to give judgment accordingly, since the girl was still under puberty. But on appeal it was held that his abandonment of the girl justified the court in "deviating" from the strict rule of Islamic law and in refusing his claim.[3]

7. PATERNITY

The Shāfi'ī Qāḍī naturally upholds the orthodox principles of his school, which are perfectly clear on this point: i.e., that a child born within four lunar years of its mother's widowhood or irrevocable divorce is always regarded as the legitimate offspring of her former husband, regardless of whether or not she has claimed that her *'idda*[4] period has come to an end, unless it is born six months after her remarriage to another man. This, moreover, is one of the matters on which he would certainly feel bound to give judgment accordingly, and leave it to the High Court to quash his judgment on appeal.[5] The normal Ibāḍī view is similar, except that (like the Ḥanafīs) they substitute two years for four: but a variant view is found in their school to the effect that this is only so if the mother claims to have had no menses and to feel pregnant. On one view, moreover, the Ibāḍīs regard a child as legitimate if born to the mother six months after her marriage contract, regardless of any question of the access of the parties to each other, unless the father repudiates the child by the *li'ān* procedure: but an alternative view reckons legitimacy only by reference to the consummation of marriage. After consummation[6] a child will be regarded as legitimate by all Ibāḍīs even if born, e.g., ten years after the father went away: but there is a further difference of opinion about second or third children born subsequently to his departure. It is clear, therefore, that in such matters the Ibāḍī view is somewhat closer than that of the Shāfi'īs to the Evidence Decree, which is of course officially binding on both Qāḍīs.

8. SUCCESSION

Here, again, the normal Shāfi'ī rules apply where the deceased was a Shāfi'ī, the only exception being the limited "return to the spouse relict" allowed under the Succession Decree (see above). In Zanzibar, moreover, the *Bayt al-Māl* still exists, so no Shāfi'ī may bequeath more than one-third of his property on the grounds that he has no heirs. The Ibāḍīs agree with the Ḥanafīs in holding that the father's father totally excludes all brothers; they commonly follow the principle of "*ahl al-qarāba*"[7] regarding the inheritance, in the absence of either sharers or

[1] She may not, however, opt for the mother if the latter is of bad character.
[2] In this context, cp. also the Juvenile Offenders Decree, 1935 (p. 63 above).
[3] *Atiya* v. *Khamis* (1941), 6 Z.L.R. 37.
[4] See Glossary.
[5] See p. 69 above.
[6] And the minimum period of six months (for pregnancy).
[7] For the technical term, see Glossary. This corresponds, in most points at least, to the principles of Abū Yūsuf among the Ḥanafīs; although the Ibāḍīs claim that their rule was even older. *Sed quaere.*

agnatic heirs, of those cognates who are not Qur'anic sharers; they allow the return to the spouse relict where no other heir exists, and also recognise the right of the "universal legatee"; but they do not recognise any inheritance right of the "acknowledged kinsman" (other, of course, than child or parent).[1] In testate succession the Ibāḍīs agree with the Sunnīs in forbidding all bequests to an heir and, of course, all bequests in excess of the "bequeathable third" unless the heirs consent; but both these restrictions can be quite simply evaded by using the formula "*'an ḍamān*" (i.e., by representing the bequest as the fulfillment of an obligation), which will validate any bequest whatever—an improper use of this formula being regarded as a sin indeed but as something into which the court is not competent to inquire.[2]

9. SLAVERY

An interesting case on this subject went as far as the Privy Council in 1947.[3] Here the Judicial Committee accepted the findings of the Chief Justice of Zanzibar that a mother had given a slave girl, Panya, to her son in 1907 to be his slave concubine; that he had accepted her in that capacity; and that the appellant was the offspring of that union: and was also willing to assume that the father's treatment of the appellant constituted sufficient acknowledgment of her paternity. It was held, however, that the Slave Trade (Prohibition) Decree of 1890, then applicable, which absolutely prohibited all exchange, sale or purchase of slaves, made the mother's gift invalid; so Panya could not be regarded as the son's true slave concubine, and her offspring could not be held legitimate. This reasoning is, of course, unassailable in English law; but it seems highly dubious from the Muslim point of view. Now, moreover, under the Slavery Decree of 1909, the very status of slavery is officially abolished, although concubines lawfully held at that date were to keep their "rights and privileges" provided they did not leave their masters (see above). It is important in this context, however, to compare the views held, e.g., among the Muslims of Northern Nigeria (p. 215); since it is more than possible that local opinion may in fact be much the same in parts, at least, of East Africa.

10. TORT

Very few actions in tort seem to be heard in His Highness' courts, where Sharī'a law is still applicable in such cases (see above). It is noteworthy, however, that in *Nasor* v. *Mohamed* (Civil Appeal No. 2 of 1935—unreported) it was held that an owner was liable for the damage caused by his animal only if he knew that it was vicious and liable to behave in that way and still failed to take reasonable steps to prevent this (e.g., to tie it up); that on another occasion it was stated that Islamic, like English, law allowed an action in tort between the owners of two adjoining buildings for the breach of the obligation to provide lateral support; and that in *Dr. Francis Charlesworth* v. *Naranji Rawji and Others* (1 Z.L.R. 186) two Qāḍīs[4] gave a full statement of what they considered to be the Islamic (or local) law of nuisance. Both here and in another case of nuisance (*L. Matthews, Binti Masood, etc.,* v. *Mancharji Pestonji, etc.* (1887) 1 Z.L.R. 26) the court, however, held that English rather than Islamic law must apply, presumably because the parties concerned were immigrants subject to the jurisdiction of the British Court and to the principles of law therein applied.

---

[1] *Saumu binti Uleidi v. Khamis bin Sorigoro* (Civil Appeal No. 7 of 1944—unreported) is very interesting in this context. For these terms see any text book on Muhammadan law as applied in India.

[2] Among the Shāfi'īs, apparently, the legatee would have to prove that the debt, etc., was in fact owed to him, if the heirs (or other heirs) disputed the point. As a result, the formula never seems to appear in Shāfi'ī wills.

[3] *Fatma binti Hafidh* v. *Admin-General.* (P.C. Appeal No. 81 of 1947.)

[4] i.e., the leading Qāḍīs of the Shāfi'īs and Ibāḍīs, respectively, in Zanzibar.

11. WAQF

The Ibāḍī law of waqf differs from the Shāfi'ī in several important respects. There must, apparently, be an express mention of the poor or of some "charity" which cannot end as the ultimate beneficiary, while the Shāfi'īs do not insist on this;[1] a dedication in favour of "X.Y.Z. and their heirs" without further specification will be held to entitle males to twice the share of females, while the Shāfi'īs give them equal shares in such cases;[2] the phrase "*awladuhu min ṣulbihi*" ("his children from his loins") will be interpreted as applying to the first generation of children only, while the Shāfi'īs will extend this to grandchildren, too;[3] the sale of waqf property is allowed, in suitable circumstances, with consent of the court, again in contrast to the Shāfi'ī view; and, while both schools agree that the founder may appoint himself as administrator of his waqf, and that he may benefit thereunder as one of a class, there is a conflict within the Ibāḍī school as to whether he may name himself first beneficiary, while the Shāfi'īs, as has been seen above, only allow this by the subterfuge of a circumlocution or indirect description.[4] Now, however, this last problem has been solved, in so far as the Zanzibar courts are concerned, by the Waqf Validating Decree of 1946, which expressly provides that an Ibāḍī waqf in which the founder makes such a reservation is to be valid.[5] In the case of waqfs created by will, revocation is, of course, allowed by both schools during the founder's life, while anything in excess of the bequeathable third is dependent on the heirs' consent; but the validity of a testamentary waqf in favour of heirs even within the third is disputed in the Ibāḍī school. Some, looking primarily at the first beneficiaries, regard such waqfs as bequests to heirs and wholly invalid; while others, emphasising the ultimate gift to the poor, uphold them, but allow all the heirs to participate in the income.[6] Judicial recognition,[7] moreover, has been given to the fact that, under Shāfi'ī law, a waqf cannot be invalidated on the grounds that its motive was to defeat the rights of creditors, provided that it was created before its founder was put under interdiction for "bankruptcy." It is interesting to observe that where the necessity for the sale of waqf property in a Shāfi'ī waqf comes before the Waqf Commissioners, the Shāfi'ī Qāḍī leaves it to his Ibāḍī colleague to take the lead in stating that this is allowable, and then himself agrees, i.e. he supports a view which he regards as a legitimate conclusion reached by some recognised authorities, although he could not himself have adopted it *ab initio*.[8] Finally, it should be noted that the local Waqf Validating Decree was made necessary by the fact that the Court of Appeal for Eastern Africa in 1945 held a waqf invalid[9] on the grounds that the gift to the poor was too remote, the

---

[1] See *Ali* v. *Zwena* (1911), 1 Z.L.R. 365.

[2] See *Wakf Commissioners* v. *Saada* (1937), 5 Z.L.R. 6.

[3] See *Shawana* v. *Ali* (1923), 3 Z.L.R. 6.

[4] See *Saleh* v. *Administrator-General* (1938), 5 Z.L.R. 8. The only authority which the Ibāḍīs whom I consulted could quote in favour of the validity of a man naming himself as first beneficiary was *Mukhtaṣar al-Khiṣāl* (by Abū Isḥāq Ibrāhīm b. Qays), vii, p. 36: "If the founder says 'for myself and then for such and such a person', it is lawful." *Sharḥ al-Nīl* (by Muḥammad b. Yūsuf Aṭfayyish), vi, pp. 288-9, however, apparently takes the exactly opposite position that it is unlawful for a founder to benefit under his waqf, except as one of a class. See also *Mwajuma binti Fundi Mgindo's case* (application for leave to appeal No. 4 of 1945 in H.H.'s Court—unreported), and *Wakf Commissioners* v. *Abdulla Hemraj* (High Court case 15/42—unreported).

[5] Sect. 3(*b*).

[6] See *Said bin Mohd bin Kassim el Riami* v. *Wakf Commissioners* (1946), 13 E.A.C.A. 32 and *Sharḥ al-Nīl*, vi, p. 204 (apparently).

[7] *Admin-General* v. *Saada binti Said and Others* (High Court case No. 18 of 1941—unreported).

[8] This is perfectly valid reasoning from the point of view of Islamic law.

[9] *Said bin Mohd bin Kassim el Riami's case*. See above.

court still considering itself bound by the regrettable decision of the Privy Council in *Abul Fata* v. *Russumoy*.[1]

12. REAL PROPERTY

It has been noted that in questions concerning real property which are not covered by local or Imperial enactments the British Court, as well as the Zanzibar Court, will apply Islamic law on the common principle of *lex loci rei sitae*. This has occasioned some most interesting cases, a few examples of which must suffice.

The local application of the Islamic law of real property was raised in both *Rhematbai binti Hirji* v. *Sonaru Ismail Mohd & Co., etc.*,[2] and *Khadija binti Masood* v. *Masood bin Seif and Abdulla bin Seif*.[3] The former concerned a claim for compensation by a man who had obtained permission to sow sugar cane on Government land, had reaped one crop, and had then received notice to cut the second crop and quit within fifteen days. It was held that in Islamic law the owner might not give such notice in the case of annual crops (e.g., wheat) but must either let the crops mature, even in the case of a trespasser, in return for reasonable rent, or must pay compensation for their premature removal; that in the case of trees, etc., the position depended on whether the land had been loaned for a fixed term, for in such cases the owner, if he demanded the land back prematurely, must again either let them remain in return for reasonable rent or pay compensation for their removal, while in other cases he could demand their removal without any such restrictions;[4] and that sugar cane, as a crop which was at its best during the first year but continued to bear for some years after, fell half-way between the two. In the case under decision it was decided, however, that no compensation was payable, as the borrower had enjoyed the first and best crop, no period for occupation had been mentioned, and the owner could not be expected to wait indefinitely. The second case concerned the question as to whether a bequest had or had not been revoked. It fell to be decided under Ibāḍī law, and the point at issue was whether digging a well, reconstructing the *banda*, repairing buildings, making a drying floor for cloves, and planting clove trees, constituted revocation of the bequest of the *shamba* concerned.[5] The authorities cited made it clear that in Ibāḍī law " if the testator . . . effected changes in the *name* of the bequest " this would constitute revocation, but not if he only " increased and perfected " it: and it was held that whereas in some localities the digging of a well would effect a radical change in the very nature of the property, this was not so in Zanzibar, where all that had been done might be regarded as of the nature of " increase and perfection."

In an interesting case (*Waqf Commissioners* v. *Abdulla Hemraj*: High Court Case No. 15 of 1942—unreported) it was held that a waqf created by a Khoja in Zanzibar must be governed by either Shāfiʿī or Ibāḍī law, since in matters of real property the *lex loci*, not that of the parties, was applicable; that on balance the Shāfiʿī law should be preferred as that of the majority; and that the reservation of income for the founder's own use therefore made the waqf invalid. Now, however, the law has been changed in this respect by the Waqf Validating Decree (section 5), since the terms of the Indian Act would be applicable in such cases. Again, it has been held that there is no right of pre-emption in Zanzibar, by local usage. As for the problem of fragmentation of land-holdings to which the Islamic law of inheritance everywhere gives rise, no limit has been introduced

---

[1] As, indeed, it has been held more recently, in a Kenya waqf. See Appendix D.

[2] Civil case No. 20 of 1942—unreported —before H.B.M.'s Court in Zanzibar.

[3] Civil Appeal No. 27 of 1946—unreported—before the Court of Appeal for E.A.

[4] Following Hamilton's *Hedaya* pp. 480-481 and the Shāfiʿī *al-Anwār*, i, p. 350.

[5] *Shamba* means estate, plantation, and *banda* a large shed.

by Decree, etc.: but common sense seems normally to prevail and the heirs will usually sell a property which cannot economically be further subdivided, while the court will in proper circumstances insist on this at the instance of any one of them. It is interesting to note, however, that this fragmentation of an estate on death was previously held to include, in the case of a deceased Sultan, what would normally be expected to be reckoned as State property—e.g., lands, palaces, forts, ships of war and even the arms and equipment of troops: all was valued and divided among his heirs, at least in theory, and his successor who took them over was burdened with the obligation to compensate the other heirs accordingly.[1] But the Islamic law of real property has been much modified in Zanzibar by the series of enactments noted above.

13. CHANGE OF SCHOOL (IN WHOLE OR PART)

The Shāfi'ī Qāḍī takes the attitude that any individual may follow whatever recognised school he wishes, in whole or in part, but that he as Qāḍī must always apply his own school. In the case of a marriage which has been consummated, however, he would recognise its validity provided it was correct according to the opinion of any recognised Sunnī Imām, regardless of the school of the parties. The Ibāḍīs, being outside the Sunnī principle of unity in diversity, naturally hold that it is a major sin for one of their sect to change his school, but that under modern conditions they can do nothing to prevent it if he does so; while to follow a different view in some isolated particular is the prerogative of their *mujtahids*[2] alone. But some of their jurists, too, hold that a marriage which is valid according to any school of Islam should be recognised after consummation; while others always hold it void if invalid *ab initio* by Ibāḍī law. The attitude of the British judiciary in this matter may be seen from a statement of the present Chief Justice: "I am quite satisfied that Muhammadan law does allow this partial change of doctrine in order to escape an inconvenient rule . . . of one's own school . . . but . . . there must be a declaration to the effect that the person concerned has transferred his allegiance—either wholly or partially—from one school to another."[3] And His Honour certainly takes the view that a marriage contract validly concluded according to the tenets of any recognised school should be upheld.

14. THE ATTITUDE TOWARDS REFORM

With regard to the basic principle of reform—that the Ruler may order his Qāḍīs to apply the view of any recognised Imām, in any particular in which the learned have differed, where the public interests demand the application of some rule other than the authoritative opinion of the school normally followed—the position in Zanzibar seems to be that the Shāfi'ī Qāḍī would accept such orders as perfectly valid, while the Ibāḍīs would regard them as wrongful in themselves, but as the exclusive responsibility of the Sultan if he insisted.

It may also, however, be remarked in this context that the Shāfi'ī Qāḍī in Zanzibar does not seem to regard himself as so exclusively tied to Ibn Ḥajar as do the Qāḍīs in Somaliland and Ḥaḍramaut, but rather to be free to consult all the commentators on the *Minhāj* (the *Tuḥfa*, the *Mughnī*, the *Nihāya*, *Maḥallī*, etc) and even other works. The Ibāḍīs, for their part, officially regard

[1] Thus in the will of H.H. Sayyid Sa'īd bin Sulṭān (d. 1856) we read: "And whatever arms or weapons of war he may possess he bequeathes to his male children. And his two ships the Feidh Alim and Caroline he gives, after his death, as a legacy to the treasury of the Muslims. And whatever other ships he possesses are to be sold after his death and their value distributed among his heirs."

[2] See Glossary.

[3] *Wakf Commissioners* v. *Abdulla Hemraj* (High Court case No. 15 of 1942—unreported); cp. Tyabji, 3rd Ed., p. 56 (there quoted).

the Sultans of both Zanzibar and Muscat as worldlings who have forsaken the true path for one of compromise; it is only the Imām who rules the interior of 'Umān from Nazwa who has maintained the law in its purity, including the *ḥadd*[1] punishments. The Ibāḍīs, moreover, still have *mujtahids*[1] in 'Umān and North Africa, although there are none in Zanzibar: and these may still use reasoning (*ra'y*) to form their own deductions from the law. In regard to the science of Traditions, too, they have their own collections, although the contents largely correspond with the Sunnī books, and they also use al-Bukhārī and Muslim; while the doctrine of consensus (*ijmā'*)[1] plays but a small part in the details of their law, although in theory they recognise the consensus of the undivided Muslim community of early Islam and also of their own '*ulamā*' in any age. It seems, moreover, that certain differences previously existed between the interpretations of Ibāḍī law current in North Africa on the one hand and 'Umān and East Africa on the other; but that of recent years there has been an increasing tendency in Zanzibar to follow *al-Nīl* and its commentaries more and more meticulously.

It will be apparent from this summary that the application of Islamic law in Zanzibar today gives rise to few problems of any urgency. It would, however, seem advisable to make the law correspond with practice by providing that the Qāḍīs may follow Islamic rules of evidence, etc., at least in cases of personal status, subject to the safeguards suggested elsewhere.[2] If and when, moreover, it seems opportune to consider any measures of unification and reform of the law as it is applied, e.g., by the Kenya Qāḍīs and the Tanganyika Liwalis, it would be preferable to include the Qāḍīs of Zanzibar in any consultations and declarations; for the opinion of the Shāfi'ī Qāḍī, in particular, would carry great weight throughout East Africa. In addition, legislation similar to the Indian Dissolution of Muslim Marriages Act[3], 1939, might well be introduced in regard to immigrant Muslims.

---

[1] See Glossary.

[2] See p. 39 above, and p. 101 below.

[3] See Appendix E, and elsewhere.

KENYA

The basis for the administration of law and justice in the Colony of Kenya may best be summed up in the words of the Kenya Colony Order in Council, 1921, which reads:—

"There shall be a Court of Record styled Her Majesty's Supreme Court of Kenya . . . with full jurisdiction, civil and criminal, over all persons and all matters in the Colony[1]. . . . Subject to the other provisions of this Order, such civil and criminal jurisdiction shall, so far as circumstances admit, be exercised in conformity with the Civil Procedure and Penal Codes of India and the other Indian Acts which are in force in the Colony at the date of the commencement of this Order[2] and subject thereto and so far as the same shall not extend or apply shall be exercised in conformity with the substance of the common law, the doctrines of equity and the statutes of general application in force in England . . . (in 1897) and with the powers vested in and according to the procedure and practice observed by and before Courts of Justice and Justices of the Peace in England . . . save in so far as (all these) . . . may . . . be modified, amended or replaced by other provisions in lieu thereof by or under the authority of any Order of Her Majesty in Council or by any Ordinance . . . for the time being in force in the Colony: Provided always that the said common law doctrines of equity and the statutes of general application shall be in force in the Colony so far only as the circumstances of the Colony and its inhabitants permit and subject to such qualifications as local circumstances render necessary."[3]

As usual, however, provision is also made that "In all cases, civil and criminal, to which natives are parties, every Court (*a*) shall be guided by native law so far as it is applicable and is not repugnant to justice and morality or inconsistent with any Order in Council or Ordinance, or any regulation or rule made under any Order in Council or Ordinance; and (*b*) shall decide all such cases according to substantial justice without undue regard to technicalities or procedure and without undue delay.[4]

As for the coastal strip, or the Protectorate of Kenya—which still remains part of the dominions of the Sultan of Zanzibar, although now administered virtually as an integral part of the Colony—the Kenya Protectorate Order in Council, 1920, provides that "The Courts now or hereafter established in the Colony shall have in respect of matters occurring within the Protectorate, so far as such matters are within the jurisdiction of Her Majesty, the same jurisdiction, civil and criminal, original and appellate as they respectively possess from time to time in respect of matters occurring within the Colony. . . ."[5]

It will be observed that none of these provisions makes any direct reference, whether explicit or implicit, to Islamic law. Yet that law is applied quite extensively in Kenya, and in the coastal strip may fairly be considered the basic law, at least in so far as its "general principles" are concerned, unless or until ousted by statute or varied by contrary native custom. So the question immed-

[1] Art. 4 (1).

[2] Those still in force today include the Indian Succession Act, 1865 (slightly amended), the Indian Contract Act and the Indian Evidence Act, both of 1872 (the latter slightly amended), the Indian Oaths Act, 1873, and the Transfer of Property Act, 1882.

[3] Art. 4 (2).

[4] Art. 7.

[5] Art. XII.

iately arises as to the statutory basis on which this application rests.

It is clear, of course, that before any British Protectorate existed in East Africa Muslim courts were enforcing Islamic law over much of the coastal region, chiefly—of later years—under the authority of the Sultan of Zanzibar, who was recognised as ruler or suzerain of most of these localities. In the Concession granted by the Sultan of Zanzibar to the British East African Association, on 24th May, 1887, regarding the administration of the Sultan's territories on the mainland "from Wanga to Kipini", it was provided that "The Judges shall be appointed by the Association, or their Representatives, subject to the Sultan's approval, but all Qāḍīs[1] shall be nominated by His Highness";[2] and an identical clause was included in the Concession granted on 9th October, 1888, to the Imperial British East Africa Company[3] (which had by then succeeded the original Association). Similarly, in the Agreement of 31st August, 1889, which concerned His Highness' territories north of Kipini, article 2 provided that "These possessions are to be held by the Company as His Highness' 'Wakīl' (Plenipotentiary and Agent) and they are to be administered according to the Sharī'a (Muhammadan[4] laws and customs). His Highness' flag, and the Liwalis, 'Askaris and Qāḍīs will be maintained"[5]; while by a later Concession dated 4th March, 1890, these more northerly territories were put on an exact par with those between the Wanga and Kipini.[6] Again, the British East Africa Company issued a Notice on 20th March, 1891, respecting the administration of Witu and the coast from Kipini to Kismayu, announcing that "all the Regulations which are now in force in the Imperial British East Africa Company's other towns and territories (lying within the British sphere of influence) shall be recognised and made equally applicable to all people resident in the above-mentioned territory."[7] When, moreover, the British Government took the place of the Company in 1895 and the new Commissioner for the East Africa Protectorate stated that although the coast would remain under the Sultan's sovereignty yet he himself would take over the administration "as its Administrator and Governor", he emphasised that "all cases and law-suits between natives will continue to be decided according to the Sharī'a."[8] He also promised that Qāḍīs and *ulamā'* would be honoured: but no clause about the appointment of Qāḍīs was included in the Agreement between Great Britain and Zanzibar signed at Zanzibar on the 14th December, 1895.[9]

The promise about the Sharī'a was implemented by the Native Courts Regulations, 1897.[10] These were promulgated under the East Africa Order in Council, 1897, which empowered the Commissioner, with the consent of the Secretary of State, to make rules and orders for the administration of justice in native courts, including the alteration or modification of the operation of any native law or custom in so far as that might be necessary. The Regulations adopted a very wide definition of the term "native", which was to include not only "any native of Africa not of European or American origin", but also "any person not of European or American origin, who, within the dominions of the

[1] Here spelt "Kathis", while the form "Cadis" prevails in Kenya Ordinances. But see Introduction regarding the policy adopted in spelling Arabic words, and why.

[2] See *Map of Africa by Treaty,* by E. Hertslet, I, p. 339.

[3] Ibid., p. 353.

[4] Spelt "Sherial" (or "Sheira") and "Mahommedan" respectively in this context, while the form "Mohammedan" prevails in most Kenya Ordinances. But see Introduction, as above.

[5] See *Map of Africa by Treaty,* by E. Hertslet, I, p. 360.

[6] Ibid., pp. 362, 363.

[7] Ibid., p. 372.

[8] Ibid., p. 381.

[9] Ibid., p. 382.

[10] Equivalent, at that date, to an Ordinance.

Sultan of Zanzibar, would be subject to His Highness' jurisdiction, even though such person should not have been born in Africa "[1]; they established two classes of native courts,[2] namely those presided over by an European officer and those presided over by a native authority[3]; they decreed that the former should, as far as practicable, " be guided by the Indian Civil Procedure Code and the Indian Penal and Criminal Procedure Codes ", but that both in civil and criminal cases they should, " within the Muhammadan Coast region, or in dealing with Muhammadans, also be guided by, and have regard to, the general principles of the Law of Islam, and throughout the Protectorate be guided by, and have regard to, any native laws and customs not opposed to natural morality and humanity ";[4] while the latter should " be guided, subject to the provisions of these Regulations, by the native laws or customs existing in their respective jurisdiction."[5] Further articles provided that the foregoing provisions should not " preclude any native court of whatever description from applying any special laws, or enactments, or modifications of existing laws, enactments, or customs, which may at any future time be made, or introduced, or sanctioned by, under, or in virtue of Her Majesty's authority "[6]; that the Qāḍīs' courts[7] should " take cognisance of all matters affecting the personal status of Muhammadans (such as marriage, divorce and inheritance) ",[8] and should follow therein, " subject to the provisions of these Regulations, the law and procedure . . . which has hitherto been observed by them in accordance with the laws of the Sultanate of Zanzibar "[9]; and that the High Court, when hearing appeals therefrom, " may take whatever steps it may deem right or desirable for satisfying itself as to the Muhammadan laws and customs applicable to the case."[10] Finally, " suits relating to the personal status of Muhammadan natives not being members of the Sunnī or Ibāḍī sects may be heard by agreement between the parties in the ordinary courts, which shall, as far as possible, ascertain or apply the particular law of their personal status."[11] And it is also noteworthy in this context that a Proclamation of 1898[12] provided that civil claims under Muhammadan law in the native courts of the coast region should be barred after twelve years, except in case of the defendant's fraud.

These Regulations, it is true, were repealed by Schedule III to the Courts Ordinance, 1907—an Ordinance which established courts subordinate to the High Court (including those of Liwalis, Qāḍīs and Mudīrs) very much on a par with those established under the Courts Ordinance, 1931, which will be described in detail below. While, however, this Ordinance clearly defined the jurisdiction of the new courts thereby established, it made no reference whatever to the substantive law which these courts were to apply. It seems clear, therefore, that the relevant provisions of the Regulations of 1897 remained in force, under article 28 (1) of the East Africa Order in Council, 1902, which provides that " where other provision is not made by Ordinance, any law, practice or procedure established by or under the said repealed Orders . . .[13]

---

[1] Art. 1 (a).
[2] i.e., courts empowered to try natives —as all courts, from the Supreme Court downwards, are today.
[3] Art. 2.
[4] Art. 3.
[5] Art. 4.
[6] Art. 5.
[7] One variety of the native courts under a native authority. The others were Wālis' courts (within the dominions of the Sultan only) and those of tribal chiefs.
[8] Art. 55.
[9] Art. 58.
[10] Art. 57.
[11] Art. 59.
[12] No. 13 of 1898. This is no longer in force.
[13] i.e., in this case the E.A.O. in C. of 1897 and the Regulations made thereunder.

shall remain in force until such other provision is made." There is nothing, moreover, in the East Africa Orders in Council of 1906, 1907, 1911, 1912, 1914, 1915, 1919, or 1920 which may be regarded as repealing this provision, while article III of the Kenya Protectorate Order in Council, 1920, expressly preserves all previous Orders in Council except in so far as they may be repugnant to its terms. Even the Kenya Colony Order in Council, 1921, moreover, although it expressly provides that all these East Africa Orders in Council shall " cease to apply to the Colony ", includes the proviso that " Where other provision is not made by Ordinance, any law practice or procedure " established thereunder " shall remain in force until such other provision is made."[1] Nor, it seems, has any other provision regarding the substantive law to be applied either " in the Muhammadan Coast region " or " in dealing with Muhammadans " in fact been made (except, of course, within their particular scope, such enactments as the Muhammadan Marriage, Divorce and Succession Ordinance and the Waqf[2] Commissioners Ordinance[3]): for the Courts Ordinance, 1931, makes no reference to this point. Nor does it seem that article 7 of the Kenya Colony Order in Council, which, as we have seen, repeats the declaration of article 20 of the East Africa Order in Council, 1902, that " in all cases, civil and criminal, to which natives are parties, every court shall be guided by native law so far as it is applicable " (and neither repugnant to justice and morality nor inconsistent with any enactment, etc.), can be construed as making any such alternative provision—if, indeed, the words are intended as more than a comprehensive expression of a general principle, of which the provisions of the Native Courts Regulations, 1897, may be regarded as a particular application. If this be true,[4] it follows that, in the absence of any relevant Ordinance or subsidiary legislation, a British court " in dealing with Muhammadans "—even in the Colony—should be guided by, and have regard to, the " general principles of the Law of Islam "; that Qāḍīs' courts should follow the " law and procedure " enforced in Zanzibar and applied in Kenya up till 1897[5]; that a British court hearing appeals from a Qāḍī's court should " satisfy itself as to the Muhammadan laws and customs applicable to the case "; and that there seems no reason why the " native laws and customs " which native tribunals apply throughout Kenya should not include " Muhammadan laws and customs " in any locality where the influence of Islam has been strong enough to substitute the latter for the former indigenous customs of the tribe or area.[6]

It must, however, be noted that in the Colony of Kenya the jurisdiction of the only two Qāḍīs who have been appointed is expressly limited by the Courts Ordinance, 1931, section 17, to matters of personal status and that Islamic law is there applied today almost exclusively under the terms of some Ordinance[7] —except, that is, in the Northern Province. But in the " Muhammadan Coast region " Islamic law should still, it appears, properly be regarded as the basic law, and is still applicable as such by the Muslim subordinate courts

[1] Art. 11, Proviso (1).

[2] Spelt " Wakf " here and throughout Kenya Ordinances: but see Introduction regarding the spelling of Arabic terms.

[3] See below, pp. 93 ff.

[4] It should, however, be noted that the Judicial Committee, in a recent judgment (*Fatuma binti Mohamed bin Salim and Another* v. *Mohamed bin Salim*: [1952] A.C.I.) assumes *obiter,* and without argument, that this is not so. See Appendix D.

[5] But as regards procedure it has been held that the field is now entirely covered by express enactments. See below, pp. 99 ff.

[6] See discussion of this controversial point in the Introduction to this Survey, pp. 3ff.

[7] e.g., the Muhammadan Marriage, Divorce and Succession Ordinance, 1920, and the Waqf Commissioners Ordinance, 1951.

and even the British courts[1] wherever it has not been ousted by some specific legislation. It would seem, however, that this distinction between the Colony and Protectorate has not of late received that notice and recognition from the Supreme Court and the Court of Appeal for Eastern Africa which was formerly the case.[2]

It should also, perhaps, be observed in this context that Bombay Regulation 4 originally applied to most of Kenya[3] in the same way in which it still applies to Zanzibar, Aden and Somaliland, under article 30[4] of the East Africa Order in Council, 1897, as amended and replaced by article 5 of the Order in Council, 1899.[5] The "law practice and procedure" established thereby might also have been regarded as preserved under article 28 (1) of the Order in Council, 1902[6]—although the application of the Bombay Civil Courts Act, 1869, to the East Africa Protectorate was expressly repealed by Schedule III to the Native Courts Ordinance, 1907—were it not for the "other provision" made under the Native Courts Regulations, 1897.

When we turn to the Kenya Ordinances, it is interesting to observe that the earliest Ordinance[7] regarding the application of Islamic law—the Waqf Commissioners Ordinance, 1900—is more radical and progressive in its concepts and principles than any other enactment except and until the Ordinance of the same name which repealed and replaced it in 1951.[8] Thus this early enactment introduced a number of reforms in regard to the administration of waqf property which were contrary to the ordinary Shāfi'ī principles normally dominant in Kenya, although most of these reforms could find support in some other school or variant opinion of Islamic jurisprudence; and it applied these eclectic provisions without distinction to all local Muslims, regardless of their school or sect. This, of course, is in the best tradition of recent reforms of the Sharī'a in almost all the Middle East countries, but antedates them by a number of years. It is also noteworthy that, apart from the implicit sanction of this Ordinance, no authority seems to exist in Kenya for the recognition of waqf at all—presumably because the application of Islamic law in the coastal area, to which early waqfs would have been largely confined, and even among Muslims generally, was never called in question.

Another early Ordinance which gives implicit recognition to Islamic law is the Muhammadan Marriage and Divorce Registration Ordinance, 1906. This Ordinance, which still remains in force, makes the registration of all such marriages and divorces obligatory under severe penalties,[9] but expressly provides that "Nothing in this Ordinance contained shall be construed to (i) render invalid, merely by reason of its not having been registered, any Muhammadan marriage or divorce which would otherwise be valid; (ii) render valid, by reason of its having been registered, any Muhammadan marriage or divorce which would otherwise be invalid." It is noteworthy, moreover, that this Ordinance gives explicit recognition to the Islamic principle of the marriage of minors by their guardians.[10]

---

[1] In so far as its "general principles" are concerned.

[2] See below, p. 107. And it is noteworthy that their Lordships of the Privy Council, in their recent judgment in *Fatuma binti Mohamed*, etc. [1952] A.C.I., treated a Protectorate case as though it originated in the Colony. See Appendix D.

[3] i.e., from the Juba to the German sphere of influence and from the (then) Uganda Protectorate to the Indian Ocean.

[4] And, *possibly*, art. 11 (a) thereof. See *Dual Jurisdiction in Zanzibar*, by J. H. Vaughan, p. 48. *Sed quaere.*

[5] See *Rana Ramji* v. *Radhabai*, 5 Z.L.R. 91, since this art. is almost identical with art. 21 of the Zanzibar Order in Council, 1884.

[6] See p. 83 above.

[7] Except, that is, for the Native Courts Regulations, 1897.

[8] Details of the earlier enactment will be given thereunder. See pp. 93 ff.

[9] Up to a fine of 3,000 shillings or six months' imprisonment, or both.

[10] Sects. 9, 10, 13, etc.

The principal Ordinance concerning Islamic marriage and divorce, however, is that promulgated in 1920 "to amend the Law relating to Divorce and Matrimonial Causes in the cases of Muhammadan Marriages and relating to Intestate Succession in certain cases"—namely the Muhammadan Marriage, Divorce and Succession Ordinance. This, as subsequently amended in 1923 and 1926, provides (*inter alia*) that: —

(1) "Muhammadan marriages[1] whether contracted prior or subsequently to the commencement of this Ordinance shall be deemed to be valid marriages throughout the Colony, and the parties thereto shall, subject to the provisions of this Ordinance, be entitled to any relief by way of divorce or otherwise which can be had, granted, or obtained according to Muhammadan law and such law shall apply accordingly."[2]

(2) "The Supreme Court and every judge thereof shall, subject to the provisos hereinafter contained and to the other provisions of this Ordinance, have jurisdiction to hear and determine all matrimonial causes and suits arising out of Muhammadan marriages,[3] wherever contracted, at the suit of either party to such marriages, whether such marriages shall have been contracted either prior or subsequently to the commencement of this Ordinance: Provided always that the Supreme Court shall not exercise any jurisdiction as is hereby conferred unless the petitioner is resident in the Colony at the time of the institution of such matrimonial cause or suit as aforesaid."[4]

(3) "In all such matrimonial causes or suits . . . the Supreme Court shall exercise its jurisdiction and act and give relief upon the principles of Muhammadan law applicable to the same respectively and not otherwise"[5]; while the onus of proving these principles "shall be on the parties alleging the same respectively.[6] . . . Provided that nothing herein contained shall abridge, prejudice or in anywise affect the jurisdiction of any court of Qāḍī as by law established.[7] . . . And provided further that nothing herein contained shall be deemed to affect the rights or obligations of any person who at the time of entering into a Muhammadan marriage was already married under any law or custom relating to marriages other than Muhammadan marriages in force in, or recognised by the courts of the Colony."[8]

(4) "Where any person contracts a marriage or, being a male, contracts marriages, in accordance with Muhammadan law, whether such marriage or marriages shall have been contracted either prior or subsequently to the commencement of this Ordinance, and such person dies after the commencement of this Ordinance, and where the issue of any such marriage or marriages dies after the commencement of this Ordinance the law of succession applicable to the property both movable and immovable of such person shall be in accordance with the principles of Muhammadan law, any provision of any Ordinance or rule of law to the contrary notwithstanding: Provided that where in any sect of Muhammadans to which the deceased belonged the law of succession differs from the ordinary law of succession in accordance with the ordinary principles of Muhammadan law then the law of succession applicable to such sect shall apply."[9]

---

[1] These are defined in sect. 2 as any marriage contracted in accordance with and recognised as valid by Muhammadan law.

[2] Sect. 3(1).

[3] Defined in sect. 2 as "all causes or suits relative to the validity of a marriage according to Muhammadan law and all causes and suits relative to or claiming any species of relief, whether by way of divorce or otherwise, in respect of Muhammadan marriages, recognised or given by Muhammadan law."

[4] Sect. 3(2).

[5] Sect. 3(3).

[6] Sect. 3(4).

[7] Sect. 3(5).

[8] Sect. 3(6).

[9] Sect. 4.

(5) " Whoever contracts a Muhammadan marriage being at the time married under the Marriage Ordinance, or in accordance with the law of any Christian country and without having first obtained a lawful divorce, shall be liable to imprisonment for a period not exceeding five years, and in such a case Muhammadan law shall have no application "[1]; while " whoever contracts a Muhammadan marriage being at the time married in accordance with native law and custom to any person other than the person with whom such marriage is contracted and without having first obtained a divorce in accordance with native law and custom shall be liable to imprisonment for a period not exceeding five years, and in such a case Muhammadan law shall have no application."[2]

Points which deserve immediate notice in this Ordinance are that, except in so far as a Qāḍī's court is concerned,[3] jurisdiction in all Muslim matrimonial causes or questions of succession belongs to the Supreme Court[4]; that the law to be applied in matters of succession is expressly stated to be the law of the " sect " of the deceased,[5] while it may, possibly, be inferred from the phrase " upon the principles of Muhammadan law applicable to the same respectively and not otherwise "[6] that the law of the " sect " of the parties will also be applied in matrimonial causes; and that the application of Islamic law is expressly excluded from any " Muhammadan marriage " concluded by one who was, at the time concerned, already married under the Marriage Ordinance or under native law and custom (unless, in the latter case, the two marriages concern the same person[7]). The definition of the circumstances in which the Islamic law of succession will be applied to the estate of a deceased person laid down in section 5 will demand more detailed notice later.

In this context, moreover, reference must also be made to the Marriage Ordinance, 1902, the African Christian Marriage and Divorce Ordinance, 1931, the Matrimonial Causes Ordinance, 1941, the Penal Code, 1930, and the Age of Majority Ordinance, 1933—each of which may be said to have some bearing on the application of the Islamic law of marriage and divorce in Kenya. Thus the Marriage Ordinance provides that " Whoever contracts a marriage under the provisions of this Ordinance being at the time married in accordance with native law or custom or in accordance with Muhammadan law to any person other than the person with whom such marriage is contracted, shall be liable to imprisonment for a period not exceeding five years."[8] Again, " Any person who is married under this Ordinance or whose marriage is declared by this Ordinance to be valid, shall be incapable during the continuance of such marriage of contracting a valid marriage under native law or custom ", while the conclusion of any such contract is punishable by imprisonment for not more than five years[9]—and the same applies equally to a marriage under Islamic law (cp.

[1] Sect. 5.

[2] Sect. 6.

[3] Sect. 3(5).

[4] Sects. 3(2) and 4 (the latter by implication).

[5] Sect. 4. The drafting of this section, however, is loose and unsatisfactory, since the law of succession of Sunnīs and Shī'īs respectively differs so fundamentally (as does also that of the different Sunnī schools to a much lesser degree) that the phrase " the ordinary law of succession in accordance with the ordinary principles of Muhammadan law " is almost meaningless.

[6] Sect. 3(3). It is doubtful, however, whether this was in fact the intention behind the use of this phrase, which probably merely betrays the draftsmen's erroneous belief that in matrimonial causes, like succession, there is an " ordinary law . . . in accordance with the ordinary principles of Muhammadan law " (see note (5) above).

[7] Sects. 3(6), 5 and 6.

[8] Sect. 51. Similarly sect. 11(*d*) forbids the registrar to proceed with the marriage of any such persons.

[9] Sects. 37 and 52. It seems, however, that no prosecutions under sect. 52 are normally instituted.

the Muhammadan Marriage, Divorce and Succession Ordinance, section 5), however valid such marriage may be thereunder. Yet again, the marriage of a non-Muslim man with a Muslim girl of not less than twenty-one years of age (or, if less, with the written consent of her father or, if he be dead, insane or absent, of her mother, etc.[1]) would be perfectly valid under this Ordinance, although null and void in the Sharī'a. Even, moreover, where the necessary consent is withheld, the Supreme Court may, where it sees fit, itself consent to such a marriage.[2] Similarly, the African Christian Marriage and Divorce Ordinance, which only applies to marriages of Africans one or both of whom profess the Christian religion,[3] provides that no marriage celebrated thereunder can be dissolved during the lifetime of the parties except by a valid decree of divorce, and that if either of them contracts another marriage, while their marriage to each other remains undissolved, they will be guilty of bigamy and punishable accordingly.[4] This, again, clearly makes invalid, in Kenya, a Muhammadan marriage celebrated in defiance of this Ordinance, whether or not the party concerned has in the meantime been converted to Islam; while it similarly preserves a marriage thereunder whether or not the wife has subsequently become a Muslim.[5] Again, the Matrimonial Causes Ordinance, 1941, lays down the only grounds on which a marriage under either of these Ordinances may be dissolved or declared null and void by the courts.[6] Similarly, while there is nothing in the Kenya Penal Code which makes it an offence for a husband to consummate his marriage with a child wife,[7] section 135 provides that " Any person who with intent to marry or carnally know a woman of any age, or to cause her to be married or carnally known by any other person, takes her away, or detains her, against her will, is guilty of a felony and is liable to imprisonment for seven years "—and this might possibly expose to prosecution, in certain circumstances, a father whose actions would be justified, under the Sharī'a, as an exercise of his undoubted right to give his virgin daughter in compulsory marriage, whatever her age,[8] to a suitable suitor. Again, the definition of bigamy in section 165 ("Any person who, having a husband or wife living, goes through a ceremony of marriage which is void by reason of its taking place during the life of such husband or wife ") is presumably broad enough to include a subsequent marriage under Islamic law during the lifetime of a wife married under the Marriage Ordinance. Finally, it is noteworthy that the Majority Ordinance, 1933, expressly excludes from its provisions " any matter of marriage, dower or divorce."

The phrase about a Qāḍī's jurisdiction in the Muhammadan Marriage, Divorce and Succession Ordinance[9] must now be related to the Courts' Ordinance, 1931, which provides for a series of courts subordinate to the Supreme Court including three classes of " Muslim subordinate courts ", namely Liwalis' courts, Qāḍīs' courts, and Mudīrs' courts.[10] It further provides that

---

[1] See sect. 19. Failing the mother, the " guardian " must consent, or, failing any such, the Governor. (See sect. 21.)
[2] Sect. 22.
[3] Sect. 2.
[4] See sect. 6.
[5] In Islamic law a wife's adoption of Islam automatically dissolves her marriage to a non-Muslim, unless he too embraces Islam.
[6] Sect. 3(5). It is also noteworthy in this context that the Subordinate Courts (Separation and Maintenance) Ordinance, 1928, applies only to " monogamous marriages "—i.e., marriages which are monogamous by law, rather than by chance or the choice of the parties.
[7] Contrast sect. 133 of the Zanzibar Penal Decree, and sect. 138 of the Tanganyika Penal Code (pp. 62 and 129: also pp. 35 and 44).
[8] In the Shāfi'ī view.
[9] Sect. 3(5).
[10] Sect. 2.

"the Governor may . . . appoint any Arab, Baluchi or African (including a Somali) to hold a Muslim subordinate court[1]; that all subordinate courts shall keep written records and furnish returns of cases tried by them to the Supreme Court"[2]; that the Governor may appoint a Liwali for the Coast, who shall be empowered (*inter alia*) "to inspect all books, records and proceedings of all courts presided over by Liwalis, Qāḍīs and Mudīrs and shall render reports to the Supreme Court relative to such inspections"[3]; and that "Subject to the provisions of this Ordinance and to rules of court, all courts shall follow the principles of procedure laid down in the Civil Procedure Ordinance and in the Criminal Procedure Code, so far as the same may be applicable and suitable"[4]—while it must also be remembered in this context that the Indian Evidence Act was applied in Kenya by the East Africa Order in Council of 1902.[5]

The respective civil jurisdiction[6] of the three classes of Muslim subordinate courts is defined as:—

"Liwalis' courts	Full jurisdiction over Arabs, Baluchis and Africans (including Somalis, Malagasies and Comoro Islanders), in all matters in which the value of the subject-matter in dispute does not exceed one thousand five hundred shillings.
Qādīs' courts	Full jurisdiction over Muhammadan Arabs, Baluchis[7] and Africans (including Somalis, Malagasies and Comoro Islanders), in all matters relating to personal status, marriage, inheritance and divorce, and, within the coast districts, over all Arabs, Baluchis and Africans (including Somalis, Malagasies and Comoro Islanders), in all matters in which the value of the subject-matter in dispute does not exceed one thousand shillings.
Mudīrs' courts	Full jurisdiction over Arabs, Baluchis and Africans (including Somalis, Malagasies and Comoro Islanders), in all matters in which the value of the subject-matter in dispute does not exceed five hundred shillings."[8]

Finally "Mixed cases, that is to say, when the defendant is an Arab, a Baluchi or an African (including a Somali, a Malagasy and a Comoro Islander) and the plaintiff is not . . . may, subject to the other provisions of this Ordinance, be brought either in a subordinate court or in a Muslim subordinate court as the plaintiff may prefer: but in any action so brought in the court of a Liwali or a Mudīr the court shall have jurisdiction to adjudicate on any counter-claim or set-off raised by the defendant by way of defence to the action."[9]

[1] Sect. 5(2).

[2] Sect. 9(1).

[3] Sect. 10.

[4] Sect. 11.

[5] Art. 13 (see below).

[6] For their criminal jurisdiction see p. 107 below: but none of this is, of course, Islamic.

[7] Of these, Baluchis alone are not Shāfi'īs, but Ḥanafīs. The Qāḍīs, however, regularly give judgment by Shāfi'ī law. See *Bimoto binti Ali* v. *Dr. Chur Khan* (1929), 12 K.L.R. 104, where the Chief Qāḍī, sitting as assessor with an English judge, declared a marriage between Baluchis dissolved on grounds not allowed in Ḥanafī law, and the judge decreed accordingly.

[8] Sect. 17 (as amended).

[9] Sect. 18.

Here it is particularly noteworthy that Muslim subordinate courts form, in Kenya, an integral part of the regular judicial system which corresponds to the position of the Qāḍīs' courts in Zanzibar, but contrasts with that of the Liwalis' courts in Tanganyika.[1] As for appeals, the Civil Procedure Ordinance, section 65(1), provides that "Unless otherwise expressly provided by this Ordinance, and subject to such provision as to the furnishing of security as may be prescribed, an appeal shall lie from the decrees or from any part of the decrees and from the orders of all subordinate courts to the Supreme Court: Provided that appeals from Qāḍīs' courts shall lie to the Supreme Court with the Chief Qāḍī as assessor." Further appeals to the Court of Appeal for Eastern Africa are also allowed in suitable circumstances.[2]

There are, moreover, certain other Ordinances which demand notice in this context as having some bearing on Islamic law. Thus the Abolition of the Legal Status of Slavery Ordinance, 1907 (as amended in 1909), provides that "From and after the 1st October, 1907, the legal status of slavery shall be and remain abolished throughout the Colony and no court shall enforce any rights claimed over the body, service, or property of any person on the ground that such person is a slave": [3] but "concubines lawfully held on the 1st October, 1907, although free, shall together with their children continue to be entitled to the rights and privileges which they had previously enjoyed under Muhammadan law, save that any concubine who shall leave her master without his consent shall sacrifice all such rights and privileges including the right to the custody of her children by him" (and for the purpose of this section the word "concubine" shall mean a "female member of the household who is an inmate of the *harīm*"[4]). It is not altogether clear, however, how this Ordinance would be applied by the courts in certain questions of inheritance. Since the Ordinance is not retrospective in its operation, a master may certainly claim the property of a slave who died before it came into effect, but it is doubtful if British courts would recognise a man's claim to inherit, by right of patronage (*walā'*), the property of an ex-slave, or of the latter's descendant, who died without other heirs after the date of the Ordinance.[5] Again, the child of a woman who became a concubine before this Ordinance would be the lawful heir of his father, regardless of the date of his birth, but not, in the British view, the child of a woman whose concubinage was of more recent date. It seems probable, however, that the Qāḍīs' courts would recognise both the right of inheritance by patronage and the legitimacy of a child born in concubinage to a woman who would have been the father's slave but for such legislation,[6] provided they were not apprehensive of British reactions to such judgments.

With regard to real property, the Crown Lands Ordinance, 1915 (as subsequently amended), defines Crown land as "all public lands in the Colony which are for the time being subject to the control of Her Majesty by virtue of any treaty, convention, or agreement, or by virtue of Her Majesty's protectorate, and all lands which shall have been acquired by Her Majesty for the public service or otherwise howsoever, and includes all lands occupied by the African tribes of the Colony and all lands reserved for the use of the members of any African tribe, save only the lands declared to be native lands by the Native Lands Trust

[1] See thereunder.

[2] Civil Procedure Code, sect. 66.

[3] Sect. 2.

[4] Sect. 6. Spelt "harem" in this Ordinance: but see Introduction regarding the spelling of Arabic words.

[5] There can, of course, be no doubt that such a man died free, but this does not properly affect the right of patronage, which refers to past slavery. But British courts might well regard this as an unenforceable incident of an abolished status.

[6] cp. the practice in parts of Northern Nigeria, and elsewhere, and the far more extreme view taken by the Qāḍī of Lamu in *Ahmed bin Abdulla* v. *Admin. of Native Estates* (1925), 10 K.L.R. 136.

Ordinance "[1]; and it empowers the Governor, "subject to the provisions of any Order in Council or to any general or special instructions of the Secretary of State", to "grant, lease, or otherwise alienate in Her Majesty's behalf any Crown lands for any purpose and on any terms and conditions as he may think fit."[2] Section 159, moreover, expressly provides that "no rights or title to the possession of land within . . . the dominions of the Sultan of Zanzibar, claimed under and in accordance with Muhammadan law, shall be recognised as against the Crown or Government, unless the person claiming such right or title shall not only establish in himself such right or title but prove . . . that he or some predecessor in title was in possession . . . prior to 14th December, 1895." Again, the Land Titles Ordinance, 1908 (as subsequently amended), lays down that "All land situate in any district . . . whereto this Ordinance shall have been applied . . . concerning which no claim or claims for a certificate of ownership shall have been made in the manner and in the period aforesaid, or if such claim or claims having been made none shall have been allowed, shall at the expiration of such period be deemed to be Crown land . . .";[3] but "If within twelve years from the date on which any property shall have become Crown property by reasons of the provisions of this section any person shall satisfy the Governor in Council that he or his predecessor in title was entitled to such immovable property at the date aforesaid and that the person entitled to make a claim under this Ordinance in respect of such property had no notice of the application of the Ordinance to the area in which such property is situate . . . the Governor may either direct (*a*) a grant to be made of the immovable property to him if practicable, or (*b*) such value as in the circumstances may appear reasonable to be paid to him."[4] The Ordinance also provides for the grant, in all suitable circumstances, of certificates of ownership to those whose "claim to an estate in fee in land shall have been upheld", certificates of mortgage to mortgagees of immovable property and certificates of interest to those "whose rights as owners of immovable property (other than land) or whose rights by way of lease, encumbrance, charge, lien, contract or other interest in any immovable property . . . or whose right in remainder, reversion, or expectancy in or to immovable property or any undivided share thereof shall have been upheld.[5]

Further enactments regarding real property include the African Property Preservation Ordinance, 1916, the Registration of Documents Ordinance, 1901 (as amended), the Registration of Titles Ordinance, 1919, the Trusts of Land Ordinance, 1941, and the Land (Perpetual Succession) Ordinance, 1923. The first of these enacts that "No building, standing coconut palm, standing fruit tree, or other standing tree situated in an area to which this Ordinance has been applied shall be sold, leased, hypothecated, mortgaged or pledged by any means whatsoever to any person who is not a member of an African tribe inhabiting such area and residing therein."[6] The second provides that "All documents conferring, or purporting to confer, declare, limit, or extinguish any right, title or interest whether vested or contingent to, in or over immovable property (other than such documents as may be of a testamentary nature) and native *vakallas* shall be registered as hereinafter prescribed "[7]; while "Any document, the registration of which is compulsory under this Ordinance, shall not, unless duly registered, be received as evidence in any transaction affecting the property to which the document relates, except with the consent of the court and upon such terms and conditions as the court may impose: Provided always that nothing in this Ordinance shall make any document inadmissible in any criminal

[1] Sect. 2.
[2] Sect. 3(i).
[3] Sect. 17(1).
[4] Sect. 17(2).
[5] Sect. 20.
[6] Sect. 2.
[7] Sect. 4.

proceeding."[1] The third provides that "trust" and "trust for sale" shall have the meaning assigned to these expressions by the Trusts of Land Ordinance, but shall not include a waqf created under the rules of Muhammadan law or trustee appointed thereunder[2]; while the fourth includes a section[3] which provides that "Nothing in this Ordinance contained shall in anywise prejudice or affect the rules of Muhammadan law relating to waqf or the operation of the Registration of Titles Ordinance." And the last, again, has little importance to Muslims in view of the Waqf Commissioners Ordinance, 1951.

Other Ordinances which demand passing reference in this context include the Adoption of Children Ordinance, 1933, the Employment of Women, Young People and Children Ordinance, 1948, the Juveniles Ordinance, 1934,[4] the Age of Majority Ordinance, 1933, and the Credit to Africans (Control) Ordinance, 1948—all of which may be said partially to restrict the scope of Islamic law regarding the rights of guardians over the custody of the persons or property of minor wards or of competent adults freely to dispose of their property in any legal manner. Thus the Adoption of Children Ordinance provides a means by which all the "rights, duties, obligations and liabilities of the parent or parents, guardian or guardians, of the adopted child, in relation to (his) future custody, maintenance and education . . . including all rights to consent or give notice of dissent to marriage" are passed to the adoptive parent or parents, while the adoptive child's own liability to support his parents is similarly transmuted into an identical liability towards his adoptive parents[5]: but an adoption order does not deprive the child of rights of inheritance, whether under intestacy or disposition, which would otherwise have been his, nor of itself give rise to any new rights of inheritance.[6] Such adoption orders, moreover, may be made not only with the consent of parent or guardian but in certain circumstances at the discretion of the court.[7] Similarly, but to a less degree, the Employment of Women, Young People and Children Ordinance, 1948, and the Juveniles Ordinance, 1934, might in some circumstances transcend the rights and powers of a guardian under the Sharī'a. The Age of Majority Ordinance, 1933, does not apply to Africans but enacts that "the minority of all non-African males and females other than Europeans shall cease and determine within the Colony at the age of eighteen[8] (or in some cases twenty-one[9]) years": but this may be regarded, in the case of Muslims, as merely defining by statute the age at which they shall be regarded as reaching *rushd,* or financial competence. The Credit to Africans (Control) Ordinance, 1948, on the other hand, in effect imposes a restriction, in their own interests, on certain contracts concluded by otherwise competent adult Africans, for it forbids the enforcement of any contract or contracts of credit in excess, in aggregate, of two hundred shillings, by a non-African against an African, unless the contract has been approved in writing by an Attesting Officer,[10] after assuring himself that the African understood the nature of the transaction,[11] except in the case of certain Africans who are exempted from these provisions. And it is also relevant in this context to observe that the highly controversial question as to who is to be regarded as an "African" and a "native" respectively receives a partial answer in the Interpretation and General Clauses Ordinance, 1934,[12] which provides that "In this Ordinance and

[1] Sect. 17.
[2] Sect. 2.
[3] Sect. 58.
[4] Omitted under the Revised Edition of the Laws Ordinance, 1948, but retaining its force and validity thereunder (see sect. 5(1)). It was amended in 1951.
[5] Sect. 7(1).
[6] Sect. 7(2).
[7] Sects. 4(3), 5(*b*) and 13.
[8] Sect. 4.
[9] Sect. 5.
[10] Sect. 2(1).
[11] Sect. 2(2).
[12] As regards the section quoted, but not the whole Ordinance

in every other Ordinance, unless there is something in the subject or context inconsistent with such construction or unless it is therein otherwise expressly provided, each of the terms 'African' and 'native' means any person who is a member of or one of whose parents is or was a member of an indigenous African tribe or community, in which expression are included the people known as the Swahili, but neither of the said terms shall include:—

(*a*) an Arab, or a Baluchi born in Africa; or

(*b*) a Somali, an Abyssinian (Amhara, Tigre and Shoa), a Malagasy or a Comoro Islander, unless it is expressly stated that such terms shall include such persons or any of them; or

(*c*) any person who, of his own motion, proves to the satisfaction of the magistrate of a subordinate court of the first or second class—

(i) that he is partly of non-African descent; and

(ii) that he is not occupying land in accordance with native tenure or native customary law; and

(iii) that he is not living among the members of any African tribe or community in accordance with their customary mode of life."[1]

But much the most interesting Ordinance in Kenya, from the point of view of Islamic law, is the new Waqf Commissioners Ordinance,[2] 1951, made necessary in part[3] by a recent decision of the Court of Appeal for Eastern Africa which will be discussed below.[4] Many points in this remarkable Ordinance deserve comment, partly for their intrinsic interest, partly because its earlier sections more closely reflect the pure Sharī'a than do the terms of the corresponding legislation in India, Aden or Zanzibar, and partly because its later sections go so much further than legislation in any other country outside the Middle East in laying down liberal principles for the administration of waqf property and funds. Thus:—

(*a*) Among the definitions in section 2 it is provided that a "waqf" means "the religious, charitable or benevolent endowment or dedication of any property in accordance with Muslim law;" that "waqf *ahlī*" means a "waqf made for the benefit of an individual or family or for the performance of rites or ceremonies recognised by Muslim law as being for the benefit of the soul of an individual (including the dedicator) or of the souls of the members of a family"; while "waqf *khayrī*" means a "waqf, other than a waqf *ahlī*, made for any religious, charitable or benevolent public purpose recognised by Muslim law, including the provision and upkeep of cemeteries and burial grounds." Here the most significant point is the care with which the definition of "waqf *ahlī*" avoids any suggestion that such waqfs are limited to the founder's own family[5]—a point in which the Kenya Ordinance is superior to the corresponding enactments in India, Aden and Zanzibar—but it is also relevant to observe that while the definition of "Muslim" for the purposes of this Ordinance as "an Arab, a member of the Twelve Tribes, a Baluchi, a Somali, a Comoro Islander, a Malagasy or a native of Africa, of the Muslim faith" does not include an Indian, section 3 provides that "any person professing Islam who is not a Muslim within the meaning of section 2 of the Ordinance" may bring his waqf within its scope by appointing the Waqf Commissioners to be trustees of any property subject to his waqf.

(*b*) In section 4 it is provided that:—

"Every waqf heretofore or hereafter made by any Muslim which is made,

[1] Sect. 4.

[2] Which was shown to me in draft, and on which I commented extensively, during my visit to Kenya in 1950.

[3] Although it also includes a number of important reforms.

[4] *Fatuma binti Mohamed bin Salim and Another* v. *Mohamed bin Salim* (Civil Appeal No. 33 of 1948—unreported). But see Appendix D.

[5] A point which I emphasised during my visit.

either wholly or partly, for any of the following purposes, that is to say—

(*a*) for the maintenance and support, either wholly or partly, of any person including the family, children, descendants or kindred of the maker; or

(*b*) if the maker of the waqf is an Ibāḍī or Ḥanafī Muhammadan, for his own maintenance and support during his lifetime,

is declared to be a valid waqf if—

(i) it is in every other respect made in accordance with Muslim law; and

(ii) the ultimate benefit in the property the subject of such waqf is expressly, or, in any case in which the personal law of the person making the waqf so permits, impliedly, reserved for the poor or for any other purpose recognised by Muslim law as a religious, pious or charitable purpose of a permanent character: Provided that the absence of any reservation of the ultimate benefit in property the subject of a waqf for the poor or any other purpose recognised by Muslim law as a religious, pious or charitable purpose of a permanent character shall not invalidate the waqf if the personal law of the maker of the waqf does not require such reservation."[1] Again, " No waqf to which sub-section (1) of this section applies shall be invalid merely because the benefit in the property reserved by such waqf for the poor or any religious, pious, or charitable purpose is not to take effect until after the extinction of the family, children, descendants or kindred of the maker of the waqf."[2] This section follows, in broad outline, the pattern of all the corresponding legislation, designed as it is to restore the right of a Muslim to make a waqf in the form of a family perpetuity[3]: but it is interesting to notice (*a*) that the Kenya Ordinance not only maintains the Zanzibar reference to " kindred " in sub-section (a) [by contrast with the Indian Act and the Aden Ordinance] but also includes the significant addition, " any person including . . . ", in order to make it clear that such a waqf may validly be made in favour of some unrelated individual or family, etc.[4]; (*b*) that it again follows the Zanzibar Decree in extending the provisions of sub-section (b) to Ibāḍīs, as well as the Ḥanafīs to which the Indian Act refers[5] ,and in the emphasis it lays on the relevance of the personal law of the founder in regard to the admissibility of implicit reservations for some permanent charity[6]; (*c*) that it differs from all the corresponding legislation elsewhere in making it clear, in the proviso to sub-section (ii), that no such reservation to a permanent charity at all, whether express or implied, is required in the case of those whose personal law does not require this.[7]

(*c*) After provisions regarding the constitution of the Waqf Commissioners, the registration of waqf property, etc., sections 11 and 12 provide for these Commissioners to take over the administration of any waqf " on the application (*a*) in the case of waqf ***khayrī***, of the trustee or trustees, as the case may be, of the waqf; and (*b*) in the case of waqf ***ahlī***, of the trustee or trustees, as the case

---

[1] Sect. 4(1).

[2] Sect. 4(2).

[3] A right of which he has otherwise been deprived by a series of judgments of British courts.

[4] See comment (*a*) on p. 93, and p. 93 footnote (5).

[5] It is noteworthy in this context that this Ordinance does not follow the Aden Ordinance in extending this principle to Shāfiʿīs.

[6] This would, presumably, cover the view of Abū Yūsuf among the Ḥanafīs that the very word waqf may be regarded as an implicit reservation of this sort.

[7] This, again, was a point to which I called attention in my comments on the original draft, since the majority of Kenya Muslims are Shāfiʿīs, and no such reservation is required by their law. The Zanzibar Decree has no corresponding section, but such waqfs are deemed valid in Zanzibar under the section which reads: " Nothing in this Decree shall be deemed to affect any other custom or usage whether local or prevalent among Muhammadans of any particular class or sect." (Sect. 6.)

may be, with the consent of the majority of the beneficiaries of the waqf "[1]: or where "(*a*) there is no properly constituted trustee of a waqf; or (*b*) any trustee is acting in an improper or unauthorised manner ", after a proper enquiry held on their own motion in the case of waqf *khayrī*, or on the motion of the majority of the beneficiaries in waqf *ahlī*.[2] Here the major points of interest are firstly that the Waqf Commissioners are authorised themselves to act in a quasi-judicial capacity and thus discharge one of the proper duties of the Qāḍī in Sharī'a law[3]; and secondly that the interest of the beneficiaries in the proper administration of a waqf *ahlī* receives explicit recognition.

(*d*) Again, after sections empowering the Commissioners to call upon any trustee of waqf property to satisfy them that such property is being properly administered,[4] compelling all trustees to obtain the sanction of the Commissioners in writing to any contract or agreement " purporting to sell, to lease or otherwise alienate any property the subject of any waqf for any period exceeding one year ",[5] and providing that no title to any property the subject of a waqf shall in future be acquired by reason of adverse possession or prescription,[6] it is enacted that " In any case where in the opinion of the Waqf Commissioners the intentions of the maker of a waqf are unlawful or unascertainable (by reference to tradition or by reference to any other evidence lawfully obtainable[7]) or are incapable of being carried out or where any surplus revenue remains after fulfilling the intentions of the maker of the waqf, the Waqf Commissioners shall, in the case of a waqf *khayrī*, apply the property the subject of the waqf or any surplus property or revenue therefrom, as the case may be, for such benevolent or charitable purposes on behalf of Muslims as appear to the Waqf Commissioners proper, and in the case of waqf *ahlī*, shall apply such property or surplus revenues aforesaid in such manner as the Waqf Commissioners think fit for the benefit of the beneficiaries of the waqf."[8] Similarly " If it appears to the Waqf Commissioners that in respect of any waqf the intentions of the maker cannot reasonably be carried into effect and that it is accordingly expedient that the property the subject of the waqf or any part thereof should be sold, the Waqf Commissioners may cause such property or part thereof to be sold and shall apply the proceeds of sale in the manner provided by sub-section (2) of section 16 of this Ordinance."[9] Here both these sections represent a more detailed extension, under the dual classification of *khayrī* and *ahlī* waqfs, of the provisions of sections 11 and 12 of the Ordinance of 1900,[10] both of which constituted a major innovation in existing practice, much along the lines of the far more recent reforms in Egypt, Lebanon, etc.

(*e*) Provision is also made that " any property of a deceased Muslim to which no claim has been established within one year[11] from the date upon which such property vested in the administrator of the estate or in the Public Trustee shall be handed over to the Waqf Commissioners . . . and shall, if not handed over

---

[1] Sect. 11. [2] Sect. 12.

[3] Unlike the position under the Ordinance of 1900, whereby reference must be made to the courts in such circumstances.

[4] Sect. 13: cp., sect. 8 of the Ordinance of 1900.

[5] Sect. 14: cp., sect. 8 of 1900.

[6] Sect. 15. This is wholly new.

[7] Sect. 16(1).

[8] Sect. 16(2).

[9] Sect. 17 (but land used for a cemetery or mosque is excepted). It is noteworthy, however, that this major reform was much facilitated in East Africa by the fact that the Ibāḍī law allows the sale of waqf property in such circumstances.

[10] cp., Zanzibar Waqf Property Decree, sects. 13 and 14.

[11] Provided that subsequent claims thereto may be heard up to twelve years after such handing over (see sect. 18(2)).

in the form of money, be converted into money and paid by the Waqf Commissioners into a special fund created for the purpose to be known as the Surplus Fund "—to be "utilised by the Waqf Commissioners for such benevolent or charitable purposes for the benefit of Muslims as the Waqf Commissioners may consider proper."[1] This, again, rests on section 13 of the original Ordinance and is, of course, designed to take the place of the *Bayt al-Māl* of the pure Sharī'a.

(*f*) Once more, authority is given—as an exception to the general rule—for the Commissioners to utilise the revenue arising from property the subject of a waqf *khayrī* in order to finance repairs, etc., urgently needed by another waqf *khayrī* where they are satisfied that such revenue is not then required in connection with the first, and that the amount so utilised will be repaid within five years.[2] This section is wholly new, but corresponds to similar provisions in recent Egyptian legislation.

(*g*) Finally, it is provided that if, in respect of any waqf,

" (*a*) the intentions of the maker—

(i) are unlawful or unascertainable, or

(ii) are incapable of being carried into effect, or

(iii) cannot reasonably be carried into effect; or

(*b*) the beneficiaries are unascertainable; or

(*c*) any surplus revenue remains after . . . carrying into effect the intentions of the maker of the waqf,

the Waqf Commissioners shall pay into the Surplus Fund created under section 18 of this Ordinance the proceeds of sale of any such property the subject of a waqf as is mentioned in paragraphs (*a*) and (*b*) of this section and any such surplus revenue as is mentioned in paragraph (*c*) of this sub-section "[3]—while they shall also have power " to place on deposit in any bank or to invest in and upon such investments and securities as are allowed by law for the investment of trust funds any monies standing to the credit of the Surplus Fund and income derived therefrom shall be paid to the credit of the General Administration Fund "[4] (which shall be used " first in defraying the expenses of management, and the surplus shall be used for such charitable purposes as the Waqf Commissioners may consider proper "[5]). These provisions, again, represent major innovations along lines broadly similar to the Egyptian legislation of 1946.

Some of the cases decided by the courts in Kenya and by the Court of Appeal for Eastern Africa are so interesting, illuminative and even controversial from the point of view of Islamic law that they demand mention in this Survey. Thus in *Fatuma binti Mohamed bin Salim and Another* v. *Mohamed bin Salim* (see above),[6] the Court of Appeal held that a Shāfi'ī waqf in favour of the founder's two daughters and their children in perpetuity—and in the event of their total extinction for the benefit of certain other relations or, failing them, of three mosques—was void; on the grounds that the court was bound by the Privy Council decision in the case of *Abul Fata* v. *Russomoy*[7] and by its own decision in *Said bin Muhammad bin Kassim, etc.* v. *the Wakf Commissioners, Zanzibar* (1946), 13 E.A.C.A. 32. This was, perhaps, inevitable—in spite of the fact that the Privy Council decision has been almost universally recognised as

[1] Sect. 18.

[2] Sect. 19.

[3] Sect. 21(1).

[4] Sect. 21(2). This authorised existing practice.

[5] Sect. 22(2).

[6] pp. 84 and 93 above: see also Appendix D.

[7] (1894) 22 I.A., 76.

contrary to the pure Sharī'a[1] and has been virtually reversed in India by the Mussalman Waqf Validating Act, 1913, and that considerable evidence was produced to show that the court's own decision in 1946 was contrary to the Muslim authorities, and was indeed promptly avoided in Zanzibar by the Waqf Validating Decree, 1946 (which purported to declare the true law of waqf as it had always existed throughout the Sultan's dominions)[2]—unless it had been possible for the court in some way to " distinguish " the Privy Council decision from the case before them. In the event, however, this would have been entirely justified, since the waqf in question was created by a Shāfi'ī, while the Privy Council decision concerned Ḥanafī law (and the court's own previous decision concerned Ibāḍīs), had the Court of Appeal not, apparently, been misled by two Indian cases into the belief that " there is no difference in the law of waqf between the Shāfi'ī and Ḥanafī schools ": for while this is true in the sense that the waqf concerned would have been equally valid in both schools, it is misleading both in its absolute form and also in the sense that the Shāfi'ī law in such cases, unlike the Ḥanafī, does not even insist on any ultimate gift to a permanent charity whatever, whether express or implied. In the circumstances, therefore, it seems, with great respect, that this was a somewhat unimaginative decision[3] which missed a clear opportunity to distinguish a precedent which the court must have known to be contrary to the Muslim authorities.

This case, moreover, is also noteworthy for a remark of Nihill C. J. *obiter* that " It has always been regarded in this court and in the Supreme Court of Kenya that in cases affecting personal status arising between Muhammadans the law to be applied is Muhammadan law as interpreted by judicial decision. Whether this rests upon a secure statutory basis in Kenya is, however, by no means easy to discover. . . . If our consideration of this appeal should result in the attention of the executive being directed to the law regarding waqf as it now obtains in Kenya, I make the suggestion that any such consideration might well include this wider suggestion." In a subsequent case[4] this *obiter dictum* was

[1] Although upheld as correct, with little reference to the mass of Islamic authorities to the contrary, by their Lordships of the Judicial Committee in their recent judgment on this very case (*Fatuma binti Salim*) on appeal. See Appendix D.

[2] These, of course, include the Kenya Protectorate: but it is natural that this Decree, which would of itself have no effect in territory administered by H.M.G., was not allowed to affect the authority of a previous decision.

[3] Contrast Hamilton J. in *Talibu bin Mwijaka*, etc. (1907) (2 E.A.L.R. 33), when he even went so far as to say " These points taken together define the law which is to be applied by this court in such cases . . . that is to say, that while on the one hand the court is to 'have regard to and be guided by the general principles of the Law of Islam,' on the other, whatever respect it may pay to the decisions of the Privy Council, it is not bound by those decisions." He then described how the " pure Muhammadan law " of waqf had been " profoundly modified " in India by certain decisions of the Privy Council, and continued: " The Muhammadan law in East Africa has, however, not been subjected to the same modifying influence . . . and remains the same as when the Minhaj was written in the sixth century of the Hijra." This argument, however, has not appealed to their Lordships of the Judicial Committee in their judgment in this very case (*Fatuma's case*) on appeal [1952] A.C.1. since they could not " accept the theory . . . that the interpretation of Muhammadan law given by this Board in a series of cases is confined to that law as applied or administered in India. On the contrary, it has not been suggested that, apart from the differences existing among the Shāfi'ī, Ḥanafī and other sects, which have no present significance, Muhammadan law is not the same in East Africa as in India. The appellants have themselves relied on its universality and invoke the text of the Qur'ān and the writings of learned commentators who expounded the law not of East Africa or any part of it but of the whole Muslim world. In these circumstances their Lordships are as little justified in reviewing Abdul Fata's case in an appeal from the courts of Kenya as they would be in an appeal (if that were now possible) from the courts of India." In this connection cp. Mr. G. W. Bartholomew's notes on this case in the International and Comparative Law Quarterly, i., July, 1952, pp. 392 ff. and Appendix D.

[4] Civil Case No. 40 of 1949 (unreported). See below.

quoted in support of a fantastic contention that "Muhammadan law does not run at all in this Protectorate area of the Colony", in spite of the fact that even the broadest interpretation of this *dictum* cannot be held to throw doubt on more than the statutory basis on which that law is applied. It seems much more probable, however, that the learned Chief Justice was calling in question, not the applicability of Islamic law as such, but whether it should be applied "as interpreted by judicial decision",[1] as would appear from his references to counsel's argument that the court ought not to feel itself bound by the decision of the Privy Council in *Abul Faṭa's case*—or their own previous decision—in view of the fact that these decisions were contrary to the weight of Muslim authority.[2] In pure Islamic law, of course, no doctrine of the binding authority of precedents exists: on the contrary, the Caliph 'Umar is credited with the famous saying, when advised that the decision he had just given was directly contrary to one he had given on similar facts on a previous occasion, that "It is better to return to the truth than to persist in error." This would, of course, run counter to the training and practice of English lawyers and lead to greater uncertainty as to the law the courts are likely to apply: but it would at least prevent the *impasse* in which a judgment universally recognised as mistaken must be blindly followed, in territory after territory, until such time as the Legislature sees fit to reinstate, as nearly as possible, the original law.

Said bin Abdulla and Sabuhu binti Ali v. *The Waqf Commissioners and the Registrar of Titles, Mombasa*[3] is another somewhat unsatisfactory case. Here it was held, *inter alia*, that the creation of a waqf of land was either a "transfer" of land or a "dealing in land" under the terms of the Registration of Titles Ordinance, and therefore "null and void and of no effect" if not effected in accordance with its provisions.[4] It had previously been found, moreover, that the Registration of Titles Ordinance was not wide enough to cover many dealings in land under trusts, so the Trusts of Land Ordinance, 1941, had been introduced: but this was, expressly, not to affect the "rules of Muhammadan law relating to waqf",[5] as was also the case with the Registration of Titles (Amendment) Ordinance, 1941.[6] Under the Registration of Titles Ordinance, moreover, a registrar must not register "any instrument purporting to transfer or otherwise deal with . . . land . . . except in the manner herein provided nor unless such instrument be in accordance with the provisions hereof, but any instrument in substance in conformity with the forms annexed hereto shall be sufficient."[7] No suitable form for transfer of or dealing in registered land by way of *waqfīya*[8] had, however, been provided, so every *waqfīya* relating to such land amounted to "an attempt to deal with registered land outside the provisions of the Ordinance and so . . . is null and void and of no effect." Here the contrary argument that this reasoning leads to an obvious *reductio ad absurdum* does not appear to have been strongly pressed, in spite of the manifest incongruity of the view that waqfs in themselves are valid dealings in land; that every such dealing must be registered in that one of several specified forms which exactly or approximately corresponds with its terms; that any dealing in land not so registered is ineffectual; and that since no form exists appropriate to the registration of a waqf this dealing cannot be registered at all and therefore can never be valid and effective. Such reasoning seems to run counter to the cardinal principle in the interpretation of statutes that where the language is general, doubtful or obscure it may, if susceptible thereto, be modified or varied by

[1] Although it is certainly difficult to know what "statutory authority" could be expected for this.
[2] He may well, in fact, have had Hamilton's words in mind (see p. 97, note 3).
[3] Civil Case No. 40 of 1949 (unreported).
[4] Sect. 20.
[5] Sect. 58.
[6] Sect. 2.
[7] Sect. 33.
[8] Waqf deed. Spelt "Wakfieh": but see Introduction for the spelling of Arabic words.

interpretation, in order to avoid manifest absurdity, repugnance, mischief or injustice.

Baraka binti Bahmishi v. *Salim bin Abed Busawadi* (1939), 20 K.L.R. Pt. I. 34, concerns a still more pressing problem, namely the rules of procedure and evidence which must be followed by Muslim subordinate courts. Here the whole argument turned on the proper interpretation of section 11 of the Courts Ordinance, 1931 (see above) which reads: — " Subject to the provisions of this Ordinance and to rules of court, all courts shall follow the principles of Procedure laid down in the Civil Procedure Ordinance and in the Criminal Procedure Code, so far as the same may be applicable and suitable." In a previous case[1] it had been held that the words " so far as the same may be applicable and suitable " must be construed to allow Muslim subordinate courts to follow Muhammadan rules of procedure and evidence, on the grounds (i) that the courts concerned are specifically named Muslim courts, (ii) that the presiding officers are qualified only in Muhammadan law, (iii) that for " many years these courts have in substance administered only Muhammadan law in the exercise of their jurisdiction and have known no other code ", and (iv) " that the Protectorate where they function is in effect a part of the Sultan of Zanzibar's Dominions where Muhammadan law is recognised and practised by subordinate courts." In the case under discussion, however, the learned Judge disagreed with this former decision and held that section 11 of the Courts Ordinance must be construed not as allowing the use of Muhammadan rules of procedure and evidence in place of the Civil Procedure Ordinance and Evidence Act but, instead, as meaning that these latter enactments are to be followed except in special circumstances. As for the arguments under (i) to (iii) above, it was held that these, however cogent they might be, could not be regarded as over-riding the express provisions of section 11, while (iv) was weakened by the fact that the " Muhammadan Law of Evidence " had been specifically excluded from all Zanzibar Courts by the Zanzibar Evidence Decree.[2] If, therefore, the Legislature did not intend Muslim subordinate courts to be bound, in normal circumstances, by the statutory rules of evidence and procedure, it should have said so clearly. And this conclusion was held to be supported by section 19 of the Courts Ordinance, wherein it is enacted that mixed cases, that is to say cases where the defendant is a native and the plaintiff a non-native, may be brought in a Muslim subordinate court if the plaintiff so chooses, since it was argued that " it would be difficult to apply one of the peculiar and inherent principles of Muhammadan Procedure, i.e., the administration of the *yamin* (oath), if one of the parties were a European." Similarly, the Indian Evidence Act of 1872, having been applied to Kenya by the East Africa Order in Council of 1897,[3] retained by the East Africa Order in Council of 1902[4] and again by the Kenya Colony Order in Council of 1921,[5] must be held to override the Muhammadan law and to be binding on all subordinate courts, Muslim or otherwise. It should, however, be added that the learned Judge expressly remarked, at the end of his judgment: " In arriving at this judgment I am merely interpreting the law as I see it and I must not be taken to be expressing in any way any opinion on the question, a matter which is quite separate and distinct from the legal questions, namely, which is the more appropriate or desirable procedure for Muslim subordinate courts to follow. Upon this question there would doubtless be some divergence of view, and I am not concerned with that."

In view of this unequivocal judgment it is curious to find that in a subsequent case[6] the same learned Judge seriously discussed whether the evidence of a mother regarding the date when her child was born was admissible in the

[1] *Hussein* v. *Abdulla* (1936), 17 K.L.R. Pt. 2, 95.

[2] Sect. 2. [3] Art. 11(b). [4] Art. 28. [5] Art. 11.

[6] *Said bin Salim* v. *Masood bin Said and Hafsa binti Said.* Civil Appeal No. 15 of 1945 (unreported).

Muhammadan law of evidence. When, however, this case was taken to the Court of Appeal for Eastern Africa[1] the basic question examined was whether the Qāḍī who first heard the case had erred in following—or professing to follow—Muhammadan rules of evidence in excluding the testimony of all the witnesses called by the plaintiff, when he ought really to have followed the Indian Evidence Act, or whether he was in fact still entitled to apply the Muhammadan rules: and it was held that the wording of section 2 (1) of the Act [which specifically repeals "all rules of evidence not contained in any Statute, Act, or Regulation in force in any part of British India"] clearly includes the repeal of the Muhammadan rules of evidence previously followed; that the "decision of the East Africa Court of Appeal in *Athman bin Mohamed* v. *Ali bin Salim*, 6 E.A.L.R. 91 . . . that on a question of marriage between Muhammadans in a Muhammadan Court the Muhammadan rules of evidence apply" was not a binding authority in this regard since the wording of the Evidence Act had not been adequately discussed therein nor the issue decided on its merits; and that "it follows therefore that the rulings of the trial court . . . being based entirely on alleged Muhammadan rules of evidence were entirely on a wrong basis." The Chief Justice of Kenya did, however, remark that he "could have wished that this question had been much more fully argued before us than was done and that we had had the assistance of the Attorney-General as amicus curiae, for . . its determination raises questions of great importance to the Muslim community. I am well aware that the conclusion this court has reached may have serious and possibly embarrassing repercussions on the administration of justice in Muslim subordinate courts in the coastal district of Kenya, but that is a matter which if it is thought expedient must be set right by the Legislature."

In the event, it seems that the Indian Evidence Act is in fact now followed, in general, in both Liwalis' and Mudīrs' courts, for the dual reason that present-day Liwalis and Mudīrs commonly know English (and are thus in a position to apply it) and also because the cases they hear do not normally concern those questions of personal status and family law which are regarded by Muslims as so vitally partaking of the essence of their religion that the strict rules of the Sharī'a are particularly binding therein. But in the Qāḍīs' courts, on the other hand, no such attempt is made; partly, again, because the Qāḍīs could not, from their training, education and background, follow the Evidence Act even if they wished, and partly because it is in any case against their consciences to do so. Instead they apply a somewhat loose approximation to the rules laid down in the Islamic texts. In regard to the burden of proof, the putting of oaths, and the number of witnesses, for instance, the normal rules are strictly observed: but witnesses are sworn and questioned by the court in place of the orthodox screening, and the other party is not allowed to impugn their characters. All non-Muslim witnesses, on the other hand, are, it seems, rigidly excluded, at least in questions of personal status[2]; as also, of course, are any "interested" witnesses (see above). When reminded that the Evidence Act was supposed to govern all their proceedings, the Kenya Qāḍīs merely chuckle.

This state of affairs is obviously unsatisfactory, as it makes a farce of the law. The gulf between English and Muhammadan rules of procedure has, of course, been partially bridged, in Kenya as elsewhere,[3] by an Oaths Act. Even so, however, there remains a considerable residuum of problems where Qāḍīs will certainly continue to apply the Islamic rules of evidence and where their decisions

[1] 14 E.A.C.A. 32.

[2] They profess, however, to be rather more liberal in regard to such financial cases as come to their courts.

[3] In Kenya the Indian Oaths Act of 1873 was applied by the E.A.O. in C. of 1897 (Art. 11(*b*)), while in Zanzibar, Aden and Uganda local enactments along the same lines have been introduced. But apart from a passing reference to this Act in *Baraka* v. *Salim* (1942), 20 K.L.R. Pt. 1 at p. 38 as permitting "a measure of reconciliation between the English and the Islam [*sic*] Law of Evidence", I never heard it mentioned.

should therefore, technically at least, regularly be overruled on appeal.[1] One solution, of course, would be to equate Qāḍīs' courts with native tribunals rather than with the subordinate court system, as has been done in the case of Liwalis' courts in Tanganyika, for in that case the Evidence Act would no longer be obligatory upon them. But this would probably be regarded as a retrogressive step and an insult to Muslim dignity, as matters now stand in Kenya. It would be preferable to introduce legislation to the effect that Qāḍīs' courts, when deciding questions of personal status only, need not be bound by the Act but might follow their own rules of evidence and procedure. Even so, however, it would probably be wise, in the interests of justice and equity, to add a proviso that whenever the testimony of some witness is excluded on the grounds of his religion, or " interest " in the case, his testimony must be recorded in full and the record sent to the Supreme Court for review, so that cases in which the application of these rules appeared to have caused a miscarriage of justice could be reheard or otherwise corrected.

A somewhat similar problem concerns the applicability of the Shāfi'ī rule that a child born to a widowed or irrevocably divorced woman within four lunar years of her widowhood or final divorce—unless she has already been validly remarried for at least six months—is deemed the legitimate issue of her former husband.[2] In a comparatively early case[3] it was held that this must be regarded as a substantive rule of Islamic law rather than a mere presumption to be over-ridden by section 112 of the Evidence Act. But it seems clear that this is no longer good law in Kenya, since the East African Court of Appeal has apparently held, in an unreported case,[4] that the provisions of sections 112 and 114 of the Evidence Act set forth the presumptions now applicable in questions of legitimacy. In another early case,[5] again, it was held that where a fraudulent title had been pleaded in court to defeat a claim, the executor of the one who pleaded it was estopped, both in equity and Muhammadan law, from thereafter pleading the true title as against a bona fide purchaser for value. In Islamic law this dictum rested, of course, on the doctrine of *iqrār* or acknowledgment: but it seems certain that such a case would now be decided exclusively under section 115 of the Evidence Act.[6]

Cases which concern the authority and scope of Islamic law in the coastal strip—over and above the provisions of such enactments as the Muhammadan Marriage, Divorce and Succession Ordinance—are comparatively numerous. To take real property first, the famous case of *Secretary of State* v. *Charlesworth, Pilling & Co.* (see p. 60 above) established the proposition that, since the basic law in the Sultan's dominions was the law of Islam,[7] this must be applied by British courts—in the absence of any enactment to the contrary—in all questions of real property, whoever the parties thereto might be, on the common law principle of *lex loci rei sitae*. Again, in the *Jibana case*,[8] Hamilton J. remarked: " It has been argued on the basis of the proposition that Muhammadan law applies to sales of land within the Sultan's dominions and that as the British Government is administering those dominions on behalf of the Sultan . . . this court would recognise a title which would have been recognised by the Sultan's courts before the Agreement . . . I have no fault to find with either of these propositions." But in a much more recent case[9] concerning a piece of land

[1] cp. the Zanzibar section of this Survey, pp. 69, 70, and Appendix.
[2] Unless, being alive, the husband repudiates him by the *li'ān* procedure (see p. 21, etc.).
[3] *Sheriff Abdulla* v. *Zuena binti Abedi* (1912), 4 E.A.L.R. 86.
[4] Civil Appeal No. 21 of 1947, I am told: but I have not seen the record.
[5] *Abdi Nuri* v. *B.E.A. Corporation and Rukiya* (1909), 3 E.A.L.R. 12.
[6] Concerning estoppel by conduct. See *Masood bin Said and Hafsa binti Said* v. *Said bin Salim* (1946), 14 E.A.C.A. 32.
[7] cp. the remark " Zanzibar law, which is Muhummadan law " (p. 111).
[8] See below, pp. 102 f. and 5 E.A.L.R. 141.
[9] *Said bin Seif* v. *Shariff Mohamed Shatry* (1938), 19 K.L.R. Pt. 1, 9.

leased with permission for the tenant to build and subsequently reclaimed by the landlord, it was emphasised that *Charlesworth's case* only laid down that Islamic law was applicable where an applied Act or other legislative enactment " does not fit ", and that the case under decision was clearly governed by the Indian Transfer of Property Act.[1] It was, however, observed *obiter* that the Shāfi'ī law concerning a landowner who lends his land for building purposes without a time limit and then reclaims it provides that the borrower need not demolish his buildings unless this has been stipulated: instead, the owner might either let them stand in return for rent, himself demolish them for compensation, or (perhaps) appropriate them against payment of their value.[2] Again, where one party agreed to sell to the other, " subject to the claims, if any ", of his relatives, 10,000 acres of land " to the North of Kilifi Harbour ",[3] it was held that Islamic law was applicable and that the contract to sell was therefore void on the triple grounds of futurity, uncertainty, and because it contained a condition; while, where a property was pledged[4] by its owner and duly delivered to the pledgee, returned by him to the pledgor that the latter might reap its benefits, and then attached in execution of a decree against the pledgor in favour of a third party,[5] it was held that the pledgee had a lien on such property and was entitled to have the sale made subject to such lien. Both these comparatively early judgments seem good Shāfi'ī law: but it must be emphasised that of recent years legislation has tended to encroach on the Sharī'a to an ever increasing extent.[6]

The Law Reports also include some fascinating studies of the relation between Islamic law and native customary law in matters concerning land tenure in this coastal strip. Thus in *Parenti* v. *Barclay and the Crown Advocate* (1910), 4 E.A.L.R. 80, the court discussed the validity of a private purchase of land within the Duruma territory from an Arab family, and observed: " By the custom of the tribe no member of the tribe can sell land in the tribal occupation but on the other hand it was always recognised under Arab rule that a Muhammadan subject of the Sultan by making a shamba on the "barra"[7] acquired a title to it and the right to deal with it as private property without regard to the customs of the tribe amongst whom he settled." It was held, therefore, that the British Government was under the obligation of recognising the title in question, which extended back some ninety years, on the grounds that it would have been recognised by the Government of the Sultan, " Duruma custom to the contrary notwithstanding." But, where certain members of the Jibana tribe had purported to sell some of their tribal land,[8] it was shown that they—like the Duruma —had no title to ownership of land but only to its use and to the ownership of trees planted thereon: they might sell the trees, but properly only to a fellow tribesman; they might mortgage their rights to anyone, subject to a right of redemption at any time; and they might sell the right to sow on a plot which they had cleared for agriculture. In this case it was held, therefore, that Islamic law could not give them the right to sell what they did not themselves possess,

[1] Applied in Kenya by E.A. Orders in Council of 1897 and 1902, and Kenya Colony Order in Council of 1921.

[2] See *Minhaj* (E. C. Howard's translation), p. 196.

[3] *Edward Powys Cobb* v. *Rashid bin Salim* (1909), 3 E.A.L.R. 35.

[4] To adopt the common nomenclature.

[5] *In re Mwana Mkame* (1909), 3 E.A.L.R. 48.

[6] Although the Indian Acts (Amendment) Ordinance, sect. 9 (virtually repeating the Application to Natives of Indian Acts Ordinance, 1903) severely restricts the application of such Acts to natives, so that they are not bound by, e.g., the Indian Contract Act, 1872, and the Transfer of Property Act, 1882, this does not, of course, apply to Kenya Ordinances and subsidiary legislation.

[7] i.e. an estate or plantation on the mainland.

[8] *Muluwa Gwanombi and Others representing the Jibana tribe* v. *Abdulrasool Alidina Visram* (1914), 5 E.A.L.R. 141.

namely, the ownership of the land; and that the sale of the trees did not give any title to the land on which they stood, as land, buildings, trees, etc., might well be owned by different persons in Islamic law. It seems, then, that here the claim to have bought the land was held to vitiate what might have been regarded as a valid title by settlement and cultivation (*iḥyā' al-mawāt*).

In questions of contract in general it has been held that a stipulation to pay interest is not itself enforceable between Muslims (except, of course, in a contract concluded under some Ordinance, applied Act, etc.), but that no such stipulation should be read into a document by which a person who has received a certain sum undertakes to repay a larger sum at a future date.[1] This, of course, represents the judicial enforcement of the common device to evade the Islamic law of usury by which the borrower acknowledges the debt of a sum which really, but not expressly, includes both capital and interest. But in a later case[2] it was held that in a mortgage in which the mortgagors covenanted that if they had not repaid the sum borrowed by a specified date they would pay the mortgagee Rs. 50 per month as *nadhr*[3] until they did repay it, this covenant was void; on the grounds that the *nadhr* was made a condition of the loan, which was therefore usurious. This case too, of course, represents a common device to surmount the rules of usury, and might have been enforceable in Muhammadan law if the parties had not made their mortgage in English form and expressed the part dealing with the *nadhr* as a covenant, a point which led the learned judge to regard the latter as a condition of, and consideration for, the whole transaction. Finally, in a case of quasi-contract,[4] where an executor paid a creditor of the deceased out of funds belonging to the latter's widow, and the widow recovered against the executor, it was held that the latter might recover against the creditor—the then " Sheikh al-Islam " quoting the *Minhāj* in support of the proposition that a man who has received something from one who had obtained it wrongfully was responsible therefor, regardless of whether or not he knew the circumstances. In any case, it is clear that the Muslim subordinate courts in the coast region still regularly decide such petty cases of contract as come within their competence under the title of " debts ", and that the Qāḍīs at least do this under the Sharī'a.

In regard to tort, a case is reported where one of two neighbours opened windows in the wall of his house and the other, six months later, heightened his own walls and thereby blocked these windows.[5] Here it was held that the first party had no means of redress, the commentary of Ibrāhīm al-Bājūrī on Ibn Qāsim[6] being quoted to the effect that " it is lawful to open . . windows on one's own property for the purpose of light, even if by so doing one can see one's neighbour's family . . . In this case the neighbour must erect a wall opposite the windows. . . . Everyone may deal with his own property in any way that does not damage his neighbour's property, although it may harm him by opening such windows: but not so as to cause (actual) damage, such as to dig a pit. . . . " In another case,[7] where a trespasser on another's land had erected boundary pillars and the landowner broke them, the latter was held liable to make good the difference in value between that of their original and of their broken condition, while the trespasser must remove them. And once more it may be noted that the Qāḍīs in the coast region would decide such cases of tort as come within their competence—again under the general title of " debts "—under the Sharī'a.

[1] *Abdulrahim* v. *Hatiji* (1905), I E.A.L.R. 86.

[2] *Sheriff Abdulla* v. *Bwana Nasibu and Mzee* (1910), 3 E.A.L.R. 90.

[3] Spelt " Nathiri ", but see Introduction: the word means " vow ".

[4] *Abdulla bin Athman* v. *Abdulla bin Masood* (1910), 3 E.A.L.R. 76.

[5] *Athman b. Mahd* v. *Ahamed b. Ali* (1911), 4 E.A.L.R. 30.

[6] Vol. 1, p. 408, apparently.

[7] *Sheriff Jaffer and Co.* v. *Bwana Mzee* (1912), 4 E.A.L.R. 94.

Another and smaller group of cases concern what we may term the application of principles of equity in matters of Sharī'a law. Thus in an early case[1] it was held that the question whether a waqf had been created to defraud creditors must be deduced from all the circumstances; that a waqf made with this purpose is invalid against the creditors if no other assets are available; and (*obiter*) that the High Court[2] as a Court of Equity was not precluded from modifying the strict rules of Muhammadan law where their application would be inequitable. In this connection the Native Courts Regulations of 1897 were quoted to the effect that it was only the *general principles of the law of Islam* . . . which the High Court, as the highest Court of Appeal in civil and criminal matters from the "Native Courts", was to apply. The pure Shāfi'ī law on this point, of course, holds the waqf valid, whatever its motive, unless the debtor had been put under interdiction for bankruptcy before he made his waqf[3]: but the Mālikīs, together with the Ḥanbalī reformer Ibn al-Qayyim, deny this.

With regard to gifts—a matter concerning which Islamic law is still clearly applicable in the coastal region[4]—the only points of particular interest concern what is termed, in the law reports, *nathira, nathra* or *nathiri*—i.e., the use of the *nadhr* or vow. Unlike both *hiba* and *ṣadaqa*, a *nadhr* is valid and enforceable without delivery.[5] There is, however, a difference of opinion within the Shāfi'ī school regarding the validity of a *nadhr* by a parent to one child to the exclusion, in whole or in part, of his other children,[6] for while Ibn Ḥajar holds it valid, al-Ramlī (and even Ibn Ḥajar's pupil Zayn al-Dīn al-Malībārī)[7] holds it invalid—and the latter view has been upheld by the Kenya courts, in spite of the predominant position usually given to Ibn Ḥajar among "Southern" Shāfi'īs.[8] Similarly, in a more recent case,[9] the Chief Qāḍī stated that gifts to children during their parents' lifetime need not be identical, but that a *nadhr* which gives all the property to one or more children to the exclusion of the others must, in the absence of special circumstances, be held sinful; and that a sinful *nadhr* could be revoked by its author or upset by the courts. It is also noteworthy that a *nadhr* may be both conditional and future, may concern the use rather than the *corpus* of property, and is in each of these cases equally enforceable: this is illustrated by a case in which a *nadhr* to the effect that a woman might have the use of a room for the rest of her life was upheld.[10] The use of a *nadhr* as a means of enforcing the payment of interest has been noted above.[11]

Turning to matrimonial causes, a case has been decided[12] in which a Christian man gave notice of his intention to marry under the Marriage Ordinance a Muslim girl of fifteen whose father was dead and whose mother had given her consent in writing. Her uncle thereupon entered a caveat and pleaded that Muhammadan law utterly forbade such a union; but it was held that Muhammadan law did not apply to a marriage under the Ordinance and (*obiter*) that

[1] *Talibu b. Mwijaka* v. *Executors of Siwa Haji* (1907), 2 E.A.L.R. 33.

[2] Now Supreme Court.

[3] cp. the Zanzibar case (H.C. case No. 18 of 1938—unreported) where it was held that in Shāfi'ī law a waqf is valid if created with all due requirements before a declaration of bankruptcy, and that it cannot be set aside in such circumstances on the ground that it was intended to defeat or delay payment of a debt.

[4] Or, possibly, among Muslims everywhere, cp. pp. 83 f.

[5] *Mohd b. Abdulla* v. *Mwana Mkuu binti Hussein* (1903), 1 E.A.L.R. 55. For these technical terms, see Glossary.

[6] See *Joha binti Rashid* v. *Mwana Iki binti Salim* (1911), 4 E.A.L.R. 27.

[7] Author of the *Fatḥ al-Mu'īn* (p. 68). Contrast *al-Tuḥfa*, x, p. 79.

[8] See above, in the Aden section of this Survey (p. 22 note (3)).

[9] *Mwana Arafah binti Jambeni and Others, etc.* (1930), 14 K.L.R. 69.

[10] *Fatuma binti Mzee v. Ali Hirji* (1921), 9 K.L.R. 49.

[11] See p. 103. For the Shāfi'ī law, cp. *Fatḥ al-Mu'īn*, p. 69.

[12] Civil Case No. 408 of 1921 (unreported).

the girl, being a Ḥanafī and having reached puberty, could marry "whom she liked." The latter remark, of course, was clearly wrong, as the Ḥanafī law in such cases gives the agnatic guardian the right to forbid, or even claim the annulment of, a marriage between his ward and one who is her social inferior[1]—as a Christian spouse, in the Muslim view, is emphatically regarded: but the case was perfectly correctly decided on the first grounds. Where, however, a father did petition for the dissolution of his daughters' marriage[2] with a man of whom he did not approve, it was held that the Muhammadan Marriage, Divorce and Succession Ordinance only provided for the dissolution of a marriage at the instance of one of the parties thereto. This is a striking instance of relief being refused not because it was inapplicable in Muhammadan law but under the precise wording of the Ordinance concerned. Again, in an early case[3] where a decree of restitution of conjugal rights had already been granted to a husband and the wife had suffered six months' imprisonment for her recalcitrance, it was held that no fresh decree could be passed on the same facts (on the grounds of *res judicata*) and that the wife, as mother, was entitled to the custody of a young child which was decreed to be the legitimate child of her husband. Points which call for notice here are that the decision departs from Sharī'a law both because a decree of restitution of conjugal rights (*ṭā'a* or obedience) can thereunder be made as often as the facts warrant it, and also because a wife who unjustifiably refuses to live with her husband is disqualified from claiming the custody of his children—while it is also noteworthy that decrees of "obedience" are now no longer executed by the courts, whether by dragging the wife back to the matrimonial home (as under the pure Sharī'a) or by sentences of imprisonment on recalcitrant wives.

An interesting case of paternity concerned the child of a woman who had been a concubine slave and was then given in marriage to another, who went straight from her master to her husband without waiting the requisite period of *istibrā'*, and who gave birth to a child just eight months later.[4] Here the Qāḍī held that the child, having been born more than six months after the marriage, belonged to the husband, while the then Sheikh al-Islam laid it down that, if the woman was in fact pregnant at the time of her marriage and her husband knew this, then the marriage was void and the child must be attributed to the master; while, if she was in fact pregnant but the husband had no knowledge of this, the marriage was valid but the paternity of the child must be decided either on grounds of resemblance or by the child's own option when it reached the necessary age.[5] And this last point was echoed in another case[6] where it was held that, when a child was acknowledged by two different men neither of whom could prove paternity, it might choose which he or she preferred as a father.

---

[1] It is, however, noteworthy that in a Uganda case (*Fazalan Bibi* v. *Mahomed Din Kashmiri* (1921), 8 K.L.R. 200) the Court of Appeal for Eastern Africa supported the view that the Ḥanafī rule of "equality" in marriage was now obsolete in Uganda (or, apparently, any non-Muhammadan country), in the sense that where a major woman married herself, without her guardian's consent, to an inferior, the court would not annul the marriage.

[2] *Mirza Amir Beg* v. *Saadat Begum and Mohamed Bashir* (1946), 22 K.L.R. 12. But whereas it was decided in *Gulam Mohamed* v. *Hadayat Bibi*, 9 K.L.R. 76, that the Supreme Court was precluded by that Ordinance from entertaining a case regarding dowry, it was expressly stated in *Ex-Officio Agent* (*etc.*) v. *Shahasi binti Sheikh Terro* (1930), 12 K.L.R. 129, that "According to the Courts Ordinance, sect. 20, the Qāḍīs' courts are stated to have full jurisdiction over Muhammadan natives in all matters relating to personal status, marriage, inheritance and divorce . . . The decision in Gulam (etc.) is not intended to limit the jurisdiction of the Qāḍīs' courts on the question of dowry."

[3] *Sheriff Abdulla bin Mohamed* v. *Zuena binti Abedi* (1912), 4 E.A.L.R. 86.

[4] *Aisha binti Vali and Nyanya binti Hamis* v. *Fatuma binti Shaabek* (1902), 1 E.A.L.R. 44.

[5] Today, however, such a case would presumably be decided under the Evidence Act.

[6] *Abdureman bin Khamis and Aisha binti Safi* v. *Khamis bin Malim* (1918), 7 E.A.L.R. 110.

Finally, in regard to guardianship, a distinction must be made between the guardianship of property and the guardianship or custody of a minor's person. In the former, it seems, Islamic rules will normally be applied, as where it was held that a mother might sue, in Shāfi'ī law, for debts due to her minor child whose father and grandfather were dead, but that she had no right to use or dispose of the property so recovered,[1] since she was not the proper guardian of his property. It has, however, been held that the court may make the Administrator-General trustee of an infant's property instead of the grandfather, who intended to trade with it, in spite of the normal rules of Muhammadan law—on the grounds that the court has a discretion in such cases to act in accordance with the best interests of the minor.[2] But in cases regarding the custody of minors it is clear that, while it was previously held that Muhammadan law would apply in regard to Muhammadans[3], the British courts in Kenya will now apply English and not Muhammadan law in all cases.[4] Recent decisions on this subject have largely followed the ruling of the Court of Appeal for Eastern Africa in an unreported case[5] that "questions of guardianship are part of the common law of England and have always been determined by the English Courts and accordingly form part of the jurisdiction of the Court here. In our opinion the right to determine this question in accordance with the principles of the common law of England has not been ousted by the Ordinance referred to" (i.e., the Muhammadan Marriage, Divorce and Succession Ordinance). And this decision was supported in a comparatively recent case—with the proviso that due regard should be had to the customs of the race and community concerned in deciding what would, in all the circumstances, be in the best interests of the minor, for the common law right of the parent could only be ousted by considerations of the welfare of the child.[6] It must, however, be observed that the logic on which these decisions rest seems distinctly questionable, since the true point at issue does not appear to be whether the Muhammadan Marriage, Divorce and Succession Ordinance has ousted the principles of the common law of England but whether any specific enactment has ousted the duty of the courts, "in dealing with Muhammadans"—and especially "in the Muhammadan coast region"—to follow the "general principles of the Law of Islam",[7] except, of course, in a case where the welfare of the child exonerates them from following the letter of the law on equitable principles,[8] or where the Islamic law might be held contrary to justice, humanity and good conscience. In any case it is clear that Qāḍīs still regularly decide such cases under the Sharī'a, although they are liable to be overruled on appeal.

It may be added that in 1926 a special Ordinance regarding the custody of children was promulgated[9] in Kenya, which laid down, *inter alia*, that "where a parent has (*a*) abandoned or deserted his child; or (*b*) allowed his child to be brought up by another person at that person's expense for such a length of time and under such circumstances as to satisfy the court that the parent was unmindful of his parental duties . . . the court shall not make an order for the delivery of the child to the parent unless . . . satisfied . . . that, having regard to the welfare of the child, he is a fit person to have the custody."[10] This

[1] *Fundi b. Hamadi Saburi* v. *Mpunga binti Abubakar Mzee* (1941), 20 K.L.R. Pt. 1, 44.

[2] *Adamji Abdulali* v. *Admin-General and Sherifali Mohamedali* (1918), 7 E.A.L.R. 206.

[3] *Mbaruk bin Diwansap* v. *Hamsini bin Jumbe Kimemeta* (1927), 11 K.L.R. 56.

[4] e.g., *Hamisi bin Ali* v. *Mariamu binti Ali* (1929), 12 K.L.R. 51, and *Nana binti Mzee* v. *Mohamed Hassan* (1932), 20 K.L.R. Pt. 1, 3.

[5] *Shariff Abdulla* v. *Zwena binti Abedi*, quoted in *Mohamed Hassan* v. *Nana binti Mzee* (1943), 11 E.A.C.A. 4.

[6] *Mohamed Hassan* v. *Nana binti Mzee* (1943), 11 E.A.C.A. 4.

[7] cp. pp. 83 f. above.

[8] cp. p. 104 above.

[9] Custody of Children Ordinance, 1926.

[10] Sect. 5.

Ordinance was "omitted" in 1948, presumably on the grounds that its terms were sufficiently inherent in the English law now held to be alone applicable in such cases. But it has, in any case, the same force and validity as if it had not been omitted.[1]

It is important to notice in this context, again, that while many of the cases in the earlier Law Reports shown a clear appreciation on the part of the courts concerned of the difference between the law applicable in the Muhammadan coast region or the dominions of the Sultan of Zanzibar on the one hand and the rest of Kenya on the other—i.e., between the Protectorate and Colony—this distinction seems to have become blurred or even partially forgotten in more recent years.[2] This may be due partly to the increasing intrusion of legislation and partly to the virtual identification of the Protectorate with the Colony: but it remains a point which seems to demand authoritative and up-to-date elucidation.

The Muslim subordinate courts actually established in the coastal Protectorate include those of the "Liwali of the Coast",[3] the Assistant Liwali[4] of Mombasa, and the Liwalis of Vanga, Malindi and Lamu; those of the Qāḍīs of Mombasa, Malindi, Lamu, Takaunga, etc.; and those of various Mudīrs. On paper all Liwalis' courts and those Qāḍīs' courts established in the coast districts have the same powers in all criminal matters with respect to Arabs, Baluchis and Africans (including Somalis, Malagasies and Comoro Islanders) only, as a subordinate court of the second class, and Mudīrs' courts those of a subordinate court of the third class[5]; while their civil jurisdiction is as set forth at p. 89 above. In practice, however, it seems that Qāḍīs' courts exercise criminal jurisdiction only in places where no Liwali's court has been established: and that where Liwalis' and Qāḍīs' courts exist side by side the jurisdiction of the latter is chiefly confined to matters of personal status under Islamic law.[6] Elsewhere, however, the Qāḍīs apparently exercise such criminal jurisdiction as falls within their competence, nominally at least under the Penal Code and other appropriate enactments, although they are in fact little qualified to do so. Outside the "Coast districts" there are no Liwalis' or Mudīrs' courts, but Qāḍīs' courts have been established both at Isiolo in the Northern Province and at Mumias trading centre in Nyanza Province, with jurisdiction expressly limited to "matters of personal status, marriage, inheritance and divorce."[7] This jurisdiction is generally regarded, it seems, as limited to the application of the terms of the Muhammadan Marriage, Divorce and Succession Ordinance,[8] although it is not at all clear why they should not also hear any matters of personal status (such as those concerning the custody and guardianship of children) which fall outside the terms of that Ordinance under the relevant principles of Islamic law.[9]

---

[1] See Revised Edition of the Laws Ordinance, 1948, sect. 5(1).

[2] cp. p. 84 above.

[3] Who, in addition to his ordinary powers as a Liwali, is "empowered to exercise jurisdiction . . . in all districts in which Liwalis exercise jurisdiction by virtue of this Ordinance" and also has "power to inspect all books, records and proceedings of all courts presided over by Liwalis, Qāḍīs and Mudīrs and . . . render reports to the Supreme Court relative to such inspection" (Courts Ordinance, sect. 6(1)).

[4] Now "Acting" Liwali.

[5] With respect to the same categories of persons only. See Criminal Procedure Code, 1930, sect. 10. An appeal lies to the Supreme Court in suitable circumstances.

[6] The Courts Ordinance, sect. 6(2) provides that "where there is more than one subordinate court in the same district the Supreme Court may direct the distribution of business between such courts."

[7] See Courts Ordinance, sect. 17.

[8] This Ordinance also, of course, binds the Qāḍīs in the coast districts in so far as a case falls within its terms; but there Islamic law is also clearly applicable on somewhat broader terms (see above).

[9] Except, of course, for the attitude of the Supreme Court regarding custody and guardianship. See p. 106.

It may be added that the Liwalis and Mudīrs of the Protectorate almost all know English; that the Mudīrs in particular used to be recruited from local notables but are now in some cases trained for their duties from an early age; and that the predecessors of the "Chief Qāḍī"[1] at Mombasa used to have the title "Sheikh al-Islam" (as, indeed, the present holder of the office is still regarded by the Liwalis in Tanganyika). It should, moreover, be noted that both Liwalis and Mudīrs and also those native tribunals which have been established both inside and outside the Protectorate may all on occasion apply the provisions of Islamic law, the former as the basic law in the Protectorate in the absence of any specific enactment or well established custom, and the latter as "native law" when the latter has in fact been assimilated thereto.

From conversations with several Liwalis, Qāḍīs, Mudīrs, members of Native Tribunals, Chiefs, Registrars of Marriages, etc.—and, of course with Administrative Officers—from Mombasa, Malindi, Kwali, Takaunga, Kalifi and Lamu, the following facts also emerged.

In the coastal towns the proportion of Muslims is comparatively high, but is mostly composed of Arabs, Swahilis, Somalis, Baluchis, Indians, etc. The only African tribe in the vicinity of Mombasa which has accepted Islam on any scale is the Digo, although a few of the Duruma and Giriama have also become Muslims. Further north, in the River Province, Islam is, perhaps, making slightly more progress;[2] while the great majority of the population of the Northern Province is Muslim. For the rest, Islam in Kenya is largely limited to Muslim communities in the towns and in the district around Mumias trading centre in Nyanza Province.

In the coastal towns Muslims normally go to the Qāḍī to make their marriage contracts, and "tribal marriages" contrary to Islamic law are not common. Where they do occur the issue are apparently regarded as illegitimate, unless formally acknowledged. Not infrequently, however, Africans marry by tribal custom first and then resort to the Qāḍī for the Islamic contract later. Muslims also usually go to the Qāḍī in questions of divorce; while in matters of guardianship and custody,[3] testate and intestate succession, gifts, vows, etc., the Qāḍīs endeavour to apply the ordinary Shāfiʿī principles. Cases concerning real property are today almost all covered by Ordinances, as are also most cases of contract of any sort (except, e.g., gifts). Some actions in tort, however, still go by Sharīʿa law: but complaints of adultery go to the native tribunals, where injured husbands may either sue the "co-respondent" for compensation (*malu*)[4] or may now bring a criminal prosecution against him,[5] while there is no penalty for the wife—and Muslim Africans, as well as pagans, may (and do) avail themselves of customary law in this respect. Actions may also be brought in native tribunals by both pagans and Muslims for return of bride-price, where, e.g., a wife runs away from her husband.

Additional points which deserve mention are that the marriage of girls who have not reached puberty appears to be rare, as does also the marriage of a girl by her father directly against her will: but such marriages would be upheld by the Qāḍīs if they occurred and would only be annulled on grounds of "inequality" or "hostility"[6] (and not hardship in general).[7] Several Qāḍīs, however, alleged that they would willingly annul the compulsory marriage

[1] Whose duty it is to sit as an assessor in the Supreme Court when an appeal from one of the Qāḍīs' courts is being heard. See above p. 90.

[2] Though not very much, according to the ex-Liwali of Lamu, who says that converts frequently revert when they return to tribal life.

[3] By contrast with the view now taken by the Supreme Court (see above p. 106).

[4] e.g., 60 shillings.

[5] e.g., 100 shillings' fine or 3 months' imprisonment.

[6] This last point was not known or understood by some.

[7] See discussion at p. 25 above.

of a young girl to a very old or blind husband if they could be shown a text which justified such action. The rules applied in regard to the marriage of a girl in the absence of her guardian are as in Somaliland,[1] but are less well understood; and a marriage is liable to be annulled if no one acted as the woman's guardian, even by a correct use of "*tawlīya*."[2] The Qāḍī of Mombasa mentioned that a formal acknowledgment of marriage by both parties would never avail where the guardian had not in fact consented,[3] and opined that a mistake concerning the law was only allowable in the case of a new convert. Stipulations in favour of a wife inserted in marriage contracts are always regarded as null and void; the principal of " equality " in marriage is apparently applied according to the texts by all Qāḍīs,[4] questions of religion, family, trade and character all being taken into account; and no dissolution of marriage is ever granted for cruelty, however extreme: but several Qāḍīs said they would be prepared to accept the " weaker " Shāfi'ī rule that the two arbitrators advocated by the Qur'ān in cases of matrimonial disputes should be regarded as empowered by the court rather than the parties (and therefore that their decision, if all else failed, that the marriage should be dissolved by *ṭalāq* or *khul'*[5] should be enforceable, whether or not the parties consented), if they could be shown good authority for so doing. Where a husband who is present can be proved to be indigent the wife can apparently obtain dissolution of marriage after seven days,[6] in Mombasa; where he is absent in, e.g., Lamu the demand will be recorded and letters, etc., will be written, and if there is no result within a period of about two months the marriage will be dissolved; while if he has disappeared and no one knows his whereabouts notices concerning him will be posted in the court, in a public place, and at his last known abode, and if these prove fruitless the marriage will be dissolved after thirty days.[7]

Divorce is extremely common. I was told that among African Muslims only one or two out of every ten marriages last until death, among Arabs some fifty per cent., while among Indians divorce is rare. Most divorces are for a money consideration, whether return of " dower " or some other sum; the dissolution of marriage by the *li'ān* procedure is very rare, and *īlā'*, *ẓihār* and *tafwīḍ* unknown; but suspended divorce (*ta'līq al-ṭalāq*)[8] is common, among Ḥaḍramīs especially.

For the rest, cases of *nadhr* not infrequently occur; and obligations so undertaken are enforceable as soon as they have been expressed, and may be conditional, future, etc.[9] The contract known as " *bay' al-khiyār* "[10] (a redeemable sale, used as a device to evade the Islamic rules of usury in regard to interest on a loan) is used by Ḥaḍramīs in particular, but the Qāḍī of Mombasa had never dealt with a case (although he remembered that his father, when Qāḍī, had upheld such, while the then Sheikh al-Islam had taken the contrary view).[11] There is no right of pre-emption (*shuf'a*) in Kenya. Inheritance among town Muslims goes by Sharī'a law—with no return to the spouse relict[12]; bequests are

---

[1] See pp. 51 f. above.
[2] See p. 52 note (3) above, and Glossary.
[3] But this is very doubtful.
[4] Contrast the attitude of the Court of Appeal: see p. 105 above.
[5] See pp. 29, 54, 74 above, and Glossary.
[6] Instead of the normal three.
[7] For the usual Shāfi'ī rules, see Appendix C.
[8] For all these terms, see above, pp. 21, 29, 54, 74, and Glossary.
[9] As noted above from the Law Reports: see pp. 103, 4.
[10] See p. 66 above, and Glossary.
[11] Such cases used almost always to go to the Supreme Court, not the Muslim subordinate courts, because of the monetary limit on their jurisdiction. But since the introduction of the Land Titles and Registration of Titles Ordinances such contracts cannot be registered and are therefore unenforceable before the courts. Previously, however, their validity was fully discussed in *Sheikh Burhan* v. *Khalfan bin Salim* (1929), 4 Z.L.R. 90.
[12] By contrast with the special provisions in Zanzibar and Tanganyika.

usually reduced to writing; the property of minors, and the administration of estates of deceased persons, are normally supervised by the Public Trustee[1]; only official documents are accepted in evidence without oral testimony; but periods of limitation are apparently observed. Regarding the fragmentation of estates which commonly results from the Islamic system of inheritance, it seems that division into entirely uneconomic holdings is normally avoided by the sale of the property concerned by mutual consent, or its appropriation by one heir against compensation to the others. As for the adoption of some opinion other than the " authoritative " Shāfi'ī rule, the Chief Qāḍī considered that any Qāḍī may follow a " weaker " Shāfi'ī view in case of need; while he agreed that such—or the view of any other Sunnī school—would become obligatory on the courts if, e.g., Judicial Circulars were issued specifying which view was to be followed in particular cases. He also, it may be observed, supported in all cases the legitimacy of the offspring of a marriage between two Muslims even if concluded in tribal rather than Islamic form, on the ground both that it was incumbent to " cover up " (*satr*) any such irregularities and that the " semblance " (*shubha*) of marriage would suffice.[2] Where, however, the woman was a pagan the children would be illegitimate unless formally acknowledged.

Among the Duruma and Giriama, as has been noted, very few have accepted Islam, and those few have become largely detribalised and have adopted Islamic law.[3] Such Giriama pay only a small bride-price,[4] which is not returnable on divorce unless by agreement; they conclude their marriage contracts before the Qāḍī (otherwise the union is regarded as illegal, and the children belong to the mother); and their inheritance goes by Islamic law, and not to the eldest brother, etc., according to tribal custom.[5] One Muslim Giriama whom I met told me that he had left his relatives, after his father's death, of his own volition; that he had married before the Qāḍī; and that, should he divorce his wife, he would try to recover the bride-price only if he considered the failure of the marriage to be her fault. Among pagans, the wives of a deceased Giriama are at the disposal of his eldest brother; but levirate marriage is not, apparently, practised among those who have become Muslims. Where a Muslim Giriama had died leaving a Muslim wife and a son of fourteen who denied being a Muslim, the Qāḍī had advised the latter to state that he was a Muslim so as not to forfeit his right, and had allowed him to inherit when he did so. I also interviewed a pagan Duruma who had contracted both a *ki-duruma* and *ki-ngombe* marriage; in the former, which is matrilineal, a mature girl chooses her own husband, subject to the veto of her father and uncle[6]; while in the latter, which is patrilineal, co-habitation starts as

---

[1] cp. The Public Trustee Ordinance, 1925, sect. 4(1) whereof reads: "When a person (other than an African living in a communal state in a tribe within the native lands or other area set apart for Africans who has no property purporting to belong to him as an individual) dies in the Colony, the district commissioner . . . shall report the death with full particulars as to the estate, as far as ascertainable, to the Public Trustee." Also sect. 16, etc.

[2] This view is of doubtful validity in Islamic law, although eminently beneficial: cp. Appendix C.

[3] In *Muluwa Gwanombi and Others representing the Jibana Tribe* v. *Abdulrasool Allidina Visram* (1914), 5 E.A.L.R. 141, it is stated that "members of the tribe converted to Islam (known as Mahaji), having assumed an individual status incompatible with the customary communal tribal life, and in order, no doubt, also to live with members of their own faith, always leave the tribal land and go to live nearer to the coast." (p.144.) My own enquiries confirmed this.

[4] The reason given for this was that marriage was so very unstable that it would not be reasonable to pay more.

[5] If there is no Muslim relative, it apparently goes to the one who " converted " the deceased.

[6] See Phillips' Report on Native Tribunals, para. 383.

soon as the payments are complete.[1] This, of course, applies to the vast majority of the tribe, which is predominantly pagan.

It is among the Digo[2] that the chief problem of the Protectorate arises. This tribe has accepted Islam, nominally at least, on a large scale, some eighty per cent. claiming to be Muslims. But the sincerity of their profession, judged in terms of their understanding of Islam and their observance of its tenets, varies enormously as between the truly islamicised element in the coastal towns and those living a tribal life further inland. Among the "Swahili" Digo of the coast marriage contracts are, apparently, normally concluded before the Qāḍī according to Islamic law, although it is noteworthy that astrologers are usually consulted; that the bride's father insists on the payment to himself, nominally for "expenses", of what corresponds to the old bride-price, over and above the official dower; and that other payments, such as the "*haki*" or virgin-price, and the *ṣubḥīya* or gift on the morning after consummation, are also customary. Among the more tribal elements, however, the marriage seems originally to be concluded according to tribal custom, either with certain initial payments by the bridegroom's father to the bride's father for liquor, etc., with a regular "*hunda*" or bride-price, *haki* or virgin-price, etc.; or, more commonly still, by the bridegroom taking the girl and the couple starting to live together until found by her father[3], whereupon either *hunda* must be paid and the marriage recognised or a fine paid and the couple separated—and it is only subsequently, often at a considerably later date, that the marriage is regularised, in Muhammadan law, by a contract in the Islamic form, the original bride-price usually being named therein as dower. And even in the towns a few follow this custom; while some, Arabs included, never regularise their unions at all. Most Muslim marriages, on the other hand, are said to be registered.

It is interesting to note in this context that where a man marries a woman first by tribal custom and then by a contract performed by the Qāḍī and the woman later runs away with another man (as is, apparently, far from rare), the father must, in Digo customary law, repay the former husband the original bride-price, while the Qāḍī, it seems, will regularise the second marriage on condition (nominally at least) that the former is first dissolved. The first husband, in such cases, can first demand restitution of conjugal rights and then, if his wife refuses to return to him, the return of *hunda*; while the Qāḍī on his part will virtually force return of *hunda* as consideration for *khulʿ*.[4] Matrimonial disputes are often referred to the local registrar of marriages; while he, if the case proves beyond him, writes a letter to the nearest Qāḍī. Similarly, the President of the Kwale Native Tribunal said that he usually asked spouses who brought their disputes to his tribunal if their marriage was Muhammadan and, if so, referred the matter either to the registrar who had concluded the contract or direct to the Qāḍī. It seems, moreover, that if a Digo marries in the Muslim form before the Qāḍī he will normally divorce in the same way. But the local custom is for such divorce to be pronounced before two witnesses, while—an interesting point —a divorce pronounced in drunkenness is apparently not regarded as binding.[5]

In matters of inheritance, it seems, the Digo fall into three divisions. Their original tribal structure was matrilineal, and the *mjomba* (uncle or nephew)

[1] In theory. But in practice it probably starts as soon as the arrangement is complete and the preliminary payments are made, for these payments may continue for a number of years before they are complete.

[2] These are said not to be an autocthonous tribe, but to have been brought to Mombasa by the Portuguese as slave labour. This may account for their more widespread acceptance of Islam.

[3] Although this elopement is today more a matter of form, it seems, than of real secrecy.

[4] This illustrates how Islamic law may be made to reinforce custom.

[5] This—in the case of "culpable" drunkenness—is, of course, contrary to normal Shāfiʿī law.

was the normal heir.[1] This still prevails among the pagan elements, among Muslims inland from the coast, and among, it seems, large numbers of all Digo outside the towns. In some places, however, Muhammadan law has had enough influence to make the sons, rather than the *mjomba,* the primary heirs; while in the case of Digo who are detribalised Muslims the Sharī'a law of inheritance is applied in full. Viewed from a different angle, it may be said that where questions of inheritance are taken to the Qāḍīs Sharī'a law is applied; that where they are taken to the Digo native tribunals the matrilineal system is still normally followed; but that the feeling that sons should inherit—i.e., that the patrilineal system should be adopted—is spreading near the coast and the eldest son sometimes at least contrives to oust the *mjomba* and divide the inheritance with his brothers, or even brothers and sisters. Bequests are extremely rare, except in the towns: but any bequests which are recognised at all go by Sharī'a law.

It is, however, in regard to the question of inheritance among some of the Digo that the conflict between Islamic and customary law in Kenya has come into greatest prominence. Thus in Mr. Arthur Phillip's valuable Report on Native Tribunals, section 379, it is stated: " One of the most difficult problems connected with the administration of this (Digo) district arises from the conflict between native law and custom on the one hand and Muhammadan Law on the other. . . . It is in connection with inheritance that the consequences of the conflict of laws are most serious."

This problem came before the Court of Appeal for Eastern Africa in the case of *Ali Ganyuma* v. *Ali Mohamed* (11 K.L.R. 30), where it was decided that section 4 of the Muhammadan Marriage, Divorce and Succession Ordinance, 1920, must be applied, and that Muhammadan law must, therefore, prevail. It was also held that the proviso to that section—that, should the deceased have belonged to " any sect of Muhammadans " among whom the law of succession differs from the ordinary principles of Islamic law, the law of the sect should be applied—could not be extended to cover a tribal group. And this decision was commonly accepted as establishing the fact that Muhammadan law must invariably prevail in any conflict with native law and custom regarding the disposition of the estate of a deceased African who had at any time professed Islam, in however shallow or ignorant a fashion. An extreme example of such conflict is provided by a pagan tribesman (whose whole immediate family is pagan) who in his old age visits a distant cousin resident in Mombasa who is a Muslim, and who persuades him to make a profession of Islam before his death. Here the native tribunal of his locality would unquestionably award his property according to tribal custom either to his children or his maternal uncle, etc.; while a Muslim subordinate court would equally certainly award his whole estate to the distant cousin, who could rightly claim to be the deceased's sole Muslim relative and that every other claimant was excluded in Islamic law by the principle that there can be no inheritance between those who differ in religion. It seems to be generally believed, moreover, that if this conflict were referred to a British court the Muhammadan view would always be upheld. It was in this belief that the District Commissioner, Kwale (Mr. Marchant) stated in his Annual Report for 1928 "The elders still continue to find in accordance with tribal custom, but on appeal their decisions have to be revised in accordance with the ruling of the Court of Appeal for Eastern Africa, which held that Muhammadan law prevails to the exclusion of tribal law in cases where the deceased was a Muhammadan." Fourteen years later the then District Commissioner (Mr. A. C. M. Mullins) could still write "This question probably causes more discontent than any other in the Digo District. There is a mass of correspondence and cases which have been referred to the Supreme Court. I cannot do better than quote Minute No. 119/40 of the Digo Local Native Council

[1] But the sons of the deceased might come to him for bride-price, etc.

which is as follows:— 'According to Muhammadan Law no pagan could inherit from a Muhammadan. There had been cases of pagans on their death beds being bullied into accepting Islam. When they died their nearest Muhammadan relatives—usually undesirables from Mombasa whom they had not seen for years—arrived and claimed all their property. According to law these persons were entitled to the property. It was iniquitous. Were they to get it pagan wives and children would be left absolutely destitute. So far the property had been kept out of the way of the Muhammadan relative and he had returned to Mombasa empty-handed. Sooner or later one of these persons would claim in the courts and be awarded the property unless the law was changed. It was a very bad state of affairs when all the leading people of the district had to conspire to prevent what everybody knew to be unjust but what was upheld by the law. Could immediate steps be taken to alter this most unsatisfactory state of affairs?' "[1]

Nor must it be thought that the Digo alone are involved. The Digo are indeed unique among the coastal tribes of Kenya in that they have accepted Islam on a large scale while still in part retaining their customary system of inheritance. But the District Commissioner, Tana River District, wrote in 1942: "Hitherto it has been the Pokomo practice for native inheritance to follow tribal law, but I anticipate trouble in the near future owing to the activities of the young Muslim element, who wish to insist on a strict application of Muhammadan law. This would be strenuously opposed by the tribal elders, many of whom are Muslims."[2] Similar problems apparently occur from time to time even in the Northern Frontier District; while instances have also been reported from Nyanza (see below).

It must, of course, be observed that the administrative officers and the local native council quoted above took an exaggerated view of what the law actually was—although not, indeed, of the law which would in fact have been applied by any Muhammadan subordinate court. A reference to section 4 of the Muhammadan Marriage, Divorce and Succession Ordinance reveals that its terms do not by any means provide that "Muhammadan law prevails to the exclusion of tribal law in cases where the deceased was a Muhammadan." In reality, the relative passage lays down that "Where any person contracts a marriage . . . in accordance with Muhammadan law . . . and such person dies after the commencement of this Ordinance, and where the issue of any such marriage . . . dies after the commencement of this Ordinance the law of succession applicable to the property both movable and immovable of any such person shall be in accordance with the principles of Muhammadan law, any provision of any Ordinance or rule of law to the contrary notwithstanding. . . ."[3] In other words, those principles shall only be applied where the deceased not only made some profession of Islam but was either the child of a regular Muslim marriage or else had himself or herself contracted such a marriage. And while it is not, perhaps, altogether apparent why those who drafted the Ordinance hit on these particular terms, presumably the conclusion of a valid Muhammadan marriage was considered the simplest test of whether one professing conversion to Islam really intended to live according to the tenets of that religion. Only if he did—or if he were the child of parents who had done so—was it thought right that the law of Islam should be applied to his estate at death.

No reference to this question of marriage was, however, made by the Court of Appeal for Eastern Africa in the case of *Ali Ganyuma* v. *Ali Mohamed,* except that section 4 of the Ordinance was quoted in full. Presumably the court was satisfied that the case came properly within the terms of the section; but it seems unfortunate that the point was not mentioned, since it has certainly escaped the notice of many of those who have commented on the decision and its applicability. If the terms of this section were in fact consistently applied some

[1] cp. Phillips' Report, sect. 381.
[2] Ibid, sect. 397.
[3] See p. 86 above.

of the more extreme cases of conflict of law could never arise, since a death-bed conversion to Islam would have no effect on the inheritance of the convert unless either his parents had been practising converts or he himself followed his death-bed conversion with a death-bed contract of valid Muhammadan marriage (having previously dissolved any previous customary marriage: see section 6 of the Ordinance)—both of which contingencies seem sufficiently remote.

But not only have these rules about marriage been absent from the minds of administrative officers and local native councils, but they represent a closed book to Qāḍīs (and even, it would seem, to other Muslim subordinate courts). No Qāḍīs whom I questioned had so much as heard of them, while none of them would be willing to apply these restrictions even if they knew and understood them, for they unquestionably run counter to the pure Sharī'a (under which anyone who makes profession of Islam is normally regarded as a Muslim and subject in all respects to Islamic law). While, therefore, the Ordinance in fact includes safeguards against the more extreme cases of injustice noted above, these safeguards are not known, understood or accepted by the courts which are primarily concerned. Admittedly any judgment of a Qāḍī's court contrary to the terms of the Ordinance concerning this question of marriage is liable to be reversed on appeal: but it seems most improbable that the parties concerned would appreciate this point, or that anyone would necessarily notice the error from a mere perusal of the record of the case.

It may be asked, then, how this problem can best be solved. Some four possibilities seem to present themselves.

(*a*) That, in the terms of the Phillips' Report, " native inheritance should follow tribal not religious law ", as recommended in 1942 by the local native council delegates of the Central Province (see section 936). This proposal receives the support of Mr. Phillips himself in section 938, where he argues that " there should be a clear delimitation of frontiers between the civil and religious spheres. . . . The title to property should not, in my opinion, be liable to be affected by purely religious distinctions. Now the rule of Muhammadan law that a pagan may not inherit from a Muhammadan is based entirely on a religious distinction, and its introduction into the legal system of a community of mixed religions seems to me to be indefensible. It is interesting to speculate what the reactions would be to a proposal that no pagan Kikuyu or Kavirondo native should be allowed to inherit property from a Christian! "

This argument has much force. The Islamic law was intended to be the dominant legal system in a State in which Islam was supreme, and there the rule that there could be no inheritance between those who differ in religion would work both ways (i.e., would exclude Muslims from succeeding to non-Muslims as well as vice versa). In Kenya, on the other hand, it is entirely one-sided, for the principle of exclusion is applied only where the deceased was a Muslim. The suggestion as it stands, however, goes far beyond the mere question of exclusion: for the Islamic law of inheritance lays down (*inter alia*) precisely what share in a deceased's estate shall go to his or her sons and daughters, father and mother, and spouse relict—or, in suitable circumstances, to grandchildren, grandparents, collaterals, etc. These rules, moreover, are regarded by Muslims as peculiarly sacred, since the great majority of them are governed by the express text of the Qur'ān, while the study of the laws of inheritance is considered equal to half the whole range of human knowledge. To decree categorically that " native inheritance should follow tribal not religious laws " would thus be regarded by the pious Muslim as nothing less than an attack on his religion, and as depriving him of a God-given right and privilege.

(*b*) Less drastic than this would be the introduction of an enactment to the effect that difference of religion should be no bar to inheritance in Kenya. This would leave untouched the detailed provisions prescribed in the Qur'ān for the division of a Muslim's estate between his heirs, and, indeed, the whole structure of the Islamic law of inheritance, except for one single particular—that none of those prescribed heirs would be debarred from his rights merely by reason of his not being a Muslim. In defence of such an enactment it could be pointed out that in a State where Islamic law was accorded general application the Muslim rule of exclusion would work both ways and reciprocity, and thus substantial justice, be ensured; that as things now stand in a country such as Kenya the reverse is true; and that the innovation was designed merely to restore such reciprocity and justice. Even so, it would no doubt arouse opposition—although on a long view it would probably provide the most equitable and satisfactory solution. A partial precedent for such a rule can be found in the Indian Caste Disabilities Removal Act, 1850, and also in section 18 (4) (b) of the Tanganyika Administration (Small Estates) (Amendment) Ordinance, 1947, and in section 6 (1) (a) of the Nyasaland Asiatics (Marriage, Divorce and Succession) Ordinance, all of which provide that no one shall be deprived of a right to succession to property solely by reason of his having renounced, or been excluded from, the communion of any religion: in other words, none shall be excluded from his rights of inheritance to a deceased Muslim solely by reason of his having renounced Islam and become either a Christian or pagan—a provision diametrically contrary to the Sharī'a, where an apostate is rigidly excluded from such rights. It seems, however, that no great opposition was aroused by these enactments. The measure under discussion is, of course, wider in its scope, since it extends to all who follow a different religion, whether by birth or conversion. But to allow an apostate to inherit must be even more abhorrent to Muslim sentiment than to extend that right to one who has never embraced Islam; so the precedents at least cover the most controversial point. But to these enactments Kenya has, as yet, no parallel.

(*c*) A less controversial although less comprehensive solution to the problem might be found in a redraft of section 4 of the Muhammadan Marriage, Divorce and Succession Ordinance.[1] In such a redraft the references to marriage might be omitted in toto and the section concerned might simply read "Where any person has made a profession of Islam, the law of succession . . ."; while the proviso at the end might be expanded by the addition of the words "or native tribe of which he was a member" after the words "any sect of Muhammadans", and "or tribe" after the words "applicable to such sect." This would have the effect of making the test of applicability of Islamic law no longer dependent on the question of marriage but rather on the mere profession of the deceased, except where his sect or tribe followed customary laws of their own, when these alone would be applicable. In such circumstances the native tribunals would have exclusive competence, and Qāḍīs would have to inform would-be suitors that they were unable to entertain such cases.

(*d*) It may be thought, however, that this solution, though simple, is somewhat too sweeping and makes no provision for individual liberty. However convinced a Muslim an African might be, his estate would only be divided according to Islamic principles if he had become completely detribalised—or if, of course, his whole tribe had become so islamicised that their customary law had embraced the Sharī'a. It might be well, therefore, to provide that where any such member of a tribe makes a formal application to an administrative officer to the effect that his estate should be divided on his death according to Islamic law, his estate should be removed from the competence of the native tribunal and lie within the exclusive competence of the Qāḍīs or the Supreme Court. Such a provision would safeguard personal liberty; would give the administrative officer the opportunity to call the applicant's attention to the needs of his family, if not Muslims; would prevent the abuses sometimes resulting from death-bed conversions; and would in all cases clarify the issue as to the competence of the different courts, for where a tribesman made no such application

[1] cp. p. 86 above.

the native tribunal would alone be competent, while where he had made such application only the Qāḍī's court (or Supreme Court), could entertain the case.[1]

Again, moreover, certain precedents exist. Thus the relevant clause in the Tanganyika Administration (Small Estates) (Amendment) Ordinance, 1947, reads: "The estate of a member of a native tribe shall be administered according to the law of that tribe unless the deceased at any time professed the Muhammadan religion and the court exercising jurisdiction over his estate is satisfied from the written or oral declarations of the deceased or his acts or manners of life that the deceased intended his estate to be administered, either wholly or in part, according to Muhammadan law, in which case the estate shall be administered, either wholly or in part as the case may be, according to that law."[2] In Tanganyika, therefore, the purport of the existing legislation is that the intention of the individual concerned should be the governing factor, and that this intention must have been expressed by word or deed. Even so, however, the test proposed is rather vague and difficult of application; while the criterion now suggested—namely a formal application to an administrative officer—not only avoids this vagueness but would provide an opportunity for the relatives of the applicant to be called (where necessary) and his decision and its implications questioned, explained and publicised.

Another precedent for the suggestion may be found in the Sharī'a[3] Act passed by the Indian Legislature in 1937. This Act, the primary purpose of which was to substitute the Sharī'a for the customary law of certain sects of Muslims (e.g., the Ismā'īlī Khojas) includes one section which allows an Ismā'īlī Khoja to make a formal declaration that he desires to be bound by Sharī'a law in the matter of testamentary bequests. Where he makes such a declaration he and his minor children are bound thereby; while, where he does not, he still enjoys an unrestricted right of bequeathing his personal, as distinct from any joint-family, property to whomsoever he pleases.

It may well be, moreover, that this illustration is helpful in yet another particular, namely in the distinction between joint and personal property which pervades Hindu law. As things now stand in Kenya a similar distinction should, perhaps, explicitly be made between private property and tribal land. Thus the tribesman who declares his desire to have his estate governed by Islamic law should be expressly debarred from any attempt to include tribal land in the estate so divided: instead, this would continue to be dealt with on purely tribal principles.

The amended section 4 of the Ordinance might, therefore, read somewhat as follows: —

"Where any person professes the Muhammadan religion and such person dies, the law of succession applicable to his property, both movable and immovable, shall be in accordance with the principles of Muhammadan law, any provision of any Ordinance or rule of law to the contrary notwithstanding. Provided that where, in any sect of Muhammadans to which the deceased belonged or in any African tribe of which he was a member, other rules of succession are habitually followed, then the law of succession applicable to such sect or tribe shall alone apply. Provided always that if any such person shall make application in the appropriate form to an administrative officer that he desires that his estate on death should be divided according to the rules of any particular school of Islamic law, those rules alone shall apply to all his private property, whether movable or immovable, but not to any tribal land over which he has any right of usage."

It should be noted that the final proviso, as thus drafted, would allow not only

[1] With the alternative of settlement out of court by mutual agreement, in cases where the issue is particularly complex because of differences of religion.

[2] Sect. 18 (1) (*a*).

[3] Spelt "Shariat": but see Introduction regarding the spelling of Arabic words.

an African tribesman but also a member of a Muhammadan sect which followed special rules of inheritance to make a declaration that he wished the rules of some other school of Islamic law to be applied to his property after his death. This may or may not be thought advisable. The "sect" primarily concerned is, of course, the Ismā'īlī Khojas, whose intestate succession is now governed in India (unlike East Africa)[1] by the Shī'ī (Twelver) school of Islamic law, while their testate succession is also so governed only if they make a declaration of their wishes to that effect. Whether the community in East Africa would welcome, or acquiesce in, their members being granted a legal right to make a declaration under this Ordinance that they desired their estate to be divided according to some other school of Islamic law, is a point that could best be solved by reference to them; but it seems probable that their members would in practice follow their own "party line" whether or not the legal right to make such a declaration were available. Alternatively, of course, the last proviso might read "Provided also that if any such member of an African tribe . . ." and thus limit its applicability to Africans.

It may also be remarked in passing that the proviso to section 4 as now worded constitutes almost the only indication in the Ordinance that Muslims differ greatly among themselves as to their systems of "Muhammadan law" and that the courts would apply—at least in matters of inheritance—the system of the school or sect to which the party or parties belonged. If this is a fair interpretation, then the word "sect" would here not only include the obvious and extreme case of the Ismā'īlī Khojas but also the Ithnā 'Asharīs, the Bohoras, the Ibāḍīs and, indeed, the four recognised schools of Sunnī orthodoxy. It must be remarked, however, that the Ordinance might well be re-worded in this respect also, i.e., to make it clear that the principles of Muhammadan law to be applied in any original suit before a British court would be those principles as expounded by the school of the parties or, if they differed, of the suitable party. The only possible indication that this would in fact be done in matters of marriage and divorce is the phrase "principles of Muhammadan law applicable to the same respectively" in section 3 (3); but it seems extremely doubtful if this is the meaning the words were intended to convey.[2] In appeals from Qāḍīs' courts, on the other hand, the Supreme Court would presumably only be concerned to ascertain whether the Qāḍī had correctly applied his own school of law, while persons whose personal law differed from that of the Qāḍī would have the option of bringing their cases straight to the "ordinary courts."[3]

It may be asked, of course, how the Ordinance if so amended would work out in practice. Is there any reason to suppose, for instance, that the Qāḍīs would take any more notice of the law in its amended form than they do of the terms of the present Ordinance? To this the best reply seems to be that the principle now suggested is much more simple to explain, understand and apply than the existing provisions, and that, e.g., a Judicial Circular could be issued to Qāḍīs pointing out that questions concerning the estate of African tribesmen who had not made the proposed declaration were within the exclusive competence of the native tribunals, whether or not the deceased had made any profession of Islam; while questions concerning the estates of those who had made such a declaration were within the exclusive competence of their own courts or the Supreme Court. If, in spite of such a Circular, Qāḍīs were to exceed their jurisdiction, their judgments should, of course, be quashed.

It is interesting to observe that the present suggestion corresponds in principle (and indeed puts into concrete form) the view expressed by Chief Justice Hamilton as long ago as 24th June, 1916, in a Judicial Circular (now apparently largely forgotten) to officers holding subordinate courts and subordinate native courts. Sections 3 and 4 of that Circular read: "In the Muslim Coast area mere

[1] cp., *In re Kassum Premji* (1924), 1 T.T.L.R. 53, and *Fatmabhai d/o Jafler* v. *Mahomed Ladha* (1928), 1 T.T.L.R. 55.

[2] See pp. 86, 87 above.

[3] See p. 83 above.

professing Muslims who retain tribal customs are to be considered as subject to the jurisdiction of those Native Tribunals to which, apart from any question of religion, they would be subject under the Native Tribunal Rules. A native convert to Islam, or Haji, in the Muslim Coast area who has renounced native custom for the Sharī'a shall seek his remedies in matters of marriage, inheritance and divorce in the Qāḍīs' courts." I only discovered this Circular after my own opinion had been formed, but it served as an agreeable confirmation.

It may be added that it would, of course, be possible to combine this suggested amendment to section 4 of the Ordinance with an enactment that difference of religion should be no bar to inheritance. The latter alone would solve most problems but might still leave the door open for Qāḍīs' courts to upset tribal principles of inheritance (particularly matrilineal ones) in the case of professing Muslims, though not to the extent of excluding non-Muslims from their proper shares. The proposed amendment alone, on the other hand, would not prevent the exclusion of pagan children or spouses from rights of inheritance in the case of a Muslim prepared to go through with the suggested declaration in spite of any dissuasion by his relatives or even the administrative officer concerned, nor would it secure the result already attained in India, Tanganyika and Nyasaland of preventing a convert from Islam from exclusion from rights of inheritance.

It is, however, probable that an enactment that difference of religion should be no bar to inheritance would meet opposition in the Kenya Legislative Council. So to some extent, of course, might the proposed amendment to section 4. But here it could at least be argued: (1) that the proposed limitation of the scope of Muhammadan law was only being substituted for another and less satisfactory limitation (that of the Muhammadan marriage of the person concerned or of his parents); (2) that the proposed amendment could scarcely be regarded as other than consonant with natural justice in a country such as Kenya; (3) that some such clarification of a very confused issue was imperative. Most of these arguments, it is true, apply almost equally to the other suggestion, but two differences remain: (*a*) that the suggested amendment would leave the question of jurisdiction crystal clear (and would never require a Qāḍī to give judgment against his conscience), while the more radical suggestion, at least if accepted alone, would leave the question of jurisdiction somewhat confused and difficult; and (*b*) that the latter might be regarded as an attempt to change Muhammadan law, while the proposed amendment only represents a partial restriction of its scope. And to the Muslim mind it is far less heinous to restrict than to amend.

Where inheritance is matrilineal, the problem of legitimacy in regard to the issue of marriages which are not validly concluded according to Islamic principles does not, of course, arise. Where, however, a detribalised Muslim marries two wives, the one by Islamic law and the other by tribal custom, the case is more difficult. If the second wife was a pagan her children would not inherit unless formally acknowledged; and the same is probably true even where she was a Muslim. But the children of Muslim parents are apparently presumed to be Muslims, whatever their age; so exclusion by reason of "difference of religion" is rare in such cases. As for claims to inherit by right of patronage (i.e., as the descendant of the emancipator of the deceased, or of his father, etc.) or to inherit as the child of the deceased born in concubinage with a woman who would have been his slave but for the abolition of slavery, it seems probable that the former and certain that the latter would not be allowed in Kenya today, whatever the Qāḍīs themselves may consider right and proper.[1]

[1] See *Ahmed bin Abdulla* v. *Admin. of Native Estates* (1925), 10 K.L.R. 136. In this case the Qāḍī of Lamu upheld a claim by an ex-owner to inherit from his emancipated slave to the exclusion of the latter's own grandsons, on the grounds that the latter, only having been freed by the Slavery Ordinance, were still technically slaves. This decision, of course, has no direct bearing on the claim to inherit by patronage, from an admittedly free man, in default of other heirs: but it has a direct bearing on the concubinage problem.

The inhabitants of the island of Lamu are almost solidly Muslims, of very mixed nationalities, and Islamic law is there strictly applied in matters of personal status, etc. Muslims from the adjacent mainland, moreover, apparently come to the Qāḍī of Lamu to settle matters of marriage and divorce. But where a tribe is only slightly islamicised, tribal custom still normally prevails in matters of inheritance.

The inhabitants of the Northern Province are again mixed. About half are Somalis, chiefly of the Isāq and Dārōd tribal groups: and these are solidly Muslim, although their customs differ from the Sharīʿa in many respects. The Rendille, on the other hand, are almost all pagans. The Boran and Gabbra are Galla tribes, most of whom are really pagans, although one group has recently turned Muslim; while the Gurrah, who are a mixture of Galla and Somalis, are Muslims. The Adjuran are Somalis of the Hawiya tribal group, and all except two sections are Muslims. There are also certain riverine Bantus, into whose paganism Islam is slowly infiltrating.

There are only some two native tribunals in the whole of this Province, and even they have little work to do. Most disputes are settled by *ad hoc* arbitration "tribunals", which apparently apply an admixture of tribal and Islamic law,[1] as they see fit. There is only one official Qāḍī[2], at Isiolo, the headquarters of the Province; but there are registrars of marriages (who act as unofficial Qāḍīs) at Wajir, Moyale, Garissa, etc. There are also a few "holy men"—i.e., local leaders of dervish orders—who sometimes act in a semi-judicial capacity.

In general, tribal law undoubtedly prevails, but in a dispute between two tribes whose customary law differs, administrative officers sometimes, it seems, force them to accept Muhammadan law as arbiter, unless they agree to some other compromise.[3] In marriage a bride-price (*yarad*) is paid to the bride's father, and a dower (*mahr*) to the bride herself—but the latter is usually paid only on divorce or the death of one of the parties.[4] Cases of divorce within a tribe are normally arranged between the families concerned; while cases which concern two different tribes not infrequently lead to fighting. Often, however, such matters are referred to the arbitration of the registrars of marriages or "*haji*" traders, etc.: and in certain circumstances administrative officers will enforce such decisions in order to preserve the peace. Inheritance (which scarcely involves anything but stock) normally goes by tribal custom, and mostly to sons: while the occasional problems which arise are dealt with by arbitration and mutual arrangement.[5] Blood money is payable for homicide or injury at scales which vary among the tribes; and even murder is so commuted unless the Government is in a position to prosecute. Compensation is also payable for adultery, which the Somalis regard with gravity.

There is an interesting pocket of Muslims in Mumias trading centre in Nyanza Province. The inhabitants of the town are almost all Muslims (Arabs, Somalis, Nubis[6] and local converts); while there are a few Muslims also in the

---

[1] Which sometimes, of course, virtually coincide.

[2] See above, p. 84. He was gazetted under Government Notice No. 22 of 1946—presumably under the Courts Ordinance, although this is not mentioned. He has jurisdiction over Muslims, be they Arabs, Baluchis, Somalis, Comorians, Malagasies or Africans, in the Northern Frontier District, but only in matters of personal status, marriage, inheritance and divorce (see Courts Ordinance, sects. 6 and 17).

[3] This is particularly interesting, since there appears to be no juristic justification for this whatever except the virtually forgotten rule, emphasised in this Survey, that courts should, when "dealing with Muhammadans," be "guided by the general principles of the Law of Islam."

[4] For all such points, however, see the Somaliland section of this Survey (p. 46), since Somali customs do not differ greatly between the two territories.

[5] Even the Qāḍī is said to administer "a judicious mixture of law and custom."

[6] ex-ʿAskaris from the Sudan, the descendants of Emin Pasha's troops, etc.

surrounding country. And in addition to the usual native tribunal a Qāḍī[1] has been gazetted—the only Qāḍī in the Province or, indeed, in the whole Colony, except for Isiolo.

In matters of procedure this Qāḍī again, it seems, follows the Islamic rules in general, but not very strictly. Tribal marriages are not unknown; but the Qāḍī maintained that the issue of such unions would not be legitimate, even if both parties were Muslims, unless the customary marriage had preceded their conversion. He was vague about the grounds on which a marriage by compulsion could be set aside; but when adequately prompted he gave approximately the right answers. He also maintained that a marriage could be dissolved on account of certain diseases, failure of support or even continuous cruelty—but again he was somewhat vague about details, as also as to whether he, or the arbitrators advocated by the Qur'ān in cases of matrimonial discord, could ever insist on divorce or *khul'* in any other circumstances. But the native tribunal will always insist on the return of bride-price in suitable circumstances, and will also deal with questions of adultery. Matters of inheritance, it seems, here commonly go to the Chief or tribunal, not the Qāḍī: but if a Muslim were determined to dispute the decision he could presumably take his case to the Qāḍī and thence, if need be, to the Supreme Court, provided always that the circumstances were such as to make Islamic law applicable under the terms of the Muhammadan Marriage, Divorce and Succession Ordinance.

The members of the native tribunal of Mbale said that there were not many Muslims in their district. Such as there are follow Sharī'a law in matters of marriage, divorce and the custody of children, by reference to the Qāḍī of Mumias. Bride-price in cattle is paid under customary law to the girl's father and then "*mahari*" in shillings is payable to the bride, under the Sharī'a, but is in practice normally handed over to her father: and the cattle, unlike the *mahari,* can be demanded back in suitable circumstances (e.g., if the wife refuses to live with her husband). In questions of inheritance some Muslim families allegedly apply to the Qāḍī for a ruling, but if this is not accepted by the parties the native tribunal will apparently enforce customary law: and in the case of tribal land, etc., the latter would, of course, always prevail.

Similarly, in Kakamega (where I met the Muslim elders) Muslims represent a small minority, although they include a few of the leading personalities. African converts to Islam do not here become detribalised: so the ordinary bride-price in cattle is arranged according to tribal custom and then a *mahari* in cash paid nominally to the bride but really to her father. In marital disputes and questions of divorce the Muslim elders first arbitrate; but if this is not effective the case is sent to the Qāḍī of Mumias. In cases of inheritance there seems to be no uniformity of practice. I talked to a man who was the only Muslim among seventeen children of a Muslim father, and he told me he intended first to take his share under customary law and then present his claim to the whole estate to the Qāḍī and thence, if necessary, to the Supreme Court: but the native tribunal was much opposed to such procedure, and tribal land, at any rate, was in their exclusive competence. It seems, however, that customary law normally prevails in matters of inheritance and that Muslims in this locality have only very occasionally contrived to get more than their customary share. In cases of adultery, husbands can bring their complaint to the native tribunal—and "Arabs" too, but not Somalis, apparently avail themselves of this procedure.

In the town of Kisumu there are a number of Yemenīs (mostly Shāfi'īs, but including a few Zaydīs) and groups of Ismā'īlī Khojas, Bohoras, and Ḥanafī

[1] See above, p. 84. He was gazetted under Government Notice No. 1068 of 1947, under the Courts Ordinance. His jurisdiction extends to the whole of the Nyanza Province, " with full jurisdiction over all Muhammadan natives in all matters of personal status, marriage, inheritance and divorce—i.e., over Africans (including Swahilis) but not over Arabs, Baluchis, Somalis, Comorians or Malagasies.

Indians, in addition to certain African Shāfi'īs. There is a registrar of Muslim marriages acting under the supervision of the Qāḍī of Mumias, while the Imām of one of the Mosques, a Ḥaḍramī, has much influence as an arbitrator. Disputes about marriage, divorce, inheritance, etc., are settled in one of three ways: by the arbitration of the Community Councils, with or without the advice of the said Imām; by reference to the Qāḍī of Mumias, on the part of those who are subject to his jurisdiction; or by reference to the Supreme Court, on the part of those not so subject. It is noteworthy, moreover, that some of the Kisumu Indians expressed their regret that the Indian Dissolution of Muslim Marriages Act, 1939, had not been applied in Kenya, at least to Indians.[1]

In Nairobi, I interviewed the President of the Tribunal, who is also the registrar of marriages. He told me that Muslims in Nairobi normally conclude marriage contracts with the help of a local *mwalimu* to see that all is in proper form, and then register them with him. Litigation regarding dissolution of Muslim marriage, etc., goes to the Supreme Court[2]—as do all questions of Muhammadan law in places where there is no Muslim subordinate court; but questions of bride-price go to the native tribunals. Disputes regarding the custody of children, waqfs, inheritance and bequests all go to the Supreme Court, while the Public Trustee deals with estates, etc. Cases of adultery go to the Tribunal, where the co-respondent is fined some 200 shillings, or sentenced to three months' imprisonment in default, if he is well to do, or fifty shillings, or one month (apparently), if he is poor.

The points regarding Islamic law which chiefly seem to demand solution in Kenya are the rules of procedure applicable in Qāḍīs' courts and the conflict of law in certain questions of inheritance, both of which have been discussed in some detail above. But there are also a number of other points in which either uniformity or reform might well be introduced into the law now applied by the Kenya Qāḍīs. Such, it seems, could best be effected by means of some form of Judicial Instructions or Circulars issued, perhaps, by the Chief Qāḍī—as the leading Muslim authority—with the approval of the Chief Justice, and made binding by some legislative enactment. To this the procedure adopted in the Sudan would seem to provide the nearest and most appropriate parallel: but on this whole subject reference may be made to several sections of this Survey,[3] as it is applicable (*mutatis mutandis*) to a number of different territories.

[1] cp. reference to this point in the Aden section of this Survey, pp. 37 and 39, and see Appendix E.

[2] And conversion to Aḥmadī tenets is not, therefore, regarded as apostasy—by contrast with the view taken, e.g., by some Liwalis in Tanganyika.

[3] e.g. pp. 16-18, 22-23, 30, 32-33, 38-39, 55-56, 79-80, 146-147, 311 ff, 339 and 363.

TANGANYIKA

The Tanganyika Order in Council, 1920, makes substantially the same provisions for the administration of justice in that territory as does the Kenya Colony Order in Council, 1921, quoted above.[1] This means that "civil and criminal jurisdiction shall, so far as circumstances admit, be exercised in conformity with the Civil Procedure, Criminal Procedure and Penal Codes of India and the other Indian Acts and other laws which are in force in the territory at the date of the commencement of this Order or may hereafter be applied or enacted, and subject thereto and so far as the same shall not extend or apply shall be exercised in conformity with the substance of the common law, the doctrines of equity and the statutes of general application in force in England at the date of this Order . . . save in so far as (all these) may, at any time before the commencement of this Order, have been or may hereafter be modified, amended or replaced by other provision in lieu thereof by or under the authority of any Order of Her Majesty in Council, or by any Proclamation issued or by any Ordinance or Ordinances passed in and for the Territory: Provided always, that the said common law, doctrines of equity and statutes of general application shall be in force in the Territory so far only as the circumstances of the Territory and its inhabitants . . . permit, and subject to such qualifications as local circumstances may render necessary."[2] But "In all cases civil and criminal to which natives are parties every court shall (*a*) be guided by native law so far as it is applicable and is not repugnant to justice and morality or inconsistent with any Order in Council or Ordinance or any Regulation or Rule made under any Order in Council or Ordinance; and shall (*b*) decide all such cases according to substantial justice without undue regard to technicalities of procedure and without undue delay."[3]

It is clear, then, that these provisions, like those which we have examined in Kenya, make no direct reference whatever to Islamic law as such. Yet again, as in Kenya, that law is applied quite extensively in Tanganyika, particularly by the Liwalis who hold courts right along the coast and in certain inland centres. So the same question confronts us as to the juristic basis on which this application rests.

By contrast with the position in Kenya, of course, the Tanganyika Order in Council of 1920 was the first of its kind, so no prior "law, practice or procedure established by or under" some previous repealed Order in Council may here be held to have remained in force until some other provision is made. But it is evident that Muslim judges—whether Liwalis or Qāḍīs[4]—were applying Islamic law, to a greater or lesser extent according to locality, at least in those coastal districts (and inland centres such as Tabora and Ujiji) where Kitchener, as the British representative on an International Delimitation Committee, had found the Sultan of Zanzibar to be exercising sovereignty in 1886.[5] It was, of course, only over a much narrower area that the Germans—and eventually the full Committee—acknowledged his sovereignty to exist,[6] and his claims even over that were the subject of a permanent cession to the Germans in 1890.[7] But while it seems clear that the German Administration paid little regard, in general, to

---

[1] See p. 81.

[2] Art. 17(2).

[3] Art. 24.

[4] "At Tungi, Mikindani, Lindi, Kilwa, Kikunga and Kisiju there were Governors or *wālis*, all Omani Arabs. At Lindi and Kilwa there was also a Qāḍī . . ." (K. to R., 10, ii, 1886. K.P. xii, pt. iv, p. 102). See *Exploitation of East Africa*, by R. Coupland, p. 452. The quotation adopts the spelling "Cadi": but see Introduction for policy adopted in regard to Arabic words.

[5] (Report enclosed in H.K. to R., 30, vi, 86. K.P. xiii, pt. vi, p. 33). See *Exploitation of East Africa*, p. 467.

[6] See *The Map of Africa by Treaty* by E. Hertslet, I, p. 304 and iii, p. 882.

[7] Ibid, iii, p. 907.

native law and native institutions, it is certain that Muslim Liwalis continued to exercise jurisdiction in many localities, and it seems equally clear that they continued to apply Islamic law, at least in so far as the personal status of Muslims was concerned.

Precisely the same holds true, moreover, from the time of the British Occupation. Thus the Courts Ordinance, 1920,[1] expressly provided for "Courts of a Liwali, Qāḍī, Akida, Chief, Headman (etc.) . . . to be called Native Courts",[2] although—like the Kenya Ordinances of 1907 and 1931 noted above—it makes no reference whatever to the law which these various courts were to apply. An even earlier Ordinance, however, had given an unmistakable indication that this must include Islamic law, for the Muhammadan[3] Estates (Benevolent Payments) Ordinance, 1918, had provided that "In any case in which, according to the law of Islam, the whole or part of an estate is payable to the Public Treasury (*Bayt at-Māl*) a District Officer may, in his discretion, order that the whole or a part of the amount . . . not exceeding Shs. 1,000 be distributed, in such proportions as he may think fit, among the husband, wife or wives, or any other dependents of the deceased."[4]

It seems obvious, then, that the juristic basis for the very considerable application of Islamic law which is in fact found in Tanganyika must be sought, in so far, of course, as it is not covered by the terms of some specific Ordinance, either in the principle that the laws of a conquered or ceded country remain in force until they are altered,[5] or else under the comprehensive phrase "native law" and the relevant provisions in the Order in Council. In favour of the latter alternative may be urged the arguments discussed at length in the Introduction to this Survey, together with the fact that in the vicinity of those centres on the coast such as Lindi, Mikindani, Dar es Salaam, Pangani and Tanga—and, to a lesser extent, inland centres such as Tabora and Ujiji—where Arab colonies had been long established, the Arabs had succeeded, partially at least, in ousting the indigenous African law and custom and virtually replacing it by the Sharī'a, at least in so far as the general principles of marriage, divorce and inheritance are concerned.[6] On this basis the Order in Council may be held to cover the whole administration of justice in Tanganyika, providing as it does for the application of both "English" and Indian law on the one hand and, on the other, of "native law" in its dual form of indigenous custom and what has elsewhere been described as "Muhammadan laws and customs"[7] where these

[1] Repealed in 1930, and now partially replaced by the Local Courts Ordinance, 1951.

[2] Sect. 3(4).

[3] Spelt "Mohammedan" in all Tanganyika Ordinances: but see Introduction regarding the policy adopted throughout this Survey in spelling Arabic words.

[4] Sect. 2.

[5] cp., *Campbell* v. *Hall* (1774), 1 Cowp. 204. This, it might be argued, is covered in the Order in Council by the phrase: "provided always that the said common law, doctrines of equity and statutes of general application shall be in force in the Territory so far only as the circumstances of the Territory and its inhabitants and the limits of Her Majesty's jurisdiction permit, and subject to such qualifications as local circumstances may render necessary": but it would seem more natural to interpret these words as authorising the occasional variation or exclusion of the sources of law already named rather than the application of a whole system of law to which no direct reference is made whatever. (Cp., in this context, the argument in *Baraka binti Said* v. *Salim bin Abed* (1939), 20 K.L.R. Pt. 1, 34, regarding the interpretation of the words "so far as the same may be applicable and suitable" in the Courts Ordinance, sect. 11, in reference to the Civil Procedure Ordinance, 1924, and the Criminal Procedure Code: cp. p. 99 above).

[6] But it is noteworthy that an International Delimitation Commission which visited Mikindani in 1886 found in that locality an Arab colony, with a Liwali appointed by the Sultan of Zanzibar, together with an islamicised population of mixed Swahili and Makonde blood which recognised matrilineal succession and other non-Islamic customs.

[7] See Kenya Native Courts Regulations, 1897, art. 57.

have in fact replaced the former or become identified therewith. And this interpretation seems to be conclusively proved correct, in so far as Tanganyika is concerned, by the fact that the Local Courts Ordinance, 1951—which covers Liwalis' courts as well as Chiefs' courts, etc.—expressly excludes from the jurisdiction of such courts " any proceedings in connection with marriage, other than a marriage contracted in accordance with customary law, except where the claim arises only in regard to bride-wealth or adultery and is founded only on customary law,"[1] while it limits the law they are to administer, apart from certain Ordinances, Orders etc., to "the customary law prevailing in the area of (their) jurisdiction."[2] But it must be emphasised that while this Ordinance shows clearly that Islamic law is frequently identified in Tanganyika with customary law, yet the Administration (Small Estates) (Amendment) Ordinance[3] and the Land (Law of Property and Conveyancing) Ordinance[4] show equally clearly that it is sometimes distinguished therefrom. Nor can this inconsistency be resolved by the suggestion that while Islamic and customary law have remained separate and distinct in matters of inheritance they have become fused and assimilated, among Muslims, in questions of marriage and divorce—as some of the cases discussed below will amply indicate. It would seem, indeed, that the explanation of this inconsistency can only be sought in the confusion of thought on this whole subject discussed in the Introduction to this Survey.

When we turn to those Ordinances which expressly provide for the application of Islamic law, we find the outstanding examples of such in Tanganyika in the Marriage, Divorce and Succession (Non-Christian Asiatics) Ordinance, 1923, and the Administration (Small Estates) (Amendment) Ordinance, 1947; in addition, of course, to the Muhammadan Estates (Benevolent Payments) Ordinance quoted above. The first of these provides that " The marriage in the Territory of non-Christian spouses either of whom is an Asiatic,[5] whether domiciled in the Territory or not, who are not related to each other in any of the degrees of consanguinity or affinity prohibited by the law of the religion of either party to the marriage, shall, if the marriage is contracted in the manner customary in the Territory among persons professing the religion of either of the parties . . . be deemed for all purposes to be a valid marriage."[6] This provision is to apply also to marriages contracted before the commencement of the Ordinance, except where any such marriage has been declared invalid by some competent court or where either party has lawfully contracted a subsequent marriage which would be avoided by the validation of the previous one.[7] It was similarly provided that " The dissolution in the Territory of the marriage of non-Christian spouses either of whom is an Asiatic . . . shall, if the divorce is on grounds which are recognised as valid grounds for divorce by the law of their religion, if it be the same, or, if they profess different religions, by the law of the religion in accordance with which the marriage was solemnised and if effected in the manner customary in the Territory among persons professing that religion, be deemed

[1] Sect. 13(*b*). The relevance of this point is obvious when it is realised that the Liwalis in fact deal with a great deal of litigation regarding the marriage and divorce of Muslims under Islamic law. And it is also noteworthy in this context that the corresponding clause in the Native Courts Ordinance, 1929, sect. 12(*b*) read: " cases in connection with marriage other than a marriage contracted under or in accordance with Muhammadan or native law or custom . . ."

[2] Sect. 15.

[3] Sect. 18, see below.

[4] Sect. 15(1).

[5] These now include Arabs, who were previously included (in so far as the administration of their estates were concerned) in the Deceased Native Estates Ordinance, 1922, now repealed and replaced by the Administration (Small Estates) (Amendment) Ordinance. See below pp. 126 ff.

[6] Sect. 2(1).

[7] Sect. 2(2).

for all purposes to be a valid divorce."[1] Nothing, however, in this Ordinance was to affect the provisions of the Marriage Ordinance or permit the dissolution of a marriage contracted under that Ordinance.[2] Provisions regarding registration follow. Finally, it is provided that "Subject to the provisions of this or any other Ordinance or applied Act . . . the succession to the movable property in the Territory of a deceased non-Christian Asiatic who at his death is domiciled in the Territory and to the immovable property in the Territory of such an Asiatic, whether domiciled in the Territory at his death or not, shall be regulated by the law of the religion professed by him at his death: Provided that (*a*) so much of the law of any religion as deprives any person of a right of succession to property by reason of that person having renounced or having been excluded from the communion of any religion or having been deprived of caste shall not be in force in the Territory; and (*b*) every creditor shall have the same rights and remedies against the estate of a non-Christian Asiatic (including the right to follow assets) as he has against the estate of a deceased Christian."[3]

In Fatuma Bachoo v. *Majothi Kara Juma Bolia* (1946), 5 T.T.L.R. 163, however, it was decided that there was no court in Tanganyika which had jurisdiction to hear non-native matrimonial causes under Islamic law or to dissolve a marriage between immigrant Muslims.[4] So in 1947 an amendment to this Ordinance repealed sections 3 and 4 above and replaced them by sections providing that "The High Court[5] shall have jurisdiction to hear and determine all matrimonial causes and suits arising out of the marriage of non-Christian spouses either of whom is an Asiatic, if at the time of the institution of any such cause or suit the petitioner is domiciled in the Territory: Provided always that nothing in this sub-section shall confer or be construed as conferring upon the High Court jurisdiction to hear or determine any such cause or suit if recourse to a judicial tribunal is not permitted by the law of the religion of the parties to the marriage, where their religion is the same, or, if they profess different religions, by the law of the religion in accordance with which the marriage was solemnised."[6] Again, "Subject to the provisions of this Ordinance in all matrimonial causes or suits to which this section relates the High Court shall exercise its jurisdiction and act and give relief upon the principles of the law of the religion of the parties to the marriage, where their religion is the same, or if they profess different religions by the law of the religion in accordance with which the marriage was solemnised: Provided that where such law is repugnant to justice or morality or inapplicable to the circumstances of the Territory or inconsistent with any Order in Council or Ordinance . . . it shall be deemed to be varied accordingly"[7]—while "a cause or suit under this section may be instituted by either party to a marriage."[8] Similarly, the new section 4 provides that "Nothing in this Ordinance contained shall (*a*) affect the provisions of the Marriage Ordinance; or (*b*) permit the dissolution of a marriage contracted under that Ordinance or under any other law (other than a law to which section 3 relates) in force in the Territory or recognised by the courts thereof; or (*c*) affect the rights or liabilities of any person who is a party to such a marriage."

Several points in this Ordinance demand notice. In the first place it only applies to marriages between parties one, at least, of whom is a non-Christian Asiatic, and has no reference, therefore, to marriages between "natives" of

[1] Sect. 3.
[2] Sect. 4.
[3] Sect. 6(1).
[4] Presumably because Bombay Regulation 4 of 1827 was not applicable to Tanganyika. See above, pp. 2, 6, 33, 40, 60, etc.
[5] Or any subordinate court, as authorised. See sect. 3(4).
[6] Sect. 3(1).
[7] Sect. 3(2).
[8] Sect. 3(3).

Africa. Secondly, it makes no express mention of Islam or Muslims, since it applies to Asiatic adherents of any non-Christian religion: but it may be presumed that in questions of marriage or divorce the law of the sect or school of Islam to which the parties belong or under which the marriage was celebrated will in each case be applied, and that in matters of succession the law of the sect or school of the deceased will, equally, be followed. Thirdly, no mention is made of the Islamic prohibition of marriage between those within the prohibited degrees of foster relationship, although it is possible that the courts would read this extension of the prohibited degrees of consanguinity and affinity into the Ordinance. Fourthly, while provision is made for the registration of such marriages and divorces, no doubt is thrown on the essential validity of marriages and divorces which the parties thereto have failed to register. Fifthly, it is noteworthy that section 2(1) provides for the validity of a marriage in which the parties are not precluded from marriage in the law of the religion of either party and which is celebrated according to the law of the religion of either—a provision which is obviously stricter than Islamic law in the first point and more lenient and comprehensive in the second. Sixthly, in the case of a divorce the principle has been adopted that, where the parties follow the same religion (whether originally, or by conversion subsequent to the marriage, it may be presumed) the law of that religion is to apply, while where they differ (again, presumably, whether at the time of the marriage or by subsequent conversion) the law under which the marriage was celebrated is to govern the case: and this provision would run counter to Islamic law in, e.g., the case of a Hindu marriage in which either husband or wife subsequently embraced Islam and claimed the dissolution of the marriage on the grounds that for a Muslim husband to be married to anyone who does not follow a " Scriptural " religion, or for a Muslim wife to be married to any non-Muslim, is utterly precluded in Islamic law—or, indeed, where the husband tried to exercise his unilateral and almost unrestricted right of repudiation under that law. Seventhly, the provision forbidding the disinheritance of anyone who renounces or is excluded from the communion of his religion protects a convert from Islam to, e.g., Hinduism from the relevant rule of Islamic law, yet it would not allow the Hindu relatives of one who embraces Islam to inherit from him: that is, like the Indian Caste Disabilities Removal Act, 1850 (by which, no doubt, it was inspired), it protects the convert himself from losing his rights of inheritance from his unconverted relations but does nothing to protect those relatives from exclusion from inheritance from him[1]—nor, indeed, does it in any way benefit the children of the convert or outcaste, or any other persons claiming through him. Finally, the proviso about the rights of creditors protects the latter from the rule of Anglo-Muhammadan[2] law whereby, although they may always bring their claims against the heirs of the estate in person in proportion to their shares therein, yet they have no right to follow its assets if alienated by the heirs.

But it is the Administration (Small Estates) (Amendment) Ordinance of 1947[3] which provides the statutory basis for the application of the Islamic law of succession in the case of specified " natives "—here interpreted as members of African tribes, Swahilis and Somalis. This provides that " The estate of every deceased native to which this Ordinance applies by virtue of an order or direction under section 16 of this Ordinance shall be administered according to

[1] But this would not signify in the case of a convert to Christianity, since under the law applicable to his estate on death his unconverted relatives would not be excluded on grounds of religion.

[2] By contrast with the pure Sharī'a.

[3] Which replaces, *inter alia,* the Deceased Native Estates Ordinance of 1922, which made very similar provisions for the application of Islamic law (sect. 4(1)), but also expressly provided for the application of that law to Arabs (now included as Asiatics in the Asiatics Ordinance).

the law following: —(*a*) The estate of a member of a native tribe shall be administered according to the law of that tribe unless the deceased at any time professed the Muhammadan religion and the court exercising jurisdiction over his estate is satisfied from the written or oral declarations of the deceased or his acts or manner of life that the deceased intended his estate to be administered, either wholly or in part, according to Muhammadan law, in which case the estate shall be administered, either wholly or in part as the case may be, according to that law.

(*b*) The estate of a Swahili[1] shall be administered according to Muhammadan law unless the court exercising jurisdiction over his estate is satisfied from the written or oral declarations of the deceased or his acts or manner of life that he intended his estate to be administered, either wholly or in part, according to any tribal law, in which case the estate shall be administered, either wholly or in part as the case may be, according to that tribal law."[2]

Provisions similar to those we have already noticed follow, e.g., "(*a*) every creditor, whether a native or not, shall have the same rights and remedies against a native estate (including the right to follow assets) as he has against the estate of a deceased European, and (*b*) a person shall not be deprived of a right to succession to property by reason of that person having renounced or having been excluded from the communion of any religion."[3] It is also provided that "In the administration of the estate of a deceased native by virtue of an order or direction under section 16 of this Ordinance any testamentary disposition purporting to dispose of any part of that estate shall be recognised as a valid will . . . where the estate is to be administered according to Muhammadan law, if the disposition is recognised as valid by that law."[4] Finally, by the Somalis (Miscellaneous Provisions) Ordinance, 1949, a further section was added to this Ordinance which reads: "The provisions of sections 18 and 19 shall apply in respect of the estate of a deceased Somali to which this Ordinance applies by virtue of an order or direction under section 16 as they apply in respect of the estate of a deceased Swahili."[5]

The most noteworthy feature in this Ordinance—besides the provision in favour of the convert, etc., on which comment has already been made above—is the attempt which it makes to solve the difficult problem of the conflict between Islamic and tribal law. It provides, in this connection, that in the case of Swahilis or Somalis, to whose estates this Ordinance has been applied, Islamic law shall prevail unless a contrary intention on the part of the deceased is explicit or implicit, while in the case of a member of an African tribe customary law shall prevail unless the contrary intention has been expressed or implied. Both these provisions seem fair enough in a territory of such diverse religious affiliations, and such various degrees of attachment thereto, as Tanganyika; although both run counter, of course, to Islamic law. More serious than this, however, is the fact that the test adopted both in this Ordinance and in the now repealed Deceased Native Estates Ordinance,[6] 1922, is far neater on paper than in practice, where it may be somewhat difficult to apply; while the requisite orders[7] or directions[8]

[1] Originally "and Somali," until the Somalis Ordinance of 1949 changed this.
[2] Sect. 18(1).
[3] Sect. 18(4).
[4] Sect. 19(1).
[5] Sect. 3.
[6] In this Ordinance sect. 4(1) (*a*) and (*b*) correspond verbatim to sect. 18(1) (*a*) and (*b*) of the Administration (Small Estates) (Amendment) Ordinance, and sect. 4(4) (*a*) and (*b*) to sect. 18(4) (*a*) and (*b*).
[7] No such orders have, it seems, ever been made by the Governor.
[8] Only a very few such directions have been given by district courts. But interested parties could, of course, always make suitable application, if they had any knowledge of the law concerned.

seem very seldom to have been given in regard to the estates of deceased natives The present Ordinance is not applicable by Liwalis or other local courts: but where the former administer the estates of deceased natives, as they do in most townships, they are said to "continue to act as though the Deceased Native Estates Ordinance had never been repealed." But the fact remains that no Liwalis whom I questioned seemed either aware of these provisions or willing to apply them if they were—including, of course, the proviso about the convert, etc. To this whole problem we must recur: but it is also noteworthy in passing that although this Ordinance, unlike the Kenya Muhammadan Marriage, Divorce and Succession Ordinance, makes no reference to the Islamic law of marriage, yet the provision that certain estates are to be "administered according to Muhammadan law" necessarily implies and involves the applicability of the Muhammadan law of marriage, divorce and paternity at least in so far as such considerations determine who are or are not entitled heirs. It should also be observed that the Muhammadan Estates (Benevolent Payments) Ordinance, 1918, is not only remarkable for the recognition which it gives, in the earliest days of the British administration of the territory, to the applicability of the "law of Islam,"[1] but also for making partial provision for that "return" (*radd*) to the spouse relict, in the absence of any other heirs, which the Ibāḍī law [and the law now followed in India, Egypt, the Sudan, etc.] regularly allows, but concerning which the Shāfi'ī law normally applicable in East Africa makes no concession; and even for extending this principle to cover "other dependants" who, in some cases at least, would not otherwise be entitled to inherit at all.[2]

There are, however, several other Ordinances which have some bearing, direct or indirect, on the question of the degree to which Islamic law is to be applied. Thus several references have already been made to "natives" and non-natives, so it is relevant to note that the Interpretation and General Clauses Ordinance, 1928, provides that where not otherwise provided—and it might almost be said that in this respect every Tanganyika Ordinance is a law unto itself[3]—"native" means any member of an African race and includes a Swahili but not a Somali[4] (or, of course, an Arab). Again, it is noteworthy that the Indian Acts which have been applied in the Territory include the Indian Evidence Act, 1872, the Indian Code of Civil Procedure, 1908, the Indian Succession Act, 1865, the Indian Probate and Administration Act, 1881, the Indian Majority Act, 1875, the Indian Oaths Act, 1873, the Indian Contract Act, 1872, and the Indian Limitation Act, 1908.

The applicability of the Islamic law of marriage is, moreover, in Tanganyika as elsewhere, partially modified by the terms of the Marriage Ordinance, 1921, for while it is provided that "Nothing in this Ordinance shall apply to any marriages to which each of the parties is a Muhammadan" it would presumably provide a way in which a Muslim girl of over twenty-one, or under that age with the consent of her father or (if he be dead, insane or absent from the territory) her mother, etc., could marry a Christian husband, in spite of the fact that such a union is utterly void in Sharī'a law. Again, a man married under this Ordinance may neither divorce his wife nor marry a co-wife (even under "any native law or custom"—which, whatever the primary reference of the words, must certainly here be held to cover a marriage under Islamic law[5]) except as provided under the Divorce Ordinance, 1929, nor may a woman so married claim dissolution of her marriage except under the latter Ordinance—however much Islamic law may accord these rights to either party, whether *ab initio* or as a result of the conversion thereto of the party concerned. At the same time, however, the Divorce

[1] Sect. 2.
[2] cp. in Zanzibar, the Succession Decree, sect. 327, and the Administrator-General's Decree, sect. 12(3).
[3] See below, p. 132.
[4] Sect. 2(1)—as amended by the Somalis Ordinance, 1949.
[5] cp. the references at p. 124 above to the Local Courts Ordinance, 1951.

Ordinance authorizes a wife to petition the court for the dissolution of her marriage if, " since the solemnisation thereof, her husband has changed his profession of Christianity for the profession of some other religion and gone through a form of marriage with another woman "—or, indeed, committed adultery in any circumstances whatever.[1] But before concluding a marriage under the Marriage Ordinance the Registrar should satisfy himself that " neither of the parties to the intended marriage is married by native law or custom to any person other than the person with whom such marriage is proposed to be contracted"; and whatever the proper meaning of a marriage by native law and custom may be elsewhere it must here again (for want of any direct provision whatever regarding the marriage of " native " Muslims[2]) be held to include the marriage of natives by Muhammadan law. And it is also noteworthy in this context that the District Courts (Separation and Maintenance) Ordinance, 1949, is only applicable to monogamous marriages—i.e., marriages necessarily monogamous, not ones which happen to be so by the circumstances or choice of the parties.

Indirect recognition of the application of Islamic law to the marriages of African Muslims is, moreover, forthcoming in the Penal Code, 1945, section 138(*b*), which provides that " Nothing in this section shall render it an offence for any person of African or Asiatic descent to marry or permit the marriage of a girl under the age of twelve years in accordance with the custom of their tribe or religion where it is not intended that the marriage shall be consummated before the girl attains the age of twelve years." But it is noteworthy in this context that the preceding parts of the same section had decreed, in a manner to which Islamic law provides no parallel, that any attempt on the part of a husband to consummate such a marriage before the girl has attained, or he has reasonable cause to believe and does in fact believe that she has attained, the age of twelve years shall be a misdemeanour punishable by imprisonment with or without corporal punishment, and that any parent or other person having custody of a girl under the age of twelve who disposes of her with the intention, or knowing it to be likely, that her marriage would be consummated before she has reached twelve, shall be similarly guilty of a misdemeanour and punishable by imprisonment with or without corporal punishment.[3] Again, it seems that the Shāfiʿī law which gives a father the right to give his virgin daughter, whatever her age, in compulsory marriage would be no defence, in suitable circumstances, to a charge under section 133,[4] which provides that "Any person who with intent to marry or carnally know a woman of any age, or to cause her to be married or carnally known by any other person, takes her away, or detains her, against her will, is guilty of a felony and is liable to imprisonment for seven years."

Similarly, the Adoption of Infants Ordinance, 1942, transcends the relevant provisions of Islamic law, which recognises no legal consequences of adoption. This Ordinance provides on the one hand that " Upon an adoption order being made, all rights, duties, obligations and liabilities of the parent or parents, guardian or guardians of the adopted child, in relation to the future custody, maintenance and education of the adopted child, including all rights to appoint a guardian or to consent or give notice of dissent to marriage shall be extinguished, and all rights, duties, obligations and liabilities shall vest in and be exercised by and enforceable against the adopter as though the adopted child was a child born to the adopter in lawful wedlock and in respect of the same matters and in respect of the

---

[1] Sect. 5(2). But it seems that in practice persons who conclude a further marriage under native law are not normally prosecuted, although such subsequent marriage would be recognised, at most, only by the local courts.

[2] Except for the phrase about a " marriage contracted under or in accordance with Muhammadan or native law or custom " in the Native Courts Ordinance, 1929, which was not reproduced in the Local Courts Ordinance, 1951. See above.

[3] cp. p. 88 above. The Islamic rule is simply that the wife must be able to bear this.

[4] This provision is common to the Penal Codes of all the territories in East Africa.

liability of the child to maintain its parents the adopted child shall stand to the adopter exclusively in the position of a child born to the adopter in lawful wedlock." But at the same time it also decrees that "An adoption order shall not deprive the adopted child of any right to or interest in property to which, but for the order, the child would have been entitled under any intestacy or disposition . . . or confer on the adopted child any right to or interest in property as a child of the adopter, and the expression "child," "children" and "issue" . . . shall not, unless the contrary intention appears, include an adopted child."[1] And a somewhat similar case is provided by the Affiliation Ordinance, 1949, which provides that the court may make orders regarding the support of illegitimate children by those whom it sees adequate reason to believe to be their natural fathers.

In matters of contract little trace of Islamic law can be found in Tanganyika. It is noteworthy in passing, however, that the unlimited contractual rights accorded by Muhammadan law to the adult who is not under any form of legal interdiction have been limited in Tanganyika in the case of natives, in their own interests, by the Credit to Natives (Restriction) Ordinance, 1931, which provides that, subject to certain exceptions and exemptions, "no debt for money lent, goods supplied or services . . . rendered by a non-native shall be recoverable from a native unless either (*a*) the transaction creating the debt is in writing and approved in writing by an administrative officer or (*b*) the native holds a permit in writing from an administrative officer to contract such debts . . ."[2]

There is no legislation whatever in Tanganyika regarding waqfs. To this we must recur later; but here it may be sufficient to observe that any case of waqf which reached the High Court or subordinate courts would presumably be dealt with under the Religious and Charitable Societies (Disposal of Land) Ordinance, 1929,[3] the Land (Perpetual Succession) Ordinance, 1927, and legal principles of a general character. An Ordinance to set up a board of Waqf Commissioners and otherwise provide for the better administration of public waqfs is, however, under tentative consideration. Meanwhile Liwalis' courts deal with matters of waqf under Shāfiʿī law (see below).

The preamble to the Land Ordinance,[4] 1923, rehearses that "Whereas it is expedient that the existing customary rights of the natives of the . . . Territory to use and enjoy the land . . . and the fruits thereof . . . should be assured and preserved. And Whereas it is expedient that the existing native customs with regard to the use and occupation of land should as far as possible be preserved. And Whereas it is expedient that the rights and obligations of the Government in regard to the whole of the lands within the Territory and also the rights and obligations of cultivators or other persons claiming to have an interest in such lands should be defined by law." It then proceeds to enact that "The whole of the lands . . . whether occupied or unoccupied . . . are hereby declared to be public lands. Provided that subject to the provisions of sub-section (2) of this section nothing in this Ordinance shall be deemed to affect the validity of any title to land or any interest therein lawfully acquired before the date of the commencement thereof,"[5] and to authorise the Governor to grant rights of occupancy for definite periods not exceeding ninety-nine years[6] to natives and non-natives, and to demand and revise rentals, etc.,[7] after any native authority established in

[1] Sect. 7(1) and 7(2), respectively.
[2] Sect. 3.
[3] As amended in 1949 (now Cap. 120). But in *Omar Fakirmohamed and Gulam Mohamed, etc.* v. *Remtulla Talab and Another* (1927), 1 T.T.L.R. 38, the court quoted as relevant a Privy Council judgment concerning an Indian waqf, under the title of a "public religious trust."
[4] As repeatedly amended.
[5] Sect. 3.
[6] Sect. 7.
[7] Sect. 6.

the area has been consulted.[1] Further sections provide that the devolution of the rights of an occupier upon death shall be regulated, in the case of a native, by the provisions of sections 4 and 5 of the Deceased Native Estates Ordinance[2] —and in this Ordinance, again, the term " native " is to include a Swahili but not a Somali.[3]

It is apparent, then, that the use and occupancy of land in Tanganyika was, and is, in the main regulated and governed by customary law. This normally recognises no private property in land as such, but tribal lands are distributed by the elders, chiefs, etc., to individuals whose right to cultivate their plots— and to pass this right to their heirs—is secure only so long as they make full use of them. But in most areas an individual right of ownership is recognised in the trees a man plants or the buildings he erects.

It is by no means certain, however, how far this applied in the areas of Arab settlement. On one theory this system was prevalent " when the Arabs came," whereupon the latter settled amicably among the natives, giving presents to the tribal elders for permission to do so; while *shambas* were bought and sold for the value of the crops thereon, since land *per se* was regarded as valueless. This state of affairs only changed on the arrival of the Germans, with their western ideas of individual ownership: for if the latter wanted a piece of land they bought it, and chiefs and elders soon " cashed in " on this state of affairs by providing land for sale as freehold, although in reality, of course, they had no such title to convey. Later, the German Government became alarmed at the course things were taking and under Imperial Decree of 1895 took over all land not actually claimed by anyone at that date. It was in such circumstances that the Flurbuch was compiled as a preliminary survey— and complicated matters still further by giving quasi-official sanction to individual claims to land—while the Grundbuch was to represent registered titles after proper investigation.

It is sometimes argued, however, that this reconstruction of the position is far from accurate. Arabs, Persians and Indians have been making descents on the coast of Tanganyika for some two thousand years, and at the height of the slave trade it has been suggested that in some areas (e.g., Kilwa, Bagamoyo, Pangani, Tanga, etc.) the coast was almost denuded of the indigenous tribes.[4] In large part, therefore, these immigrants simply seized abandoned land; while when the natives drifted back to the coast as security improved the old principle prevailed among them that coconut trees could be owned, together with the land on which they stood, but that over land devoted to annual crops they enjoyed a mere right of " user." In any case, however, there can be no doubt that lands occupied by Arabs, however acquired, were frequently regarded as privately owned under Islamic law;[5] while under the German survey " Crown land " was entered as " Herrulos," and although largely, no doubt, occupied by natives, was not claimed by them in any individual sense.

Again, the Land (Law of Property and Conveyancing) Ordinance of 1923[6] provides that " A disposition of land belonging to a native in favour of a non-native . . . shall not be operative unless it is in writing and unless . . . it is approved

[1] See Land (Amendment) Ordinance, 1947-9, sect. 4.

[2] Sect. 12. Now, of course, replaced by the Administration (Small Estates) (Amendment) Ordinance.

[3] Sect. 2, as amended by the Somalis Ordinance, 1949.

[4] This seems distinctly doubtful, however, as many of the coast tribes participated in the trade as middle-men.

[5] Especially in the case of grants of land in Tanganyika by the Sultan of Zanzibar. But see also two early Kenya cases in this context, *Parenti* v. *Barclay and the Crown Advocate* (1911), 4 E.A.L.R. 80, and the *Jibana case* (1914), 5 E.A.L.R. 141: cp. pp. 101, 2 above.

[6] Amended in 1948.

by the Governor,"[1] and this is to include a sale, conveyance, mortgage, lease, sub-lease, or transfer of possession, etc.[2] But "Nothing in this Ordinance shall affect any native law relating to the succession to property on death or to the rights of a native husband or wife in the property of the other, or any rule of Muhammadan law, as applied to natives, relating to succession to property on death, waqfs, or gifts."[3]

It seems to have been the policy of the British Administration in the past to grant freehold titles to natives (*a*) under section 20(a) of the Land Ordinance, which reads: "Notwithstanding anything contained in this Ordinance the Governor may make such grants and leases of public land as he may consider expedient (*a*) to give effect to any contract or undertaking by the former German Government" and (*b*) under section 11 of the Land Registry Ordinance, 1923,[4] which in effect provides for registration of title in the case of any who have held public land for thirty years prior to January, 1923, or any period which would bar an action under the Indian Limitation Act of 1908. But to such a policy there are certain objections, since in Africa the grant of freehold title to plots of land tends to foster speculation, fragmentation (especially where the Islamic law of inheritance prevails) and the growth of a landless peasantry. The present tendency, therefore, is against the grant of freehold except where "adverse" possession for 60 years, or 30 years prior to 1923, can be proved, while an entry in the Flurbuch only entitles the claimant to the "favourable consideration" of his claim.

Complications arise in this connection, however, from the lack of consistency in the use of the term "native" in Tanganyika Ordinances.[5] A good example of the confusion which this may cause is provided by the problem raised by some plots of land said to have been sold to Saidi Abed, an "Arab" of Dar es Salaam, at such a ridiculously low price that it was contended that the transactions concerned were really mortgages, subsequently foreclosed. But under the Land (Law of Property and Conveyancing) Ordinance an Arab is a native,[6] so no consent to the alleged sales would have been required; while under the Credit to Natives Ordinance he is a non-native, and may not give credit to a native without an administrative officer's consent. As for Somalis, the changes of view concerning them which have transpired may best, perhaps, be illustrated by reference to the Somalis (Miscellaneous Provisions) Ordinance, 1949, which provides for the deletion of the word "Somali" from section 2 of the Interpretation Ordinance, section 18(1) (a) of the Administration (Small Estates) (Amendment) Ordinance and section 2 of the Land Ordinance; the deletion of the whole definition of "native" in ten other Ordinances[7]; the addition of a clause about Somalis in section 19(2) of the Administration (Small Estates) (Amendment) Ordinance and in section 23(2) of the Births and Deaths Registration Ordinance; and the amendment, in so far as Somalis are concerned, of clauses regarding "non-natives" in the Crops (Increased Production) Ordinance and the Non-Native Education Tax Ordinance.

In any case it seems clear that land law in Tanganyika is now almost entirely governed by the relevant Ordinances, only some of which have been mentioned

[1] Sect. 11(1).
[2] Sect. 11(2).
[3] Sect. 15(1).
[4] Amended in 1949.
[5] See above, p. 128.
[6] As also under the Land Registry Ordinance, 1923, sect. 63.
[7] i.e., the Porters (Restriction of Employment) Ordinance, sect. 2, the Destitute Persons Ordinance, sect. 2, the Native Authority Ordinance, sect. 2, the Native Liquor Ordinance, sect. 4, the Native Food-stuffs Ordinance, sect. 2, the Master and Native Servants Ordinance, sect. 2, the Animals (Native Livestock) Ordinance, sect. 2, the Marriage Ordinance, sect. 2, the Intoxicating Liquors Ordinance, sect. 2, and the Divorce Ordinance, 1929, sect. 3.

above.[1] However the original titles were acquired there is now considerable freehold along the coasts, and particularly around the major towns; while for the rest the land has been declared "Public" and remains for the most part at the disposal of the native tribes in accordance with ancient custom, but it is within the discretion of the Governor to grant rights of use over[2] appropriate areas for definite terms not exceeding ninety-nine years to individuals or companies, natives or non-natives, as he considers would tend, directly or indirectly, to the public good. Islamic law is no longer applicable in this field except in so far as it may represent the local customary law or coincide with—or at least not contravene—the terms of any relevant Ordinance. Moreover, some of the ordinary rules of Islamic law regarding the powers of administrators of waqfs and guardians of the property of minors, etc., are transcended by section 6 of the Land Acquisition Ordinance, 1926 (amended 1948), which provides that "It shall be lawful for the persons being seized, possessed of or entitled to any lands or any estate or interest therein, to sell and convey the same to the Governor, and particularly it shall be lawful for all or any of the following persons to sell or convey, that is to say—all guardians, managers of the estates of lunatics, trustees for charitable or other purposes, executors and administrators, and all persons for the time being entitled to the receipt of the rents and profits of any lands . . ."

Scattered about Tanganyika, but particularly in the major towns, can be found an extremely wide assortment of Muslims whose schools of law differ widely from each other. The predominant school, as elsewhere in East Africa, is of course that of the Shāfi'īs, and the only other Sunnī school with any considerable number of followers is that of the Ḥanafīs, as represented by Indian and Baluchi immigrants. But there are also Ibāḍīs from Zanzibar and 'Umān; Ithnā 'Asharīs from Iran, India, etc. (including those Khojas who have severed their connection with the Agha Khan and declared themselves Ithnā 'Asharīs, not Ismā'īlīs); Ismā'īlīs of both the Khoja and Bohora sects; and Aḥmadī "heretics." Notes on some of these communities will be found in Appendix B to this Survey.[3]

Very few cases from any of these non-Shāfi'ī communities find their way into the courts. The vast majority of the people concerned are, of course, non-natives whose cases of personal status, etc., would normally go to the High Court or some authorised subordinate court under the Asiatics (Marriage, Divorce and Succession) Ordinance, where an attempt would always be made to apply the law of the parties concerned. But provision has been made in section 10(2) of the Local Courts Ordinance, 1951, for a local court (i.e., here a Liwali's court) to hear civil cases where any of the parties concerned, and criminal cases where the accused, is an "Arab, a Somali, a Comorian, a Baluchi or a Malagasi"—i.e., persons who are not normally under the jurisdiction of such courts[4]—with their consent: and this provision, it seems, merely authorised existing practice. Most of these immigrants are, of course, Shāfi'īs, so no problem as to their school of law arises: but the Baluchis are almost all Ḥanafīs, while some of the Arabs are Ibāḍīs. When such take their cases to the local Liwalis, however, it is always Shāfi'ī law which is applied. Furthermore, it is not at all unknown for a Shī'ī "Shirāzi" to find his way to these courts.

I heard of occasional cases in which a Shāfi'ī African wife had petitioned the local Liwali for the dissolution of her marriage on the grounds that her husband

[1] Others include the Land Registry Ordinance, 1923, and the Registration of Documents Ordinance, 1924 (amended 1948).

[2] But not now any freehold estate.

[3] See also pp.6-8.

[4] See Local Courts Ordinance, sect. 10(1).

had adopted Aḥmadī tenets as a result of the missionary activities of Indian Aḥmadīs, that this was equivalent to apostasy from Islam, and that her marriage was thereby automatically dissolved unless the erring husband immediately returned to the faith: and most Liwalis concerned were disposed to grant such petitions. British and Indian courts, it is true, have refused dissolution of marriage in such circumstances[1] on the ground that Aḥmadīs recite the Muhammadan creed and must therefore be regarded as Muslims: but there seems to be considerable justification for the Liwalis' view that membership of the Qādiānī sect of Aḥmadīs involves a denial that Muḥammad is the last of the prophets and therefore amounts to apostasy from orthodox Islam. This, however, seems to be the only juristic problem to which the Aḥmadīs of East Africa[2] give rise. As for the Ibāḍīs, their tenets are discussed in the Zanzibar section of this Survey. Suffice it to say here, therefore, that elsewhere in East Africa disputes on matters of personal status involving Ibāḍīs are settled either by the arbitration of members of their community, by correspondence with the Ibāḍī Qāḍī of Zanzibar, by reference to some local Sunnī Qāḍī or Liwali, or even before an " infidel " judge.

Prior to 1941 the Liwalis' courts in Tanganyika, like the Muslim subordinate courts of Kenya and the Qāḍīs' courts in Zanzibar, were part of the High Court system as a particular type of subordinate court (see Courts Ordinance, 1920). But in 1941 this was changed, and they were instead incorporated in the native (now " local ") courts system and ceased to have any direct connection with the High Court. This decision had two main results: firstly, that the Liwalis' courts in Tanganyika are not bound, like the Muslim subordinate courts in Kenya and the Qāḍīs' courts in Zanzibar, by the Evidence Act, etc., but are free to follow customary or Islamic rules of procedure in the absence of any specific rules to the contrary under section 44 of the Local Courts Ordinance; and that appeals therefrom go first to a local court of appeal, then to a District Commissioner or Provincial Local Courts Officer, and then, with leave of the Provincial Commissioner, to the Central Court of Appeal[3] (formerly termed the Governor's Appeal Board). A tenuous link with the regular judicial hierarchy has, however, been provided by the inclusion of one High Court Judge, as president, sitting with two Administrative Officers, on this Central Court of Appeal.[4] In addition, all proceedings of local courts, original or appellate, are subject to the revisionary powers of the appropriate Provincial Commissioner, Provincial Local Courts Officer or District Commissioner—or, indeed, of the Local Courts Adviser—any of whom may transfer such proceedings to another local court or to a district court, quash them and order the case to be reheard, or vary the decision given, etc.[5]; while any court in the Territory may order the transfer to and trial by a local court of any civil or criminal proceedings which " are of such a character as to be more properly cognisable by a local court."[6]

The local courts covered by this Ordinance comprise, of course, not only Liwalis' courts but various types of Chiefs' courts. In some cases the court is constituted by the Liwali alone, as in most of the coastal districts, while in others the court is constituted by the Liwali or Chief sitting together with elders. But the present policy is to separate, in so far as is practicable, the judiciary from the executive. This means that any opportunity may be taken to relieve chiefs of as much court work as possible and encourage them

[1] cp. *Hakim Khalil Ahmad* v. *Malik Israfi* (1917), 2 Pat. L.J. 108; and *Narantakath* v. *Parakkal* (1922), 45 Mad. 986; etc.

[2] But see under Aḥmadīs in W. Africa pp. 265, etc., and Glossary.

[3] Local Courts Ordinance, 1951, sect. 38(1) and sect. 39.

[4] Ibid, sect. 39(2).

[5] cp. sects. 34, 35 and 42.

[6] cp. sect. 36.

to appoint judicial deputies for this purpose who will in time become the ***primi inter pares*** of panels of selected elders. Similarly the tendency is to relieve Liwalis of their executive responsibilities so that they may devote themselves exclusively to judicial work. But in Africa the age-old association of executive and judicial powers always dies hard.

The jurisdiction of all these local courts is comprehensively defined as extending, to the extent defined in their respective warrants of establishment, " over causes and matters, civil and criminal, in which the accused or parties is or are Africans "[1]—i.e., persons whose tribe is a tribe of the Territory or of the Colony and Protectorate of Kenya, the Uganda Protectorate, Zanzibar, Northern Rhodesia, Nyasaland, the Sudan, the Belgian Congo, Ruanda Urundi, or Portuguese East Africa, including Swahilis[2]—provided the offence occurred, the cause of action arose, the defendant is ordinarily resident, or the immovable property is situate, within the area of jurisdiction of the court concerned.[3] The only general limits on the jurisdiction of these courts are that no local court may entertain: " (*a*) any proceedings in which a person is charged with an offence in consequence of which death is alleged to have occurred, or which is punishable under any law with death; (*b*) any proceedings in connection with marriage, other than a marriage contracted in accordance with customary law, except where the claim arises only in regard to bride-wealth or adultery and is founded only on customary law; (*c*) any proceedings affecting the title to or any interest in land registered under the Land Registry Ordinance or any Ordinance amending or replacing the same; (*d*) any proceedings in relation to witch-craft, except with the approval of the Provincial Commissioner . . . ; (*e*) any proceedings removed from the jurisdiction of such court by the terms of any warrant or order; (*f*) any other class of proceedings which the Governor may, by order published in the Gazette, remove from the jurisdiction of local courts."[4] As for the law they are to administer, this consists of " the customary law prevailing in the area of the jurisdiction of such court, so far as it is applicable and is not repugnant to natural justice or morality or is not, in principle, in conflict with the provisions of any law in force in the Territory ",[5] together with " rules or orders made in accordance with the provisions of the Native Authority Ordinance "[6] and the "provisions of any Ordinance or other law which such local court is authorised to administer or enforce."[7] It is also noteworthy that it is provided that " Notwithstanding anything to the contrary in any law for the time being in force in Tanganyika no civil proceedings in respect of—(*a*) customary marriage or inheritance; and (*b*) immovable property, other than freehold land, leasehold property or land held under a right of occupancy for a term of years, shall be commenced by any African in any court other than a local court having jurisdiction "[8]; while the prohibition of usurpation of judicial powers is not to be " deemed to prohibit any customary arbitration or settlement by the tribal elders in any matter arising out of any minor infringement of customary law if such arbitration or settlement is conducted in the manner recognised by local customary law."[9]

In the case of Liwalis, particularly in the more strictly Islamic districts, the " customary law prevailing in the area " is interpreted as being Islamic law in regard to all that concerns the personal status and family law of Muslims, but

---

[1] Sect. 10(1). For the right of certain non-Africans voluntarily to submit to their jurisdiction, see above (p. 133) and sect. 10(2).
[2] Sect. 2.
[3] Sects. 11 and 12.
[4] Sect. 13.
[5] Sect. 15(*a*).
[6] Sect. 15(*b*).
[7] Sect. 15(*c*) and (*d*).
[8] Sect. 12(3).
[9] Sect. 26.

pagan and even " Christian " customary law in the case of others; while in matter. of contract and tort the " customary law " applicable may not infrequently conform to, or at least have been greatly influenced by, the Sharī'a. In less islamicised localities, on the other hand, the local tribal law is almost always applied, particularly in the Chiefs'[1] courts: although such courts not infrequently include a " Muslim member " who may sometimes give advice regarding the dictates of Islamic law.

From conversations with the Liwalis of Dar es Salaam, Bagamoyo, Lindi, Mikindani, Tabora, Mwanza, Tanga and elsewhere, with the local *shehes*[2] in most of these places, with various Chiefs and, of course, with Administrative Officers— together with the perusal of a large number of case records, files, etc.— the following facts emerged.

The procedure followed by Liwalis' courts is basically Islamic, but greatly modified on common-sense principles. Thus the question of the burden of proof is decided, in general, according to the ordinary rules; but witnesses are regularly put on oath, are not " screened " and are accepted without regard to their religion; while evidence, if any, is heard from both sides and the court then decides which is the more credible. Most Liwalis, on the other hand, tend to insist either on two witnesses or, in financial cases, on one supported by the plaintiff's oath, although some would apparently accept a single witness if thoroughly convinced that his testimony was true; but written and even—on occasion—circumstantial evidence is accepted. In default of sufficient evidence the defendant in his turn may be put on oath,[3] and some Liwalis allow him the option of returning this oath to the plaintiff, while others do not; but all such oaths must be taken in the mosque—in the case of Muslim litigants—at the request of the other party. There are no exact periods of limitation, but any party who delays over-long in bringing his suit is asked why he has not brought it sooner; and if he has no adequate reason the suit may well be refused.

Islamic law, then, is virtually confined today to questions of marriage, divorce, legitimacy, guardianship, maintenance, bequests, inheritance, waqfs, gifts, etc. (and even here in a somewhat modified form, on occasions) with regard to Muslims only: but Liwalis may still occasionally hear a case of contract or tort thereunder. The *bay' al-khiyār*[4] is, apparently, almost unknown, but most Liwalis, it seems, will enforce a contract of pledge [*sic*] or mortgage according to whatever terms were agreed between the parties, although one or two alleged that they would not enforce a manifestly usurious contract of this sort. But even these would, of course, admit one of the recognised evasions, such as an acknowledgment of a debt which really includes both capital and interest.

It seems that Muslims in the towns generally, but not invariably, marry by Sharī'a law; while in the country some conclude a proper Islamic contract, whereas others content themselves with following tribal custom. In the latter case the usual procedure, apparently, is for the prospective bridegroom to send two men to the father of the girl he wants to marry, with a gift, to ask his consent; and if all goes well they proceed to fix the "*mahari*" (properly Islamic dower, but here used for the customary bride-wealth) and the time when it must be

[1] The essential difference between a Liwali and a Chief in Tanganyika is that the former is purely a Government official whereas the latter owes his position primarily to native custom, subject to confirmation by Government. Not all Liwalis are Muslims, however, today; although they no doubt originally were, and still are so in most coastal districts.

[2] Arabic *shaykh, shuyūkh,* etc.: a learned man.

[3] But Administrative Officers are said to dislike cases decided on oath in default of evidence.

[4] See above, p. 109.

paid, whether in whole or in part. The "ceremony" follows soon after, when the couple are seated opposite each other and anointed with oil, and much beer is drunk. It is clear, therefore, that the Islamic requirements of the guardian's consent, the payment of dower, and the presence of two witnesses are regularly fulfilled: but there is considerable dispute concerning the matter of that *ījāb* and *qabūl* (declaration and acceptance) which is also regarded by Muslim jurists as essential.[1] In general, it seems, these are not pronounced, at least in any formal way, in a tribal marriage—except, of course, where Muslims call in a *shehe* or *mwalimu*[2] who dictates the appropriate words, pronounces the *khuṭba,* etc. But there is much disagreement, in Tanganyika and elsewhere, as to the effect of a marriage by tribal custom in Islamic law. Some maintain that some sort of *ījāb* and *qabūl,* however rudimentary, must be presumed in such cases, and that this—provided both parties are Muslims—will suffice[3]; while others maintain that such a marriage can never be regarded as a legal union, and that the children, unless formally acknowledged by the father,[4] are illegitimate and excluded from all rights of inheritance. To the argument that such a marriage at least raises such a "*shubha*" (semblance, or doubt) as to make the children legitimate they reply that such a *shubha* is only raised in Shāfi'ī law by a marriage which is valid and legal according to the view of one of the recognised Imāms; that a union of the tribal variety would only have been recognised by 'Aṭā' or by Dā'ūd al-Ẓāhirī; and that Ibn Ḥajar (as opposed to al-Ramlī) said that their view was too eccentric to be included in this principle. Those who are sufficiently learned, however, admit that not only the children but the marriage itself can be validated by formal acknowledgment. Others, again, introduce distinctions, and allow the children of such marriages to inherit where the parties thereto are first generation Muslims, but not where they have been brought up in a Muslim family.[5] In general, however, it seems that such children are often excluded from inheritance on the coast, but not (in general) inland. Where a Muslim marries a pagan wife she will never inherit (unless she accepts Islam, and the marriage is subsequently validated), but minor children[6] are regarded as following the religion of their father and will inherit if formally acknowledged. But the Liwali of Tabora[7] would allow both wives and children of a tribal marriage to inherit, whether the wives were Muslims or pagans—as would also, of course, almost all the Chiefs' courts, whether the Chiefs themselves are Muslims or not.[8]

A study of the cases in which appeals have been made from the Liwalis' courts reveal several which turn on this point. A good instance is provided by the case of *Seleman bin Sudi* v. *Hassan bin Ali.*[9] Here the father's brother claimed that Seleman had no claim to inherit from his father since he was the offspring of only a tribal marriage. The Liwali held that "according to Muhammadan law this child is a legal child," since his mother had been given to his father as wife, for a dower and before witnesses, by her Muslim father. The District Commissioner, on the contrary, held that "according to Muhammadan law, the respondent is debarred from inheriting . . . as his parents had not been married by Muhammadan

[1] See Glossary. But the precise procedure differs from tribe to tribe.

[2] Arabic *mu'allim* or teacher. The Swahili plural is commonly written *walimu.*

[3] Advocates of this view included Ali bin Hemedi, the ex-"Qāḍī" of Tanga, and quite the most learned Sharī'a lawyer in Tanganyika; the Chief Qāḍī of Mombasa; and others.

[4] And the Liwali of Bagamoyo even denied that they could be legitimated by acknowledgment: *sed quaere.*

[5] The Liwali of Dar es Salaam takes this view.

[6] At least, see below.

[7] Who is far less strict than most of his confrères whom I met.

[8] As also, probably, most Liwalis in inland districts.

[9] Secretariat File 13879/246.

law "[1]; that according to tribal law the marriage was perfectly valid and the child entitled to inherit; that both systems of law were of equal validity in the Territory[2]; and that customary law must in these circumstances be preferred. This was duly upheld by the Provincial Commissioner; while the Governor's Appeal Board boldly declared: " The evidence . . . clearly shows that the respondent is the lawful heir . . . There is no doubt that the father recognised the respondent as his son, and accordingly he is entitled to inherit."

It seems that girls are seldom married in Tanganyika before they reach puberty. The right of the father or grandfather to give his virgin daughter compulsorily in marriage under Shāfiʿī law is, of course, recognised, but Liwalis and *shehes* differ considerably between themselves as to their understanding, and application, of the detailed rules. Some say that a girl married by her father or father's father has no redress; others, by way of contrast, maintain that, if the girl can prove that the marriage is injurious to her, the court will in all cases annul it;[3] while a few are aware that such a marriage can always be dissolved if the husband is not the girl's equal, or cannot afford her proper dower, or if "manifest hostility" exists between guardian and ward—and that annulment for other reasons (e.g., the fact that the husband was old or blind, etc.) is accepted by some Shāfiʿīs but not by Ibn Ḥajar.[4] The problem of a girl given in marriage by a more distant guardian without the consent of the nearer seldom, it seems, arises in Tanganyika, since it the father or nearest guardian who in fact, if not in law, takes the *mahari*: but it is held that such a marriage, if it occurred, might be annulled.

Stipulations inserted in marriage contracts in favour of wives are rare and would, in any case, be disregarded, in normal Shāfiʿī fashion. But the only reported case I saw on this subject[5] concerned a girl of fourteen who was given in marriage by her father and then, two days after the marriage was consummated, left her husband and went back to school. Her husband claimed the return of her *mahari* on the grounds of her neglect of her wifely duty; but the Liwali held that she was not yet sufficiently mature in mind to be competent to agree to *khulʿ* (the only basis on which the dower would be returnable in Islamic law), since financial majority is delayed in Tanganyika until eighteen by applied Act.[6] The girl on her part offered to return to her husband if he would allow her to continue her education, as, she claimed, had been expressly stipulated (and witnessed) in their contract of marriage. On appeal, the District Commissioner ordered that the girl be paid "*arsh*" (i.e., compensation) for consummation of the union, that the balance of the bride-wealth be returned, and that the husband divorce his wife—a judgment which represents a rough and ready justice which departs from Sharīʿa law in almost every particular. But the position is complicated in all such cases by the fact that in Tanganyika—as elsewhere in East Africa—no decree of restitution of conjugal rights is (naturally) now executed by force.[7] Not all Liwalis, moreover, are at all clear regarding the principles governing conditions in marriage contracts.

---

[1] i.e., no *shehe* had been called in, nor *khuṭba* said; and there was, therefore, doubt regarding *ījāb* and *qabūl* (which is the real point at issue, although it seems doubtful if this was appreciated).

[2] An interesting statement, in view of the discussion on pp. 122-4 above.

[3] This was the view both of the Liwali and *shehes* of Tabora, the latter quoting a Tradition in justification of their attitude.

[4] Ali Hemedi knew this, and was prepared to follow the " weaker " view; while the Liwali of Tanga said he would annul a marriage for blindness, but not for old age.

[5] *Juma Shamte v. Mohamed Safr* [D.C. Dar es Salaam Appeal No. 1 of 1942]. The correct decree in Shāfiʿī law would have been full dower to the bride and restitution of conjugal rights (including the right to prevent her going to school) to the husband. Only in Ḥanbalī law would she be entitled to dissolution of marriage for his breach of a condition (if proved)—or at least to continue going to school without becoming *nāshiz*.

[6] Indian Majority Act, 1875.

[7] See p. 105, etc.

Most Liwalis seem to know (and allegedly apply) the usual Shāfiʿī rules about the dissolution of marriage at the instance of either party if they find the other afflicted with one of certain grave diseases at the time of the marriage or even subsequently. But in a case[1] where a wife claimed annulment of marriage on the ground of her husband's impotence the parties were ordered to live together for a month (instead of the orthodox year); and, when the husband, instead, stayed away from his wife entirely for the next three or four months, the marriage was dissolved.

Whether a wife may claim dissolution of marriage for repeated acts of cruelty occasions much difference of opinion in the Territory, and this is reflected not only in the practice of Liwalis but in those appeal cases which I was able to study. Thus in one case[2] the Governor's Appeal Board committed itself to the statement that a Muslim wife "cannot divorce her spouse at will . . . and she can only secure a judicial divorce . . . on the grounds of cruelty, which include failure to maintain her." In another—and a confused—case[3] both parties tired of a marriage in which the wife also alleged cruelty, but the husband stood out both for *khulʿ* at a higher price than mere return of *mahari* and also for the children. In first instance the Jumbe of Korogwe decided, by customary law, that the husband could have either bride-price or children, but not both. The District Commissioner on appeal ordered return of dower, divorce, and that the children should go to the wife permanently. The Provincial Commissioner, on further appeal, upheld the divorce, but decreed that because of the cruelty there should be no return of that part of the dower which had already been paid, while the children must go to the father after the usual time of mother's custody (*ḥaḍāna*). The Governor's Appeal Board first requested more evidence regarding the alleged cruelty, but finally upheld the Provincial Commissioner's judgment. In yet another case[4] in which a wife wanted a divorce (but this time without any express allegation of cruelty) and offered return of *mahari* which the husband refused, the Acting Provincial Commissioner of Dar es Salaam gave judgment that arbitrators were to be appointed either to effect reconciliation or to arrange a divorce. Again, where a husband demanded a decree of restitution of conjugal rights and the wife replied by demanding a dissolution of marriage for cruelty,[5] the Liwali decreed that the wife was *nāshiz* (disobedient) and not entitled to either maintenance or divorce, but gave no decree of restitution; the District Commissioner ordered that the wife must either return to her husband within ten days or return her bride-price in consideration of a divorce (or *khulʿ*); the Provincial Commissioner upheld this judgment; while the Governor's Appeal Board held that the wife could only claim divorce for cruelty, and sent the case back to the Liwali for more evidence. The latter heard further witnesses and appointed arbitrators who agreed on a sum for *khulʿ*, but the husband still stood out for more: so the Liwali summoned him to appear and, when he refused to come, lost his patience and decreed a judicial divorce, without payment, on grounds of cruelty and repeated allegations of adultery—and this was upheld by the Governor's Appeal Board. Finally, where a wife complained two or three times about her husband's promiscuity to the Baraza of Nampunga[6] and

[1] *Matar Ismail* v. *Asha binti Ukashi* (Secretariat File 13879/71). But this case was complicated by a further claim of divorce for cruelty, which was stated to be inapplicable in Shāfiʿī law, and by a problem concerning jurisdiction.

[2] *Enzi binti Mohamed* v. *Saidi Larusai* (File 13879/158).

[3] *Hamisi Kallaghe* v. *Nemkondo binti Ali*—a case somewhat further complicated by allegations that the husband had apostatised from Islam (File 13879/268).

[4] *Ramadhani Simba* v. *Fatuma binti Ali* (P.C. Dar es Salaam Appeal Case No. 3 of 1949).

[5] *Mohamed bin Juma* v. *Mtumwa binti Mohamed* (File 13879/111).

[6] *Mohamed Ahmad* v. *Baraza Nampunga*, Lindi Cases 1/336.

the husband ignored all summonses to attend and then went off to the coast, the court gave her leave to remarry without divorcing her, and only issued a divorce when the husband returned and complained. The District Commissioner held that the Baraza had plainly erred in giving permission to remarry without a prior divorce, but committed himself to the surprising statement that "a Muhammadan marriage can be dissolved at the wish of either partner." When this case came to the Provincial Commissioner, the wife alleged that her husband had had relations with her niece and first cousin, and this—without distinction—was termed "incest" by the Provincial Commissioner and upheld as an adequate ground of divorce. This case represents, *inter alia*, an interesting instance of a Chief's court dealing with a question of Muhammadan marriage on totally un-Islamic principles.

The opinion of Liwalis and *shehes* on this controversial subject may be summarised as follows. The Liwali of Bagamoyo insisted that there was no judicial divorce for cruelty in Shāfiʿī law, but the local *shehes* disagreed, and said that where the two arbitrators recommended in the Qur'ān decided that a marital dispute was the husband's fault the Liwali might dissolve the marriage.[1] In Tabora, on the other hand, both the Liwali and the *shehes* held that divorce could be granted on such grounds. The Liwalis of Lindi and Mikindani stated that in their view a husband guilty of cruelty should be warned twice (perhaps with a small fine), fined or imprisoned for the third offence, and if again guilty should be persuaded, if possible, to accept *khulʿ* but forced to do so if obdurate: they knew this was not orthodox Shāfiʿī doctrine, but felt that justice demanded it. The Liwali of Mwanza alleged that he advocated the appointment of arbitrators in such cases and that he would somehow contrive to induce the parties to give them adequate powers of attorney. The Liwali of Tanga also advocated this procedure, after the husband had been warned; but was apparently prepared to enforce the decision of the arbitrators without them being granted any power of attorney by the parties. The Liwali of Dar es Salaam maintained that no dissolution of marriage for cruelty was allowable in the Shāfiʿī school, but that a Qāḍī might follow the Mālikī school in this respect in very pressing circumstances—as also if the husband, even after punishment, continually harassed his wife with groundless taunts of adultery.[2] Ali bin Hemedi[3] advocated warning, the appointment of arbitrators, and—as a last resource—the enforcement of their decision, relying on a view accepted by many Shāfiʿī authorities but not dominant in the school.[4]

A closely allied question—partly covered in the preceding paragraph—is whether *khulʿ*, at what seems a fair figure, can ever be enforced by the courts. In the pure Sharīʿa only the dominant Mālikī and a variant (but "weak") Shāfiʿī opinion allow a judicial decree of *khulʿ* for a specified consideration based on the recommendation of arbitrators in cases of marital discord, the other schools insisting that the husband must, in all such cases, agree to the divorce and the wife to the compensation. But complications are bound to arise where no decree of restitution of conjugal rights is executed by force, for a wife may simply desert her husband and refuse either to return or refund her prompt dower, while a husband may always, of course, refuse a *khulʿ* except at an exorbitant figure. In tribal law the common-sense[5] solution is adopted that bride-price must be returned and the marriage dissolved, and this is in fact decreed in Chiefs' courts

---

[1] They thought this view was supported by *Fatḥ al-Muʿīn*, the *Minhāj* and the *Mughnī*!

[2] Other Liwalis disagree, and would never dissolve a marriage on this ground. Instead, they would leave the wife to bring an action for slander.

[3] In such names no attempt has been made to use the true Arabic spelling, owing to the local mispronunciation.

[4] For a discussion of this problem see Appendix C.

[5] Since, that is, no lofty view is taken of marriage in any case.

even in the case of Muhammadan marriages.[1] The Liwali of Tabora would also follow this practice, but the local *shehes* disagreed (in contrast to the case of cruelty). But most of the coastal Liwalis take the orthodox view that the woman can only be decreed *nāshiz* and therefore disentitled to maintenance in such cases, and that events must then be left to take their own course (except for advice and persuasion) until the parties themselves come to some agreement.

Further questions regarding *khulʿ* are whether the divorce is immediately effective and the consideration merely a debt enforceable against the wife or whether the divorce is conditional on the payment of the consideration. This, of course, really depends on the exact import of the words used: but this seems to be little understood in Tanganyika, except by a few Liwalis and *shehes*. But in one Lindi case[2] I found a *fatwā*[3] (opinion from a Muslim jurist) written in Arabic stating, in perfectly orthodox form, that a *mubāraʾaʾ*[4] was valid provided the wife was of sound reason and understood the consideration involved.

The practice regarding dissolution of marriage for failure of maintenance seems to be as follows. If the husband is present but fails to support his wife most Liwalis will order the husband to maintain her and then, if he fails to do so, dissolve the marriage—allegedly after the orthodox three days[5]—even, apparently, if the husband could support her if he would, or claims to have property in some other locality.[6] Where the husband is absent but of known whereabouts letters are written, and the marriage is only dissolved (allegedly, again) three days after it has become known that he refuses to maintain her or if there is no news whatever for some ninety days. Where the husband's whereabouts are unknown the matter is given as much publicity as possible, and if there is no news for ninety days the marriage is dissolved.[7] Several Liwalis realised that there was no textual authority for this period of ninety days but that the orthodox Shāfiʿī view held either to three days on the one hand or to an almost complete denial of relief on the other; but they maintained that this period had been adopted as reasonable in Tanganyika in all the circumstances.[8] But other variant views appear, as where two *shehes* testified in a Dar es Salaam case that "even a period of six months' absence without maintenance is sufficient to enable a wife to sue successfully for divorce!"

The Liwali of Tabora, alone, opined that he could and would dissolve a marriage at a wife's request if her husband had deserted her physically for a period of not less than three months. But Ali bin Hemedi and the Liwali of Dar es Salaam, among others, were perfectly aware that the orthodox Shāfiʿī opinion gives no relief on these grounds.[9]

It seems that dissolution of marriage by means of *liʿān* is rare, but not unheard of,[10] that *ẓihār* is even rarer,[11] and that *īlāʾ*[12] is unknown. The triple divorce

[1] As also in the case of cruelty, or any circumstances in which a wife refuses to go on living with her husband.

[2] *Mohamed Selemani* v. *Mohamed Saidi Allay* (File No. 1/355).

[3] Administrative officers, however, are said to dislike the use of written *fatwās* in court cases and much prefer the *shehes* to attend, give evidence as expert witnesses and submit to questioning, etc., by the other party.

[4] A special form of *khulʿ*. See Glossary.

[5] Although others said five or seven days or even in some cases a month. So it may well be that three days represents only a "book" answer. cp. note (8) below.

[6] Ali bin Hemedi, especially, was quite clear on this last point.

[7] But here Ali bin Hemedi opined for waiting only three days.

[8] And virtually replaces the three days, I suspect, in almost all circumstances.

[9] See Appendix C.

[10] See Glossary. The Liwali of Dar es Salaam claimed to have known some three instances; and it had also, apparently, been known in Lindi.

[11] See Glossary. The Liwali of Dar es Salaam claimed to have known two instances and said that, if the husband refused expiation, the marriage might be dissolved after some four months. This is not the normal Shāfiʿī view (and seems confused with *īlāʾ*).

[12] See Glossary.

formula is apparently in common use, and is officially regarded (quite regularly) as valid and binding even when used as an oath or threat. Most of those questioned regarded it as binding, too, if used as a jest, but some thought not.[1] Neither *ta'līq al-ṭalāq* (suspended divorce) nor *tafwīḍ al-ṭalāq* (delegated divorce), seem to be commonly used, but the *taḥlīl* procedure after a triple divorce is not unknown.[2] It seems, moreover, that divorce is exceedingly common in Tanganyika. I was told in Bagamoyo that most old women, if questioned, would be found to have been married as often as, e.g., ten times, and most old men to have had from twelve to twenty wives; that there is no concubinage which is now—officially, at least—regarded as legal,[3] although much illicit concubinage exists; and that most local Muslims have two or three wives, and many have four. It may be added that registration of both marriage and divorce is voluntary in many districts, although attempts are made to encourage it; while in a few localities it is now compulsory.[4]

Suits in respect of adultery may be brought before Liwalis in Tanganyika, as well as before other local courts. The guilty man is fined and, in default of payment, sometimes imprisoned, but the value of the fine and the length of the sentence varies from place to place. In some places the guilty wife seems to go scot free;[5] in others she is liable to a fine, and imprisonment in default; while in yet others she is made to sweep out the court house or some other task which exposes her to public censure.[6] Among non-Muslims the fines, or part thereof, are normally paid to the husband by way of compensation, but in the case of Muslims the fines are paid into court in some localities,[7] while elsewhere Muslims have the option of taking part of the fine as compensation where such an order has been made by the court. In some localities, again, imprisonment, etc., in default of payment is regarded as a punishment under Islamic law (by way of *ta'zīr*—or a punishment at the discretion of the court); but the full Islamic proof of guilt is never required, nor is the Islamic punishment for slander (*qadhf*) ever imposed where accusations are made without such evidence. It seems, moreover, that charges of adultery may be brought among Muslims in Tanganyika by either husband or wife, although accusations by husbands are far more common.[8]

Out in the " bush " local courts seem to apply customary law, in the great majority of cases, without regard for whether the parties are Muslims or not. But in a few instances they claim, particularly where the chiefs concerned are themselves staunch Muslims, to pay some attention to Islamic law—e.g., should the parties to some matrimonial cause demand the application of the Sharī'a (which is itself unlikely) some chiefs will ask a local *shehe* for his opinion, or discourage a divorce of which he disapproves. But it is clear that customary law in general prevails, even among such inland tribes as are predominantly Muslim.[9]

Regarding legitimacy, again, some curious cases occur. The normal Shāfi'ī rule, of course, is that a child born within four years of a woman's widowhood or

---

[1] e.g., the leading *shehe* of Tabora, etc.

[2] See Glossary.

[3] But see above, pp. 22, 27, 30, 48, 76 and 118.

[4] Yet even there an unregistered marriage or divorce would be perfectly valid.

[5] e.g., Tanga, unless (I was told) the husband demanded her imprisonment.

[6] e.g., Dar es Salaam. This, apparently, is very effective, is welcomed by husbands, corresponds with certain customary punishments, and is considered very much preferable to the moral dangers of imprisonment.

[7] Because local Muslim opinion rightly regards it as incorrect to accept financial compensation in such circumstances.

[8] So I was informed by the Liwali of Mwanza, for instance.

[9] In some districts compensation for adultery may only be claimed twice, after which the aggrieved husband may make no further claim in regard to the same offender. In other localities the compensation in respect of a first offence usually represents one-quarter of the bride-price, and for the second offence one-half.

irrevocable divorce is regarded as the legitimate child of her former husband unless she has either remarried (after claiming that her *'idda*[1] period has come to an end) at least six months before its birth or already given birth to a child during the intervening period. In a country where Islamic law was applied in its entirety such a rule would, no doubt, serve as a valuable, if somewhat fantastic, protection for both mother and child. But in a country such as Tanganyika divorced wives who give birth to a child some two years after the dissolution of their marriage often vehemently maintain that this was a child of adultery, and therefore theirs alone, against their former husband's claim of paternity. In one case,[2] for instance, a husband who had divorced his wife claimed a child who was born to her sixteen months later; while the woman's brother maintained that the spouses had in fact been separated for two years before the divorce,[3] that the woman had aborted subsequently, and that the child under dispute was a child of adultery. On appeal the Governor's Appeal Board held that the four-year rule of Shāfi'ī law amounted to a mere matter of presumption and was a very different thing from saying that " the child belongs to the ex-husband " in such circumstances. " It is clear to the Board (*sic*) that the law is concerned to *presume* legitimacy and not to *deem* it, and, where clear evidence is forthcoming that the child was not born of the union, then the presumption is rebutted." But although this judgment can derive some support from judgments in India and Zanzibar to the effect that the four-year rule can no longer be applied by the courts in places where the Indian Evidence Act is in force, yet there can be little question that their summary of the basis and nature of this rule is incorrect according to the pure Sharī'a, where it must be regarded as an extension of the rule that any child born to a married woman is regarded as her husband's[4]; while it has already been noted that the Evidence Act, etc., are not applicable in the local courts. The only point in doubt in Sharī'a law in this particular case concerned the question of the alleged abortion, for if a real abortion or miscarriage could have been proved then the child under dispute would have been regarded as the second child born to his mother since her divorce, and would not, therefore, be attributed to her former husband. Quite a different type of dispute regarding legitimacy, on the other hand, concerned two Muslims[5] who lived together out of wedlock and had two daughters. When these approached puberty the father wished to pay the sum customary among non-Muslims in such circumstances and claim the daughters as his, but his Muslim wife's non-Muslim father rejected this claim on the grounds that Islamic law was applicable and gave no such privilege (although it seems that he was willing to agree at a black-market price!). Here the native court concerned decided according to customary law; the District Commissioner decided according to Islamic law; the Provincial Commissioner upheld the native court; and the Governor's Appeal Board, apparently, upheld the District Commissioner's judgment. It seems, moreover, that the parties continued to live together, and that the " husband " had paid dower for his " wife " after the birth of the children. In general, moreover, it seems clear that the Liwalis insist that an acknowledgment of paternity must be formal to be effective, although the test upheld by assessors in one Dar es Salaam appeal case was whether a father had " during his lifetime treated (her) as his daughter and arranged her marriage " —i.e., the test of implied acknowledgment, by behaviour. This corresponds to

[1] See Glossary.

[2] *Omar bin Mihombo* v. *Abdulla Ali* (Secretariat File 13879/82).

[3] This, of course, was quite irrelevant.

[4] Except in very rare circumstances. It is, however, noteworthy that in Ibāḍī law this rule (which they in any case limit to two years) is regarded as a rebutable presumption in certain circumstances. See p. 75 above.

[5] *Abdulla Juma* v. *Kaluli Kashaga* (Tabora case).

the attitude taken by the courts in India, while the insistence on formal acknowledgmen[4] represents the pure Sharī'a.

I came across very few cases regarding slavery. In one such a daughter had been born to a father from a slave wife,[1] and the father subsequently "assisted his nephew to buy (his daughter) as his wife." When, therefore, the father's heirs denied that this daughter was entitled to inherit on the grounds that she was a slave, it was held that the fact that her father had helped his nephew to buy her was sufficient indication that she must have been set free. In another[2] a mother had owned a slave woman, by whom, on the former's death, one of her sons had a child: and when the other heirs tried to exclude this child from inheritance as illegitimate it was held that she was in fact legitimate, as her father had been part-owner of her mother. There can be little doubt, however, that claims to inherit as patron, or as descendant of the liberator of the ancestors of the *de cujus,* would still be upheld in most Liwalis' courts,[3] as would also, I suspect, the claim to inherit of a child born to a man in concubinage with a woman who would have been his slave but for the abolition of slavery.[4]

In regard to the custody of children, the usual Shāfi'ī rule seems to be generally known that both boys and girls go to the mother, unless she be disqualified for some reason, up till the age of discernment (e.g., seven), after which they have an option; and most Liwalis profess to apply this: but it seems distinctly doubtful how genuine an option is really given to the children in such cases.

Again, the normal Shāfi'ī rules regarding inheritance are widely known, a fact which can be largely attributed to an excellent booklet on the subject in Swahili by Ali bin Hemedi, with an English translation by Mr. (now Sir Philip) Mitchell.[5] But continual difficulties and problems arise from the fact that Christianity, Islam and paganism are often professed in Tanganyika by different members of a single family, and also by the fact—already noted—that Muslims frequently contract marriages which are of very doubtful validity in Islamic law. It is quite clear, moreover, that the Liwalis as a whole have little knowledge—and less regard—for the clauses of the Administration (Small Estates) (Amendment) Ordinance which decree that, "where the Governor in Council has made an order or the district court has given a direction" that the provisions of this Ordinance are to apply to the estates of certain deceased natives, then the estate of a member of a native tribe shall be administered by tribal law unless he not only professed Islam but gave some explicit intimation that he wished his estate to be distributed under Muhammadan law, while in the case of a Swahili, on the other hand, Islamic law must be applied unless the deceased had given some explicit or implicit indication of a desire to the contrary.[6] Instead, they adopt the uncompromising attitude (which is, of course, perfectly correct in Islamic law) that if the deceased professed Islam at all then his estate must be administered accordingly. Similarly, most of them seem not to know, and none of them would be willing to apply, the provisos designed to protect one who has renounced Islam.[7]

---

[1] *Mohamed bin Issa* v. *Njanja bin Hamisi,* Lindi Case No. 1/283.

[2] *Mohamed Atiki* v. *Mohamed Salim Mohamedi,* Lindi Case No. 1/356.

[3] But it seems much more doubtful whether British courts, or even the Central Court of Appeal, would uphold such decisions [see above p. 118]—and some Liwalis might reflect the British attitude in such matters. But cp. *Mirathi* p. 13 (note): see below.

[4] See above, p. 142 note (3). But this is by no means certain in Tanganyika.

[5] *Mirathi.* Reprinted in Nairobi, 1949.

[6] See p. 127 above. And whereas the application of this Ordinance is not within the jurisdiction of any local court, the now repealed Deceased Native Estates Ordinance, with its identical provisions in this respect, was within the Liwalis' competence for a number of years.

[7] But such a convert could, of course, apply to the district court for relief—in the somewhat unlikely contingency that he had any knowledge of the relevant legislation.

In practice, however, some Liwalis are less uncompromising than in theory. Thus the Liwali of Dar es Salaam adopts the attitude that in the case of first generation Muslims the full force of Islamic law cannot reasonably be applied and that where, in particular, they have expressed a clear intention which transgresses its terms their wishes should be respected.[1] But other Liwalis will have none of this distinction. It seems, however, that almost all of them try to settle difficult cases by informal arbitration,[2] and that it is only if they are driven to give a formal judgment that they feel bound to follow the letter of the law. Another way out of such difficulties in the case of the new convert, moreover, is that minor children are regularly regarded as following the religion of their father, and some Liwalis would extend this even to the major children of a convert to Islam if they have not been formally—and unsuccessfully—summoned to accept that religion; while in such cases a marriage which was valid according to their former "*mila*"[3] would, of course, normally be unchallenged.[4] It also seems clear that Chiefs' courts regularly follow tribal and not Islamic law in all matters of succession, in the case of Muslims and non-Muslims alike. In most parts of Tanganyika the tribal system is patrilineal and patrilocal, and a man's estate goes exclusively to his children (the boys taking the lion's share), while widow and parent have no legal claim: but there are a few tribes which follow the matrilineal system.[5] Similarly, tribal marriages are, naturally, regarded as valid by these courts, virtually without distinction of religion. And in Tabora even the Liwali seems to take scarcely any account of the religion of the claimants to an estate.[6]

Bequests seem rare, but in regard to the few there are the ordinary Shāfi'ī rules are apparently applied.[7] There is, moreover, no statutory limitation to that excessive fragmentation of estates in land to which the Islamic law of inheritance so often gives rise, but I was told that in the towns (where alone, practically speaking, this would occur) the heirs usually agree to obviate uneconomic fragmentation by selling the land and dividing the price, or by one taking it over and compensating the others.

Waqfs exist in the coastal towns, mostly of the "public" or "charitable" variety, but there seem to be few, if any, inland. I heard some demand for the appointment of Waqf Commissioners, to take general oversight over all waqfs; but not very much. A vital point in any Ordinance to set up such a Commission would, of course, be the powers it was to wield. Only Ali bin Hemedi, when questioned, seemed to stand by the orthodox Shāfi'ī view that no waqf property may be sold, even with consent of court, although even he admitted that the court might authorise a very long lease, etc., in any case of need. But the Liwalis of Dar es Salaam, Lindi, Mikindani, Bagamoyo, etc., held that such property might even be sold if this seemed necessary (except in the case of mosques, cemeteries, etc.), by consent of court, although some of them realised

---

[1] e.g., in a case where a first generation Muslim asked that one-third of her estate should go to relatives who happened to be Muslims, and two-third to relatives who were not, he allowed this to be done.

[2] An example given to me was that where the two claimants to an estate were a sister of whose claim there was no question and a daughter whose claim was questionable the sister might be persuaded to accept $\frac{5}{8}$ and leave $\frac{3}{8}$ to the daughter.

[3] Swahili: presumably, from the Arabic *milla*.

[4] Where, however, a Muslim in a coastal town marries, e.g., a Muslim, a Christian and a pagan wife—as occasionally seems to happen in Tanganyika—but only the first by regular Islamic contract, the children of the other two will be regarded as illegitimate and as following the religion of their mother.

[5] e.g., the Yao, in the South West (cp. the Nyasaland section of this Survey).

[6] e.g., he told me that if a Muslim died leaving only two brothers, one a Muslim and one a pagan, he would grant them equal rights. And this may well be typical of inland Liwalis.

[7] See the Administration (Small Estates) (Amendment) Ordinance, sect. 19(1).

that this was a view derived from other than the orthodox Shāfi'ī opinion.[1] Very few family waqfs seem to exist in the Territory, so the complications raised by the unfortunate decision of the Privy Council in the Indian case of *Abul Fata* v. *Russomoy,* which has necessitated the promulgation of Mussalman Waqf Validating Acts in India, Aden, Zanzibar, Kenya, etc., have not yet made themselves felt. But it is noteworthy that by Shāfi'ī law a "family" waqf is valid even without any ultimate dedication whatever to charitable purposes which cannot fail; and that after the failure of named beneficiaries the income would be paid to the nearest relative of the founder in such circumstances.

In many parts of the Territory there are *shehes* or *walimu* who earn a living, in most cases, by teaching groups of pupils and by giving *fatwās*. Even Liwalis will sometimes call them to court to give their opinion on some knotty point, and usually accept this opinion when given[2]—and the same applies, occasionally, to Chiefs' courts. Some of these *shehes* are reasonably learned, while others are extremely ignorant. It seems, however, that both Liwalis and *shehes* in Tanganyika are less tied to Ibn Ḥajar's opinion than those in, e.g., Somaliland and Aden, and most of them appeared to put the *Mughnī* and the *Nihāya* much on a par with the *Tuḥfa*.[3] Many maintained, moreover, that not only might an individual Muslim follow which of the great Imāms he pleased in each particular point, but that even a Qāḍī or Muftī might in case of need forsake the most authoritative view in his school in favour of the rule laid down by some other recognised authority which seemed to provide the solution required by the circumstances of the case. And I found a ready acceptance of the principle which upholds the validity of any instructions issued by the Ruler as to which of certain variant views the courts are to apply.[4]

There are, in fact, a number of points which seem to require such elucidation in Tanganyika. Such include the legality of dissolution of marriage for repeated acts of cruelty; the permissibility of forced *khul'* where a wife deserts her husband[5] and refuses to return, or where the parties prove incompatible, etc.; the conditions under which a wife whose husband fails to support her can obtain dissolution of marriage; the position of the children of Muslim parents by a "tribal" marriage; and various inheritance problems—regarding all of which considerable uncertainty and lack of uniformity prevails. This situation could almost certainly be remedied by the issue of, e.g., Judicial Circulars along the lines indicated in Appendix A and C to this Survey—issued either in Tanganyika alone or in all the East African territories. In addition, it is suggested that questions of inheritance would be much clarified if in place of the express or implied intention for which section 18 of the Administration (Small Estates) (Amendment) Ordinance now provides it were clearly laid down that, in the case of members of an African tribe, tribal law must be applied unless the deceased had made an express declaration to some administrative officer that he wished his estate to be governed by Islamic law; and, in the case of a Swahili, etc., that Islamic law would be applied in the absence of an express declaration of a desire to the contrary. This would not only provide a far more definite test—and one applicable, perhaps, by the Liwalis and other local courts—but would also give the administrative officer concerned the opportunity to ask the applicant a few pertinent questions about his non-Muslim relations and about any issue by tribal marriages.[6] Again, an enormous amount of useful information relevant to both Islamic and customary

[1] Almost certainly, in their case, from the Ibāḍīs (see above).
[2] Administrative officers, etc., regard this as expert testimony to the law.
[3] cp. above, p. 22 note (3), etc.
[4] This is the basis on which all the recent reforms of Sharī'a law in the Middle East have been promulgated, for all (in theory, at least) represent no more than an authoritative choice between variant opinions.
[5] The present position makes adultery almost certain in such circumstances.
[6] See above, pp. 115 ff., in the Kenya section of this Survey.

law could be obtained in Tanganyika, particularly, by the issue of a suitable questionnaire to all District Officers regarding the extent to which Islamic law (real or professed) is in fact applied and the precise provisions included thereunder; the extent to which customary law prevails and the local variations in its content; and the extent, if at all, to which these two systems have become fused or intermingled.

It is also worthy of consideration whether the Indian Dissolution of Muslim Marriages Act, 1939, should not be applied to Indians domiciled in the Territory.[1] Alternatively it might, of course, be given general application: but this would probably be too rapid a reform for local Shāfiʿī opinion, and cause consternation to the Liwalis who would in most cases have to apply it. Finally, it seems essential that the Central Court of Appeal should come to a clear decision as to the attitude it intends to adopt towards certain cases of conflict between Islamic and customary law on the one hand, and towards some of the variant opinions even in the Shāfiʿī school—to say nothing of the other schools of Islamic law—on the other. Only then will it be in a position to give consistent and authoritative decisions.

[1] Again, see Appendix E.

UGANDA

The statutory basis for the application of any Islamic law which may in fact be applied in the Uganda Protectorate must be sought either in the express provisions of some relevant Ordinance or in the usual reference, in the Uganda Order in Council, 1902, to the applicability of " native law "—in so far, that is, as Islamic law may be held to have become the " native law " of any section of the community.[1] For the rest, the provisions of the Order in Council correspond so closely to those of the Kenya Colony Order in Council, 1921, and the Tanganyika Order in Council, 1920 (for both of which it evidently served as a model), that no quotation of its terms seems to be necessary.

The outstanding Uganda Ordinance which concerns Islamic law is the Marriage and Divorce of Muhammadans Ordinance, 1906. This provides that the Marriage Ordinance and the Marriage of Africans Ordinance shall not apply to marriages between persons both of whom profess the Muhammadan religion and neither of whom is a party to an existing marriage, under or declared valid by the said Ordinances, with any person other than a Muhammadan[2]; that every marriage previously celebrated between Muhammadans shall be deemed to have been a legal and valid marriage[3]; and that for the future " All marriages between persons professing the Muhammadan religion, and all divorces from such marriages celebrated or given according to the rites and observances of the Muhammadan religion customary and usual among the tribe or sect in which the marriage or divorce takes place, shall be valid and registered as herein provided."[4] Provisions concerning registrars, records, applications and enquiries follow, the only points of particular interest being that the Ordinance expressly provides that in the case of a divorce between " persons of the Shī'a[5] sect " there must be two witnesses,[6] that a divorce of " the kind known as *khul'* "[7] is clearly distinguished from other forms,[8] and that the right of guardians to act for minors is recognised.[9] But, although parties become liable to punishment by fine or imprisonment if they fail to register their marriages and divorces,[10] it is expressly stated that "Nothing in this Ordinance shall be construed to (*a*) render invalid, merely by reason if its not having been registered, any Muhammadan marriage or divorce which would otherwise be valid; (*b*) render valid, by reason of its having been registered, any such marriage or divorce which would otherwise be invalid ".[11] Again, " Nothing in the Divorce Ordinance shall authorise the grant of any relief under that Ordinance where the marriage of the parties has been declared valid under this Ordinance: provided that nothing herein contained shall prevent any competent court from granting relief under Muhammadan law; and Her Majesty's High Court of Uganda, and any court to which jurisdiction shall, by notice, be specially given by the Governor, shall have jurisdiction herein."[12] Schedules for the registration of both marriages and divorces are provided, regarding which it need only be remarked that provision is made for the marriage of minor boys and girls by their guardians[13]; that the name

[1] See the discussion of this controversial point in the Introduction to this Survey.
[2] Sect. 2. [3] Sect. 2.
[4] Sect. 3.
[5] Spelt " Shiah ": but see Introduction regarding the spelling of Arabic words in this Survey, to avoid confusion and possible misunderstanding.
[6] Sect. 9. This is perfectly correct law.
[7] Spelt " Khula ": but see Introduction for spelling of Arabic words.
[8] See sects. 6(2) and 9(*b*) (i). In this case the wife, as well as the husband, must register the *khul'*.
[9] Sect. 6(1) (Proviso). [10] Sect. 18.
[11] Sect. 17.
[12] Sect. 19. Jurisdiction has in fact been given to all First-Class Magistrates.
[13] But see pp. 152, 3.

of the guardian of the bride need not be specified if she is major;[1] that full details concerning dower, both prompt and deferred, etc., must be provided; and that, in the case of divorces, the manner in which they were effected must be recorded.

The points which call for immediate comment in this Ordinance are, firstly, that, unlike its counterpart in Kenya, it is confined to questions of marriage and divorce and makes no mention of succession—a matter to which we must return later; secondly, that the phrase in section 3 " according to the rites and observances of the Muhammadan religion customary and usual among the tribe or sect " gives ample scope for the recognition of the different schools of law,[2] together with local variations (if any), and the phrase in section 19 about any competent court " granting relief under Muhammadan law " must presumably be construed accordingly; but, thirdly, that it is not altogether clear whether a woman married by customary law could, on embracing Islam, conclude a valid marriage with a Muslim under this Ordinance.[3]

It must, however, also be observed that the Marriage of Africans Ordinance, 1903, formerly applied where the parties both professed either the Christian or Muhammadan religion, until replaced in the latter case by this Ordinance. But the Marriage Ordinance, 1902, would still be applicable to Muslims in certain circumstances, e.g.—

(1) A Muslim man who marries a Christian woman under the Marriage Ordinance may neither contract another legal marriage nor divorce his wife except under the terms of the Divorce Ordinance—although he would be free to marry up to three more wives or divorce his wife for any or no reason under Islamic law.

(2) A Muslim girl who has reached twenty-one may marry a non-Muslim under the Marriage Ordinance, and so may a girl of under that age if her father, or (if he be dead, insane or absent from the Protectorate) her mother, etc., gives consent in writing—although such a union is utterly precluded under Muhammadan law.

(3) A non-Muslim man married under either the Marriage Ordinance or the Marriage of Africans Ordinance who subsequently embraced Islam would not thereby be in a position to divorce his wife or remarry (or, indeed, to regard his marriage as automatically dissolved) except as provided in the Divorce Ordinance, regardless of the position under Islamic law.

(4) Similarly, a non-Muslim woman married under either of these two Ordinances who subsequently embraced Islam would still be bound by her former marriage, although this is regarded as automatically dissolved, if her husband be a non-Muslim and refuses to accept Islam, under the Sharī'a.

(5) It may be added that bigamy under this Ordinance includes the act, on the part of one married thereunder, of contracting a marriage under native law and custom and is punishable by imprisonment for up to five years[4]: and here this wording would presumably include a second marriage under Muhammadan law, whether registered or not. However this may be, moreover, the definition of bigamy in the Penal Code, section 161, which reads: " Any person who, having a husband or wife living, goes through a ceremony of marriage which is void by reason of its taking place during the life of such husband or wife, is guilty of a felony . . ." is clearly applicable to a Muhammadan marriage. And it seems

---

[1] See pp. 152, 3.

[2] Contrast the Kenya Muhammadan Marriage, Divorce and Succession Ordinance.

[3] cp. sect. 2 of this Ordinance with sect. 11(*d*) of the Marriage Ordinance and sect. 10 of the Marriage of Africans Ordinance.

[4] Sect. 52.

equally clear that sections 160 and 162 of the Penal Code, which concern fraudulent pretence of marriage, would similarly apply to such a marriage under Muhammadan law; while it is also noteworthy in this context that although the Uganda Penal Code provides no penalty for the premature consummation of a child marriage, yet section 130, which provides that "Any person who, with intent to marry or carnally know a woman of any age, or to cause her to be married or carnally known by any other person, takes her away, or detains her, against her will, is guilty of a felony . . . ", might possibly expose to prosecution a Muslim father whose actions might have been quite unexceptionable under the principles of Islamic law governing his right to give his minor, or in some schools[1] major,[2] daughter in compulsory marriage.

Matters, however, are far less clear with regard to succession. The Succession Ordinance, 1906, provides that "Except as provided by this Ordinance, or by any other law . . . the rules herein contained shall constitute the law of Uganda applicable to all cases of intestate and testamentary succession"[3] and proceeds to lay down detailed rules for the distribution of estates on intestacy in Parts IV and V, for wills, codicils and bequests in Parts VII-XXVII, for gifts made in contemplation of death in Part XXVIII, and for the grant of probate and letters of administration in Parts XXIX-XXXIV; while the only mention of Muslims throughout the Ordinance is in section 50, where it is merely provided that the rules about the signing and witnessing of wills shall in no way "affect the validity of any will made by a Muhammadan or a native according to the provisions of Muhammadan law or native custom, as the case may be." But by a separate Order (dated 22nd January, 1906) the estates of all the natives of the Protectorate were exempted from the operation of the Succession Ordinance "and the estates of Muhammadans from the provisions of Part V of the Ordinance" (a phrase which was presumably intended to include the initial provisions regarding the distribution of an estate on intestacy in Part IV as well as their continuation in Part V).

The position, then, is somewhat confused. The Ordinance does not apply to natives of the Protectorate at all, whether Muslims or not, whose testate and intestate succession is in all cases governed by customary law; but to this we must recur later. As for such Muslims as are not natives, one would suppose that they were specifically exempted from the relevant provisions of this Ordinance in order that their own personal law with regard to intestate succession—a matter very dear to their hearts—might be applied; and this interpretation, which must admittedly rest on a rather unsatisfactory argument of implication, seems to find strong support in the express reference to "Muhammadan law" regarding the validity of wills in section 50. But in *Re Mahomed Habash. Vasila* v. *Worsta Sophia* (1920), 3 U.L.R. 26, the High Court of Uganda held that, in so far as the immovable property of deceased non-native Muslims was concerned, the rules as to intestate succession were those laid down by English law, while the report also states that the law as to intestacy in regard to the movable property of such Muslims is that of their domicile.[4] This decision presumably rests on the dual consideration that the exemption of non-native Muslims from the relevant provisions of the Succession Ordinance leaves the law as it was before that Ordinance was passed, and that no statutory authority for the application of Islamic law in such cases exists: but it seems most unlikely that the Governor expressly excepted non-native Muslims from rules of succession applicable to all other non-natives in Uganda just in order that the relevant provisions of the law of England should in their case be retained. Again, it seems that such Muslims

[1] cf., the Shāfi'ī and Mālikī schools.
[2] Provided she was still a virgin, etc.
[3] Sect. 2.
[4] i.e., again, English law, in the case of those domiciled in the Protectorate.

may make wills which are Islamic in form but need not be so in content—i.e., that they may make them orally in the presence of two witnesses, on the one hand, but may thereby bequeath, e.g., the whole of their estate, whether to an "heir" or to a non-heir, on the other. Again, section 105 provides that "No man, having a nephew or niece or any nearer relative, shall have power to bequeath any property to religious or charitable uses, except by a will executed not less than twelve months before his death"; and this would presumably have the somewhat curious effect that where a Muslim made a bequest which was perfectly valid in Islamic law but which contravened this section, the bequest would be void and the property so bequeathed would be distributed according to English rules for intestate succession (or Muhammadan rules, in the intention of the Governor?).

The meaning of the exemption of "natives of the Protectorate" from the above Ordinance is elucidated by the Interpretation (Definition of "Native") Ordinance, 1945. This provides that the term "native" means "any person who is a member of, or any one of those parents is or was a member of, an indigenous African tribe or community, but the term "native" shall not include:—

(*a*) an Arab, an Abyssinian (Amhara, Tigre and Shoa), a Somali, a Seychellois, a Baluchi born in Africa, a Malagasy or a Comoro Islander: Provided that any of the said persons may for the purposes of this Ordinance be declared a "native" . . . if of his own motion he proves . . . that he is living among members of any indigenous African tribe or community in accordance with their customary mode of life;

(*b*) any person who, of his own motion, proves

(i) that he is partly of non-native descent; and

(ii) that he is not living among members of any indigenous African tribe or community in accordance with their customary mode of life."[1]

No comment need be made here on the Crown Lands Ordinance, 1903, the Crown Lands (Declaration) Ordinance, 1922, the Crown Lands (Amendment) Ordinance, 1949, the Land Regulations Ordinance, 1897, the Registration of Titles Ordinance, 1922 (as amended), the Buganda Land Law of 1908 (amended 1942)[2] and Land Succession Law of 1912, or the Land Transfer Ordinance, 1944; as there is no question, in Uganda, of the application of the provisions of Islamic law in regard to immovable property: but it is, perhaps, worth notice in passing that the last named Ordinance precludes any "non-native or person acting as his agent," without the written consent of the Governor, from occupying or entering into possession of any land of which a native is registered as proprietor or from making any contract to purchase, lease or accept as a gift or bequest any such land or any interest therein "other than as a security for money." It is also sufficient to observe that the Oaths Ordinance, 1907, is virtually identical with the Indian Oaths Act applied in Kenya and the Oaths Decree promulgated in Zanzibar.[3]

With regard to the courts, the Subordinate Courts Ordinance, 1940, provides that the subordinate courts thereby constituted "shall exercise both criminal and civil jurisdiction and shall have concurrent jurisdiction with any native court established in accordance with the Native Courts Ordinance, 1940, unless by the said Ordinance or other law express provision is made to the contrary: Provided that, subject to any directions of the High Court . . . the practice relating to the distribution of work as between subordinate and native courts in the

---

[1] Sect. 2.

[2] In order to bring it into line with the policy later laid down in the Land Transfer Ordinance, 1944 (see immediately below).

[3] See above, pp. 101 and 60.

Protectorate . . . shall continue to be observed."[1] Similarly, the Native Courts Ordinance, 1940, provides that " Subject to any limitation contained in its warrant or in this or any other law," a native court may exercise jurisdiction over all causes and matters where, in civil cases, all parties are natives or, in criminal cases, the accused is a native[2]—and the term native is here to include any person whose tribe is a tribe of the Protectorate or of the Colony or Protectorate of Kenya, the Tanganyika Territory, Nyasaland, the Sudan, the Belgian Congo, and the Trust Territory of Ruanda-Urundi, and includes a Swahili.[3] It may also be authorised to " exercise jurisdiction over classes of persons who are not natives within the meaning of this Ordinance but who, having regard to their general mode of life, may . . . be made amenable to the jurisdiction of such court."[4] But offences in consequence of which death is alleged to have occurred, proceedings concerning marriage or divorce under the Marriage Ordinance, the Marriage of Africans Ordinance, or the Divorce Ordinance " unless it is a claim arising only in regard to bride-price or adultery and founded only on native law and custom " (and the same, apparently, is true of cases under the Marriage and Divorce of Muhammadans Ordinance, although not mentioned here, under section 19 thereof), proceedings affecting the title to or any interest in land registered under the Registration of Titles Ordinance, and proceedings under any Ordinance or English or Indian law in force in the Protectorate (except by special authorisation) are expressly excluded from the jurisdiction of native courts.[5] The law they are to enforce may be summed up as (*a*) the native law and custom of their area so far as this is applicable and not repugnant to natural justice and morality or in conflict with any other law; (*b*) the provisions of rules and orders by Provincial Commissioners, District Commissioners or native authorities; and (*c*) any Ordinance or other law where so authorised,[6] under a system of practice and procedure " in accordance with native law and custom."[7] Both magistrates and authorised chiefs[8] have the right of access to the native courts in their areas, and magistrates have wide powers of revision.[9] Appeals are allowed as specified in the warrants establishing the native courts concerned[10]; while the High Court may itself exercise powers of revision regarding original, revisional or appellate proceedings where it deems this necessary.[11] In Buganda, however, a special Ordinance, the Buganda Courts Ordinance, 1940, replaces this Ordinance: but the provisions are very similar except in matters of detail and regarding the special powers granted thereunder to the Lukiko court (now termed the " Principal Court ").

The Law Reports include very few cases in which the High Court of Uganda has applied Muhammadan law. From these few, however, two points of interest seem to emerge, namely that it has been authoritatively ruled that the law regarding marriage equality (*kafā'a*) is " obsolete " in Uganda, in the sense that if an adult woman marries herself without her guardian's consent to a husband who is not her " equal " the court will not annul the marriage at the guardian's request[12]; while it has also been held that " parents in Uganda have no authority

[1] Sect. 4(1).
[2] Sect. 8(1).
[3] Sect. 2.
[4] Sect. 8(2).
[5] Sect. 10.
[6] Sect. 11.
[7] Sect. 18.
[8] Chiefs may in suitable cases forward the record, with their remarks, to the court to which an appeal lies.
[9] Sects. 23 and 24.
[10] Sect. 25.
[11] Sects. 26 and 27.
[12] *Fazalan Bibi* v. *Tehran Bibi and Mahomed Din Kashmiri* (1921), 8 K.L.R. 200.

to contract for the marriage of their children whether Muhammadans or not."[1] The latter case concerned an action brought by a prospective husband to enforce a betrothal concluded by a father without his daughter's consent, but from the tenor of the judgments delivered it may, it seems, be inferred that an actual contract of marriage concluded in such circumstances by a father's right of compulsion would have been annulled—particularly, perhaps, in the case of an adult but virgin daughter under Shāfiʿī law.

Circumstances did not permit me to visit any parts of Uganda outside Buganda. Elsewhere there are pockets of Muslims, such as at Arua, on the borders of the Congo north of Lake Albert, and Gulu and Kitgum, both in Acholi. Islam reached Uganda, of course, both from the coast of East Africa, whence Arab traders began to penetrate the country more than a century ago and gained considerable influence, and from the Sudan, through the armed forces of Emin Pasha and others, some of whom settled in the country. The descendants of these *ʿaskarīs* and those who, from long association with them, have lost all connection with the tribes from which they originally sprang, are termed "*nūbīs* "; while recognised settlements of these *nūbīs* are termed " *mulkīs*." Some of these ex-soldiers were formerly, at least, regarded as having the right to claim to be tried by British courts, while it was also suggested[2] that in *mulkī* settlements special " *nūbī* native courts " should be established. But it seems that the former privilege is never claimed and that the latter recommendation has never been put into effect, largely because no exclusively *mulkī* settlements appear to exist. Those natives of Uganda whose attachment to Islam can be traced to the coast might be expected to be Shāfiʿīs, and those whose attachment can be traced to the Sudan Mālikīs, but the distinction, if it ever existed, has tended to become more and more blurred, and little trace of genuinely Mālikī principles appears to have survived.

The only *mulkī* settlement which I was able to visit was in Bomba, where I interviewed the two Imāms in the presence of many of the leading *nūbīs*. The Imāms maintained that marriages in Bomba were concluded according to Sharīʿa law, but that they would decline to conclude a marriage contract by " *jabr* "[3] directly against the bride's wishes, however correct this might be under Shāfiʿī law, because of Government disapproval. If, moreover, a wife were to claim dissolution of marriage for failure of maintenance or for persistent cruelty the senior of the two alleged that he would grant this; and he even averred that he had in fact done so, once for each of these reasons, during the last eight years. But questions of intestate succession go by *nūbī* custom, the children being the sole heirs (and the boys getting the lion's share), for neither spouse relict nor parent gets any share at all: and where there is no child the brother takes his place. Legacies are apparently unknown. This means that even here customary rather than Islamic law prevails, except in certain matrimonial causes. There is, moreover, no *nūbī* court in Bomba, although the Imāms act as unofficial arbitrators whose decision, in matters of marriage in particular, would generally be accepted. But elsewhere, as we have seen, it has been recommended at least that *mulkī* settlements should have their own courts to apply their own customary law, which has unquestionably been influenced to some extent by the Sharīʿa. And it may be added in this context that I understand that in the considerable Arab and Swahili colony of Mbale there used previously to be a person recognised by the community as their Qāḍī who disposed of matrimonial affairs, and even, perhaps, matters relating to inheritance, under Islamic law, but who had no

---

[1] *Fazaldin Satardin* v. *Din Mahomed and Hajra Begum* (1928), 11 K.L.R. 41.

[2] *Handbook on Native Courts,* 1941.

[3] A father's right of compulsion. See Glossary.

official *locus standi* under any Courts Ordinance or similar legislation. Presumably, however, Islamic law was regarded as " native law " in such circumstances, since in such colonies the latter would be largely assimilated to the former.

From conversations with the Kabaka, with Prince Badru Kakunguru (the leading Muslim of Buganda), with the Omulamuzi (Chief Justice) with certain Saza and Gombolola chiefs, and with several imāms, teachers and leaders of rival factions (in addition, of course, to several British officers), the following facts emerged.

Out of the twenty Sazas (counties) into which Buganda is divided, the chiefs of two are regularly Muslims, while every county has its quota of those who profess Islam. There are no Muhammadan courts, for even the courts of those chiefs who are themselves Muslims apply the same customary law as do those of the other chiefs: but there is a Muslim Religious Council in Kampala which has certain rather nebulous functions.

Muslim marriages are normally concluded with the help of a *mwalimu* and therefore in a form which is at least approximately correct; and in general they are registered by a registrar, as provided in the Ordinance. If a Muslim contracts a " customary " marriage which is not in the proper Islamic form, this is regarded as an irregular union in the eyes of Islamic orthodoxy but not, of course, by the people at large: and since inheritance goes by customary law the children of such unions would not be disinherited, although among Muslims the " principal heir " is, normally, said to be the son of a regular marriage.[1] The right of fathers to give their virgin daughters compulsorily in marriage (*jabr*) is said not to be exercised in Buganda today. The Omulamuzi quoted one instance of a girl so married who escaped and reported the matter to the Gombolola court, which referred the case to the District Commissioner, whereupon the marriage was declared null and void. More, girls used, apparently, sometimes to go so far as to hang themselves in such cases, while others resolutely demanded the dissolution of their marriages. So although the right of *jabr* is recognised in theory, and most daughters would no doubt acquiesce, yet fathers would seldom persist if their daughters were adamant, partly because it would be against custom and partly because most *walimu* and registrars would in such cases refuse their services for fear of Government disapproval. If such a contract were in fact performed and a dispute arose the case would apparently be referred to the Muslim Religious Council, which would probably arrange a dissolution of marriage for return of dower: but the case might also be taken to the District Commissioner or the High Court, which would almost certainly annul the marriage. Marriage before the age of about fifteen is, apparently, contrary to custom.

Since, however, the dower, even among Muslim Baganda, is always paid to the father, his consent is virtually essential to his daughter's marriage—and most *walimu* at least would refuse to conclude a contract of marriage without it. Not infrequently, of course, the daughter of an obstinate father will elope with her lover; and in such circumstances the father will in most cases eventually see reason and agree to regularise the union: but only if she is under twenty can he recover her by force of law.[2] Disputes about marriage " equality " are virtually unknown, largely no doubt because the consent of both the girl and her father are normally regarded as essential to a marriage; while when I asked if a bride might claim the dower as her own property I was told that this never actually happens, as women do not know the Sharī'a!

If a Muslim woman runs away from her husband, and he desires restitution of conjugal rights (*ṭā'a*), it is to the registrar of marriages that he will usually go

[1] It seems very doubtful, however, how much substance there is in this claim.

[2] The Buganda Adultery and Fornication Law, sect. 7.

in the first place. If, however, the latter fails to arrange matters and the husband demands either restitution or return of dower, the case will probably be referred (whether by the registrar or the husband's chief, if he takes his complaint to him) to the Muslim Religious Council, which will first tell the wife to return to her husband and then, if she refuses,[1] will tell her father to refund the dower (or bride-price). Should he do so and the husband decline to accept it the latter would be persuaded to relent: but if he proved adamant, or the wife's father persisted in refusing to pay up, the case would have to be referred to the Protectorate courts—unless an action for return of bride-price under purely customary law were brought in the Buganda courts. And the Protectorate courts, apparently, will usually order the wife to return to her husband or pay suitable compensation (whether this represents an exact refund of the bride-price or not), chiefly, it seems, on the ground that this accords with local custom, even among Muslims.

Where a wife claims dissolution of marriage on grounds either of cruelty or failure of support, the case will again go first to the registrar: but if he, or the chief concerned, cannot settle matters it will, again, be referred to the Muslim Religious Council. The Omulamuzi assured me that this Council had the right to dissolve Muslim marriages[2]: but well-informed Saza chiefs affirmed that its powers were in fact purely conciliatory, although parties would seldom refuse to accept its decisions—which would no doubt be strongly pressed, and based, fundamentally, on the *khulʿ* procedure.[3] Certain *walimu* also maintained that they had the right to "cancel" a marriage, although they admitted this was in a religious rather than a judicial sense—i.e., they claim to declare a marriage dissolved according to the sacred law, but have no authority to enforce their decisions. In reality, however, not only the ordinary Muslim but even the avowed teachers in Uganda are extremely ignorant of the Sharīʿa; and the only judicial authority, in all Muhammadan matrimonial causes, is the Protectorate courts.

In regard to divorce, it seems that the normal Shāfiʿī view that a divorce formula spoken in a state of culpable drunkenness is binding, but not one uttered under compulsion, is known by some; as are also the rules about the triple divorce and the intervening marriage which is thereafter necessary before the couple can come together again. But such refinements as *tafwīḍ al-ṭalāq, taʿlīq al-ṭalāq, īlāʾ, ẓihār, liʿān,* etc., are virtually unknown.[4]

Questions of guardianship and the custody of children are, apparently, usually arranged by mutual agreement: otherwise, the Buganda Guardianship Law of 1904 is applied by the courts. This provides for a boy to be in the custody of his mother, if alive, up to the age of seven, and then that of his father (or, if dead, his uncle) up till eighteen—as also before seven if the mother be dead; while a girl, on the other hand, will stay with her mother until eighteen or marriage, when she will go either to her father, uncle or husband, as the case may be. But the Omulamuzi may give other orders in special circumstances. If an appeal were to reach the High Court it is clear that Muhammadan law would never be applied in such circumstances.[5]

Inheritance is governed by customary law, for Muslims as for others. In Buganda there is a Land Succession Law, 1912, under which no one may deal with a deceased man's land without a certificate of succession from the Lukiko; and such certificate (which does not entitle the holder to *all* the land) will

---

[1] Since this order will in no case be executed by force.

[2] Perhaps, however, he merely meant declare them dissolved in the sacred law.

[3] More than once I was told that double the dower was a figure which a husband would almost certainly accept! For *khulʿ*, see Glossary.

[4] For all these technical terms, see Glossary.

[5] See the Kenya section of this Survey p. 106 above.

normally be given to the "principle heir" designated in the deceased's will or by the custom of succession among the Buganda. This is usually the eldest son; but it is in the discretion of the head of the clan (in consultation with the family or clan elders, etc.) to select the "principle heir," and this must be confirmed in all cases by the Kabaka himself. A Muslim, therefore, may in theory make whatever will he likes (under the Buganda Wills Law of 1916, which prescribes that the testator must sign the document and that there must be two witnesses, etc.) whether or not he thereby seeks to apply the Islamic law of intestate succession—or, indeed, keeps within the terms of the Islamic law of bequests. But while he may bequeath property to anyone, he may never designate as his "successor" one who is not a descendant or, in default of any such, at least a relative; while in all cases the successor-designate must be confirmed as such by the clan chief and the Kabaka himself. In general, however, the terms of a will which is properly made are likely to be observed, and if (which is unlikely) a Muslim were to make a will to the effect that the *shehes* were to divide his estate according to the Islamic rules of succession, this would probably suffice. The *shehes,* would, allegedly at least, like Sharī'a law to be applied in its entirety to the estates of deceased Muslims, but to this the Kabaka, very sensibly,[1] would never agree—and under the Uganda Agreement (Clan Cases), 1924, the Protecting Power has conceded that no native court shall take cognisance of any case relating to headship, membership or other matters affecting the clans, but that the clan council shall in each case lay its recommendations before the Kabaka and the Lukiko Council, whose decision shall be final (even with reference to an appeal lodged with the High Court). This last point has recently been upheld in *In re succession to Sepiriya Bingo Kadumukasa, deceased* (1949)[2] where the Kabaka's use of his prerogative was challenged, but it was held that this question was outside the jurisdiction of the court. It was also stated in the judgment that the law of succession among the Buganda was mainly customary; that the clan head chose the "successor" with the help of the family members and perhaps his clan elders; that the ultimate right of choice lay with the Kabaka alone, as the head of all the clans; that the "successor took the lion's share of realty and, usually, of personalty too"; and that the remainder, in the absence of a will, was distributed "as appeared right and proper."[3]

The "principal heir" or "successor" is largely explained by the Buganda system of land tenure, which owes nothing, of course, to Islam. Originally, there seems to have been no "ownership" of land, except, perhaps, in the Kabaka himself; for land was regarded as either too sacred, or probably too valueless, to be owned in itself. Instead, each chief was granted the lordship—during the Kabaka's pleasure—over a certain area, which primarily meant ' rdship over those resident therein; and where this was regarded as clan land a relative, selected by the clan, might succeed him on his death, but only after presentation to and confirmation by the Kabaka. Now, however, the Buganda Land Law of 1908 restricts individual holdings of "*mailo*"[4] land, except with the written consent of the Governor and Lukiko, to thirty square miles; allows

[1] Since, *inter alia,* the Islamic law of inheritance leads to much dispute and injustice in a land of such mixed religions, because of the rule that difference of religion is an absolute bar to inheritance.

[2] Miscellaneous Appeal No. 13 of 1949 (unreported).

[3] cp. also *Marko Kajubi* v. *Kulanima Kabali* (1944), 11 E.A.C.A. 34, where it was held that succession to estates belonging to natives is regulated in Uganda by native law; and that in Buganda the custom on intestacy is for the clan head to distribute the estate, subject to confirmation by the Kabaka.

[4] A word derived from the English "mile" and meaning land allocated under the Uganda Agreement of 1902 to be held by a tenure resembling freehold, but with certain restrictive incidents imposed by law.

them to be sold, given or bequeathed to another subject of the Protectorate, but not to anyone else, without the consent of the Governor and Lukiko, etc.; and forbids a bequest thereof to a church or religious society to the disherison of lawful heirs: while where a Muganda dies intestate the successor to his *mailo* land shall be ascertained " according to the rules of succession of the Baganda."

There are, apparently, no family waqfs in Uganda, and such public waqfs as exist (e.g., mosques) are recognised, but not governed by any special Ordinance. Instead, the Trustees Incorporation Ordinance, 1939, and the Public Trustee Ordinance, 1937, are presumably applicable.

Questions of adultery go to the native courts or, in the case of Muslims, even the Protectorate courts. Damages can be obtained in any native court by a husband against the man who commits adultery with his wife, according to the law of the tribe concerned—regardless, normally at least, of whether the marriage was Muhammadan or customary. Adultery is also a criminal offence under customary law and the third party concerned is liable to fine or imprisonment, while under the law of some tribes the woman is also punished. In Buganda these matters are governed by the Adultery and Fornication Law, 1918, which covers the whole law of sexual offences as now applied by the native courts.

The Administrator-General is only concerned with Muhammadan law in cases involving the movable property, situated in Uganda, of, e.g., Indian Muslims domiciled in India or Pakistan, or involving the estates of persons such as Muslim postal officials seconded from Kenya, Tanganyika, etc. If in doubt on any point he applies to the High Court for a ruling.

But the burning question among Muslims in Buganda is not the Muhammadan law of marriage, divorce or inheritance, but a controversy regarding the Friday prayer.[1] This controversy started about 1924, when what seems to have been the normal practice in Uganda of repeating the ordinary noon prayer (*al-ẓuhr*) after the *jum'a* prayer was challenged by a party who maintained that there was no need for this, since the *jum'a* prayer took the place of the noon prayer. The opposite faction—which seems to have remained the larger—made much of the fact that many Shāfi'ī books laid down extremely strict conditions for the validity of the *jum'a* prayer, insisting (on the basis of Shāfi'ī's later pronouncement) that it must be performed by at least forty adult, male Muslims who were all regularly domiciled in the vicinity, were able to speak Arabic correctly, understood the obligatory character of the ceremony, observed the correct time and manner of prayer, and were neither deaf nor dumb, etc. Further complications arose, where the prayer was performed in several mosques in the same vicinity, as to which of these performances must be regarded as the valid one, for in the strict Shāfi'ī view the *jum'a* prayer must never be said in two different mosques in the same locality at one and the same time; while it has also been held that it cannot properly be performed at all in villages where the houses are too scattered.

The two factions became known as the " Juma " and the " Juma-Zukuli " (or, more properly, Juma-Zuhuri) parties and their disagreement became sharp. So in 1927 the Muslims of Buganda requested the Protectorate Government to arrange for a learned man from Zanzibar to come and advise them on this matter. This was arranged, and the learned visitor gave it as his opinion that things were not yet ripe in Uganda for the noon prayer to be omitted: but the leaders of the Juma party would not accept his verdict, and the split continued.

More recently, however, the younger and better educated Muslims of both parties began to demand that this senseless dispute be brought to an end. So arrangements were made to send two *shehes,* one from each party, to consult

[1] The *jum'a* prayer.

the Shāfi'ī Muftī of Mecca and other Meccan authorities. They returned with a salutary homily to the effect that the purpose of the Friday prayer was to promote unity, not discord; with much encouragement to compose their differences; and with a signed agreement that they should (*a*) unite to build a large mosque for the *jum'a* prayer, the existing mosques being kept for congregational prayers at other times, (*b*) try to persuade any dissidents that there was no need to repeat the noon prayer after the *jum'a* prayer had been properly performed by forty or more people, (*c*) inform Prince Badru of this agreement. It is evident that this represents a compromise settlement wherein the middle item leaves the real point at issue undecided: but on the return of the delegates Prince Badru summoned a great meeting to which Muslims assembled from many different localities, where it was decided by the considerable majority (allegedly the vast majority) of both parties to unite, bury the hatchet and accept the settlement.[1]

But not all were willing to unite. Some of the Juma party still stood aloof, presumably on the grounds that the *jum'a* prayer alone was perfectly valid even if attended by less than forty worshippers. Similarly some of the Juma-Zukuli party also refused the compromise, on the grounds that the proper conditions for a valid performance of the *jum'a* prayer were so difficult and doubtful of fulfilment in Uganda that the noon prayer should always be repeated afterwards as a precaution.[2] I was presented with several Memoranda on this subject, extracts from three of which are appended below, in translation: the first represents the Meccan agreement, the second the view of the protagonists of the "New Juma" (or United) party, and the third that of the Juma-Zukuli dissidents.

It must, however, be added that, as usual in such cases, it seems probable that the basis of the dispute is more personal than theological. That personal rivalries and antipathies are now involved there can be no doubt whatever; and it seems probable that part at least of the reason for the persistence of the dispute is the attitude of the dissident leaders that it is better to reign in hell (or gather a living, however poor, in Buganda) than serve in heaven.

If it becomes necessary for the Government to express any view in this matter, the safest attitude would seem to be that each individual must be left perfectly free to follow his own conscience as to whether he repeats or omits the noon prayer after that of the *jum'a*; that this constitutes no reason for disputes, divisions or demands for separate mosques, since those who feel the *jum'a* prayer as performed in Uganda to be of doubtful validity may quieten their misgivings by repeating the noon prayer as well, while those who are satisfied of its validity should have no objection to the performance of an additional prayer by those who are more scrupulous or less enlightened. On such a basis it should at least be possible to deal promptly with any breach of the peace. But it is unlikely that this would of itself end the discord, on account of the personal rivalries and interests involved.

For the rest the only immediate need in Uganda, as regards the application of Islamic law, seems to be the introduction of some legislative enactment providing for the application of the Islamic law of intestate succession in respect of non-native Muslims domiciled in the territory.[3] Whether it will also be

[1] The present leaders of what we may call the united party, under the Prince, are Haji Abdulla Sikimwanyi and Haji Ahmadu Nsambu, two of the chief protagonists of the Juma party, on the one hand, and Sheikh Shwaib Semakula and Haji Lubowa, two of the leading men in the Juma-Zukuli party, on the other.

[2] The present leaders of thought in these dissenting factions, which still cause considerable discord, seem to be Sheikh Mugenyasoka and a certain Yusufu Mutenda of the Juma party and Sheikhs Abdul Rahman Mivule and Yusuf Kasujja of the Juma-Zukulis. But, according to his Memorandum, further points in which Sheikh Mugenyasoka differs from the other parties are (1) in following the Meccan calendar; (2) in not playing "religious drums"; (3) in explaining the Qur'ān in the vernacular.

[3] See above, pp. 149-151.

necessary, in course of time, to make any similar provision—with suitable safeguards—for indigenous Muslims, depends entirely on how far local customary law continues to prevail in such matters.

THE MECCAN AGREEMENT (SUMMARY)

1. The two parties shall choose a piece of land for a large mosque for the *jum'a* prayer, other mosques already in existence being used for congregational prayers other than the *jum'a.*

2. If any who attend the *jum'a* wish to pray the noon prayer afterwards, those of both parties will try, gently and with courtesy, to explain that the *jum'a* prayer, when properly performed by forty or more people assembled in one place, should not be followed by the noon prayer, since it fulfills all the necessary conditions.

3. In order to put this agreement into effect, Prince Badru must be informed, etc.

FATWĀ TO THE EFFECT THAT THERE IS NO FIXED MINIMUM FOR THE JUM'A PRAYER

(Extract only—handed to me by the " Uganda Jamiat al Islam, of Kawempe ".)

1. Several (Shāfi'ī) doctors have mentioned that there is no minimum number for the *jum'a* prayer established by the Traditions, while all agree that this prayer is a binding command on every eligible person. When, therefore, the numbers in a village are inadequate and they cannot (or cannot easily) go to a place where the number of persons is sufficient, they must (or may) perform the *jum'a* prayer in their own locality. These views are attributed to Sulaymān al-Shaṭṭī and Aḥmad bin Zayn al-Ḥabashī.

2. Sulaymān al-Shaṭṭī was once asked whether the *jum'a* prayer was valid when performed by less than forty even if a sufficient number were available in the town; whether a minimum number was in fact laid down; whether, if the prayer was held valid with less than forty, those concerned must consciously follow (by *taqlīd*)[1] the authorities who support this; what, if there are any conditions attached to such *taqlīd,* the position of the *profanum vulgus* would be in such circumstances; whether the congregation should repeat the noon prayer as a precaution; whether, if so, they should repeat it congregationally or individually; whether all the inhabitants of the town will incur guilt in default of the proper number being present, or only those who did not take part in the *jum'a* prayer; whether one visiting the town may join in the prayer with them; and whether they should pray it at the beginning of the specified time or delay as long as would still allow them time to say the *jum'a* and the noon prayer. To all these questions he replied: " Our school maintains that the *jum'a* prayer is not valid with less than forty who fulfil the conditions mentioned in the books of *fiqh.*[2] But this represents Shāfi'ī's later *dictum*; while he also expressed two earlier *dicta,* one of them to the effect that the minimum number was four, and that with four the *jum'a* was valid; and the basis for this *dictum* is more convincing than that concerning the forty. So you can adopt this, without following any other authority and without repeating the noon prayer, since God has given you the opportunity to follow your own Imām. The basis for this *dictum* is what al-Dāraquṭnī reported from Umm 'Abdallāh al-Dūsīya, who said: " The Prophet of God said: ' The *jum'a* prayer is incumbent on every village even if there are only four persons therein.' Shāfi'ī's third *dictum* was twelve, . . . which al-Nawawī accepted as the best view.

---

[1] i.e., the acceptance of some doctrine on the authority of someone else.

[2] Sharī'a law: see Glossary.

OBJECTIONS TO THIS VIEW (SUMMARY)

(Handed to me by Abdul Rahman[1] Mivule)

God knows that I (Mivule) am determined to hold to this right way because of the teaching I have seen in the books of leading Shāfi'ī jurists regarding the incumbency of repeating the noon prayer after the *jum'a* prayer. I am pained by this dispute and by the fact that my brothers do not follow the right path. But the elucidation of this matter is enough explanation of my own position.

It is stated in *al-Bājūrī* (i, p. 232): "We must pray the *jum'a* prayer first, in case it may prove to have been performed by the requisite number, then we must pray the noon prayer, in case it (the *jum'a*) was not performed by the requisite number, the presumption being that a satisfactory *jum'a* prayer has not been performed."

It is stated in *I'ānat al-Ṭālibīn* (p. 88): "a number of learned men—a large number—have declared the performance of the *jum'a* prayer allowable. So if any company follows those who hold this view, they will pray the *jum'a* prayer. But if as a precaution they pray the noon prayer too, they do well."

It is stated in *Bughyat al-Mustarshidīn* (p. 84): "He who says that the *jum'a* prayer should never be followed by the noon prayer, because God has not commanded the performance of six obligatory prayers in twenty-four hours, is at fault."

These texts prevent us from praying the *jum'a* prayer without repeating the noon prayer as well, while the factors which prevent us praying the *jum'a* prayer at all[2] when the conditions which govern its validity are lacking are also explained as follows: —

It is stated in *al-Bājūrī* (i, p. 234): "The second essential is that the number who perform it together must be forty men who fulfil the necessary conditions —i.e., that they are sane, adult, male, free and regularly domiciled in the locality (i.e., they do not leave it by winter or summer except for some such reason as trade, etc.)." It is stated in *Bughyat al-Mustarshidīn* (p. 84): "The conditions of the *jum'a* prayer are fulfilled when all the required forty are males, free, adult and sane; domiciled in the locality; do not omit any element or condition of the prayer nor regard it as (merely) *sunna*[3] and as needing repetition; do not substitute one letter of the alphabet for another; do not omit a letter or add anything which changes the meaning; do not speak incorrectly in such a way as to change the meaning; and do not fall short in knowledge, as Ibn Ḥajar said. But if the conditions of the *jum'a* prayer according to Shāfi'ī's teaching are lacking, it is not obligatory, but rather forbidden in such circumstances, for it becomes an invalid act of worship."

It is stated in the *Umm* (i, p. 171): "Shāfi'ī says that even in a town with a large population and many officials and mosques, the *jum'a* prayer must only be prayed in the largest mosque. Even if the town has many large mosques, the *jum'a* prayer must be prayed in one only. So in whichever the *jum'a* prayer is prayed first after the declining of the sun, this represents the true *jum'a;* and if it is subsequently prayed in another mosque also, then those who took part in this prayer will not be deemed to have performed the *jum'a* and must repeat the noon prayer of four *rak'as*."[4]

It is stated in *I'ānat al-Ṭālibīn* (p. 52): "If there are several localities and each is distinguished by a name, then each will stand alone for this purpose if they be customarily regarded as independent villages in the sense that one who

[1] The usual Arabic spelling does not seem suitable for Baganda names, on account of the local pronunciation. See here and above.

[2] The Arabic is only "*faqaṭ*" but the sense requires the stronger term.

[3] i.e., something which is praiseworthy but not strictly commanded.

[4] i.e., prostrations.

leaves one of them for another is customarily regarded as a traveller; or if there is a gap between two of them, even of two cubits, if this be customarily regarded as a gap—such as a cemetery, or children's playground, or cinder dump, or kneeling-place for camels, etc.; or if there is no gap but the houses do not adjoin each other as houses in a town usually do. But if the buildings are scattered to the extent that they are not customarily regarded as forming a village, the *jum'a* prayer must not be performed."

Another quotation—this time from *Anwār al-Masālik* (p. 26)—follows, concerning (*a*) the difference between one who is domiciled in a place and one who is merely resident therein, for however long a time; and (*b*) concerning the invalidity of the *jum'a* prayer in any place where the houses are scattered and separate. Mivule then adds: "Our houses are scattered, and there are not among us any who are united in a group of adjacent houses such as to fulfil the conditions of the *jum'a* prayer—while others like the Arabs and the Indians are not domiciled here, so they do not count in this respect. So in all these circumstances the *jum'a* prayer is not valid in this country of ours according to the school of our Imām Shāfi'ī: and he who studies this will arrive at the truth of the matter."[1]

[1] It will, of course, be noticed that even from the above quotations two different views emerge: (*a*) that the noon prayer should be repeated after the *jum'a* prayer in case the former was not valid, and (*b*) that when the conditions laid down for the *jum'a* prayer are lacking it should not be performed at all. These can, of course, be reconciled quite simply on the basis that when the conditions of the *jum'a* are clearly not fulfilled it should be omitted entirely, while where there is some doubt about whether or not they are fulfilled it should be duly performed and the noon prayer added as a precaution. But the matter is complicated by the exceedingly diverse views held by the jurists of the past about these necessary conditions. It seems, then, that few if any in Buganda go so far as to maintain that the *jum'a* prayer should be entirely omitted: instead, those who have scruples normally content themselves with adding the noon prayer as well.

NYASALAND PROTECTORATE

The British Central African Order in Council, 1902 (as amended in 1907 and 1912) includes provisions regarding both the jurisdiction of the High Court and the application of " native law " which are almost identical with those already noted in the case of the East African territories.[1] With regard to the application of Islamic law, therefore, the position is that it will only be applied (*a*) in so far as this is specifically provided, or at least implied, in any Ordinance; (*b*) in so far as it may have become the " native law " of any locality, tribe oı community[2]; and (*c*) in so far as this may be necessary, on ordinary principles, in regard to the movable property situated within the Protectorate of a deceased Muslim domiciled elsewhere.[3]

It is noteworthy that the only Ordinance in Nyasaland which directly concerns Muhammadan marriage is the Asiatics (Marriage, Divorce and Succession) Ordinance of 1929. This, clearly, like the Tanganyika Marriage, Divorce and Succession (Non-Christian Asiatics) Ordinance, is at once narrower and wider than the corresponding Ordinance in, e.g., Kenya: narrower, in that it concerns Asiatics exclusively and is not applicable to Africans at all; and wider, in that it does not confine itself to Muhammadans but covers all Asiatics who are not Christians. Under this Ordinance " The marriage in the Protectorate of non-Christian Asiatics, whether domiciled (therein) or not, who are not related to each other in any of the degrees of consanguinity or affinity prohibited by the law of the religion of either party to the marriage, shall, if the marriage is contracted in the manner customary in the Protectorate among persons professing the religion of either party to the marriage, be deemed for all purposes to be a valid marriage."[4] Similarly, " The divorce in the Protectorate of either party to a marriage of non-Christian Asiatics, whether domiciled (therein) or not, shall, if the divorce is on grounds which are recognised as valid grounds for divorce by the law of the religion of the person divorced and is effected in the manner customary in the Protectorate among persons professing that religion, be deemed for all purposes a valid divorce."[5] Again, " Subject to the provisions of this or any Ordinance or applied Act for the time being in force in the Protectorate, the succession to the movable property in the Protectorate of a deceased non-Christian Asiatic who at his death is domiciled in the Protectorate and to the immovable property in the Protectorate of such an Asiatic, whether domiciled in the Protectorate at his death or not, shall be regulated by the law of the religion professed by him at his death: provided that: —(*a*) so much of the law of any religion as deprives any person of a right of succession to property by reason of that person having renounced or having been excluded from the communion of any religion or having been deprived of caste shall not be in force in the Protectorate; and (*b*) every creditor shall have the same rights and remedies against the estate of a deceased non-Christian Asiatic, including the right to follow assets, as he has against the estate of a deceased Christian."[6] In addition, it is provided that " For the purposes of this Ordinance, the law of the religion of any person shall be that law subject to any special custom recognised and adopted by his co-religionists domiciled in the Protectorate ";[7] and that the court " may ascertain the law of any religion or any custom by any means which it thinks fit, and may act on information which appears to the court to be credible though it is not legal evidence, and

[1] Arts. 15(1) and 20. See pp. 81 and 122, etc. above.

[2] See discussion of this controversial point in the Introduction to this Survey.

[3] See also legislative provisions regarding succession, below.

[4] Sect. 2(1).

[5] Sect. 3(1).

[6] Sect. 6(1).

[7] Sect. 8(1).

in case of doubt or uncertainty may decide as the principles of justice, equity and good conscience may dictate."[1]

There are several points of interest in this Ordinance. It is noteworthy, in the first place, that its wording not only covers, by implication at least, the application of the different systems of law followed by the various sects and schools of Islam, but also expressly includes any local variants which may become customary.[2] Again, the provisos to the section governing the law of succession protects the convert or outcast in a way to which only Tanganyika among the East African territories provides a parallel,[3] although both are, of course, inspired by the Indian Caste Disabilities Removal Act of 1850. It is for this very reason that the provision, though admirable in intention, may be somewhat inequitable in its application, for it retains the defect inherent in the Indian Act that where, e.g., a Hindu or Christian Asiatic renounces his religion and embraces Islam, he is not thereby deprived of his rights of inheritance from his Hindu or Christian relations,[4] whereas they are deprived of any right of inheritance from him: but it is noteworthy that this does not happen in the case of a convert to Christianity, for while the proviso protects him from the exclusion that would otherwise be his under Islamic law, the " Christian ", or rather English, law which will govern his own estate would not exclude his unconverted relatives.[5] It is also noteworthy that the Ordinance excludes from application the rule of Anglo-Muhammadan law[6] whereby the creditors of an estate may only press their claims against the heirs personally, in proportion to their shares therein, and may not follow the assets into the hands of bona fide purchasers for value. Further points of interest are that no mention is made in section 2(1) of the specifically Islamic bar of fosterage (although it seems possible that the courts would regard this as implicit and enforceable); that the prohibition of marriage between those whose union is precluded by the law of the religion of either party is stricter than Islamic law, while the recognition of a marriage contracted in the manner customary to adherents of either religion is more lenient;[7] that the criterion adopted in the case of divorce is not the religion under which the marriage was celebrated but that of the party divorced, although it is not altogether clear whether the original religion or the one he or she may have subsequently embraced is intended;[8] and that section 8(2) not only provides a safeguard but might even, in certain circumstances, prove a possible means of reform. But most important of all, perhaps, it must be noted that this Ordinance, like the corresponding Ordinance in Tanganyika before it was amended in 1947, makes no provision for the judicial dissolution of a Muslim marriage or, indeed, for the hearing of any matrimonial cause under Islamic law. And in default of such provision it would doubtless be held that there is in fact no court competent to exercise such jurisdiction,[9] since nothing corresponding to Bombay Regulation 4 of 1827 is applicable in Nyasaland.

---

[1] Sect. 8(2).

[2] See sect. 8(1) above. This represents a great improvement on many similar enactments.

[3] See Marriage, Divorce and Inheritance (Non-Christian Asiatics) Ordinance, sect. 8, and Administration (Small Estates) (Amendment) Ordinance, sect. 14(4) (*b*): also discussion at p. 126 above.

[4] Among Christians this would, of course, be true even without the Act.

[5] It is also noteworthy that this provision, like its Indian model, does nothing whatever to help the children of the convert or outcaste, or any other persons claiming through him.

[6] cp. p. 125 note (4) above.

[7] Islamic law is, of course, only concerned with its own rules, in both of these cases.

[8] Contrast the Tanganyika Administration (Small Estates) (Amendment) Ordinance, sect. 18(4) (*b*). The wording of the Nyasaland Ordinance runs counter, of course, to Islamic law in that a divorce uttered by a Muslim husband in valid legal form would not be effective thereunder if contrary to the personal law of his divorced wife.

[9] cp. *Fatuma Bachoo* v. *Majothi Kara Juma Bolia* (1946), 5 T.T.L.R. 163.

For practical purposes, however, it seems that the Muslim Asiatic community in Nyasaland is almost exclusively composed of Indians of the Ḥanafī school, and that all that concerns their personal status is normally settled by their own Community Council. I only found the record of one case of inheritance under Islamic law which had come before the High Court, and this had been decided on strict Ḥanafī principles as propounded by a local Indian. There are virtually no Arabs, Somalis, Comoro Islanders or other immigrant Muslims in this Protectorate.

Other Ordinances which have some bearing on our subject include the Marriage Ordinance, 1903, under which a Christian man may validly marry a Muslim girl, in spite of the total invalidity of such a marriage in Islamic law; a Muslim man—or a man who subsequently embraces Islam—may not, if married thereunder, exercise his undoubted right under the Sharī'a to divorce his wife or marry one or more co-wives, while neither party may claim dissolution of marriage on the grounds that the petitioner has embraced Islam or the other party "apostatised" therefrom; and the intestate succession of parties to such marriages, and even of their children, is governed by the "laws of England."[1] Such marriages may, of course, only be dissolved under the terms of the Divorce Ordinance, 1905, as amended: but it is noteworthy that the latter provides that "A wife may apply by Petition to the Court for the dissolution of her marriage on the grounds that since the solemnisation thereof her husband has changed his profession of Christianity for the profession of some other religion and gone through a form of marriage with another woman . . ."[2]—or, indeed, been guilty of adultery in any circumstances whatever; while cruelty, desertion or insanity also provide grounds on which a wife may petition for the dissolution of her marriage. It is also relevant in this context to observe that the Penal Code of Nyasaland has no section making it an offence for a husband prematurely to consummate a marriage with a child wife, but does include the usual section[3] about abduction ("Any person who, with intent to marry or carnally know a woman of any age, or to cause her to be married or carnally known by any other person, takes her away, or detains her, against her will, is guilty of a felony")—and this, as has been noted elsewhere, might possibly expose to prosecution a Muslim father whose actions would be unexceptionable under the provisions of Islamic law which allow him to give his daughter in compulsory marriage, under conditions which differ according to his school. Again, the definitions of bigamy and fraudulent pretence of marriage in sections 162, 161 and 163 are presumably wide enough to include a void or pretended ceremony of Islamic marriage.

The Native Courts Ordinance, 1947, provides for native courts to exercise jurisdiction, within their respective territorial limits,[4] "over all causes and matters where, in proceedings of a civil nature, all parties are natives, or where, in proceedings of a criminal nature, the accused is a native"[5]—i.e., "any person whose tribe is a tribe of the Protectorate or of the Colony of Southern Rhodesia, the Territory of Northern Rhodesia, the Tanganyika Territory, the Belgian Congo or the Trust Territory of Ruanda-Urundi, the Union of South Africa, Basutoland, the Protectorate of Bechuanaland, Swaziland and includes a native of Portuguese East Africa."[6] The law they are to apply is "the native law and custom prevailing in the area . . . so far as is applicable and not repugnant to natural justice or morality or is not, in principle, in conflict with the provisions

[1] For a fuller treatment, see under corresponding legislation elsewhere.
[2] Sect. 5(2).
[3] Sect. 134.
[4] Sect. 10.
[5] Sect. 9(1).
[6] Sect. 2.

of any law in force in the Protectorate,"[1] together with "the provisions of all rules or orders made in accordance with the provisions of the Native Authority Ordinance"[2] and such Ordinances or other laws as they are authorised to administer or enforce[3]: but "any proceedings in which a person is charged with an offence in consequence of which death is alleged to have occurred"[4] and "any proceedings concerning marriage or divorce regulated by the Marriage Ordinance, or the Divorce Ordinance, unless it is a claim arising only in regard to bride-price or adultery and founded only on native law and custom,"[5] are expressly excluded from their jurisdiction. As for practice and procedure, these, subject to any express provision to the contrary, "shall be regulated in accordance with native law and custom."[6] The Native Courts Adviser or a Magistrate may, at any time before judgment, transfer cases to another native court or to a subordinate court,[7] the Native Courts Adviser may, upon the application of an aggrieved party or of his own motion, revise any original or appellate proceedings of a native court,[8] while appeals lie sometimes to another native court, sometimes to a Magistrate and sometimes to the Native Courts Adviser.[9] It is also provided that "Where a case comes before the Native Courts Adviser on revision or appeal and a question of law is involved, the Native Courts Adviser may state a case for the opinion of the High Court"[10] which (when given) "shall be final and conclusive"[11]: but "no proceedings in a native court and no summons, warrant, process, order or decree issued or made thereby shall be varied or declared void upon appeal or revision solely by reason of any defect in procedure or want of form," but such cases shall instead be decided "according to substantial justice without undue regard to technicalities."[12]

Again, the Nyasaland Protectorate (African Trust Land) Order in Council, 1950, follows normal modern principles in vesting in the Secretary of State as "African Trust land"[13] the whole of the lands of the Protectorate except public land and land claimed under one of several types of title going back to before 1936[14]; in providing that the Governor shall "administer and control all African trust land for the common benefit, direct or indirect, of Africans, and in so doing shall have regard to African law and custom in so far as they are applicable and not repugnant to justice or morality"[15]; and in empowering the Governor to acquire such land for public purposes "for the benefit, direct or indirect, of Africans"[16] or to grant leases or rights of occupancy therein, on such terms and conditions as he may think fit, with certain provisos[17]—after, in each case, consultation with the appropriate native authority[18]; while it also provides that the whole of the proceeds of any such disposal is to be paid either into the treasury of the native authority concerned or into a central fund established

[1] Sect. 12(*a*).
[2] Sect. 12(*b*).
[3] Sects. 12(*c*) and (*d*).
[4] Sect. 11(*a*).
[5] Sect. 11(*b*).
[6] Sect. 19.
[7] Sect. 22.
[8] Sect. 24(1).
[9] Sect. 25.
[10] Sect. 26(1).
[11] Sect. 26(2).
[12] Sect. 30.
[13] Art. 5.
[14] Art. 4.
[15] Art. 6(1).
[16] Art. 8(1).
[17] Art. 7(1).
[18] Arts. 7(1), (*a*) and 8(1).

under the Native Development and Welfare Fund Ordinance, etc.[1] As for minerals, the "entire property in and control of minerals in, under, or upon any African trust land are, save in so far as any part thereof may have been the subject of alienation duly ratified by the Crown, or in relation to which prospecting or mining rights subsist by virtue of express grant made by the Governor, hereby vested in the Secretary of State, and shall be administered by the Governor for the use and common benefit, direct or indirect, of Africans.[2] For the rest, however, it is expressly provided that "a native authority may, subject to the general or special directions of the Governor, authorise the use and occupation by an African of any African trust land within the native authority's area in accordance with the African law and custom prevailing in that area"[3]; but that "No title claimed by any person other than an African to the use or occupation of African trust land shall be valid unless it has been granted or confirmed by the Governor."[4] The purpose of the policy adopted has been summarised as the protection of the interests of the indigenous population in the land and the securement that they can "neither dispose of it against their own interests, nor stand in the way of it being temporarily disposed of to their own real advantage." In any case it is clear that Islamic law is equally inapplicable in Nyasaland in the case of such land as is privately owned, whether by Muslims, Christians or pagans, under some title recognised by Ordinance or in the case of land declared to be African trust land and administered on the principles outlined above.

From talks with the Provincial Commissioner of the Southern Province, with some of his District Commissioners, with Dr. Sanderson (a retired Medical Officer who has made a special study of the Yao) and with various chiefs and local Muslim authorities, the following points emerged.

Virtually the only Muslims in Nyasaland, except for the Indian community referred to above, are members of the Yao tribe, which has largely accepted Islam[5] through its historical connection with the slave traders. In the main, however, the Yao are extremely ignorant of their professed religion[6] and their sex morals, by any European or even Islamic standards, are extremely lax. Conversion to Islam chiefly means the acceptance of complete (instead of the customary partial) circumcision; the imitation of a few ritual practices, postures and prayers without any real knowledge of their meaning (and pre-eminently the abstention from pig-flesh or that of any animal not slaughtered by a ritual cutting of its throat); and the observance of the Ramaḍān fast—all of which acts of conformity confer a certain sense of superiority and are regarded as a passport to Paradise. The major points of dispute among Yao Muslims seem to be such questions as the legality of hippopotamus meat and the propriety of drumming and singing at funerals. But in matters of law Yao custom almost entirely prevails, for in general terms it seems that the law of Islam exercises a considerable, but by no means basic, influence in matters of marriage, a very minor influence in questions of divorce, and virtually no influence whatever in any other matter cognisable before the courts.

The Yao are by custom matrilineal and also (except in the case of chiefs) matrilocal. The girls never, it seems, marry before puberty (although they are often as young as ten to fifteen years old) and are never now married by compulsion.[7]

[1] Arts. 9 and 1(*a*).
[2] Art. 5(2).
[3] Art. 6(1) (Proviso).
[4] Art. 6(2).
[5] About 70 per cent., apparently.
[6] Although they are intelligent and possessed of a beautiful and flexible language and a highly developed code of behaviour.
[7] Confusion often, however, arises—among Europeans—from the fact that the title "spouse" (*asonogo*) is often used by a man in reference to a girl, however young, whom he has, in Yao custom, a prescriptive right to marry by reason of relationship, even though he may have no intention of bespeaking her.

Instead, the normal procedure is for a young couple to come to a private understanding and to start to sleep together (although this is, of course, not "official," especially among Muslims), and for a formal marriage only to be concluded at a later date. Among both Muslims and non-Muslims marriage "sponsors"[1] are an essential feature: but in the case of Muslims the local *mwalimu* always attends the formal marriage, recites the appropriate prayers, etc., and dictates some form of declaration and acceptance; while dower of some sort is also commonly given.[2] It seems, however, that a rudimentary offer and acceptance is usual on such occasions even by non-Muslim Yao custom; that any large payment to the parents of the bride is contrary to Yao traditions and deprecated among Muslims, too; but that presents to the bride are, of course, on a different footing. Registration of marriage at the Chiefs' courts is voluntary, but encouraged. Marriages between Muslims and non-Muslims often take place, but the non-Muslim party is said usually to accept Islam, although the marriage is of course regarded as valid by customary law in any case. In general terms, therefore, it seems that most of the essentials of the Islamic contract of marriage (declaration and acceptance, witnesses and dower) are present in cases where two Muslim Yao formally contract a marriage, although it is noteworthy that the sponsors who act for the bride are not her father or grandfather but the heads of her sorority group. Men often, moreover, have more than one wife, either in the same or, more frequently, different villages, with whom they live either in rotation or according to circumstances, and there are occasional complaints that a man has even exceeded the four which Islam allows: it was apparently for this reason, *inter alia,* that a Yao chief was recently deposed.

Dissolution of marriage is almost entirely by customary law. If it is the husband who tires of the marriage he reports to his sponsors, who meet those of the woman to arrange a divorce, while if it is she who tires of him, *vice versa.* If it is his fault, he commonly has to pay compensation, over and above the dower which, as a Muslim, he may either have paid or undertaken to pay; while if it is her fault, her family must pay compensation (which may or may not include the return of any dower she has received). If the sponsors fail to agree the case will go to the Chief's court, which will probably first urge the parties to be reconciled (especially if both the chief and the parties are Muslims) but, if this proves abortive, will assist the sponsors in reaching agreement; while the chiefs are now trying to secure that all divorces, even when arranged by sponsors, should be reported to their courts for "confirmation", in the interests of both prestige and revenue. *Shehes* and *walimu* are not, it seems, consulted in such cases except by certain chiefs who are prompted thereto either by particular zeal for Islam or on analogy with Roman Catholic practice. Where they are so consulted, however, it appears that most *walimu* would allow a divorce for repeated acts of cruelty or continual marital discord, after efforts to induce the offending party to reform; but that they would not normally advise a divorce for physical desertion, provided maintenance was forthcoming. All this, however, seems to correspond tolerably well with non-Muslim Yao custom: and it is significant that all agree that even the triple divorce formula would be disregarded, and the marriage continued or renewed, if the sponsors should succeed in reconciling the parties. Even where the religious authorities would advise against a divorce, however, the court will regularly arrange one[3] if the wife persists in her refusal to have anything more to do with her husband, however much she might be anathematised by the *walimu* thereafter.[4] In effect, then, a Muslim

[1] Two from each side.

[2] This, however, does not seem to be universal.

[3] Only one chief, Chikumba, denied this.

[4] It seems doubtful, however, whether they would in fact be particularly shocked by her behaviour in Nyasaland.

wife among the Yao is in almost, if not quite, as favourable a position as her husband in regard to securing the dissolution of an unsatisfactory marriage: and no other form of dissolution or divorce (e.g., *khulʿ* or *mubāraʾa*, properly so-called; *īlāʾ* or *ẓihār; faskh;* or suspended, conditional or delegated *ṭalāq*)[1] is known. The fact that customary law normally at least finds general acceptance in all such matters, in default of the mutual agreement of the parties, is shown by the fact that no complaints that the courts have given a decision which is contrary to the law of Islam ever seem to reach administrative officers.

Any question of maintenance, etc., would be decided entirely by customary law. In cases of adultery (which is said to be exceedingly common) the injured husband may bring an action for compensation against the offending man, while the wife must also, today, pay a fine to the court (or in some districts, it seems, compensation to her husband). A husband's adultery, on the other hand, is not normally actionable by his wife, but only by the " owner " of the other woman. Such charges, moreover, are usually proved among the Yao, it seems, by confession of the guilty parties, for there is little or no sense of shame and the unfaithful wife is often quite prepared to confess her intrigue[2] in the hope that her husband will divorce her and she will be able to marry her lover. Neither the *ʿidda* of divorce nor even that of widowhood[3] is observed; while on divorce or the death of either party the children, as in all matrilineal systems, go to the mother and her sorority group.

Inheritance almost invariably follows tribal custom—i.e., a deceased man's name, title, office (if any) and property will go to the *mwipwa,* or his eldest sister's eldest son, who may divide the property with other claimants within the sorority group; but something, it seems, is frequently left to the children, and even their mother, in suitable circumstances today, partly as a result of the influence of Islam and partly as a result of that of Christianity. No native authority, it appears, would dare to oppose the customary claimant in such cases. But a son may, of course, succeed his father as *mwalimu,* etc., by right of training and ability, and I was told of one case where a son apparently succeeded even to the property of his *mwalimu* father. Bequests, it seems, are extremely rare, follow no fixed rules, and are by no means always honoured. As a consequence of the matrilineal system legitimacy is largely immaterial in matters of succession. A woman, technically at any rate, owns no property, as even her dower is commonly taken by her male relatives; while if a wife dies or is divorced her husband and his sorority group will normally take away even the doors and windows from the house which he had built for her. In places, however, it seems to be becoming customary among Christians, and even Muslims, that when the wife dies or the marriage is ended by mutual consent the house and its chattels should be left intact for the children of the marriage.

For the rest, it seems that " apostasy " does not normally cause dissolution of marriage; that Muslim boys are usually circumcised, with various initiation ceremonies,[4] at about seven years of age, while girls undergo similar initiation, but without circumcision, at about the same age; and that a number of pagan

[1] For all these technical terms, see Glossary.

[2] Particularly if pregnant by her lover, since a failure to confess the child's true paternity is held to occasion a hard or abortive labour.

[3] Although it used to be customary for widows not to remarry at once, but to remain *tabu* until released by intercourse with a *litunu* (literally " hyena," or special night visitor) after a specified period of isolation.

[4] Partial circumcision was a feature of the customary initiation ceremonies (*unyago*), or fertility rites, among the Yao. Though still performed in many districts, these ceremonies (and the corresponding rites for girls) seem to be gradually dying out in their original form in favour of those imported from the coast. The latter purport to be Islamic, but often retain much of their pagan flavour.

ceremonies have survived, either intact or in Islamicised form, such as the "*sadaka*",[1] the prayers and oblations offered to ancestral spirits,[2] and the purely customary *litiwo* procedure on the occasion of a woman's first pregnancy. In the main, not only the ordinary tribesmen but even the recognised Muslim teachers in Nyasaland are incredibly ignorant of both the law and theology of Islam, and few even know that they are Shāfi'īs.[3] Far better known than the schools of law are a few rudimentary differences between the Ṣūfī fraternities of the "Shaziriya" (Shādhilīya) and the "Khadiriya" (Qādirīya) or, more particularly, between a sub-section of the latter, called the "Zukutis" (Sukūtīs), and the rest of its local adherents. It is on such questions as the differences between these two groups that local Muslim opinion has at times run high. Very few can read Arabic; and although Dr. Sanderson thought it worth-while to translate the first three Sūras of the Qur'ān into their local dialect he soon desisted, because of the lack of interest which this aroused.[4]

The situation may, perhaps, best be illustrated by a short list of the chief differences which seem to have divided the "Zukutis" from the rest of the "Khadiriya." Such were: —

1. the propriety at funerals of eating cooked food before the burial;
2. the propriety of singing and dancing on such occasions;
3. the propriety of carrying flags at funerals;
4. the propriety of dancing at graves at the yearly visit (*ziyāra*) thereto;
5. the legality of eating hippopotamus meat;
6. the legality of building new mosques where others already exist;
7. the legality of certain special prayers.

The "Zukutis," it seems, forbade the first six but observed the seventh; while the rest of the "Khadiriya" allowed the first six but forbade the seventh.

These differences, trivial although most of them were, led to considerable religious friction and some political unrest, for such questions as the succession to at least one chieftainship became involved. It was arranged, therefore, that a *sharīf*[5] from Zanzibar should come and try to reconcile the parties: and in course of time Sharīf 'Abdūh Ḥasan duly arrived, some three thousand persons assembled to meet him, and the leaders of the contending parties proceeded to argue their case. To the "Zukutis" the arbitrator conceded that funerals are reported as having been conducted in silence in the time of Muḥammad, but he maintained, none the less, that singing, dancing and carrying flags thereat were permitted by the Qur'ān and sanctioned by most modern authorities, including the "Muftī of Zanzibar", as preferable to the irrelevant conversation and inattention which commonly took their place. Eventually, however, he gave a

[1] This term, as used by the Yao, has no reference to alms, but means a funeral feast held at the time of burial and at stated intervals thereafter and typically associated with a special dance (*cindimba*) and the brewing of special beer. This has been partially islamicised by the *dhikr* (*sikiri*), which is locally regarded purely as a dance. Fervour in performing this is evidence of enjoyment of rhythm rather than religious ecstasy, for its true purpose is quite forgotten.

[2] This, too, has been partially islamicised and is "explained" by the more zealous Muslims as the gift of food to passers-by in order that God may forgive and bless the spirit of one's ancestors.

[3] Far the best informed native of Nyasaland whom I met was Sheikh Abdulla Sabiti (Thabiti), who had studied in Zanzibar.

[4] Partly, perhaps, because the Qur'ān and Arabic formulae derived therefrom are regarded as "words of power" whose magic would be destroyed by translation.

[5] Descendant of the Prophet.

compromise judgment that the eating of cooked meats before a burial was allowable; that a certain amount of singing, but no dancing, might be permitted at a funeral; that flags might be brought as far as the house of the deceased, but not used in the procession to the grave except at the funeral of chiefs or *shehes*; that dancing should not be allowed at the yearly visit to the grave; that the eating of hippopotamus[1] meat was not permitted; and that the legality of building new mosques where others already existed and of using certain special prayers were matters for local decision. This compromise was accepted by both parties, and an agreement was duly signed and witnessed by the District Commissioner and others.

Since this dispute was resolved no particular problem or difficulty seems to have arisen in Nyasaland regarding Islamic law. The religion of Islam is today making little or no progress in the country and even among the Yao appears to be generally only skin-deep. There are, perhaps, some signs of a greater recognition of Islamic law by certain chiefs in matters of divorce, and a certain tendency for matrilineal succession to make some concessions to the claims of the deceased's children: but elsewhere administrative officers report a contrary tendency. Certainly there is little in the moral or social condition of the Yao to recommend Islam to the Protectorate as a whole. The missionary agencies active in Nyasaland are, moreover, exclusively Christian, for even the Aḥmadīya do not seem to have extended their activities to the Protectorate. The only legislation concerning Islamic law which might, conceivably, be required in Nyasaland in the foreseeable future is an amendment to the Asiatics (Marriage, Divorce and Succession) Ordinance, along the lines of the amendments to the corresponding Ordinance already introduced in Tanganyika, providing for the High Court to dissolve such marriages, in suitable cases, according to the relevant personal law.[2]

NOTE.—No provision whatever seems to exist in either Northern or Southern Rhodesia for the application of Islamic law, whether among indigenous or immigrant Muslims—except, of course, in so far as any parts of the Sharī'a may have become native law and custom, and may be applied as such, in the case of any local Muslim tribe or area. These territories are, therefore, omitted from this Survey.

[1] The legality of hippopotamus meat, of course, turns on two different but related questions: whether the hippo is to be regarded as primarily a denizen of land or water, on the one hand, and whether, if the former, its throat was cut in the correct manner, on the other—and this, it seems, can virtually never occur, as the hippo is normally killed in the water and almost always sinks immediately.

[2] See pp. 125 f. above.

Part II. West Africa

NIGERIA

It would at first sight seem somewhat of an anomaly that the Ordinances of a territory in which, so far as its Northern Provinces are concerned, Islamic law is in fact applied more widely than in any other part of the British Empire, except the Aden Protectorate, should include virtually no reference whatever to that law. Perhaps the only[1] exception to this generalisation occurs in the Sheriffs and Enforcement of Judgments and Orders Ordinance, 1945, where section 53 reads: —

"(1) In the application of sections 43 to 52[2] to the Northern Provinces the following provisions shall apply: —

(a) where all parties to a suit are Muhammadans,[3] or

(b) where in any other suit the person applying for a writ of execution and the person against whose property the writ is to be directed are Muhammadans, the court to which application is made shall be guided by the principles of Muhammadan law relating to the levying of execution of immovable property and any writ issued against immovable property shall in such a case as aforesaid be issued subject to Muhammadan law and the person applying for such writ shall prove the Muhammadan law on the point whether or not such Muhammadan law is to his benefit.

(2) For the purpose of this section any firm, body of persons or company . . . the members of which are all Muhammadans, shall be deemed to be a Muhammadan . . ."[4]

The explanation of this anomaly, however, is not far to seek, for Islamic law is in fact applied throughout Northern Nigeria under the provisions concerning the application of "native law and custom". The propriety of this nomenclature has already been discussed in the Introduction to this Survey: but it seems that in Nigeria at least its advantages outweigh its disadvantages. Among the latter must, of course, be numbered the obvious objection, to the purist, to regarding a system of law worked out in meticulous detail in innumerable compendiums in Arabia, Spain and Morocco as the indigenous law and custom of Northern Nigeria, and the manifest anomaly of an Alkali[5] enforcing any provision of these

[1] For the former Oaths and Affirmations (Amendment) Ordinance, 1922 [now repealed] provided no real exception, since this made no mention of Islamic law as such but merely provided that a Muslim witness might give evidence on affirmation rather than oath (sect. 3A), provided that he must repeat all or part of his evidence on oath if so required either by court or accused. This may, clearly, be regarded as no more than a partial concession to Muslim aversion to sworn testimony: but it also, as we shall see, corresponds tolerably well with the attitude which prevails in most of the Northern Provinces regarding the vexed question of whether, and in what circumstances, the Sharī'a permits witnesses to be put on oath.

[2] Which concern execution against immovable property.

[3] Here spelt "Mohammedan": but see Introduction to this Survey concerning the liberty I have taken in spelling Arabic words, even in quotations, to avoid chaos and possible misunderstanding.

[4] It seems that this particular piece of legislation was introduced under pressure from the Chief's Conference, which had protested against cases, in centres such as Kano, where a magistrate ordered the sale of a debtor's only house to settle the debts of a creditor who had been ingenious enough to apply to his court in circumstances where the local Alkali would refuse such an order.

[5] The Hausa form of the Arabic "al-Qāḍī".

texts which runs counter to normal local practice under legislation providing only for the enforcement of " native law and custom ". But against these disadvantages must be set the fact that the phrase covers equally the application of Islamic law in those areas of the Muslim Emirates where it has in fact been accepted as the law of the locality, and of pagan customary law where this still prevails; that it provides an adequate legal justification for those modifications of the pure Sharī'a in favour of local custom which are noticeable, in greater or less degree, in the day to day work of even the most staunchly Muslim courts; and that it emphasises the territorial rather than personal basis on which the law is intended to be applied in Nigeria—thus avoiding, in the main, the confusion consequent on every individual being subject to the personal law of his own religion.[1]

It is both curious and illuminative to notice the degree to which Islamic law is identified with, and yet at the same time differentiated from, native law and custom in such a book as Lord Lugard's *Political Memoranda*. Thus on page 84 he distinguishes them in the following terms: "The fundamental law in the Native Muslim[2] Courts of Nigeria is the Mālikī Code of Muhammadan Law, and in the Native Pagan Courts it is the local native law and custom. Both are subject to the proviso that all judgments and sentences must not be repugnant to natural justice and humanity, or to any Ordinance of Nigeria." Yet four pages later he observes that "The Native Courts . . . administer native law and custom only . . ."; while four pages later still he half identifies and half distinguishes them, when he remarks that "It is very essential for Political Officers, in Provinces where there is a considerable Muslim population, to have some knowledge of Muhammadan law, both in order that their supervision of the Native Courts may be intelligent and effective, and in order that they may know how to 'observe and enforce native law and custom' in Civil cases which come before Provincial Courts . . ." and that "The administration of Muslim law is modified by the local law and custom in Pagan Districts, provided that by so doing the Judge does not directly oppose the teaching of the Qur'ān.[3] There is no doubt that even in Muslim Districts, the law, as administered today, especially in the Emirs' Judicial Councils, is often modified by recognition of the native law and custom which has been much influenced by the system the Fulani found in operation at the time of their conquest."[4]

From this it appears that at least three strata of law—the indigenous pagan customs of the country; the pagan or semi-pagan customs introduced by its different conquerors, ending with the Fulani; and Islamic law (or "the teaching of the Qur'ān") as adopted, at different stages and to different degrees, by a certain proportion of both conquerors and conquered—are all now enforced, with more regard for the situation already existent at the time of the conquest than for any logical consistency or precise nomenclature, under the all-inclusive aegis of "native law and custom". Lord Lugard himself suggested that the best criterion by which the latter could be tested was whether it was "admitted as such by the community and its competent spokesmen": but it must be admitted that in practice the question whether the orthodox but "foreign" doctrines of the text books, or the indigenous customs of the tribe or locality, are enforced by the courts frequently turns chiefly on the relative orthodoxy or realism of the Emir or Alkali concerned.

For this application of "native law and custom" throughout the Protectorate (and, within much stricter limits, the Colony) ample authority exists. Thus the Royal Instructions issued in 1946 retained the usual provision that "In the making

[1] Certain exceptions to this generalisation are now apparent (see below); while difficult cases were previously solved by transfer to the old Provincial Courts.

[2] Here spelt "Moslem": but see p. 171, note 3.

[3] Spelt "Koran": but see above.

[4] p. 92.

of Ordinances any native laws by which the civil relations of any native chiefs, tribes or populations under Our protection are now regulated shall be respected, except in so far as the same may be incompatible with the due exercise of Our power and jurisdiction, or clearly injurious to the welfare of the said natives."[1] And the immediately subsequent clause[2] in the same Instructions, that "Nothing in any Ordinance contained shall take away or affect any rights secured to any natives in the Protectorate by any treaties or agreements made on behalf or with the sanction of Her late Majesty Queen Victoria, Her Heirs and Successors, and all such treaties and agreements shall be and remain operative and in force, and all pledges and undertakings therein contained shall remain mutually binding", may be regarded as covering the undertakings given by Lord Lugard to several of the Northern Emirs that Her Majesty's Government would not in any way interfere in their "religion"; an undertaking which the Emirs naturally, and usually successfully, try to press to the furthest possible limits and regard as including all the ramifications of the law which that religion[3] enjoins. It is this, of course, which explains the almost unique phenomenon that in those Northern Emirates which represent roughly one-half of the whole territory the jurisdiction exercised by the Emirs and their Alkalai under "native law and custom"—i.e., a slightly modified form of the Mālikī school of Sharī'a law, at least in the more staunchly Muslim areas—extends even to matters of crime (including, in many Emirates, capital offences) and to the infliction of the punishments therein prescribed, except for such penalties as mutilation, lapidation and crucifixion, which were prohibited from the inception of the British Protectorate.

The Supreme Court Ordinance, 1943, also contains the usual reference to native law and custom when it provides that "Nothing in this Ordinance shall deprive the Supreme Court of the right to observe and enforce the observance, or shall deprive any person of the benefit of any existing native law or custom . . . not being repugnant to natural justice, equity, and good conscience, nor incompatible either directly or by necessary implication with any law for the time being in force. Such laws and customs shall be deemed applicable in causes and matters where the parties thereto are natives and also in causes and matters between natives and non-natives where it may appear to the court that substantial injustice would be done to either party by a strict adherence to the rules of English law."[4] Matters in which "native law and custom" are particularly applicable, moreover, are expressly excluded from the original jurisdiction of the Supreme Court, for section 12 provides that "except in so far as the Governor in Council may by order otherwise direct and except in suits transferred to the Supreme Court under the provisions of section 25 of the Native Courts Ordinance, the Supreme Court shall not exercise original jurisdiction in any suit which raises any issue as to the title to land or as to the title to any interest in land which is subject to the jurisdiction of a native court nor in any matter which is subject to the jurisdiction of a native court relating to marriage, family status, guardianship of children, inheritance or disposition of property on death." And similar provisions also appear in the Magistrates' Courts Ordinance, 1943.[5]

Again, the Native Courts Ordinance, 1933 (as amended several times), provides that "By warrant under his hand . . . a Resident may establish within his province such native courts as he shall think fit"[6]; that

[1] Art. 17 (1).

[2] Art. 17 (2). But these articles were omitted from the Instructions of 1951.

[3] On the widest application, for instance, this undertaking would clearly run counter to the usual provisos regarding any native law or custom "contrary to natural justice or humanity" or "inconsistent with any Ordinance". But it appears essential to keep a sense of proportion in interpreting such undertakings: cp. the part of this Survey dealing with the Aden Protectorate, p. 39.

[4] Sect. 17(1) and (2).

[5] Sect. 19(1).

[6] Sect. 3(1).

such native court "shall consist of—(*a*) head chiefs or a head chief, chiefs or chief or any other person or persons (who may include non-natives) or a combination of any such . . . sitting with or without assessors; or (*b*) in the Northern Provinces only, an alkali, with or without assessors,"[1] and shall have "full jurisdiction and power, to the extent set forth in its warrant and subject to the provisions of this Ordinance, in all civil and criminal cases in which all the parties belong to a class of persons who have ordinarily been subject to the jurisdiction of native tribunals"[2]; and that "the Governor[3] may by order grade native courts and prescribe the jurisdiction and power . . . of each grade"[4], and "the Governor in Council may with the approval of the Secretary of State by order direct that any person or classes of persons not being persons or classes of persons who have ordinarily been subject to the jurisdiction of native tribunals shall be subject to the jurisdiction of any particular class of native court or of any particular native court", whether with or without their consent.[5] Such courts are, in practice, graded A, B, C and D (grades B, C and D being distinguished by the maximum penalties they may impose and the maximum sums to which their civil jurisdiction extends), and are further sub-divided into "limited" and "unlimited". Thus Grade A (limited) courts are excluded from hearing cases of homicide, ju-ju or witchcraft, while Grades B, C and D (limited) are excluded from exercising jurisdiction in homicide, counterfeiting, slave dealing, child stealing, judicial corruption, fraudulent false accounting, obtaining goods by false pretences, official corruption, defilement of girls, procuration, rape, defamation (documentary), forgery, corrupt practices, conspiracy, knowingly making untrue statements before a court, and cases involving witchcraft or ju-ju.[6] Again, no native courts have jurisdiction in matters of treason, sedition, trial by ordeal, official corruption by Government officials, offences against the revenue of the Government, offences concerning posts, telegraphs or railways,[7] or official secrets.[8] Only the courts of the leading Emirs are graded A (unlimited) and thus have jurisdiction in cases of homicide; but it is expressly provided that where such cases are heard by an Alkali's court "such court may refrain from pronouncing sentence and may transmit the evidence recorded by it to the court of the head chief . . . and such court of the head chief, upon considering such evidence, may pronounce sentence . . ."[9]

As for the law to be applied, section 10(1) defines this as "(*a*) the native law and custom prevailing in the area . . . so far as it is not repugnant to natural justice or morality, or inconsistent with any provisions of any . . . Ordinance, (*b*) the provisions of any Ordinance which the court may be authorised to enforce . . . (*c*) the provisions of all rules or orders made under the Native Authority Ordinance." For offences against any native law or custom, moreover, "a native court may, subject to the provisions of this Ordinance, impose a fine or imprisonment or both, or may inflict any punishment authorised by native law or custom,

[1] Sect. 4(1).

[2] Sect. 8(1).

[3] His powers under this section have been delegated.

[4] Sect. 8(2).

[5] Sect. 8(3).

[6] It is open to question, however, whether some at least of these restrictions should not now be removable at the recommendation of the Resident; while it may be noted that cases of false pretences, defilement, rape, etc., are in fact sometimes handled by such courts without any questions being raised.

[7] These latter exceptions are, it seems, sometimes pressed to the point of excluding cases of damage to telegraph wires or theft of railway sleepers from the competence of native courts, rather than those more complex or technical offences in respect of these services which such courts would not, of course, be competent to handle.

[8] See Schedule for Native Courts, Northern Provinces, substituted by Government Notice 1723 of 1938 (as amended).

[9] Sect. 9—but only, of course, where the Emir's court has such powers.

provided it does not involve mutilation or torture, and is not repugnant to natural justice and humanity."[1] It is, however, expressly provided that "In any matter relating to the guardianship of children, the interest and welfare of the child shall be the first and paramount consideration."[2] As to practice or procedure, section 14 provides that "Subject to such rules as may be made under section 49, the jurisdiction conferred on native courts shall (as regards practice and procedure) be regulated in accordance with native law and custom."[3]

Detailed rules follow as to the procedure to be observed when a sentence of death is passed by a native court having jurisdiction in capital offences, and as to the Governor's powers in such cases (when no right of appeal to the Supreme Court or to the Court of Appeal any longer remains) to order a retrial either by a native court or by any other court of competent jurisdiction, to order further evidence to be taken, or, after consultation with the Executive Council, to confirm the sentence, commute it to any other punishment, or decline to confirm it (in which case the person concerned "shall be forthwith set at liberty").[4] Similarly, with regard to corporal punishment, "no sentence of corporal punishment shall be carried out until it has been confirmed" by the emir (etc.) if imposed by a native court of Grade A, or by the district officer if imposed by a native court of a grade other than A.[5] Detailed provisions, moreover, cover the supervision of native courts by the Resident or the district officer in charge of a division,[6] who may review any proceedings (except a sentence of death), whether civil or criminal, and make such order or pass such sentence therein as the native court could itself have made or passed[7]; set aside the conviction and sentence and order any case to be retried either before the same native court, any other native court of competent jurisdiction, the Supreme Court, or any magistrate's court; or order the transfer of any cause or matter either before trial or at any stage in the proceedings to another native court, a magistrate's court or the Supreme Court[8]—but any order so made or sentence so passed by a Resident or district officer is susceptible to the same right of appeal, if any, as if the order or sentence had proceeded from the native court concerned.[9] Again, provision is made for the appointment of native courts as courts of appeal[10] and for appeals thereto, to a "Final Native Court of Appeal", to a magistrate's court or to the Supreme Court, as the Governor may prescribe, provided that "except in so far as the Governor may . . . direct, no appeal shall lie to a magistrate's court or to the Supreme Court or to a district officer or a Resident from any order or decision of a native court in any matter relating to marriage, family status, guardianship of children, inheritance, testamentary disposition or the administration of an estate"[11]; for a second appeal in certain circumstances[12]; for assessors, if required, to assist in appeal cases[13]; and for such appeal court, after rehearing the whole case or not, to make any such order or pass any such sentence as the court of first instance could have made or passed,[14] order any such

[1] Sect. 10(2).
[2] Sect. 11(1). But I never heard of this sub-section being invoked in the Northern Emirates.
[3] Sect. 14.
[4] Sect. 15(5).
[5] Sect. 16.
[6] Sects. 23, 26.
[7] Provided that there shall be no increase in penalty, etc., without the party concerned being heard.
[8] Sect. 28(1).
[9] Sect. 28(7).
[10] Sect. 29(1). But a party who has asked for a review loses thereby the right to appeal against the resulting order or sentence (see sect. 30(4)).
[11] Sect. 30.
[12] Sects. 30(2), 34, 38.
[13] Sect. 39.
[14] But the meaning of this phrase has been called in question: cp. pp. 182, 3.

cause or matter to be reheard before the court of first instance or before any other native court or magistrate's court, or (in the case of the Governor alone[1]) order a rehearing of the case before the Supreme Court.[2] In practice, it seems, appeals from the courts of district Alkalai lie to the court of the Chief Alkali and thence to the Emir's court (which would always in such circumstances necessarily be a Final Native Court of Appeal) or to the district officer, where there is no suitable Final Native Court of Appeal; that appeals from the Chief Alkali's court or from the Emir's court in first instance, if Grade A in each case, go straight to the Supreme Court in all circumstances; and that where these courts are of an inferior grade an appeal from the Alkali may lie first to the Emir's court and thence to the appropriate administrative officer.[3] Finally, it is decreed that "Any person who shall exercise or attempt to exercise judicial powers within the area of the jurisdiction of a duly constituted native court" shall be punished; but that "Nothing in this section contained shall be deemed to prohibit any chief, headman or any other person from adjudicating as an arbitrator upon any civil matter in dispute where the parties thereto have agreed to submit the dispute to his decision".[4]

It should be added that by Nigeria Order in Council No. 16 of 1934 under section 8 of this Ordinance it is provided that "Every native court in the Northern Provinces, in addition to having jurisdiction within such territorial limits as may be defined by its warrant over persons and classes of persons who have ordinarily been subject to the jurisdiction of native tribunals, shall within such limits have jurisdiction over the following classes of persons:—

(*a*) All persons—

(i) who permanently reside on land within the area of jurisdiction of a native authority with the permission, express or implied, of the native authority . . .

(ii) whose general mode of life is that of the general native community.

(*b*) All persons not permanently resident within the area of jurisdiction of a native authority but who are within such an area and whose general mode of life while therein is that of the general native community.

(*c*) All natives of Nigeria—

(i) who reside or are on land within the area of jurisdiction of a native authority as tenants or employees of any person holding such land . . .

(ii) whose general mode of life is that of the general native community."

From this it is clear that the dominant consideration in all cases is whether or not the mode of life of the persons concerned conforms to that of the general native community.[5] But it is interesting to observe that a recent tendency

---

[1] Or by delegation.

[2] Sect. 40.

[3] Appeals from native courts thus go sometimes to native courts of appeal (final or otherwise), sometimes to a magistrate's court or to the Supreme Court, sometimes to administrative officers. The question is decided by what is prescribed on the warrant of the court concerned.

[4] Sect. 43.

[5] It is, however, noteworthy that persons whose "mode of life" is superior to that of the "general native community", such as Syrians and Lebanese, often have recourse to such courts in the Northern Emirates, e.g., to recover trading debts, probably for the dual reason that this may save them time and money on the one hand and be considered "better form" by the native community on the other.

is to decide questions of jurisdiction by the dual criteria of the competence of the court and of the law to be applied, rather than the test, previously favoured, of the persons "subject to the jurisdiction" of this court or that: so it is to the resultant question of the law to be applied that the status of the parties—together with their intention, in such matters as contract—would be relevant.[1]

Other Legislation

There are several other Ordinances which have a distinct bearing, direct or indirect, on the application of Islamic law in Nigeria, and it will be convenient to discuss these at this point in order to preserve the sequence followed in other parts of this Survey. It should, however, be stressed that most Nigerian Ordinances seem to have little impact on the day to day life of the Muslims of the North outside urban areas—drafted, as such legislation often is, by those whose experience of the powerful native authority, native court and native authority police systems of the Northern Emirates is strictly limited.[2]

Thus the Interpretation Ordinance, 1939 (as repeatedly amended), defines the term "native" as including a native of Nigeria and a native foreigner, the latter phrase including "any person (not being a native of Nigeria) whose parents were members of a tribe or tribes indigenous to some part of Africa and the descendants of such persons, and shall include any person one of whose parents was a member of such tribe".[3] Again, both the Supreme Court Ordinance and the Magistrates' Courts Ordinance include almost identical clauses providing that "The court shall not enforce against a native living in any area specified by order in Council . . . any obligation incurred by him towards a non-native in respect of a commercial transaction, so far as it is based on credit, if it appear to the court in its discretion that it was not reasonably probable that the native was fully aware of the nature of the transaction and the consequences of failure to perform the same."[4] Similarly, the Native Children (Custody and Reformation) Ordinance, 1917, and the Children and Young Persons Ordinance, 1943 (as amended), include provisions which run counter, in certain circumstances, to the normal rules of guardianship in Islamic law.[5] But it is noteworthy that, unlike some other Codes, the Criminal Code Ordinance has no provision making it an offence prematurely to consummate a child marriage,[6] although it is a felony or misdemeanour to defile girls under the age of eleven and thirteen respectively: but section 361, which provides that "Any person who, with intent to marry or carnally know a female of any age, or to cause her to be married or carnally known by any other person, takes her away or detains her against her will" is guilty of a felony and punishable accordingly, might in certain circumstances expose to prosecution a Muslim father, or his executor, whose actions might have been unexceptionable under the Mālikī principles regarding marriage by compulsion (*jabr.*).

[1] See below, p. 284.

[2] For example, the native authority police, which police almost the whole of the Muslim North, and the native authority prisons were not recognised by Ordinance until 1943; while references in other Ordinances to, e.g., the "public service", or to persons who may authorise this or give permission for that, largely ignore the native authorities which administer the overwhelming majority of the public services of the North.

[3] Sect. 3.

[4] Sect. 34 of the Supreme Court Ordinance, sect. 37 of the Magistrates' Courts Ordinance.

[5] See sects. 3 and 4 of the former, Parts II and V of the latter. But the latter Ordinance has not been made applicable to the Northern Provinces; while the former no longer applies to the Colony.

[6] Government recently attempted to amend the Code in this respect, but the Muslim members of the Northern House of Assembly voted almost unanimously against it.

More important than these, however, is the Marriage Ordinance, 1914 (as amended), which may be said to run counter to pure Islamic law in the following respects: —

(*a*) in providing a way in which a Muslim girl of over twenty-one years of age, or under that age if already a widow or she has obtained suitable consent, could validly marry a non-Muslim, in spite (i) of the complete nullity of such a marriage under Islamic law, with or without consent, (ii) of the fact that the Mālikī law locally applicable denies a woman of any age the right to contract herself in marriage, and (iii) of the fact that in default of the father the right to consent to the marriage of a girl under twenty-one rests under this Ordinance with the mother instead of the agnatic guardian of Islamic law[1];

(*b*) in providing (presumably) a way in which two Muslims, debarred from intermarriage under Islamic law by foster relationship, could validly marry[2]—unless, that is, the phrase " any other lawful hindrances to the marriage " is to be construed, in the case of Muslims alone, as including foster relationship;

(*c*) in making any person so married, or whose marriage is declared valid thereunder, " incapable, during the continuance of such marriage, of contracting a valid marriage under native law and custom "[3] (including, of course, Islamic law), however little a marriage under this or any other Ordinance would, under the Sharī'a, deprive a Muslim of his right to contract further marriages;

(*d*) in precluding a Muslim so married from exercising his right in Islamic law unilaterally to repudiate his wife, since a marriage under this Ordinance can only be dissolved by a court of competent jurisdiction under " English " law;

(*e*) in precluding the dissolution of such marriage by reason that either spouse had subsequently embraced Islam or " apostatised " therefrom, however much such change of religion would *ipso facto* have that effect in Islamic law;

(*f*) in making a man already married under Islamic law who contracts a marriage with another woman under this Ordinance, or a woman who so contracts a marriage with a man whom she knows to be already married to another under Islamic law,[4] liable to imprisonment for five years, in spite of the fact that for a Muslim to marry more than one wife is no offence under the Sharī'a;

(*g*) in having the effect, in the Colony alone, that where one so married dies intestate leaving a widow or husband, or where the issue of such marriage dies intestate, his or her personal property and any real property of which he or she might have disposed by will must be distributed according to the law of England, any native law or custom (including Islamic law) to the contrary notwithstanding.[5]

Again, with regard to slavery, the Slavery Ordinance, 1916, which repealed and replaced an Ordinance of 1908 applicable to the Southern Provinces and one of 1910 applicable to the Northern Provinces, declares the " legal status of slavery . . . hereby . . . abolished throughout the Protectorate "[6] and (as amended in 1936) "All persons heretofore or hereafter born in or brought within the Protectorate . . . hereby . . . free persons ".[7]

[1] See sect. 11(*b*) and 18.

[2] See sect. 11(*c*).

[3] See sects. 35 and 48 and cp. sect. 370 of the Criminal Code Ordinance, concerning bigamy in such circumstances.

[4] Sects. 47 and 40 respectively. The subsequent marriage under the Ordinance is, moreover, invalid (under sect. 33(1)).

[5] Sect. 36(1).

[6] Sect. 2.

[7] Sect. 3. Before amendment this section read " born in or brought within the Northern Provinces after the 31st March, 1901."

There are also, of course, several Ordinances regarding land. Thus the Crown Lands Ordinance, 1918, defines " Crown land " (in both Colony and Protectorate) as " all public lands in Nigeria which are for the time being subject to the control of Her Majesty by virtue of treaty, cession, convocation or agreement, or by virtue of Her Majesty's protectorate ", except lands subject to the Land and Native Rights Ordinance[1] and provides that, except with the consent of the Secretary of State, the Governor shall not sell any Crown lands[2] but may " grant leases (thereof) for any term, or in the case of a lease to a native of Nigeria for an indefinite term, and may also grant licences for the temporary occupation of Crown lands ".[3] Similarly the Land and Native Rights Ordinance, 1916 (as repeatedly amended), was expressly based on the expediency both of protecting and preserving the " existing customary rights of the natives of the Northern Provinces and of the Cameroons under British Trusteeship[4] to use and enjoy the land of the Protectorate and the natural fruits thereof in sufficient quantity to enable them to provide for the sustenance of themselves and their families " and also of defining by law " the rights and obligations of the Government in regard to the whole of the lands within the boundaries of the Northern Provinces of the Protectorate and of the Cameroons under British Trusteeship and also the rights and obligations of cultivators or other persons claiming to have an interest in such land ".[5] The term " native " in this Ordinance is expressly defined as including any person " whose parents were members of any tribe or tribes indigenous to the Northern Provinces or the Cameroons under British Trusteeship and the descendants of any such persons ", including (*a*) any person one of whose parents was a member of such tribe, and (*b*) any person, being a native of Africa, who shall have obtained a certificate from the Governor, after declaring his intention of making the Northern Provinces or the Cameroons under British Trusteeship his permanent domicile and satisfying the Governor that he has obtained the consent of the native communities concerned.[6] The Ordinance then proceeds to provide that save and except (*a*) scheduled lands, (*b*) all land to which a title shall have been established in accordance with the provisions of section 22, (*c*) all land or interests therein in respect of which a title has been granted under the provisions of section 23, " the whole of the lands of the Northern Provinces and the Cameroons under British Trusteeship, whether occupied or unoccupied, are hereby declared to be native lands "[7]; that " All native lands, and all rights over the same, are hereby declared to be under the control and subject to the disposition of the Governor, and shall be held and administered for the use and common benefit of the natives: and no title to the occupation and use of any such land shall be valid without the consent of the Governor "[8]; and that the latter " in the exercise of the powers conferred upon him . . . shall have regard to the native laws and customs existing in the district in which the land is situated ".[9] Subsequent sections enact that the Governor, or those to whom he delegates his powers, may grant rights of occupancy to natives and non-natives,[10] for definite or indefinite terms,[11] and may demand[12] and revise[13] rentals, provided no single right of occupancy

---

[1] Sect. 2, as amended in 1945.
[2] Sect. 3.
[3] Sect. 4.
[4] As amended.
[5] Preamble.
[6] Sect. 2.
[7] Sect. 3.
[8] Sect. 4.
[9] Sect. 5.
[10] Sect. 6(*a*).
[11] Sect. 7.
[12] Sect. 6(*b*).
[13] Sect. 6(*c*).

granted to a non-native exceeds a certain maximum acreage[1]; that "Except as may be otherwise provided by the regulations in relation to native occupiers, it shall not be lawful for any occupier to alienate his right of occupancy, or any part thereof . . . without the consent of the Governor"[2]; that the "devolution of the rights of an occupier upon death shall be regulated, in the case of a native, by the native custom existing in the locality in which the land is situated . . . Provided that the land shall not be divided into two or more parts on devolution by the death of the occupier, except with the sanction of the Governor"[3]; that disputes and claims under this Ordinance are to go to the Supreme Court or, in some cases, to magistrates' courts[4]; that "Nothing in this Ordinance shall be deemed to affect the validity of any title to land granted to a non-native or any interest therein acquired by such non-native before the 25th of February, 1916", in the Northern Provinces or 4th of February, 1927, in the Cameroons under British Trusteeship[5]; and that "It shall be lawful for the Governor to delegate to any native authority all or any of the powers conferred on the Governor by this Ordinance."[6] Similarly, in the Southern Provinces, the Native Lands Acquisition Ordinance, 1917 (as amended), enacts that "No alien shall acquire any interest or right in or over any land within the Southern Provinces from a native, unless such alien has been approved in writing by the Governor in that behalf".[7] And the Land (Perpetual Succession) Ordinance, 1924, provides that "Trustees or a trustee may be appointed by any community of persons bound together by custom, religion, kinship or nationality or by any body or association of persons established for any religious, educational, literary, scientific, social or charitable purpose, and such trustees or trustee may apply . . . to the Governor for a certificate of registration . . . as a corporate body"[8]; and that, if the Governor sees fit to grant such certificate, the body corporate so formed "shall have perpetual succession and a common seal, and power to sue and be sued in such corporate name, and . . . to hold and acquire and . . . convey, assign and demise any land or any interest therein now or hereafter belonging to, or held for the benefit of, such community, body or association".[9]

As for procedure, it is noteworthy that even in litigation before a British Court the Oaths and Affirmations Ordinance, 1942, enacts that if any party to any judicial proceedings of a civil nature offers to be bound by an oath or affirmation "common amongst or held binding by persons of (his) race or persuasion . . . and not repugnant to justice or decency"[10] made by the other party or any witness in such proceeding, "the court may, if it thinks fit, ask such party or witness . . . whether or not he will make the oath or affirmation",[11] whereupon "The evidence so given shall, as against the person who offered to be bound as aforesaid, be conclusive proof of the matter stated".[12] Where, however, the party or witness refuses, he shall "not be compelled to make it, nor be asked his reason for refusal, but the court shall record . . . the nature of the oath or affirmation proposed, the fact that he was asked whether he would make it and that he refused it, together with any reason which he may voluntarily assign for his refusal".[13] This provision clearly goes a certain way—but not very far—towards bridging the gulf between the English and Islamic rules of procedure and evidence.

---

[1] Sect. 8.
[2] Sect. 11.
[3] Sect. 15.
[4] Sect. 21.
[5] Sect. 22.
[6] Sect. 26(1). This has been widely done.
[7] Sect. 3(1).
[8] Sect. 2(1).
[9] Sect. 2(3).
[10] Sect. 7.
[11] Sect. 8.
[12] Sect. 10. But I did not hear of any instance of this Ordinance being invoked in a magistrate's court or the Supreme Court.
[13] Sect. 11.

Finally, it is noteworthy that the problems raised by the trial of homicide cases under Islamic law when committed within the jurisdiction of an Emir whose powers are of the grade A (unlimited) variety, and under the Criminal Code before the Supreme Court in all other cases,[1] led in 1948 to a highly controversial amendment of the Native Courts Ordinances[2], which provided, *inter alia*: —

(*a*) That " Subject to any limitation imposed on its jurisdiction by or under the Native Courts Ordinances, but notwithstanding anything contained in the Criminal Code Ordinance, where any person is charged with an offence against native law or custom, a native court may try the case in accordance with native law or custom even though the act or omission constituting the offence may also constitute an offence under the provisions of the Criminal Code or of any other enactment ".[3] This provision was designed to give statutory authority to what had previously been current practice which had never been called in question, but was completely upset by the decision of the West African Court of Appeal in *Tsofo Guba's case*[4]—which was, in fact, the *raison d'être* of this amendment Ordinance as a whole.

(*b*) That " Subject to any limitation imposed on its jurisdiction by or under the Native Courts Ordinances, a native court may try and punish a person for any act or omission constituting an offence against the provisions of the Criminal Code as if jurisdiction in that behalf had been conferred upon the court by Order in Council under the Native Courts Ordinance "[5]—i.e., provided that the offence and punishment concerned do not exceed its jurisdiction, it may abandon its normal application of native law in favour of the Criminal Code, where the offence concerned is punishable thereunder.

(c) That any court or other authority exercising appellate jurisdiction in criminal matters under the Native Courts Ordinances may, where it " considers that there is sufficient ground for interfering with the decision appealed against, set aside that decision and either—(i) acquit the appellant; or (ii) retry the appellant on the same charge or on any charge which might have been laid on the facts as disclosed by the evidence, and make such order or pass such sentence as to the court or other authority may seem just; or (iii) order the retrial of the appellant before a court of competent jurisdiction on the same charge or on any charge which might have laid on the facts as disclosed by the evidence; or (iv) substitute any other decision (whether as to guilt or punishment) which the court of first instance could have made on the facts disclosed by the evidence, but so that, by the decision so substituted, the appellant shall not be found guilty of any offence with which he was not charged before the court of first instance, unless the appellate court or authority is satisfied that the defence of the appellant before the court of first instance would not have been substantially affected if he had been so charged; or (v) substitute a special finding to the effect that the appellant was guilty of the act or omission charged, but was insane . . ."[6]: and any of these powers may be exercised " notwithstanding that the verdict of the court of first instance was correct by native law and custom ".[7] All these somewhat cumbersome provisions were primarily designed to cover the case of an appellant found guilty of wilful homicide and sentenced to death by a Grade A (unlimited) Emir's court in circumstances which, while justifying that verdict under Mālikī law, would only amount to manslaughter under the Criminal Code,[8] and to enable the appellate court or authority to substitute in such cases a term of imprisonment for capital punishment.

[1] For detailed discussion, see below (pp. 198 ff.).
[2] No. 36 of 1948.
[3] Sect. 3(1).
[4] *Tsofo Guba* v. *Gwandu Native Authority*, W.A.C.A. 5.5.1947—unreported.
[5] Sect. 3(2).
[6] Sect. 4(1).
[7] Sect. 4(2).
[8] See below (p. 198).

(*d*) That "As soon as practicable after the determination of a trial for homicide before a native court, and in the case of a trial before a native court for any other offence if the Attorney-General (of his own motion or on the application of any person) so directs . . . , the court shall send to the Registrar of the Supreme Court . . . copies of all documents, minutes and notes of evidence taken in the case"[1]; and if, on the perusal thereof, a Judge of the Supreme Court is "satisfied that, by reason of the application to the case of native law and custom, the decision of the court of first instance is not satisfactory having regard to the provisions of the Criminal Code applicable in the circumstances, he shall, by order, set aside the decision" and act in any of the ways[2] open to an appellate authority under (*c*) above, "Provided that, in the case of a conviction by a native court, a Judge shall not make any (such) order . . . unless the time limit for appeal has expired"[3] (while he shall also "if he is of the opinion that justice so requires, afford an opportunity to be heard to the Attorney-General and to the person convicted or acquitted and to any other person or authority who the Judge considers should be heard"[4]).

It may be added that opinion has varied considerably as to the correct construction to be put on the words "not satisfactory having regard to the provisions of the Criminal Code applicable in the circumstances". It was originally urged on behalf of the Attorney-General that where the accused, if tried by the Supreme Court, would have been sentenced to death and the native court only imposed, e.g., five years' imprisonment, this was "not satisfactory within the meaning of section 5(2)"[5]: and this was accepted, with some reluctance, by the Judge concerned and upheld by the West African Court of Appeal as a legitimate interpretation of that section. Later, however, the Crown Counsel of the Northern Provinces applied in the Kano Division of the Supreme Court[6] to set aside seven orders for the retrial under this section of persons convicted by a native court of intentional homicide, amounting to murder under the Code, but only sentenced to a term of imprisonment, on the grounds that "the only case contemplated" when the section was drafted was "where a native court had sentenced a person to death for what, under the Criminal Code, would be manslaughter only": and it was held that, the Attorney-General having withdrawn his previous submission, the Court was free to adopt the narrower interpretation of the section, on the grounds that "it is a well-known canon of interpretation that the mischief which a law was enacted to remedy may be considered in interpreting the law", while the decision of the Court of Appeal that its former discretion was "not wrongly exercised" did not debar it from now exercising it differently. In other words, it was finally accepted both by the law officers and the Supreme Court that the discretion conferred by section 5(2) should not be exercised "otherwise than in favour of the accused".

Yet another matter of controversy, moreover, concerns the proper interpretation to be put on the clause[7] which empowers an appellate authority to "substitute any other decision . . . which the court of first instance could have made". Here the point at issue is whether an Emir's court could in fact have found the offender guilty of manslaughter and sentenced him accordingly when the Mālikī law, by which such court in fact regards itself as bound, allows no such verdict or

[1] Sect. 5(1).

[2] i.e., acquit the appellant, direct his retrial before the Supreme Court, substitute a conviction for manslaughter for a sentence of death, substitute a special finding or confirm the decision.

[3] Sect. 5(2).

[4] Sect. 5(3).

[5] *Rex* v. *Usman Acida* [K/381/49—unreported].

[6] Under sect. 45 of the Supreme Court Ordinance.

[7] See (*c*) at p. 181 above.

sentence. It seems clear, however, that the phrase was intended, and must be understood, to include any sentence within the powers conferred by Ordinance on the court concerned,[1] however little the passing of any such verdict would have been within the self-imposed competence of that court.

This Native Courts Ordinance (No. 36 of 1948) has, however, now been repealed and the vacuum temporarily filled by another amendment to the Native Courts Ordinance, 1934, dated 12th April, 1951. This omits entirely the provisions of section 5 of the above-quoted Ordinance,[2] leaving the problem of cases which would be capital under the Mālikī law but only amount to manslaughter under the Criminal Code to be dealt with not by review by the Supreme Court but by transfer thereto by the Resident or district officer concerned, or by order of retrial thereby, or indeed the immediate commutation of the sentence, under the Governor-General's prerogative. Section 4 of the 1948 Ordinance, on the other hand,[3] is repeated in the 1951 Ordinance, as a new section added to the 1934 Ordinance.[4]

As for the native court itself, its right to try a case under native law and custom even though it also constitutes an offence under the Criminal Code or some other enactment is retained,[5] but with the simple proviso that the punishment imposed in such circumstances must not exceed the maximum punishment permitted by the Criminal Code or other enactment concerned.[6] This means, of course, that the death penalty must not be imposed for a homicide which would only constitute manslaughter under the Code; so the native court has the choice in such cases either of complying with the Ordinance and disregarding the Mālikī texts or of following the Sharī'a and leaving it to the Supreme Court or the Governor to quash or commute the sentence. In the stricter areas they will probably choose the latter alternative, initially at least.

Personalities

During my tour of the Northern Provinces I was able to meet and talk with the Sultan of Sokoto, the Shehu of Bornu, the Etsu of Nupe, and the Emirs of Kano, Gwandu, Katsina, Zaria, Argungu, Dikwa, Fika, Bauchi and Ilorin—usually in the company of some, at least, of their Council members. These Emirs naturally vary a good deal in their relative ability, their interest in developments in other Muslim lands, and in the complexion (ranging from extreme conservatism to mild liberalism) of their general outlook on the one hand and the rigidity of their adherence to the letter of the Mālikī texts on the other. I was also able to have long and detailed discussions, sometimes on several occasions, with the Sudanese lecturers at the School of Arabic Studies at Kano; the Walis of Kano and of Bornu; the Waziri of Sokoto; the Chief Alkalai of Kano, Sokoto, Birnin Kebbi, Argungu, Katsina, Maiduguri, Bama, Potiskum, Bauchi, Zaria, Bida and Ilorin; with assistant or district Alkalai in a number of different localities; and with leading local authorities on the law in several centres, but particularly in Katsina. Individuals, again, varied greatly in their relative erudition, intelligence and conservatism: and I was particularly impressed with Sheikh 'Awaḍ of the School of Arabic Studies, a man of character and erudition with judicial experience in the Sudan[7]; the Chief Alkali of Zaria, probably the outstanding jurist of the old school among the present Alkalai; the

[1] See (*b*) at p. 181 above.

[2] cp. (*d*) at p. 182 above.

[3] cp. (*c*) at p. 181 above.

[4] Sect. 40A.

[5] Sect. 2, now sect. 10A of the original Ordinance.

[6] Much in the terms of (*a*) at p. 181 above.

[7] As, indeed, has been true of all those seconded from the Sudan to teach in the Kano Law School (now the School of Arabic Studies).

Chief Alkali of Bida, who struck me as the best example of the more modern type of jurist produced by the Kano School; and the Wali of Bornu, whose conservatism in law is matched by an active interest in the problems of reform. Several others—including the Chief Alkali of Birnin Kebbi and two or three of the younger district Alkalai who are recent products of the School—also deserve honourable mention. To the attitude of these and others to modern developments in the Sharī'a reference will be made *passim* in several contexts and *seriatim* later in this Survey; but the following summary of the law as applied in Northern Nigeria today is chiefly derived from detailed questioning of these native jurists (mostly in Arabic, but occasionally by interpretation into the vernacular), augmented, of course, by conversations with administrative officers and by the perusal of numerous files, case records and other material.

Land Tenure

It is in the matter of land tenure that native law and custom has won its most decisive victory over the general ascendancy of the Sharī'a in the Muslim Emirates of Northern Nigeria. Yet even here the victory is not complete, and the situation remains somewhat fluid.

It is obvious that in Nigeria, as elsewhere in Africa, rights to land originally partook of the " character of a privilege based on membership of a community, entitling every member to the beneficial use of the community lands . . . rather than a right over specific areas identified with the holder.[1]" Thus most land was held on a tribal, kindred or at least family basis: and partly for this reason, and partly because there was no land hunger and so no intrinsic value in land *per se*, the sale or permanent alienation of land was virtually unknown. And whatever the theory may have been, the function of the chief with regard to land did not in practice exceed an administrative control over vacant lands in the interests of the community, whereby he would grant to family groups an usufructuary right not permanently alienable, over such land as they needed, and might demand the return of any excess; but even the temporary introduction of a stranger commonly required his consent.[2]

These conditions, moreover, still obtain throughout many areas of Northern Nigeria, particularly among the pagan communities, although they have become modified in some localities. Thus even in pagan areas there has been a tendency—very strong in parts—for kindred tenure to break up into that of the biological family or even the individual[3]; for land in densely populated or particularly fertile areas to acquire a commercial value, so that its temporary,[4] or even permanent,[5] alienation has become increasingly common[6]; and for the control of the chief or village head to become progressively looser. In general, however, it seems clear that even where rights in land may be alienated with almost complete freedom these rights are normally conceived as those of user rather than the English " freehold "—a fact illustrated *inter alia* by the circumstance that in some districts rights of wet and dry season farming over the same land may be respectively exercised, and alienated, by and to different persons.

---

[1] Lord Hailey's *African Survey*, p. 830.

[2] See *Land Law and Custom in the Colonies*, by C. K. Meek, p. 149.

[3] Factors which have favoured this development are settled conditions, which minimise the need for a family to stand together, and the passing of the old communal sanctions against an unsatisfactory member of a family enterprise.

[4] e.g., by loan (often merging into lease), pledge, etc.

[5] e.g., by sale, gift or pledge merging into sale.

[6] While it is noted in Lord Lugard's *Political Memoranda* that " proprietary rights in building sites in the large cities have long been recognised, and also transfer or lease of lands for valuable consideration " (p. 353).

In the Muslim areas, also, custom in fact reigns supreme, with minor but interesting exceptions. True, certain local purists now[1] maintain that the land in Sokoto and Gwandu (originally part of Sokoto) should be regarded as *'ushr*[2] land or private property[3]; that the land in Kano and Zaria, for instance, was captured by force (*'anwatan*) at the time of the Fulani *jihād*, and thus became either *kharāj* land[4] over which its possessors or their successors held only a right of user (as is postulated of most of Kano Province) or was granted outright to the conquerors as fiefs[5] (as, it is now argued,[6] was the case with parts of Zaria Province, although other parts were left to their original possessors, where Muslims, allegedly as *'ushr* land). But this theoretical pattern is further complicated by the circumstances of the British conquest, for in Katsina, for instance, the Emir maintains that, although this Province submitted by treaty (*ṣulḥ*) at the time of the Fulani *jihād*, yet the British captured it by force of arms, whereupon the ultimate ownership passed to the conquerors; while in the case of Zaria, on the other hand, local jurists argue that the British entered by treaty,[7] so the *status quo* (particularly with regard to fiefs and *'ushr*, even if not *kharāj*, land) was preserved.

But local theory regarding land tenure seems to vary in details from locality to locality and even jurist to jurist,[8] and a few examples must suffice. Thus in Kano the Emir is emphatic that land—or rather its user—may not be sold without his permission,[9] while the Islamic laws of inheritance are at least modified to the extent that only males normally succeed to the user of land and houses.[10] In Katsina, on the other hand, the jurists argue that land is "owned", may be freely sold or bequeathed, and is subject to the Islamic rules of inheritance[11], while the Emir maintains the British attitude that it may be sold only with his permission (delegated to village headmen) and that every effort is made to limit inheritance to one heir, who should compensate the rest. In Sokoto and Gwandu

[1] For the older view, see *Ta'limu Radthi*, composed by Mallam Abdullahi, which may be said, however, to enshrine the Fulani view, at the time of the *jihād*, of what land tenure ought to be, rather than to record existing practice. According to this compilation private rights in land may be acquired either by occupation and improvement, etc., or by assignment by the Imām. In the former case all claim is lost by abandonment; while all land "privately" owned may be given away, bequeathed, etc. But cultivated land captured in war may not be so assigned as private property by the Imām: it must remain as a waqf in favour of the state, and only its use may be assigned. Even so, however, it is expressly stated that the authority in disputes about land is the executive, not the judiciary. But it is noteworthy that the theories recorded in this and the following paragraphs of this Survey appear to be largely of recent inspiration an inspiration not wholly unconnected, it seems, with the payment by Government of large sums of money by way of compensation in respect of the site of the Gaskiya Corporation, etc.

[2] i.e., land owned by Muslims before the *jihād*, in respect of which the ordinary *zakāt* must be paid.

[3] *Sed quaere.* The Sultan himself, it seems, told the Northern Nigerian Lands Committee in 1910 that there was no private right to land in Sokoto.

[4] As a waqf in favour of the State, or Muslim community. This is the true Mālikī doctrine.

[5] But this appears to be against the thesis of *Ta'limu Radthi* and the true Mālikī law: see note (1) above.

[6] e.g., by the Chief Alkali of Zaria. But see the last sentence of note (1) above.

[7] Zaria in fact, it seems, asked for a British garrison as a protection against Kontagora.

[8] For only jurists and interested parties, it seems, bother their heads about such theories in Nigeria today.

[9] An unauthorised sale would be stopped, I was told, if discovered in time, but not rescinded if the vendee had already started to cultivate the land—and the rule, it seems, is more honoured in the breach than the observance.

[10] In other words, custom, not the Sharī'a, in fact prevails.

[11] Although the Sultan came out strongly in the 1939 Conference of Chiefs against this theory.

the sale and bequest of land is allegedly unrestricted in some areas[1] and the Islamic rules of inheritance are said to be applied, except that local custom normally prevails at least to the extent that females are excluded from succeeding to rights in land[2]: but in Argungu neither sale nor bequest is allowed.[3] In Bornu land in the neighbourhood of Lake Chad is, it seems, privately owned, freely alienated and subject to the Islamic rules of inheritance[4]; while elsewhere only a right of user is recognised,[5] control rests (by delegation) in the hands of the village headmen who will redistribute abandoned land, and females have only rights in produce, not to a division of the land. In Fika (whence, like Bornu, the Fulani *jihād* was repulsed) neither sale nor bequest is allowed; while in Bauchi, too, land is plentiful, alienation virtually unknown, and the eldest son or senior member of the family group usually continues to cultivate after his father's or brother's demise—and the same is true of "family" houses, only those privately built by some individual being alienable by him (and then only with the Emir's consent). In Jos, as in most towns, houses represent individual property in some cases and family compounds in others.[6] In Zaria sale of land is officially prohibited, but bequest and inheritance are alleged to go by the Sharī'a, except that only males normally succeed to land or houses—and that, too, usually on a communal basis.[7] In Nupe, again, there are two main ways of acquiring the use of land[8]: in virtue of membership in a kinship group or village community holding corporate rights, and in virtue of a contract between individual landowners. Under the former various "rights of access" may in turn be distinguished, such as the grant of temporary and restricted access to a small portion of family land which is allotted to each male for private cultivation; the claim to a farm by adult members of a family group; and the general right of management vested in the family head: and it is expressive of the position of the chief as trustee of all land on behalf of the community that it is only in the case either of succession to the position of family head or of additional land being needed by a family group that reference must be made to him. Under the latter, however, must be classified the short term loan, which often merges into a lease; the lease for life (in "conquered" lands only), under which the tenant makes a substantial initial payment in cash followed by a fixed annual rental in kind[9]; and the tenure of a "client" on the lands of the big fiefholders, under which certain visits, ceremonies and tithes of produce were formerly due to the patron—but the last-named were reluctantly forbidden by the Etsu, under British pressure, in 1945, although the practice no doubt continues to some extent *sub rosa*. In both Nupe and Ilorin, moreover, family lands and houses are inalienable and pass, as we have seen, to the senior or ablest member of the family, whereas houses or farms built or cleared by individual effort would pass to a man's sons, as a new sub-section of the family,

---

[1] *Seq quaere*, for the Sultan stated in the 1939 Conference of Chiefs that he was opposed to this (see above).

[2] Which again shows that it is customary law, not the Sharī'a, which in fact prevails.

[3] Argungu, of course, was never conquered in the *jihād*.

[4] Except that females are probably even here normally excluded from actual succession to land, but receive (perhaps) compensation from other assets.

[5] And land is held to vest in the Shehu himself.

[6] While in a town such as Kano many are owned by the Native Authority.

[7] This, of course, again means that the Sharī'a is not fully applied in practice, whatever the theory may be. The Chief Alkali maintained that if a female claimed her rights he would grant them, provided there was no "confusion of rights" in the property concerned (which would, of course, in practice always be the case in regard to a family compound, etc.).

[8] cp. *A Black Byzantium*, by S. F. Nadel.

[9] And may "sell" his lease for a fixed sum, after which the assignee becomes responsible to the landlord for the annual rent.

or might even be bequeathed to a servant or adopted son in default of natural heirs.

But whatever theories may be put forward in different localities and by different local jurists, the two points of major significance which everywhere emerge are firstly that cases concerning land seldom find their way to the courts at all, and secondly that throughout Northern Nigeria, with the solitary exception of Zaria Province, any actual litigation concerning land is in the hands of the executive, not the judiciary.[1] Regarding the former point it may be observed that the vast majority of all transfers of land or its use, whether by inheritance, loan, gift or even sale, go by local custom without involving any form of dispute or litigation, and Lord Hailey justly observes: " there is in Northern Nigeria often an open divergence between the concepts of Muslim law and the current practice in such matters as the sub-division of landholdings by succession, the holding of land by women, and the specific character of pledges of land as security for debt "[2]. And this independence of the Sharī'a is maintained, in general, even in the small minority of cases which give rise to disputes, since these are almost invariably decided by the executive—whether village head, district head or Emir's court[3]—in accordance with local custom; while, conversely, the comparatively recent transfer of jurisdiction in such cases to the Alkalai in Zaria alone is significant of the increasing influence of Islamic law in regard to land tenure in parts of that province.[4]

Again, whatever local theorists may say, it is clear that in British law no distinction whatever is recognised between Emirates which capitulated with or without fighting. Thus Lord Lugard records that " When Northern Nigeria was conquered in 1902-3, each of the present Emirs was appointed by me on terms embodied in a 'Letter of appointment' publicly read and translated, and accepted by him and his people,[5] in which *inter alia,* the ultimate rights in the land, in so far as they were held by the Fulani dynasty as conquerors, were transferred to the British Crown[6] ". But he goes on to say that " no attempt was made at the time to define those rights . . . It may be argued that under the Law of Islam the right of the conqueror to unrestricted ownership of the land is recognised,[7] but Muhammadan law in Nigeria has been modified by native law and custom, though to what precise extent it is impossible to define ".

Prior to 1910, moreover, it seems that the official attitude of Government can best be summarised, again in the words of Lord Lugard, as " the recognition of the advantage of individual occupation rights, combined with the right of Government, as Suzerain and conqueror, to dispose of lands not in actual occupation, and to control all lands leased to aliens. The right of a native to acquire such rights in land, as were his by native law and custom, and to dispose of them, even to an alien, was not denied in principle, but in order that the Government might be the sole landlord of all aliens, and to protect the natives in their dealings with them, no non-native could acquire land except with the consent of the Governor, and the land would be acquired by Government and disposed of (by lease only) to the intending purchaser. No rentals were charged to native occupants, and all rents from non-natives were paid into Revenue "[8].

---

[1] See Report on *Land Tenure in Zaria Province,* by C. W. Cole, pp. 49 ff.; although it must be observed that certain cases which partially at least concern land are not infrequently heard in practice by district Alkalai.

[2] *Native Administration in British African Territories,* Vol. III, p. 95.

[3] Acting here, really, in an executive rather than a judicial capacity.

[4] See *Land Tenure in Zaria Province,* by C. W. Cole, pp. 50 ff.

[5] i.e., his Council.

[6] *Political Memoranda,* p. 344.

[7] But this in fact would depend on the circumstances of the conquest and the terms of any treaty concluded between the parties.

[8] *Political Memoranda,* p. 350.

There was thus a clear distinction between Crown lands, which were claimed in absolute title, and public land, which was only controlled by the Government administratively.

All this was changed, however, as a result of the work of a Committee appointed in 1908, which decided that the "ultimate ownership of land, whether occupied or not, was vested in the heads of the Community, and now vested in the Governor, to be held and administered by him for the use and common benefit of the natives, but that the Governor's powers must be exercised in accordance with native law and custom". As a result the Land and Native Rights Proclamation of 1910 was promulgated, to be replaced (with alterations) by the Land and Native Rights Ordinance of 1916 summarised above. This abolished all distinction between Crown and public lands; and it was no longer necessary for Government to pay for any lands it might hypothecate for public use or for lease to aliens, except by way of compensation for any "improvements" attributable to their previous holders.[1]

Not unnaturally, this Ordinance has been attacked in some quarters[2] as an "expropriation" of all native lands, as invalidating customary native land tenure, and as contrary to native law and custom in requiring rent for those rights of occupancy to be granted by the Governor. But while some of these criticisms may find partial justification in the terms of the Ordinance, Lord Hailey has justly remarked that "As regards the first point raised, the Crown has used its powers to make only a very limited number of alienations, mainly connected with the tin mines. On the second point, the security of customary rights has been maintained by leaving the settlement of land disputes in the hands of the native authorities and their courts; in practice, their control is complete, subject to the power of revision exercised over all decisions of native courts. The native authority also deals with land transactions between natives: there is no restriction on sale, transfer or bequest to a blood relation, but the approval of the administration is needed[3] for the transfer of land to a native not resident in the district.[4] Finally, no rent is taken by the Crown in respect of native lands, nor is the imposition of any such charge by native authorities contemplated in the regulations. In this respect, therefore, the form adopted by the law would also appear to be of less significance than its operation in practice; it would not appear that its working has tended in any way to invalidate customary rights, while it provides machinery for the evolution of native tenures in response to altered economic conditions."[5] And it may be added that any idea that customary land tenure is disregarded, even in theory, by the Ordinance receives no support from a comparison of section 9 with the definition of "occupier" in section 2.[6]

Under the Ordinance, then, the rights of persons occupying land in the Northern Provinces fall into two categories: namely (*a*) those persons (natives or non-natives) who have been granted rights of occupancy by the Governor, whose rights are defined by the Ordinance or by their contract of lease, whose

---

[1] Op. cit., p. 351.

[2] But not, it seems, in the Northern Provinces themselves, where the Ordinance is normally regarded as the charter of local land rights, and the chief bulwark against the disastrous litigation and alienations of the south and of parts of the Gold Coast, as a result of the importation of alien principles and practices; while the Minutes of the 1908 Committee show that it follows local concepts in declaring that the ultimate right to land is now vested in the conqueror.

[3] Nominally, but not now, it seems, normally in practice, since it is no longer necessary in most localities, as in Lord Lugard's time, to protect the Northerners against immigrants.

[4] See Schedule 3 to the Ordinance. But parts of this seem somewhat artificial, and are "not even honoured in the breach" in Kano Province (see Report on *Land Tenure in Kano Province* by C. W. Rowling, p. 7), although apparently enforced in Zaria.

[5] *An African Survey*, pp. 773 and 774.

[6] i.e., that it "includes a native or native community using or occupying land in accordance with native law and custom" (Added by No. 23 of 1926).

occupancy can only be prematurely terminated for "good cause" under section 12, and who must normally pay rent; (*b*) those natives who occupy land under native law and custom, whose rights are governed by local custom except as modified by the Ordinance and its dependent regulations, whose rights can be determined at any time by the Governor for the general benefit of the community[1] (with due regard for native law and custom) and who are not required to pay rent. The basic principle, moreover, everywhere prevails that the land is held in trust for the people by the native authority in Muslim areas, by the tribal land authority in Benue Province, and by the chief or council of elders in other pagan areas, all as agents of the Governor. But in a country consisting of many administrative units with widely different conditions (e.g., density of population, amount of land available, social organisation of the people, proximity to large towns, system of cultivation, suitability of soil for cash crops, and influx of immigrant elements) the degree to which customary practices are being, and are likely to be, modified by the march of modern progress and of alien ideas must necessarily vary.

It may be asked, then, in what respects and to what extent Islamic law has in fact influenced or replaced native law and custom in regard to land in Northern Nigeria? A good example is provided by the matter of inheritance. It has already been noted that in the main inheritance to land still goes by custom rather than Islamic law, for normally either the senior member of the family or the male agnates collectively take over any land farmed by the deceased, without any necessity to compensate other heirs, on the grounds that he or they are now going to lead and support the family previously led and supported by the deceased. But this is no longer universally true; for in the region of Lake Chad and the areas contiguous to the cities of Kano, Sokoto and Zaria farms are now valuable commercial assets which may be (and sometimes are) reckoned in the estate, which is not infrequently divided on strictly Islamic principles.[2] Again, Sir Richmond Palmer is reported[3] as having remarked years ago, that the influence of Islamic law could be seen in increasing claims to individual proprietorship of houses, wells and valuable trees, leading, in certain localities, to individual ownership of the land itself. More, the fact that land can be privately owned, alienated and inherited in Islamic law much on a par with movables has proved one factor,[4] among others, in promoting the growth of individual ownership of farms and the claim that they should be susceptible to commercial (and other[5]) alienation which underlies this whole development. Again, Islamic law is often invoked, as has been seen, by interested persons to validate some claim—e.g., claims of descendants of alleged fiefholders in Zaria to compensation for expropriated land, instead of this being paid to the actual occupiers who would be so entitled under customary law; claims to an inherited ownership of valuable swamp lands, or even of a piece of bush cleared by someone else, because some ancestor once farmed that piece of bush or in the vicinity of that swamp land, whereas any such claim in customary law would have long lapsed from non-use;[6] and the claims of absentee owners to retain the "title" to abandoned lands and houses.[7] Mr. C. W. Cole also traces the increased stress on Islamic law regarding land in Zaria to the virtual ban on

[1] With appropriate compensation, unless the occupier is himself at fault.

[2] Except that females, even here, would not normally take their share of farms as such but rather compensation from other assets (e.g., fruit-bearing trees).

[3] *Political Memoranda*, p. 359.

[4] Or, possibly, an argument to bolster up a tendency which is basically economic.

[5] e.g., outright gift in perpetuity before witnesses, now recognised in Zaria City under the direct influence of Islamic law. (See Report on *Land Tenure in Zaria Province*, p. 67.)

[6] But the Emirs have ruled that such claims cannot be entertained where the alleged farm has genuinely reverted to bush; while sometimes a period of, e.g., ten years, or a test such as the disappearance of all signs of old furrows, has been applied.

[7] But these claims, too, are almost invariably refused.

the sale of farms in that province which results from a stricter insistence on Schedule 3 of the Ordinance than is found, e.g., in Kano.[1] And the argument of certain jurists and interested persons that the "native law and custom" applicable in Northern Nigeria even in questions of land is in fact the law of Islam finds superficial support in the general similarity of the Islamic system with regard to *kharāj* and *waqf* land, to unoccupied or *mawāt* land, and to the possibly diverse ownership of trees and buildings from that of the land on which they stand, on the one hand, to certain customary concepts of user, waste land and fruit-bearing trees, respectively, on the other.

A few more points, of a somewhat heterogeneous variety, must be given passing notice in this connection. Thus the influence of Islamic law may be plainly traced in the attitude of the native courts to pledges[2]—although it must be noted that in many parts of Nigeria the latter more commonly consist of articles such as pieces of clothing than of land and houses. While, therefore, the usufructuary mortgage is everywhere practised, the attitude of the courts thereto differs according to their relative orthodoxy. In general it may be said that the usufructuary mortgagee is allowed to use the property for his own benefit but not to put it to hire: but whereas in some courts no notice would be taken of past benefits derived thereunder, although present or future benefits would not be enforced,[3] in others even past benefits would be reckoned against the debt, if the mortgagor so claimed[4]; while in yet others custom would prevail and the contract be enforced as a whole.[5] Again, it is directly on the basis of the Sharī'a—although entirely, it seems, for economic reasons and under administrative influence—that the Emirs some years ago placed a ban on the sale of immature crops: but it is interesting to note that, again presumably for economic reasons, this ban has never applied to the premature sale of growing sugar-cane. It seems somewhat anomalous, therefore, that it is in connection with swamp land used for the cultivation of sugar-cane that Islamic concepts of tenure have been most intrusive; partly, no doubt, because such land is scarce, extremely valuable and so expensive to cultivate that hired labour is almost always used. A further instance, moreover, of the Emirs in Council making a pronouncement on land law is provided by their agreement in 1939 that where the application of the Islamic law of inheritance would result in uneconomic subdivision of land, or insanitary conditions in compounds, the property might be sold and the proceeds divided among heirs or legatees; while in the following year the Conference also agreed that local native authorities might determine the minimum area into which any estate might be divided on inheritance.[6] Finally, it is only in the Tripolitanian Arab ward of Kano, it seems, that houses and building sites are regarded as passing by inheritance to absent owners who may never appear in the locality at all, for among the Arab community the full Islamic law is applied in this matter—although, incongruously enough, it is apparently distinctly doubtful whether these same Arabs have any title at all which would be recognised under the Ordinance.[7] A propos of houses, moreover, it is relevant to observe both that many of these, throughout Northern Nigeria, partake more of the nature of family compounds than of individual dwellings, and that outside the major towns they are usually too ephemeral in structure to have any appreciable commercial value.

[1] Report on *Land Tenure in Zaria Province*, p. 52.

[2] It should, however, be noted in passing that in Ilorin I read the case-record of a "foreclosable mortgage" in which the Emir refused the mortgagor's claim to redeem his house after the date for foreclosure—or, indeed, even to claim the balance in its value.

[3] e.g., in Bornu.

[4] e.g., in Zaria, so the Chief Alkali claims.

[5] e.g., in Fika, and by certain district Alkalai of Dikwa.

[6] But there seems to have been little effect given to these agreements in practice.

[7] See Report on *Land Tenure in Kano Province* by C. W. Rowling, p. 25.

Procedure and Evidence in Alkalai's Courts.

In 1950 some six hundred and forty-two native courts of first instance, and eighty-one native courts of appeal, had been established in the Northern Provinces of Nigeria, of which seventeen were of the grade A (unlimited) variety.[1] Roughly speaking, about half of these courts are those of Muslim Emirs or Alkalai, while the remainder are "pagan". These last apply the local law and custom according to customary methods of procedure, almost entirely uninfluenced by Islamic ideas: so they fall outside the scope of this Survey. It is noteworthy, however, that where a litigant claims to be a Christian or Muslim a pagan court will usually swear him on the Bible or Qur'ān instead of the local fetish. In some localities, moreover, either the court President is himself a Muslim[2] or a Muslim member is appointed to assist[3] him; and in such circumstances it is possible that local pagan custom would be varied to some degree in the case of Muslim litigants in favour of rudimentary Islamic law.[4] Elsewhere a Muslim Alkali will take pagan as well as Muslim cases, either in his normal court or on circuit. The propriety of this procedure has been called in question, on the grounds that an Alkali is always inclined, both from training and prejudice, to apply his own law and that it is anomalous, to say the least, to impose the Sharī'a on pagans in the name of native law and custom.[5] As a consequence, a considerable number of "pagan" courts have been established of recent years; but it is noteworthy that pagans seem sometimes to prefer the Alkalai, as trained and unprejudiced jurists, and that the latter—particularly in predominantly pagan areas—often prove remarkably broad-minded and willingly apply pagan law and custom with the aid of pagan assessors.[6] Elsewhere, however, they apply the Sharī'a, although sometimes with considerable concessions[7] both to local customs and to those of non-Muslim immigrants. But in more rigidly Islamic centres most such concessions would not be tolerated and all will depend on whether non-Muslim litigants are willing to accept judgment by the law of Islam: if so, Alkalai will proceed with the case accordingly; while, if not, they will advise the litigants to seek justice elsewhere.[8] In the case of litigation between a Muslim and a pagan, moreover, an Alkali will almost always apply the Sharī'a[9]: but little difficulty is normally encountered in such cases, since they very rarely concern family law.

---

[1] See above, p. 174. Also *Native Administration in British African Territories,* Vol. III, p. 82.

[2] e.g., in Gwoza.

[3] e.g., in the newly established Jarawa court.

[4] In the Jarawa court, for instance, it was interesting to observe that while cases of marriage, divorce, inheritance, etc., all normally follow customary law the President and members all professed themselves willing to accept and apply the Muslim member's interpretation of Islamic law regarding succession to the property of such few Jarawa as have embraced Islam (even to the extent of allowing the exclusion of non-Muslim relatives) and also regarding certain of the matrimonial precepts of Islam. It seems, moreover, that this attitude is comparatively common elsewhere.

[5] The official Muslim attitude is that where a Muslim Emir conquered the pagans they must submit to his courts, but that where they remained unconquered they may be allowed to apply their own customs in their own courts. And the practice may also be defended to some extent, in the case of a small pagan pocket in a Muslim area, on the grounds that native law and custom is regularly enforced in Nigeria on a territorial rather than a personal basis.

[6] This is true in Gwoza district, in Bornu (if they refuse the Sharī'a), Bauchi, etc.

[7] e.g., the district Alkalai of Dikwa, who in such cases ignore the rules concerning *'idda* and apply the customary law of marriage, inheritance, etc.

[8] e.g., in Kano, Sokoto, Katsina. "Elsewhere" may, according to circumstances, mean a pagan native court, a "mixed" native court, or a magistrate's (or district officer's) court. But it is noteworthy that in Nupeland custom is, to a considerable extent, independent of religion.

[9] But not too strictly in, e.g., Bauchi, while in Jos the Alkali professes to apply either Sharī'a or custom if the litigants both agree, but to refuse the case if they disagree.

A different problem has been posed by the conglomeration of mixed races and religions found in the "Sabon Gari" areas of the larger cities of the Northern Provinces.[1] To meet their needs "mixed" native courts have been devised. These constitute, of course, a major exception to the principle that the administration of justice in Nigeria is on a territorial rather than personal basis (see above): but prior to their establishment Christian and pagan inhabitants of these townships were faced with the bleak alternative of submitting their matrimonial or other personal causes to the judgment of the Sharī'a or travelling hundreds of miles to their own native tribunal, for magistrates have no jurisdiction in such matters. The law these courts apply is a mystery (described as "common sense", a gleaning of common law and Muhammadan law, and bits of tribal custom) under a procedure which represents a rough adaptation of British practice, so they are anathema to the purists: but others maintain that they fill a clamant need with considerable distinction. Appeals go to the Chief Alkali where Muhammadan law is involved, but otherwise to the magistrate. In those Emirates, moreover, where pagan courts have been established appeals therefrom go not to the Chief Alkali but to the Emir's court, where pagan custom is again (professedly) applied, with the assistance of assessors.[2] Even in cases of homicide—which normally go straight to the Emir's court—it is noteworthy that some Emirs are prepared to modify the strict application of the Sharī'a in the case of pagans,[3] in suitable circumstances. Wherever, moreover, non-Muslim litigants are involved they are allowed to take their own form of oaths, although some courts insist on the prior mention of the name of God[4] or even the prior swearing of an oath somewhat in the Islamic form.

As regards witnesses, again, the attitude of the Alkalai varies greatly from place to place. Thus in most localities non-Muslim witnesses are only accepted in cases which involve non-Muslims—and then only on the ground of "necessity"[5]: but in some districts non-Muslim witnesses are accepted even against Muslims,[6] while in a few localities they are scarcely accepted at all.[7] In some places, moreover, it was admitted that less stringent rules concerning witnesses might be applied in cases involving man-made law than in those under the Sharī'a—even to the extent of accepting the testimony of a single witness, where the court felt convinced of his credibility.[8] Everywhere, moreover, the screening of witnesses (*tazkiya*) is now limited to the right of the defendant to

---

[1] e.g., in Kano, Kaduna, Zaria, Jos, Makurdi, Minna, etc. That of Kano was established in 1932. Its President was recently a Christian from Sierra Leone, with a Hausa and a Yoruba Muslim as members, assessors being called where desired. In 1943 records show that 1,830 cases were tried with only ten appeals and seven applications for review, which must be reasonably typical.

[2] e.g., in Zaria, Ilorin and elsewhere. And this is also true of the Emir of Fika, who deals with such cases in first instance. But where one party is a Muslim, and the original case has been decided by customary law, most Emirs' courts would no doubt incline to Islamic law on appeal.

[3] e.g., the Emirs of Zaria and Bauchi, the Lamido of Adamawa, and the Shehu of Bornu.

[4] e.g., in Birnin Kebbi.

[5] e.g., in Kazaure, Hadejia, Sokoto, Birnin Kebbi, Katsina, Maiduguri.

[6] e.g., in Gumel, some parts of Bornu and Dikwa, in Fika, Bauchi, Jos, Zaria (formerly, when the Alkali used to hear pagan cases), Nupeland and Ilorin—but here one Alkali said that he could not accept them, while others emphasised that they could only be accepted on oath and where their testimony seemed trustworthy.

[7] e.g., in Kano, where they are normally only accepted in cases involving the proof or denial of defects in merchandise, etc. (in default of Muslims). In this connection, see remarks of Ames J. re admissibility of only Muslim witnesses in the court of the Chief Alkali of Kano in *Isa* v. *Okoye* (K/18A/1943). The rigidity professed in Kano in this matter may, perhaps, be partly explained by the fact that there are so few pagans in the vicinity; while it seems distinctly possible that the district Alkalai of the Emirate are less rigid than this in practice.

[8] e.g., in Sokoto—and that not only in "financial" cases.

attack the plaintiff's witnesses; while it seems that this in turn is limited in practice to alleging that they are prejudiced (as friends, relatives, etc.) or notorious liars, rather than any attempt to discredit them on grounds of general character or laxity in religion.[1] And the cleavage of opinion between locality and locality is particularly manifest in the question whether witnesses are to be put on oath: for in some parts this is never done,[2] in accordance with the dominant Mālikī opinion; in others an oath is applied where the court is in doubt or the other party particularly requests this[3]; while in others the defendant will nearly always demand that a hostile witness be put on oath (to confirm the testimony which he has already given[4]). Almost everywhere, moreover, the court will cross-examine the witnesses, one by one, in suitable circumstances; while questions will also be put to them by the court at the request of the other party, wherever it seems likely that this might throw light on the case.[5] This, indeed, would in many courts be regarded as the normal method of resolving a case where the defendant wished to bring evidence (e.g., of an alibi) to rebut that of the plaintiff: but in others it was stated that the "most trustworthy" (*aʿdal*—i.e., by general repute, etc.) of the two conflicting bodies of testimony would be accepted,[6] elsewhere that they would be regarded as cancelling each other out and recourse would be had to oaths,[7] and elsewhere again that only that of affirmation, not denial (i.e., *ithbāt,* not *nafy*) would be accepted [8]—while the special rules regarding such cases as where a vendor and vendee differ with regard to the price on which they agreed would also be followed.

Circumstantial evidence is accepted in most localities, if sufficiently strong. Where, for instance, a wife can produce adequate testimony that she was well and happy just before her husband came home, but that soon after he entered the otherwise empty house her neighbours heard cries and saw her run out with the signs of violence on her person, almost all courts would regard this as adequate proof that he had beaten her, in, e.g., a suit for divorce for injury.[9] There was only occasional hesitation or reserve on this point; while the Chief Alkali of Zaria remarked that this should be placed in the "*qaṭʿī*" or conclusive category and that it should be given general application[10] (as in the stock illustration of a homicide established by the testimony of witnesses to having

---

[1] e.g., in Kano, Sokoto, Katsina, Maiduguri, Bauchi, Zaria, Bida, Ilorin. In Bama and Jos the Alkalai specifically stated that they would not pay attention to an attack on witnesses' general character or piety, since "times were bad", and one must accept the best witnesses available. Elsewhere the more orthodox view was held in theory, but I was assured that no such attempts to discredit witnesses are made in practice. But it is largely under this heading that the testimony of "accomplices" in, e.g., homicide will often be rejected (except as constituting *lawth* and thus a basis for *qasāma*—see below): and this is even more true of the "con-complainant" (e.g., several men who state that they collectively bribed an official).

[2] e.g., in Sokoto, Katsina, Bauchi, Zaria and Jos.

[3] e.g., in Kano, Bida, Ilorin. This is supported by a variant Mālikī view.

[4] e.g., in Bornu, Bama, Fika.

[5] e.g., in Sokoto, Katsina, Maiduguri, Bama, Fika, Bauchi, Jos, Zaria, Bida and Ilorin. The Chief Alkalai of Zaria and Bida were particularly emphatic about this. See also remarks of Brooke J. in *Katsina Native Authority* v. *Abdullahi Kogo (and others)* that "There is strictly no right of cross-examination under Muhammadan law: questions are put by the court but in this case the right of questioning not only the witnesses but also the co-defendants was allowed" (14 *N.L.R.* 54).

[6] e.g., at Maiduguri, Bama, Fika, Bauchi.

[7] e.g., at Katsina.

[8] e.g., at Kano and Zaria—except in case of an accusation based on *tuhma* (suspicion), when proof of alibi would end the case.

[9] e.g., at Sokoto, Katsina, Maiduguri, among district Alkalai of Dikwa, at Fika, Bauchi, Zaria, Bida and Ilorin.

[10] This, in view of his great repute and general conservatism, is a point of considerable significance.

seen a man running from a house with a knife in his hand, having promptly entered the house and found a man bleeding to death, and having discovered no sign of any other possible assailant[1]); and the Chief Alkali of Bida remarked that such evidence was " better than testimony ". In a similar problem concerning an accusation of theft supported only by testimony to the fact that a brief case was lying beside its owner's chair one minute and was recovered the next from the hands of a boy running from the building, most courts, again, would regard the charge as proved: but elsewhere it was remarked that this must be classified as "*ikhtilās*" rather than "*sariqa*"[2]—a distinction which has largely lost its significance now that the amputation of hands for *sariqa* has been forbidden, and the latter, like the former, only occasions a discretionary (*ta'zīr*) punishment; otherwise this answer would probably have been much more general.

It is also noteworthy in this context that the orthodox rules about the minimum number of witnesses are generally applied in Northern Nigeria, including the requirement of four adult male witnesses to the very act in charges of illicit sex relations (*zinā*), although a charge on the same facts couched in different terms[3] can be sustained by the normal minimum of two witnesses—or even less, in localities where custom largely prevails in such cases.[4] Again, the usual Mālikī rules are normally followed in cases of a partial or qualified acknowledgment, i.e., the part of the plaintiff's case thus confirmed is regarded as proved, and the burden of proving the points on which the acknowledgment differs from the plaint passes to the defendant[5]—but important controversies have arisen concerning this point in certain prosecutions for homicide.[6] Cases are not decided *ex parte* in most localities if the whereabouts of the defendant are known,[7] since he will be arrested for contempt of court if he fails to appear after a repeated summons[8]: but where his whereabouts are unknown judgment may be passed after the plaintiff has produced the necessary proof and taken the oath normal in such circumstances in confirmation of his plaint[9]; although this judgment is liable to be upset[10] if the defendant subsequently appears and proceeds to impugn the witnesses, etc. (whereupon the latter may be punished for false testimony, or be held financially liable for any loss sustained by the defendant). Finally, bail is not very commonly allowed: but it is noteworthy in this context that the different types of suretyship known to Mālikī law include guarantees (*a*) to pay a debt if the debtor is unable (not merely unwilling) to do so; (*b*) to produce the debtor, alive or dead; and (*c*) merely to do one's best to find him—and that many courts will allow type (*b*) in minor cases other than debt.

---

[1] This is regarded by some as a "*qarīna*" (context, circumstance) sufficient to establish the homicide without the need for *qasāma* (compurgation), on the authority of *Tabṣirat al-Ḥukkām*. But this would never be extended to cases of *zinā* or *sariqa* (or any *ḥadd* punishment), where the minimum number of witnesses must testify, in detail, to having witnessed the very act of intercourse or theft (see below).

[2] i.e., at Sokoto, Kano, etc. But the difference between the two offences, in the Mālikī view, lies in the absence of stealth in the former, rather than in the matter of proof. See Ibn Rushd's *Bidāyat al-Mujtahid*, ii, p. 369.

[3] e.g., of an attempt to seduce, rather than the act of adultery.

[4] e.g., in Nupeland and Ilorin, see below.

[5] e.g., in an acknowledgment that the debt alleged by the plaintiff did once exist, but had been repaid, etc., the burden of proving the repayment passes to the acknowledger.

[6] See below.

[7] But in Bida, it seems, they will be heard provided there is proof that the defendant has been summoned, in which case he will not be allowed subsequently to attack the witnesses unless he had adequate excuse for non-appearance.

[8] Although failure promptly to compel the appearance of one or other of the parties appears to be one of the commonest complaints against native courts.

[9] *Yamīn al-qaḍā'*. See Glossary.

[10] And is, in fact, very rare, except in certain divorce cases.

Crime

The Islamic law of crime set forth in the recognised law books is largely limited to those offences—illicit sex-relations (*zinā*), theft and brigandage (*sariqa* in its dual form), slander of a chaste person's continence (*qadhf*), and drinking alcohol (*shurb*)—for which a prescribed punishment (*ḥadd*) is expressly laid down in the sacred texts.[1] Apostasy from Islam (*irtidād*) is sometimes added to this list: but homicide and wounding are in the main treated as torts rather than crimes. The punishment of other wrong-doing is largely left to the discretion of the Ruler: and where this punishment is imposed in the normal jurisdiction of the courts, in regard to offences which do not amount to those specified above, and conforms to the ordinary principles of the law, it is termed *ta'zīr;* while where it transcends such limits and proceeds from the ultimate right and duty of the Ruler to safeguard the moral and material welfare of the community, it is termed *siyāsa*.[2] History, moreover, shows that the very limited scope of the *ḥadd* offences and the extremely exacting form of proof prescribed thereunder, together with the inadequate severity of the normal *ta'zīr* punishments, have resulted in the fact that criminal jurisdiction has seldom, if ever, been vested in the ordinary courts or administered according to the rigid principles of the texts.

In Northern Nigeria, however, the *ḥadd* offences remain, in most localities, within the jurisdiction of the Alkalai, while homicide alone is reserved for the Emir's court (if of the Grade A unlimited status) or the Supreme Court. This can be traced to the fact that the British Protectorate was imposed at a time when the puritanical reforms introduced by the Fulani *jihād*—including an attempt largely to confine jurisdiction to the regular courts and the letter of the law[3]—were still operative,[4] and the advent of the Protecting Power served, almost inevitably, to crystallise the situation and retard those modifications which might otherwise have supervened.[5] Only those punishments regarded by the British as inhuman, such as lapidation, crucifixion and mutilation, were prohibited: for the rest "native law and custom"—but here, largely, because it was regarded as the divine law—was allowed to continue in force.

It is difficult to determine how far the *ḥadd* punishments were in fact imposed in Northern Nigeria before the Protectorate was established. For the most part, of course, here as elsewhere, the requirement[6] of four competent male witnesses to the very act in the case of *zinā,* and of two competent male witnesses in the case of *sariqa,* would effectively debar in the first and limit in the second the imposition of the prescribed punishments, since it would be a brave offender who would incur these penalties by sustained[7] confession (*iqrār*): but it must be remembered that the Mālikī law—unlike the Ḥanafī or Shāfi'ī—allows the punishment to be imposed on an unmarried or divorced woman by reason only of her pregnancy,[8] unless she can produce adequate evidence that she was

[1] Although that of *shurb* is not, in fact, so prescribed, but rather derived by deduction therefrom, in the majority view.

[2] The terms are, however, often used interchangeably.

[3] Even so, this attempt was not wholly successful, or—in all probability—intended to be so. The Emirs still retained jurisdiction concerning land in their own hands, and the pure law was still modified by local custom in a number of respects (see below)—while most Emirs and their district and village headmen probably also exercised criminal jurisdiction when they chose.

[4] Since there had been little contact between Northern Nigeria and the outside world in the intervening century.

[5] These points have been well developed in a (unpublished) Paper on the legal position in Northern Nigeria by Dr. J. Schacht.

[6] The minimum requirement unless the accused "confesses" the offence.

[7] For in such offences (*ḥuqūq Allāh*) even a confession can at any time be withdrawn.

[8] Provided, of course, it cannot still be attributed to her former husband.

deceived or forced.[1] But it seems very doubtful whether lapidation was in fact imposed in Nigeria even before the British came, except perhaps in an occasional instance; while even amputation for theft was imposed, it seems, only by certain Rulers, in certain centres and at certain periods, when considerations of public order reinforced (or perhaps replaced) the motive of orthodoxy.

The crime of *zinā,* where adequately proved, is now punished—in the strictly Muslim centres—by one hundred lashes and one year's imprisonment (as the modern equivalent of one year's banishment) in the case of a man who has never been validly married, and by a sentence of one hundred lashes commuted to imprisonment or fine in the case of a woman who has never enjoyed a valid marriage.[2] Where either party has been so married the more orthodox courts will sentence him or her to be " stoned to death ", and will then add that " as stoning to death is not allowed nowadays " a sentence of imprisonment is to be substituted. And it is noteworthy in passing that, while the year's imprisonment for the unmarried male is regarded as a divinely prescribed penalty in which no remission may be granted for good conduct, this does not apply to the discretionary punishment substituted for the prescribed lapidation.[3] Elsewhere (e.g., Birnin Kebbi) the usual sentence for both adulterers seems to be one hundred lashes and three months' imprisonment: but here, as throughout the country, the infliction of those lashes is officially forbidden in the case of females. Where, moreover, a husband finds his wife in compromising circumstances in these strictly Muslim areas, most know enough of the law not to make an open accusation of *zinā* (which would, in the absence of the adequate testimony from four witnesses, or resort to the *li'ān* procedure,[4] make him liable to the penalty for *qadhf*) but rather to accuse her lover of " seduction "; whereupon the court will impose a discretionery punishment on both parties, usually a fine, on the basis of any adequate testimony[5]—and it often happens that the husband will himself pay his wife's fine if he wants to keep her. But in less orthodox areas, such as Bida and Ilorin, customary law entirely takes the place of the Sharī'a in such matters; and the gravity of the offence depends primarily on whether pregnancy ensues, while the " seduction " of a virgin is in some parts considered much more serious than that of a married woman. In Ilorin, for instance, the usual punishment for one who causes the pregnancy of an unmarried girl (proved by the paramour's confession or the girl's statement on oath) is a fine of £5 or six months' imprisonment, while the girl herself is fined £2 10s. or imprisoned for three months (which usually means that her father has to pay the fine, virtually as a penalty for not looking after her better); and the same fine is here imposed on the seducer of a married woman, but in this case half goes to the husband by way of compensation. In many places, moreover, " seduction " (" *khalwa* ", i.e., being alone together in suspicious circumstances) is often proved by the production of articles of clothing belonging to the guilty pair—as, for instance, in Bida, where the normal punishment for seduction of a virgin, when pregnancy ensues, is one or two years' imprisonment for the man and a fine of £5 for the girl; while that for seduction of a married woman is only a lesser fine for both parties. It is also interesting to notice that the suggestion has been made in Bida that in cases of persistent adultery between the same persons the woman should be forbidden by court to enter the man's compound and he

[1] It is the possibility of this which very properly prevents the imposition of the punishment in such cases by the Ḥanafīs and Shāfi'is.

[2] Or, in reality, enjoyed sexual intercourse in a valid marriage. This test applies to both parties.

[3] An admirable example of the above is provided by the case record of *Katsina Native Authority* v. *Gaude and Ramatu of Mayana in Kogo District* (unreported), where they confessed to killing their illegitimate child.

[4] See below (p. 213) and Glossary.

[5] e.g., two witnesses to the parties entering an empty house together, etc.

to receive her: and, should they disobey, they would then become liable to an increased penalty for "contempt".

Theft requires little comment here, for the abolition of the penalty of mutilation has largely obliterated the distinction between the *ḥadd* offence of *sariqa*—to establish which either two competent witnesses to the very act or a sustained confession is required, together with the fulfilment of all the necessary conditions regarding the value of the thing stolen, its "safe-keeping", the nature of the act, and the relationship of the parties—and some similar offence punishable by *ta'zīr* (with much greater laxity regarding both the nature of the offence and the degree of proof required), since both alike are now punishable mainly by imprisonment. In many localities,[1] moreover, the normal way for the offence to be established is for the accused to be found in possession of stolen goods without being able to provide any adequate explanation.[2]

For the offence of wine-drinking (*shurb*) witnesses to the very act are not required in Mālikī (unlike Ḥanafī and Shāfi'ī) law, since testimony to the smell of drink or the effects of intoxication are, in the absence of proof of some extenuating circumstances[3] on the part of the accused, enough to establish guilt. Officially, the penalty is eighty lashes, in orthodox Mālikī fashion, in the stricter areas but more commonly (it seems) a fine or imprisonment in practice; while in the laxer atmosphere of, e.g., Bida or Ilorin drinking does not constitute any offence at all. Much the same, too, is true of the offence of *qadhf*, for in the stricter areas a distinction is drawn between the *ḥadd* offence of *qadhf*, which is confined to accusations or remarks which involve the imputation of incontinence to a Muslim who cannot be proved unchaste and which involves the statutory penalty of eighty lashes, and the *ta'zīr* punishment (usually a fine) due for any other proved and unjustifiable defamation. But in the laxer areas, again, the *ḥadd* offence is unknown; and a general charge of defamation is the remedy, if any, for slander of any kind.

It is, moreover, most important in this connection clearly to distinguish the lashes imposed under the Sharī'a from any form of corporal punishment permitted under the Criminal Code. The former must be inflicted with a cow-hide whip held only between certain fingers of the hand, while the one who inflicts it must also hold some object under his arm throughout. It is clear, therefore, that this punishment, at least in modern Nigeria, is to be regarded as a disgrace, and sometimes even as a sort of religious penance, rather than a very severe physical ordeal.

For wounding another wilfully the orthodox punishment is retaliation—an eye for an eye and a tooth for a tooth—except in such wounds as defy exact reciprocity. I met no one, however, who could remember having heard of this being put into practice in Nigeria even before the British came.[4] Instead, wounding is punishable, where wilful, by a discretionary sentence of imprisonment or fine and gives rise, in all cases, to award of compensation. In those wounds for which a specific proportion of the full blood-wit is prescribed all is straightforward, except that the differences between locality and locality both as to the amount of this blood-wit and the proportion thereof due in respect of pagans require careful notice: but in the case of those wounds for which the compensation

---

[1] e.g., Bida, etc.

[2] It may be added, in this connection, that in the court of the Chief Alkali of Zaria I saw several men, who had been ordered (as strangers known as undesirables) to leave the Emirate and not return, sentenced to six months' imprisonment for being found again in Zaria. The Chief Alkali emphasised that this was a *siyāsa* punishment: and it appears that it was in fact imposed under the Native Authority Ordinance, sect. 29.

[3] It is the possibility of such which prevents the imposition of the penalty, in such cases, in Ḥanafī and Shāfi'ī law.

[4] The more orthodox tried to explain this on those grounds of the fear of exact reciprocity being unattainable which the strict law applies only to certain types of wound.

is not so prescribed the calculation required is more complex, and is said to be reached by first valuing the injured person, as though a slave, before and after the injury and then allotting him that proportion of the full blood-wit which would correspond to the resultant decrease in value.[1]

But it is cases of homicide which have caused, and do cause, the most difficulty.[2] The major problems concern (*a*) the definition of wilful homicide (*'amd*); (*b*) the right normally inherent in the heirs of blood to demand retaliation in such cases, to accept blood-wit instead, or to forego either; (*c*) the inadequacy as a punishment for wilful homicide of both blood-wit and the prescribed *ta'zīr* which accompanies it—or is often the sole penalty, if the heirs forego their rights altogether; (*d*) those factors which preclude retaliation and greatly reduce blood-wit; and (*e*) certain matters of proof and procedure such as confession, compurgation and evidence of insanity, etc. It will, perhaps, be best to consider these *seriatim*.

(*a*) The definition of wilful homicide. This is much wider in the Māliki school than in any other, for it includes (i) death resulting from any unjustified assault, whether intrinsically likely to kill or not, and (ii) death caused by any means intrinsically likely to kill, even in play or chastisement.[3] It will be immediately apparent, therefore, that the Māliki definition of wilful homicide, for which the death penalty is normally allowed, includes many circumstances which would only amount to manslaughter under the Criminal Code: and it was this, brought to a head in *Tsofo Guba's case,* which led to the legislation of 1948 discussed above. This same issue was raised previously[4] in a dissenting judgment by Ames J. in the West African Court of Appeal, when he asked " Can it be the law of this large British Protectorate . . . that in many parts of it a man can be sentenced to death for what is shown by the evidence to have been at the most manslaughter and not murder? . . . Muhammadan Law has no privileged position[5]: it prevails, where it does prevail, because it is there the local law and custom "—provided always, therefore, that it is not inconsistent with any Ordinance, etc.

(*b*) The right normally inherent in the heirs of blood to demand retaliation in such cases, to accept blood-wit instead or to forego either. Under this heading three subsidiary problems arise. (i) The definition locally accepted of those types of homicide, *ḥirāba* and *ghīla,* in which this option is not open to the heirs but the Emir must always impose the death penalty. Of these the former, homicide in the course of brigandage, presents little difficulty: but the latter has been variously defined in the texts as homicide in order to facilitate robbery (or, e.g., some sexual offence) and homicide by trickery and stealth—or even, perhaps, with planned and obvious premeditation. The narrower definition is alone accepted in Katsina, Maiduguri, Bama,[6] Zaria, etc.,[7] while in Bauchi, Jos and Bida the Alkalai would include homicide by trickery—and in Bauchi even homicide with obvious premeditation such as laying the victim down and cutting his throat—in this category. This difference of interpretation is not very satisfactory, particularly when it involves a matter of life or

[1] More commonly, however, the figure appears to be assessed by reference to a rough table on which most Alkalai seem to rely, or else as the result of what amounts to bargaining.
[2] Although these seem, in the main, to be well and carefully tried by Emirs' courts, according to the relevant principles.
[3] i.e., by one entitled to chastise. But see under ascendants below.
[4] In 1946, in *Bornu Native Authority* v. *Abatcha Magudama*—unreported.
[5] This statement is, as we have seen, justified in so far as Ordinance law is concerned, but scarcely so as a matter of policy and practice.
[6] But here the Limam seemed prepared to accept the wider definition of trickery and stealth.
[7] Also probably in Kano, Sokoto and Birnin Kebbi, but I did not ask.

death.[1] (ii) In all other cases, except those treated under (*d*) below, the fate of the killer depends on the heirs of blood, who may choose retaliation (but may no longer, as formerly under the pure Sharī'a, execute this in person in exactly the same way, if feasible and not expressly precluded by the texts, in which the original homicide was committed), may accept blood-wit instead if the culprit agrees,[2] or may waive their rights *in toto;* and in this case the texts only allow for the imposition of a prescribed[3] *ta'zīr* (regarded by some jurists in Nigeria, incorrectly, as a *ḥadd*[4] punishment) of one hundred lashes and one year's imprisonment. But it is obvious, again, that it is unsatisfactory for the imposition of the death penalty, in what may amount to a foul and brutal murder, to rest on the mere whim of some relative of the deceased.[5] (iii) A further problem arises where one of the heirs is a minor or insane, etc., at the time when this option must be exercised. Here again a divergence of view appears in Nigeria if the heirs of blood consist, e.g., of adult brothers and minor sons: for some jurists maintain that the brothers may insist, in their own right, on retaliation in such circumstances without awaiting the consultation, on majority, of the sons as the primary heirs[6]; others give them this right only as guardians of the sons, whether by appointment under the deceased's will or by right of agnatic relationship[7]; and others say that the decision of the sons must be awaited[8]—while all, of course, exclude the death penalty entirely if any primary heir consents to forego it.

[1] I found an interesting discussion of the difference between conspiracy and *ghīla* in *Kano Native Authority* v. *Gwandai Bembem and Ahmadu Shokana* (28/5/50). The facts were that the accused went to deceased's house, broke some gourds to make him come out, and then shot him. This was held not to constitute *ghīla*—by reference to the *Tuḥfa* of Ibn 'Aṣim, p. 351.

[2] Whether he must agree is in dispute in the Mālikī school, but the above is the view accepted, e.g., in Bornu.

[3] It is a matter of debate, in reality, whether this penalty should be regarded as a prescribed *ta'zīr,* as most Nigerian jurists maintain, or merely as an example of a penalty which may in fact be varied to suit the circumstances.

[4] e.g., at Katsina.

[5] It comes as a surprise in this connexion to find a statement of a former Chief Commissioner (dated 4/7/1933, on file 11454/105) which reads: "The fact is that the formal question is put at the end of the proceedings to the blood relations, who are in form the prosecutors, as a part of the regular formal procedure under Muhammadan law; but that it is a formality . . . The usual procedure whereby what is in effect a preliminary investigation is held by the Native Court and scrutinised by the District Officer, to whom reference will again be made before sentence is passed, should ensure that no murderer escapes his punishment because the blood relations have claimed *dīya* in place of *qiṣāṣ*. I have already written to the effect that our influence over a course of years has resulted in criminal law in Native Courts in all important matters coming into accord with our criminal law to the extent that there cannot be said any longer to exist in practice a separate and distinct Muhammadan criminal law". Here the middle sentence is both true and important, for it means that the case can and should be transferred to the Supreme Court, for trial by a different law and procedure, in suitable cases; but the first and third sentences are fantastic.

As an extreme instance of the ramifications involved in Islamic law in this matter cp. *Bornu Native Authority* v. *Yusus and Dauna of Marte.* Here the court held the two accused guilty of deliberately killing one who was himself the deliberate killer of another deceased (Kyari by name). So the decision as to whether the accused should die rested with the heirs of blood not of their victim but of his (Kyari's). Since, however, the latter's sole heir was a niece, the decision passed to the Emir, who was bound to choose talion (cp. Kaduna file 11454/S/178).

[6] e.g., at Sokoto, Bama, Zaria. This view can claim the authority of *Al-Mudawwana 'l-Kubrā,* xvi, p. 238.

[7] e.g., at Maiduguri.

[8] e.g., at Bauchi and (?) Katsina. But it seems doubtful how far this represents practice, as distinct from theory: since the normal procedure is for the senior heirs of blood to be sent in by the district head, and asked for their decision by the court, without any enquiry about minor sons.

(*c*) The inadequacy of either blood-wit or the prescribed punishment—or, indeed, of both, since it should be noted that the latter is also imposed where the heirs choose blood-wit as compensation for a homicide for which talion would have been in order. Under this heading, again, four distinct points arise. (i) The total inadequacy of even the full rate of blood-money payable in Nigeria, which varies between £12 10s. at Ilorin[1] and £60 at Maiduguri. In this connection it is noteworthy that the blood-wit payable in Sokoto was recently doubled by order of the Sultan on the grounds that the previous tariff (£12 10s.) was less than the price of a mare. But even £25 is fantastically small compared with the rates of early Islam.[2] (ii) The wide differences between Province and Province concerning the proportion of the full blood-wit payable in the case of a pagan, which varies from one-fifteenth[3] in, e.g., Maiduguri and Zaria, to one-fifth in, e.g., Bauchi, and one-half in, e.g., Nupe and Ilorin, where pagans are reckoned on the same tariff as Christians (whose blood-wit is everywhere in Nigeria regarded, in normal Mālikī fashion, as half that of a Muslim). (iii) The fact that the statutory punishment of one hundred lashes is far less drastic than it sounds, as the rules governing its application preclude any severe pain and reduce the penalty largely to a matter of disgrace.[4] (iv) Much controversy has arisen, in Nigeria, concerning the question whether the Emir may add a further *siyāsa* punishment, where he considers that the interests of public security require this, in order to discourage the culprit, and others, from a repetition of the offence. The legality of such a penalty is rather half-heartedly accepted now in the majority of Provinces provided it does not amount to the death penalty[5]: but in some places this, too, would be accepted,[6] while in others the mention of a year's imprisonment and one hundred lashes in the texts is regarded as excluding any greater penalty whatever.[7]

(*d*) Factors which preclude retaliation and greatly reduce blood-wit. Such, in the old days, was the fact that the victim of a free Muslim happened to be a slave; and such, even today, is the fact that his victim happens to be a

[1] And £16 13s. 4d. in Nupe. But it is noteworthy that homicide cases in both these Provinces in fact go to the Supreme Court—in spite of the fact that in Ilorin they are technically within the competence of the Emir's court.

[2] But not so, perhaps, for the type of man commonly arraigned on such a charge. The paramount need seems to be longer sentences, rather than more money.

[3] This, however, is the orthodox view. See 'Abd al-Bāqī al-Zurqānī, viii, p. 37, regarding the *dīya* of the Zoroastrian (*mājūsī*) and, according to one view, the apostate (*murtadd*).

[4] See p. 197 above.

[5] All agreed on this at Katsina (while some jurists there were even prepared to accept the death penalty, too, in such cases), Bama, Bauchi, Jos, etc. But there is often considerable hesitation about inflicting any such punishment in practice.

[6] e.g., some Katsina jurists, and the chief Alkali of Bida. The case record of *Katsina Native Authority* v. *Yakudi of Hadaba and Danboko of Rimage*, moreover, shows that when Yakudi was found guilty the deceased's brother first requested talion and then retracted his request. Thereupon the chief Alkali of Zaria and the Sheikhs of the Law School advised that his second opinion was binding: but the Emir gave judgment to the effect that "I and the members of my court having heard this legal opinion then considered the nature of Yakudi's crime having regard to the instructions of Government that in cases of wilful murder the wishes of the blood relatives should not influence the judgment of the court. Therefore I and the court pass sentence of death on Yakudi. He should die as Barmo (the deceased) died, as a warning to the public"—and the prisoner was duly hanged. Again, in *Adamawa Native Authority* v. *Koji of Cike,* where a pagan woman brutally murdered the two daughters of a woman she believed to have caused the death of her son, death sentence was passed without any mention of *ghīla* or reference to the heirs of blood. I understand, moreover, that this used to happen frequently in the court of the Lamido of Adamawa: but it is noteworthy that the discussion of such points in the Conferences of Chiefs tends to make the more orthodox views everywhere prevail. (c.p. Katsina file 3341 and Kaduna file 11454/S/176).

[7] e.g., in Bornu and Zaria.

non-Muslim or that the killer, in a homicide which was not self-evidently premeditated (such as holding the victim down and cutting his throat), is an ascendant of the deceased. In all these circumstances only blood-wit, together with the statutory penalty, is normally applicable, and even that is greatly reduced in the case of a non-Muslim (and used to be reckoned on the basis of the victim's market value in the case of a slave). While, however, local jurists undoubtedly still regard ex-slaves as of slave status,[1] it seems unlikely that talion would be excluded or the normal blood-wit varied today on this account, since all know that any such judgment would be upset. Unfortunately, however, the same cannot be said with regard to non-Muslims: for the majority of native courts would still exclude talion in such cases except in homicide by *ghīla* or *ḥirāba,* and all would impose a reduced blood-wit; and while many Emirs add a *siyāsa* term of imprisonment in suitable cases, the death penalty could in most Emirates[2] only be imposed by the case being transferred to, or retried by, the Supreme Court.[3]

(*e*) Matters of proof and procedure. Here again three different points arise.

(i) An accused man may be convicted in Islamic procedure on his bare confession of guilt, without the need for confirmatory evidence of any kind: and since a trial for homicide is regarded as essentially a civil action between the accused and the heirs of blood, such confession once made may not be retracted.[4] And not only did I hear of one case where such a confession proved entirely false,[5] but homicide cases provide the outstanding instance of the unsatisfactory nature of the Mālikī attitude to partial or qualified confessions (see above). Of this, two instances (culled from many) must suffice. Thus in *Katsina Native Authority v. Gambo of Katantu*[6] a man originally confessed to having caused the death of his wife by misadventure (through slashing her throat with an axe aimed at a bird). When, however, an Alkali accused him, after witnesses had given evidence to the type of wound which had been inflicted, of having in fact slit her throat with a knife, and ordered him to be struck on the face several times when he denied this, he eventually agreed that this was what he had done: and the Emir's court duly found him guilty on the basis of both confessions.[7] The Resident thereupon ordered his retrial before the Supreme Court, which acquitted him on the grounds that there were no witnesses to the actual homicide, that his story of how it happened was not impossible in the absence of satisfactory medical evidence, and that the subsequent confession was improperly obtained. Again, in the case of *Zaria Native Authority* v. *Gamco of Matakarka,*[6] the accused confessed to having killed the deceased in a fight after, allegedly, finding him

---

[1] cp. the question of concubines, below. But Lord Lugard gave express orders that "Alkalai must be instructed, should occasion still arise, that slave status must in no way be considered as affecting the administration of justice and the penalties inflicted . . . If there should be any fear of a Native Court showing such discrimination in such cases, it will be tried by the Provincial Court." (*Pol. Mem.* p. 94).

[2] But to this there have been certain exceptions in the past: see above.

[3] As is, of course, commonly done in such cases.

[4] This applies to all offences which primarily involve human rights, as opposed to those "crimes" in which the right of God is considered predominant. See p. 195, note (7).

[5] Here a householder was knifed by a thief with whom he struggled in the dark, and before his death told his wife and father that "Musa did it". Thereupon Musa, who was known as a criminal, confessed and was condemned. But it subsequently transpired that he was engaged on another robbery, miles away, on the night in question: and when asked why he had confessed, he replied, "Well, what could I do? The right people had heard the deceased's dying accusation." (See below)

[6] Unreported.

[7] The first, presumably, on the grounds that he had confessed to the homicide, and that whether this were wilful or accidental must be decided not only by his story but by the nature of the wound, etc. In this case the heirs did not in fact demand either talion or blood-wit, but the Emir imposed a *siyāsa* punishment of six years' imprisonment.

in the act of adultery with his wife under a tree; while the wife alleged that she and the deceased were only sitting together, that her husband had followed the latter when he ran away, and had shot him with an arrow (which was found near the scene of the "fight"). Here, too, the prisoner was convicted of wilful homicide on the basis of his confession coupled with circumstantial evidence; and this time talion was demanded. An appeal to the Supreme Court was dismissed, on the grounds that the native court had correctly applied Islamic law: but the West African Court of Appeal ordered a retrial on the grounds that the element of provocation, which might well have reduced the offence to manslaughter, had not been adequately considered—and it is noteworthy in this context that the more rigid of the Nigerian native courts regularly refuse to consider a plea of the deceased having been found *in flagrante delicto* with the killer's wife in mitigation of the latter's offence or sentence unless the alleged adultery is supported by four competent witnesses to the very act.[1] This seems to have been the first case in which the Court of Appeal refused to uphold a judgment of a native court on what may, from one point of view, be regarded as a matter of procedure: but it is obvious that in these circumstances "procedure" merges into substantive law.[2]

(ii) In the absence of either confession by the accused or the testimony of two competent witnesses to the very act, the further possibility exists, in homicide cases only, of a conviction based on the system of *qasāma* or compurgation. Under this procedure the prosecution must establish one of the various types of incomplete proof (*lawth*) known to Mālikī law: and this, if supported by fifty oaths to the accused's guilt, divided between the deceased's male agnates, is sufficient to justify the infliction of the death penalty where wilful homicide is alleged, or the exaction of blood-wit in cases of accident.[3] It is, however, noteworthy that only agnates may take these oaths, not, e.g., the Emir on behalf of one who has no blood relations; that there must be at least two such agnates in cases of talion; and that only one of several accomplices may be executed in a case so established: while the oaths so proferred will be "returned" to the accused if the agnates cannot or will not take them (whereupon he, on

[1] i.e., the same proof as would be needed to establish the offence of adultery *per se*. This was in fact demanded in this case: but some Nigerian courts take a less extreme attitude on this point, as was emphasised by the Wali of Bornu.

[2] For the policy of non-interference previously followed in such cases, see *Bornu Native Authority* v. *Abatcha Magudama*, where the appeal was based on a plea of self-defence. The judgment reads: "In this case it is Mālikī law and the procedure followed may be archaic but it is sanctioned by sect. 12 of the Native Courts Ordinance. The verdict was, as it appears on the record, based on a judicial confession which under Muhammadan law constitutes full proof . . . The confession must be spontaneous and voluntary but it does not cease to be so because the court puts questions to elucidate the statement of the accused in what is the equivalent of a plea: the system of procedure is of a more inquisitorial nature than our own". But on appeal to the Supreme Court in *Bornu Native Authority* v. *Abba Gaha of Mastaram in Geidam District*, where the assessors advised that the case be returned to the native court for the *qasāma* procedure to be followed, the Judge substituted a sentence of imprisonment on the grounds that provocation had been proved. It may be added that the Chief Alkali of Zaria maintains that, if a man confesses to killing another but pleads self-defence, and there are no witnesses, his defence may be accepted only if the deceased was known as a thief or personal enemy and the homicide occurred, e.g., in the prisoner's house. This is significant of the difference between the Muslim and British attitudes.

[3] And this has been insisted on by the Supreme Court in their appellate jurisdiction. Thus in *Babayi of Wandie* v. *Bornu Native Authority* (1936), 13 N.L.R. 18, it was held that the Muhammadan, not the English, law of evidence was applicable; that the evidence produced was enough to justify resort to the *qasāma* procedure, but not for a conviction without it; and that the case must be remitted to the native court for this procedure to be applied: if the oaths were duly taken, the appeal would stand dismissed, while if the heirs refused the oaths the sentence must be one year's imprisonment and one hundred lashes. And *Katsina Native Authority* v. *Abdullahi Kojo and others* (1930), 14 N.L.R. 49, is very similar.

swearing, will escape both talion and blood-wit but will still, incongruously enough, be liable to the prescribed penalty of one hundred lashes and to one year's imprisonment[1]). There is, moreover, yet another use for the *qasāma* procedure, namely that of establishing the offence of homicide where the death does not immediately follow the assault but might conceivably have been due to some intervening factor—e.g., where the wounded man is not "mortally" wounded (*munfadh al-maqātil*), recovers consciousness or manages to eat, drink or talk between the assault and his demise.[2] Here, again, it is obviously unsatisfactory for a prisoner's life or death to hang, not on the intrinsic strength of the case against him, but merely on the presence of one of the recognised categories of *lawth* together with the largely fortuitous circumstance that his alleged victim has at least two agnatic heirs prepared to take what may be a blind oath to his responsibility.[3] And the form of *lawth* which consists in a dying statement by the deceased is among the most unsatisfactory of all.[4]

(iii) Again, there is the old problem of insanity. Here, however, it may be sufficient to observe that Islamic law contents itself with excluding talion if there is adequate testimony to the fact that the accused was so insane at the time of his assault as not to know what he was doing, while the refinements insisted on by the Government (of medical evidence to the deceased's and his parents' general mental antecedents, etc.) are not infrequently criticised by local jurists.[5]

Three or four more points deserve passing mention in this connection. Firstly, local Nigerian opinion echoes the two conflicting views in the Mālikī school as to the liability of a man who means to kill A but actually kills B instead, for some regard this as deliberate and others as accidental homicide. Secondly, some courts maintain the orthodox Mālikī view that if a man digs a hole in his compound as a trap for a thief, or keeps a dog he knows to be dangerous, and the thief is in fact killed thereby, then the householder is liable to retaliation if he had that particular victim in view, but otherwise only to blood-wit: but a few courts[6] take the less orthodox but more British attitude of asking whether the hole was actually meant to kill or to capture. Thirdly, it is noteworthy that the old pagan customs concerning homicide were even less satisfactory than Islamic law: for among the Jarawa, to take a single instance, the deliberate killer had to supply a boy to serve as a son to the parents of the deceased, while an accidental killer merely had to supply a goat for sacrifice before the fetish shrine. Fourthly, it has been observed above that where the heirs of

---

[1] Why, it is hard to see.

[2] i.e., there is no need for *qasāma* where some vital part of the body has been pierced or the victim has never recovered consciousness. But the mere fact that he has not eaten, etc., will not exclude the need for *qasāma* where other plain signs of life intervened.

[3] Here it is interesting to note that in *Katsina Native Authority* v. *Abdullahi Kogo and others* (1930), 14 N.L.R. 49, the West African Court of Appeal upheld the decision of Brooke J. in the Supreme Court to refer the case back to the native court for the *qasāma* procedure, previously omitted, to be completed; whereupon the appeal was to stand dismissed. *Qasāma* was required in Islamic law in this case because this particular accused, unlike others, had not confessed; while the evidence against him was tainted and such as to constitute *lawth* only.

[4] See footnote (5) to p. 201 above. See also the discussion in the Court of Appeal in *Bornu Native Authority* v. *Abatcha Magudama*, where it is stated that "It was also argued that the statement of the deceased should not have been given in evidence, but this dying declaration is admissible under Muhammadan law . . . We do not feel that we should be justified in interfering with the verdict of the native court in which it was held that wilful homicide had been committed and full proof was constituted under native law and custom." (C.A.W.A. 11/1/1946—unreported).

[5] It is, however, noteworthy in this connection that the Emirs raised little objection, in homicide cases, to such modifications of the normal Islamic procedure as a written preliminary investigation and a medical report.

[6] e.g., in Bama, where both the Chief Alkali and the Limam took this view.

blood pardon a murderer his case may be transferred to[1] or retried by the Supreme Court: but it is obviously unsatisfactory for the accused to have to undergo the ordeal of another trial, and ultimate conviction, after the strain of the original trial and the relief consequent on pardon.[2] Finally, it is noteworthy that the majority of homicide cases in Northern Nigeria concern peasants and occur in the bush, where neither police nor doctors—nor, indeed, expert witnesses of any kind—are available.

Marriage and Divorce.

Throughout most of Northern Nigeria a father[3] is regarded as entitled to conclude marriages on behalf of his minor sons, or his virgin daughters up to any age, at his unilateral[4] discretion. The three chief dangers in this wide application of the father's right of compulsion (*jabr*) are the possibilities it involves of child marriage, with all its attendant evils; of adult women being forced into odious unions, with the misery—or, more commonly, facile divorce—which this promotes; and of the system being used as a cloak for what is almost, if not quite, a traffic in slaves. Each of these deserves separate mention.[5]

In the first a clear distinction must, of course, be drawn between contracts of marriage concluded on behalf of child spouses and the actual consummation of marriage with a child wife. In Nigeria as a whole the latter seems uncommon, but it is by no means unknown in the extreme North. Thus the Wali and Chief Alkali of Kano expressly stated: " We pay no attention to puberty in regard to marriage, but only to the circumstances of the girl's father and husband and to what they mutually agree "—while the marriage of a minor girl may be consummated as soon as she is " able to bear this "[6], which will be judged by her " type, condition and physical strength " but will often precede puberty. Similarly, the Waziri of Sokoto told me that child marriage is very common among the upper classes, and sometimes takes place when the girl is as young as five, whereafter she is often brought up in her husband's house, and the marriage consummated as soon as he considers her able to bear it. And the frequent marriage of minor girls on much the same terms in Bornu[7] was confirmed by the Wali of Maiduguri.

It is not suggested that this practice is nearly so widespread, or quite so vicious, in Nigeria as it used to be in India. There seems to be no doubt, however, that it is distressingly common among the richer families of the North[8]; that both the law and practice sanction consummation at an age when

[1] i.e., if judgment has not yet actually been given.

[2] Although it would not be common, in some parts of the country, for the heirs of blood to waive talion in a case where a British court would sentence to death; while it must also be remembered that, e.g., in parts of Bornu, it may still be important to allow the death penalty to be waived in some cases to avoid murderous vendettas.

[3] In Potiskum, at least, this right is regarded as passing to, e.g., a brother, where the father is dead. And although this is contrary to the pure Mālikī law, except as the father's executor (*waṣī*), it seems probable that it would also, in practice, be recognised elsewhere.

[4] Although frequently the whole family will have a say in such matters (see below), particularly the mother on whom most of the work involved will fall. The pure Mālikī law permits this right to the father unless the virgin daughter has been expressly emancipated from tutelage or (some say) has reached a comparatively advanced age.

[5] Although it may be noted that the lower social classes seem more and more to avoid such unions, because of the trouble they so often cause.

[6] *Mutīqa.* This is the orthodox Mālikī law.

[7] Where the father of a daughter so married often, it seems, sends an older woman with her to look after her property, etc., until she becomes adult.

[8] A particularly regrettable fact is that this practice is followed by many of the younger class of educated Northerners, when their salaries permit. This is, perhaps, partly attributable to a desire to advertise their improved social status; partly to the motive of reassuring the older generation; and allegedly to a determination to protect their own health in the existing state of society. *Sed quaere.*

serious physical injury may be done to immature wives[1]; and that there is no guarantee that husbands do not sometimes abuse child wives at an even earlier age than the law allows.[2] It is on record that the Acting Resident of Sokoto remarked in 1946 that he found child marriage "increasingly prevalent and deleterious"; that Nigerian legislation to prohibit the transfer of immature wives to the custody of their husbands or their relatives would in his view be justified; and that the native authorities would, he believed, be willing to enforce such legislation if enacted, but not—in view of the lamentable precedent of 'Ā'isha—to introduce it themselves. It was partly to remedy this evil, moreover, that a proposed amendment to the Criminal Code Ordinance was debated in the Northern Regional House of Chiefs and House of Assembly in 1950, whereby the "age of consent" was to be raised from thirteen to fifteen years and was to be applied not only to extra-marital relations but even to the consummation of marriage. But although it was supported by the Etsu of Pategi and the Provincial Member for Ilorin, respectively, the great majority of the unofficial members in both Houses opposed this reform, partly on the grounds that extra-marital relations were punishable at any age, and with or without consent, under the Sharī'a, but chiefly because they regarded any restriction of the age at which a marriage might be consummated—other than the bride's capacity to bear it—as contrary to the divine law.[3] This provides a good example of the fact that such reforms must be introduced in countries such as Nigeria either without the concurrence of the Muslims themselves[4] (who will thus be absolved from all responsibility, and will in most cases then be prepared to enforce the law with a free conscience) or by one of the indirect and administrative means used to such good effect in Egypt and elsewhere.[5] Meanwhile, public opinion should be influenced as widely as possible through medical and educational channels.

As for the forcing of adult wives into uncongenial unions, a comparatively recent questionnaire on this subject elicited the following replies. In Sokoto it was admitted that marriages by compulsion were common, but it was claimed that any girl who strongly resisted such a marriage and appealed to authority would be granted relief. Similarly, in Katsina, it was emphasised that an aggrieved girl could always—in theory, at least—apply to the Alkali, who would thereupon, if conciliation failed, give orders that any marriage payments be refunded and the girl set free. In Kano, Zaria, Bauchi, Niger and Adamawa Provinces it was stated that forced marriage was becoming increasingly rare from fear that the girl would only run away, bride-wealth have to be returned, and adultery perhaps result, while appeals from misused girls for judicial relief would be granted: and in Ilorin coercion was said to be unknown today, since the right of a girl to claim her liberty was common knowledge. While, therefore, there can be little doubt that many of these replies were tinged with wishful thinking—not only in Muslim areas, but in pagan enclaves where both exchange of brides and levirate marriage (which often involve some coercion) are still not wholly extinct—it seems clear that Native Authorities in most cases discourage parents from riding too rough-shod over their daughters' feelings and would usually support a girl who was willing, and able, to appeal to them: but neither the legal right of fathers under the Sharī'a, nor the strength of what may

[1] See statistics quoted, e.g., in K. Mayo's *Mother India* for injury to wives of ten, eleven and twelve years of age.

[2] cp. instances of consummation between seven and ten in *Mother India*.

[3] A further reason is that young girls are said to be so easily seduced in many parts of Nigeria today that Northern opinion will not at present agree to prohibit the transfer of a child wife to her husband's house and custody—after which the control of consummation of marriage becomes virtually impossible in practice.

[4] But the day for this seems now to have passed in Nigeria.

[5] See below (pp. 218, 9) and Appendix A and C.

euphemistically be termed "moral suasion" in African families, may either be doubted or denied.

Thirdly, the possibilities of what amounts to a traffic in slaves under the cloak of such marriages are as obvious as they would be difficult to check.[1] The major safeguard in Nigeria, however, is that no decree of restitution of conjugal rights may be executed by force, so a runaway "wife" would never be dragged back to her "husband". True, her guardian might be ordered to refund the husband's "dower"[2]: but in cases approximating to a traffic in slaves this would usually amount to rescinding the bargain, if the "guardian" could be found. As for cases of "slave"-concubinage in contemporary Nigeria, these will be discussed below.

Local opinion with regard to marriage equality (*kafā'a,* i.e., that a woman may be given in marriage to one who is not her equal only if both she and her guardian consent) differs a good deal from place to place. In Kano and Bornu, it seems, considerations of religion, lineage, employment and wealth are all taken into account; in Sokoto the main emphasis is apparently put on religion, although lineage and wealth are also customarily considered; in Zaria I was told that religion and employment—and occasionally lineage—were the relevant points; while in Potiskum, Bauchi, Jos, Bida and Ilorin the only criterion is that the bridegroom must be a Muslim.[3]

Mixed marriages—i.e., those between Muslims and non-Muslims—are, however, not unknown. The Mālikī law, of course, utterly precludes the marriage of a Muslim to a pagan (but not a Christian) woman or of a Muslim woman to any non-Muslim.[4] In the vast majority of cases it seems that where a North Nigerian Muslim wants to marry a pagan woman she will embrace Islam, nominally at least, and all will be well[5]: but should she openly remain a pagan the contract would be regarded as invalid (*fāsid*), she would only be entitled to dower if and when the union was consummated[6] and there is a conflict of opinion about the legitimacy of any issue.[7] A mixed-marriage the other way round is, of course, even more seriously regarded: but in a number of cases Muslim women have been formally given in marriage to Christian Southerners,[8] and in some Provinces such unions, although considered invalid *per se,* have been regarded as giving rise to a civil action for debt for the return of bride-wealth if the "wife" subsequently deserts her "husband".[9] In order further to discourage such unions the Emir of Zaria proposed at a Conference of Chiefs

[1] It seems, however, that in fact little, if any, of this exists in Nigeria today.

[2] See below (p. 209).

[3] It is noteworthy that while some Mālikī jurists have regard to six criteria of marriage equality (blood, religion, employment, freedom, absence of defects and wealth), the most authoritative doctrine limits these to two only (religion and "condition", i.e., freedom from physical defects). "Religion" here means piety.

[4] But I saw it stated on files (e.g., 21235) that the leading jurists of Bornu regarded "mixed marriages" as "legal, provided that cases of divorce follow the Muhammadan Code" (letter from Acting Resident, dated 1/1/1934). *Sed quaere.* Again, the Alkali of Muri is reported to hold a mixed marriage with a Christian (*either* way) to be valid.

[5] This is quite common in some parts.

[6] Thus, the Chief Alkali of Zaria. Some, however, would not enforce it even then. But in the orthodox view dower is due on consummation. (This, however, is disputed: see al-Dasūqī, ii, 372). For *fāsid,* see under *ṣiḥḥa* in Glossary.

[7] They are regarded as always legitimate, by the Chief Alkali of Zaria; as legitimate provided they are formally acknowledged, by the Chief Alkali of Bida and the Alkalai of Ilorin (while the Chief Alkali of Bida would include acknowledgment by "actions"); as illegitimate, by the Chief Alkali of Bauchi; and as not even legitimate if specifically acknowledged, by the Alkali of Jos and the Chief Alkali of Bornu. The dominant view seems to be that they are illegitimate unless specifically acknowledged as legitimate.

[8] Who normally submit in such cases to a Muslim ceremony of marriage.

[9] e.g., at Katsina, where the husband may recover his disbursements less the minimum dower of ¼ *dinār* (often reckoned in Nigeria at 5s.).

held in 1941 that unions between Christian men and Muslim women should be forbidden by Proclamation; that the courts should not assist any recovery of money in such cases, since the contract was wholly invalid; and that the women's guardians should be punished: while the Chief Commissioner, reversing the policy previously followed in some Provinces, agreed that no assistance should be given by the courts in recovering disbursements made in respect of such unions. Yet another problem, moreover, is occasionally raised by a pagan wife of a pagan husband embracing Islam—for this automatically dissolves the union, unless the husband, too, accepts Islam, under the Sharī'a; and most Alkalai will not even enforce refund of bride-wealth in such cases[1]: but here again practice differs.

Customs with regard to marriage payments, etc., are by no means uniform, and differ not only from locality to locality but from tribe to tribe.[2] In Bauchi, for instance, the prospective husband will first send a money gift to the girl's father, who will keep this while he discusses the proposal with other members of the family. Next, if all goes well, discussion will begin with regard to the amount of "*sadaki*"[3] which must be paid, and how much is expected in advance, while the groom will begin to send or give[4] small presents to his future bride. A further sum must be provided for her trousseau, etc.[5] When both these are paid a day will be fixed for the contract; and this will involve further disbursements for kola nuts, etc., for guests, relatives and neighbours and a small fee for the *mallam* who will not only recite the appropriate prayers, but ensure that the contract is in proper Islamic form. Thereafter the bride will be sent to her husband's house almost at once. In Zaria local custom prescribes seven different payments by the groom—some to the girl herself, some to her guardian, and some for distribution to members of her family—including the "*sadaki*", which is handed to the guardian but is intended, nominally at least, for the bride herself; while all those relatives who have received a share in these payments will contribute towards her *tajhīz*. In Bida the couple usually come to a mutual understanding first, after which a formal approach is made to the girl's father, with two shillings and kola nuts. A further payment of six shillings and eight pence (with nuts) to the father follows, and gifts to the girl. Next the *sadaki* is fixed, followed by two further payments—which may be termed respectively "Big Thanks" and "Little Thanks"; while the groom must also provide his bride with clothes, or money in lieu.

Further differences occur if for any reason the contract is not in fact completed, although some at least of the payments have already been made. Where it is the girl or her family who fail to complete the union all payments (including gifts) may normally be recovered; but where it is the man who backs out of the arrangement opinion differs, for in some places he may by custom recover

[1] But the Chief Alkali of Zaria said that he would ignore a professed conversion which was only a pretence; while the Alkalai of Ilorin and Bida held dower recoverable in such circumstances.

[2] Where it is customary for certain gifts to be given to a betrothed woman or bride before consummation of marriage, one view in the Mālikī school regards these as on a par with other gifts, as only complete by delivery, and as lapsing by prior divorce or death; while the other opinion holds them binding and enforceable in full on death, or in half on divorce by the husband before consummation of marriage.

[3] i.e., the Arabic *ṣadāq* or *mahr*.

[4] According to whether she is "purdah" or not.

[5] *Tajhīz* or *jihāz,* wider than the English trousseau. This is provided in Bauchi partly out of this sum, partly out of the *sadaki,* and partly (perhaps) by the father from his own resources. It is noteworthy that the normal Mālikī view is that *jihāz* must be provided, at the customary scale, from the dower, where the husband pays the father before the marriage is consummated. Where, however, he does not, then no *jihāz* may be demanded, unless it were expressly stipulated or locally customary. See al-Dasūqī, ii, p. 364.

half his disbursements,[1] in others none,[2] and in others all.[3] It is interesting to compare this with the situation when a marriage once consummated, is dissolved at the instance of the wife (see below).

A special variety of marriage not uncommon in Northern Nigeria is *ṣadaqa* marriage—i.e., a marriage in which a father gives his daughter in marriage to a *mallam*, student or orphan and himself bestows a gift upon his daughter as her dower. This is said to be the correct form[4]· the father merely calls men together as witnesses, announces the name of the man to whom he is giving his daughter in *ṣadaqa* marriage and the amount of dower (in Hausa, *sadaki*) which he has given her, and has her escorted to her bridegroom's house. But in practice, it seems, the *sadaki* is often handed to the bridegroom rather than to the girl and he is simply named, at the ceremony, " Muḥammad ", whatever his real name may be (i.e., the girl is regarded as given in alms-marriage to the Prophet himself). If such a marriage breaks up, then the correct procedure, apparently, is for the Alkali to investigate on which side the fault lies: if it is the wife's, she should be ordered to pay into court the dower which her father gave her, and this should be handed to her husband, while if the fault be his no action is required, as she already has her dower. Where, however, the Alkali finds that, although the girl's parents claimed to be giving their daughter in *ṣadaqa* marriage, certain payments were in fact made by the bridegroom, that the latter himself received the " alms-dower " and that the marriage was celebrated in the name of Muḥammad, he will at once annul the contract, since the groom " cannot get both the alms-dower and the girl " and the marriage was not celebrated in his own name and was therefore invalid; while if the marriage was consummated " proper " dower must be provided.[5] It is said, moreover, that strict families tell the groom not to provide a wedding feast at a *ṣadaqa* marriage; but that here again custom differs and in practice he commonly does so.

It seems that nowhere in Northern Nigeria are conditions inserted in marriage contracts in favour of the bride, and that they would everywhere be regarded as legally invalid even if they were. This is the normal Mālikī law. The maintenance due to a wife, on the other hand, is everywhere calculated by exclusive reference to the husband's means: and this, while reasonable enough, is directly contrary to the normal Mālikī rule, as the better jurists in Nigeria fully realise. This provides a good example of a point on which customary law has everywhere triumphed. Finally, it is relevant to observe that while there are no appeals from native courts in cases of marriage and succession,[6] and no other courts have original jurisdiction in such causes under native law and custom,[7] yet the right is reserved to administrative officers to review them[8] or even to order their transfer to the Supreme Court or to a magistrate's court.[9] It is, moreover,

[1] e.g., at Bauchi.

[2] e.g., in Ilorin.

[3] e.g., at Jos. The pure Mālikī law allows him to recover advance payments of dower, but not gifts, in such circumstances.

[4] For this description I am indebted to the Chief Alkali of Bauchi (through Mr. L. C. Giles). There may, of course, be differences in detail elsewhere.

[5] This, it seems, is only £1 for a virgin wife and ten shillings for a previously-married woman in Bauchi: but the rate, of course, differs from place to place. It is noteworthy, however, that it is commonly a fixed or flat rate in Nigeria, and does not normally vary according to the lineage or charms of the woman concerned.

[6] Native Courts Ordinance, sect. 30(1), Proviso 3, as amended in 1936 (the only exception being if and in so far as the Governor otherwise directs by endorsement on the court warrant concerned).

[7] Supreme Courts Ordinance, sect. 12, Proviso, and Magistrates' Courts Ordinance, sect. 19, Proviso.

[8] Native Courts Ordinance, sect. 28(1) (*a*).

[9] Native Courts Ordinance, sect. 28(1) (*c*), with Supreme Courts Ordinance, sect. 12, Proviso, and Magistrates' Courts Ordinance, sect. 19, Proviso.

probable that a maltreated wife could in some cases obtain relief under the Criminal Code Ordinance: for while her husband might plead his right under native law and custom (or Islamic law) to give her personal chastisement within specified limits, this might well be held to be ousted by the terms of the Ordinance, to be contrary to "natural justice", or to be allowed only the most restricted application.

In general, wives seem to enjoy more freedom in Nigeria, and throughout West Africa, than in most Muslim lands. Only among the upper classes of the Northern Emirates are they kept in seclusion[1]: but where this is enforced it is very strict, and the women are scarcely allowed out by day at all. The majority of women are much less restricted, but commonly lead a hard life; and I was told that opulent husbands frequently keep their wives hard at work in comparative squalor, while any real companionship between the sexes is extremely rare. The chief weapon in the hands of an ill-used wife is the danger—very real, it seems, today—that she will abscond, for decrees of restitution of conjugal rights (*ṭāʿa*) may never be executed by force in Nigeria.

It is no doubt partly for this reason that a discontented wife can almost always get release from an unhappy marriage if she can provide suitable financial compensation, for a husband whose wife runs away and cannot be recovered by force will normally agree to release her for a sum which will enable him to replace her. Sometimes a woman will be able to provide this from her own resources; but more often it will be paid either by her guardian or family (who will hope for reimbursement by remarrying her for the same dower) or, secretly, by some other man who wants to marry her.[2] In reality, however, this situation is helped rather than caused by the British refusal to countenance the forcible return of wives to their husbands, for it represents one of the major examples of the triumph of customary law—under which a marriage can almost always be dissolved by return of bride-wealth, etc.—over the Sharīʿa. And it is assisted, again, by the fact that Mālikī law, alone in Sunnī Islam, allows for compulsory *khulʿ* (release of a wife in consideration of a money payment), although only after two family arbitrators appointed by the court to investigate the causes of matrimonial discord have reported that reconciliation seems impossible, that the fault is at least partly that of the wife, and that dissolution of marriage on this basis seems the only feasible solution.

It is significant that the vast majority of divorces in Northern Nigeria are at the instance of the wife.[3] They may be broadly classified as those in which some justification for judicial divorce known to Mālikī law is alleged, and proved, in support of the demand, and those in which no such justification exists. A very few of the stricter jurists[4] maintain that where the husband is not himself at fault they will never force him to accept a *khulʿ*, but will only grant repeated postponements of the case to allow the parties to reach mutual agreement[5]: but the vast majority admit that, after more or less protracted efforts to reconcile the parties, or at least to arrange a dissolution by mutual consent, they will finally

---

[1] i.e., *purdah* or *taḥajjub*.

[2] However this may be, women in Northern Nigeria today generally seem to be able to raise the money somewhere.

[3] Those at the instance of the husband do not, of course, normally come to court; while husbands who want divorce commonly try to provoke their wives into taking action.

[4] Such as, e.g., the Chief Alkali of Zaria.

[5] No doubt this would normally come to the same thing, since a husband who found his wife adamant would usually, sooner or later, accept compensation and release her.

order a suitable refund of marriage payments and dissolve the union.[1] There is a difference from locality to locality, however, regarding what this refund entails: the commonest view is that only the "*sadaki*" is involved; but in some places this is liable to be increased on occasion,[2] while elsewhere all or most of the disbursements made by the husband in contemplation of marriage, whatever their name, are included.[3] In some districts, moreover, the Qur'anic injunction about the appointment of two family arbitrators is apparently followed,[4] whether in cases of alleged ill-treatment or other disputes; while in others this procedure is never used.[5] And it is also noteworthy that some courts[6] are much stricter than others in preventing a woman so released from marrying a lover who persuaded her to take this action (and may even have supplied the necessary funds).

Where the husband is present and not impecunious, but refuses or fails to support his wife, he will be ordered to do so: then, if he disregards this order, he will not be forced to support her by imprisonment or distraint but the marriage will be judicially dissolved[7] without any repayment by the wife. This seems to be general throughout the Northern Emirates.[8] Where, however, the husband is present but unable to support his wife and she demands divorce, a respite of one month[9] is usually allowed him, after which the marriage will be dissolved—usually, but not invariably, without any refund.[10] A more difficult

[1] This was admitted *inter alios* by the Waziri of Sokoto, the Wali of Bornu and the Chief Alkalai of Argungu, Birnin Kebbi, Katsina, Fika, Bauchi, Bida and Ilorin and the Alkali of Jos. But there are minor differences as to whether they merely put pressure on the husband or, in case of need, either pronounce the divorce themselves or let the woman do so—although it seems that much the most usual form is for the Alkali himself to utter the words of divorce.

[2] e.g., by some of the district Alkalai of Dikwa (who say that husbands will always accept an increased sum unless they merely want to prevent their runaway wives from remarrying, in which case the Alkali should intervene in the interests of public morality).

[3] e.g., at Bida, Ilorin, etc. But differences in detail abound. A reasonably typical example may be found in the practice of the Chief Alkali of Bauchi, which may be summarised as follows. (*a*) Where the husband is gravely at fault, he gets no refund whatever; (*b*) where the wife insists on divorce within three months of marriage without accusing her husband of any fault, he may recover both *sadaki* and other costs of the marriage, including all presents given formally to or through her parents from the time of his first formal approach to them (but not the casual presents of courtship), less the value of *tajhīz* received; (*c*) where the wife insists on divorce later, without attributing any fault to the husband, he will be entitled to recover the *sadaki* only, and will often waive even this.

[4] e.g. (allegedly), in Bama, Fika and elsewhere. *Sed quaere.* It is noteworthy that orthodox Mālikī doctrine leaves the compensation which these arbitrators may order to their absolute discretion, which might coincide with any of the alternatives mentioned above.

[5] e.g., in Jos and, curiously enough, Zaria.

[6] e.g., at Bida, where such marriage is not allowed so long as the first husband is alive. The man concerned will be summoned and warned, and should the parties nevertheless marry the contract will be dissolved and all concerned will be punished. And much the same is true in some other localities.

[7] This represents one of two Mālikī views (while the other allows for imprisonment first), except that any available property (*māl ẓāhir*) should first be taken in execution of a maintenance order.

[8] Except, e.g., in Bida, where the "*sadaki*" (only) is reclaimable even then.

[9] But the Chief Alkali of Birnin Kebbi said that about two months would be allowed, while a wife unwilling to wait so long would have to refund *sadaki*. And there were other variations. The orthodox view leaves the period of "*talawwum*" to the discretion of the court.

[10] But in Bida, again, *sadaki* (only) is refundable, while in Ilorin all marriage payments are reclaimable in such circumstances—which is supported by the argument that women there are free and could support themselves by trade. This is, of course, entirely contrary to the Sharī'a.

problem arises when a husband is able to provide only the bare necessities of life and a wife who is accustomed to ease and luxury complains that this is inadequate. In such circumstances most Nigerian jurists[1] deny her right to a judicial divorce—although she can almost everywhere get a compulsory *khul'* if she wants it.

Where, again, the husband is absent in some known locality and his wife claims dissolution of marriage for failure of maintenance, the usual procedure is either for his relatives to be instructed to contact him and tell him to support her or else for letters to that effect to be sent to the Alkali of the place where he is staying; and if he fails to respond within a reasonable time (usually about one month) he will be treated as though present and recalcitrant.[2] Where, again, the husband is of unknown whereabouts his relatives will be instructed to find him and enquiries will be made in likely quarters; and if these precautions prove abortive and the wife insists on divorce the Alkali will require proof of the marriage, make her swear the suitable oath in support of her claim[3] and then dissolve the contract.[4] It is apparently rare in Nigeria for absent husbands to have left property in the hands, e.g., of their brothers: but should this happen most Alkalai say they would dissolve the marriage but neither seize nor sell property to provide maintenance, although a few allege that they would order a wife's maintenance, out of movable property only, for a limited period[5]—if this would content her—before dissolving the marriage, and particularly if she were pregnant or had a young child. This principle that marriages should be dissolved rather than property taken to provide the wherewithal to preserve them represents another triumph for customary law.[6]

A further problem may arise in such cases if the husband of a wife who has claimed (and sworn) that she was left without maintenance, has obtained her divorce, and has subsequently remarried, ultimately returns, denies and wishes to disprove her statement, and reclaims her. Here there is a difference of opinion in Northern Nigeria as to whether the second marriage should stand or the first husband, if he can prove his case, be allowed to recover his wife. In Maiduguri, for instance, the second marriage is regarded as invalid and the woman ordered to return to her former husband,[7] although the second husband may keep as his legitimate offspring[8] any children she has borne him; while in Bauchi both the divorce and the second marriage are allowed to stand.[9]

[1] But not, it seems, the Chief Alkali of Bauchi, who asserts that to eat means to eat adequately and that a wife of noble family cannot be expected to eat the coarsest food. And the Alkali of Jos was inclined to agree, and even the Chief Alkali of Zaria doubtful. The orthodox view, it seems, differentiates between the quality and the quantity of food provided: for however poor the former may be, no divorce is allowed (unless, presumably, the husband could and should do better, but refuses), while where the latter is insufficient divorce is allowed, even if the wife's life would not have been endangered.

[2] But in Ilorin all payments made in contemplation of marriage are reclaimable (see p. 210, note (10)), except where the husband is ordered to support his wife and wilfully refuses, when nothing is refunded. Elsewhere, moreover, the summons is sometimes repeated, etc., before action is taken.

[3] *Yamīn al-qaḍā*, or *yamīn al-istiẓhār*—i.e., that she does not know where he is, and that he has not left or sent her maintenance, etc. See Glossary.

[4] But *sadaki* (only) would again be reclaimable in Bida, and all marriage payments in Ilorin, if the husband subsequently returned.

[5] e.g., the Chief Alkalai of Sokoto, Katsina, Bama, Bauchi and Zaria: but they differ between themselves in matters of detail (e.g., whether this is to last for three or six months, or even for a year). But this seems largely theoretical: see below (note (6)).

[6] Since the orthodox Mālikī view allows for any "*māl ẓāhir*" to be seized in such circumstances. But Nigerian wives seem always to prefer divorce.

[7] And this is the orthodox doctrine. See al-Dasūqī, ii, p. 544.

[8] Because of the "*shubha*" of a valid marriage. See Glossary.

[9] In Ilorin the Alkalai even suggested that the woman might choose whether to return to her first husband or refund all his marriage payments and stay with the second!

A further difference of opinion prevails regarding a wife's right to demand dissolution of marriage, even though her maintenance may be forthcoming, on the grounds that she is suffering injury from her husband having gone away and deprived her of his company. In such circumstances the classical Mālikī jurists allow divorce only after one or even three years' separation and on the ground that she is afraid of falling into adultery, and a very few jurists[1] in Nigeria try to insist on the one year rule: but the vast majority will, in theory,[2] grant a divorce in such circumstances after only about one month's separation or delay, if the wife is sufficiently pressing,[3] although they would probably allow the husband to reclaim his *sadaki* if he returned in the comparatively near future[4]—while a few jurists say that they try to insist, as a compromise, on a few months' delay, before they allow divorce in such cases.[5] Where the absent husband is of known whereabouts most, of course, will insist on giving him warning and a reasonable respite to return or to send for his wife,[6] although a threat that she may fall into adultery sometimes works wonders in such cases; while where his whereabouts are unknown others confuse the relevant rules with those providing for a "missing" husband[7] to be presumed dead, in so far as his wife is concerned, after a suitable period of absence. It is again noteworthy that the grant of divorce after, e.g., only a short desertion represents another obvious triumph for African customary law.

Dissolution of marriage for *ḍarar* (injury) is allowed in cases of physical ill-treatment or deliberate sexual desertion, provided, in either case, that they cannot be regarded as lawful punishment under Sūra 4. 38.[8] Where the wife, for instance, has been very severely or repeatedly beaten, most Alkalai will grant divorce without any refund; but where ill-treatment is alleged but cannot be proved, or is regarded as insufficient to justify such action, a wife determined to obtain her release must resort to the procedure for a compulsory *khulʿ*.[9]

Three further points deserve mention in this connection. Firstly, the number of divorces which occur in Northern Nigeria today is causing widespread anxiety among all thinking men and many suggestions have been made as to how the situation might be remedied. In cold fact, however, no juristic device would be likely to prove effective unless decrees of restitution of conjugal rights were to be executed by force, and to this the Government, very properly, would not agree. Many of the Nigerian jurists themselves realise, moreover, that the basic reason for the present situation is that most husbands do not treat their wives sufficiently well, and that the only cure is to extend education and improve social conditions.[10] Secondly, in 1937 the Sudanese teachers at the

[1] e.g., the Chief Alkali of Zaria. For this rule see al-Dasūqī, ii, p. 488.

[2] But in practice most courts, it seems, try to insist on a few months' delay (e.g., from three to six).

[3] Some even say at once, where adultery is feared.

[4] Or even all marriage payments, e.g., in Ilorin.

[5] e.g., the Chief Alkali of Bauchi. And this appears to be common practice.

[6] Unless the wife can produce some representative of the husband, who will agree to the divorce on his behalf.

[7] i.e., the "*mafqūd*" (see below).

[8] The orthodox Mālikī doctrine allows a divorce, with no refund, where the wife can prove that she has been punished wrongfully or excessively in either of these ways, or that she has been abused, etc. See al-Dasūqī, ii, p. 391.

[9] It seems that in Northern Nigeria a wife seldom in practice gives her reason for demanding divorce, except when it is her husband's absence, lack of maintenance, or his failure to follow her when she ran home. She rarely alleges cruelty, a second wife, favouritism, etc., but merely repeats interminably: "No reason, only I do not love him."

[10] It is, moreover, a vicious circle. The wives will not take marriage more seriously until the husbands do, and the husbands feel they cannot until the wives do. The parent-child relationship is, of course, far stronger than the conjugal one.

School of Arabic Studies at Kano produced a memorandum emphasising that it would ameliorate the situation if it became widely known that husbands who maltreated their wives, failed to support them, or refused to fulfil their marital duties were liable to have their marriages dissolved without any financial compensation whatever[1]; that wives who sought a dissolution of marriage just because they wanted to marry other men would be prevented from marrying their paramours[2]; and that courts could and should resort more frequently to the system of appointing a family council of arbitration to investigate the causes of marital discord. This memorandum was circulated to Muslim courts in Kano, Zaria, Benue, Katsina, Niger, Bornu, Sokoto, Bauchi, Plateau, Ilorin and Adamawa Provinces, was generally regarded as "beneficial", and has almost certainly had some—although probably a very limited—effect in influencing the local practice and interpretation of the law described above: but it seems that the family council suggestion has not been implemented. Thirdly, the Etsu of Nupe had under consideration, when I visited Bida, the issue of a series of instructions regarding divorce designed to tighten up present practice among the Nupe.

It has already been noted that divorce by the husband is far less common in Nigeria than dissolution of marriage at the instance of the wife. Suspended divorce (*ta'līq al-ṭalāq*) and delegated divorce (*tafwīḍ al-ṭalāq*) are virtually unknown, as is also the vow of continence called *īlā'*.[3] "Injurious comparison" (*ẓihār*—i.e., where a man likens his wife to his mother, etc.) is almost unknown in some localities but comparatively common, it seems, elsewhere: but such cases seldom come to court.[4] Mutual imprecation (*li'ān*) is rare, but not unknown in some localities, where it is occasionally used by a husband who wishes to disown the child conceived by his wife.[5] Where a triple divorce, or the word *ḥarām*, is uttered in the heat of anger without any real desire to end the marriage, the position varies, of course, according to the relative orthodoxy of those concerned: most couples would no doubt ignore the incident and continue their relationship, but should such a case come to court some Alkalai would in all cases declare the marriage dissolved,[6] others would allow the continuance of the union provided the wife confirmed the fact that divorce was not really intended,[7] others would disregard the incident if the husband were prepared to declare on oath that he did not mean it,[8] while yet others state categorically that a divorce uttered in passion would never be regarded.[9] And much the same is also true of a formula of divorce uttered as an oath or threat.[10]

---

[1] This shows that the customary law under which a husband could always insist on return of bride-wealth where the wife refused to continue the marriage, regardless (to a great extent) of his own short-comings, still frequently prevails in practice, in some quarters at least, whatever the purists may say.

[2] This is an important point, since otherwise a woman may go from man to man, provided only that each can produce the necessary sum.

[3] For all these technical terms, see Glossary.

[4] But where they do the husband is apparently ordered to make expiation (by feeding sixty poor persons for one day, etc.) or to divorce his wife, while if he does neither the marriage will be dissolved after the period of *īlā'* (four months). This was alleged to be the practice at, e.g., Potiskum and Bama; while at Bauchi expiation is never ordered but divorce, it seems, decreed.

[5] After the mutual oaths the Alkali will formally dissolve the marriage. This is said, e.g., to have happened twice during the service of the previous Alkali of Fika (Potiskum).

[6] e.g., at Bauchi, where children subsequently born, if the parties continued the union, would allegedly be regarded as illegitimate.

[7] e.g., at Maiduguri.

[8] e.g., at Potiskum.

[9] e.g., the Chief Alkali of Bida and the Alkali of Doko; while the Alkalai of Ilorin said they would always "attempt reconciliation" in such cases.

[10] This was specifically stated by the Chief Alkali of Bida.

Where the triple divorce is uttered deliberately (or in anger in those localities where no concession is made in this matter), or where, indeed, a wife is divorced by a single pronouncement but for the third time, the question of the legality of remarriage not infrequently arises. Here the orthodox Mālikī law insists on the wife having previously consummated an intervening marriage, not expressly concluded with the purpose of making her again lawful to her former husband, and then concluding a new contract, after in each case observing the full *'idda* of divorce or widowhood; while certain purists would insist that the intervening marriage must not be concluded with even the secret intention of validating a subsequent remarriage. In Nigeria all this, again, turns on the relative orthodoxy of the parties. Many couples, as we have seen, simply ignore the triple divorce and continue their marriage, while others arrange what amounts to a remarriage without any intervening union: but were such a case to come to court most Alkalai would declare an intervening marriage to be necessary and such intervening marriage invalid if expressly contracted for the purpose of validating a subsequent remarriage (*taḥlīl*), or if an agreement to that effect between the former husband and either his wife or the second husband[1] could be proved. But while such collusion might often be suspected, it could seldom, of course, be established.

Other Matters of Personal Status

The orthodox Mālikī rule that five years[2] should be regarded as the maximum period of gestation is widely acknowledged in principle, but seldom, if ever, applied in practice. The *'idda* period of a widowed or divorced woman is correctly regarded as either three menstrual periods or three lunar months if she is past child-bearing; while where a widowed or divorced woman who normally menstruates fails to do so, her *'idda* lasts one year[3] unless she claims, is alleged, or appears to be pregnant. It is only in such cases that the five years' rule could possibly apply: but even then the continuance of the *'idda* (with consequent entitlement to lodging and, in such cases, to support) would be made dependent, if challenged, on periodical inspections by doctors or knowledgeable women, and only so (and if the woman gave birth to a child within five years and without having been remarried for at least six months) would the question arise of following the letter of the law even in theory. In reality, however, Nigerian women of child-bearing age can normally find a new husband so easily that the tendency is for the *'idda* to be curtailed rather than fraudulently protracted.

The matter of the care and custody (*ḥaḍāna*) of the children of divorced parents or of widowed women provides an important example of a deviation from the orthodox Mālikī doctrine which is common throughout West Africa. The texts provide that boys should remain in the custody of their mothers, unless the latter remarry outside the immediate family, etc., until they reach puberty, after which they are to be given an option as to which parent they will live with; whereas girls should stay with their mothers, on the same conditions, until they go to their husbands' houses. But while some courts in Nigeria allegedly apply this rule,[4] others frankly follow the variant Mālikī view, which corresponds more closely to local custom, that a boy may be claimed by his

[1] But I was told in Maiduguri that women often arrange a second marriage with this end in view and then provoke divorce, or even come to a secret arrangement with the second husband: and provided the first husband is not himself involved this is not regarded as invalidating the union.

[2] This is, in reality, a middle view between a number of variant Mālikī opinions.

[3] This, it seems, is regarded as the absolute maximum at, e.g., Potiskum.

[4] e.g., at Maiduguri, Bama, etc.

father or other guardian at between five and seven years of age[1]; while in some parts boys (and even girls, in theory at least) may be taken from their mothers after the period of weaning.[2] But this departure from the orthodox view is made largely academic by the fact that Nigerian women almost always do remarry (and that levirate marriage is becoming increasingly the exception rather than the rule); while the question of the custody of children is usually arranged by mutual agreement. The fact remains, however, that children are frequently taken from their mothers at much too tender an age—chiefly, perhaps, as a result of the application of the orthodox rules depriving a mother of their custody if she remarries outside the family,[3] but also on what are really customary grounds. As for financial majority,[4] a boy is usually regarded as attaining this at about eighteen years of age, provided he is competent (*rashīd*): but the only cases of this nature which seem to come to court are where the son of a deceased father claims that he is competent but his guardian denies this, when the Alkali, it appears, will normally put the boy to the test. Where a father does not appoint a guardian by will (*waṣī*) the natural guardian under the Sharī'a will usually act, or be appointed, on his demise: but in a few places I was assured that, e.g., the mother's brother or some other relative would be preferred by the court to the father's brother if better qualified for the responsibility.[5]

We have seen above[6] that the legal status of slavery was finally abolished in 1916, after rather more tentative legislation in the preceding years. No enactment, however, can obliterate at a stroke the social status of slavery in public opinion, or some of the implications of that status in the religious law. An interesting example of this, in Nigeria as in other Muslim lands, is provided by the institution of legal concubinage, which is restricted in Islamic law to concubinage between an owner and his own female slaves. Such relationships are not obtruded today because of what is regarded as British prejudice in this matter; but I was frankly told in a number of different Provinces[7] that it is still common for a man to have this relationship with, e.g., a daughter of his parent's ex-slaves or with the descendant of a friend's ex-slaves "given" to him for the purpose, although it was emphasised that nowadays the girl must in all cases herself consent.[8] In such circumstances the issue of these unions are regarded as perfectly legitimate. Except in the case of the "owner" himself or by his gift, however, any union with a girl of "slave"-status would be regarded as either marriage or *zinā* in the stricter districts, although in some localities opinion is probably laxer in this respect—and in Nupe, for instance, the Etsu may take even free-born girls as "concubines" by the agreement of their parents. It is only where a man gives a "present" to an "owner" for the "gift" of his ex-slave or, in the less orthodox districts, to parents of "slave"-status for their daughter, that any trouble with the

[1] The age at which they begin to change their teeth. This is true at Zaria (where the Chief Alkali frankly admitted that this was not the orthodox Mālikī view), Fika, Bauchi, Jos, Ilorin, etc.

[2] e.g., in Nupe.

[3] And also, allegedly, if she wants to leave the father's locality.

[4] i.e., the age at which a young person is regarded as entitled to manage his own property, make contracts, etc.

[5] e.g., at Maiduguri and Bauchi.

[6] p. 178.

[7] Thus the Wali of Maiduguri maintained that this practice was common among the ruling classes throughout Northern Nigeria; the Chief Alkali of Zaria assured me that it was common in Kano and Sokoto but not in his Province; while it was commonly admitted to be widespread in Dikwa, Nupe, etc. Elsewhere it was denied, alleged to be "rare" (e.g., Katsina), or stated to be only by gift of the Emir himself (e.g., Bauchi).

[8] i.e., not expostulate, run away, or appeal to authority.

Government, on the grounds of what amounts to a traffic in slaves, is likely to arise: so information on this aspect is much more difficult to get.[1]

The other respect in which the old status of slavery is legally relevant today is in the matter of inheritance. Here the Sharī'a not only provides that any property acquired by a slave belongs to his master[2] but that where an ex-slave, or even a descendant of an ex-slave, dies without natural heirs his estate shall go to his former master or the latter's agnatic heirs. Since the formal abolition of the status of slavery the former of these rules is, of course, no longer enforceable; but there seems no objection in principle to the latter, which carries no implications whatever of slavery in the present but merely recognises the historical fact of past slavery. It is not surprising, then, that most native courts in Northern Nigeria will decree inheritance by *walā*, ("patronage") in such cases; but I was told that even this had been discontinued under British pressure in, e.g., Bauchi and Zaria.

For the rest, the orthodox Mālikī rules of testate and intestate succession are, it seems, applied throughout the Muslim Emirates[3] except in pagan areas, although they are only rarely applied to immovable property (see above). In these Emirates the *Bayt al-Māl* (public treasury) of Islamic law is regarded as not only existent but properly administered, so where a deceased has no agnatic heirs, and the rights of his Qur'anic heirs (*aṣḥāb al-furūḍ*), if any, do not exhaust his estate, this goes to the *Bayt al-Māl*: thus no question of the doctrine of the "return" or of the inheritance of uterine relatives arises. Testamentary bequests, moreover, are comparatively common in some localities but almost unknown elsewhere. Problems caused by difference of religion between the *de cujus* and non-Muslim members of his family are at present comparatively rare,[4] since pagan converts to Islam are usually poor and there have as yet been few converts from Islam to Christianity or vice versa. Difficulties of this sort springing from the rigid exclusion of all rights of inheritance between Muslims and non-Muslims in Islamic law must, however, increase; but it is noteworthy that an intelligent Chief Alkali suggested solving one problem of this sort by the payment of the share to which a convert to Christianity would otherwise have been entitled into the *Bayt al-Māl* and then the grant thereof, as an *ex gratia* payment, to the claimant. It is also noteworthy that the property due to orphans is commonly paid into the *Bayt al-Māl* under the administration of the Native Authority Treasurer, but that disbursements therefrom for their maintenance, etc., are made by order of the Alkali until they reach their majority, when the balance is paid to them.

Little remains to be said. With regard to "missing persons" (the *mafqūd*) the normal Mālikī rule about a presumption of their death, as regards the remarriage of their widows but not the distribution of their estates, four years after their disappearance, is known and allegedly applied; and the four years' period is

---

[1] Although the practice was admitted in Bama: but the girl could always, of course, resist the arrangement if she wished.

[2] With certain exceptions.

[3] Should a Nigerian Muslim make a will in the English form this would, presumably, be upheld by British courts, even if its provisions were contrary to the Islamic law in substance as well as form: but it was held in *Gbadamosi Apatira's case* (17 N.L.R. 149) that a will made by a Nigerian Muslim in English form which did not comply with the requirements of the Wills Act regarding signature and attestation could not be regarded as valid under Islamic law. *Sed quaere,* if such will in fact fulfilled all the relevant requirements.

[4] But it is noteworthy that in *Mallam Abba* v. *Mary T. Baikie* (K/20A/1943) Ames J. reversed the finding of the Chief Alkali of Kano on the grounds that the exclusion of a Christian daughter from inheritance was contrary to natural justice.

regarded as commencing, it seems,[1] from the date when enquiries concerning the missing person prove abortive. A form of slavery known as the "pawning" of men, women and children—and a variety of the same practice in the form of self-pawning—was very common in Niger Province up till the middle "thirties"[2]: but many such were released in 1933, and today no cases of this sort come to light. Contracts and torts officially follow the Sharī'a, but the more technical Islamic contracts such as *salam, istiṣnā', muzāra'a,*[3] etc., are little known; and there are no endowments or trusts of the sort termed *aḥbās* or *awqāf,*[4] except in so far as mosques are concerned. Gifts in the form of *hiba* and *ṣadaqa* are common, but cases of gift by means of a vow (*nadhr*) seem never to come to court. "Usury" is in fact widely practised, in Nigeria as elsewhere; in some localities without subterfuge, and in others under the usual devices of an acknowledgment (*iqrār*) of a debt which really, but not expressly, includes both capital and interest, a "double sale" in the form of a purchase on credit followed by a quick re-sale for a lesser price either to the original vendor or some third party, or the usufructuary mortgage ("*rahn*") of farms, houses or, still more commonly, clothing. Where such cases come to court, however, undisguised "usury" is nowhere enforceable although seldom punished, while the attitude to these different devices varies according to the relative orthodoxy of the court[5] concerned. To the practice termed "*soke*" different meanings are attached in different localities, for it is sometimes interpreted as an act of intervention in a sale between two other parties, e.g., by disparagement of the goods concerned, for one's own or another's benefit; sometimes as the cornering of some commodity in order to profiteer thereby; and sometimes as the interception of country people on their way to the market in order to buy their goods cheaply and then sell them at a large profit. On the first interpretation the practice is commonly regarded as disgraceful; on the second as legitimate if only partial and moderate but illegal if carried too far; and on the third as illegal if near the market but legitimate if far afield. Instances are on record of the more extreme forms of this practice being punished by flogging or even imprisonment; while the excess profit is, if possible, prevented or even returned.

It is interesting to notice how rigidly orthodox the Emirs and their Alkalai are on some points and how comparatively lax they can be in others. Thus in the 1945 Conference of Chiefs any idea of introducing a period of limitation for the recovery of debts was rejected as "contrary to Muhammadan law and impossible in Muhammadan areas"; while at the 1941 Conference it was decided that the suggestion previously accepted that Emirs should telegraph to the Sultan of Sokoto as soon as the new moon was sighted at the end of Ramaḍān, and that he should then inform everyone else by telegraph, should be abandoned because many of the Sultan's learned men refused to celebrate the feast until they had themselves seen the moon or had received news of its having been sighted by the oral report of two reputable witnesses. Yet at the same Conference the explanation

[1] So, at least, the Chief Alkali of Sokoto maintained, and this is orthodox Mālikī doctrine. But in view of the facility of divorce described above the question is largely academic.

[2] But is quite alien to Hausa and Fulani culture.

[3] See Glossary.

[4] This is a remarkable thing, in such a very Islamic environment, and throws further light on the fact that the land law has always been customary rather than Islamic. The Land (Perpetual Succession) Ordinance, 1924, would, of course, enable a Nigerian Muslim who was an owner of land or houses in individual title to achieve some of the ends secured by a waqf elsewhere. For the terms, see Glossary.

[5] Thus the *iqrār* is almost everywhere accepted (except allegedly in, e.g., Sokoto, if there is evidence as to its true nature or the party concerned is known for usury), and the double sale usually so (except, e.g., in Bauchi, if the re-sale is to the vendor and obviously a mere device); while the usufructuary mortgage has been discussed above.

that interest on War Savings Certificates was not "usury" but merely "rent" paid for the money lent was accepted without comment[1]; while the almost universal disregard of orthodox doctrine in such matters as forced *khul'*, the calculation of a wife's maintenance, the age of *ḥaḍāna*, inheritance of immovables, the amount of blood-wit, retaliation for wounds, the recovery of marriage payments, divorce for desertion, and no distraint on a husband's property to provide his wife's maintenance, etc., have already been noted. It is highly probable, moreover, that the deviations allowed in practice are far more numerous than those admitted in conversation.

It is obvious, therefore, that the rigid orthodoxy professed by the Emirs and their jurists when faced with some reform desired by the Administration is by no means maintained under pressure from local custom: on the contrary, the willingness of these courts to adapt themselves to the latter is one of the secrets of their success, while it also in large part explains the wide-spread differences between court and court in their treatment of a number of heterogeneous points. It is noticeable, for instance, how frequently Bida and Ilorin on the one hand and Bornu and Fika on the other provide exceptions to the general rule—a fact which is clearly due to the comparative absence of Hausa-Fulani influence in these localities; while, in more detail, the emergence of pagan customs in such places as Bauchi, of Nupe custom in Bida, and of Yoruba custom in Ilorin can be plainly traced. It is partly for this reason that any attempt to promote uniformity is to be deprecated. Again, it is clear that both the Emirs and their Alkalai tend to give the orthodox or "book" answers to any questions raised in the House of Assembly or in reply to official enquiries, so any general airing of a point of law is apt to produce a greater orthodoxy as well as uniformity: it is a mistake, therefore, to put them in this position unless it can be shown that the orthodox rule is preferable in the case in point. It is when they are left to themselves to face the practical problems of their own localities that they feel most inclined to make concessions to local customs and day to day requirements. Nor, let it be said, are some of these jurists either as learned or as hide-bound as they have often been considered. Future developments depend, in great part, on the School of Arabic Studies at Kano (Legal Section); for not only will the centralisation of the training of most future Alkalai lead to greater uniformity between district and district, but it may also be hoped that the graduates of this School will evince a breadth of outlook which has not infrequently been lacking in the past.

Conversations about the progress which has been made in the administration of Sharī'a law in other Muslim countries frequently developed. Several Emirs and Alkalai were particularly interested in the device, commonly adopted in the Near and Middle East, of avoiding any attempt to amend the substantive law but merely precluding the courts, by administrative orders, from granting judicial relief in certain types of cases—a device which has been used in Egypt and elsewhere to limit, *inter alia*, child marriage, to exclude certain claims frequently based on false testimony,[2] and to introduce periods of limitation.[3] But I found almost equal interest in the principle, still more extensively used throughout these countries, that the Government may decree which of the many

[1] This, of course, was to foster the war effort, but all Native Treasuries apparently draw interest on their invested reserves. True, in neither case is the money so invested in order to get the interest, as no Northern Nigerian would consider anything under about twenty per cent. a proper return: the interest is merely an accident, as it were, arranged by the Europeans, of which they do not scruple to avail themselves.

[2] e.g., the claim of a legacy by word of mouth, brought after the death of the alleged testator.

[3] i.e., the debt, or whatever it be, is still regarded as extant and binding on the conscience, but may not be recovered by process of law by one who neglects his claim, without lawful excuse, for a specified period.

variant opinions held by the great jurists of the past, whether inside or outside the dominant school, is to be applied by the courts in any specified particular. Among those especially interested may be mentioned the Emirs of Gwandu, Katsina and Bauchi, the Wali of Bornu, and the Chief Alkalai of Katsina, Zaria, Bida and Ilorin; while it is significant that even such a staunch conservative as the Chief Alkali of Zaria admitted that Northern Nigeria must make progress in such matters or find herself left behind by the rest of the Muslim world, that the denial of jurisdiction in certain cases was justifiable, and that the issue of decrees as to which of variant opinions are to be followed by the courts was at least worthy of consideration. But as soon as closer and more frequent contact is established between Nigeria and other Muslim lands it will not be a few cautious reformers, but the educated youth of the country, who will hasten the path of progress; for the religious leaders, here as elsewhere, will realise that they must either move with the times or completely forfeit their influence.

The Future

On any long term view it seems clear that Northern Nigeria must eventually come into line with the rest of the Muslim world[1] in the establishment of two distinct sets of courts—Sharī'a courts concerned almost exclusively with matters of personal status and family law in respect of Muslim litigants, and "civil" courts administering a criminal code (whether western or hybrid in its origin) and a law of contract, tort, and commerce adapted to the complications of modern life and applied under rules of procedure and evidence free from the rigidity of the Sharī'a. This will be fostered in Nigeria not only by expansion of trade and industry and the increasing use of bills of exchange and similar refinements, but also by the paramount need, as the unification of the country grows, for a criminal law applicable to all Nigerians without distinction.

At present, as has been seen, Islamic law is more widely, and in some respects more rigidly, applied in Northern Nigeria than anywhere else outside Arabia. This is due to the fact that the orthodoxy of the Fulani *jihād* has been preserved first by a century of virtual isolation and then by half a century of colonial administration[2]; for the Muslim Emirates have naturally tended to take refuge in an almost fictitious orthodoxy and rigidity in face of any unwelcome demands or innovations, while the Protecting Power has almost invariably respected this attitude in return for the willing co-operation otherwise forthcoming. While, therefore, it seems to have been the original intention of Lord Lugard and others that the Alkalai's courts should increasingly administer the Criminal Code and Nigerian legislation alongside the Sharī'a, and that the Emirs' courts should develop into *siyāsa* tribunals free from the rigidity of the *fiqh*,[3] this has only partially been realised in practice: and the recent attitude of both Emirs and Alkalai appears to have hardened rather than the reverse. The partial integration of the native courts system with that of the Supreme Court, effected by the replacement, in 1933, of the old Provincial courts, with their very simple procedure and system of transfer of complicated cases, by the more institutionalised Protectorate courts, and of these, in 1943, by the Supreme Court itself, has naturally accentuated those particulars in which Islamic law, whether substantive or procedural, runs seriously counter to British concepts of justice—particularly, as we have seen, in cases of homicide. And with the increasing internal integration of Nigeria and its widening contacts with the outer world, it seems essential that plans should be made without delay for such further developments as can scarcely be long delayed. It was partly for this reason, no doubt, that the Brooke Commission was recently appointed to investigate the whole position

[1] With very few exceptions. [2] See p. 195, note (5).

[3] i.e., the books of law. For *siyāsa*, see p. 195, and Glossary.

with regard to native courts in Nigeria and make suitable recommendations for their future.

It is, of course, of the utmost importance that nothing should be done to weaken the framework of those Native Authorities on which the success of the new Constitution largely rests. To this end, therefore, it is essential that the "civil" courts required in the Northern Provinces should be carried on the budget of the Native Authorities, staffed with Northern personnel, and introduced in a way acceptable to Northern opinion.[1] It is with this purpose in view that the Brooke Commission has apparently recommended that the "civil" courts system of the future should be developed out of the present Emirs' courts. This seems eminently sound: but the basic need will be the training of Northern personnel in a combination of Islamic and "English" law and procedure, so that adequately qualified judicial members—whatever their nomenclature—may act for the Emirs in this capacity; for not only are the Emirs themselves becoming increasingly immersed in administrative work, but their courts will inevitably tend to become more and more specialised. Initially, of course, these courts will have to follow predominantly Islamic rules of procedure and evidence: but their progressive adoption of more liberal rules,[2] together with their gradual absorption of all non-Sharī'a jurisdiction now exercised by Chief Alkalai, would probably prove a comparatively natural development. It is essential, however, that the introduction of "foreign" elements to preside over these courts should be avoided.

Another clamant need investigated by the Commission is the increasing number of cases for which "mixed" courts are required. It will clearly be impossible for the Northern Provinces to maintain, or rather restore, their former isolation, and litigation involving immigrant elements will inevitably assume more and more importance. Opinions regarding the existing "mixed" courts differ widely, as between those administrative officers who extol their usefulness and the lawyers who deplore the nebulous nature of the law they apply. The Commission has apparently proposed, therefore, that a single, well-trained native magistrate should preside over such courts, assisted by assessors who advise, rather than members who participate in the verdict. Such courts would also be extended to cover the needs of those areas where Muslims and indigenous pagans intermingle; while it is also proposed that the definition of "native law" should be widened to include both the law prevailing in the area and the law applicable to the particular cause or matter at issue.[3]

It is also noteworthy that the unsatisfactory position with regard to homicide cases now prevailing in the Northern Provinces has led to demands for a Muhammadan court of appeal. To set up such a court presided over by Muslim judges and bound by the Sharī'a in both law and procedure would, of course, be fatal: for it would not only cut right across the jurisdiction of the Supreme Court but would serve to perpetuate the privileged position of Islamic law in the North. A possible compromise, however, would be the formation of a special division of the Supreme Court, presided over by a British Judge sitting with Muslim assessors, which would hear appeals in homicide cases from Emirs' courts under Islamic law—except where a miscarriage of justice, whether in regard to procedure, substantive law or sentence, would be likely to result, when it would order a retrial under the Criminal Code or take other suitable action. This, it seems, is one of the alternatives suggested by the Commission:

[1] This should not, it seems, prove impossible in practice, provided the need for the change and the method of implementation is sufficiently carefully explained.

[2] Whether by means of some modernised code of Islamic procedure and evidence, such as those introduced in Egypt, the Sudan and even Laḥej, or by the increasing adoption of a simplified form of English practice.

[3] cp. pp. 174 and 176-7 above.

and so long as Islamic law is to be applied in homicide cases, some such expedient seems essential. Such a court, moreover, could also be empowered to hear appeals from the native courts of the Northern Provinces in matters of family law and personal status—cases in which no appeal to the Supreme Court is at present permitted at all. And it is understood that the Commission has recommended that, should such a court be formed, the powers of review at present enjoyed by administrative officers over all cases tried by native courts should be limited to circumstances where a grave miscarriage of justice or an obvious clerical error demands adjustment, while their powers of transfer should still be widely used, particularly where the case should be governed by pagan customary law rather than the Sharī'a, where it seems doubtful what system of law is applicable, or where the Sharī'a runs seriously counter to British ideas of justice[1]; and also that the system of appeals should be simplified by the abolition of those to district officers or Residents and by the regulation of those to the Muhammadan division of the Supreme Court, and to the Court of Appeal for West Africa, by providing suitable ceilings.

If these recommendations are accepted, therefore, the district Alkalai will be progressively replaced, in pagan areas, by new courts—as and when qualified personnel becomes available—sitting with Muslim assessors in Muhammadan cases; while where the present Alkalai must be retained in those areas and take pagan cases under customary law, their courts will, apparently, cease to be called Alkalai's courts. In localities where Muslims predominate the district Alkalai will, of course, continue, as at present, to act in a dual capacity, applying the Sharī'a on the one hand and Native Authority rules, etc., on the other—for the country could not afford a double system of courts in rural districts.[2] Again, in those pagan areas where customary courts are already established these will continue, but with a steady reduction in the size of the benches.[3] In urban areas and commercial centres, on the other hand, the present mixed courts will be replaced by a new "civil" court with one well-qualified "judge" (Hausa, where possible, in the Hausa Emirates) conversant with English as well as Islamic principles of law. Appeals, when of sufficient importance, would go from the appropriate Native Court of Appeal[4] to the Muhammadan division of the Supreme Court on matters of Islamic law and to the Supreme Court as at present constituted on matters of customary law, Nigerian Ordinances or Native Authority rules; while cases of all sorts, if of sufficient importance, would go on to the Court of Appeal for West Africa.

The question remains, however, whether the trial of cases of homicide under Islamic law should not be discontinued. On any long view it is clearly intolerable that a homicide committed on one side of a somewhat ill-defined boundary line between two Emirates should be tried under one system of law, while one committed a few yards away on the other side of that line is triable under a totally different system—particularly when one of those systems decrees that the Muslim who brutally murders a non-Muslim is never, in normal circumstances,[5] liable to the death penalty: so eventual unification appears inevitable. There may, however, be sufficiently strong political and moral reasons[6] for

[1] e.g., homicide cases where the offender is a Muslim and his victim a non-Muslim; or any case which turns on the rigid exclusion of non-Muslim witnesses.

[2] i.e., in country areas where Muslims and pagans intermingle the type of court will depend on what is to be regarded as the territorial law.

[3] So here, again, the tendency would be towards the development of trained and even professional "magistrates".

[4] i.e., that of the Chief Alkali, in appeals in matters of Islamic law from district Alkalai, and that of the Emir, in customary, and most other non-Muslim, cases.

[5] Except, that is, in cases of *ghīla* and *ḥirāba*: see above, p. 198.

[6] Including, of course, the promise apparently given in 1933 that this jurisdiction would not be further curtailed.

maintaining the capital jurisdiction of the leading Emirs for the present at least, while it will certainly be some time before the judicial members of their courts will be capable of trying any such cases under the Criminal Code. In such circumstances some of the unsatisfactory factors in the present position would no doubt be mitigated by the creation of the proposed division of the Supreme Court: but the basic need would remain for cases involving non-Muslims (etc.) to be transferred at an early stage to the Supreme Court, as at present constituted, to be tried under the Criminal Code.

As for training, this might usefully be extended not only to young Northerners selected from the School of Arabic Studies at Kano and elsewhere but also to a few of the younger Alkalai. All such would profit greatly from a course of instruction in comparative jurisprudence (Islamic law on the one hand, and the basic principles of the English law of contract, tort, evidence and crime on the other),[1] which could best, it seems, be provided in the United Kingdom for the present: and this would not only train the basic personnel for the civil courts of the future but would also have an excellent effect in predisposing the Emirs and their people in favour of such a development.

The Eastern and Western Provinces, and the Colony of Lagos.

Islamic law, as we have seen, is applied in Nigeria only as " native law and custom " and, generally speaking, on a territorial rather than a personal basis. As a consequence, its judicial application is confined to the Muslim Emirates of the North; and no specifically Muslim court nor any formal application of Islamic law is known throughout the South, even in those areas where the proportion of Muslims is high (as, e.g., among some sections of the Yoruba). In general, moreover, there seems little desire or demand for either, for the majority of local Muslims appear content to follow the religion of Islam more or less closely in matters of doctrine and ritual but to adhere to their tribal customs in such matters as marriage, divorce, adultery, guardianship and succession—deferring to the law of Islam, if at all, only to the extent that a *mallam* is usually invited to recite prayers and formalise a contract of marriage otherwise arranged in customary manner or, very occasionally perhaps, to give his advice in matters of divorce. Northern Muslims living in the South, on the other hand, will normally settle their disputes informally by reference to the local headman of their community or occasionally, in the more difficult questions of family law, by repairing to the Alkali of their home locality.

There are, however, a few signs that Muslims in the Western Provinces are becoming more conscious of their religious law and disturbed by their disregard for its precepts. Thus the " Muslim Congress of Nigeria " recently addressed a letter from its Secretariat in Ijebu Ode to the Chief Secretary to the Government complaining that " Muslims in the Southern Provinces of Nigeria have long been deprived of the use of the . . . just and moral code prescribed for use by our Holy Prophet Muḥammad . . . for our guidance from generation to generation " and that they felt it " high time " that this should be changed, since " our religion has been greatly corrupted . . . and many of our Muslim brothers have gone astray", while "al-Qur'ān, the Holy Book of Islam, has been badly and wrongly used by men who have no knowledge of it." They therefore requested the establishment of a " Muslim Judiciary (Sharī'a) for Southern Nigeria ". This was followed by a longer letter from the same organisation to the Brooke Commission stating that they would wish such judiciary to deal, initially, with matrimonial causes and questions of inheritance.

[1] It is noteworthy that at the Conference of Chiefs in 1945, when the provision of higher education for Alkalai was under consideration, it was emphasised that they should be taught English and should have some knowledge of English as well as Islamic law.

The first category, they said, would include matters of marriage, divorce and adultery, which represented the greater part of the cases tried by native courts, where the Islamic requirements in regard to such questions as judicial divorce at the instance of a wife or the obligation of a husband to support her were disregarded by non-Muslims. In Ibadan, it was maintained, over four thousand cases of divorce, ninety-five per cent. of them between Muslims, were handled annually by two native courts which separated couples " like dogs, without regard to the instructions laid down by the Holy Qur'ān. Any man or woman who wants divorce will simply walk into the Native Authority court and pay the fee of £2 1s. 6d., whereupon the summons will be issued and the next thing is that on the date for hearing the case divorce is granted. . . . We therefore pray this Commission to grant our request for a separate Muslim court. . . . The condition of our courts is even worse in the case of the law of inheritance. Our Native Authority civil court that grants letters of administration does not know any Muslim Law governing this matter. . . . In conclusion, we have to say here that in almost all the towns and villages in the Western Provinces Muslims are in the majority. For this fact, we request you kindly to consider our case sympathetically and to grant our request."

It seems, however, that there is little real support for this demand, for the influence of tribal custom is still strong with the Yoruba as a whole. In any locality where Islam became so dominant that tribal custom became assimilated to the Sharī'a the courts would no doubt enforce this as " native law "[1]; but the establishment of specifically Muslim courts would inevitably result in the judicial enforcement of Islamic law on a purely personal, rather than a loosely territorial, basis. This would not only cause much confusion in a community so sharply divided in matters of religion but would also raise a formidable obstacle to the ultimate fusion of " native " and English law.

In the Eastern Provinces, on the other hand, Muslims are less numerous. It seems, however, that a Muslim member sometimes sits in the native courts: but his function is more to protect the interests of Muslim litigants than to demand or attempt any formal application of Islamic law.[2]

In Lagos itself I visited several different communities of Muslims and had conversations with their leaders. Sunnī Yoruba are in the majority but seem, in the main, strangely ignorant of the most elementary precepts of Islamic law. Like their fellow tribesmen in the Protectorate, they make some attempt to give an Islamic tinge to marriages which really follow Yoruba custom[3]; but in questions of divorce the law of Islam is seldom, if ever, considered; matters of inheritance are normally settled within the family by tribal custom, although particularly staunch Muslims may occasionally vary this somewhat in accordance with such knowledge as they possess—or can glean from others—of the precepts of Islam; the right to the custody of the children of divorced parents belongs to the father after the period of suckling; wills are very occasionally made, but only in English form; while such questions, e.g., of divorce and inheritance as cannot be settled out of court go to the magistrate.[4]

There are three different groups of Aḥmadīs in Lagos, all professing to belong to the Qādiānī rather than the Lahore party. The differences between them are

[1] See the Introduction to this Survey.

[2] But see p. 191 note (4).

[3] One Yoruba whom I questioned said he had only known two Yoruba marriages in Lagos in "Arabic form": all the rest had been by tribal custom.

[4] In Lagos, unlike the Protectorate, certain magistrates' courts have been expressly authorised to exercise jurisdiction in matters which are subject to the jurisdiction of native courts relating to marriage, family status, guardianship of children, inheritance and disposition of property on death, up to a specified maximum sum. (Order in Council 33 of 1947 under sect. 19(1) of the Magistrates' Courts (Extended Jurisdiction) Order in Council [of Nigeria].)

primarily the result of personal rivalries and have little doctrinal and no juridical basis. The initial split apparently centred round the question of the authority of the senior Indian missionary, as the local representative of the Khalīfa, *vis-à-vis* an African leader of the movement[1]; and when the Khalīfa upheld his official representative certain members of the movement refused to comply and were duly excommunicated—or "repudiated their full allegiance to the Khalīfa", as they themselves prefer to put it. The second split took place within the ranks of these dissidents: and this time it was still more frankly one of personalities and leadership, for certain seceders, who now style themselves "The Muslim Mission", felt that their African leader was himself proving too autocratic. Each of the three groups—the original Aḥmadīs who still owe full allegiance to the Khalīfa and the two dissenting movements—now have a written constitution. But it was a dispute about properties owned by the local Aḥmadīya which, as usual, brought matters to the test, and in the litigation which ensued the Court of Appeal for West Africa duly held that the dissenters must be regarded as having seceded from the original movement.

Almost all these Aḥmadīs, except for a handful of Indians, are of Yoruba origin and seem friendly, frank and reasonably well-educated. Both dissenting groups confirmed that among their communities, as elsewhere, such questions as dower, repayment of dower, divorce, etc., all go by Yoruba custom.[2] The same is true of small estates if distributed by mutual agreement; while any larger estate would be administered by the Administrator-General under English law. It is only in the actual ceremony of marriage, and possibly in attempts to reconcile discordant spouses, that Islamic precepts exercise any influence: and only one of these communities made a very half-hearted plea for the establishment of Muslim courts.

Much the same information was again confirmed by the Anṣār al-Dīn Society, another group of well-educated Yoruba which maintains several schools. Their "missionary" informed me that he tried to make people follow the law of Islam in marriage, divorce and inheritance, but that it was a very uphill fight. As one called to celebrate marriages he made sure that the contract was concluded in true Islamic form; but he admitted that in questions of dower or its return, inheritance, etc., customary law in fact prevailed.

There is also, of course, quite a large Hausa community in Lagos, and these conform far more closely and generally to the dictates of Islamic law. Disputes, however, have to be settled by the arbitration of their elders or the advice of some man of learning: for actual litigation they have only the choice between British courts applying English law, local native courts applying alien customary law, or resort to their own Northern courts for the application of Islamic law as locally adopted and adapted.

Finally, it is noteworthy that most Nigerian Muslims (even including Southerners such as the Yoruba) are more or less closely attached to either the Qādirīya or Tijānīya Ṣūfī brotherhoods. The Shehu Usmano was a Qādirī; his son Bello turned Tijānī; later Sultans returned to the Qādirīya; while today the Emirs of Kano and Katsina are Tijānīs and the Shehu of Bornu a Qādirī. But this division, which persists throughout Nigeria among the rank and file, has no legal repercussions and therefore does not fall within the scope of this Survey. It is, however, noteworthy in passing that while the Qādirīs add certain of their special prayers (*wurūd*) after each of the set prayers and hold no special meetings for the *dhikr*, the Tijānīs say their *wurūd* (which are generally longer) after the morning and evening prayers only and hold special meetings for *dhikr*, especially on Fridays.

---

[1] One Martin by name.
[2] Outside Lagos dower goes by flat rate according to locality, and is almost always returnable on divorce. But in Lagos itself this is now by no means invariable.

THE GAMBIA

From some points of view the Gambia is the most Muslim of all the British territories in West Africa. It cannot, of course, compare with parts of Northern Nigeria in the number and erudition of its scholars, in the strictness of its attachment to the practices and precepts of Islam, or in the extent to which the substance and procedure of the Sharī'a are enforced by the courts. But in the Gambia there are very few Christians outside Bathurst, and comparatively few who are frankly pagan; while the Laws of the Gambia include provisions for the application of Islamic law as such which are without parallel in any of the sister territories in West Africa.

LEGISLATION *(Colony and Protectorate)*

The earliest of these provisions is the Muhammadan[1] Law Recognition Ordinance, 1905. This provides: —

(1) That "Marriages between Muhammadan natives[2] duly contracted in accordance with Muhammadan law shall be as valid and effectual for the purpose of establishing the status of legitimacy within the Colony in favour of the children of such marriage as if solemnised in accordance with the requirements of the Christian Marriage Ordinance, 1862[3] ".

(2) That "There shall be a Court at Bathurst to be known as the Muhammadan Court[4]", which shall be "constituted by a Qāḍī[5] to be appointed by the Governor: Provided that—(*a*) Whenever in the opinion of the Governor the Qāḍī is not a man of uncontested ability the Court shall be constituted by the Qāḍī and two Assessors. (*b*) Whenever the office of Qāḍī is vacant or the Qāḍī is unable . . . to perform the duties of his office the Court shall be constituted by two or more Assessors and the Senior Assessor shall give the judgment of the Court[6] ".

(3) That this Court is to " have jurisdiction in all causes and matters, contentious or uncontentious, between or exclusively affecting Muhammadan natives, relating to civil status, marriage, succession, donations, testaments and guardianhip[7] ".

(4) That " Save in so far as may be prescribed, the procedure and practice of the Court shall be according to the rules of Muhammadan law[8] "; while " Subject to such restrictions as may be prescribed, appeal shall lie from any decision of the Muhammadan Court to the Supreme Court " with " A Tamsir or person learned in the Muhammadan law " sitting, for advisory purposes only, as assessor to the Judge.[9]

(5) That " The recognition by this Ordinance granted to Muhammadan law shall not extend beyond the matters specified . . . ; and in particular, but without prejudice always to the foregoing generality, shall not import the recognition of any rules of Muhammadan law relating to: (*a*) Any religious practices or disabilities save in so far as such may form an essential part of the law relating to the matters specified . . . (*b*) The constitution of religious trusts. (*c*) Civil

[1] Here spelt " Mohammedan ", but see the Introduction to this Survey regarding the liberty taken in the spelling of such words, to avoid the chaos, and possible misconception, which would result from continual variations from territory to territory, and sometimes even within a single territory.
[2] Defined in sect. 2 as " natives of West Africa ".
[3] Sect. 3.
[4] Sect. 4.
[5] Here spelt " Cadi ": but see (1) above.
[6] Sect. 5(1).
[7] Sect. 6.
[8] Sect. 7.
[9] Sect. 8(i) and (ii).

contracts other than marriage. (*d*) Any criminal or quasi-criminal matter whatsoever."[1]

(6) That the Judge of the Supreme Court, with the consent of the Legislative Council, may "make, and when made vary, amend or revoke" Rules regulating (*inter alia*) the practice and procedure of the Court, limiting and defining its jurisdiction in "questions relating to land, and in other cases where it may appear desirable", making such provisions as may be necessary to avoid conflicts of law or jurisdiction between the Court and any other Court of Law or Tribunal in the Colony or Protectorate, and regulating appeals to the Supreme Court and the procedure to be followed in connection therewith.[2]

Again, the Kombo Saint Mary Division Ordinance, 1946, which provides, *inter alia*, for the establishment of a Qāḍī's Court at Kombo Saint Mary, now an integral part of the Colony, contains the same provisions, almost *verbatim*, in a slightly different order, except that an additional section[3] enacts that the "Governor in Council may by order confer upon the Muhammadan Court jurisdiction to enforce within the limits of its jurisdiction all or any of the provisions of any Ordinance or Ordinances specified in such Order and to impose penalties on persons subject to the jurisdiction of the Court who offend against such provisions". It does not seem, however, that any such Order has ever been made, and all jurisdiction outside the scope of the Sharī'a is in fact exercised by the neighbouring Magistrate's Court. The only Rules which have been made under the Muhammadan Law Recognition Ordinance, moreover, appear to be those of 1917 (as amended in 1927 and 1948) which provide, *inter alia*, for a Beadle of the Muhammadan Court to "serve all summonses and execute all writs issuing from the said Court in like manner as summonses are served and writs executed under the Rules of the Court of Requests",[4] and that "No barrister, advocate, solicitor or proctor shall appear or act for any party before the Court or in any appeal from any order or judgment of the Court except by special leave of the Judge of the Supreme Court".[5]

These two Ordinances cover the jurisdiction of the two Qāḍīs' Courts in the Colony. In the Protectorate, on the other hand, there are no specifically Muhammadan Courts and no official Qāḍīs. Instead, the Native Tribunals Ordinance, 1933, which provides for the establishment of "such Native Tribunals as the Governor shall think fit", defines the law they are to administer as[6]: —

"(a) the native law and custom prevailing in the area of the jurisdiction of the Tribunal, so far as it is not repugnant to justice and morality or inconsistent with the provisions of any Order of the Queen in Council or with any other law in force in the Protectorate;

(b) the Muhammadan law relating to civil status, marriage, succession,[7] divorce, dowry, the rights and authorities of parents and guardianship whenever the parties are Muhammadans"—together with the provisions of rules or orders made by a Native Authority or a Commissioner under the Native Authority Ordinance, 1933,[8] and the provisions of such Ordinances, etc., as the Tribunal

[1] Sect. 9.
[2] Sect. 10 (*d*), (*e*), (*f*) and (*g*).
[3] Sect. 65.
[4] Rules 8 and 9.
[5] Rule 11.
[6] Sect. 11 (originally sect. 12).
[7] The word "succession" was added by the Native Tribunals (Amendment) Ordinance, 1935 (sect. 2(*c*)).
[8] Sect. 11(*c*). It is also noteworthy in this connection that the Native Authority Ordinance, 1933, sect. 17, provides that "No Court shall be precluded from trying an offence under this Ordinance by reason of the fact that such offence, if committed, was a breach of an order . . . issued by the Court as a Native Authority . . ."

is authorised to administer.[1] It is also provided that " For offences against native law and custom a Native Tribunal may . . . impose a fine or may order imprisonment with or without hard labour or both fine and imprisonment, or may inflict any punishment authorised by native law and custom . . . not repugnant to natural justice and humanity . . ."[2]; that " Subject to such Rules as may be prescribed, the practice and procedure of Native Tribunals shall be regulated in accordance with native law and custom"[3]; that although "Any unauthorised person who shall exercise . . . judicial powers within the area of the jurisdiction of a duly constituted Native Tribunal . . ." shall be severely punished, yet " Nothing contained in this section shall interfere with the amicable settlement of disputes by arbitration or otherwise "[4]; that " Every Commissioner shall at all times have access to any Native Tribunal in his Division[5] . . . and on the application of any person concerned or of his own motion " may revise any proceedings, order any case to be retried before the same or other Native Tribunal, or transfer any cause or matter to a Protectorate Court[6]; and that " No legal practitioner may appear or act for any party before a Native Tribunal ".[7] From this it is clear: —

(1) that Native Tribunals are authorised to apply Muhammadan law to Muhammadan litigants within the same limits as those assigned to Muhammadan law in the Qāḍīs' Courts of the Colony[8];

(2) that the " practice and procedure " of the Tribunals is that of native law and custom[9];

(3) that such Tribunals are extremely unlikely, in the nature of things, to draw any sharp distinction between Muhammadan law and customary law[10]; and

(4) that there is no system of appeals,[11] but Administrative Officers have wide powers of revision in all types of cases.

It is also noteworthy in this context that the Protectorate Ordinance, 1935, after decreeing that " so far as is consistent with the Protectorate System, and without prejudice to any such reasonable native laws and customs as are hereinafter mentioned, all laws, statutes, Ordinances and rules for the time being in force in, and being of general application throughout the Colony, shall extend and apply to the Protectorate ", continues " all native laws and customs existing in the Protectorate whether relating to matters of succession, marriage, divorce, dowry, the rights and authorities of parents, the tenure of land or any other matter, shall, where not repugnant to natural justice, nor incompatible with the principles of the law of England or with any law or Ordinance of the Colony applying to the Protectorate . . . continue and remain in full force and effect, and shall be taken cognisance of and enforced in all Courts of law,

[1] Sect. 11 (*d*) and (*e*).

[2] Sect. 13. But sentences of corporal punishment, or of more than fourteen days' imprisonment, were to be reported to the Commissioner, who must in all cases confirm the former before being carried out (sect. 21). Now, however, corporal punishment has been totally prohibited in the case of those aged sixteen or upwards, by the Native Tribunals (Amendment) Ordinance, 1947, sect. 2.

[3] Sect. 20.

[4] Sect. 22.

[5] See Protectorate (Amendment) Ordinance, 1944, sect. 3(2) (*a*).

[6] Sect. 23 (as re-worded by the Protectorate (Amendment) Ordinance).

[7] Sect. 30.

[8] Except, perhaps, in regard to " donations ".

[9] By contrast with that of the Qāḍīs' Courts.

[10] Nor, indeed, is any sharp distinction probably intended, since it seems most unlikely that it was ever envisaged that the law of the books, as distinct from the practice of the people, would be enforced under sect. 11(*b*).

[11] But see p. 238 below.

whether in the Colony or the Protectorate, in all causes and matters whatsoever arising in or relating to the Protectorate."[1]

The only other Ordinance which expressly concerns Muhammadan law is the Muhammadan Marriage and Divorce Ordinance, 1941,[2] which originally applied only to the Island of Saint Mary[3] but has been regarded as also applying to the Kombo Saint Mary Muhammadan Court, since the absorption of the Kombo Saint Mary Division in the Colony by virtue of the Colony Ordinance, 1946.[4] This provides, *inter alia*, that " all Muhammadan marriages and all divorces from such marriages celebrated or given according to the rites and observances of the Muhammadan religion customary and usual among the community or sect in which the marriage or divorce takes place shall be valid and registered "[5]; that Registrars shall be appointed[6] each of whom shall, on application, first " satisfy himself as to whether or not such marriage or divorce has been effected by or between the parties "[7] and then make the appropriate entry in the prescribed book[8] and deliver to each of the parties a certified copy thereof[9]; and that such register or certified copy shall be good evidence of the facts recorded.[10] But it is expressly provided that[11] " Nothing in this Ordinance shall be construed to— (*a*) Render invalid, merely by reason of its not having been registered, any Muhammadan marriage or divorce which would otherwise be valid. (*b*) Render valid, by reason of its having been registered, any such marriage or divorce which would otherwise be invalid . . . (*c*) Affect the provisions of the Muhammadan Law Recognition Ordinance, 1905, or of sections 30 and 31 of the Protectorate Ordinance, 1935 "[12]: and, conversely, " Nothing contained in section 16 of the Supreme Court Ordinance, 1889, shall authorise the grant of any relief under that Ordinance when the marriage of the parties has been declared valid under this Ordinance; provided that nothing herein contained shall prevent any court of competent jurisdiction from granting relief under Muhammadan law ".[13]

In addition, there are a few Ordinances in the Gambia which, while they make no direct reference to Islamic law, impinge to some degree on its application. Thus both the Christian Marriage Ordinance, 1862, and the Civil Marriage Ordinance, 1938, provide a way in which a Muslim girl could marry a non-Muslim,[14] in spite of the utter nullity of such a marriage under the Sharī'a; while anyone validly married under either of these Ordinances would be precluded

[1] Sects. 30 and 31. The phrase " all native laws and customs " in this context is presumably intended to include Muhammadan law. See above, especially p. 227 note 10.

[2] For which the corresponding Uganda Ordinance seems to have served as a model.

[3] See sect. 1. This means, in practice, the Bathurst Muhammadan Court.

[4] I could, however, find no authority for this.

[5] Sect. 4. Sect. 3 similarly provides that such marriages celebrated prior to this Ordinance shall be deemed valid.

[6] Sect. 6.

[7] Sect. 9.

[8] Sect. 10.

[9] Sect. 11.

[10] Sect. 14.

[11] Sect. 16.

[12] For these sections see p. 227 and note (1) above. But it is not altogether apparent what effect this proviso, presumably inserted *ex abundanti cautela,* is intended to have.

[13] Sect. 17.

[14] The girl would, of course, have to be over twenty-one, or else obtain the consent of her father, guardian or mother (Christian Marriage Ordinance, sect. 11), or father, mother or guardian (Civil Marriage Ordinance, sect. 7(*b*)). The latter, it will be noticed, further departs from Islamic law in ousting the right of the agnates to marriage guardianship, in default of the father, in preference to the mother. In the case of the Christian Marriage Ordinance it is possible that the girl would also have to make some profession of Christianity, but this would depend on the rules of the denomination concerned; while the Civil Marriage Ordinance would also, presumably, provide a way in which two Muslims, debarred from intermarriage under the Sharī'a by foster relationship, could—in theory, at least—validly marry in the Gambia (see sect. 16(b)).

from exercising any right to dissolve or claim dissolution of marriage except under the local law relating to divorce,[1] or of contracting any other marriage until the former were so dissolved—regardless of their rights to do any of these things under the Sharī'a, as a result of his or her conversion to Islam, the other party's apostasy therefrom, or any other cause whatever.[2] Similarly, the Criminal Code Ordinance, 1933, enacts that " Any person who, having a husband or wife living, goes through a ceremony of marriage which is void by reason of its taking place during the life of such husband or wife, is guilty of a felony."[3] And the Criminal Code also provides that[4] " Any person who, with intent to marry or carnally know a woman of any age, or to cause her to be married or carnally known by any other person, takes her away, or detains her, against her will, is guilty of a felony "—a provision which might possibly expose to prosecution a Muslim father whose actions in the course of giving his daughter in compulsory marriage would be unexceptionable under the Sharī'a. Unlike the Criminal Code in some territories, however, that of the Gambia provides no penalty for the premature consummation of a child-marriage. Again, the Children and Young Persons Ordinance, 1949, may be said somewhat to limit, in appropriate circumstances, the unfettered application of the Sharī'a principles concerning guardianship: but it is noteworthy that the Intestate Estates Ordinance, 1909 (as amended in 1940), expressly provides that " nothing in this section[5] contained shall be deemed to affect . . . the provisions of the Muhammadan Law Recognition Ordinance, 1905, the Native Tribunals Ordinance, 1933, and the Protectorate Ordinance, 1935."

THE COLONY

The Muslims resident in the Colony are mostly composed of those members of tribes found in the Protectorate—Mandingo, Serahuli, Jola, Fula and especially Wolof—who happen to live therein, but also include a number of Aku, or descendants of liberated slaves who were settled in the Colony. In the case of those living in Bathurst and its immediate environs, tribal custom does not loom very large,[6], and the Qāḍīs' Courts apply a law not very remote from pure Mālikī doctrine, influenced as much, perhaps, by British concepts as by tribal customs. All Gambia Muslims belong to the Mālikī school of law, while the vast majority are also loosely attached to either the Tijānīya or Qādirīya Ṣūfī brotherhoods, with the Tijānīs, in the Colony at least, in the ascendancy. A man learned in the Islamic disciplines is termed a *tamsīr* among the Wolof, a

[1] cp. Order XLVIII of the Rules of the Supreme Court, 1928.

[2] This, however, has never been judicially decided in the Gambia and is a matter on which opinions are divided. See note (3) below.

[3] Sect. 155. This would, presumably, include a second marriage by a woman already married under the Muhammadan Marriage Ordinance. Whether it would also include a second marriage under Islamic law by a man already married under either the Christian or Civil Marriage Ordinances is a difficult point, since it might well be argued that such a marriage would be perfectly valid in Islamic law and therefore recognised as such under the terms of the Muhammadan Marriage Ordinance—so it could not be regarded as " void " within the meaning of the Criminal Code. But even more cogently, perhaps, it might be urged that a marriage under either the Christian or Civil Marriage Ordinance is essentially a monogamous union (cp. the words prescribed to be addressed to the parties by the Registrar solemnising the latter in sect. 15), so a further marriage, while such marriage remains undissolved, is necessarily void and bigamous in English law; and that this remains true despite the concession to Islamic law expressed in such unguarded terms in the Muhammadan Marriage Ordinance. In any case it is clear that this legislation has not been adequately integrated in the Gambia.

[4] Sect. 125.

[5] Sect. 14. (cp. sect. 3 of No. 19 of 1940.)

[6] Thus no recognition is given to marriage by native law and custom, but only marriage under one of the three Marriage Ordinances.

fode among the Mandingo, and an *alpha* among the Fula: and in Bathurst itself there are a few, including the two Qāḍīs,[1] whose knowledge is considerable.

Procedure

In matters of procedure the Muhammadan courts adopt a compromise between Islamic and English principles. Thus the Muslim rules about burden of proof, the minimum number of witnesses and the total exclusion of the testimony of ascendants, descendants or spouse, on the one hand, or of personal enemies, on the other, are regularly applied; but all witnesses are put on oath and may be cross-examined not only by the court but by the other party, circumstantial evidence is sometimes considered sufficient,[2] and non-Muslim witnesses—or Muslims who are slack in their religious observances[3]—are accepted. Again, while the ordinary oath which all witnesses take is an oath on the Qur'ān in the English form, the " perishable oath " is used when a defendant is challenged by a plaintiff who lacks adequate evidence or when the defendant " returns " such oath to the plaintiff; and this is sworn by the party concerned, after the performance of ceremonial ablutions, putting his finger on the first radical of the Sūra in the Qur'ān entitled *al-Ṭūr* and repeating there times after the Qāḍī the first eight verses of that Sūra.[4] And many who would otherwise lie without a qualm are, it seems, frightened by this oath into veracity.[5]

Marriage

In the Colony, girls are seldom contracted in marriage, and never sent to their husbands' homes, before they have reached puberty, although they are sometimes still very young when the marriage is consummated. Should they be contracted in marriage by their fathers when immature, and subsequently refuse to consummate the marriage, their parents would no doubt put considerable pressure upon them: but, if they remained adamant, the court would annul the contracts after ordering the refund of all the husband's disbursements. Should a girl, on the other hand, conclude a marriage without her guardian's consent, this would be annulled by the court at the latter's request.[6]

In Bathurst the following marriage customs[7] are, it seems, reasonably typical. A man who sees a girl who attracts him will in most cases make his first approach to the girl herself. Next, he will get some friend or relative to approach her

---

[1] The Qāḍī of Bathurst, in particular, is much respected for his learning, culture, dignity and moral integrity. In addition, he is quite a facile author of Arabic verse, and composed a poem in my honour.

[2] e.g., the fact that a husband had beaten his wife would be held proved by the evidence of those who could testify to seeing her happy and uninjured just before her husband joined her in an otherwise empty house, and to her exit soon after, bruised and weeping.

[3] Attempts to discredit witnesses on the ground of such slackness are virtually unknown throughout West Africa. It is also noteworthy in this context that witnesses are not discredited merely because they are friends, or even collateral relations, of the party concerned, provided they are of good character.

[4] In Bathurst this takes place in the court, but in the Protectorate in a mosque.

[5] It is not uncommon, for instance, for a party, previously adamant, to refuse at the last moment to take this oath in support of his statement—while bystanders frequently shuffle away somewhat self-consciously when it is taken, so as not to become in any way involved.

[6] Unless, that is, the Qāḍī decided to overrule the guardian and confirm the marriage in those circumstances in which he would have married the girl to the man of her choice, in spite of the guardian's objections, had she applied to him (as she ought to have done) in the first place. This is an instance of the way in which the Qāḍīs of Bathurst exercise an intelligent discretion in applying the law, since a more wooden interpretation would lead to the dissolution of a marriage wrongfully contracted even where the Qāḍī would originally have interposed in favour of the girl had she appealed to him and where she could demand " re-marriage " to the same man.

[7] These are Wolof in origin.

father, with a gift of kola[1] nuts; whereupon her father will normally ask for time to consult his daughter and the other members of his family. If all agree, he in his turn will send a friend to request more kolas, which will signify his willingness to discuss financial arrangements. The customary dower for a young, unmarried girl is £20, and for a widowed or divorced woman some lesser sum fixed by mutual agreement: but the would-be husband must also produce a further £17 17s.—in the case of a virgin[2]—to cover various payments to his bride's parents and relations and hospitality for the wedding guests,[3] etc.; and this includes a sum of sixteen shillings paid to the bride as "prompt" (or "minimum") Islamic dower (*ṣadāq* or *mahr*)[4] and one shilling to the *mallam* who performs the ceremony. Where, however, the bridegroom cannot produce £37 17s. all at once he may be allowed to pay part in advance and the remainder by instalments during the next few years. When an initial payment, whatever it be, has been made,[5] a day will be fixed for the marriage ceremony, at which someone delegated by the groom will always say "We are asking the hand of so and so for such and such on terms of so much dower and so much expenses", while a delegate of the bride's father will reply "We accept such and such as the husband of so and so for so much dower and so much expenses" (including mention of the terms of deferred payment, if any).[6] Next, a later date will, usually, be fixed for the bride to be conducted to her husband's house: on which occasion speeches will be made at both houses regarding the marital duties of the spouse concerned, and hospitality will be provided—at the bride's house partly out of the sum paid by her groom for "expenses" and partly at her father's cost, and at the groom's house at his own expense (including fees for musicians and entertainers). Finally, if the bride proves to be a virgin[7] her groom will leave £2 under her pillow for those who come to see her next morning; while he will also provide trinkets, etc., for the bride and payments for minstrels for seven days' festivities.[8] All this, of course, is in addition to the presents which he will have made both to the girl and to her family during the time of courting.[9]

[1] Which play a most important part in many social customs.

[2] Or some £7 2s. in the case of a widow or divorcee.

[3] Among the Wolof these "expenses" will be distributed as follows: (*a*) £2 to the bride's mother, to be shared with her relatives; (*b*) £2 to the bride's father; (*c*) £2 for entertainment of the bride's club-mates; (*d*) £2 for ginger-beer for wedding guests; (*e*) £2 for mosquito-net for the bride; (*f*) £4 to her parents for keeping other suitors at bay; (*g*) £1 for kola nuts to be sent to relatives, even if abroad; and (*h*) £2 for fee in respect of application to marry. In the case of a widow, etc., items *a, b, c, d, e* and *g* are halved; item *f* omitted entirely; and item *h* reduced to £1 12s.

[4] It is not at all easy to decide what terms to employ for these different payments. It seems, however, that Muslims in the Gambia regard both the larger payment (of £20, etc.) and the smaller payment (of sixteen shillings) as constituting the Islamic dower (*ṣadāq* or *mahr*)—the latter representing the "minimum" dower of Mālikī law, on the payment of which they insist at the time of the contract, and the former the balance of the dower customarily payable, which may be deferred. In the pure Sharī'a there is, of course, no need for minimum dower to be paid where a larger sum is also provided; but the Mālikīs regard it as reprehensible for a bride to permit consummation of marriage before she has received at least minimum dower. This may be the origin here; while it is also possible that the £20 represents an Islamicised form of the normal African "bride-wealth". But however that may be the Islamic terms have been retained throughout this section of this Survey, out of deference for Muslim practice in the Gambia.

[5] Eight shillings is traditionally returned by the bride's father, "for their journey", to those who bring the money.

[6] This is the actual contract of marriage, but neither bride nor groom are present, in the Gambia.

[7] If not, he may divorce her immediately: but often he will pretend she is a virgin, even if she is not, to avoid a scandal and an inter-family quarrel.

[8] Or only three, in the case of a widow or divorced woman.

[9] It may be added that among the Mandingo in the Colony the dower payments are similar to those of the Wolof but commonly rather smaller (e.g. £16 and £6 12s.).

From the legal point of view the importance of these details is as follows. Should the bridegroom make these payments and then the girl, or her parents, refuse to complete the marriage, he is entitled to reclaim all that he has spent. Where, on the other hand, the marriage is duly consummated and then, at some later date, the wife claims divorce without adequate justification, only the sum of £20 (i.e., the major dower payment) and not the further sum for " expenses " or any other payments,[1] is returnable in the Colony.

Divorce

One of the chief ways in which the law of divorce as administered in the Qāḍīs' courts of the Gambia differs from the pure Sharī'a is that here, as elsewhere in West Africa, a wife can always obtain dissolution of marriage, however little justification she may have, provided she or her family will pay adequate financial compensation.[2] The court, of course, will make every effort to effect a reconciliation: but in the last resource, and if she proves adamant, it will order what amounts to a compulsory *khul'*,[3] but without recourse to the method of arbitration favoured in pure Mālikī law. This represents a triumph for West African customary law,[4] as the Qāḍī of Bathurst fully realises. Where, on the other hand, the husband proves impotent, beats his wife cruelly or repeatedly, continually abuses her parents,[5] or wantonly refuses to support her, the court will—in true Mālikī fashion—grant her a judicial divorce without any repayment; but if the alleged cruelty is deemed inadequate, then she can only get release by means of the compulsory *khul'* described above. Where a husband goes away and leaves his wife without maintenance, both Qāḍīs profess that they would take any movable property he might have left behind and provide maintenance from it or its price[6]: but they will never take immovables. Divorce will only be granted in such circumstances after attempts have been made to contact the husband, or after a delay of up to three months if his whereabouts are unknown.[7] Where the wife of an absent husband claims divorce not on the grounds of having been left without maintenance but of injury by desertion and loneliness, and of consequent fear of falling into adultery, this will be granted without any insistence on the minimum period of one year's desertion laid down in the Mālikī texts; but dower must in such cases be repaid. This represents a further concession to customary law. Finally, where the wife of a husband who is present complains that he does not support her adequately he will be ordered to pay a fixed sum: and if he fails to provide this his property will not be taken in execution but his wife will be granted a divorce without any repayments.[8]

When a husband decides to divorce his wife the triple formula is little known and seldom used, but the word *ḥarām* is known and regarded as having the same irrevocable effect. In practice many will become reconciled and continue their marriage—or at least remarry without an intervening marriage—even after such

---

[1] Except loans, or payments towards the funeral of any of her relatives. But in the Protectorate a husband may commonly claim the repayment of much more than this.

[2] In the Colony this is—normally, at least—limited to return of dower (see above).

[3] See Glossary.

[4] Except that " expenses ", too, are often repayable thereunder.

[5] Or even repeatedly accuses her herself of adultery, according to the Qāḍī of Bakau (Kombo St. Mary), but the Qāḍī of Bathurst disagrees. From the viewpoint of Sharī'a law, of course, this question turns on whether this constitutes sufficient *ḍarar*, or injury.

[6] In reality, however, this seems to be extremely rare.

[7] For the relevant provisions of the pure Mālikī law, see Appendix C.

[8] As also, it seems, if an absent husband fails to obey a letter ordering him to return to his wife, send for her to join him, or send her supplies. But where the wife presses for dissolution prematurely in such circumstances refund of dower may subsequently be demanded.

expressions have been used; but if such a case comes to court the orthodox rule will be applied that they must not remarry unless the wife has first consummated another marriage and then been widowed or again divorced, and a second marriage especially arranged for this purpose by agreement with the first husband will not count.[1] The triple formula uttered in anger counts as triple according to the Qāḍī of Bathurst,[2] but single according to the Qāḍī of Bakau.[3]

Divorce suspended on a condition (*ta'līq al-ṭalāq*) is apparently fairly common, but delegated divorce (*tafwīḍ al-ṭalāq*) is virtually unknown. *Li'ān* is very rare, but would, apparently, be treated according to the books; *īlā'* is unknown; while *ẓihār*, again, is most unlikely to occur (but, if it did, the wife could apparently claim divorce if the husband refused to perform the necessary expiation[4]). A husband's renunciation of Islam would terminate the marriage,[5] but not, apparently, a wife's conversion to Christianity. It seems that just after the war divorce was very common in the Colony, but that this has now returned to normal; and I was told that at present roughly one-third of all marriages end in this way, rather more often at the instance of the husband than of the wife. This is in contrast to the situation in the Protectorate, where at least half the marriages end in divorce, but almost invariably at the instance of the wife.

Married Life

A wife's maintenance is here, as throughout West Africa, reckoned by exclusive reference to her husband's resources (again by contrast with the pure Mālikī doctrine, which postulates the mean between the financial standing of the married parties). A husband is regarded as having the right to chastise his wife when she deserves it, but a beating which draws blood or causes excessive bruising would be regarded as *ḍarar* (injury) and a good cause for divorce; as would also the desertion of one wife in favour of another after an order by the court that he should distribute his time impartially.[6] No actions for adultery[7] are heard in the Colony, since the Qāḍīs' courts are not competent to apply either the criminal law of Islam or native law and custom, while adultery is not punishable in the Gambia in the magistrates' courts as an offence under the Criminal Code. The rules concerning the period of retreat (*'idda*) both on widowhood and divorce are strictly applied,[8] except that Mālikī dicta about the maximum period of gestation are disregarded: but in practice it seems that no women in the Gambia falsely protract their *'idda*, since women of child-bearing age (who alone can practice such deception) almost invariably remarry as soon as possible, while any claim of pregnancy which lasted unusually long would be submitted to medical opinion. Should a widowed or divorced wife claim to be an *ama* (i.e., of slave status) and that her *'idda* should be reckoned accordingly,[9] this would be accepted: but, where such woman acknowledged that she was so born but claimed that she was now of free status under the laws of the Gambia, the Qāḍī of Bathurst would accept the latter plea and rule that she must keep the *'idda* of a free wife, while the Qāḍī of Bakau would decree

[1] But only, of course, where such an arrangement can be proved: cp. *taḥlīl* in Glossary.

[2] In orthodox Mālikī fashion. So, too, the *ḥarām* formula.

[3] In accordance with the law now applicable in Egypt, the Sudan, and Jordan—but in Bakau probably on general considerations rather than any juristic authority.

[4] For all these technical terms, see Glossary.

[5] cp. p. 235 below.

[6] Both these points represent the orthodox Mālikī doctrine.

[7] But it is noteworthy in this connection that a wife's adultery would, in Bathurst, normally mean divorce, by contrast with the Protectorate (see below).

[8] i.e., a second marriage before the *'idda* had ended would be regarded as invalid, the issue illegitimate, and the parties as permanently debarred from intermarriage (if intercourse took place).

[9] i.e., at one and a half instead of three months, or two periods of legal purity.

the *'idda* appropriate to a slave.[1] The Qāḍī of Bathurst assured me that he had no first-hand knowledge of men keeping " slave "-concubines in the Gambia in the Nigerian fashion,[2] although the practice survived in the Senegal: nor had the device, common in the Protectorate,[3] of having " slave "-wives in excess of the legal four ever come to his notice.

Custody of Children

The right to the care and custody of children (*ḥaḍāna*) belongs to the divorced or widowed mother in the case of a girl until she is married, but in the case of a boy only until he is seven years of age (although the Qāḍī will often try to persuade the father to let him stay with his mother rather longer than this). This represents a " weaker " Mālikī view, preferred to the more authoritative doctrine on customary grounds.[4] The father is regarded, quite regularly, as responsible for his children's maintenance during this period; while the mother's remarriage outside the family[5] causes her right to such custody to lapse in the legally correct view of the Qāḍī of Bathurst, but not that of the Qāḍī of Bakau; and although the latter knows that the mother must not take the children to live far away from the father, without his permission, he maintains that such permission is almost always forthcoming in the Gambia (while a father, it seems, would not be allowed to claim his children under these ages, even if he were about to emigrate in order to settle elsewhere[6]). But the Children and Young Peoples' Ordinance, 1949, is also relevant in this connection, and may be said to override the Islamic principles regarding the custody and guardianship of minors in so far as its provisions provide otherwise in respect of those exposed to danger or neglect. As for guardianship of property, the usual practice is that one who has reached puberty and given evidence of competence (*rushd*) is allowed to manage his own affairs.[7]

Inheritance

Questions of succession normally go by the pure Sharī'a, including inheritance by patronage (*walā'*) in the case of the descendants of slaves. The only exceptions which I discovered concerned the allegedly posthumous or post-marital child, who would not be regarded as entitled to inherit from his father if born more than a year after his mother's widowhood or divorce unless his mother's claim were supported by medical opinion (see above), and the fact that the Qāḍī of Bathurst applies the doctrine of the " return " to the spouse relict as well as to other sharers.[8] The application of the doctrine of the return

[1] Although he would not for a moment, of course, question her personal liberty.
[2] See p. 215.
[3] See p. 237 below.
[4] See *ḥaḍāna* in Glossary.
[5] Actually, outside the prohibited degrees of marriage in respect of the child concerned.
[6] See below. This, again, represents a partial triumph of customary law.
[7] While the Public Trustee Ordinance, 1939, sect. 8, provides that where " any infant or lunatic is entitled to any gift, legacy or share of the assets of a deceased person, it shall be lawful for the person by whom such gift is made or the executor or administrator . . . or any trustee . . . to transfer the same . . . to the Public Trustee."
[8] He asserted that Khalīl contented himself in this context with observing that where there was no proper Public Treasury (*Bayt al-Māl*) then the "return" should be granted to " sharers ", without further specification. This would mean that all sharers would first take their shares and then, in default of agnates, the residue of the estate would be " returned " to them in proportion to their shares. In reality, however, Khalīl never meant this doctrine to be applied to the spouse relict at all. But it is important also to notice in this context that the right of the spouse relict to the " return "—or residue of the estate—might also be recognised in the Gambia on " equitable or moral grounds " under the Intestate Estates Ordinance, 1909, sect. 15(i)—while the claim of an illegitimate child to inherit from his natural father, for which there is no authority whatever in the Sharī'a, may be similarly recognised (sect. 15 (vii)).

at all, together with the recognition of the rights of cognates to inherit in default of either agnates or sharers, is also, of course, an exception to the original Mālikī doctrine; but one which may now be regarded as virtually regular where there is no *Bayt al-Māl*.[1] Strong moral pressure is, it seems, brought to bear upon heirs to induce them to pay the debts of the deceased even where these exceed his assets; but the Qāḍi of Bathurst denied that this would actually be enforced by the courts against a recalcitrant heir. Bequests must not exceed the bequeathable third nor be made in favour of heirs, in accordance with orthodox doctrine—except under a will made in the English form, when English law will prevail. And since, on the one hand, land and houses within the Colony are governed by the English[2] rather than customary law and, on the other, Islamic law is expressly applicable to the estates of deceased Muslims, any interest in such property would pass by the same rules of testate and intestate succession as would apply to the rest of his estate. But in Kombo Saint Mary—although now included in the Colony—there is little or no freehold, for the ownership of land largely follows the Protectorate pattern.[3]

One day I had the good fortune to hear the Qāḍī of Bathurst give judgment in an unusually interesting case. Judgment had been reserved, and he read it first in Arabic and then again in the vernacular, while an interpreter translated the latter into English. The defendant was alleged to have professed conversion to Islam; to have married a Muslim girl; to have consummated the marriage; and to have really remained a Christian throughout: but he, on his part, denied each of the first three allegations and claimed that he and the girl were only friends. The Qāḍī held that he had in fact professed Islam, on the solitary testimony of the Imām before whom he had repeated the Islamic creed (*shahāda*), supported only by circumstantial evidence[4]; that he had also married the girl, on the testimony of her guardian supported by two other witnesses; and that he had subsequently consummated the marriage, on the testimony of the girl, the evidence of gifts made, and the assertion of her father. Judgment was given, therefore, that he must make up the sum of some twelve pounds which had already passed hands (as part payment of dower, as the bride's father alleged, or as a loan, as the defendant maintained) to the normal figure for a virgin wife (i.e., twenty pounds), and that the marriage must stand dissolved—on the grounds[5] that his profession of Islam was enough to make the marriage valid, that consummation established the bride's right to full dower, and that his " apostasy " had of itself dissolved the marriage.

THE PROTECTORATE

In the Protectorate the dominant tribe is that of the Mandingo,[6] almost all of whom profess Islam, although some are lax in such matters as the number of wives they allow themselves. But the strictest Muslims in the territory are the Serahuli,[7] of whom there are comparatively few in the Gambia, almost all in the Upper River Division. For the rest, the Wolof[8] almost all profess Islam

[1] i.e., no Public Treasury administered by Muslims, or none adminstered according to the appropriate rules [cp., in this connection, the Intestate Estates Ordinance, 1909, sect. 17(1)].

[2] See Colony Lands Ordinance, 1945.

[3] See Protectorate Lands Ordinance, 1945.

[4] Although he had presumably " acknowledged " this to the girl and her family ?

[5] Presumably; but this point was not brought out in the judgment.

[6] These come from the Upper Niger, and formed a great empire in the 13th and 14th centuries A.D. Those of the Gambia represent, therefore, only a western offshoot of a larger group of tribes. In the Gold Coast, Nigeria, etc., they are termed " Wangara " by the Hausa and others. They are also, and perhaps more correctly, named " Mandinka ".

[7] These stretch eastward into French territory.

[8] These stretch north into French territory, up to St. Louis and beyond.

and are reasonably strict in matters of religion; the Fula[1] fall into various sub-tribes, some of which are predominantly Muslim and some pagan, with the pagan elements slightly more numerous, it seems, in the Gambia; while the Jola[2] were until recently almost entirely pagan—but among them, too, Islam is now spreading fast, so that the young people usually profess to be Muslims, while their elders remain frankly pagan. But all this is complicated by two other factors: firstly, that the tribes do not occupy distinct and separate tribal territories but are much intermingled, and often villages populated by two different tribes will alternate with each other; secondly, that memories of the "Marabout-Soninki War"[3] in the nineteenth century still survive almost everywhere, in the Central and Western Divisions, in mutual animosity between villages which were on different sides, while the same distinction partially accounts for the marked variation in the fervour of local adherence to the precepts and practices of Islam from locality to locality. Here and there one chances upon a village where the elders know and apply the Sharī'a in comparative purity; and this can almost always be traced to the influence and teaching of some *marabūṭ*[3] who lived and taught there.

The centres I visited were Basse, where the Chief is a Mandingo and the people a mixture of Mandingo, Serahuli and Fula, all except the last-named being solidly Muslim, in name at least; Gambisara, a *marabut* village which is exclusively Serahuli and strongly Muslim; Bansang, where the Chief and most of the people are Fula, but interspersed with Mandingo, Serahuli and Wolof, all except certain sections of the Fula being Muslim; Georgetown, where the majority are Mandingo and Fula, but there are a few Serahuli and Wolof, all predominantly Muslim; Kuntaur, where the Chief is a Wolof and his people a mixture in which the Wolof—and Islam—predominate; N'Jau, where the people are both Wolof and Fula, and almost all Muslims; Kaiaf, where the Mandingo preponderate; Batteling, where the Mandingo majority is leavened by both Jola and Fula, including, of course, many pagan elements; Bwiam, where the Jola predominate; Brikama, where the Mandingo are in the majority but interspersed with Jola and Fula elements; and Gunjur, Faraba, and Sukuta, in each of which the Mandingo preponderate. Almost all the Muslims of the Protectorate, again, owe some sort of allegiance to either the Qādirīya or Tijānīya Ṣūfī brotherhoods: the latter completely holds the field in Gambisara and predominates in such places as Basse, Bansang, Georgetown, Kuntaur, N'Jau and Sukuta, while the former is in the ascendancy in such localities as Bwiam, Brikama and Gunjur.

Attitude to Islam and its Precepts

Yet the distinction between Muslims and non-Muslims outlined above is much more clear-cut than the facts warrant, for the one often shades into the other in such a way that no sharply drawn division is possible.[4] Even professed "pagans" will often attend a Muslim funeral, keep Muslim feasts, and say

---

[1] Termed Fulani in Nigeria and the Gold Coast, they are scattered throughout the whole of West Africa: some sections are settled, and others still nomadic.

[2] These are the northern fringe of a large tribe of southern origin which stretches from Portuguese Guinea through the French Cameroons up the southern bank of the Gambia River.

[3] See *A History of the Gambia,* by J. M. Gray, pp. 328-330, 388-398, 416-430, 444-455, etc. *Marabūṭ* is a common colloquialism for the correct Arabic form *murābiṭ,* which may be loosely translated "holy man". The division between *marabuts* and *soninkis* in the Gambia represented a distinction between those who wished to be strict Muslims and those who did not.

[4] For Islam in the Gambia today may not inaptly be compared with the Roman Church in Western Europe in the Middle Ages, in the sense that many pagan practices are being brought within the fold of respectability by means of toning down the more uninhibited parts and interspersing the rest with suitable prayers.

Muslim prayers; while professed Muslims will not only be exceedingly lax about the precepts and practice of their religion but will retain many pagan beliefs and practices—and this, in all probability, more in the less accessible villages which I did not visit than in the more strongly Muslim centres on my schedule. Charms and amulets abound, some Islamic[1] and some animistic, and seem to be worn almost indiscriminately; while the relatives of one who is seriously ill will frequently seek the help of some local Muslim renowned for holiness and occult powers on the one hand and a pagan "witch-doctor" on the other, with little or no sense of incongruity. Learning in the Islamic sciences varies greatly from locality to locality. In some parts, where a *marabūṭ* has had a school, quite a number can read Arabic and several of the usual Mālikī law books are known and consulted; while in others almost complete illiteracy prevails. "Higher" studies are normally pursued in French territory, where several centres are locally renowned.

A good example of laxness with regard to the precepts of Islam is provided by the matter of the number of wives which a rich man, and more particularly a chief, will permit himself. Some, particularly in the Upper River Division, are quite uninhibited in this matter, and I heard of one recent chief[2] who had sixty; while fifteen would be regarded in some localities as almost moderate. Others, less indifferent to Islamic law, content themselves with four "free" wives, whom alone they profess to regard as legal wives in the full meaning of the term, but add one or more "concubines" or, more accurately, "slave"-wives. These women are not necessarily drawn from the number of those who would have been their husbands' slaves but for the abolition of slavery, or, e.g., those of a friend who has "given" them for the purpose (like the concubines who survive in Nigeria today), but consist of any women of "slave"-status[3] whose fathers will give them in marriage for a suitable dower and in a regular contract of marriage. As such, of course, they should count towards the legal maximum of four, quite apart from the prohibition of a man marrying a slave-wife at all in such circumstances, and they are in fact treated exactly as other wives: yet the device serves to quieten pricks of conscience on the part of those whose knowledge of and adherence to Islamic law is just sufficient to make them hesitate unequivocally to flout the rules limiting polygamy. But the majority keep to the legal maximum in fact as well as in theory, whether on economic or religious grounds.

It will be clear from the above that the distinction between "slaves" and freemen still persists in the minds of Muslim jurists in the Gambia, fundamental as it is to large parts of the Sharī'a, in spite of its total abolition under the law of the Protectorate. It is interesting to observe, moreover, how the social status of slavery is clearly recognised in some villages, while in others scarcely a trace seems to remain.[4] In the former each "slave" knows his "master", and vice versa: but the services which the former pay to the latter, while clearly defined, are normally restricted to the ceremonial. I heard[5] details, moreover, of a ceremony of manumission as recent as in 1950. This concerned a "slave" who,

[1] Consisting of verses of the Qur'ān, etc., including "mumbo jumbo" words written in Arabic script, and other forms of "white" magic.

[2] In this case in the Macarthy Island Division.

[3] i.e., socially. The status has, of course, been utterly abolished in so far as British law is concerned. See the Affirmation of the Abolition of Slavery Ordinance, 1930, sect. 2. Previous legislation included the Slave Trade Abolition Ordinances of 1894 and 1906, the former declaring all slaves to be free on the death of their masters and the latter providing for the freedom of all persons born thereafter.

[4] While in some localities the public imputation of slave ancestry is regarded as criminal slander under customary law.

[5] My informant was Mr. D. P. Gamble, an anthropologist working in the Gambia, to whom I am also indebted for other information incorporated in this section. He witnessed this ceremony himself.

in the course of his study of the Qur'ān and the Sharī'a, became so concerned that he had not fulfilled his duties to his " master " that he broached the matter to his teacher, who was astonished to discover the status of his pupil and nearly turned him out of his school—on the grounds that it was unusual in the Gambia for a " slave " to receive more than elementary instruction in such subjects. On reflexion, however, he suggested that his pupil should seek manumission: and this he did, not only on his own account but also on behalf of his mother and two brothers. A not inconsiderable sum, apparently, was first tendered and accepted; but this was not mentioned at the actual ceremony outside the mosque, when the heads of the ex-slaves were shaved, they were given new names, and pious speeches were made by all concerned.

As for the practice of circumcision, this again varies from tribe to tribe. Among boys it is almost universal, usually between the ages of seven and ten; while female clitoridectomy is practised by the Mandingo and Jola, but not by the Wolof and Fula. This illustrates once more the way in which Islamic practice and pagan custom merge into one another in the Gambia. Muslims, again, seem commonly still to pay their religious alms (*zakāt*) in the Protectorate, but on a voluntary basis and from subsistence, but not cash, crops. It is paid by persons of slave origin to their " patron ", as the head of the family which originally owned them is now considered; by younger men to the head of their compound; and by the latter to the *almami*,[1] to elderly men of learning, or sometimes to elderly female relatives.

Courts

As regards courts, the system in the Protectorate is quite simple. In each District there is a Tribunal in which the Chief himself sits as President assisted by a number of members, who usually represent the different tribes settled in his District. Apart from the right of the High Court to intervene in criminal cases which originate in these Native Tribunals, there is no system of appeals, but provision exists in the Native Tribunals Ordinance, as we have seen, for the appropriate Commissioner to exercise powers of revision in any type of case, either of his own motion or " on the application of any person concerned "; and in the latter case this operates, in practice, much as an appeal, but by grace rather than right. In such circumstances the Commissioner will normally hear both parties and some or even all of the witnesses, for the extent to which he will re-hear the whole case *de novo* depends both on the extent to which the original hearing is challenged and on his own judgment as to how much may be taken as proved. The Senior Commissioner also now has the same powers of revision, with regard to the Protectorate as a whole, as each Commissioner in his own Division[2]; but he has no power further to revise a case in which a Commissioner has already exercised his powers of revision. There is no formal court below the level of the Chief's Tribunal; but village cases are frequently taken to the headman sitting with his " elders ", and in most cases their decision, although it has no formal coercive power, will no doubt be accepted by the parties. But this varies, of course, from village to village: in some, particularly if they are very close to the Chief's village, litigation will regularly go direct to his Tribunal; while in others, where the sense of village solidarity is strong, almost everything will be settled locally.[3]

---

[1] i.e., Imām.

[2] See the Protectorate (Amendment) Ordinance, 1944, sect. 4—supplying a new sect. 9A to the principal Ordinance.

[3] This is particularly true of certain *marabūṭ* villages; e.g., in the Serahuli village of Gambisara I was told that appeal from the headman and elders to the Chief's Tribunal was unknown.

Procedure

In general, these Tribunals follow a common-sense system of evidence and procedure. Testimony is normally given without the witness being put on oath; but where a particular and important point is in doubt, he is made to swear the "perishable" oath.[1] Judgment may, moreover, be based on the testimony of a single witness if his testimony appears worthy of credence, or on circumstantial evidence; while non-Muslim witnesses are regularly accepted, and cross-examination of an informal character is practised both by the court and by the other party to the case.

Marriage

In most parts of the Protectorate a girl is promised in marriage at any time from birth upwards,[2] and from then on periodical presents[3] will be given both to her and to her parents. In many parts, again, the actual contract of marriage will be concluded when she reaches the age of about ten years[4] or even earlier[5]: but elsewhere it is uncommon for this to take place until she reaches puberty,[6] and in some places I was told that the latter had become customary because so many disputes arose regarding marriages contracted prematurely. Everywhere, however, it is most uncommon for the bride to be sent to her husband's house before she reaches puberty, except, it seems, among some of the Fula. Where the girl has reached puberty at the time of the contract she may be sent to her husband immediately: but this will normally depend on whether he has paid her dower and the other customary payments in full, or part payment in advance and the remainder by instalments has been mutually agreed; while in some parts, it seems, intercourse is permitted after the contract has been concluded, but the girl must continue to live in her father's house until the payments are complete.[7] If a girl who had been promised or even contracted in marriage subsequently refused to complete or consummate the union she was previously forced to do so, and strong pressure from both families would still, no doubt, normally be brought to bear upon her: but if she were to remain adamant[8] and appeal to the Chief's Tribunal or the Commissioner, they would both today support her right to refuse.[9] If the contract had already been concluded in such cases the two main payments of dower and "expenses" must everywhere be refunded,[10] and in some localities any presents in cash,[11] or even all presents whatsoever, must also be returned if demanded[12]—although many husbands would not insist on this out of regard for public opinion. Normally, moreover, the marriage would be regarded as dissolved in such cases by the agreement of the families concerned and by the act of repayment: but in some cases the Tribunal will decree that repayment must take place and then declare the marriage dissolved. Where, moreover, the girl has only been promised in marriage and no contract has been concluded

[1] See p. 230 above.

[2] e.g., at Basse, Bansang, Gambisara, Kuntaur, N'Jau, Kaiaf, Batteling, Bwiam, Brikama, Sukuta, etc.—but not (apparently) in Georgetown, for instance.

[3] But no formal payments.

[4] e.g., at Basse, Bansang, Kuntaur.

[5] e.g., at Gambisara and Bwiam.

[6] e.g., at Georgetown, N'Jau, Kaiaf, Batteling, Brikama, Gunjur and (usually) Sukuta.

[7] e.g., at Georgetown.

[8] This, however, has "never happened" in, e.g., Gambisara.

[9] This, in the case of many Chiefs' Tribunals, is largely, no doubt, because she might otherwise appeal to the Commissioner.

[10] But these only, apparently, in, e.g., Bansang.

[11] e.g., in Basse, Bwiam, Brikama, for instance.

[12] e.g., in Sukuta, for instance. Marriage by native custom often consists of what may be described as a succession of little ceremonies. But among Muslims in the Gambia the final ceremony usually takes place in a mosque on a Friday, and includes the *ījāb* and *qabūl*. See Glossary.

only "presents," etc. will have changed hands: and whether these are returned will depend both on custom and demand.[1] This is particularly applicable, of course, in localities where the contract is normally postponed until puberty; and in these parts marriage by compulsion (*jabr*) in the technical sense is now rare.

In most parts, at least, a true Islamic contract of marriage seems to be customary, with a declaration (*ījāb*) and acceptance (*qabūl*) much as described above.[2] The amount payable for dower and "expenses", etc., differs from place to place: but these regularly constitute the two main payments, although certain other gifts and services are also customary; while it is noteworthy that the sum due for "expenses" normally includes an item of some shillings due to be given to the bride herself at the time of the contract.[3] It may be added that the actual disposal of the dower also differs from place to place: always handed in the first place to the father or guardian, it is sometimes distributed among the family, and sometimes ultimately handed over, in substance or kind, to the bride herself.

Again, questions of "marriage equality" (*kafā'a*) vary according to locality and, still more, from tribe to tribe. It is regarded as especially important among the Wolof, where goldsmiths, leather workers, minstrels and "slaves" (of whom there are a high proportion) are regarded as castes into which a girl must never marry—and, indeed, a man[4] would seldom marry a wife from any of these castes, except for a "slave"-wife. Throughout the country, moreover, it would be entirely contrary to custom for a girl to get herself married to anyone without her guardian's consent: but, were such a thing to happen, the marriage would be regarded as invalid in most districts[5] and would normally be dissolved at the demand of the guardian. Where, however, a guardian refuses to allow his ward to marry a suitable suitor she may appeal to the Chief's Tribunal, which will normally order her guardian to comply and, in default, tell the Imām to act in his place. This procedure is, in fact, of fairly common occurrence.

Divorce

Divorce, as has been noted, is common in the Protectorate, and almost always occurs by the action or at the demand of the wife. In most cases a discontented wife will run away from her husband, either to her old home or with another man: but sometimes she or her father will go to the court and demand dissolution of marriage. When she absconds to her father the deserted husband will normally follow her and demand her return; and the father will usually advise her to comply. If, however, she remains obdurate, a family palaver will ensue, and protracted attempts to reconcile the parties will normally be made; while in the last resort the wife was formerly compelled to return to her husband unless her family was prepared to pay up all the marriage payments[6] which the husband had incurred. The chief differences which obtain from locality to locality and tribe to tribe concern three points: the extent to which such marriage expenses must be refunded by the family of a recalcitrant wife; the circumstances in which a wife is regarded as justified in demanding dissolution of marriage; and the degree, if any, to which such circumstances limit or exclude the refund normally required.

[1] See p. 232.

[2] See p. 231.

[3] See p. 231 note (4) above.

[4] Although the Islamic rules of *kafā'a* do not apply in his case.

[5] Only at Kuntaur, N'Jau and Sukuta did I find hesitation on this point; and at Sukuta alone did the Chief say that he would not dissolve such a marriage even if the guardian tried to insist.

[6] And any loans, or payments towards funeral expenses of the wife's family. All these must still be refunded in most cases (see below), but the alternative of compulsion no longer subsists, officially at least.

A husband's impotence, it seems, is universally regarded as justifying a wife in demanding dissolution of marriage, and no repayment whatever is normally due in such cases. Almost everywhere, moreover, the same applies with regard to a husband who contracts, or proves to be afflicted with, some serious disease such as leprosy or insanity. In the majority of centres which I visited, again, the Chief's Tribunal would decree[1] dissolution of marriage without any financial return if the husband had been guilty of giving his wife a severe flogging[2] (although this would normally have to be extremely severe or repeated on more than one occasion), of refusal[3] to provide her with food and clothing, of continual abuse of her parents,[4] or of persistent refusal to cohabit[5]—although in many localities refund of marriage payments would normally be exacted from a wife who ran away from her husband even for one of these reasons unless she or her father took the matter to the Tribunal, while in some localities no such claim has, it seems, ever been heard in court.[6] Still more controversial is the case of the wife who demands dissolution of marriage on the grounds that her husband has gone away and left her either without support or in danger of falling into adultery on account of physical desertion. Wives left without maintenance are normally, it seems, supported by their families while letters or messages are sent to their husbands: it is only if they have no one at all to support them, or if their husbands either cannot be traced or stay away an unconscionable time, that a matter of this kind is likely to be brought to court. And in such circumstances the attitude adopted by the Tribunals differs widely from place to place. Where the husband has left personal property in the hands of, e.g., his brother, some Tribunals will order the latter to support the wife or even, allegedly, take the husband's movable property and sell it to provide her maintenance.[7] Where, again, she has no means of support whatever the marriage would in most places be dissolved at once, or after about a month's delay: but usually, as we have seen, the woman will be supported by her family while efforts are made to contact her absent husband and get him to return, to send for her or to provide maintenance; and the marriage will not be dissolved until a suitable time has elapsed, ranging from one to six months (according both to how far he is away and how long the wife has been deserted before she brought her case to court) in some localities, and up to a maximum of three years, in cases which are not urgent, elsewhere. Much the same, too, applies to cases where the husband's whereabouts are unknown, provided the circumstances are not pressing. And in general it seems that where a wife waits for the whole period which the Tribunal feels suitable, and the husband is felt to be gravely at fault,[8] she will normally get dissolution of marriage without repayment; while where she insists on getting her freedom prematurely, or the husband proved to have been delayed through no fault of his own, the latter may, on his return, demand a refund

[1] Allegedly.

[2] But in, e.g., Gunjur the court members insisted that a woman who claimed dissolution of marriage because she had been beaten, however severely or repeatedly, must always refund the husband's marriage payments; and this would certainly obtain elsewhere whenever the treatment complained of was not considered sufficiently cruel—or proven—to justify her claim; while in Sukuta a distinction is made in doubtful or borderline cases and refund of dower, but not of expenses, is decreed in such circumstances (allegedly).

[3] Or inability.

[4] But not allegations of the wife's own adultery; for which accusation, if unfounded, he can, however, be fined.

[5] Although this seems virtually unknown in the Gambia.

[6] e.g., Batteling, Bwiam, etc.

[7] e.g., at Basse, N'Jau, Kaiaf and elsewhere. But at, e.g., Gunjur the brother would only be requested, not commanded, to support her; while nowhere would immovable property be sold for this purpose (or, for that matter, for any other purpose—see below).

[8] e.g., if he fails to return when summoned (at Kuntaur, for instance).

of his marriage payments. Somewhat the same is also true of a demand for dissolution of marriage on the part of a wife who does not lack maintenance but who complains of desertion, loneliness and fear of adultery. Here, too, a period adequate for correspondence with the absent husband, if his whereabouts are known,[1] is usually allowed; little, if any, notice is taken of the normal Mālikī rule that a divorce may only be granted after from one to three years' desertion[2]; and a dissolution is usually granted without delay if the wife is sufficiently insistent, although some Tribunals profess to be less forthcoming in this matter: but in the vast majority of such cases the absent husband may reclaim his dower and expenses, etc., on his return.[3]

Where, again, a woman demands dissolution of marriage with no such justification whatever, where the justification she pleads is not thought adequate, or where—as is more usually the case—she simply runs away from her husband and refuses to return, the only problem that now arises is what refund she must make to her aggrieved husband—for the old rule of forcible return, never universal, is now a dead letter, officially at least. In some localities all marriage disbursements are reclaimable in such circumstances, even down to such items as kola nuts[4]; in others the dower, "expenses" and cash presents, but not perishable items, must be repaid[5]; in others only the dower may be insisted on[6]; while in a few places even this is subject to deductions according to the number of children she has borne and the number of years the couple has been married.[7] It may be added that where the dissolution is arranged between the families concerned no special form of words is used, and suitable repayments, according to custom, are normally made, largely regardless of the merits of the case: but where a dispute of this nature is taken to the Chief's Tribunal or to a village headman the marriage will, where necessary, be declared dissolved by him, and refund of such disbursements will in some cases be excluded.[8]

Finally, where a wife becomes involved with another man three different lines of action are open to the husband. He may, of course, divorce her and cut his losses; but this would be extremely rare in the Protectorate. Far more commonly he will do all he can to get her back, and will probably bring an action for seduction against her lover. If, in such circumstances, the husband can "prove" misconduct by his own testimony, supported by at least one other witness, to his wife having been alone in a house with the alleged adulterer, or by the testimony of a witness that he found the husband fighting a man apparently caught in the act of seduction, or by the production of articles of clothing seized from the guilty pair, the paramour is liable to a fine ranging up to £10 (the

[1] e.g., one to three months (at Basse and elsewhere).

[2] Although some Tribunals allegedly try to insist on some such periods (e.g., Kaiaf, one year; Gunjur, three years; etc.). *Sed quaere.*

[3] And where the wife, her family, or some other man (secretly, or in some localities even openly) are prepared for such refund, the wife can usually get dissolution of marriage whenever and however she likes (see above and below). But in a few localities the Tribunal professes to resist this (e.g., in Gunjur).

[4] e.g., at Gambisara, where this was specifically mentioned; while elsewhere it was stated that the husband might claim refund of all disbursements which he could prove (Georgetown); or of "everything" (Kaiaf and Sukuta, for instance).

[5] e.g., at Basse, and elsewhere. At, e.g., Bwiam the husband may claim refund of the bull normally paid as bride-wealth, of his expenses, but not of the sum of sixteen shillings paid to the bride at the ceremony, since this has become the wife's absolute property on consummation of marriage: and much the same is true at, e.g., Brikama and Gunjur, where bride-wealth and a sum of £2 are reclaimable, but not the mat and kola customarily supplied, nor the sum of four shillings given to the bride.

[6] e.g., Kuntaur, if the case is brought to court; and at Kaiaf, provided the parties have been married at least one year, etc.

[7] e.g., at Kuntaur. Also Kaiaf, in some circumstances, where the deduction is normally £2 for each son and £1 for each daughter (allegedly).

[8] As specified above.

maximum within the competence of Native Tribunals) or, in default, to imprisonment. This fine, the size of which apparently varies according to circumstances (e.g. it is increased if the paramour sedulously sought to seduce the wife or persisted therein after warning, and decreased if the wife is regarded as largely to blame; while it may also, in some places, be reduced on the plea of the offender's previous good character,[1] etc.), is normally divided between the Tribunal and the husband[2]: in some localities the division is equal,[3] in others the Tribunal takes the greater part,[4] in others the husband gets most,[5] while in yet others the share of the husband will, it seems, depend on whether he was guilty of what may be termed "contributory negligence"![6] In most localities the woman escapes without punishment, from the Tribunal at least; but in a few she too is fined,[7] usually at half the rate of her lover: and this fine is not infrequently paid by the husband himself, if he succeeds in getting her back.[8] Where, however, the woman absolutely refuses to return to her husband he has the further alternative of demanding a repayment of all his marriage disbursements, etc., from her parents.[9] If these are forthcoming the husband or the Tribunal will normally dissolve the marriage forthwith, although some Tribunals[10] allegedly try to insist on the wife waiting for a certain time before dissolution is granted. Once the marriage is dissolved there is in most places no objection to the woman marrying her paramour, provided her father agrees: but in some localities this is forbidden,[11] and a marriage in defiance of this rule (except after elopement to some distant part) would be dissolved and the parties thereto punished. In a strict *marabūṭ* village such as Gambisara, moreover, such cases of seduction are apparently unknown.

Although the vast majority of divorces in the Protectorate are at the instance of the wife, husbands do at times divorce their wives even here. Again, however, there are marked differences from place to place, and here custom, there Islamic law, but more often a mixture, seems to prevail. The triple formula is little known and seldom used; but expressions based on the word "*ḥarām*" are somewhat more common and are regarded as having the same implications. In some parts the use of such an expression—even in a fit of anger—means that reconciliation is impossible, and that the parties cannot remarry unless the wife has first gone through an intervening marriage[12]: but even in these stricter districts such matters seldom get to court, and in any case the Tribunal cannot forcibly separate the parties nor do more than declare a child subsequently born to be illegitimate—which, again, would only affect his rights of inheritance if they too were the subject of litigation (which is unusual). In progressively less strict localities the use of such words is regarded as necessitating a new contract and dower, but no intervening marriage[13]; as inoperative, if said in sudden anger[14]; or even as no barrier whatever to reconciliation.[15] Again, where (as is usual) some

---

[1] e.g., at Brikama.
[2] i.e., is treated as partly a fine and partly damages.
[3] e.g. at Basse.
[4] e.g., at Kuntaur.
[5] e.g., at Georgetown and Kaiaf.
[6] e.g., at N'Jau.
[7] e.g., at Gunjur and Sukuta.
[8] e.g., at Gunjur.
[9] Who will usually recover such from the paramour in such circumstances, if he is allowed to marry the woman.
[10] e.g., at Sukuta.
[11] e.g., at Basse, Bwiam and Sukuta.
[12] e.g., allegedly at Basse, Gambisara (where parties who disregard the law would be asked to leave the village), Kuntaur, N'Jau, Sukuta, etc. But one wonders whether the law is really applied as strictly as all that.
[13] e.g., at Batteling and Gunjur (allegedly).
[14] e.g., at Georgetown.
[15] e.g., at Kaiaf, Bwiam, Brikama.

lesser expression is used and the wife is just sent home (with or without a letter to her father, or a gift of kola nuts), reconciliation is regarded in most places[1] as permissible, even after six months' or a year's separation, without any new contract or dower: all that is necessary is some gift of kolas or other form of "compensation" to persuade the wife to return. Where divorce is at the instance of the husband, of course, he has no right to claim any refund: instead, any unpaid balance of marriage commitments must still, in theory at least, be paid. It may be added that in the Gambia husbands occasionally, it seems, address their wives in such phrases as "I take my mother's cloth and put it on you": but here, again, reconciliation is normally encouraged, apparently without any question of the expiation properly required under the Sharīʿa in cases of "*ẓihār*".[2]

Remarriage

The *ʿidda* period during which a widowed or divorced woman may not remarry is, it seems, well known[3] and usually observed throughout the territory. In the case of the *ʿidda* of widowhood this seems almost invariable: but no such emphatic terms can be used regarding the *ʿidda* of divorce, since divorced women do sometimes, in certain localities[4] at any rate, remarry almost at once. In theory at least a child so born would be regarded as illegitimate and not entitled to inherit; but no such case ordinarily comes to court and no action, beyond pressure of public opinion, would normally be taken against an offending couple.[5] Divorced or widowed women are, indeed, in great demand in the Gambia, and suitors regularly court them beyond the limits prescribed by the Sharīʿa during their *ʿidda* periods: but since most marriages are celebrated in the mosques the actual conclusion of a new contract of marriage is, it seems, usually postponed until immediately after the *ʿidda* has terminated.

Mixed Marriages

"Mixed" marriages (i.e. marriages between a Muslim and a non-Muslim) are said to be completely unknown in some localities. In others, however, Muslim men do marry non-Muslim women; and while in some districts these will almost invariably embrace Islam, in others some at least remain pagans. It is only in the last case, of course, that any problem arises, and that chiefly in regard to inheritance; for in the stricter localities the marriage would, of course, be regarded as invalid and any children as precluded from inheriting from their father, while in the laxer areas this would not obtain.[6] It is much rarer for a Muslim girl to be given in marriage to a non-Muslim[7]: but where this happens customary, not Islamic, rules of inheritance would almost invariably be applied.

Paternity

When we turn to the matter of children, we find that problems of legitimacy, etc., seldom come before the Tribunals. If a woman bears a child to her paramour

---

[1] e.g., at Kaiaf, Batteling, Bwiam, Brikama, Gunjur, and even Sukuta and elsewhere: but in a few places like Gambisara the rules regarding *ʿidda*, revocation of divorce, new contract of marriage, etc., are known and observed.

[2] See Glossary.

[3] Although in Bwiam the court members seemed to think that the *ʿidda* on widowhood lasted for four months only, instead of four months and ten days, and the distinction between the reconciliation of divorced couples during, and after, the *ʿidda* is largely ignored (see above).

[4] This was admitted in, e.g., Gunjur, Sukuta and Bwiam.

[5] Except, perhaps, in a village like Gambisara, where the headman and elders assert that they would declare the marriage dissolved.

[6] e.g., at Brikama such children are apparently entitled to inherit if themselves Muslims, and at Bwiam without any such restriction.

[7] Only at Bwiam did the court elders admit that this happened; mostly, they said, in the case of relatives. But it must really be less rare than this.

before her marriage is dissolved this child should belong to her husband, if he claims him: but if the woman has meanwhile been divorced and has married her lover this might be difficult to enforce. Where a man has more than four wives the children of supernumerary wives are normally regarded as legitimate and treated on the same footing as those of the first four: and while most Tribunals[1] maintain that they would be excluded from rights of inheritance from their father if challenged, no such cases seem in practice to come before them.[2] The usual Mālikī rules about the legal paternity of posthumous or post-marital children are, it seems, everywhere ignored. Instead, a child born within nine (or possibly ten) months of a woman's widowhood will be allowed to inherit from her deceased husband, but not one born after a longer period; in the case of divorce much the same would apply, except that here the prime factor would normally be whether the husband claimed the child and the woman confirmed that he was the father: and in general it may be said that unless a woman were known to be pregnant during her *'idda* the child would normally never be regarded as belonging to her former husband.

Custody of Children

After widowhood or divorce, the care and custody (*ḥaḍāna*) of the children of the marriage is regarded as belonging to the mother, throughout most of the Protectorate, until a boy reaches seven and a girl her marriageable age. This corresponds to what we have already seen to be the case in the Colony, except that in the Protectorate a mother is never regarded as forfeiting that right by, e.g., returning to her father's house in a distant part of the country[3] or even by remarrying outside the family, while the father is never allowed to claim his infant children even if he intends to emigrate and settle permanently in some distant place. In some parts of the Gambia, however, the above rules give way to the custom of a mother's right being limited, in the case of both sons and daughters, to the period of suckling.[4] During this period of *ḥaḍāna* the father is, of course, properly responsible for his children's maintenance; and this is followed and enforced at least in the more strongly Muslim areas. A child is regarded as attaining financial majority,[5] in most localities,[6] when he not only reaches puberty but has shown himself as capable (*rashīd*), and his capacity is said to be tested by the Tribunal[7] in any case of dispute; while neither men nor women, whatever their age, normally marry in the Gambia without their father's or elder brother's consent.[8]

Inheritance

When we turn to the question of succession, it must first be remembered that farms and dwelling compounds are not normally regarded in the Protectorate as individual, but village or family, property. As such they can neither be sold

[1] But not at Bwiam. At Brikama the Chief admitted to having ten free wives and regarding all his children as on the same level; but he alleged that those of supernumerary wives would be disinherited if challenged (which would, it seems, never happen).

[2] And, even if they did, would the Tribunals really prove so doctrinaire, by Gambia standards ?

[3] Not even in so strict a village as Gambisara. But for her to leave the territory altogether is regarded as on a different footing, and usually not allowed.

[4] e.g., at Bwiam.

[5] i.e., the right to take over the management of his own property, make contracts, etc.

[6] In Bansang I was told that this was usually at about sixteen, when the Fula regard a boy as able to look after cattle unaided.

[7] In most districts.

[8] In the case of a woman such a marriage would be invalid, and would usually be dissolved (see above): but in the case of a boy who had reached puberty it would be contrary to custom, but not dissolved by court.

nor pledged (except, e.g. a house[1] which does not form part of a family compound); but a farm may be lent for a year or two's farming or "leased" for a token payment rather than a fixed rent. As a consequence, real property is virtually never divided up when a man dies, but passes intact to the next senior member of the family, who holds as trustee for the family as a whole, each member of which continues to farm the land and inhabit the compound. A deceased's wives, again, were formerly taken over by his brother, but this is dependent today on their consent. Where they are so taken over (as still happens in the vast majority of cases) a new contract must, apparently, be concluded, but for greatly reduced dower; while if they insist on marrying outside the family their new dower goes to their own family and not to the deceased's brother.

It is only in regard, then, to cattle, money, clothes and sometimes trees that problems of inheritance arise. Even so, moreover, very few disputes of this nature ever get to court. In the majority of cases, it seems, the family comes to some mutual agreement, either maintaining the estate as a whole as family property under the care of the senior or ablest member as trustee for the rest,[2] or dividing it as seems suitable[3] (as usually, one presumes, happens in the case of clothing, etc.). Sometimes, however, among comparatively strict Muslims, the family prefers to consult some learned man as to the Islamic rules of inheritance and apply these, in whole or in part, with regard to some or all of the movable property. On the rare occasions when a dispute of this sort reaches the Tribunals the general rule is for Islamic law, as interpreted by the local *almami* or other man of learning, to be applied in the more Muslim localities; and this would also be the case where the headman of a strictly Muslim village such as Gambisara was concerned. Elsewhere, however, customary law would prevail even in court, as was admitted in, e.g. Bwiam,[4] where females are excluded from inheritance. A reasonable knowledge of the Islamic rules of inheritance was shown by at least one of the members of most of the Tribunals which I visited, but this naturally varied from place to place.[5] In the case of an ex-slave who dies without natural heirs, the descendants of his owner still inherit everywhere by right of patronage (*walā'*); while in the absence of any proper *Bayt al-Māl* even the strict Mālikī law, as we have seen, now allows both the doctrine of the "return" to sharers and rights of inheritance to cognates, in default of agnates in the first case and of either agnates or sharers in the second.

Testamentary bequests of any sort are unknown in some localities,[6] particularly in the country districts, while in other centres both oral and written "testaments" are known and enforced. In some places, again, these must conform to the proper Islamic rules and neither exceed the "bequeathable third" nor favour an heir[7]; in others these rules are not so strictly applied, but some limitations—either by custom or through the influence of the Sharī'a—are put upon

[1] This may be sold or pledged. In the latter case it is not handed over; but if the debt is not repaid by the agreed date the house may be taken by the creditor, provided he gives compensation for any excess value, or alternatively it may be sold.

[2] This would apply where all the members of a family compound work on a communal basis, which is still common.

[3] Thus among the Fula, for instance, a man who has two or more wives normally divides his cows among them to be milked, etc., and when he dies each wife's herd passes to her children.

[4] Or in Bansang in the case of Fula, if some of the family are either pagans or lax Muslims, when Fula custom would be applied; or in Brikama, it seems, but here it was difficult to decide whether the Chief and court members were primarily unorthodox or ill-informed.

[5] e.g., in Basse the Chief and members were somewhat vague on such points, as also in Batteling, Brikama, Gunjur and Faraba; while in Gambisara, Sukuta and N'Jau, for instance, they were very well informed.

[6] e.g., in Bansang, Bwiam, Brikama.

[7] e.g., in Gambisara and N'Jau.

a man's right to dispose of his estate by bequest[1]; while in yet others his bequests will allegedly be enforced without restriction.[2] It must, of course, be remembered that all this applies to personalty only; while in the stricter areas a man who wishes, e.g., to favour one son at the expense of another will normally effect this by means of a gift *inter vivos*.

It may be added that a perusal of the records of Native Tribunals reveals that, besides petty criminal cases and those matrimonial causes already discussed, one of the commonest types of case is a charge of using " abusive language " about either the complainant or his parents—an offence normally punishable by a fine. Other charges which recur with comparative frequency are those of seducing a virgin girl, which is punishable by a fine (part of which may be given to the father, if he has not been negligent in looking after his daughter, by way of compensation); of " giving the complainant's wife in marriage to another ", an action brought by a husband against a father-in-law who arranges another marriage for his daughter either before she is sent to her first husband's house[3] or after a period of separation; and of " breaking a daughter's marriage without her consent ", a charge which may be brought against a father who drives his daughter's husband from his compound or drags her away from her marital home. All these, however, are plainly of a customary nature and bear no relation to Islamic law[4]: and they indicate clearly how far the former has in fact survived, in spite of the lip-service paid to the latter.

Finally, it is noteworthy that the degree to which different Tribunals adhere to Islamic law is not only traceable to the comparative orthodoxy or laxity of the locality and its tribes, but also—and to a marked degree—to the personality and education of the Chief or any outstanding member of his Tribunal. Of this a single instance must suffice: for the close adherence to the Sharīʿa, in most respects, of the N'Jau District Tribunal is chiefly due to the preponderant influence of a comparatively young, well-educated and progressive Chief who strongly inclines to orthodoxy in matters juridical; while the laxity of certain other courts can largely be explained by the lower standard of intelligence and education of their Presidents and members.

Suggestions

The application of Islamic law in the Protectorate of the Gambia seems to raise no particular problems, for the present at least, nor call for any immediate action. Only the future can show which way the Native Tribunals will develop, how they will reconcile the rival claims of Islamic and customary law (which itself largely depends on whether the local attachment to the religion and social system of Islam waxes or wanes) and how they will ultimately fuse both, or the amalgam of both, with certain basic English principles. In the meantime the present system permits the local elasticity which is needed: and what seems chiefly required is for administrative officers to keep a watchful eye on any cases of conflict of law due to difference of religion, or any attempt on the part of a staunchly Muslim Chief unduly to force the Sharīʿa on an unwilling people.

In the Colony, too, the present position seems, in the main, perfectly satisfactory. The Qāḍīs appear to apply the Sharīʿa with both knowledge and discretion, making suitable concessions to " English " principles in matters of procedure and to African custom in some matrimonial causes. A certain lack of uniformity,

[1] e.g., in Basse, where a man may apparently bequeath something, but not everything, to one son, while a man whose only heir is a brother may bequeath up to half his estate

[2] e.g., in Kaiaf.

to a stranger, etc.: and somewhat similarly in Kuntaur and Batteling, for instance.

[3] Whence the sum included in marriage expenses which the groom gives to the bride's parents for " keeping other suitors at bay " (see p. 231 note (3)).

e.g., except the matter of seduction, if regarded as involving *taʿzīr*.

moreover, in the opinions of the two Qāḍīs on various points of detail seems preferable to the rigidity in which any attempt to secure strict uniformity would almost certainly result; and any point which may from time to time demand action can best be treated on an *ad hoc* basis. It might, however, be advisable, at some suitable juncture, to introduce legislation (*a*) providing for the distribution of the estate of an immigrant Muslim under Islamic law (for the Muhammadan Marriage and Divorce Ordinance, like its counterpart in Uganda—but unlike most such Ordinances elsewhere—makes no mention of succession), and (*b*) along the lines of the Indian Caste Disabilities Removal Act, 1850 [and the relevant clauses[1] in the Asiatics (Marriage, Divorce and Succession) Ordinance in Nyasaland, and both the Marriage, Divorce and Succession (Non-Christian Asiatics) Ordinance and the Administration (Small Estates) (Amendment) Ordinance in Tanganyika] to protect the interests of converts.

[1] Sects. 6(1)(*a*), 6(1)(*a*) and 18(4)(*b*) respectively.

THE GOLD COAST

At first sight the Gold Coast appears to resemble Nigeria in the distribution of the Muslim, pagan and Christian elements in its population and in the areas where Islamic law might be expected to prevail. Like the Southern Provinces of Nigeria, the Colony and Ashanti were largely pagan until a considerable proportion of their peoples embraced Christianity; while the Northern Territories, like the Northern Provinces of Nigeria, are a mixture of Muslim and pagan elements. But the resemblance is superficial only, for Islam is in fact incomparably weaker in the Gold Coast than in Nigeria. Thus the Muslim elements in the Colony and Ashanti are largely limited to immigrants from the north or from outside the territory, and there is nothing comparable to the growth of Islam among the Yoruba of the Western Provinces of Nigeria; while the impression—prevalent in the south—that the Northern Territories are largely Muslim is chiefly derived from the fact that most northerners seem to profess that religion if and when they come south, whereas in their native setting the overwhelming majority are frankly pagan and the Islam of the minority largely skin-deep.

The reason for this is not far to seek. In Nigeria Islam has to a great extent been imposed from above, through the Fulani *jihād* and the Muslim Emirates; while the Gold Coast has seen no *jihād* and knows nothing comparable to the Hausa-Fulani Emirates. But if this is true of the influence and spread of Islam in general it is still more relevant to the prevalence and application of Islamic law, for only to a very limited extent can this system be said to have become identified, anywhere in the Gold Coast, with native law and custom, while it has never there been imposed by Muslim rulers, as a matter of religious conviction, on an indifferent or unwilling people.

Unlike Nigeria, again, there exists in the Gold Coast one Ordinance which gives a specific status—quite apart from that of "native law and custom"— to the Islamic law of marriage, divorce and inheritance, namely the Marriage of Muhammadans[1] Ordinance, 1907 (as amended in 1935). This provides that the Commissioner of each district shall be local registrar of Muhammadan marriages and divorces and shall keep a book called the Muhammadan Marriage and Divorce Register[2]; that it "shall be lawful for the Governor to grant a licence in the form of Schedule A to any Muhammadan priest applying for the same who in his opinion is a fit and proper person to perform the duties imposed by this Ordinance on licensed priests"[3]; that "Every Muhammadan marriage celebrated in the Gold Coast after the commencement of this Ordinance shall be registered"[4]; and that the register and certificates must be signed by the bridegroom, the bride's *walī*[5], two witnesses and a "Muhammadan priest licensed under section 3", who must certify that the marriage is "valid according to Muhammadan law".[6] Similarly, with regard to divorces, it is decreed that "Every Muhammadan divorce effected in the Gold Coast after the commencement of this Ordinance shall be registered",[7] and that the register must again be signed by the man, the woman's *walī*, two witnesses and a "Muhammadan priest" licensed under section 3, who must certify that the divorce is "valid

[1] Here spelt "Mohammedans": but see the Introduction to this Survey regarding the liberty taken in the spelling of Arabic words, etc., to avoid the confusion and possible misunderstanding which would result from constant changes and inconsistences.
[2] Part 2, sect. 2.
[3] Part 3, sect. 3.
[4] Part 4, sect. 5.
[5] i.e., marriage guardian.
[6] Part 4, sect. 6.
[7] Part 5, sect 7.

according to Muhammadan law".[1] Finally, it is expressly stated that thenceforth "No marriage contracted or divorce effected in the Gold Coast . . . by persons professing the Muhammadan faith shall be valid unless registered under this Ordinance"[2]; that the proof of every marriage or divorce under this Ordinance shall be by the production of the register, an extract therefrom, or the relevant certificates[3]; and that "On the death of a Muhammadan whose marriage has been duly registered under this Ordinance, the succession to his or her property shall be regulated by Muhammadan law".[4]

This Ordinance, however, remains, or has become, largely a dead letter. In some centres which I visited neither the District Commissioner nor any one else seemed aware of its existence; in most localities no marriages or divorces are in fact registered thereunder; and even where the machinery exists the marriages so registered represent only an inconsiderable fraction of the total number of marriages celebrated between Muslims in the district. All these unregistered marriages and divorces, moreover, are regarded by the people as perfectly valid and binding both under native law and custom and according to the law of Islam: but it remains largely a matter of speculation how they would be regarded by the British courts, since the proper interpretation of this Ordinance is obscure in the extreme.

Section 9, as we have seen, provides in the most sweeping terms that "No marriage contracted or divorce given in the Gold Coast after the commencement of this Ordinance by persons professing the Muhammadan faith shall be valid unless registered under this Ordinance". But does this merely mean that a "Muhammadan marriage"[5] not so registered will not be recognised as such by British courts and will not have the effect regarding the devolution of property on death specified in section 10? Or does it mean that "persons professing the Muhammadan faith" may not, since the commencement of this Ordinance, validly contract a marriage under the Marriage Ordinance on the one hand or according to native law and custom on the other? It is comparatively common, whether in Colonial territories or independent Muslim states, for legislation to be introduced providing that Muhammadan marriages and divorces must be registered, and even imposing penalties in default of such registration; while it has been decreed, e.g., in Egypt that the courts may not entertain any matrimonial or other cause (except a claim of paternity) based on a marriage which was not so registered: but it is quite a different thing to decree that a marriage or divorce which has not been registered is invalid *per se*.[6] Presumably, therefore, the section can only be interpreted as meaning that such marriages will not be regarded as valid and operative by British courts. But the problem remains as to whether they would be so regarded thereby not only as "Muhammadan marriages" within the meaning of the Ordinance but even as customary marriages under native law and custom, for it must be remembered that the majority of marriages between Muslims in the Gold Coast partake of both these elements. Again, it is curious to observe that whereas a native who marries under the Marriage Ordinance will not thereby deprive

[1] Part 5, sect. 8.

[2] Part 6, sect. 9.

[3] Ibid.

[4] Part 6, sect. 10. But what if the deceased has made a will in the English form bequeathing all his property to a stranger, or to one only of his heirs?

[5] It is noteworthy, however, that while sect. 5 refers to "every Muhammadan marriage", sect. 9 distinguishes marriages not by reference to their form but to the faith of the contracting parties. If, as must be presumed, this distinction is intentional, it is difficult to assess its implications. And the same may perhaps be true of the terms "celebrated" and "contracted" in sects. 5 and 9 respectively. Again, is it to be inferred that both parties must necessarily be Muslims?

[6] And this has, in fact, been specifically denied, either in the original Ordinance or a subsequent amendment, in several other territories.

his customary heirs of a right to one-third of his estate,[1] one who marries under the Marriage of Muhammadans Ordinance will thereby exclude any non-Muslim relatives, however intimate and needy, from any right of inheritance whatever.[2] The Ordinance, moreover, is defective in other respects, for while it provides for the courts to recognise the validity of a marriage or divorce registered thereunder it gives no indication (*a*) how a wife can obtain such judicial divorce as Mālikī law allows her in appropriate circumstances; (*b*) where and how other matrimonial causes, such as demands for maintenance or restitution of conjugal rights, are to be decided; (*c*) what is to happen if the certificate of validity under Muhammadan law of a marriage or divorce so registered is subsequently challenged; and (*d*) how far the courts will recognise a divorce, if so registered, between foreign Muslims whose marriage was celebrated outside the Gold Coast. In practice, however, cases under (*a*) and (*b*) never, it seems, reach the Supreme Court at all and will be discussed later in this Survey; cases under (*c*) have never apparently arisen as yet but would presumably be decided by the Supreme Court, as a matter of "foreign" law, with the help of expert witnesses; while under (*d*) there is one reported case [*Mohammed Wahib Huzaifeh v. Hussein Saba and Maria Elina Sabeh* (1939), 5 W.A.C.A. 181] in which a father and daughter appealed against a judgment for damages given by the trial Judge in favour of the daughter's husband on the grounds that a contract of marriage concluded in Syria had never been consummated; that, instead, the father had registered his daughter's divorce[3] under the Marriage of Muhammadans Ordinance and she had subsequently been married to another man; and that dower and gifts were therefore reclaimable. This judgment had apparently been based on "expert" testimony given by one whose claim to any knowledge of the Ḥanafī law under which the marriage had been contracted was doubtful in the extreme, and the Court of Appeal very properly quashed the decision.[4] But the judgment of the Court of Appeal seems to imply that had the respondent claimed refund of dower, or half dower, under Islamic law, and produced adequate evidence in support of his claim, the Court would have applied Islamic law in his favour—but under what legislative authority it is extremely difficult to determine.

For the rest, however, Islamic law is applied in the Gold Coast, where it is applied at all, either as "native law and custom" or as a factor which is regarded by certain native courts as modifying the normal native law and custom in so far as Muslim litigants are concerned.[5]

For this application of native law and custom throughout the territory the usual authorities exist. Thus the Royal Instructions, 1950, include the words: "In the making of Ordinances, any laws by which the civil relations of any chiefs, tribes or population under Our protection are now regulated shall be respected, except in so far as the same may be incompatible with the due exercise of Our powers and jurisdiction, or clearly injurious to the welfare of the said chiefs,

[1] While two-thirds will go by English law, in certain circumstances: see Marriage Ordinance, sect. 48.

[2] Sect. 10.

[3] But how this could be regarded as "valid according to Muhammadan law" is not apparent, and the Court of Appeal realised it was not so.

[4] The correct action for the husband in this case, according to the Sharī'a, would have been one for conjugal rights—or for return of half the dower, etc., if he divorced her.

[5] See below—especially regarding "any law binding between the parties". But it is startling to find that in *Ali Buzu* v. *Suli Shardow*, etc. (1929) F. Ct. '26-'29 p. 357, both the Chief Justice in first instance and the Full Court on appeal treated a claim to declaration of title to property by virtue of being an adopted son of the deceased as wholly "governed by Muhammadan law".

tribes and population."[1] Similarly, the Courts Ordinance, 1935 (as repeatedly amended), provides that the Supreme Court and magistrates' courts shall not normally exercise jurisdiction in matters properly cognisable by a native court—e.g., the paternity and custody of the children of a non-Christian marriage, divorce and matrimonial causes under native law and custom, and claims to land[2] and succession to a deceased native under customary law.[3] And it is relevant to notice that for the purposes of this Ordinance the term " native " is defined as " a person of African descent: provided that the expression shall not include any person who does not belong to a class of persons who have ordinarily been subject to Native Tribunals ".[4] Again, the same Ordinance provides that " Nothing in this Ordinance shall deprive the Courts of the right to observe and enforce the observance, or shall deprive any person of the benefit, of any native law or custom existing in the Gold Coast,[5] such law or custom not being repugnant to natural justice, equity and good conscience, nor incompatible either directly or by necessary implication with any Ordinance for the time being in force. Such laws and customs shall be deemed applicable in causes and matters where the parties thereto are natives, and particularly, but without derogating from their application in other cases, in causes and matters relating to the tenure and transfer of real and personal property, and to inheritance and testamentary dispositions . . .".[6] And in deciding questions of native law and custom, the courts may " call Native Chiefs or other persons whom the Court considers to have special knowledge . . . and may require them to give evidence on oath.".[7]

Native Courts

There are four different Native Courts Ordinances in force in the Gold Coast—namely the Native Courts (Colony) Ordinance, 1944, the Native Courts (Ashanti)

[1] Art. 10(1). In previous Instructions, the word " native " occurs before " laws " and " chiefs " respectively, while the section ends with the words " injurious to the welfare of the said natives ": cp. Instructions of 1946, art. 17(1).

[2] It is noteworthy that provision has also been made for land cases to be tried by a special division of the Supreme Court: but the distinction between this and other divisions of the Supreme Court has been almost lost in practice.

[3] See sects. 17 and 42 and relevant sections in the various Native Courts Ordinances (below).

[4] Sect. 2.

[5] It is particularly noteworthy how much wider this definition is than that in the different Native Courts Ordinances (see below), for this form of words would presumably include the customary law of immigrant communities. But later in the same sub-sect. the phrase " any local law or custom " occurs, and it is not altogether apparent if this far more restricted phrase is intended as a synonym of the former.

[6] Sect. 74(1). For the rest the Supreme Court is to administer, subject to local legislation:—
(*a*) common law, equity, and statutes of general application in force in England on 24th July, 1874 (sect 70);
(*b*) Imperial Statutes declared to extend or apply to the Gold Coast, in so far as local circumstances permit (sect. 72);
(*c*) native law and custom " not repugnant ", etc. (sect. 74);
(*d*) the principles of justice, equity and good conscience (sect. 74);
(*e*) the law and practice in force in England in probate, divorce and matrimonial causes and proceedings.

The position may conveniently be summarised as follows:—
(i) In cases between native and native, customary law is the normal rule, except where it appears that their intention was otherwise.
(ii) In cases between native and non-native, English law is basic, but customary law may be applied where " substantial injustice would be done to either party by a strict adherence to the rules of English law ".
(iii) In cases between non-native and non-native, English law is basic.

So the question turns (1) on the parties concerned and (2) on the nature of the case at issue.

[7] Sect. 74(2).

Ordinance, 1935, the Native Courts (Northern Territories) Ordinance, 1935, and the Native Courts (Southern Section of Togoland under United Kingdom Trusteeship) Ordinance, 1949 (as variously amended). It would be tedious in this Survey to summarise these *seriatim*, and it will suffice for our purpose to pick out points of particular interest from the Colony Ordinance, with brief references to the major differences thereunder in the other three Ordinances. Thus it is noteworthy, *inter alia*: —

(1) That it is provided that the " following persons or classes of persons shall be subject to the jurisdiction of Native Courts:

(*a*) Persons of African descent, provided that the mode of life of such persons is that of the general community and, that such persons are in their country of origin subject to African customary law, howsoever that customary law may be modified or applied.

(*b*) Any persons or class of persons whether of African or non-African descent whom or which the Governor in Council may with the approval of the Secretary of State direct to be subject to the jurisdiction of any particular class of Native Court or of any particular Native Court, or to be subject to such jurisdiction in certain causes or classes of causes only . . .

(*c*) Persons whether of African or non-African descent who have at any time instituted proceedings in any Native Court ".[1] And it is similarly provided that " Every Native Court shall have full jurisdiction and power to the extent set forth in the order of the Governor in Council establishing it and, subject to the provisions of this Ordinance, in all civil and criminal causes in which the parties are persons subject to the jurisdiction of Native Courts ".[2]

(2) That the law a Native Court is to administer is defined as: —

" (*a*) the native customary law prevailing within the jurisdiction of the Native Court so far as it is not repugnant to natural justice, equity and good conscience nor incompatible either directly or by necessary implication with any Ordinance for the time being in force: Provided that in regard to criminal offences by virtue of native customary law the Native Court shall take cognisance only of those offences set out in the first column of the First Schedule to this Ordinance and no Native Court shall impose in respect of such offences penalties heavier than such Court is, according to its grade, authorised to impose by virtue of the relevant provisions of the First Schedule[3];

(*b*) the provisions of any law binding between the parties subject to the jurisdiction of Native Courts: Provided that in any civil cause or matter a Native Court shall not, unless the parties agree thereto, have jurisdiction to determine any cause wherein it shall appear . . . that the parties agreed either expressly

[1] Sect. 10 (as also in the Togoland Ordinance, *verbatim*). In the two earlier Ordinances the only parallel is the definition of " Native " in their sect. 2 as " a person of African descent: Provided always that the expression shall not include any person who does not belong to a class of persons who have ordinarily been subject to the jurisdiction of Native Tribunals ".

[2] Sect. 13 (as also in the Togoland Ordinance, *verbatim*). These provisions are substantially covered by sect. 7 of each of the earlier Ordinances, but with the term " natives " (within the definition already given) substituted for " persons subject to the jurisdiction of Native Courts ", and other minor differences.

[3] Sect. 15(*a*) (as also in the Togoland Ordinance, *verbatim*). These provisions are substantially covered by sect. 8(*a*) of each of the earlier Ordinances. It is particularly noteworthy that all four Ordinances limit the native law and custom which these courts are to administer to that prevailing within the area of their jurisdiction.

or by necessary implication that the obligations arising out of such transactions should be regulated exclusively by English law[1];

(*c*) the provisions of any Ordinances which such Native Court is by or under such Ordinance authorised to administer;

(*d*) the provisions of any Ordinance which a Native Court may be authorised to enforce by an Order made in accordance with section 16;

(*e*) the provisions of any orders or rules in force by virtue of the Native Authority (Colony) Ordinance, 1944, and in force in the area of the jurisdiction of the Native Court."[2]

(3) That the procedure and practice of these courts, subject to any express provision to the contrary, is to be " regulated in accordance with native customary law "[3].

(4) That appeals from Native Courts lie either to a Native Appeal Court, a Magistrate's Court, or the Land Court, according to circumstances, and that further appeals are allowed under appropriate conditions.[4]

(5) That any cause or matter determined by a Native Court may be reviewed by the Judicial Adviser or, under certain conditions, by the District Commissioner[5] concerned, who may either (*a*) make such order or pass such sentence therein as the Native Court itself could have made or passed[6]; (*b*) order any cause to be retried either by the same Native Court or any other Native Court of competent jurisdiction; (*c*) order costs awarded to be disallowed or reduced; (*d*) order that any execution process be disallowed; or (*e*) make such other order as may be necessary.[7]

(6) That " Whenever it shall appear to any Court that any civil cause or matter brought before it is one properly cognisable by a Native Court, the Court shall

---

[1] Sect. 15(*b*) of the two more recent Ordinances. The only parallel to these provisions in either Ashanti or the Northern Territories is found in the Native Courts (Ashanti) (Amendment) Ordinance, 1943, which provides that " a Native Court shall not unless the parties shall agree thereto, have any jurisdiction in any cause or matter where it appears . . . that the parties expressly or by implication agreed that their obligations in connection with such transaction should be regulated substantially according to the provisions of some law or laws other than native customary law, or where otherwise some other such law or laws is or are properly applicable thereto ". It is a matter for speculation how far the phrase " any law binding between the parties " in the two more recent Ordinances may be held to authorise, in certain circumstances, the application of Islamic law in the Colony and Southern Togoland respectively: although the Ashanti parallel, if parallel it be, tends to discount any such contention and to limit the application of the words to transactions under English law, etc. But the wider wording may, of course, have been designed to be more comprehensive in its scope.

[2] Sect. 15(*c*), (*d*) and (*e*) in the two more recent Ordinances (*mutatis mutandis*). These provisions are covered by sect. 8(*b*), (*c*) and (*d*) of the older Ordinances.

[3] Sect. 23 of the two more recent Ordinances: cp. sect. 10 of the two earlier ones.

[4] Sects. 46-53 in the two more recent Ordinances. In the two older Ordinances sects. 24-29 correspond, but with considerable differences—which are, however, scarcely relevant to this Survey.

[5] Acting in an administrative capacity, rather than the magisterial capacity in which he hears certain appeals.

[6] But no sentence in a criminal cause must be increased without an opportunity being given to the convicted person to be heard.

[7] Sects. 59-66 of the more recent Ordinances: compare sect. 22 of the older Ordinances, as amended. But again there are important differences, for there is no Judicial Adviser in the Northern Territories, while the Judicial Adviser in Ashanti has no powers of review; District Commissioners in Ashanti have no powers in land cases; and the powers of Chief Commissioners also vary, being least restricted of all in the Northern Territories.

stop the further progress of such civil cause or matter before it, and refer the parties to a competent Native Court "[1]—provided that the latter is functioning, etc.[2]

(7) That any person not duly appointed who shall " hold himself forth as having or shall falsely pretend or claim to have, any authority to take part in any proceedings of a Native Court shall be guilty of an offence ".[3] This provision corresponds to section 30 of the two older Ordinances, but the latter also expressly provide in section 32 that " Nothing in this Ordinance contained shall be deemed to affect the power of any native or Native Authority to act extra-judicially as an arbitrator in any dispute of a petty nature in respect of which the parties . . . consent to his so acting under native customary law; but recourse shall not be had for the purpose of enforcing the award to the powers or facilities provided by this Ordinance ". This is, moreover, a matter of vital moment in regard to the position of the headmen of Zongo communities in the major towns of Ashanti and the Colony on the one hand, and of *limams* and *mallams*[4] in the Northern Territories on the other, when they " arbitrate " or act in a quasi-judicial character, in causes referred to them by Muslim litigants, in accordance with, or at least influenced by, the appropriate provisions of Islamic law. To this subject fuller reference must be made later.

Other Legislation.

As elsewhere, moreover, there are certain other Ordinances which may impinge on the application of Islamic law. Thus the Criminal Code, 1892, provides in section 173 that " Whoever carnally knows any female under ten years of age, whether with or without her consent, shall be liable to imprisonment for life "[5]; and it is noteworthy that since this section is expressed in absolute terms it would presumably include the consummation of child marriage. By contrast section 174 only provides that " Whoever unlawfully and carnally knows any female, being of or about ten years and under thirteen years of age . . ." shall be liable to punishment; for here the word " unlawfully " clearly excludes the consummation of marriage. But section 183 (" Whoever takes away or detains against her will any female of any age, with intent to marry or carnally know her, or to cause her to be married or carnally known by any other person, shall be liable to imprisonment for fourteen years "), section 184 (" Whoever by duress causes any person to marry against his or her will shall be liable to imprisonment for two years "), and section 185 (aiding and abetting the above) might clearly run counter to the Mālikī doctrine of a father's right to give his minor son, or virgin daughter, in compulsory marriage, and might expose to prosecution the father, suitor or even husband for acts which might be unexceptionable under the Sharī'a: cp. also section 189 (" If a female is compelled to marry another person by such duress as avoids the marriage or makes it voidable, the marriage is of no effect for the purpose of Book 1 with respect to consent "). Similarly, the provisions in section 66 with regard to the right of correction, including personal chastisement, which are accorded, in suitable circumstances and under appropriate conditions, to parents, masters, etc., make no reference whatever to the Muslim husband's right to chastise his wife, minor or adult, under Islamic

[1] Sect. 58 of the more recent Ordinances, together with sect. 35 of the older Ordinances, which are substantially the same.

[2] Sect. 58(*a*).

[3] Sect. 6(2) of the newer Ordinances.

[4] These terms represent the Arabic *imām* and *mu'allim*, prayer-leader and teacher, respectively. They are widely used in this form in the Gold Coast.

[5] Or, prior to Ordinance 21 of 1951, at the discretion of the court, to flogging.

law[1]; while the Courts (Amendment) Ordinance, 1946, which repealed and replaced the Children (Care and Reformation) Ordinance, 1928, might, under certain circumstances, prove at variance with the Islamic rules regarding the guardianship of children.

Again, the Marriage Ordinance of the Gold Coast, which dates as early as 1884, may be said to run counter to pure Sharī'a law at least in the following respects: —

(1) That it provides a way in which a Muslim girl could validly marry a non-Muslim, in spite of the complete nullity of such a marriage in Islamic law. Provided she were over twenty-one or a widow, moreover, she could conclude such a marriage without the intervention or consent of any guardian[2]; while if she were a virgin under twenty-one years of age the consent of father or, in default, of her mother or, again in default, of her guardian, must be obtained[3]: and these provisions run counter both to the Mālikī insistence that a woman may never give herself in marriage and also to the proper order of priority of marriage guardians.

(2) That it may possibly[4] provide a way in which two Muslims, prevented from intermarriage in Islamic law by the bar of fosterage, could validly conclude a marriage—unless, indeed, the phrase "any other lawful hindrance to the marriage[5] is to be construed as including fosterage, in the case of Muslims only.

(3) That a man married thereunder is debarred from exercising his right under Islamic law unilaterally to repudiate his wife or to marry a second, third or fourth wife.[6]

(4) That a marriage concluded thereunder is not dissolved by reason that either party may have embraced or renounced the religion of Islam, however much such change of religion would have that effect under the Sharī'a.

(5) That the estate of one married thereunder, if he or she dies intestate leaving a widow or husband or any issue of such marriage, together with the estate of any issue of such marriage, shall be distributed, in so far as personal property and any real property of which the intestate might have disposed by will is concerned, not in accordance with either Islamic law or native law and custom but (*a*) as to two-thirds in accordance with the provisions of the law of England in force on 19th November, 1884, and (*b*) as to one-third in accordance with the "provisions of the native customary law which would have obtained if such person had not been married under this Ordinance".[7]

As for land, the relevant Ordinances are the Survey Ordinance (Gold Coast), 1922 (as amended), the Land Registry Ordinance (Colony and Ashanti), 1895 (as amended), the Public Lands Ordinance (Colony and Ashanti), 1876 (as amended), the Land (Perpetual Succession) Ordinance (Colony and Ashanti), 1932 (as amended), the Land and Native Rights Ordinance (Northern

[1] It is, perhaps, possible to argue that a Muslim wife has, by contracting her marriage under Islamic law, given such implicit consent to her husband exercising his rights under that law as to protect him from criminal liability, in cases of reasonable chastisement, under sect. 56(10) of the Code. But such consent may at any time be revoked, except, in the case of spouses, "for the purposes of marriage" (sect 67(4)).

[2] See sect. 14(2).

[3] See sect. 27.

[4] On the assumption that sect. 9 of the Marriage of Muhammadans Ordinance is not to be interpreted as forbidding such parties to marry under any other Ordinance: see above, p. 250.

[5] See sect. 14(3).

[6] See sect. 44.

[7] Sect. 48.

Territories), 1931 (as amended), the Courts (Amendment) Ordinance, 1944, and the Public Lands (Leasehold) Ordinance, 1950. The only comments which seem called for here are, however, as follows:—

(1) That the Land (Perpetual Succession) Ordinance might be used by a Muslim of the Gold Coast in order to secure some of the objects for which a waqf might be created in, e.g., most of the East African territories.

(2) That the Land and Native Rights Ordinance follows the usual pattern of such Ordinances (cp. that of Northern Nigeria) and declares the "whole of the lands of the Protectorate, whether occupied or unoccupied," to be "native lands: Provided that—(*a*) nothing in this Ordinance contained shall be deemed to affect the validity of any title to lands or any interest therein lawfully acquired before the date of the commencement thereof . . . ; and (*b*) nothing in this Ordinance contained shall be deemed—

(i) to affect the validity of any mining lease or other right acquired or hereafter to be acquired under the Mineral Rights Ordinance, 1904, or the Minerals' Ordinance . . . , or

(ii) to affect the acquisition of land for the public service, or

(iii) to apply to lands or any interests therein vested in the Crown or in any public office."[1] Similarly, it also provides that "All native lands and all rights in or over the same shall . . . be under the control and subject to the disposition of the Governor, and shall be held and administered for the use and common benefit, direct or indirect, of the natives . . .";[2] that "The Governor in the exercise of the powers conferred upon him by this Ordinance in respect of any native lands shall have due regard to the native customary law existing in the locality in which such lands are situated"[3]; that it shall be lawful for the Governor to grant rights of occupancy to natives and to non-natives, to exact a rent in respect of rights of occupancy so granted, and to revise such rents,[4] but such rights of occupancy shall be for any definite term not exceeding ninety-nine years . . .[5]; that "It shall not be lawful, without the consent of the Governor—(*a*) for any native to purport to alienate any estate, right, or interest in, or with respect to, any land lying within the Protectorate to a non-native; (*b*) for any occupier to purport to alienate his right of occupancy granted under this Ordinance, or any part thereof, or interest therein, either (i) to a non-native, or (ii) otherwise than in accordance with regulations" made under the appropriate section,[6] and "any conveyance, grant, mortgage, transfer of possession, lease, bequest or other instrument or transaction . . . which purports to effect an alienation in contravention of this section shall be void of effect"[7]; and that the "devolution of the rights of an occupier upon death shall be regulated, in the case of a native, by the native customary law existing in the locality. . . . Provided that a right of occupancy granted under this Ordinance shall not be divided into two or more parts on devolution by the death of the occupier, except with the sanction of the Governor."[8] But it is also relevant in this context to note that section 2 provides that a "right of occupancy means a title to the use and occupation of lands, and includes the title of a native or native community lawfully using or occupying lands in accordance with native customary law"; while "native," so far as this Ordinance is concerned, means a "person whose parents are or were members of some tribe or tribes indigenous to the Protectorate, or . . . the Northern Section of Togoland under British Trusteeship, and any descendant

[1] Sect. 3.
[2] Sect. 4.
[3] Sect. 5.
[4] Sect. 6.
[5] Sect. 7.
[6] i.e., sect. 24.
[7] Sect. 17.
[8] Sect. 20.

of such a person, and includes—(*a*) any person one of whose parents was a member of such tribe, and (*b*) any person who shall have obtained a certificate from the Governor " (being a native of Africa who has declared his intention of making the Protectorate his permanent domicile and has obtained the consent thereto of the native communities concerned).

(3) That the Courts (Amendment) Ordinance, 1944, provides for a Land Court which shall have " exclusive original jurisdiction to hear and determine any cause or matter relating to the ownership, possession or occupation of land—(*a*) where there is no Native Court competent to try the cause or matter; (*b*) where the cause or matter has been transferred . . . from a Native Court in accordance with the provisions of the Native Courts (Colony) Ordinance,[1] 1944."[2]

(4) That it is abundantly clear that Islamic law has no influence whatever on land tenure as such in the Gold Coast, and that it is only in regard to such questions as testate and intestate succession—and then only in a small minority of cases, and almost exclusively with regard to self-acquired as distinct from " family " property (see below)—that that law is ever applied in respect of farms and compounds.

The following summary of the application of Islamic law in the Gold Coast is based on visits to Prang, Salaga, Kpembe, Yendi, Tamale, Larabanga, Wa and Bole in the Northern Territories; to Wenchi, Kintampo, Kumasi and Obuasi in Ashanti; and to Accra in the Colony. In each of these places I had talks with the chiefs and native court members, with leading members of the Muslim communities, and with British officers, and I consulted numerous files. It is obvious that generalisations based on visits to certain centres alone may be dangerous, but it seems probable that the places named provide a reliable and reasonably complete cross-section of the country as a whole.

The Northern Territories

In so far as it is possible to select one centre as " typical " of the Northern Territories in regard to the local influence of Islamic law (and it will appear from this Survey that the term typical is an euphemism where conditions differ so widely from place to place), Yendi would, perhaps, appear the best choice. Here Islam is more strongly entrenched than in most of the north, but remains largely indigenous; whereas a centre such as Prang is largely dominated by Hausa and other extraneous elements, while in Wa the missionary influence of the Aḥmadīya is strong. It seems best, then, to start with Yendi, and to relate the other centres roughly thereto.

Yendi

My informants in Yendi were the Ya-Na, a colourful chief with wide-spread influence, the Yidan Baba or chief butcher, said to be the richest man in the town and a staunch Muslim, a group of *limans* and *mallams*, and some native court members—besides, of course, the District Commissioner, and an anthropologist, Mr. Tait, who was working in the vicinity.

It seems that the number of Muslims among the Dagbamba (usually termed Dagomba) is on the increase, particularly in Yendi—at least to the extent that far more people than formerly now recite Muslim prayers. For years the Muslims have occupied an honoured place in the Ya tribal system, with various *limams* and other functionaries appointed by the Ya-Na each to some special duty: yet the whole has been strangely blended with that paganism which is still frankly

[1] Etc., *mutatis mutandis*.
[2] Sect. 6(4).

professed by the Ya-Na and the majority of his people, while such subject races as the Komkomba are solidly pagan. An interesting illustration of the position is provided by the members of the Ya-Na's court. All eight with whom I talked denied that they were Muslims, yet all performed Muslim prayers (learnt by heart in Arabic). When asked why, therefore, they did not claim to be Muslims, they first said that this was because they could not read the Qur'ān: later, however, they admitted that they still believed in paganism, which they regarded as more powerful than Islam, but they added Muslim prayers as a sort of insurance policy, because Muslims assured them that he who prayed five times a day was sure of Paradise. Those who had really turned Muslim, they added, abandoned the fetish—except, perhaps, in times of special stress. As for circumcision, all boy Dagbamba are circumcised between the age of five and seven: while an 'Aqīqa ceremony,[1] at which a baby is named and shaved on the eighth day, is also common to pagans and Muslims alike. But in the Ya-Na's court customary law almost invariably prevails, whoever the litigants may be.

Marriages, again, are normally arranged in accordance with local custom, whether between Muslims or non-Muslims. The stricter Muslims, however, add a ceremony at which the principal *mallam* present, besides saying suitable prayers, will three times ask the leading representative of the bride's and bridegroom's families (for the spouses are never themselves present) whether they give and accept the girl in marriage to her suitor, and will in each case proclaim their answers to the assembled guests in a loud voice.[2] This is known locally as an "*Amalīya*"[3] marriage, and is peculiar to Muslims; and I was told that the principal *mallam* present would tell all concerned that in such marriages the groom must never have a mistress in his room and drive away his wife, while should he do so the fathers of the parties must call in the *mallam* to dissolve the marriage; that the wife must not go about the town, except on her lawful business; that the husband must be patient and not quarrel with his wife; that the wife must obey her husband; and that the father of the groom must ensure that both regularly recite their prayers. Muslims alone, moreover, add to the customary marriage payments (of money and kola nuts, in instalments, to the girl's father, and clothes to the girl herself) a "*sadaki*"[4] of eleven shillings, given to the father on behalf of the bride. But mixed marriages between Muslim men and pagan women, and even between Muslim women and pagan men, also occur; and the issue of such marriages are regularly regarded as legitimate—as are also the children of Muslim wives in excess of the four to which alone a Muslim is properly entitled.[5] Official Muslim concubinage,[6] however, is said no longer to exist.

Girls are sometimes, but not always, promised in marriage when very young, but are never, it seems, sent to their husbands' homes until between fifteen and eighteen years of age, and the actual contract or ceremony[7] is not performed until the same day. The father's promise, however, is normally regarded as binding, and a girl who refused to comply would formerly have been forced to submit or be thrown out of the family, in which case the *mallams* assert that

---

[1] Fowls are killed and the baby's hair is given to the mother, who often makes a talisman of it to be hung round the baby's neck for some years. Others, however, bury it. Such Naming Ceremonies are widespread.

[2] This covers that declaration (*ījāb*) and acceptance (*qabūl*) which constitute the essence of the contract in Islamic law. The other essentials, i.e., consent of the bride's guardian, and the necessary witnesses or publicity, are also present.

[3] Presumably from the Arabic *'amalīya,* in the sense of "ceremony".

[4] A corruption of the Arabic *ṣadāq* (or dower) employed throughout most of the Gold Coast among Muslims, and used throughout this section.

[5] All this is, of course, contrary to the Mālikī law, under which a marriage between a Muslim and a pagan is invalid, as also a marriage with a fifth wife.

[6] cp. the practice still current in parts of Nigeria, see p. 215.

[7] i.e., the "*Amaliya*": see above.

they would refuse to marry her to anyone else. She might, however, sometimes persuade her father to marry her to some one else and refund the payments made by the one to whom she had been promised; for where the parents promise a daughter to one man and then marry her to another the former may always claim a complete refund of all his disbursements. The court members affirmed, however, that nowadays a girl who persistently refused a promised match would get her own way, while her father would try to supply her suitor with another bride: but they admitted that much pressure would be brought to bear upon her first. There is no custom of levirate marriage, and a widow returns to her own family.[1]

Men, it seems, frequently divorce their wives. Normally, they simply tell the wife's parents why they are sending her home; but sometimes the triple formula, or an oath on the Qur'ān, is apparently used. But even such expressions are commonly disregarded afterwards if spoken in anger or if the parties become reconciled. If, however, the wife holds back or some other difficulty arises, a re-marriage may, it is said, very exceptionally be arranged; but an intervening marriage to legalise this is quite unknown.[2] When a husband divorces his wife he can of course claim no refund, but any deferred payments may sometimes lapse.[3]

It may be added that the stricter and wealthier Muslims frequently, it seems, "repudiate" wives who are past child-bearing, in the sense that they no longer sleep with them, although the women may continue to live in their husbands' compounds, enjoy high status, and remain on excellent terms with them. Such "repudiation" is, of course, designed to permit the husband to have four younger wives without exceeding the legal maximum. But others, as we have seen, are less meticulous in this matter. Again, while instances of adultery on the part of the young wives of elderly chiefs are said to be so common as scarcely to provoke comment, cases of divorces in such circumstances appear to be unknown.

Where a married woman is unhappy or ill-treated she will commonly abscond to her parents or elope with a lover. In the former case her father will usually attempt to effect a reconciliation, failing which the husband may claim a refund of his marriage payments (if he has "no great respect for his father-in-law"): but the *mallams* say that the *sadaki* payment is not properly included,[4] although the ignorant claim and obtain this also. Where, however, matters cannot be mutually arranged the case must go to the native court—for a *mallam* may do no more than investigate, advise and attempt reconciliation: so the question whether the woman has any valid justification for refusing to continue the marriage[5] is only relevant with regard to the terms which may be arranged between the families or if the question is so taken to the native courts. Even so, such "justification" is, it seems, restricted to cases where she bears the marks of whipping, was not given adequate food and clothing, or had been left

[1] In Mālikī law a father may give his virgin daughter in compulsory marriage, but a widow may not be so compelled.

[2] Under the Sharī'a a divorce under the triple formula, etc., is not only irrevocable but the parties are also precluded from concluding a new contract unless or until the wife has completed her *'idda,* been validly married to another husband who has consummated the marriage, and then again been divorced or widowed; while a divorce expressed in any suitable words becomes irrevocable at the end of the wife's *'idda,* after which a new contract and dower is incumbent before marriage relations may be resumed. See Glossary.

[3] Although always payable, except by agreement, under the Sharī'a.

[4] Unless the woman had no adequate grounds for divorce, the *limans* add. but they admit that the distinction is largely academic, as the native court has no knowledge of such matters.

[5] Without which there can be no judicial divorce in Mālikī law, except on the recommendation of family arbitrators: see Appendix C.

without maintenance[1] (and letters requesting this had been repeatedly ignored or the husband's whereabouts were unknown). In such circumstances the court will apparently tell the husband, if present, that it has granted his wife a divorce, and the wife, if he is absent, that she is free. Normally, moreover, it seems that the husband may recover his marriage payments even in these circumstances, but these may be reduced by the court where his wife has borne him children, served him for years, or by way of set-off for any gifts she has given him. No distinction whatever is made by the court as to whether the litigants are pagans or Muslims: no *mallam* is consulted, and the *sadaki* is apparently treated as any other payment. Similarly, where it is the husband who brings the matter to the Native Authority because his wife has absconded and will not return, the Native Authority will again attempt conciliation. Where, however, the woman remains adamant the husband will bring the matter to court, where he will normally be advised to wait until she goes to some other man—unless, that is, her father voluntarily refunds the husband's marriage expenses, which will always be regarded as ending the union.[2]

If and when the woman goes to another man, the situation will be much the same as if she had run away with him from the first. The husband will in both cases appeal to the court, which will order the wife to return to her husband. Where she complies the case will resolve itself into one of simple adultery, and the paramour will be liable to pay a fine (none of which is claimed as compensation by Muslim husbands in this area).[3] If, on the other hand, she refuses, her husband may recover his marriage gifts and payments, and any funeral expenses incurred on her behalf, from her father,[4] and the marriage will be regarded as ended.[5] But in these circumstances, too, the husband's claims may be reduced if she has borne him children. The *'idda*[6] period during which a divorced wife may not properly remarry is, moreover, regularly disregarded, with the result that a married woman who runs away with another man is considered to be married to the latter as soon as the first husband has recovered his expenses and her father has consented to her remaining with the second. In such circumstances, moreover, a *mallam* will willingly solemnise the second marriage.[7] Children properly belong to their physiological father, and in this respect the woman's word is final: but they must stay with their mother

---

[1] And, apparently, has no other means of supply. If her father maintains her, in other words, the court would not act in this way—although she might, of course, take the law into her own hands by going off with some other man. For Mālikī law, see Appendix C.

[2] Without, it seems, any formal divorce; which is quite contrary to the Sharī'a. It is significant that here and elsewhere the African regard for the family or community rather than the individual overrides the entirely individualistic concept of divorce in Islamic law.

[3] It is noteworthy in this context that in the Northern Territories sexual connection with another man's wife is an offence under native law and custom punishable by native courts—see Order by Governor No. 43 of 1936, under sect. 8(*a*) of the Native Courts (Northern Territories) Ordinance. It is everywhere punished by fine (or imprisonment, in default), but part of the fine may be awarded to the injured husband by way of compensation. In the Colony and Southern Togoland, on the other hand, only sexual connection with a chief's wife is a criminal offence, while sexual connection with another's wife is a civil wrong for which a compensation fee (only) may be claimed. In Ashanti, again, sexual connection with any wife whose marriage has been "registered" with the Native Authority is an offence—although this seems to be contrary to indigenous custom, except in regard to chiefs—while the civil remedy is open to all, whether the marriage is registered or not. For Ashanti, see Native Courts (Offences under Native Law and Custom) Order No. 7 of 1935, as amended by No. 24 of 1943.

[4] Who will normally recover from the other man, as the price for consenting to his marriage to the daughter.

[5] Again, without further formalities: see (2) above.

[6] Of three menstrual periods, etc.: see Glossary.

[7] i.e., regardless of the absence of any formal divorce under the Sharī'a.

until weaning, at the age of two, and commonly stay rather longer—while during this period she may take them wherever she likes. This, again, is clearly a matter of customary rather than Islamic law.[1]

It is interesting to note, however, that while the *'idda* of divorce is regularly disregarded that of widowhood is normally observed. The reason, it seems, is that the *mallams* have no means of enforcing the former, while in regard to the latter they secure compliance through fear that the spirit of the dead husband would not tolerate his widow having premature sexual relations with another man. This is no doubt much facilitated by the fact that the Muslim *'idda* of widowhood, which normally lasts for four months and ten days, closely corresponds with local custom, which forbids a wife to remarry until her late husband's funeral rites are complete—which may, apparently, take anything from, e.g., two to six months in this locality.

The local law and custom with regard to inheritance gives all to the senior member of the family,[2] who will act as a sort of trustee or manager for the family as an whole. This applies to property of all sorts, whether personal or the use of a farm or compound. But the court members admitted that very few such cases come to court, since the vast majority are arranged between the family; while Muslims frequently consult *mallams* on this subject. The latter, when questioned, averred that the stricter Muslims usually consult a certain Ḥājj 'Abdulai,[3] the most learned of local *mallams,* and that he bases his distribution of all personal property on the text of the *Risāla*: but land and houses are excepted from such treatment, as family rather than personal property. Laxer Muslims, of course, still follow customary law in all such matters: but the *mallams* assured me that the Na would not support the senior member of a strictly Muslim family if he tried to enforce customary law against the desire of the rest of the family to follow Ḥājj 'Abdulai's interpretation of Islamic law.[4] Inheritance by patronage[5] (*walā'*) is known and applied where there is no natural heir. Bequests are rare: but the *mallams* claim to uphold them, if properly witnessed, without regard to the " bequeathable third " or the rule that there must be no bequest to an heir,[6] although they say that they would try to reduce a bequest which seemed excessive. In customary law, on the other hand, bequests are never, it seems, enforced if the senior member of the family disputes them: and this principle would no doubt be followed by many Muslims too, and would probably always be enforced in any case pressed to formal litigation in the native court.

Oaths are regularly imposed, both here and elsewhere in the Gold Coast, on the claimant and on all witnesses, as is also the decisive oath, in default of adequate testimony, on the defendant. Such are taken by pagans on their fetish, by Muslims on the Qur'ān and by Christians on the Bible; and it is left to each individual to say which religion he professes. The records of the

[1] Since the latter prescribes that a boy should remain in the custody of his mother until he reaches puberty and a girl until she goes to her husband's house; that a mother's right should be forfeit if she remarries outside the degrees of relationship prohibited to the children concerned, whereupon the right of custody passes to the maternal grandmother, etc.; and that the mother may not take the children further from their father's home than would allow him to visit them and return home in one day.

[2] But in default of either brother or son property may, apparently, go to daughters or sisters, in some cases at least.

[3] Unfortunately absent at the time of my visit.

[4] *Sed quaere.* The *Risāla* is that of Ibn Abī Zayd al-Qayrawānī.

[5] That is, the right of the ex-owner of a slave, or the descendants of the ex-owner, to inherit the estate of his ex-slave, or that of the latter's descendants, in default of any prior heirs.

[6] Islamic law, of course, limits a man's testamentary powers to one-third of his net estate; while the Sunnī schools forbid any bequest whatever to one entitled to inherit on intestacy.

native court show that the commonest cases concern "sexual connection with" or "seduction of" another's wife, theft, assault, slander, burning of grass, and failure to pay tribute. I noticed that in one case (*Native Authority v. Nlebe Konkomba*—unreported) where the accused was alleged to have severely beaten his wife who thereupon took refuge at the District Commissioner's flag, the court's judgment read "Kopie Konkomba to divorce her husband Nlebe Konkomba this day, since not any woman is to be forced against her will on marriage". But it is questionable how far this may be regarded as customary law or was influenced by the interest the District Commissioner had evinced in the case.[1]

It is apparent, then, that Islamic law is never enforced by the Yendi Native Court, with the possible exception that it might uphold the distribution of the estate of a strict Muslim according to Islamic principles, as advised by local *mallams,* if the majority of the family desired this.[2] The stricter Muslims, however, certainly follow its precepts regarding the actual contract of marriage,[3] the distribution of personal property on intestacy, and even, in some cases, the maximum number of wives and the proper formulae of divorce[4]: but the legitimacy of the children of "mixed" marriages or of wives in excess of the legal four is never questioned, the normal restrictions on a man's testamentary powers are disregarded, and "divorces" by customary law are recognised as valid.

Tamale.

Tamale[5] is under a sub-chief who is subordinate to the Ya-Na, so need not detain us long. I had talks with the chief, the *limam,* most of the leading Muslims and several pagans. On the whole my informants were vaguer and less educated than those in Yendi and we covered much the same ground: so I shall confine myself to points on which their answers were different, for what these may be worth.

Something like fifty per cent. of those in Tamale, it seems, say Muslim prayers, but not more than twenty per cent., at most, have broken with their fetish. Girls are not normally promised in marriage so young as formerly and are not now forced into unwelcome unions, if they resist sufficiently strongly, lest they take refuge at the Chief Commissioner's flag. Again, the chief maintained that if a woman came to court demanding a divorce "for a good cause" only part of the husband's marriage expenses must be refunded,[6] while where she had borne him children he could in no case claim his expenses too.[7] Such "good cause," moreover, would apparently include severe and repeated beatings, failure of support, desertion, or the fact that her husband was afflicted with some grave and infectious disease. But these assertions were mitigated by the remark that the *sadaki* must always be repaid where it is the wife who demands divorce, regardless both of her justification for so doing and of the number of children she had borne him: so it is apparent that the alleged concessions in the case of a maltreated wife are, at most, of limited application. Inheritance among Tamale Muslims seems to follow the Sharī'a even less than in Yendi[8]: instead,

[1] Under Mālikī law she might or might not have been entitled to a divorce for *ḍarar* (injury), according to the circumstances.

[2] Even this, however, is distinctly doubtful, if challenged by the customary heir.

[3] i.e., questions of *ījāb, qabūl, sadaki,* etc.: see above, p. 259.

[4] More rarely.

[5] The administrative capital of the Northern Territories. As such, it has a more mixed population than Yendi.

[6] But this seems doubtful: see under Yendi above.

[7] But this statement, too, did not pass unchallenged; and it seems probable that her husband could really reclaim both, at least if and when she remarried—except where she had borne him several children, when suitable deductions would probably be made.

[8] But this may mean no more than that my informants in Yendi happened to be stricter Muslims.

the senior member of the family normally, it appears, gives something to younger males, but nothing to daughters, mothers or widows. Bequests are not unknown, and the chief asserted that they would always be enforced; but this can scarcely be true if the primary heir resists: and the local Muslims, on their part, know the rule about the bequeathable third, but never attempt to apply it.

Wa.

In Wa I unfortunately missed the Na, who was on tour. He is an Aḥmadī, and seems to be a remarkable man. Islam has been firmly established at Wa for many years[1]; but it is the presence of a strong and active Aḥmadī community which chiefly distinguishes it from every other Northern centre. In the town itself Muslims outnumber pagans, but in the surrounding countryside pagans are in the overwhelming majority: and the Wa Native Court consists of two orthodox Muslims, two Aḥmadīs and four pagans.

Marriages follow local custom, with a series of gifts to both father and bride, some of the former being widely distributed among the family: but Muslims always end with a ceremony which includes a formal contract,[2] whereat a *sadaki* of five shillings is given to the bride[3] (regardless of the customary payments, which may well amount to some £20 in all); while further expenses for entertainment, etc., follow the wife's move to her husband's house. But it is noteworthy that while the contract of marriage is never concluded before the girl is nubile, she may well have been promised in marriage in infancy; and this promise is virtually binding, for a girl who persistently refused to comply would be disowned. Muslims will marry pagan women provided the latter will make some profession of Islam, but Wa Muslims assert that they never give their daughters to non-Muslims. They also affirm that no one has more than four wives, and that the legal status of concubinage is now extinct.

On the rare occasions when men divorce their wives they first complain to their fathers-in-law, who will in turn warn their daughters. The triple formula is not unknown but is seldom used; and if this, or any other form of words, is used in anger, the marriage will be allowed to continue. A woman dissatisfied with her husband will usually run away to her father, whither her husband will in due course follow her; whereupon the affair will frequently be settled. If, however, she remains adamant, or this happens repeatedly, the husband may well divorce her or, more likely still, her father may tell him to let her marry another man, perhaps supplying him with another girl in her place. Where, on the other hand, she elopes with a lover the latter may be fined for " seduction "; but the local Muslims, in contrast to pagans,[4] claim none of this as compensation. Where, moreover, she refuses to return to her husband the question as to whether this second union is to be regarded as a valid marriage depends entirely on her father's consent: for in the last resort it is the father who is regarded as dissolving his daughter's marriage with an unsatisfactory husband and giving her in marriage to another.[5] The former husband may reclaim his expenses if he wishes (although most Muslims in Wa seem to forgo any claim in regard to kolas or entertainment, and only reclaim clothing and half the money payments), and these the father will in turn recover[6] from the second husband, as the price of his consent to the marriage. Provided the father does so consent, moreover,

[1] They have a tradition that their original ancestor came from Baghdad (!) via Mende. Two brothers are said to have set out from the latter place on pilgrimage to Mecca, but never to have got beyond Wa.

[2] i.e., *ījāb* and *qabūl*: see above.

[3] By the hand of her father or other guardian.

[4] Who use it for purification ceremonies.

[5] This clearly demonstrates the dominance of customary over Islamic law.

[6] Even in court, it seems, in Wa—unlike most other places.

a *mallam* will solemnise the subsequent union and the children, who will belong to their physiological father in any case, will be regarded as perfectly legitimate. The fact that the decision finally rests with the woman's father naturally results in a general haziness as to what precisely justifies a woman in seeking divorce.[1] The *'idda* of widowhood is rigidly observed, but not that of divorce: if, however, a second husband finds his wife to be pregnant, he will always, it seems, if a Muslim, send her away; while a mother's statement as to the paternity of her children is regarded as final. The custody of the children of divorced parents may be claimed by the father after they are weaned; but in practice they usually stay with their mother a little longer, while the latter may take them, so long as her right of custody lasts, wherever she likes.[2]

Cases of inheritance seldom come to court at all; and never, it seems, from the Muslim community. Instead, all is settled within the family, and customary law in practice prevails. Thus the senior member of the family succeeds to all except clothing, which usually goes to the children. Wives remain in the custody of their deceased husbands' brothers, but a new contract is needed if they want to marry them; and this is no longer *de rigeur*. Succession by patronage is recognised, in default of natural heirs[3]; but no bequests are known, except that of a daughter in marriage. And it may be added that the orthodox all profess to follow the Tijānīya Ṣūfī brotherhood; that they observe the 'Aqīqa[4]; that both males and females are circumcised; but that the Zār[5] is apparently unknown.

The Aḥmadīya movement started in Wa when one of the "orthodox", Ṣāliḥu by name, went to Saltpond on business, was converted, and returned to Wa as an Aḥmadī in about 1933. The orthodox regard them as Muslims in appearance only; and where a husband turns Aḥmadī, his wife's father will give her the option of following her husband or being married to another man. This provides a good example of the way in which a woman's father in Wa takes the place properly occupied by the court. The Aḥmadīs in Wa are thus an off-shoot of the mission in Saltpond.[6] They number some two hundred and thirty men, have their own Indian missionary, their own school and mosque, and pay considerable deference to their founder and leader, Ṣāliḥu. On the whole, moreover, they seem to observe Islamic law rather more strictly than do the orthodox, but coloured, of course, by their own tenets. Where they marry non-Aḥmadīs they follow the usual local customs, but when they intermarry they profess to follow " Islamic law "—which seems to amount to adding a substantial *sadaki* (of from £3 to £6) to the customary preliminaries, and includes, of course, a ceremony at which a formal contract is concluded.

With regard to divorce Ṣāliḥu and my other informants were far from lucid. Normally, it seems, a man who wants to divorce his wife must not only inform her family but also the Aḥmadī leader: and without the latter's permission the divorce will not, apparently, be recognised. But Ṣāliḥu was very vague about such points as the triple divorce, its rules and application. Again, where it is the woman who demands divorce, consultations between the parents and Ṣāliḥu are also needed. In the last resort, however, the decision of the girl's father will apparently prevail, as among the orthodox: but the husband may recover

[1] A consideration which is largely alien to customary law in any case: see below.
[2] See above p. 262, note (1).
[3] See above, p. 262.
[4] On the eighth day after a baby's birth a meeting is held in the house of the head of the family. A sacrifice is made; and the baby's hair is shaved, weighed against silver, and then buried. Cp. Naming Ceremonies elsewhere.
[5] A procedure, animistic in origin, practised in many Muslim lands in order to exorcise the evil spirit which is regarded as having taken possession of some individual. It is usually confined to women.
[6] See below, pp. 283 f.

both expenses and *sadaki*, largely without regard for his own behaviour, where dissolution of marriage is at the instance of the wife. The only difference, then, seems to be that where an Aḥmadī woman insists on leaving her husband without justification (such as his impotence, failure to maintain her, sexual desertion, cruel ill-treatment, etc.) she is liable to be turned out of the Aḥmadī community.

In cases of adultery Aḥmadīs, as others, go to the native courts, although they profess a desire that the British would allow them to impose the full law of Islam.[1] Where the woman refuses to return to her husband all depends, as with the orthodox, on her father's attitude; for where he consents to the second union and repays the husband's disbursements the latter is recognised as a valid marriage. Where he does not consent, on the other hand, the Aḥmadīs assert that the parties will somehow be separated. The *'idda* of widowhood is as usual observed, and the Aḥmadīs apparently try to insist on that of divorce also; while the custody of children goes to the father after weaning, which Ṣāliḥu believes to be the law of Islam.[2]

In intestate succession Ṣāliḥu is, it seems, usually called in to divide the estate. But he himself is very vague regarding the details of Islamic law in this respect. When in doubt he claims to consult his headquarters at Saltpond[3]; while any case of dispute would go to the native court and be decided by customary law. In practice, however, it seems that Aḥmadī families compromise between custom and rudimentary Islamic law in such matters. Bequests, apparently, are not unknown; but Ṣāliḥu is none too sure of the relevant rules, except that bequests must not be made, e.g., to a son.

One interesting case of which I heard in Wa concerned an Aḥmadī convicted of adultery who was sentenced by the Wa-Na, his co-religionist, to the maximum penalty which the court was competent to inflict, on the grounds that he should properly have been executed by stoning. The District Commissioner, not unnaturally, considered this unfair, since it greatly exceeded the usual penalty and amounted to a religious rather than a customary punishment: and I understand that a compromise was reached by which the penalty was reduced, although still left higher than usual.[4]

Larabanga

When we turn to the Gonja areas, which extend right across the Northern Territories further south, from Kpembe to Bole, we find that Islamic law exercises even less influence, except in the market town of Prang, where it is stronger than anywhere else in the Gold Coast. But before turning to Kpembe and Bole the interesting village of Larabanga, some ten miles west of Damongo, in the north of the Gonja areas, demands passing reference. In this village the population is solidly and exclusively Muslim, although the surrounding countryside is almost entirely pagan. The chief, the *limam*, the *mallams* and village elders told me that they traced their origin to "Madina"—i.e., one of the numerous towns of that name in the Mende district; that their village had been Muslim as long as memory went back; and that all their people believed in the God of Islam, while none followed any local fetish. The nearest native court is at Damongo and is, of course, pagan; but the village headman settles all minor disputes. In these circumstances it was both surprising and instructive to discover that Islamic law seems to be almost completely disregarded in Larabanga, in all but certain matters of ritual.

[1] i.e., death by stoning, in the case of an offender who has ever enjoyed a valid marriage, and a beating, in the case of one who has never enjoyed married life.

[2] See above, p. 262, note (1).

[3] Or, more probably, the local Indian missionary.

[4] Which may be regarded as an instance of the African *penchant* for compromise in such matters, however dubiously the purist may regard it.

Thus prayers are said at a wedding ceremony but, unlike the practice among Muslims elsewhere, there is no formal contract of marriage[1] and no formal "*sadaki*" (although various customary gifts and payments are, of course, made). The men never, it seems, divorce their wives; while wives wanting divorce simply inform their husbands and, if attempts at conciliation fail, that is that, regardless of justification or any refund of expenses.[2] No *'idda* of divorce is observed, and a wife who goes straight from one husband to another will observe no restrictions, but the union will none the less be recognised as valid.[3] Children go to the physiological father, and the woman's word is accepted as final in this matter. But an injured husband may, of course, always prosecute one who has "seduced" his wife in the Damongo Native Court, where the offender will be duly fined. The custody of children may be claimed by the father after weaning, although here as elsewhere they are often in practice left with the mother until the age of six or seven. But not even the *'idda* of widowhood is here observed, and a widow may remarry as soon as her husband's "funeral custom" is complete, which may, apparently, vary, according to circumstances, from about one month to one year after his death. The property of one who dies goes to his nearest male kinsman: no one else will take, except as a sort of gratuity from the primary successor; and bequests are quite unknown.

The solitary indications which I could find that Islamic law exerts the slightest influence in Larabanga except in ritual was that its inhabitants never, they say, give their daughters in marriage to outsiders, while when they marry pagan woman the latter always make some profession of Islam. None, again, seem to have more than four wives. The headman alone confessed to having a concubine, whose parents, he said, had been bought by his father: so she might be regarded as "legal" on the Nigerian model,[4] although it seems extremely doubtful if he would have had any scruples in this respect.

Kpembe, Salaga and Bole.

In the area of jurisdiction of the Kpembe Native Court there are many Muslims, for the market town of Salaga, with its immigrant Muslim elements from Hausaland and elsewhere, is close at hand. Islam, in fact, is here spreading rapidly, through the preaching of certain *mallams* who extol the future bliss of those who observe the ritual prayers. In Bole, on the other hand, there is less Hausa influence. But throughout the Gonja areas Islam is largely confined to the towns and paganism reigns supreme in the countryside; for Christianity has made little headway, as yet, in the Northern Territories. In both Kpembe and Bole marriage customs follow the general Gonja pattern among both Muslims and pagans, except that Muslims include a final ceremony which comprises both prayers and a formal marriage contract, while a special "*sadaki*" payment is added to the customary gifts and other disbursements. This ceremony never takes place before the bride is nubile; but a promise of marriage is often made almost from birth and becomes virtually binding by the series of gifts and payments which follow, and only if the girl proved exceptionally stubborn, or the father himself had cause to change his mind, could the marriage be avoided by a full refund of these disbursements. Where a Muslim marries a pagan woman she usually makes some profession of Islam,[5] while Muslim girls are not normally given in marriage to non-Muslims except in the case of close

[1] i.e., no proper *ījāb* and *qabūl.*

[2] Or, of course, such judgment of court as Islamic law demands.

[3] Which is wildly contrary to Mālikī law.

[4] i.e., concubinage between a man and his own ex-slaves, or another's ex-slave "given" to him by her "owner" for the purpose. See p. 215.

[5] Failing which the stricter Muslims would regard the marriage as invalid, although it would be perfectly valid in customary law.

relations, and even then the purists profess to regard the children as illegitimate[1]: but this makes little or no difference in practice.

On the rare occasions when men divorce their wives the usual method is to inform their parents and swear an oath—a method used when the wife is held to have been gravely at fault and no compensation is paid to her. Very occasionally, however, the husband, it seems, will offer some form of compensation, whereupon the divorce is not regarded as valid until this is paid.[2] The triple formula is little used; and reconciliation is always regarded as possible.

Where it is the woman who wants to end the marriage she will, as elsewhere, normally either abscond to her father or elope with another man. The Kpembe Court members alleged, however, that should a woman demand divorce from the court this would be granted if she had adequate cause, but that the husband might still reclaim his expenses, on her remarriage at least. Where she absconds to her father the husband will commonly take no action, except attempts at conciliation, until she remarries[3]; while where she elopes with a lover the latter may be summoned and fined for "sexual connection with" or "seduction of" another man's wife (according, it seems, to whether she subsequently returns to her husband or not), and in Gonja even Muslim husbands commonly take part of this fine by way of damages. Where she refuses to return to her husband, moreover, the latter may recover his marriage expenses from her father, who will normally re-imburse himself by making her lover provide these as the price for authorising their marriage. Where the woman has borne children, however, a husband may not always be allowed to claim a full refund; while in Bole it seems that in the past at least he would sometimes refrain from claiming any financial refund but demand instead the first issue of the new union, which would frequently be granted him.[4] The *'idda* of divorce is not observed, and a woman who elopes with a paramour can always, it seems, get her position regularised by arranging the repayment of her husband's marriage expenses through her father: thereupon the strictest *mallam* will apparently solemnise the new marriage, regardless of any formal divorce. In Kpembe, however, the court members allege that they take no interest in the actual "*sadaki*", as a specifically Islamic payment, but leave it to the *limam* to advise on this point[5]; while they also maintain that they would not allow a woman to claim a divorce while pregnant. Some of the *mallams* of Salaga, moreover, profess that they try to insist on three months' delay between the end of one marriage and the solemnisation of another, and that where a woman has good grounds to claim divorce (the impotence of her husband, failure of maintenance, unjustifiable ill-treatment, etc.) no refund whatever is really due; but these are voices crying in the wilderness. Similarly the Muslims of Bole maintain that where a woman complains of ill-treatment the *limam* will caution her husband and, if this recurs repeatedly, will declare the marriage dissolved, allegedly without any refund[6]; and that the native court will uphold this. It may also be noted in passing that adultery or "sexual

[1] Except where one of them is given to the wife's father to bring up in the faith, when he is regularly regarded as legitimate.

[2] I was told that this method is common in Cape Coast and not unknown in Salaga. But it seems somewhat odd—as the very reverse of the Islamic *khul'*—and probably represents the "send-off" money of Fante customary law.

[3] This is partly in order not to close the door to reconciliation, and partly because he feels that a father-in-law who has not encouraged his daughter's action is not to blame and should not be embarassed until he is in a position to come down, in his turn, on a new suitor.

[4] And much the same used to be true of a woman promised to one man who ran off with another, for in the past the promisee could claim a child or children of the union. Today, however, children commonly go to their physiological father.

[5] *Sed quaere.* This is certainly not true of Bole.

[6] But it seems doubtful if the native court would uphold this point, anyway: some of my informants, moreover, obviously disagreed with the *limam* in this opinion, which was probably a dictum from the books.

connection " may be proved by testimony to the couple being alone in a room or by the production of articles of their clothing, etc.; that the woman escapes all official punishment in such cases; that the *'idda* of widowhood, unlike that of divorce, is regularly observed; and that the custody of the children of divorced couples may be claimed by the father after the period of suckling.

Inheritance, again, normally goes by customary law, even among Muslims. Such cases scarcely ever come to court, however, for they are regularly settled among the family: so the " immigrant " elements in Salaga may sometimes, perhaps, follow the books. Bequests are not, it seems, unknown, for in Kpembe a man will sometimes specify, e.g., who is to succeed him[1] (although bequests to strangers do not, it appears, occur), while in Bole bequests are allegedly allowed[2] without regard for the " bequeathable third ": only among the immigrant Muslims in Salaga are the Islamic rules both known and, possibly, observed. In Bole, at least, the levirate marriage of widows used to be compulsory and is still extremely common; but today a widow who is sufficiently determined to avoid such a marriage can always appeal to a British administrative officer.

Prang.

It is only in Prang, it seems, that Islamic law has to some degree come into its own. Here the foreign influence of Hausa and other immigrant elements is strong, and while the Pranghene is a pagan the present President of the Native Authority is himself a definite Muslim. The town is, in fact, divided into an indigenous and pagan group under the Pranghene, and a largely immigrant and Muslim community under the " Chief ".[3] And it is the latter who presides over the native court, with the help of the Pranghene in pagan cases—whence, of course, the unique influence of Islamic law in Prang.

Marriages, as usual, follow local custom, with the Islamic additions common to the Muslims of the Northern Territories. All marriages in Prang, it seems, are informally " registered,"[4] and all gifts, payments, etc., recorded in writing. Should a promised marriage be cancelled at the last moment at the instance of the bride or her family all disbursements may be reclaimed; while where it is the groom who defaults half the *sadaki* (only) must, apparently, be refunded.[5] But any marriage by compulsion is said to be rare.

Where a husband pronounces the triple divorce, even in anger, the Muslim leaders regard this as final and any continuance of the relationship as a sin. Where, on the other hand, a woman wants a divorce she will make application to the Chief,[6] accompanied by a fee of one guinea. Attempts will then be made by both the Chief and his *limam* to reconcile the parties; but if the woman proves obdurate the Chief will eventually decide the matter. Where he considers she has good cause for her demand (e.g. maltreatment after warning, or being left without either maintenance or any address to which correspondence might be addressed) he will allegedly grant a divorce without any refund; but in all other circumstances both *sadaki* and other disbursements may be reclaimed. My informants, however, were somewhat vague on points of detail. Again, the *'idda* of both widowhood and divorce is here alleged to be observed, while " mixed " marriages are apparently unknown (except where the non-Muslim party is prepared to profess Islam). Adultery, on the other hand, is treated exactly as elsewhere, and compensation is claimed even by Muslim husbands.

---

[1] Which specification, while not binding on the family, will be accorded due weight in their choice of the primary successor.

[2] Among the Gonja ruling caste.

[3] i.e., the President of the Native Authority.

[4] i.e., jotted down by the Chief, not registered under the Ordinance.

[5] If already paid in full; presumably on analogy, or by confusion, with divorce after the contract but before consummation.

[6] i.e., in this instance, the President of the Native Authority—at least among Muslim litigants.

Where a Muslim dies the *limam* will, it seems, often be called in to record his estate and divide it on Islamic principles, which I found to be well-known and understood by local leaders. Bequests, moreover, are sometimes made, and here too the orthodox rules are professedly applied. Should a brother, for example, challenge the distribution of an estate on Islamic principles on the ground that he alone was the customary successor, the Chief would apparently question the *limam* and then, in regard to members of the Muslim community, uphold his decision.

The points, then, in which the Prang Native Court will apply Islamic law, in litigation between Muslim litigants, where other native courts in the Northern Territories would not normally do so, may be summarised as follows: (1) that a genuinely misused wife will apparently be granted a divorce without repayment; (2) that the *'idda* of divorce is allegedly enforced (and as a consequence, presumably, of both these considerations, it is noteworthy that in Prang Muslim women who desire divorce seem far more frequently than elsewhere to apply to the court rather than simply abscond to their fathers or elope with their lovers); (3) that the orthodox rules concerning both testate and intestate succession are apparently not only followed in private by the stricter Muslims but even upheld by the court.

To all these points parallels may, indeed, be found in the Zongos[1] of the major towns of Ashanti and the Colony. The difference is that in Prang the statutory court powers have been given to the immigrant Zongo people, not to the autochthonous or "native" Prangs. So instead of the Prang court enforcing the Zongo headman's decisions the latter himself gives the formal judgment of the court.[2] All the same, the precise juristic basis for such application of Islamic law as the Prang court may in fact administer is a matter for speculation. In the Native Courts (Northern Territories) Ordinance there is no clause authorising these courts to apply "any other law binding between the parties"—whatever that phrase may be held to mean in the Native Courts Ordinances of the Colony and Southern Togoland— so it must clearly be applied on the basis of native law and custom. But the Ordinance only authorises native courts to apply the native law "prevalent in the area of their jurisdiction": and it seems extremely unlikely that the immigrant community of Prang, large and influential although it is, could properly be said to have succeeded in making their customary law "prevalent"[3] within the area served by the court. It would seem, then, that a form of words similar to that employed in the Courts Ordinance, section 74 (1)—i.e., "any native law or custom existing" within the area of the court's jurisdiction—would much more satisfactorily cover what must be regarded as a perfectly reasonable and salutory practice.

Ashanti

In Ashanti Islam is even weaker than in the Northern Territories, for here it is Christianity which constitutes the chief challenge to paganism. The Muslim elements may be said to fall into four different categories. The most influential of all are those colonies of immigrants from the Northern Territories, Nigeria and French territory which form the Zongos in all the major towns; next, there are certain sections of the Banda tribe settled in northern Ashanti (but with roots still farther north) elements of which have become Muslims and are to be found in Wenchi, Kintampo and elsewhere; while there are also small groups of Akan[4]

---

[1] Suburbs or quarters occupied by immigrants.

[2] In so far as this is an apt description of the award of any native court. See pp. 280 f.

[3] If this is to be interpreted in the sense of being dominant, rather than merely to exist. *Sed quaere.*

[4] The Akan comprise about ninety per cent. of the one million inhabitants of Ashanti and about seventy-five per cent. of the two million in the Colony. They are matrilineal, by contrast, e.g., with the Ga, who are primarily, but not wholly, patrilineal.

converts both to the Aḥmadīya movement, who form a community of their own, and also to orthodox Islam, most of whom seem to become more or less identified with the Zongo communities. It will be possible, then, to give a fairly comprehensive account of the application of Islamic law in Ashanti, such as it is, by reference to four different localities—namely Kintampo, Wenchi, Obuasi and Kumasi.

Kintampo

In the town of Kintampo the majority of the population are Muslims, although there are few such in the surrounding countryside. Their predominance in Kintampo itself is chiefly due to the large number of Hausa, Dagbamba and Wangara[1] immigrants. All are " orthodox " Mālikīs, and a large number follow the Tijānīya Ṣūfī brotherhood.

Arrangements for marriage, as in the north, follow tribal customs, but all Muslims also observe a ceremony on the day when the bride is to go to her husband's home, which includes prayers, a triple repetition of a formal offer and acceptance and specific mention of a "*sadaki*" (usually, in Kintampo, £1 2s. 0d.) which is additional to the customary gifts and payments. This never happens before the girl is nubile, but often when she is still very young: and although girls are frequently promised in marriage at a very tender age, they may, apparently, today resist the union if sufficiently determined, as a result of British influence and possible interference.

Men occasionally divorce their wives, but seldom follow any set formula; and reconciliation is always, it seems, considered allowable. Where it is the woman who is dissatisfied she may either send one guinea to the headman, or " *sarki* ", with a request for divorce[2], or simply abscond. In the former case the headman will call the parties together and attempt conciliation. Where this succeeds he will advise the husband to refund the wife's guinea, while where the woman remains adamant he will try to arrange a divorce: but nearly always, it seems, the wife will have to refund the husband's marriage expenses, except that if he is impotent half only are regarded as returnable, while some reduction, at least, may be made where he has failed to support her (but not, apparently, where she complains of beating or sexual desertion). Where, on the other hand, the woman simply absconds, her husband will usually approach her father to try to get her back. Thereafter the issue rests largely in her father's hands, for he may either send her back to her husband or support her refusal to return; while if he refunds the husband's expenses, either at once or when he can himself recover them from a new suitor, the marriage is regarded as dissolved. Occasionally, however, a husband will appeal to the headman in such cases, and it will then be for him to declare that the former's marriage expenses must be repaid, either at once or if, and when, the woman finds another suitor. But the headman, of course, has no power to enforce such decisions, which must be referred to the nearest native court in case of need.

The *'idda* of widowhood is faithfully observed in the vast majority of cases, as in the north, but that of divorce very seldom. There are recognised " fees "[3] for seduction, etc.; while the children begotten by a lover technically belong to the husband unless or until he accepts the refund of his expenses: but the British are regarded as opposed to children being allotted to other than their physiological fathers. Inheritance is arranged within the family, but the senior member normally succeeds; while bequests are, it seems, unrestricted in their

[1] The Hausa name for Mandingo.

[2] For a discussion of such " arbitration fees ", see p. 280 below.

[3] Not fines, as in the Northern Territories, for here only sexual connection with a chief's wife, or with a wife whose marriage has been registered, is a criminal offence: cp. p. 261, note (3).

scope, to heirs or strangers, on the principle that a man may do what he likes with his property—possibly under the influence of English law.

Wenchi

In Wenchi there is a native court which includes the headman of the Zongo, a Banda Muslim, as one of its members, but applies customary law to all litigants; while the Zongo as usual comprises immigrants from the Northern Territories and elsewhere, but also a considerable Banda element.[1] Marriages among Muslims follow much the pattern described above, but the whole Muslim community commonly attends the prayers and formal contract[2] on the final day, while a *sadaki* of twelve shillings is handed to the bride's father on her behalf. " Mixed " marriages are said to occur only between Muslims and such non-Muslim women as are prepared to make some profession of Islam. No marriage, moreover, is concluded before the bride reaches puberty, but girls are sometimes virtually forced to fulfil promises made on their behalf in infancy: otherwise, of course, a full refund must be made of all marriage gifts and payments.

Where a husband wishes to divorce his wife he merely tells her that he no longer wants her, which he usually repeats three times; but where he afterwards thinks better of it the marriage may be continued provided he observes certain rites (allegedly because he " acted under the influence of Satan "). Where it is the woman who wants divorce she will normally abscond to her father: then, if efforts to arrange matters prove abortive, an appeal may be made to the Zongo headman, who is prepared, where all else fails, to declare the marriage dissolved. Should the husband have proved impotent no refund is, it seems, incumbent, while in cases of ill-treatment (such as failure of support, sexual desertion, or cruel beating) the *sadaki* and some three garments are alone reclaimable: but in all other circumstances a full refund may be demanded. Where, moreover, a husband goes away and cannot be traced, the headman says that he and his elders will declare the marriage dissolved, at the request of the wife, after about three months' delay.[3] If, on the other hand, the wife elopes with another man, the case will usually be taken to the native court, where her paramour will be made to pay the suitable " fee "; while if she refuses to return to her husband he may demand a refund of all his expenses from her father—who will endeavour to recoup himself from the other man, but not by formal litigation. A child begotten by the paramour technically belongs to the husband, unless the latter's expenses are refunded before its birth. Both the *'idda* of widowhood and of divorce are said to be observed, but my informants appeared vague about the latter.[4]

Inheritance by customary law among the Akan goes first to the maternal brother,[5] and then to the maternal nephew. Akan Muslims largely follow this, while with others, particularly immigrants from the north, either the paternal brother or eldest son is the primary successor (the choice between these largely turning on how far the brothers had worked together in partnership, and other family considerations). When the family has reached agreement this will be approved by the Zongo headman; while in case of dispute he alleges that he will himself distribute the estate according to Islamic law. In such cases the customary successor could sometimes, perhaps, successfully assert his right in the native court, particularly if an Akan convert; but in others the headman's decision would be upheld. This is an interesting instance of the fact that native courts

[1] There are also a few local converts to orthodox Islam.

[2] Each part of which is repeated three times.

[3] For the capacity in which a Zongo headman acts in this way, see pp. 278, 9 below.

[4] The length of which they identified with that of the former!

[5] Or, technically, first to the mother herself, and then—as almost always in practice—to the uterine brother or nephew.

are usually perfectly prepared to enforce the customary law of an immigrant community, in spite of the narrow definition of the native law and custom which they are authorised to administer under the Native Courts Ordinances[1]; while it is also noteworthy that they often see nothing incongruous in varying the local customary law in the case of converts, particularly when a whole family has adopted Islam, since the concept of special family customs is in no sense alien to their mode of thought. As for testamentary dispositions, these are not unknown, particularly in the form of a designation of the primary successor[2]: but while the Sharīʻa is neither known nor applied in this matter, no excessive bequest to a stranger would, it seems, be enforced.

Files which I perused included the following points of interest regarding " complaints " lodged with the District Commissioner.

(1). Dated 18.5.50. A girl was promised in marriage in infancy, and was subsequently contracted in marriage by her grandfather against her will and without her knowledge. This marriage had never been consummated, and the woman eventually bore a child to a lover: but the husband still refused to release her. The case was referred to the Zongo headman, who held that the husband had been at fault in ignoring her and failing to support her for four years, and proceeded to dissolve the marriage.

(2). Dated 27.7.50. A woman alleged that her husband " forced me and shaved the hairs of my head with razor which results brought the marriage to an end before the headman Kintampo, and two days after the marriage separation (he) claimed all the personal properties he bought for me and . . . my mother." She thereupon insisted that it had been decided in 1935[3] " in the Ashanti Confederacy Council that any person who divorce his wife has no right to claim personal effects from the woman, except gold trinkets, gold chain, gold ear-rings, etc., and not personal effects such as this . . . "

(3). Dated 22.9.50. A wife claimed that she had been treated " as a slave " and not supported by her husband, who had already recovered his effects. The marriage was thereupon dissolved by the headman, and the wife's re-marriage approved.

It should be added that this method of bringing a " complaint " to the District Commissioner is often adopted, as free of all charge, in preference to litigation in the native court—especially among immigrants whose customs are different from those known to the court members. Where the complaint concerns some matter of marriage, divorce or inheritance concerning Northerners, or other immigrants, the probability is that the District Commissioner will write a note to the appropriate headman asking him to investigate the matter; and in the vast

---

[1] See p. 253 above.

[2] Which, among the Akan, would be given due weight, but not regarded as binding and conclusive, by the family concerned.

[3] This presumably refers to the recommendations of a committee, " adopted and accepted " by the third meeting of the Ashanti Confederacy Council, that where a husband divorces his wife he should have no claim to the return of "any article of dress, nor money given for maintenance or funeral expenses "—but only of valuable trinkets or debts. But this was not, it seems, given any legislative authority until the Ashanti (Declaration of Native Customary Law) Order, 1946 (schedule), sect. 3 of which confined itself to cases where a husband divorced his wife on the grounds of her repeated acts of adultery, and specified that even in such circumstances " any properties given her during the marriage shall be claimable; these properties, however, should not include such articles or apparels and gifts given by the man to the woman or to her relatives, nor should they include monies spent on maintenance as donations given her or to any of her relatives on the death of the woman's relatives ". But this again was subsequently interpreted to mean that gifts such as a house, cocoa farm, or money (other than money for maintenance) *can* be recovered. See *A Digest of the Minutes of the Ashanti Confederacy Council*, by J. N. Matson, pp. 24, 45 and 25.

majority of cases there the matter ends, as all accept the headman's ruling. Should one of the parties prove recalcitrant, however, the District Commissioner might try to induce him to be reasonable; but where he persists the case must, of course, go to the native court, as the District Commissioner has no original jurisdiction in such cases. But the native court will itself normally uphold the headman's decision in such circumstances[1]; while there is always a right of appeal from the judgment of the native court to the District Commissioner,[2] who in the Gold Coast is in no way debarred from taking cases of marriage, divorce and inheritance on appeal, and who would no doubt normally support the appropriate headman's ruling.

Obuasi

In Obuasi and its district the Muslim elements in the population fall into two clear-cut divisions: the inhabitants of the Zongo, who are immigrants from the Northern Territories or even further afield,[3] and a few local converts to the Aḥmadīya movement, mostly living in a village about six miles outside Obuasi town.

The Zongo headman (himself a Wangara, or Mandingo) and his elders confirmed that their marriage customs included the formal contract and the *sadaki* common among Muslims elsewhere; that marriages were never solemnised until the bride was nubile; and that a girl promised in infancy could nowadays resist the marriage later (whereupon pre-marital payments and gifts must, of course, be returned). No " mixed " marriages, it seems, occur. Men sometimes divorce their wives, but use no special formulae: instead they inform the headman, who will summon and inform the woman. Where it is the wife who desires release she may appeal to the headman, who will call her husband and try to reconcile them: if, however, she insists, the marriage will in all cases, it seems, ultimately be dissolved. Should the husband have proved impotent[4] half his expenses, only, are reclaimable; where he has failed to feed or clothe her none,[5] it seems, may be reclaimed; while in all other cases, including complaints of beating, etc., all expenses (except the fee for the prayers said at the wedding ceremony and the cost of hospitality thereat) may be demanded. If, on the other hand, the woman simply runs away with another man the husband will complain to the headman who will tell the paramour to pay the husband two guineas; while, where the woman refuses to return to him, he will also, it seems, dissolve the marriage and order the suitable refund.[6]

Not only the *'idda* of widowhood is strictly observed but also, apparently, that of divorce.[7] Where, moreover, a woman bears a child to her lover without her former marriage being dissolved the child is regarded as belonging to her husband.[8] Problems of inheritance are nearly always settled within the family, but any dispute would be taken to the Zongo headman and his *limam,* who profess to follow Islamic law but are blissfully vague about its details. Bequests, too, are not unknown and are allegedly enforced without restriction, if made in health and not in fear of death.

Among the Akan converts to the Aḥmadīya movement the ordinary Akan marriage payments are followed but an Islamic *sadaki* added, together with

[1] Although there is no authority for this in the Native Courts (Ashanti) Ordinance: see above, p. 253.

[2] Except in land cases.

[3] e.g., Hausa, Wangara (originally from French territory), Dagbamba, Moshi, Zabrama, Yoruba, etc.

[4] After, it seems, three months of medical treatment.

[5] But there was some hesitation on this point.

[6] For the capacity in which the headman assumes these powers, see below, pp. 278, 9.

[7] *Sed quaere.* This probably differs from community to community.

[8] But it seems doubtful if this can be enforced.

suitable prayers and a formal marriage contract. If for any reason a promised marriage is not in fact concluded all pre-marital gifts and payments may be reclaimed in full. Where, however, a marriage is consummated and the wife subsequently demands divorce it seems that this will be granted among the Akan, quite regardless of the question of adequate justification, without any refund except of articles of dress, valuable trinkets still undamaged, or a loan[1]—in the case of both Muslims and non-Muslims alike: the only difference is that these Aḥmadī converts affirm that the specifically Islamic *sadaki* must be repaid if the wife has no adequate reason for her demand.[2] Where, moreover, she commits adultery her paramour is liable to pay a "fee"[3] and she herself to make a "pacification" payment[4] under customary law: and this, too, applies to Muslims and non-Muslims alike. If she subsequently refuses to return to her husband the marriage may be dissolved by a pronouncement by or before her family elders[5]; while children will in any case be regarded as members of her family, owing to the matrilineal structure of society (although their father may be entitled to custody, if he has asserted his claim in customary form, and provided that they are not too young to leave their mother). Where, again, she simply absconds to her father the husband will complain and the family will investigate the matter, while she may even be made to swear an oath regarding her fidelity[6] (and if she confesses to adultery no divorce will be granted until she has helped her husband to collect the adultery fee); but in other circumstances the decision of the family council of arbitration will constitute divorce. A widow used formerly almost always to be married by an heir, provided they were both of the same religion[7]: and, while this is much less common today, in such cases no new payments are required, although Muslims allege that they will meet to bless the new union, which they regard as constituting a new contract of marriage. No intercourse, however, must take place for forty days after the husband's demise. If, however, the woman persistently refuses this levirate marriage she is nowadays usually allowed to marry another, after the same period of forty days. And the *'idda* of divorce is equally disregarded, except that a woman who is known to be pregnant may not normally remarry before delivery.

Succession among the Akan is matrilineal, the maternal brother being the primary successor.[8] It seems, however, that the members of the Obuasi Native Court make a partial exception in the case of Muslims, for they assured me that while two-thirds of the estate must go to the customary successor, even among Muslims, one-third would be granted to the eldest son, if himself a Muslim, or

---

[1] See Digest of Minutes of the Ashanti Confederacy Council, p. 24. My informants simply stated that the husband's "expenses" were not reclaimable.

[2] i.e., unless her husband is impotent or she has been cruelly ill-treated (or left without support).

[3] See Native Courts (Offences under Native Law and Custom) Order No. 7 of 1935, as amended by Order No. 24 of 1943. And it is noteworthy that according to Akan custom an adultery fee may be claimed by a man to whom a girl was promised in marriage in infancy (and who had made the suitable payments), even if she had refused to cohabit, every time she has intimacy with another man. Nowadays, however, this is commonly limited to twice (see Ashanti (Declaration of Native Customary Law) Order, 1946, schedule, sect. 2—quoted at p. 26 of the Digest of Minutes of the Ashanti Confederacy Council)—after which she is apparently deemed a prostitute. As soon as the promised husband accepts a refund of his expenses, however, she is free to marry another.

[4] This usually consists of a chicken and some eggs and is paid only by way of reconciliation; i.e., not in cases where the adultery is not condoned and divorce follows. But divorce will not affect the paramour's liability for the adultery fee.

[5] And if she is adamant she will always, it seems, ultimately get her way in this matter.

[6] See the Wives Fidelity Declaration (Confederacy) Order, 1949. (Digest of Minutes of the Ashanti Confederacy Council, p. 44.)

[7] i.e., both Muslims or both non-Muslims.

[8] See pp. 270 and 272 above.

would be divided among such sons of different mothers as were all Muslims.[1] As for bequests, the normal Akan custom seems to be for the testator to call the family together, explain his wishes, secure their agreement,[2] and celebrate this with rum, whereupon the bequest becomes binding: provided the family agree, then, there is no limit on a man's testamentary power, and this appears to be applicable to Muslims and non-Muslims alike. Where, however, a written will is made in the English form individual, as opposed to family, property may, perhaps, be bequeathed without restriction.[3]

It is noteworthy in this connexion that an African Judge of the Supreme Court in Kumasi, whom I questioned about the statement of the members of the Obuasi Native Court regarding the compromise which they adopt in the case of an Akan Muslim who dies intestate, confirmed that he would uphold this compromise, on appeal, as an equitable arrangement, on the basis that an adoption of the Islamic form of marriage, with its attendant *sadaki*, showed the parties' consent to some curtailment of ordinary customary law.[4] This was in marked contrast to the attitude taken by the same Judge regarding Akan Christians whose marriage, not being under the Marriage Ordinance, had been "blessed" by the church; for in this case he holds customary law alone to be applicable, regardless of any variation or compromise supported by the churches. Where, of course, a Muslim has registered his marriage under the Marriage of Muhammadans Ordinance, any dispute regarding his estate would be governed by Islamic law throughout.[5] He was also inclined to hold that in cases of divorce a *mallam's* view might be accepted as to whether the specifically Islamic "*sadaki*" was properly reclaimable in the circumstances, whereas customary payments must be governed by customary law: even so, however, the native law and custom of the parties, not of the Akan, was applicable in regard to the Zongo communities, and this might approximate more closely to Islamic law.[6] It is also noteworthy that the concept of "family" property is far more developed in Ashanti than in the Northern Territories, and that any property which is passed by intestate succession *ipso facto* becomes "family," however much it may have been self-acquired by the deceased; that the customary successor takes as trustee for the family as a whole; and that where, in old Akan custom, there was no customary successor of free blood, the children of a slave wife—but not, of course, of a free wife—would inherit as "adopted" members of their father's family: while a master had a right to the property of a deceased "domestic" (i.e. descendant of a former slave in the female line), but would not usually exercise this where the "domestic" had descendants.[7] It is, however, surprisingly difficult to get a clear-cut answer regarding customary law from, e.g., the members of a native court even on a point of common occurrence with which they must often have dealt: and it is a matter for speculation whether this is because they are unused to conscious reasoning on principle and commonly

[1] The introduction of some such provision for the Akan in general has been much debated: see Digest of Minutes of the Ashanti Confederacy Council, pp. 26, 27.

[2] On the basis that property is "family" rather than individual. Where the item concerned is purely individual this agreement may, perhaps, be dispensed with, but the rest of the procedure is apposite.

[3] But this is contested by many.

[4] He said that he would not, however, uphold the application of Islamic law in full, even should a native court decree this.

[5] See p. 250 above—except, presumably, in the case of a will made in the English form.

[6] It has, however, been seen above that there is no legislative authority in Ashanti—by contrast, perhaps, with the Colony and Southern Togoland—for this very reasonable proposition: see pp. 253-4, 273, etc.

[7] This still applies today in the native courts, but not in the Supreme Court (where the right of the master has been held to be contrary to equity and also to the Slavery Ordinances).

arrive at their conclusions only after such mutual argument as prompts them to apply principles which are basic to their thinking but not wholly articulate, whether they deliberately avoid any such general statement as would hinder them from treating each successive case *ad hoc*[1] without laying themselves open to a charge of inconsistency, or whether—and this seems the most probable view—the concept of arbitration and conciliation is so fundamental in native litigation that it seems almost impossible to give an abstract and general rule divorced from particular considerations.

Kumasi.

The Kumasi Zongo includes Hausa, Yoruba, Moshi, Fulani, Wangara, Dagbamba, Zabrama and other elements. Some of these come from the Northern Territories, and some from Nigeria and French territory; while most make some profession of Islam. Each community has its own headman, while the senior headman of the whole Zongo[2] is a Hausa. There are also a few Ashanti Muslims in Kumasi. At least three-quarters of all the Muslim elements are "orthodox" Mālikīs (and most are also attached to the Tijānīya Ṣūfī brotherhood); but there is also a considerable Aḥmadī following.

The practice regarding marriages is very much as described above, allowing for differences of detail between the different tribes. Muslims always, it seems, observe a ceremony on the day when the bride is to go to her husband's house, which includes a formal contract publicly proclaimed. Besides the smaller customary gifts and payments, most of these Zongo Muslims seem, moreover, to pay both a substantial "bride-wealth" and a smaller sum named *sadaki*, although some regard these two sums as together constituting the *sadaki*. Consummation of marriage never precedes puberty, but girls are often promised in marriage when very young. If they subsequently resist the union much pressure is brought to bear and sometimes the contract is concluded regardless of their protests[3]: but the fear of an appeal to the Administration probably checks the worst abuses. Very few[4] of these marriages, however, are registered under the Ordinance: and this is largely, it seems, because such registration involves several persons going a considerable distance—only, perhaps, for the District Commissioner's clerks to keep them waiting or send them away until a more convenient occasion. They recognise, however, the value of registration if a simpler method could be devised.

Men sometimes divorce their wives, and the triple formula is not unknown. If used in anger most couples disregard this, but the law about the need for remarriage—and that after an intervening union—is known and understood by the *mallams*. Where it is the wife who wants release she normally repairs to her father, whither her husband follows her and attempts to compose their differences: but if this proves impossible she will send some £1 15s. 0d. to the headman,[5] who will call together his elders, send for the husband, and hold an enquiry. He will always, it seems, order at least two postponements, extending over two or three months in all, in order to give plenty of time for mutual settlement: but finally he will, if necessary, declare the marriage dissolved. Where the wife has been really maltreated or left without food and clothing,[6]

[1] Partly, perhaps, as a matter of self-interest.

[2] The "*Sarkin Hausa*", who is also the unofficial *Sarkin Zongo*.

[3] In old Akan custom such promise virtually constitutes marriage: see above.

[4] Perhaps five or six a year (out of something in the neighbouhood of six hundred).

[5] i.e., the Hausa headman, who is the unofficial Zongo headman. But others may go to their own headman.

[6] But it is noteworthy that where the wife alleges that her husband is impotent, has maltreated her or has failed to maintain her, and he denies this, the headman and *mallams* affirm that the burden of proof is his!

moreover, no refund is ordered[1]; and the same was alleged, after some hesitation, of sexual desertion. Where, again, the husband has gone away and left his wife without support the headman will send for the husband's representatives or relations, who will sometimes themselves provide maintenance and sometimes request time to contact the husband; while if this proves ineffective the headman will himself try to contact him by post. Where, however, even this proves abortive he will apparently declare the marriage dissolved, after some three months' delay, whether the husband's whereabouts are known or unknown; and this, it seems, applies whether the wife complains of destitution on the one hand or of sexual desertion and fear of adultery on the other. If she remarries after such dissolution and then her husband returns and claims her, the second marriage will stand. Where, however, the wife has no valid grounds for divorce both *sadaki* and other expenses are reclaimable, but the headman and elders will commonly order certain reductions for children borne and services rendered.

In cases of seduction the husband will complain to the headman who will, it seems, " fine " the paramour seven guineas, only two of which he will hand over to the husband by way of damages.[2] Adultery may be proved by two witnesses, including the husband, and evidence that the parties were alone together in a closed room is enough. Where the woman refuses to return to her husband her marriage will be dissolved, but the headman and *mallams* maintain that she will not be allowed to marry her paramour, in Kumasi at least. The *'idda* of both widowhood and divorce is, allegedly, observed; while the custody of the children of divorced parents may be claimed by the father after the period of suckling. The orthodox rules about the period of gestation are, moreover, ignored; and the headman said that he himself would regard some fifteen months as the very maximum.

When a man dies his estate is sometimes taken over by his brother or eldest son as trustee for the family, while in other cases it is divided up according to Islamic law (the details of which were well known by the *mallams* in Kumasi). The orthodox rules about bequests are also known, although often disregarded: but the headman professes to enforce them in any case referred to him. Where one of the family rejects the decision of the remainder (whether this is according to Islamic law or not) he will sometimes take his case to the District Commissioner, who might well remit it to one of the Zongo headmen for " arbitration,"[3] or to the Kumasi Native Court, the members of which might either apply their own customary law or ask the headman concerning the customs of the parties: but the former naturally causes much dissatisfaction,[4] while the latter, as we have seen, is, strictly speaking, *ultra vires*. Wills may also, of course, be made in the English form; while it is noteworthy that the Akan distinction between individual and family property is not applied in the Zongo, except in the case of a family compound.

It is interesting to observe that in an exchange of letters between the Hausa headman and a Hausa tailor whose marriage the former had dissolved, after repeated requests from the wife, the headman wrote: "According to the tenets of Muhammadan Law, where a woman suffers at the hands of her husband through indifference, negligence and lack of support in food and clothing, and

[1] This, however, is primarily true of the Hausa, while other communities may differ.

[2] In view of sect. 30 of the Native Courts (Ashanti) Ordinance this procedure is legal only if (*a*) the headman and elders make no pretention to being a native court within the meaning of the Ordinance and (*b*) the " fine " is regarded as compensation to the injured husband on the one hand, and a fee to the headman for his services on the other, both provided without any coercion. But see below for a discussion of these points from the native viewpoint.

[3] See above and below.

[4] The headman spoke bitterly of this.

proved satisfactorily, before a competent responsible authority which by the grace of the Almighty Allah I am privileged to hold to His glory and honour, the power is vested in me to dissolve such a marriage ". This shows clearly that the headman regards himself as having the authority of a Qāḍī in Islamic law, in fact if not in theory.[1]

THE COLONY

In the Colony, again, much the same conditions as in Ashanti seem to prevail. In Accra, for instance, there are Hausa, Yoruba,[2] Wangara, Fulani, Gurunshi and other immigrant Muslim communities, some from the Northern Territories and some from Nigeria, French territory and elsewhere. There are also a small number of Ga[3] Muslims, both orthodox and Aḥmadīs—the latter representing converts won by the headquarters of their movement in Saltpond.

The marriage customs[4] of all these communities follow much the same pattern as those described above, with minor differences, except that a few immigrant groups sometimes, it seems, conclude the actual contract of marriage before a girl reaches puberty, although the marriage is apparently never consummated before she is nubile. Compulsion in such matters, while valid under the Sharī'a, is little practised locally because of Government disapproval: so if a girl promised in marriage persistently refuses to agree, pre-marital payments are returned, while where the contract itself has been concluded, this is dissolved. Men divorce their wives by both the single and triple formula; but where one uses the triple formula in a fit of anger most *limams* regard this as single only, while the formula is continually disregarded in practice, whether used in anger or not.[5] Where a woman goes to her headman seeking divorce he and his elders (including the *limam*) will send for the husband, and if the latter refuses to come (as the headman has no coercive powers[6]) they will apparently dissolve the marriage—but they profess not to know what would happen if the husband complained to the native court or to the District Commissioner. Where the husband is absent letters will be written, etc., and the marriage will not, it seems, be dissolved until some three months have passed.[7] If the husband is impotent, has failed to support his wife, has cruelly maltreated her, or has gone away and left her to suffer from loneliness, no *sadaki* or expenses are normally returnable[8]; while where the wife has no such reason for divorce, conciliation is attempted, but eventually what amounts to a forced *khul'*[9] for the return of the *sadaki* (but not of all the marriage expenses) will be pronounced by the headman.

In cases of seduction, again, many headmen (and even *limams*) act as though they were possessed of judicial powers. The *limam* of the Fulani, for instance,

---

[1] It also provides an interesting instance of the common disregard among Africans of the English distinction between an official court judgment and an unofficial arbitration award or even an administrative order. As headman of the community the *Sarki* here felt perfectly entitled to declare a marriage dissolved, both under Islamic law and native custom.

[2] These include Muslim, pagan and Christian elements.

[3] Accra is part of the comparatively small Ga territory.

[4] My informants were the headmen and *limams* of several of the communities.

[5] While the Yoruba say the husband must either show her to be at fault, or pay some sum to satisfy her.

[6] But see below, p. 280-1.

[7] The senior *limam* said six months, but was obviously at sea, while the leading headman said three months followed by three months *'idda*. But the headman apparently in practice allows a wife to marry another without dissolution of her marriage with her absent husband, and then to return to the latter if he reappears!

[8] So, at least, the better educated *limams* affirmed, but this must vary from community to community.

[9] Dissolution of marriage in consideration of a financial consideration produced by the wife. See Glossary.

takes £5 from the man and £2 10s. from the woman; hands £2 10s.[1] to the husband as " damages "; and pockets the rest. Other *mallams* do much the same, but the senior *limam*[2] allegedly does not, out of fear of Government disapproval.[3] Where the woman refuses to return to her husband the marriage will be dissolved, but the same *limam*, at any rate, would not be willing to marry her to her paramour.[4] The *'idda* of both widowhood and divorce is, it seems, strictly observed; while something in the nature of one year[5] would, apparently, be accepted, on the woman's claim, as the maximum period of gestation. One interesting point which came to my notice was the view that, where a woman's guardian refused to marry her to the man of her choice, she might authorise another to act for her: and when I pointed out that this represents Shāfi'ī rather than Mālikī practice,[6] the local *mallams* calmly stated that where the *taqlīd*[7] of another *imām* best suited local customs and conditions this was, in their view, perfectly in order.[8] The custody of the children of divorced parents should properly remain with the mother, the *mallams* further affirmed, until the boy reached seven and the girl went to her husband's home, but the headmen admitted that in practice this rule was forsaken in favour of the right of the father to claim them at any time after weaning.[9]

In matters of inheritance most Hausa, it seems, apply the Sharī'a, while among the Yoruba the senior member of the family usually succeeds. The Islamic rules concerning bequests are known, but bequests of any sort are contrary to custom. Most such questions are, however, settled within the family, with the help of the headman and his *limam* when sought. There is, of course, no Muslim Treasury (*Bayt al-Māl*), so rights of inheritance are extended to include blood relations of all sorts. It is noteworthy, however, that wills in the English form are becoming increasingly common.

All the headmen and *limams* whom I met in Accra admitted to acting as arbitrators[10] and to taking fees for so doing. They urged that the Muslims of the Gold Coast should have their own recognised courts to deal with matters of family law, i.e., that their headmen or *limams* should have proper judicial status, or at least that their cases should go to British officers rather than the ordinary native courts. But in this context it is apposite to quote from a Judicial Circular regarding arbitration proceedings issued by the Senior Judicial Adviser in 1945. After remarking that where parties agree to go to arbitration and choose or agree to an arbitrator to settle a dispute all the elements of a submission to arbitration[10] are present, and that the essential point is that no compulsion is used by the arbitrator to bring witnesses, to compel attendance, to enforce the award or for other purposes, it continues, " If drink is given to the arbitrator, if the witnesses are asked to swear . . ., if witnesses are given some allowance . . . or even if the arbitrator or arbitrators are paid a ' judgment fee ', the proceedings still do not cease to be an arbitration. It is open to either party to withdraw

[1] This, clearly, may cancel out with the wife's " fine ".

[2] Ḥājj Imām Muḥammad 'Abbās, from Katsina.

[3] But see p. 277 above, and foot of this page.

[4] i.e., they will at least have to go elsewhere.

[5] But the senior *limam* said two years.

[6] Where, however, she applies to her headman this may be regarded as Mālikī practice, since the Mālikīs regularly allow an appeal to the Ruler or Judge in such cases.

[7] i.e., adoption of the view as authoritative. See Glossary.

[8] This opinion is particularly interesting in view of the extent to which the adoption of variant opinions has been made compulsory by express legislation in several Muslim countries, as the basis for far-reaching reforms in the administration of Sharī'a law.

[9] See p. 262, note (i) above. But the statement regarding a boy at the age of seven represents a " weaker " Mālikī variant.

[10] In the English sense: for the native view, see below.

from the arbitration at any time before the award is given, but when it is given it is binding on the parties[1] . . . Only where arbitrators hold themselves out as having the powers of a native court, or issue process for the institution of proceedings, or for the execution of judgments, or where they use compulsion at any stage, can a proper prosecution . . . be instituted."[2]

This, however, is an essentially English view of the distinction between a judicial judgment and an arbitral award, and between the processes leading to each. In the native view, it seems, there is no such distinction. This may be illustrated with reference to the concepts of submission to jurisdiction or arbitration, of judgment or award, and of *res judicata*, respectively, in each of which the native view is quite different from the English. Thus, when one African takes some grievance to his political superior, for instance, and the latter orders the other party to come and answer to the complaint, the latter can be said voluntarily to submit to that superior's arbitration, where he holds no formal judicial powers, little more than a party can be said to submit voluntarily to the jurisdiction of the appropriate native court under the Ordinance: the difference, in the native view, was originally one of degree, and that in turn was entirely dependent on the relative prestige and power of the two authorities concerned. Again, there was (and, to some extent, is) no difference in essence, in the native mind, between a judicial judgment and an arbitration award, for the former, like the latter, always primarily partakes of the nature of an attempt to reconcile the parties and suitably to adjust any differences between them—except, that is, in the case of a few major offences which run seriously counter to basic *tabus*. And as for *res judicata*, not only does native opinion reject the English doctrine that an arbitral award becomes binding when the parties have submitted to the arbitration concerned, but it also takes much the same view of a judicial judgment, for both are dependent for their acceptance on the parties' conviction of their justice or their respect for the authority which gave them: the doctrine of *res judicata* is involved, in regard to both " arbitration " awards and court judgments, only by the formal signification of their acceptance by the customary drinks or by obedience thereto[3]—and even then a change of circumstances may well be held to justify a reopening of the case. But it must, of course, be remembered that Ordinance law, and English doctrines, have already influenced the native concepts to a considerable, and increasing, extent.[4]

It is, however, impossible to generalise with any confidence of accuracy regarding the attitude taken by native courts towards appeals by dissatisfied parties against the decisions of Zongo headmen and their *limams* (and other elders) in matters of personal status such as those discussed above. Most of the *limams* to whom I spoke complained that the native courts rode rough-shod over their " decisions " and applied the local customary law, but several of the headmen denied this and affirmed that the native courts normally supported their decisions and even sought their advice regarding Zongo litigants. And the members of the Ga Native Court themselves (two Divisions of which I visited) were emphatic that they not only asked all litigants their religion before putting

[1] This, again, is the English view, which is now gaining some support in native practice, under English influence.

[2] i.e., under sect. 30 of the Native Courts (Ashanti) Ordinance: see p. 255 above. It is, however, noteworthy that this circular represents a generalisation from Akan custom.

[3] i.e., the basic question in the English view is " Did the parties submit to the arbitration?" while to a native court the question is " Did they accept, e.g., the Zongo headman's decision?" But even if they did not, of course, that decision might well be enforced by the native court.

[4] For a full discussion of this subject, see J. N. Matson's unpublished paper on " Custom in the Courts ".

them on the appropriate oath, but that when the case involved some question of marriage, divorce or inheritance concerning Muslims[1] they would call expert witnesses[2] and give judgment according to the law of the parties. Cases of seduction, on the other hand, are all governed by customary law, although even here they profess to inquire into, e.g., Hausa custom in the case of Hausa litigants.[3]

I also interviewed four Ga[4] converts to Islam, all of them from the orthodox party, who claimed that there were some two thousand such converts, mostly young, including a minority who have embraced Aḥmadī tenets. My informants alleged that in marriage they omit customary payments and confine themselves to the Islamic *sadaki*[5]; that they normally call in the senior *limam*[6] to supervise their formal contracts of marriage; and that in divorce, too, they would take the *limam's* advice, but that hitherto all their divorces had been by agreement, after discussion before the *limam*. In any case of seduction, however, they said they would go to the native court both to exact the suitable fee from the guilty man[7] and also to reclaim the *sadaki* from the father-in-law. "Mixed" marriages only occur, it seems, with women who are prepared to embrace Islam, or where Muslim girls insist on marrying non-Muslims: for there is, apparently, considerable personal freedom in their circles. The *'idda* of both widowhood and divorce are, it seems, observed. They knew of married women with absent husbands, from other Muslim communities, who were temporarily married to other men with their headman's consent,[8] but were emphatic that this never happened in their community. They affirmed, moreover, that in any case before the native court which involved some question of personal status concerning a Muslim litigant it was up to him to call a *limam* or *mallam* to give evidence of Muslim law, and that this would normally be accepted[9]; while the court sometimes sent for such testimony on its own motion. They had no idea, however, how cases of inheritance[10] would go, as only one of their number had so far died: but they professed to desire to follow the law of Islam in this also.

It may be added that this community of young converts to Islam may well grow, as more and more are becoming dissatisfied with the old paganism. Islam, moreover, is favoured in certain nationalist circles, as the religion of the quondam "indigenous" kingdom of Ghāna, at the expense of the "foreign" Christianity;

[1] Even, they allege, in the case of Ga converts to Islam.

[2] But not, it appears, the senior *limam*: instead they call the lawyer whom the parties name, the headman himself, or one of two or three regular "consultants". That they do in fact call expert testimony is confirmed by British officers: but it apparently sometimes happens that both sides call expert witnesses who flatly contradict each other.

[3] But the Native Courts (Colony) Ordinance only authorises, in sect. 15(*a*), the application of the "native law prevailing within (their) jurisdiction", as we have seen, by contrast with the Courts Ordinance. So the only juristic basis, strictly speaking, which can be found for the application of either the customary law of immigrant communities or of Islamic law in regard to Muslims (whether immigrant or indigenous) is the phrase about "any law binding between the parties" in sect. 15(*b*), if indeed this interpretation may properly be put on those words.

[4] The Ga, unlike the Akan, are primarily patrilineal.

[5] *Sed quaere.*

[6] Ḥājj 'Abbās: see above.

[7] Apparently eight guineas if the wife became pregnant, four guineas if not.

[8] See above, p. 279, note (7). They say that the Hausa, Fulani and Wangara all do this.

[9] But whether as the "law binding between the parties" under the Ordinance, or on general African principles (see below), it would be difficult to say.

[10] Bequests, it seems, are contrary to custom in Accra.

while it also, of course, combines the dignity of monotheism with a much more accommodating attitude to such subjects as polygamy and divorce.

The following information from Koforidua, a small town some forty miles north west of Accra, may also suitably be included here, although I did not obtain this in person but through the kindness of my friend Mr. A. N. Allott.[1] Here, again, the Zongo includes the most diverse elements,[2] each under their own headman and the general aegis of the *Sarkin Zongo*; while there are also a few Akan Muslims. All are Mālikīs. The formal contract of marriage and the *sadaki* follow the usual pattern, but there appear to be certain differences regarding the age of marriage. Thus girls are not, it seems, promised in infancy, but they may be married and sent to their husbands' houses at any time after about twelve years of age, although the marriage is allegedly not consummated before puberty; and at that age she may, moreover, refuse the marriage if she insists, on the grounds that she " did not know the meaning of love."

Where a man decides to divorce his wife the triple formula is not used, but the husband summons the parents of the girl before the Zongo headman and must then specify his reason.[3] Where it is the woman who demands divorce the Zongo headman will again enquire into the reason, and will grant her request if the husband has failed to support her,[4] has repeatedly ill-treated her, has left her alone for more than a year, or proves to be impotent after three months' treatment: but the husband may recover both *sadaki* and other expenses, except only where he has failed to support her. Where, on the other hand, the wife elopes with another man the latter may be made to pay a fee (as for ordinary adultery), and the husband has the choice between taking his wife back or reclaiming *sadaki* and expenses[5]; while where she refuses to return, or otherwise insists on the dissolution of her marriage without proper justification, these refunds are again incumbent. The *'idda* of both widowhood and divorce are normally observed, for the headman notes the dates of divorce and will not permit premature remarriage. Formerly there were plenty of concubines, but this relationship is not regarded as legally possible under present conditions, although the ignorant and illiterate still in fact keep them.

When a man dies leaving children they, it seems, are his heirs (to the exclusion of a brother, except in the capacity of guardian); but the Islamic rules of inheritance are only applied where the heirs decide to divide up the estate. Bequests, both oral and written, are known, but must never be in favour of children[6]; yet there is no restriction, it seems, on the amount bequeathed, provided the children agree. Most cases of personal status concerning the Zongo community go to the Zongo headman: and while any party may appeal therefrom to the native court, the Zongo headman is normally called in as an expert witness. It seems, however, that the Omanhene has for some reason ordered that Muhammadan cases should not be recorded in the court record book.

The Aḥmadīya has made considerable progress in the Gold Coast, as has been noticed *passim* above. Unfortunately, I was unable to visit their headquarters at Saltpond and meet their local Amīr, but I had long talks with two Aḥmadī missionaries, both Indians, in Wa and Kumasi respectively, and also

[1] To whose intimate knowledge of native customary law I am indebted for enlightenment on a number of heterogeneous points regarding the Gold Coast and elsewhere.

[2] Hausa, Yoruba, Moshi, Zabrama, Grunshi, Fulani, Dagbamba and others.

[3] But mere dislike is sufficient.

[4] Or, it seems, to pay up arrears of maintenance when he returns from a journey.

[5] But where a woman says that a child was begotten by the other man, he may claim him.

[6] This, of course, is the orthodox doctrine, but the latter includes any heir.

with two Aḥmadī schoolmasters in Kumasi. The Aḥmadī adherents in the Gold Coast, like those of Nigeria, are all Qādiānīs, but unlike those of Nigeria they are all united in support of the present Khalīfa (although I heard of a few dissidents in Accra). Their missionaries, it seems, usually travel to Africa at the expense of the central treasury of the movement, but are then supported by the African converts.

In matters of law Aḥmadīs do not, in theory, belong to any of the orthodox schools but are committed to following the teachings of their "Promised Messiah" and his Successors. He himself, however, is reputed to have said: "Follow my teachings and, in default thereof, those of the Ḥanafīs". But the legal pronouncements of the Aḥmadīya are, it seems, chiefly available only in Urdu, except such as are included in their official commentary on the Qur'ān. In Pakistan, of course, the community has its own "court" (*dār al-qaḍā'*) at Rabwa, and members of the community may not, it seems, litigate between themselves before the ordinary courts without permission. In West Africa, however, all this is a far cry, for the local background is Mālikī, not Ḥanafī, and many legal dicta of the Promised Messiah and his Successors are totally unknown. Even in Pakistan, moreover, the law seems at present somewhat in a state of flux, for a committee to consider the law of succession was, apparently, recently convened. In these circumstances it is not surprising that the missionaries in West Africa have concentrated much more on matters of belief and ritual than on details of family law, and have in fact done little or nothing to force their views, even in such matters as "purdah" and divorce, on their African converts. Yet, even so, a certain Aḥmadī influence can be discerned even in matters of law—chiefly, perhaps, through the tendency to refer disputed points to the "Amīr" in Saltpond (i.e., the senior of the five Indian missionaries working in the Gold Coast), who is the local representative of the present Khalīfa, or "Promised Reformer". Thus in Cape Coast, I am told, an Aḥmadī litigant before the native court would not hesitate to call suitable testimony to "Aḥmadī" law and practice on any suitable point in dispute. It is interesting, therefore, to speculate when, how and under what conditions an Aḥmadī community might be held to have evolved a new and valid Aḥmadī "native law and custom" by an amalgam of their original customary law with Aḥmadī additions, subtractions and variations.

The above summary will suffice to give some idea of the complex problems to which the conflict of laws may give rise in the Gold Coast. What law, for instance, is to be applied in a matrimonial cause which concerns a Yoruba woman and a Ga man, both living in an Akan district, when decided by an Akan native court? Presumably the phrase "any native law or custom existing in the Gold Coast" in section 74(1) of the Courts Ordinance is wide enough to allow the application of the customary law of any immigrant community provided it has persisted in its new environment: but while the law applicable within each community is thus, perhaps, satisfactorily established, what of mixed cases? In such circumstances is an equitable compromise, if any, to be effected, or is the local or territorial customary law to prevail? Again, it is only the latter which any of the native courts of the Gold Coast are in fact authorised to apply—unless, indeed, the phrase "any law binding between the parties", peculiar, in any case, to the Colony and Southern Togoland, is to be interpreted as covering immigrant customary law: yet it is the native courts which are, in general, masters of such "equitable compromise", for the very basis of their litigation is a form of arbitration which seeks to reconcile the parties by a careful and acceptable adjustment of their rival claims.

Again, what of Islamic law as such? Can the phrase "any law binding between the parties" ever be invoked to cover the application of Islamic law, as distinct from native law and custom? And at what point may Islamic law be said to have become the customary law of some locality, community or even family—for the recognition of special customs applicable to particular families is quite a common phenomenon? Supposing, for instance, that an Akan dies a Muslim and his Muslim children demand that his estate be divided up on Islamic principles, while his pagan uterine brother claims the whole property under customary law? If, moreover, it be held that the brother must triumph in these circumstances, would it make any difference if he himself had also embraced Islam; or if the whole village had become Muslim; or if it could be shown that the estates of other members of that family or locality had, of recent years, been divided up, by mutual consent, on Islamic principles?

To many of these questions a categorical answer cannot well be given. That the native customary law of Africans who have accepted the religion of Islam does tend to assimilate itself to Islamic law, in certain respects at least, is obvious: and that a law which is, in parts, substantially the Sharī'a can in such circumstances properly be administered under the title of "native" or customary law has been argued in the Introduction to this Survey—where it has also been noted that the people themselves, in such cases, frequently regard it not as native law, binding by precedent and tradition, but as religious law, incumbent upon them by divine command. The exact point at which the change from the old customary law to the new takes places is, however, an exceedingly difficult problem—as also the size of the community or locality which may be held to have adopted any new and distinctive rules. In the Gold Coast, of course, the right of, e.g., the Asanteman Council[1] to record in writing, for submission to the Governor in Council, a declaration of what it considers to be the native law and custom relating to any particular subject, or to recommend to the Governor in Council any modification of native law and custom which it considers expedient, is recognised under the Native Law and Custom (Ashanti Confederacy Council) Ordinance, 1940[2]—in addition to its powers to make orders and rules under the Native Authority (Ashanti) Ordinance, 1935.[3] But we are here concerned, in the main, with something far less tangible than such decisions.

It is just at this point that the peculiar genius of native courts is thrown into particularly clear relief. Where a British court might well feel helpless because of the absence of — and the virtual impracticability of framing — any coherent rule of law, the native system is seen, perhaps, to best advantage. It has already been noted that the judgments of any native court represent, for the most part, far less the unequivocal enunciation of firm principles of law than careful and conscientious attempts to reconcile differences, adjust conflicting interests, and restore the social equilibrium. And for such a purpose the conflict between tribal laws, local laws and religious laws is not nearly so insoluble as it might seem; for in appropriate circumstances two or even three of these may all be taken into account.

It seems probable, moreover, that this is the major explanation of the differences in points of detail, amounting at times to actual inconsistencies, in the accounts given by different courts and other informants as to the law applicable in this locality or that regarding, e.g., the repayments due to a Muslim husband whose wife demands divorce, with or without such legal justification as Mālikī law recognises. It is clear that a problem such as this is governed, in the Gold Coast, more by customary than Islamic law, except perhaps among such staunch Muslims as some of the Hausa communities; and that this itself differs in details from

[1] Formerly, the Ashanti Confederacy Council.

[2] Sects. 3(1) and 4(1). For examples of such declarations see p. 275 above.

[3] Sects. 8 and 15 respectively. And cp. corresponding Ordinances elsewhere in the Gold Coast.

tribe to tribe and locality to locality. But a baffling point is the degree to which the appropriate rules of Islamic law seem to influence or supplement local custom, in the case of Muslim litigants, to a different (and largely unpredictable) degree from court to court—as also the exasperating way in which conflicting answers seem to be given to what appears to be substantially the same problem stated in rather different terms. But the solution, in great part, appears to be this: each case is considered strictly on its merits, the general principles of the customary law being applied to the individual circumstances of the particular litigants and varied accordingly; while the relevant principles of Islamic law, as locally known and partially accepted, are thrown in as a further ingredient, to be accorded greater or lesser weight according to the court, the parties and the case at issue.

Even in the Supreme Court, moreover, Islamic law might on occasion be applied, not as native law but as required by "justice, equity and good conscience".[1] The Court, however, is only to resort to this "in cases where no express rule is applicable" to the matter in controversy; and it seems doubtful, therefore, whether this clause could properly be invoked to justify the variation of customary law in accordance with the dictates of the Sharī'a in regard to indigenous Muslims or as authorising the application of Islamic law in respect of immigrant Muslims. But, except within the terms of the Marriage of Muhammadans Ordinance, or under the principles of Private International law, no other authority for the latter exists in the Gold Coast.

---

[1] See the Courts Ordinance, sect. 74(1).

SIERRA LEONE

Like the other British territories in West Africa, Sierra Leone is divided into a Colony and a Protectorate, while the former is again sub-divided into Colony proper and Colony administered as Protectorate.[1] Thus in general terms all persons born in the Colony are British subjects, while those born in the Protectorate are British protected persons. Again, this distinction between Colony and Protectorate is reflected in the definition of the term " native "; for section 3 of the Interpretation Ordinance, 1945, enacts that this means " any person who is a member of a race, tribe or community settled in Sierra Leone (or the territories adjacent thereto), other than a race, tribe or community—(a) which is of European or Asiatic origin, or (b) whose principal place of settlement is in the Colony." It is clear, however, that this last phrase further distinguishes those members of tribes indigenous to, or settled in, the Protectorate who happen to live in the Colony from the descendants of those liberated slaves[2] and others, frequently termed Creoles,[3] who have no direct connection with the Protectorate at all. But it is noteworthy that the legal distinction between Colony and Protectorate is not so strong today as it was formerly, and is, it seems, often ignored in practice by litigants as a matter of convenience—a fact which may serve to prepare the way for ultimate fusion.

The only specific mention of Islamic law in the Ordinances of Sierra Leone is provided by the Muhammadan[4] Marriage Ordinance, 1905. This provides that " Every marriage entered into and subsisting between persons professing the Muhammadan faith and domiciled in the Colony or Protectorate which is valid according to Muhammadan Law . . . shall be valid for all civil purposes "[5]; that " Proof according to Muhammadan Law " of the existence, past or present, of a Muhammadan marriage, or of the dissolution of a Muhammadan marriage, " shall be received in evidence by all the Courts in the Colony "[6]; that " Muhammadan marriages and final divorces may be registered "[7]; that the Registrar, when requested to do so, shall enter a record of " any Muhammadan marriage or final divorce, if satisfied that such marriage or final divorce is in accordance with Muhammadan Law "[8]; that " If any party to a Muhammadan marriage and being at the date of his death a Muhammadan, or if any person being unmarried and being at such date a Muhammadan, shall die intestate, the estate real and personal of such intestate shall be distributed in accordance with Muhammadan Law "[9]; that the eldest son " if of full age according to Muhammadan Law " and, failing such, the brother, shall be entitled to take out letters of administration, " Provided always, that a creditor, not being a Muhammadan, may apply to the Court for letters of administration and, notwithstanding that letters of administration have already been granted to another person, the application of such creditor shall be granted . . . unless the previous grantee shall pay the debt, or prove to the satisfaction of the Court that nothing is owing from the estate of the intestate to the applicant "[10]; that " Save as regards distribution

---

[1] See Protectorate Ordinance, sect. 2(2).

[2] Concerning such, see also the Liberated Africans (Sierra Leone) Act, 16 and 17 Vict.

[3] In the past the term " Creoles " was largely confined to Christians and "Akus " used of Africans from Yoruba-land, who would frequently have been Muslims; but the latter term was, until recently, regarded as somewhat uncomplimentary, and " Creoles " was largely used instead. Now, however, a reaction against this attitude has set in.

[4] Spelt " Mohammedan " in this Ordinance: but see Introduction to this Survey regarding the policy adopted in the spelling of Arabic words, etc., to avoid confusion.

[5] Sect. 2.

[6] Sect 3.

[7] Sect. 5.

[8] Sect. 6(*a*).

[9] Sect. 9(1).

[10] Sect. 9(2).

or any other matter expressly provided for in this section" the estates of intestates "shall be administered in accordance with the law of the Colony"[1]; and that "In the event of there being at the time a Tribal Authority of a race which is Muhammadan, the Official Administrator shall, in the absence of any direction given by the Chief Justice to the contrary, consult such authority as to what is the Muhammadan Law as to distribution of an intestate's estate."[2] It is noteworthy, however, that this Ordinance is only applicable in the Colony, although it applies to parties whose domicile is either Colony or Protectorate; that no provision is made for any court to hear matrimonial causes under Islamic law[3] or, in particular, to dissolve a Muslim marriage, but only to receive evidence that such marriage has in fact been dissolved; that the phrase "proof according to Muhammadan Law" presumably imports all the relevant rules of evidence, eligibility of witnesses, etc., under the Sharī'a; and that the estate of an intestate who dies a Muslim but who was married otherwise than in conformity with Muhammadan Law will not be distributed according to that law, nor will the estate of a Muslim native of the Protectorate in any circumstances whatever.

Instead, the Administration of Estates Ordinance, 1945, provides in its Second Schedule detailed rules for the distribution of an intestate's estate, but decrees in section 43 (1) that "Notwithstanding anything contained in this Ordinance, where any native dies intestate leaving assets in Sierra Leone which are not within the jurisdiction of any Native Court the distribution of such assets after payment of the debts of the deceased . . . shall be according to native law and custom"; while in the Protectorate the Native Courts Ordinance, 1933, provides that these courts "shall have jurisdiction according to native law and custom . . . to administer the estates of deceased persons, so far as they are situated within the jurisdiction of the Native Courts, where such deceased persons are natives,"[4] and under the Courts Ordinance, 1945, the jurisdiction of any other court is expressly ousted in such circumstances.[5]

This Native Courts Ordinance makes provision for both Chiefs' Courts and Appeal Courts (together with "Combined Courts" to deal with petty disputes between natives and non-natives) to administer justice "in accordance with native law and custom so far as the same is not repugnant to natural justice, equity and good conscience, but subject always to the provisions of this Ordinance".[6] Their jurisdiction extends to civil cases arising exclusively between natives and triable by native law[7]; criminal cases in which the accused and the person who is, or was, primarily affected by the alleged offence are both natives and which do not fall within various categories of serious crimes which are expressly beyond their competence[8]; and "any cause or matter arising out of the provisions of any Ordinance which the Native Courts may be authorised to enforce"[9]. But provision is also made for all sentences exceeding fourteen days' imprisonment to be reported to the District Commissioner by a method which is to operate as an appeal[10] and for the Magistrate to have the full right to

[1] Sect. 9(3).
[2] Sect. 10.
[3] cp. *Salim Mustapha* v. *Lola Mustapha* [The Sierra Leone Law Recorder III. 20], where English law was applied to a matrimonial suit between Muslim spouses; although there is nothing in the report to show under what law they had solemnised their marriage.
[4] Sect. 7.
[5] Sect. 11(*b*).
[6] Sects. 3, 4 and 5.
[7] Sect. 7(2)(*a*).
[8] Sect. 7(2)(*b*).
[9] Sect. 7(*c*). It is also noteworthy that in practice Syrians and Creoles frequently go to the Chief's courts in both civil and petty criminal cases, whether involving a native or another non-native. The decisions given are, of course, *ultra vires*, but are nearly always accepted by the parties.
[10] Sect. 22(1) and (2).

review all decisions of native courts[1] and to transfer any cause or matter, either before trial or at any stage, to the Magistrate's Court.[2]

Unlike its equivalent in most territories, the Civil Marriage Ordinance, 1910, which applies to both the Colony and Protectorate, is not applicable to "natives"; but any non-native Muslim girl (including, of course, those Africans who belong to a race, etc., whose usual place of settlement is in the Colony) could avail herself of this Ordinance to marry a non-Muslim, regardless of the nullity of any such marriage under Islamic law. Whether a native Muslim girl could so marry a Christian under the Christian Marriage Ordinance, 1906, without first professing conversion to Christianity would depend on whether any church would celebrate such a marriage, since section 3 simply refers to " Persons desiring to be married according to the forms and ceremonies of a Christian denomination . . . " But it is noteworthy that the provisions in this Ordinance regarding bigamy expressly state that " For the purpose of this section, a marriage made in accordance with native law and custom shall not be deemed to be a marriage,"[3] and this would certainly include a marriage in the Protectorate which fulfilled the requirements of a valid Muhammadan marriage, but presumably not a marriage recognised in the Colony under the Muhammadan Marriage Ordinance.[4] Again, no person married under either the Civil or Christian Marriage Ordinance would, of course, be entitled to divorce, or claim divorce from, the other party merely by reason that he or she had either embraced or renounced Islam, whatever the right to which such circumstances might give rise in Islamic law.

Finally, it may be remarked in passing that neither the Children's Ordinance, 1926, nor the Young Persons and Children Ordinance, 1945 (as amended in 1949), can be said in any way to impinge on Islamic law in Sierra Leone, since the latter is totally inapplicable in regard to the care, custody and guardianship of children. Instead, this and all else is governed, under the Courts Ordinance, 1945, by " the common law, the doctrines of equity, and the statutes of general application in force in England on the 1st day of January, 1880 "[5]—except, on the one hand, that " nothing in this Ordinance shall be deemed to invest the Court with jurisdiction in regard to (*a*) any question arising exclusively between natives (i) involving title to land situate within the Protectorate,[6] or (ii) relating to marriage or divorce by native customary law or any matrimonial claim founded on such a marriage . . . , or (*b*) the administration of estates of deceased persons who are natives where such estates lie within the jurisdiction of any Native Court "[7]; and, on the other hand, that " Nothing in this Ordinance shall deprive the Supreme Court and the Magistrates' Courts when determining matters arising in the Protectorate in their civil jurisdiction, of the right to observe and enforce the observance of, or shall deprive any person of the benefit of, any law or custom existing in the Protectorate and not . . . repugnant to natural justice, equity and good conscience, nor incompatible, either directly or by necessary implication, with any Ordinance applying to the Protectorate".[8] It is, moreover, noteworthy in this context that the District Councils Ordinance, 1950, provides that " In addition to the functions of District Councils

---

[1] Sect. 22(2)(*a*). He may " Suspend, reduce or otherwise modify any sentence or decision ".

[2] Sect. 27(2)(*b*).

[3] Sects. 16 and 17, which are also applicable to the Civil Marriage Ordinance.

[4] A previous marriage under native law and custom would, however, presumably invalidate a marriage under either of these Ordinances. See Christian Marriage Ordinance, sects. 10(*b*) and 7(3); Civil Marriage Ordinance, sect. 15(*b*).

[5] Sect. 38. And cp. *In the Matter of Zenebah Mustapha, etc.* [The Sierra Leone Law Recorder III. 19].

[6] In respect to which customary law prevails.

[7] Sect. 11.

[8] Sect. 39.

herein-before set out, it shall be lawful for a District Council, with the approval of the Governor in Council, to make rules altering or modifying native customary law in the District, and all Native Courts in the said District shall take cognizance of all rules so made."[1] It is apparent then that, apart from the very limited scope of the Muhammadan Marriage Ordinance, the Sharī'a can only be applied in Sierra Leone—whether in regard to marriage, divorce, testate and intestate succession, guardianship, maintenance or any other matter whatsoever[2]—as constituting " native law and custom " in so far as it may in fact have been accepted as such by any tribe or locality, or in so far as it may occasionally be applied, to a very limited degree and as a sort of equitable exception, as the law and custom of some immigrant group or the adopted law of some family or individual.[3]

Perhaps the only express mention of Muhammadans in any Ordinance other than the Muhammadan Marriage Ordinance is in the Oaths and Affirmations Ordinance, 1930. This, however, represents a concession to Muslim sentiment and practice rather than to Islamic law as such, and simply provides that " In any proceedings a court may permit a Muhammadan witness to make an affirmation that he will, in giving evidence, speak the truth . . . Provided that, when a Muhammadan witness has given evidence on affirmation, the court may, if it thinks fit, and shall, if so required by an accused person in criminal proceedings, or by a party to civil proceedings, require the witness to repeat on oath the whole or any portion of his evidence. Provided further that any Muhammadan witness who shall wilfully give false evidence on such affirmation . . . shall be liable to be prosecuted and punished for wilful and corrupt perjury."[4]

Not less that two thirds, it seems, of those now living in the Colony represent persons of Protectorate origin, and more than half of these are probably Muslims. There are also considerable communities of Hausa and Yoruba immigrants from Nigeria and elsewhere, besides Fula and Mandingo, almost all of whom are Muslims. In addition there are a few descendants of liberated slaves who have embraced Islam. In the Protectorate, on the other hand, about one-third of the total population would probably claim to be Muslims. The strictest of these are the Fula and the Mandingo, who are both comparatively recent immigrants and never " owners of the soil ": instead they live as clients or tenants of the more indigenous tribes. Among the Fula (called Fulani in Nigeria, etc.) both the settled and nomadic elements are found: the former represent the primary stream of Islam in the territory, while even the latter are now, for the most part at least, nominal Muslims. The second stream of Islam is supplied by the Mandingo (named Wangara in the Gold Coast, etc.), who again are sometimes comparatively strict in matters of religion. Among the more indigenous tribes the Susu and the Temne are largely Muslim; and Islam may be said to pre-

---

[1] Sect. 17—which repeats sects. 5(7) of the Protectorate Ordinance, 1933, now repealed.

[2] An illustration of this may be found in *Rex* v. *Salla Silla* and *Rex* v. *M'fa Nonko and others* (1927, unreported), where the right of a slave-owner in the Sierra Leone Protectorate to recapture his runaway slaves was argued before the Supreme Court. This right was upheld, within limitations, by the majority judgment as justified by native law and custom, which had not been modified or taken away by any legislative enactment at that date. Now, however, the Protectorate Ordinance, 1933, has expressly proclaimed that " The legal status of slavery and slavery in any form whatever is abolished throughout the Protectorate " (sect. 9). While, therefore, women who were previously slaves are still, doubtless, often regarded as slave concubines in native opinion—and, in the case of the more ardent Muslims, as having that legal status in Islamic law—neither the legitimacy of the offspring of such unions nor the question of rights of inheritance by patronage, etc., are discussed in this context, since in all such cases it is native customary law, not the Sharī'a, which would always be applied.

[3] See the discussion on this whole subject in the Introduction to this Survey and at pp. 284-6 above.

[4] Sect. 4.

dominate north of the Rokel (Roquelle)—or, as it is called farther up, the Seli—river line. South of this line, again, there is a considerable sprinkling of Muslims—notably, perhaps, Mandingo traders who have become semi-permanent residents, but also including a certain proportion of the Mende and of the Gallina.[1] In the main, however, "Poro" secret societies predominate in the south, and these are disliked by the stricter or more enlightened Muslims. Even in the north, however, Islam seems, from many points of view, only skin-deep, and the Koranko, for instance, appear to be largely pagan, although some perform the Muslim prayers. In general, however, it may be said that the Muslims of Sierra Leone observe some of the ritual observances of their religion but scarcely apply—or even know—any of its social and family laws.

Girls are often promised in marriage when very young, but are scarcely ever actually given in marriage until after they have reached puberty and have undergone the form of clitoridectomy locally practised. It is this operation, with all that accompanies it, which seems to constitute the primary concern of the Bundu, or female societies; and to these even the stricter Muslims appear to have no objection, by contrast with the male Poro—although even here an exception seems to be made in favour of the Yoruba "Ojeh," which is only frowned upon by the purists.[2] If, moreover, a girl promised in infancy subsequently refused the marriage, the Chief's courts would not normally support her parents in forcing her,[3] but would content themselves with ordering a refund of any gifts or other payments disbursed by the intended husband.

Marriage customs naturally differ in form from tribe to tribe, and even seem to vary in detail from occasion to occasion. But throughout the Protectorate the essentials may be said to consist of (*a*) a mutual agreement to marry between the man and girl concerned,[4] and (*b*) an eventual meeting of the two families, at which a pre-arranged bride-wealth is counted by the principal members of the girl's family and passed to any witnesses who care to check it (as a precaution in case of divorce). Sometimes, on the other hand, only part of this sum is actually handed over and the rest promised by instalments, failure to pay which is sometimes regarded as good grounds for dissolution of marriage. There is, it seems, no rule as to which members of the bride's family take what proportion of this money, but the leading members of both the paternal and maternal side take the lion's share, with the paternal side usually in the ascendancy (although respectful attention and a certain amount of money are always paid to the oldest maternal uncle, even if senile). The bride-wealth as such is never paid to the bride herself; but the husband will normally make her presents of money and clothing in order to win her affection. All this applies both to Muslims and non-Muslims alike: and the more learned and zealous of local Muslims profess to regard these

[1] These are of more immediate Mandingo stock than the Mende, and include a higher proportion of Muslims.

[2] e.g., even some of the leaders of the Fourah Bay community are, it seems, members. The reasons behind the Muslim attitude are probably as follows. The Poro and certain other societies are quasi-religious in nature and involve beliefs and practices plainly inconsistent with Islam; so the stricter Muslims abjure them, and run a short circumcision school of their own for boys. The Bundu is regarded as less objectionable, partly because it only concerns women, and partly because the chief instruction involved is in regard to sex and housewifery, together with the clitoridectomy which local Muslim opinion thoroughly supports. As for the Ojeh, this has few religious implications, for it is largely on a par with those societies which exist almost exclusively for purposes of amusement (chiefly in the form of dancing), while it also helps to provide hired labour for farmers. Its least commendable manifestations occur in the Colony, and are due to the breakdown of tribal control and the lack of demand for massed labour.

[3] Nor, indeed, would parents be at all likely to take such a case to court; while where the suitor applies to the court the girl's refusal would be final.

[4] Either by words, or some other means of mutual understanding. But where an older man wants a young girl he will, perhaps, try to enlist the support of her family first.

proceedings as including an adequate declaration (*ījāb*) and acceptance (*qabūl*) of marriage. A small payment of "dower" to the bride herself at the conclusion of the contract is allegedly added by some of the stricter Muslims: but otherwise the bride-wealth is regarded, by any who concern themselves with such questions, as taking the place of the Islamic dower (*mahr* or *ṣadāq*)—while the requirement of witnesses to the contract or wedding is amply fulfilled. A further payment is commonly made on proof of virginity to the bride's mother, to reward her for the purity of her daughter's upbringing; while in default of this the husband may dissolve the marriage and recover any payments he has made (but would in fact be most unlikely to start an inter-family scandal of this sort, without considerable provocation).

In the south a deceased man's wives are regarded as family property, and must marry either his sons or brothers on pain of the repayment, by their families, of their bride-wealth. In the north, on the other hand, sons never marry their fathers' wives, although brothers will marry those of a deceased brother if the women consent; but where they do not consent, no bride-wealth is repayable. Both these differences are probably due to the influence of the law of Islam,[1] and are also true of the more enlightened Muslims even in the south. The degrees of consanguinity prohibited under the Sharī'a are, it appears, normally observed; but even practising Muslims often have more than four wives and are frequently married to two or more sisters at the same time.[2] Again, the *'idda* of divorce is commonly ignored[3]; while the relationship of the seducer of another man's wife with his mistress can easily be regularised,[4] with the co-operation of her family, provided the aggrieved husband's financial demands are duly met. Marriage without the consent of a woman's guardian (or family), on the other hand, is quite unknown.[5] Where a husband divorces his wife without adequate reason (e.g. repeated infidelity) no refund of bride-wealth may be claimed: but even if he were to use the triple formula or the word *ḥarām* (both of which would be most unlikely in Sierra Leone) reconciliation would certainly be allowed, as would also be the case after the *'idda* period had elapsed, without any question of a new contract, etc. It is apparent, therefore, that tribal custom is the real criterion in all these matters, and that Islamic law exercises very little influence. It is only in the case of the small minority of educated Muslims that its more detailed requirements would have any place at all; and even in such cases they would seldom (if ever) be enforced by the native courts.

Much the same is also true of dissolution of marriage at the instance of the wife. As obtains throughout West Africa, a wife can always secure the dissolution of her marriage if she or her family return her bride-wealth and such other

---

[1] Which is, as we have seen, much stronger in the north than in the south.

[2] I was told, e.g., of an upright and practising Muslim who died some seven years ago leaving at least one hundred wives, including two or three batches of sisters (for the Kissi and certain other tribes have a custom that a man who marries an elder sister may also marry any or all of her younger sisters or half-sisters).

[3] But it has been recorded that among the Susu a woman may not remarry until "a fixed and sufficient time has elapsed to allow of the birth of a posthumous or post-matrimonial child"; that "In the case of the husband's death, the wife reverts to her own family, after the usual period of mourning (four months)"; and that a divorced wife may not remarry either her former husband or another until six months after divorce, but where her family then consent to remarriage with the former husband he will pay only half the previous dowry. (See *Sierra Leone Studies* XX, Nov., 1936, pp. 67 ff.) It is possible, but by no means certain, that the author intended the Islamic waiting period of four months and ten days between widowhood and remarriage; but the connection of the alleged six months' period after divorce with the Islamic *'idda* seems even more questionable. Again, it is by no means certain how far the customs recorded in this article should be regarded as of general validity, even among the Susu.

[4] i.e., by arranging for a divorce and remarriage.

[5] Since payment of bride-wealth to the family of the bride is of the very essence of customary marriage. But a proffer of bride-wealth—especially after unauthorised cohabitation—would seldom be refused.

pre-marital expenses, gifts, etc., as local custom demands in such cases.[1] This may, of course, be regarded as compulsory *khul'*[2] (such as the Mālikīs allow when recommended by arbitrators in cases of marital dispute), but really represents tribal custom, reinforced, in the more strictly Muslim areas of e.g. Northern Nigeria, by the fact that decrees of restitution of marital rights may not be forcibly executed. But even where the wife has such reason for demanding the dissolution of her marriage as would justify a judicial divorce under Mālikī law the husband may, in Sierra Leone, still demand this full refund of his expenses, except that the Chief's courts will usually decree some deduction in respect either of the number of children she has borne or the severity of the ill-treatment she has suffered.[3] A point often discussed by would-be jurists but seldom met in practice is whether a wife can demand dissolution of marriage, without any refund, if her husband proves impotent. In the south, in all probability, the wife would have to go to his son or brother—in default of refund of bride-wealth—just as though he were dead, while in the north she would almost certainly be set free without refund: but all over the country the husband would normally let his wife go, and cut his losses, rather than face the public ridicule to which such a case would give rise. It must, of course, be realised that refund of bride-wealth is not by any means so simple a matter as it might sound, for it will normally involve either contributions from all those members of the bride's family to whom it was originally distributed or else the production of the whole sum by whatever other man wants to marry her.

An aggrieved husband may, it is true, sue his wife's lover before the Chief's court, which will award him suitable compensation. If the wife absolutely refuses to return to him he may also demand refund of expenses from her parents, who will try to force her lover to pay these or else to give her up. Where the lover pays it seems that a child subsequently born will normally go to the second husband, even if in fact begotten by the first. In all cases of dispute, moreover, the woman's word as to who was the father of her child is accepted as final, and litigation about paternity is virtually unknown; while failure to observe the *'idda* of divorce is not regarded as affecting the legitimacy of the children begotten then or thereafter. As for children born to a divorced or widowed woman who has not remarried, a purely common-sense attitude appears to be taken[4]; if born within one year the child may be allowed to inherit from the late husband, but this will normally depend on the word of the mother; for the Mālikī rules regarding a maximum period of gestation of five years, etc., are scarcely known and never applied. And the children of wives in excess of the legal four (for even the Mandingo, for instance, allow themselves considerable latitude in this respect), are always regarded as legitimate.

In practice, of course, this question of legitimacy primarily concerns the law of inheritance, and in this again customary rather than Islamic law applies in the Protectorate. Thus in most cases no division or distribution of the estate seems to occur and the deceased is simply succeeded by the next senior member of the family; while the disposal of his wives has been discussed above.[5] In those rare instances where a man makes a bequest of his property, this will seldom

---

[1] This differs much from tribe to tribe and locality to locality—but any loans or funeral expenses provided by the husband are normally included, while expenses incurred for maintenance during marriage are not. In general the Southerners, in Sierra Leone, are apt to count the last penny, while the Northerners seem to be more liberal.

[2] See Glossary.

[3] In extreme cases, moreover, no refund whatever may be ordered.

[4] It has been stated, however, that among the Susu "Any child born during the six months following on a divorce belongs to the second (first?) husband, unless the latter exercises his right of disowning it" . . . "Children born during this period belong to the first husband" (see *Sierra Leone Studies XX,* Nov., 1936, pp. 67 ff.). This, however, seems contrary to normal custom.

[5] See p. 292.

be enforced by the Chief's court, for such a procedure is regarded with great suspicion, as in most illiterate localities; but no question of such detailed rules of Islamic law as the bequeathable third or "no bequests to an heir" would in any case arise: instead, the desire and intention of the testator would probably be the sole criterion, within the general framework of the customary law, in the extremely rare cases where bequests were enforced at all.

It is possible, however, that this represents somewhat of an over-simplification of the position and that the Islamic law of inheritance is exercising a very limited influence in some quarters. Unfortunately, in Sierra Leone—unlike Nigeria, the Gold Coast and the Gambia—I was unable to investigate this and kindred questions first-hand in the Protectorate, and must rely on enquiries I made from those (Europeans, "Arabs" and Africans)[1] whose knowledge of the Protectorate is both long and intimate, and on the little I have been able to read. Thus in an article on "The Temne; Their Life, Land and Ways"[2] E. R. Langley writes: "The whole . . . law of inheritance is extremely complicated and differs in different chiefdoms: in chiefdoms which are most influenced by Muhammadanism a modified form of the Muhammadan law of inheritance is generally in vogue." Elsewhere in the same article, however, he says that "The precedence amongst heirs seems to be as follows, the sons come first, then the father's full brothers, then half brothers, then daughters and then sons of fathers, brothers"; and, again, "Real property does not descend . . . from father to son but from brother to brother and to brother's children, while personal property may descend to a son or adopted son though it often follows the rule applicable to real property." Similarly, in an article on "Laws and Customs of the Susus" translated from the French of M. Aubert,[3] it is said that where the deceased is a *man* who has left any children, "only the sons inherit, the eldest receiving the largest share[4] . . . When the property has to be divided, everything is divided including land . . . Each of the heirs is responsible for the debts in proportion to the amount of his inheritance. Where, after the realisation of the whole property, the liabilities exceed the assets, the creditors may sue the maternal relations of the debtor." Where, on the other hand, the deceased is a *woman* who "leaves sons of age, they inherit any money, jewellery, cattle and kola trees and divide them equally.[5] The other personal property passes to the deceased's sisters or half-sisters by the same father; failing them, to her mother." Where there are sons and daughters, the former, apparently, get all the money and cattle and half the jewellery and kola trees; while the latter get the other half of these and all the pots, pans and clothing. If there are only daughters, these get all except money, which the husband keeps. As for testamentary bequests, "The power of a father to devise property by will is limited: if he has sons he cannot make particular legacies except to his heirs and his daughters. . . . Women cannot make general legacies. Their particular legacies are of little importance and can be made in favour of their sisters, mother or husband: but, if the heir is a sister, more substantial legacies may be left to the husband, mother, brother or even friends." While, however, these quotations aptly illustrate the complications introduced into any generalisation by local differences,[6] they also show that the

[1] Especially Mr. J. M. Malcolm, Mr. E. F. Sayers, 'Alī 'Abd al-Qādir, and Idrīs Dayfān, to all of whom I am much indebted.

[2] *Sierra Leone Studies XXII,* Sept., 1939, pp. 68 ff.

[3] "Coutumiers Indigènes de la Guinée". See *Sierra Leone Studies XX,* No., 1936, pp. 67 ff. I have not been able to consult the original.

[4] Failing sons, the order seems to be grandchildren, eldest brother or his descendants, father, cousin (son of father's sister), nephew, etc. . . .

[5] It must, however, be very rare for a woman to leave such property; and the value of generalisations from exceptional cases seems dubious.

[6] They also, perhaps, indicate that their authors try over-much to reduce the vagaries of native law to a neat formula. See comments on this subject in the Gold Coast section of this Survey, pp. 284-6.

influence of Islamic law on tribal custom is negligible, and that it must be very much the exception rather than the rule for any Chief to have regard thereto.

In questions of the care, custody and guardianship of children, tribal custom again prevails. Thus a divorced wife has the right to the care and custody of children only during the period of suckling: after weaning, the father may always claim them. But while every young African, whether married or single, remains under the general control of his father and uncles to a degree unknown in modern Europe, guardianship in the technical sense is virtually unknown.

Islamic law in the Protectorate, therefore, seems to be chiefly limited to those cases where the stricter and better educated Muslims observe it of their own volition or by agreement of the family, whether from their own knowledge thereof or on the advice of some local authority.[1] Where a case is taken to a Chief's court customary law almost invariably prevails, although a liberal-minded Chief will often consult an expert, particularly in the case of "stranger" Muslims such as Fula or Mandingo, or if and when the parties so request—and the advice so given might represent either the litigants' own customary law or even, in some cases, certain precepts of the Sharī'a.

In the Colony, too, the position is much the same in fact, if not altogether in theory. In the first place, in spite of the full recognition given to Muslim marriages and divorces by the Muhammadan Marriage Ordinance, there is no court, as we have seen, which appears to be competent to grant a judicial dissolution of marriage under Islamic law. A Magistrate's Court might, it seems, give relief to a deserted Muslim wife under the Married Women's Maintenance Ordinance, and might also entertain an action for return of bride-wealth, etc., if a marriage between Muslims was also regarded as a marriage by native law and custom.[2] But Muslim wives desiring a judicial dissolution of marriage can go only to the headman of their particular community (or, if they prefer, to some learned and respected local Muslim). Technically, of course, these headmen have no judicial powers whatever, for the Tribal Administration (Colony) Ordinance, 1932, decrees that "No Tribal Headman shall exercise any jurisdiction, civil or criminal, of any nature whatever in respect of the members of his tribe."[3] In practice, however, they do of course act as arbitrators—a practice which the Ordinance, presumably, in no way forbids, provided they make no pretence to coercive powers. Thus a woman desiring dissolution of marriage will go to her "Almami Qarya"[4], who will then consult with his "Almami Masjid" (the Imām of the mosque) and other elders, including—among the Yoruba at least—one termed the "Alkali" whose special function it is to deal with quasi-legal problems. These elders will normally send for[5] the husband, if available, and do their utmost either to reconcile the parties or to terminate the marriage on some agreed terms. In cases where this is impossible, however (e.g., where the husband is

---

[1] e.g., the Islamic contract—and ceremony—of marriage is indulged in as a fashionable frill by a few African Muslims, but is a routine matter with Syrians. And the former would also sometimes consult a learned man about divorce, etc.

[2] i.e., it would grant this, if at all, under native law and custom, not Islamic law. It is doubtful, however, whether a magistrate's court is really competent to do this, since it is only in matters arising in the Protectorate that a court operating under the Courts Ordinance is authorised to give effect to native law and custom (under sect. 39). But the Supreme Court has given judgment in favour of an aggrieved husband, or the return of bride-wealth by the family of a wife who has left him, on a number of occasions. See *Alpha Suliman* v. *M'Balley* 199/43 and *Brown* v. *Jelaelay* 362/45: but contrast *Jackson* v. *Weeks* 363/45 (all unreported).

[3] Sect. 12.

[4] i.e., headman of her village.

[5] This procedure, while eminently sensible, perhaps sails rather near the wind as regards the Tribal Administration (Colony) Ordinance (see above).

absent, or where he absolutely refuses to agree to divorce, or the wife resists return of bride-wealth, etc.), they will sometimes declare the marriage dissolved—ordering the return of the husband's marriage disbursements, or not, according to their tribal custom, more or less influenced by the Sharī'a.[1] But it is obvious that knowledge of Sharī'a law is more developed, and tribal customs less binding, among some of the Colony Muslims (especially the Hausa, Mandingo, Yoruba, etc.) than among most of those of the Protectorate,[2] where such immigrants are much more scattered; and it seems that many would in fact apply the following principles:—

(*a*) If a husband fails to maintain his wife he will be told to do so, but no such "court" of arbitration has any power, of course, either to make a maintenance order or to seize property in execution; while where the husband is absent the wife's parents will usually support her and seek re-imbursement from the husband on his return.

(*b*) Where, however, a wife insists on dissolution of marriage—either for failure of maintenance, cruelty, or some other adequate or inadequate reason—some at least of these tribal headmen in the Colony will take advice from learned Muslims as to whether "bride-wealth" and expenses are returnable in such circumstances and will dissolve the marriage accordingly (i.e. either by *ṭalāq* or what amounts to forced ***khul'***[3]).

(*c*) This dissolution is sometimes, although by no means always, perfectly correct in Islamic law, except, of course, that the headman, etc., has no recognised judicial standing. But in the vast majority of cases his decision is accepted by the parties; and the Registrar will no doubt enter the "final divorce" in his register, as conforming to the requirements of Islamic law, under the Muhammadan Marriage Ordinance.

When, on the other hand, a Muslim man decides to divorce his wife, it seems usual, in the Colony, for him to do this before witnesses and to have it duly registered. Rather more distinction is, perhaps, recognised in the Colony than in the Protectorate between revocable and final divorces; but it seems that, except amongst a small number of purists, reconciliation will be allowed whatever formula was used and whether or not the *'idda* period had ended; for comparatively little attention is paid even in the Colony to the niceties of Islamic law in any such respect.

Among Muslims in the Colony many contract their marriages with the assistance of their tribal Imām—usually in the mosque and with a formal declaration (*ījāb*) and acceptance (*qabūl*). They also register them under the Ordinance; although "customary" marriages are also, of course, frequent, particularly among members of Protectorate tribes living in the Colony. Muslim men sometimes marry non-Muslim women, but the latter, apparently, almost always embrace Islam; while more rarely Muslim girls marry non-Muslims, usually, it seems, under the Christian Marriage Ordinance (but whether after profession of conversion, or not, I am not sure). Girls are never, officially at least, married by compulsion in the Colony; but marriage without their guardians' consent is almost equally rare. And deferment of part of their dower until divorce or widowhood (*aḥad al-ajalayn*) is, it seems, extremely rare but not wholly unknown.

In the Colony, again, property is chiefly held on an individual rather than a family basis. Problems of inheritance are normally settled within the family, either by tribal custom, by mutual agreement, or perhaps by Islamic law (as expounded by some would-be savant): and in default of such agreement the tribal headman is no doubt consulted. In many cases, of course, the Official

---

[1] It seems doubtful, however, how far they would be willing to do this in the case of an absent husband.

[2] Where Muhammadan marriage may be said to be a routine matter for Syrians, but merely a fashionable frill for Africans (see above).

[3] For these terms, see Glossary.

Administrator will take over the administration of such estates under the Administration of Estates Ordinance; while in the last resource any dispute regarding inheritance will go to the Supreme Court, where, in the case of a deceased Muslim who was either unmarried or married under the Ordinance, Islamic law, as expounded by expert witnesses, will prevail. In matters of bequests, on the other hand, English law is applied.[1] Cases of inheritance may, of course, frequently involve questions of paternity and legitimacy, and logic would seem to require that Islamic law should then apply in such matters precisely in so far as the Islamic law of inheritance is itself applicable. It seems, however, that such disputes seldom arise, even in the Colony; that such refinements of Mālikī law as the maximum period of gestation of five years are completely ignored; and that in cases of disputed paternity common-sense principles, or the word of the woman concerned, regularly prevail. And in all other types of cases (e.g. custody of children, guardianship, etc.) either English law or tribal custom are alone applicable.

During my short visit to Freetown I met most of the members of the "Sierra Leone Muslim Congress." These included a Lebanese-bred Arab of Hijāzī extraction; an "Arab" with a Moroccan father and a Mandingo mother; an Indian missionary of the Aḥmadīya movement; the Imāms of the Hausa, Fula, Mandingo (himself a Serahuli) and Timne communities; and several leading Muslims of the Creole (or Aku) community, mostly Yoruba by origin. They presented me with a petition which I at once passed on to the Secretariat, but which may be reproduced here. It reads as follows:—

> "The Sierra Leone Muslim Congress, the largest organised Muslim body, representing all sections of the Muslim communities in the Colony and Protectorate of Sierra Leone, desire once more to place on record their expression of loyalty and deep sense of gratitude to His Majesty the King, to His Representative His Excellency the Governor and all His Officers in this dependency, for the unfettered manner they have, from time to time, allowed us to observe our religious and personal laws in accordance with the teachings of Islam, since the Colony was founded over one hundred and sixty years ago.
>
> The Muslims of the Colony and Protectorate of Sierra Leone now feel that the time has arrived when they should be accorded the same privileges to practise the Muslim Personal Law (Sharī'a) as their brothers in other parts of our beloved Empire—the British Empire. E.g., in Nigeria and the Gambia, the Muslim law is applied as a *branch of the personal law* to Muslims in accordance with the principles of their own school or sub-school, modifications being made to suit present day requirements.
>
> The whole of Muslim Criminal Law has been superseded by our English Criminal Law and Criminal Procedure.
>
> The English Laws of Evidence and Contract, also, have superseded the rules of Muslim Law on these subjects in Sierra Leone.
>
> At the present time, provisions are made in the Laws of Sierra Leone whereby Muslims enjoy a branch of their personal law, e.g.
>
> (*a*) Marriage.
> (*b*) Divorce.
> (*c*) Inheritance and Succession.
>
> We desire that provisions should be specifically made in the Laws of Sierra Leone (with suitable modifications) to deal also with the following:—Wills, Gifts, Waqfs, Dower, Paternity, Guardianship, Maintenance, Trust or Trust Property.
>
> When our requests and wishes contained herein become accomplished fact, it will be very necessary to appoint someone qualified and learned in Muslim

[1] But not in the Protectorate.

Jurisprudence to administer the law. We shall be most grateful, therefore, if steps may be taken to appoint a Muslim Judge (Qāḍī) as early as possible."

The essence of this petition clearly consists in the two requests (*a*) that the whole of the Islamic personal law should be applied in the Colony (and Protectorate?) of Sierra Leone among Muslim litigants, and (*b*) that a Muslim Qāḍī should be appointed to apply it. A few comments on this petition may, therefore, be in place.

(1) It appears distinctly doubtful how representative this "Muslim Congress" can really claim to be. It seems, in any case, that the Protectorate Muslims were not consulted about this particular petition; and the same is probably true of the majority of those even in Freetown.

(2) The reference to the position in Nigeria and the Gambia is not wholly accurate. It is true that in the Colony of the Gambia there are two Qāḍīs' courts which are authorised to apply the Islamic law of personal status, that these courts do in fact, although without any express authority, make certain "modifications to suit present day requirements", and that this law is also applied to Muslims by some at least of the native tribunals of the Protectorate of the Gambia under the Native Tribunals Ordinance. It is also true that Muslim Alkalis apply Sharī'a law extensively in Nigeria: but it is noteworthy on the one hand that this is virtually confined to the North and to the juristic basis that it there constitutes "native law and custom" (rather than that Islamic law is applicable as such); and, on the other hand, that it extends far beyond the bounds of personal law and includes even cases of homicide. Nor is it true that the school or sub-school of the litigants is followed, for the law of the courts is alone applied.

(3) When the petition refers to the fact that English law has "superseded" [*sic*] the Sharī'a in matters of criminal law and procedure, this is not, it seems, intended as a complaint, but rather as an argument in favour of adopting the Islamic law of personal status. But the petitioners go beyond matters of personal status when they request, e.g., the application of the Islamic law of waqf. The very inclusion of this point, moreover, seems to show that they were acting under the influence of theory rather than facts, for the Islamic law of waqf is not applied anywhere in British West Africa, even in Northern Nigeria.[1]

(4) Again, when the petitioners allege that provision already exists for Muslims in Sierra Leone to "enjoy a branch of their personal law" (e.g., marriage, divorce and inheritance), they fail to observe that no provision has in fact been made for any court to decide matrimonial causes under Islamic law (e.g., demands for judicial dissolution of marriage by Muslim wives), and that the Islamic law of inheritance is only applicable in the Colony to Muslims who have not contracted a marriage otherwise than under Islamic law, while it is not applicable to those in the Protectorate under any circumstances whatever.

(5) When, therefore, the petitioners proceed to request that Islamic law should also be applied in regard to wills, gifts, dower, paternity, guardianship and maintenance, it is a matter of considerable doubt how serious a demand this may be. It is, of course, reasonable enough to argue that where the Islamic law of intestate succession is applicable, there the rules governing testamentary dispositions should also be applied.[2] At first sight, moreover, it might seem equally reasonable to urge that where the Islamic law of marriage is recognised, there Islamic principles with regard to dower should also be enforced—but experience shows that this is a matter in which local customs frequently prevail even in strongly Muslim areas. The same remark also applies to questions of paternity, where African custom

[1] And it is expressly excluded in the Gambia, under the Muhammadan Law Recognition Ordinance, 1905, sect. 9(*b*).

[2] Unless it is thought that the individual should have the right to dispose otherwise if he chooses.

seems far more realistic than some of the theoretical niceties of the Sharī'a.[1] It is true, moreover, that litigation regarding gifts is often included in the competence of Sharī'a courts, on the grounds that gifts usually partake either of the nature of family settlements on the one hand or of charitable dispositions on the other: but where the law of waqf is not itself applied the application of the Islamic rules regarding gifts might well be confined to the question of gifts in "death sickness" (as closely analogous to bequests) at the most. And matters concerning guardianship are still more doubtful, since they impinge so closely on local customary law on the one hand and British concepts of the welfare of the child on the other.

(6) It is noteworthy, in this connection, that the petition includes the words "with suitable modifications", although it is by no means apparent what these words are intended to imply. They would, however, provide an admirable basis for obtaining the agreement of both local and immigrant Muslims, in the event of any concession being made along the lines of this petition, to the application of the principle of legislative reform of certain points in the law—at least where authority for the desired reforms can be found in the dicta of some reputable classical jurist, on the principle now accepted and applied throughout the Middle East.[2]

(7) The petition makes no specific distinction between Colony and Protectorate, and the petitioners claim to represent both. While, however, it would be comparatively simple to set up a Qāḍī's court in Freetown to exercise jurisdiction in certain specified parts of the law of personal status, it would be a very different thing to make any attempt to apply such an innovation in the Protectorate. True, the Native Tribunals Ordinance in the Gambia provides for the application by these tribunals of the Islamic law of personal status among Muslim litigants[3]: but the degree to which the Sharī'a, on the one hand, and tribal or local custom, on the other, is in fact applied varies enormously from locality to locality—and in Sierra Leone Islam is much less strongly entrenched than in the Gambia.

(8) It would seem, then, that no valid case exists for the extension of this system to the Sierra Leone Protectorate—at least unless or until there is a real demand for this. Even as things now stand it would be perfectly possible for a whole district to abandon their present customary law, in favour of the Sharī'a or some approximation thereto, in any particular which they might wish, for provision exists, as we have seen, in the District Councils Ordinance for a district council to "make rules altering or modifying native customary law in the District".[4] As for individual Muslims of the stricter or better educated type, they are always free to follow the dictates of Islamic law in their personal lives, or even in family matters if the family consents: but it seems highly undesirable to introduce the complications inevitably raised by the enforcement, by judicial processes, of a personal law different from that of the locality and based solely on the dictates of religion, particularly in a country of such mixed faiths as is Sierra Leone today.[5] And the fact that the petition only requests the appointment of a single Muslim Qāḍī seems to point to the fact that the petitioners themselves had Freetown alone, or at least primarily, in view.

(9) Even in Freetown, however, it seems doubtful how strong a demand there really is for the establishment of a Qāḍī's court, or where, indeed, a suitably qualified Qāḍī could best be found. Even the Syrians, the strongest Muslims in the territory, seem in the main satisfied with the existing machinery. But a

---

[1] e.g., the Mālikī rule that the maximum period of gestation should be reckoned as five years.

[2] See pp. 16 ff., 22 f., etc: also Appendix A (pp. 304-5) and Appendix C.

[3] Sect. 11 (as amended in 1935).

[4] Sect. 17. See p. 292 above.

[5] Any such step would, moreover, inevitably retard the eventual fusion of native and English law—which must, surely, be the ultimate goal.

good case at least exists for an amendment to the Muhammadan Marriage Ordinance along the lines of the amendment to the Marriage, Divorce and Succession (Non-Christian Asiatics) Ordinance introduced in Tanganyika in 1947, to enable the courts to hear matrimonial causes thereunder in accordance with the relevant principles of Islamic law;[1] as also for provision to be made that where the Islamic law of intestate succession is applicable, there the broad principles of the Islamic law of testamentary dispositions should also be enforced—except, perhaps, where the deceased had made a will in the English form. It might also be thought advisable to qualify any such phrase as " matrimonial causes " in the proposed amendment to the Muhammadan Marriage Ordinance by the words " including questions of dower, except where the custom of the parties differs in this respect from the Sharī'a ", which would have the effect that those who in fact follow Islamic law in this matter could litigate thereunder before the suitable court, while those who follow some tribal or local custom could continue to deal with the matter as they do at present: but it is by no means certain whether there is any real need for such a provision, at least for the present. As for questions of paternity, custody and guardianship of children, no change in existing practice is, it seems, either necessary or desirable.

(10) If, on the other hand, it is ever decided that the time has come for the establishment of a Qāḍī's court in Freetown to try matters of personal status among Muslim litigants, whether including or excluding immigrant Muslims of the standing of the Syrian community, the following points should, it is suggested, be kept in view: —

(*a*) that while it would be useless to try to insist on such a court following other than Islamic rules of evidence and procedure, the precaution should be taken of providing that, where the decision of a case turns on the ineligibility of some witness on grounds of religion, interest in the case, or some similar consideration, the evidence of such a witness should be recorded in full and the record passed to the Supreme Court for review[2];

(*b*) that suitable " modifications ", as suggested by the petitioners themselves, should be made in the strict Mālikī law in such matters as *jabr* (compulsory marriage), *ḥaḍāna* (custody of children), etc.[3];

(*c*) that the law of waqf should not be applied, but that any mosques or other institutions or endowments should be governed by the general principles of law already applicable;

(*d*) that all this should, for the present at least, concern the Colony alone.

It should, perhaps, be added that Aḥmadī missionaries are at work both in Bo and Freetown, with their headquarters at the former; but they do not seem to have made much progress as yet. As always, their strong points are their encouragement of education, their loyalty to the administration and their advocacy of certain reforms; while their less attractive features are the controversy they invariably arouse among Muslims[4] and against Christians, regarding whose beliefs they indulge in a plethora of propaganda which is sometimes as offensive (and ill-founded) as it is dogmatic.

---

[1] Chiefly requests for judicial dissolution of marriage in accordance with Mālikī law, or that of some other school in the case of immigrant Muslims.

[2] cp. pp. 39, 101, etc.

[3] See Appendix A (pp. 304-305, 311-320) and Appendix C.

[4] Even leading to demands for dissolution of marriage by wives whose husbands turn Aḥmadī, on the grounds that they have " aspostasised " from Islam.

APPENDIX A

THE ANGLO-EGYPTIAN SUDAN

The Anglo-Egyptian Sudan does not, of course, properly fall within the purview of this Survey, for it is now in the process of passing from the status of a Condominium into that of an independent State, while it has never been a British Colonial possession. But a brief review of the application of Islamic law in that country can scarcely be omitted from this Survey, if only because of the many points of interest and comparison inevitably involved; while this is also of particular importance in that the Anglo-Egyptian Sudan may be regarded, in this respect, as a pioneer in the path of reform.

The fundamental Ordinance, in regard both to the general application of Islamic law in the Sudan and also to the principles on which a series of subsequent reforms have been based, is the Sudan Muhammadan[1] Law Courts Ordinance, 1902. This provides that "The Sudan Muhammadan Law Courts shall comprise a High Court, Mudīrīya[2] Courts, and District Courts[3]"—a more elaborate organisation than that found in any territory covered by this Survey. The District Courts consist of a single Qāḍī[4]; the Mudīrīya Courts of a single Qāḍī with a deputy to be appointed when circumstances so demand[5]; and the High Court "of the Grand Qāḍī who shall act as president, the Muftī of the Sudan, and one or more other members", with the decisions of the Court given by three members only.[6] This hierachy of Courts, moreover, is competent to decide: —

"(*a*) Any question regarding marriage, divorce, guardianship of minors or family relationship, provided that the marriage to which the question related was concluded in accordance with Muhammadan Law or the parties are all Muhammadans.

(*b*) Any question regarding waqf,[7] gift, succession, wills, interdiction or guardianship of an interdicted or lost person, provided that the endower donor or the deceased or the interdicted or lost person is a Muhammadan.

(*c*) Any question other than those mentioned in the last two sub-sections provided that all the parties, whether being Muhammadans or not, make a formal demand signed by them asking the Court to entertain the question and stating that they agree to be bound by the ruling of Muhammadan Law."[8]

The definition of the jurisdiction of the Muhammadan Courts in matters of family relationship in sub-section (*a*) above seems admirable, for the insistence that either the marriage to which the question at issue relates must have been concluded in accordance with Islamic law or the parties concerned must all be Muslims would appear to provide appropriate safeguards; and although the provision in sub-section (*b*), that all questions of succession, testate or intestate, are to be within the competence of these Courts (and therefore governed by Islamic law) provided only that the deceased was a Muslim, might give rise to considerable hardship in the case of a real or alleged conversion to Islam on the part, e.g., of an elderly person with non-Muslim dependents,[9] no other rule could,

[1] Here spelt "Mohammedan": but see the Introduction to this Survey regarding the liberty taken in re-spelling all such words, even in Ordinances, to avoid chaos and possible misconception.
[2] Here spelt "Mudiria": but see above.
[3] Sect. 2.
[4] Sect. 5: here spelt "Kadi", but see (1) above.
[5] Sect. 4.
[6] Sect. 3.
[7] Here spelt "wakf": but see above.
[8] Sect. 6.
[9] cp. the Kenya section of this Survey, pp. 112 ff.

perhaps, be expected, in view of the strongly Islamic sentiment prevalent in the Northern Sudan.[1] Even so, however, the Ordinance makes express provision for any possible conflict of jurisdiction between the Civil and Muhammadan Courts when it prescribes that any such conflict " shall be referred to a council consisting of the Legal Secretary of the Sudan or an official acting for him who will preside, the Grand Qāḍī or an official of the Muhammadan Court appointed by him, and the Chief Justice or a Judge of the High Court appointed by him. The decisions of this council, on questions of jurisdiction, shall be final ".[2] And this short Ordinance also lays the foundation for many recent reforms when it enacts that " The Grand Qāḍī shall from time to time, with the approval of the Governor-General, make regulations consistent with this ordinance regulating the decisions, procedure, constitution, jurisdiction, and functions of the Muhammadan Law Courts and other matters connected with such Courts . . ."[3]

It was in accordance with these powers that the Grand Qāḍī, with the approval of the Governor-General, issued the Ma'dhūns[4] Regulations, 1912. These prescribe, *inter alia*, that *ma'dhūns* must possess " A good knowledge of the Muhammadan Law relating to marriage, divorce, *'idda*[5] and wardship, and of all rules concerning their duties"[6]; that a *ma'dhūn* must register marriage contracts and issue divorce certificates, provided that there are no impediments to the marriage concerned either under the Sharī'a or administrative regulations, that the alleged divorce relates to a valid marriage, and that enquiries have been made as to " whether the parties are adults or minors and whether they are prodigal "; and that where the parties are not adults, and the guardian concerned is not a father or grandfather, the marriage is to be registered " subject to the consent in writing of the Qāḍī . . . after satisfying himself that the promoter of the marriage stands in the relation of legal guardian to or in the place of the legal guardian of either of the parties, that the husband is of status matching that of the wife and that the dowry is such as should be assigned to an equal ".[7] These entries on the registers shall, moreover, " be a true record of what in fact has been agreed upon " —including the names of the parties, their agents (if any), the witnesses to the power of attorney appointing the said agents, a statement as to whether the husband and wife are adults or minors, frugal or prodigal, the names of the witnesses to the contract, the date of divorce or widowhood of the wife if previously married, the amount of the dower, its value if consisting in articles and property other than a money sum, and how much is payable at once and how much at a future date. Similarly, in the case of divorce, the record must include the name of the husband or his agent who promotes the divorce, the name of the wife or her agent who promotes the *khul'*[8] (or the " name and description of the person who made the agreement without her permission "), the consideration concerned, and whether the wife is minor, adult, prodigal, etc. All such records and certificates, moreover, must be suitably signed or sealed[9]; lists of all marriage

[1] But there seems little reason why any such provision, with all the suffering it may cause, should be applied in the Southern Sudan. And even in the Northern Sudan the precedent of the Indian Removal of Caste Disabilities Act, 1850, of somewhat similar provisions in Tanganyika (see pp. 125-7) and Nyasaland (see p. 162), and of a tentative solution in the Muslim Emirates of Northern Nigeria (see p. 216), is relevant.

[2] Sect. 7.

[3] Sect. 8.

[4] Here spelt " Maazuns ": but see Introduction regarding the liberty taken in re-spelling Arabic words.

[5] Here spelt " iddats ".

[6] Sect. 2(*c*).

[7] Sect. 7. The latter provisions represent the Ḥanafī law which is the official system of the Sudan (see below), rather than the Mālikī law which represents the personal law of the vast majority of Sudanese.

[8] Divorce for a financial consideration at the request of the wife: see Glossary.

[9] Sect. 8 (as also details above).

contracts or divorce certificates issued by *ma'dhūns* are to be submitted to the Muhammadan Law Courts " to serve as registers for reference when necessary "; the appropriate fees are to be paid into the Court treasury; and the registers are to be inspected by the Qāḍīs at least three times a year[1]—while it is also provided that " It is the duty of the *ma'dhūn* to report at once to the Court any marriage or divorce which takes place in his district through any person other than himself." When, moreover, such marriage or divorce is reported to the Qāḍī by the *ma'dhūn* or any other person " he shall enquire into the matter and if it is proved to be true, the Qāḍī shall have the contract or certificate registered in the register of *ishhāds*[2] of the Court in the form of a declaration ".[3] From this it is clear that although the proper registration of marriages and divorces may be regarded as " compulsory " in the Sudan no attempt has been made to regard marriages and divorces not so registered as invalid, provided they are not in fact contrary to the Sharī'a.

Far more important than these Regulations, however, are the Sudan Muhammadan Law Courts Organisation and Procedure Regulations, 1915, similarly issued by the Grand Qāḍī, with the approval of the Governor-General, under section 8 of the Sudan Muhammadan Law Courts Ordinance, 1902. These comprise no less than three hundred sections, and closely—but not uniformly—follow Egyptian models. Thus Chapter I (sections 1-10) concerns the " Selection Appointment and Delegation of Sharī'a Officials " and calls for little comment. Chapter II (sections 11-53), on the other hand, is much more important, for it defines in detail the " Jurisdiction and Competence of Courts and Functions of the Grand Qāḍī", and thus establishes a hierarchy of courts whereby the Qāḍīs of District Courts exercise a wide but limited jurisdiction,[4] the Qāḍīs of Province Courts are competent " to try by way of appeal all cases heard by Qāḍīs of District Courts under them "[5] and also original suits beyond the competence of the latter,[6] while the High Court is competent to "rehear in appeal suits decided in first instance by the Qāḍīs of Province Courts" (with certain exceptions[7]) and also to "rehear as a Court of Revision" the decisions of Province Qāḍīs in appeal from District Qāḍīs—or, indeed, cases in which an appeal might have been made, but was either not made within the prescribed time or even expressly renounced by the party concerned, against the decisions of either Province or District Qāḍīs[8]—while it may also at any time call for and revise any case heard by any of these Courts.[9] Again, " When the circumstances so demand, the Grand Qāḍī or the judge delegated by him may hear any case not previously decided by a Muhammadan Law Court ", or rehear by way of appeal certain cases of first instance previously decided by Qāḍīs of District and Province Courts[10]; he may " order the transfer of any suit pending . . . to another Court if in his opinion there are reasonable grounds for such transfer " (which shall *ipso facto* give the decision of the Qāḍī to whom the case is transferred the effect of a decision given by a Qāḍī of a Province Court[11]); and he is the " general administrator of the estates of Muhammadan deceased persons and all complaints relating to such estates shall be submitted to him for decision in such manner as he may direct ".[12] The work of all the Muhammadan Law Courts except the High

[1] Sects. 9 and 10.
[2] See below.
[3] Sect. 11.
[4] Sects. 22, 23, 24.
[5] Sect. 25.
[6] Sects. 26-29.
[7] Sect. 30.
[8] Sects. 31 and 32.
[9] Sect. 35.
[10] Sect. 36.
[11] Sect. 37.
[12] Sect. 38.

Court, moreover, is subject to the supervision of a Committee of Supervision composed of the Legal Secretary, the Grand Qāḍī, the Muftī and the Inspector of the Muhammadan Law Courts, etc.,[1] whose object shall be to "point out judicial errors in order to prevent their recurrence but . . . not affect the judgments given or the matters decided"[2]; but if it considers any judgment contrary to the principles of the Sharī'a it may refer it to the High Court for review.[3] Provision is also made that Sharī'a suits should be "barred by the lapse of 15 years, provided the plaintiff was competent to plead and that no legal impediment prevented him from doing so, except suits relating to successions and waqfs, which are only barred by the lapse of 33 years . . . Provided, in all cases that there was no acknowledgment of the right during the above mentioned periods respectively[4] . . ."; that "The Qāḍīs of the Muhammadan Law Courts as regards their decisions under the Sharī'a and the exercise of their judicial functions are independent of and in no way subordinate to the civil authorities who must not in any way interfere with their judicial independence[5]"; and that the "Decisions of the Muhammadan Law Courts shall be in accordance with the authoritative doctrines of the Ḥanafīya jurists except in matters in which the Grand Qāḍī otherwise directs in a judical circular or memorandum in which case the decisions shall be in accordance with such other doctrines of the Ḥanafīya or other Muhammadan jurists as are set forth in such circular or memorandum".[6]

This last provision is so important that it demands further comment. The first part, of course, represents a mere enunciation of the practice of the Ottoman Empire imposed upon the Sudan by its Egyptian conquerors, whereby a predominantly Mālikī population was made subject to Ḥanafī law, while the courts were precluded from any exercise of personal discretion by the dominance accorded to the doctrines which had in each particular become established as "authoritative" in that school. But the latter part of the section opens the door wide to the application in the Sudan of the reforming principles which have exercised such an extensive and beneficial influence in Egypt and other Muslim lands, whereby it is urged: —

(*a*) that it is unreasonable for modern Muslims to regard themselves as bound in every particular by the "authoritative" doctrines of any one school, when all the wealth of the divergent views attributed to the great jurists of the past may be considered equally available;

(*b*) that even if no claim is made today to the right of *ijtihād* or independent deduction from the original sources (although many modernists in fact make that claim), yet even the ***muqallid***[7] who is bound to follow the dicta of the great jurists of the past may choose which of several variant dicta he will adopt;

(*c*) that although this unfettered choice may be limited, in general, to private persons in their individual lives rather than Qāḍīs in the public administration of justice, yet the Ruler of a State has the right to instruct his judges, as a matter of public policy and in the common interests, which of these variant opinions they are to apply;

(*d*) that this in fact constitutes only a particular manifestation of the Ruler's

---

[1] Sects. 42-44, 47-49.

[2] Sect. 45.

[3] Sect. 46.

[4] Sect. 51. This is, of course, contrary to the pure Sharī'a, which knows no such periods of limitation. But it is commonly justified by Muslim jurists as an instance not of any attempt to change the substantive law but rather of an administrative order by which the Executive refuses judicial relief in certain cases wherein perjury, etc., is particularly to be feared. See pp. 17, 217-8, etc.

[5] Sect. 52. Contrast the powers of revision exercisable by administrative officers over "native", "local" or Qāḍīs' courts in many territories covered by this Survey.

[6] Sect. 53.

[7] For these technical terms, see Glossary (under *mujtahid*).

general right to limit the jurisdiction of his judges, whether by reference to the area of their jurisdiction, its scope, or its juristic basis.

Chapter III concerns "Court Procedure" and comprises one hundred and thirteen sections (54-166). The points which call for special mention here may be summarised as follows: —

(i) Provision is made for the hearing of cases *ex parte* where summonses have been duly served but the defendant fails to appear either in person or by agent[1], or where he is of unknown whereabouts,[2] and such judgment shall be considered as given in his presence[3]; while where the appearance of the defendant in person is essential, as when judgment depends on his oath in divorce and similar cases, he may be arrested and brought before the court if he fails to respond to an order to do so,[4] or be required, in cases of hardship, to appear before some other court[5] or (where ill, infirm or a secluded woman) to make a statement on oath before a deputy appointed by the Qāḍī.[6]

(ii) Claims need not be made in any special form, so long as they clearly convey the meaning of the plaintiff, while where any omission is made or point of obscurity left by either party in his case the Qāḍī shall question him, and both question and answer shall be entered in the record[7]; and even where the plaintiff fails to correct his claim when so questioned the Qāḍī may still examine the defendant and treat him in accordance with any admission he may make.[8]

(iii) "Either party shall have the right to have the other party examined on the facts relating to the issues. The party whom it is sought to examine may claim from the Court the rejection of the whole or part of the questions put if they do not relate to relevant facts"; while "Questions to which the party does not object or which the Court admits shall be put by the President . . . in the presence of the party who demands the examination, unless the Qāḍī decides that his presence is not necessary[9]."

(iv) Third parties may intervene in a suit, but judgment in the principal suit shall not be delayed on that account unless there is a cause for such delay recognised by the Sharī'a[10]; and when an incidental question is raised in the course of a suit, the Qāḍī may either decide it when it is raised or add it to the issues and deal with it on its merits in his judgment.[11]

(v) The statements of both parties and witnesses must be included in the record of the case and signed by those responsible; and if any party or witness refuses to sign his statement, this also must be recorded.[12]

(vi) A written admission has the same force as an oral admission; official documents are accepted as conclusive evidence without any other evidence being required in support, while private documents are proof against the person or persons signing or sealing them; and in any dispute

[1] Sect. 81(*a*).
[2] Sects. 82 and 83—which include certain conditions and distinctions.
[3] Sect. 81(*d*)—where the summons has been duly served (sect. 81(*a*)).
[4] Sect. 81(*b*). [5] Sect. 81(*c*).
[6] Or, indeed, the Court itself on transfer: see sects. 86, 87. It is noteworthy that these provisions clear up several points about which uncertainty prevails in other territories.
[7] Sects. 93 and 94.
[8] Sect. 95. These provisions represent a considerable relaxation of the rigidity which characterises pleadings under the Sharī'a as usually applied.
[9] Sects. 103, 104 and 105. These provisions cover the vexed question of cross-examination.
[10] Sect. 107: cp. sect. 108.
[11] Sect. 109.
[12] Sects. 112, 113.

concerning the constitution or conditions of a waqf the fact that such waqf is established by a registered *ḥujja*[1], fulfilling the conditions of validity required by the Sharī'a, precludes any suit being entertained which purports to question such constitution or conditions: but, in general, documents and writings may be attacked either by denial of signature or seal or by allegation of forgery (the first process being admissible against private documents only, while the second is always admissible), in which case expert testimony may be called.[2]

(vii) Witnesses are to be questioned individually by the Qāḍī as to their name, profession, functions and connection, if any, with the parties to the case; they may be questioned by the opposite side through the Qāḍī; and their evidence is to be accepted " if the Qāḍī is satisfied of (its) truthfulness . . . and all doubtful points have been cleared up "—provided the evidence of one witness agrees with that of the other in meaning, even though it may differ in words, and that it conforms with the allegation of the party who called them; while to establish facts relating to maintenance, wardship, nurture or lodging allowance, or the conditions on which any of these matters depend, " the evidence of any trustworthy witness is admissible "[3]

(viii) The party who desires a witness to be summoned may be required to deposit in Court the amount estimated by the Court as sufficient to cover his expenses, and the Qāḍī shall order the unsuccessful party to repay to the successful party any such sum deposited by him.[4]

(ix) When a case is dismissed " on the ground that the plaintiff has failed to make proof or . . . has been considered to have so failed, the judgment of dismissal shall be a bar to the subsequent rehearing of the same case, subject to the right of the plaintiff to proceed against the judgment in the ways prescribed by these regulations."[5]

(x) Experts may be appointed whenever this seems necessary, but the Court shall never be bound by their opinion.[6]

Chapter IV concerns " Judgment, Appeal and Revision " and comprises fifty-one sections (167-207). The only points which seem to demand comment here are that provision is made that judgments affirming divorce, ordering divorce or declaring the dissolution of marriage shall not be delivered to the successful party until it has been ascertained, in the case of an absent defendant, that the judgment has been notified[7], and, in all cases, that the period prescribed for appeal, etc., has expired[8]; that applications to set aside judgments given in default of appearance must be made within prescribed periods to the Court which gave the judgment, and such applications shall suspend the execution of judgment, except in matters of alimony or where provisional execution has been authorised[9]; that somewhat longer periods are allowed for appeals from District Courts and Province Courts (when acting in first instance) respectively, and any such appeal shall have the same effect as an application to set aside a judgment as regards execution thereof[10]; that the appellant " shall be considered as the plaintiff so long as the Appellate Court has not ordered the cancellation of the judgment and the rehearing of the case, but when the Court orders a case to be reheard

[1] Deed.
[2] Sects. 114-133. These and certain subsequent provisions cover the vexed question of documentary evidence—and subsidiary considerations.
[3] Sects. 138-149. These provisions replace the *tazkīya* of the pure Sharī'a: see Glossary.
[4] Sects. 151-156.
[5] Sect. 161.
[6] Sects. 164, 5.
[7] Except where the person concerned is of unknown whereabouts.
[8] Sect. 170.
[9] Sects. 172-178.
[10] Sects. 179-187.

such order shall restore the case to its original condition "[1]; that "By revision of judgments is meant the re-opening of suits in which final decision has been given, for the purpose of reconsidering whether the decision is in accordance with or contrary to the Sharī'a and its recognised principles "[2]; that application for such revision may be made by either party within one year from notification of judgment or removal of any obstacle to such application[3]; that the decision of the Court of Revision is not open to any objection and shall be executory, provided that the Court of Revision may review its own decision in certain specified circumstances[4]; and that the liability of a judgment to revision does not prevent its execution.[5]

Chapter V concerns "*I'lāmāt* of Heirship and *Ishhādāt*"[6] and consists of forty-five sections (208-252). *I'lāmāt* of heirship are documents recording the date of the deceased's death, the number and description of his heirs, his estate, and the appointment of any guardians or trustees or the confirmation of any testamentary guardians—together with the grounds on which the Court reached its decisions; and such *i'lām* "shall be conclusive evidence as to the heirship of the heirs mentioned in it", unless a decision be given by a Muhammadan Law Court excluding some of them or including others.[7] *Ishhādāt,* on the other hand, are formal acts—such as the making of wills or waqfs, or the appointment of a guardian or waqf administrator—made before a judicial official, signed or sealed by the parties concerned, their witnesses, the clerk who drew them up and the official who heard them.[8] Chapter VI covers "Executions", and comprises seventeen sections (253-271). These provide that "The methods and procedure contained in the Civil Justice Ordinance respecting execution and the seizure of the judgment debtor's money, movable and immovable property and the attachment of debts due to the judgment debtor, shall apply to the execution of the judgments of the Muhammadan Law Courts "[9]; that "Executions shall be affected by the Administrative Authorities or by such official as may be appointed for this purpose by the Legal Secretary "[10]; that provisional execution may be ordered before judgments become executory in matters of alimony, custody of children, etc.[11]; and that "The execution of a judgment ordering the obedience of a wife may be repeated three times after which the husband must obtain a fresh judgment if he further desires to enforce the obedience of his wife", while all other judgments remain executory however often their execution may have to be repeated.[12] Finally, Chapter VII (sections 272-300) concerns the Registers which the Muhammadan Courts must keep. Subsequently, in 1935, the Sudan Muhammadan Law Courts Fees Regulations were similarly promulgated, but need not detain us here.

But other Courts in the Sudan may also on occasion take cognisance of Islamic law. Thus the Civil Justice Ordinance, 1929, provides[13] that "Where in any suit

[1] Sect. 188: this may be a matter of great importance under the Sharī'a.
[2] Sect. 195.
[3] Sects. 197, 198.
[4] Sect. 199.
[5] Sect. 202.
[6] Here spelt "Ilamat" and "Ish-Hadat"; but see Introduction regarding the spelling of Arabic words.
[7] See sects. 208-241, especially 227 and 228.
[8] Sects. 242-252.
[9] Sect. 253.
[10] Sect. 254.
[11] Sects. 255, 256.
[12] Sect. 259. But it is noteworthy that judgments of obedience (conjugal rights) are not now executed by force in the Sudan. Instead, the Administrative Officer charged with their execution will summon the spouses to his office and formally "hand over" the wife to her husband: but if no persuasion will induce her to accompany him, he will not be permitted to drag her away, nor will the Police be charged to escort her home with him.
[13] Sect. 5.

or other proceeding in a Civil Court any question arises regarding succession, inheritance, wills, legacies, gifts, marriage, divorce, family relations, or the constitution of waqfs, the rule of decision shall be—

(*a*) any custom applicable to the parties concerned, which is not contrary to justice, equity or good conscience, and has not been by this or any other enactment altered or abolished and has not been declared void by the decision of a competent Court:

(*b*) the Muhammadan Law, in cases where the parties are Muhammadans, except in so far as that law has been modified by such custom as is above referred to". And the dictates of Islamic law might also, conceivably, on occasion be applied under the further provision[1] that "In cases not provided for by this or any other enactment for the time being in force the Court shall act according to justice, equity and good conscience". At the same time, however, it is also provided that "Civil Courts shall not be competent to decide, in a suit to which all parties are Muhammadans, except with the consent of all the parties, any questions regarding succession, inheritance, wills, legacies, gifts, marriage, divorce, family relations, or the constitution of waqfs"[2]; while it is also laid down that "Where in a suit before a Civil Court a question within the competence of the Court cannot conveniently be determined without a decision on a question exempted from the jurisdiction of the Court by section 38, the Court shall either—

(*a*) adjourn the case to enable the parties to the suit to obtain the decision of a competent Sharī'a Court on such last-mentioned question; or

(*b*) itself refer such last-mentioned question to a competent Sharī'a Court for decision, either in the form of a stated case or as an issue for trial"—and the decision of such Sharī'a Court, subject in the first case to any right of appeal and in the second to any reference by the Legal Secretary, on the application of the Civil Court, to the High Sharī'a Court, shall be accepted and put into effect by the Civil Court.[3]

Again, the Native Courts Ordinance, 1932 (as repeatedly amended), provides for the following classes of Native Courts—

"(*a*) a Sheikh's Court, that is a Court with a Sheikh as president sitting with members;

(*b*) a Court of a Sheikh sitting in *majlis*[4], that is a Court of a Sheikh sitting with elders;

(*c*) a Village Court;

(*d*) a Court of a Sheikh sitting alone;

(*e*) a Special Court".[5]

Such Courts, moreover, are empowered to administer—

"(*a*) the native law and custom prevailing in the area or in the tribe over which the Court exercises its jurisdiction provided that such native law and custom is not contrary to justice, morality or order;

(*b*) the provisions of any ordinance, where such provisions are not part of native law and custom, and where the Court has been expressly authorised in its warrant, order or regulations to administer such provisions".[6] Again, such Court "shall have full jurisdiction and power to the extent set out in this ordinance or in the warrant or order establishing the Court or in the regulations

[1] Sect. 9.

[2] Sect. 38. This is noticeably different from the wording of the Sudan Muhammadan Law Courts Ordinance, 1902, and the divergence between the two Ordinances seems almost to invite conflicts of jurisdiction.

[3] Sect. 39.

[4] Here spelt "meglis"; but see Introduction regarding the spelling of Arabic words.

[5] Sect. 5.

[6] Sect. 9(1).

accompanying such warrant or order ".[1] And provision is also made both for appellate powers to be granted to some Native Courts[2] and for the Governor or District Commissioner to exercise powers of revision, either on the application of any person concerned or of his own motion.[3]

It is apparent, then, that the jurisdiction of these Courts does not normally include the application of Sharī'a law as such, but only in so far as it may have succeeded, in any particular tribe or locality, in having influenced or replaced indigenous custom. It is noteworthy, however, that the warrants or orders establishing some of these Courts, when situated far from any " Muhammadan Law Courts ",[4] expressly authorise them to deal with matters of personal status under Islamic law, provided (in theory, at least) that they have an *'ālim* (i.e., someone " learned " in that law) sitting as a member of the Court. To this interesting provision we must return later. But it is also noteworthy in this context that in Western Darfur the Sultan has his own courts, appeal from which lies only to the Governor of the Province: but the latter would always, in any point involving the Sharī'a, consult his Province Qāḍī, whose opinion, on any interpretation of Islamic law as such, would therefore prevail.

There are a few more Ordinances which must receive passing notice as affecting, in some degree, the application of Islamic law in the Sudan. Thus in the Penal Code, 1925 (as repeatedly amended), it is noteworthy that the definition in section 307 of the offence of kidnapping or abducting a woman to compel her to marry, etc. (" Whoever kidnaps or abducts any woman with intent that she may be compelled or knowing it to be likely that she will be compelled to marry any person against her will or in order that she may be forced or seduced to illicit intercourse . . . ") is not so wide as that in some other such Codes; and although it might in certain circumstances expose to prosecution a father whose treatment of his virgin daughter might be unexceptionable under the Sharī'a, it would not extend to any case where the daughter had actually been contracted in marriage by her father in his capacity of guardian with the right of compulsion. Again, the definition of rape in section 316 expressly excludes sexual intercourse by a man with his own wife, but only if she has already reached puberty; while the Sharī'a allows the consummation of a marriage with a child wife even earlier.[5]

A particularly interesting—and somewhat strange—Ordinance is the Non-Muhammadan Marriage Ordinance, 1926. This is expressly stated not to " affect the validity of any marriage contracted under or in accordance with Muhammadan law or any valid pagan law or custom " or in any manner to " apply to marriages so contracted "[6]; and " A marriage celebrated under this ordinance shall be null and void if either of the parties thereto at the time of the celebration of such marriage is validly married whether under this ordinance or by Muhammadan law or by any valid pagan law or custom or otherwise to any person other than the person with whom such marriage is had ".[7] The usual bars of consanguinity and affinity, but not the specifically Islamic bar of fosterage,[8]

---

[1] Sect. 8(1).
[2] Sect. 12(1).
[3] Sect. 14(1)—except in the case of a Special Court, when such powers are limited to the Governor, under sect. 14(2).
[4] And especially among bedouin tribes.
[5] See p. 35, etc., above.
[6] Sect. 4. The only exception to this rule is mentioned in sect. 12 below.
[7] Sect. 6.
[8] But it is noteworthy that should a Muslim attempt to marry, under this Ordinance, anyone related to him or her within the prohibited degrees of fosterage, the terms of sect. 26 might be invoked, since this section allows a caveat to be entered on the grounds that " there is some lawful hindrance to the marriage under the personal law applicable to either party ". In such cases the matter must be referred to the Chief Justice, who shall " make such order as shall seem to him just for the decision of the matter by himself or by such other Judge as he may appoint. ".

are applicable to all such marriages[1]; "Every marriage validly celebrated under this ordinance or under any of the ordinances hereby repealed . . . shall continue and subsist until one of the parties thereto shall die or until it shall be dissolved by a decree of nullity or of divorce pronounced by a Court of competent jurisdiction"; and "So long as such marriage subsists neither party shall be competent to contract a second marriage whether under this ordinance or otherwise".[2] So far, therefore, this Ordinance follows much the same pattern as Civil Marriage Ordinances elsewhere; but just at this point we find a most unusual proviso, for section 12 continues: "Provided always that if the husband becomes an adherent of the Muhammadan faith and by reason of such adherence his personal status comes to be governed by the Muhammadan Religious Law,

(*a*) such marriage shall continue to subsist but may be dissolved in accordance with the Muhammadan Religious Law,[3] and

(*b*) notwithstanding the subsistence of such marriage it shall be lawful for the husband to marry another wife or other wives in accordance with the Muhammadan Religious Law.

Provided also that, if the husband becomes an adherent of the Muhammadan faith but the wife does not and the husband marries or purports to marry another wife during the subsistence of such marriage, then whether or not his personal status shall have come to be governed by the Muhammadan Religious Law it shall be lawful for the High Court of Justice to dissolve such marriage on petition of the wife".[4]

This provision appears to run directly counter to the usual view of British Courts that if two parties have of their own volition concluded a monogamous marriage, then the nature of that marriage should not be susceptible to radical alteration by the unilateral decision of one of the parties to embrace another religion. True, it has sometimes (but not consistently) been held that where both parties to a "Christian" marriage, being domiciled in a non-Christian country, embrace the religion of Islam, then their marriage becomes governed thereafter by Islamic rather than, e.g., English law: but in this Ordinance the same is stipulated where the husband alone embraces that religion, save only that if he exercises his right thereunder to marry a co-wife the first wife may apply for the dissolution of her marriage. But it is noteworthy that marriages celebrated according to the rites followed by a number of specified religious communities are expressly excepted from the scope of this Ordinance: instead, marriages performed by the ministers of such communities shall "be valid and shall have the effect and involve the consequence laid down by such personal law".[5] The excepted communities include the Jews, the Greek Orthodox, the Orthodox Coptic, and the Roman, Greek, Maronite, Syrian, Armenian, Coptic and Chaldean Catholics—the last seven being regarded as one "group" of excepted communities.[6]

Both the Wills and Administration Ordinance, 1928, and the Official Administrator Ordinance, of the same date, expressly provide that "This ordinance shall not apply to the estates of Muslims nor to the estates of pagan members of pagan tribes inhabiting the Sudan".[7] Again, the Public Trustee Ordinance,

[1] Sect. 7(1).
[2] Sect. 12.
[3] i.e., by the unfettered unilateral repudiation of the wife by her husband, *inter alia.*
[4] Sect. 12. But it is not clear what the phrase "whether or not his personal status shall have come to be governed by the Muhammadan Religion Law" is intended to mean, since this, in the Muslim view at least, is a necessary corollary of his adoption of that faith.
[5] Sect. 5(1). But it is not apparent what would in fact be the position if a husband, so married, were subsequently to embrace Islam. Would he be held to the implications of his monogamous marriage, or would he in fact be allowed to contract polygamous marriages or divorce his wife under the law of Islam?
[6] Second Schedule.
[7] Sect. 3, in each case.

1937, provides that "Where any interest such as is mentioned in sub-section (1) of this section (namely, where a minor or lunatic has any vested or continuing interest in any property real or personal situate in the Sudan) falls within the jurisdiction of a Maḥkama Sharʿīya[1] any order as aforementioned vesting such interest in the Public Trustee shall be made by the Grand Qāḍī of his own motion on being satisfied that the conditions laid down in paragraphs (*a*) and (*b*) of sub-section (1) (namely, that the Public Trustee consents to undertake the trust and that it is for the benefit of the minor or lunatic that such order should be made) are fulfilled".[2] Finally, it is noteworthy that the Pre-emption Ordinance, 1928, puts the application of the Islamic principles of *shufʿa* on a statutory basis, and one which does not by any means conform to all the details of the Ḥanafī law.

But much the most interesting phenomenon regarding the application of Sharīʿa law in the Sudan is the series of judicial Circulars issued by the Grand Qāḍī under section 53 of the Sudan Muhammadan Law Courts Organisation and Procedure Regulations, 1915 (themselves promulgated under section 8 of the Sudan Muhammadan Law Courts Ordinance, 1902). Up till the middle of 1950 the Circulars so issued amounted to fifty-three (in addition to a number of Memoranda and other papers), some of which had subsequently been rescinded. Those which remain in force may be subdivided into Circulars of an administrative nature, Circulars which define the way in which the Courts are to perform some of their duties (which may be regarded as partly administrative and partly, but to a minor extent, declaratory of the law), and those which either deny judicial relief altogether in certain circumstances or define the substantive law to be applied. It is these last which constitute the chief medium for reform and which demand fuller mention.

Detailed study of the Circulars concerned reveals that in most cases, but by no means all, they have been based on reforms either already promulgated or at least under consideration in Egypt. In a considerable number of instances the wording of Egyptian legislation has been adopted *verbatim*, or with trifling alterations; in others some of the salient points in a comprehensive piece of Egyptian legislation have alone been applied; while in yet others reforms under discussion in Egypt have been put into effect in the Sudan some years before they were promulgated in the land of their origin.[3] This ready reflection of the views of Egyption reformers in the judicial Circulars issued by the Grand Qāḍī in Khartoum is party, of course, explained by the fact that the present Grand Qāḍī is the first Sudanese who has ever been appointed to that office, all previous holders having been selected from among the leading jurists of Egypt[4]: but it is also due to the intimate connection which inevitably exists between the *ʿulamāʾ*, and trends in juristic opinion, in the two countries.[5] And it is also noteworthy that some of the earliest reforms, which in large part consisted in the substitution of the Mālikī for the Ḥanafī law in regard to certain matrimonial causes, were particularly easy to effect in the Sudan, where the vast majority of the people are convinced, or at least professing, Mālikīs.

The earliest of these Circulars which need detain us here is Circular No. 13, of 5th February, 1913—a Circular to which the Egyptian reforms in the law applicable to Sharīʿa Courts provide no parallel, since the subject matter of this Circular (gifts and pledges) is no longer, in Egypt, within the competence of those Courts. But this whole subject of gifts and pledges is much complicated, in the Ḥanafī system, by the rules applicable to property held in common

[1] i.e., Muhammadan court.

[2] Sect. 8(3).

[3] It might, in fact, almost be said that Egyptian Grand Qāḍīs have "tried out" some of these reforms in the Sudan before their application in Egypt.

[4] Including Muṣṭaphā al-Marāghī, himself a leading champion of reform in such matters.

[5] And, as such, will not end with the appointment of Sudanese Grand Qāḍīs.

between two or more co-owners and to property which occupies or is occupied by something of which the donor or pledgor retains ownership. The principle involved is whether the donor has given the donee the fullest possession of which the property is capable, for it is only by possession that the ownership of the donee (or the right of the pledgee) is established: and the "authoritative Ḥanafī opinion" holds that a donor who does not divide off his own share of such common property as is susceptible to such division, and does not remove all his own possessions (e.g. crops or furniture) from the property given, has not completed his gift. Circular No. 13, therefore, was designed to allow these complicated rules (of which only a part is mentioned above) to be disregarded in the Sudan in favour of the opinion of al-Shāfi'ī and Mālik that ownership in such cases passes by the donor allowing the donee to exercise the rights of ownership. The wording of the Circular, however, betrays the concern of the Grand Qāḍī to carry his Qādīs with him in this innovation, for he supports it not only by the arguments of the needs of society, the experience of the Courts and the opinions of the two great Imāms, but also by reference to the Turkish compilation of the Ḥanafī law of obligations known as the Majalla, which itself omits all reference to these niceties. It should be added that the Circular confines itself to stating that *ishhādāt* (official deeds) of gift, or *i'lāmāt* (certificates) of heirship, may be issued in spite of the fact that they concern or include gifts or pledges which transgress the Ḥanafī rules outlined above.[1]

Again, Circular No. 17 (date uncertain, but probably 1916) includes some major reforms in matters of marriage and divorce. This Circular was inspired by projects under discussion and debate in Egypt for a considerable time, but itself antedates by four years the first Egyptian reform of this nature. Thus section 1 provides that a maintenance order in favour of a wife may be executed out of any of her husband's property, whether money, movables or immovables. This is a departure from the Ḥanafī rule—which, in the case of an absent husband, only provides for execution out of property which can itself be used for maintenance, or for judicial permission for the wife to find her own maintenance on her husband's credit—in favour of the more liberal view of the other three schools. This was only introduced in Egypt by Law No. 25 of 1920, which provides in section 4 that such decree shall be executed out of the husband's "property", without further specification.

Sections 2—9 provide for the judicial divorce of a wife whose husband, whether present or absent, fails to provide her with even the poorest scale of maintenance (after a limited delay in his favour in certain circumstances). These provisions, which are also of Mālikī origin, were promulgated in Egypt, with trifling differences but considerable abbreviation, by sections 4—6 of Law No. 25 of 1920. Similarly, sections 10—12 provide for the remarriage of the wife of a "missing" husband, even if he has property out of which she can obtain her maintenance: she must bring his disappearance before the Courts, which will thereupon institute enquiries; then, if these fail, she will be told to wait four years, after which she may keep the *'idda* period prescribed for widows and then remarry. If, however, the missing husband subsequently appears she will be his, unless her second marriage has been consummated with no knowledge, on the part of her second husband, of the survival of the first (in which case the second marriage will stand). These provisions were enacted in Egypt by sections 7 and 8 of the Law of 1920, except that the four years' delay was there to date from reference to the Courts rather than the failure of subsequent enquiries: but section 7 (not 8) was subsequently replaced by the more comprehensive provisions concerning missing persons enacted by sections 21 and 22 of Law No. 25 of 1929. The Sudanese and earlier Egyptian legislation is

[1] Here and in the following pages certain passages from my article "Recent Developments in Sharī'a Law in the Sudan" [Sudan Notes and Records, 1950, Part I] are transcribed either *verbatim* or with minor alterations.

Mālikī, while the later Egyptian legislation is Hanbali in origin.

Section 13 concerns the right of a wife whose husband deserts her for more than a year to claim a judicial divorce on the grounds of hardship and fear of falling into unfaithfulness—and is based on Mālikī authority. According to section 1 of Circular No. 28, of 1927, however, this is only available in cases where a claim to divorce for failure of maintenance is not applicable. The Court will serve notice on the husband, if he can be contacted, allowing him an opportunity to return to his wife or send for her to join him: and if he does neither, or if he cannot be contacted, the Qāḍī will dissolve the marriage. This reform was not adopted in Egypt until the Law of 1929, sections 12 and 13, when it was simply termed " divorce for absence ", was based on hardship without any specific reference to fear of unfaithfulness, and is not, apparently, excluded by the possibility of claiming divorce on the grounds of failure of maintenance. It should also be noticed that Egypt allows a divorce to a wife whose husband is under final sentence of not less than three years' imprisonment after she has suffered not less than one year's separation; while no such provision has been introduced in the Sudan.

Similarly, section 14 concerns judicial divorce for proved cruelty,[1] while section 15 provides for the reference of matrimonial disputes to a council of two arbitrators, preferably one from each family. These two reforms were not introduced in Egypt until 1929[2], and then with certain minor differences. The Sudan provision mentions that the arbitrators should be learned, or else specially instructed, in the law of wifely disobedience, whereas the Egyptian legislation stresses the need for ability in effecting reconciliation; and while both provide for every effort to be made to bring the parties together and, if this is impossible, for a judicial divorce if either the husband or both parties seem at fault, the Sudan Circular alone provides for a decree of *khul'* (or purchase of her freedom by the wife) if it appears that she is the chief offender. These provisions, again, are all of Mālikī origin.

The subject of missing persons (*al-mafqūd*) is given further treatment in judicial Circular No. 24, of January, 1921. This rehearses that there are many different opinions regarding missing persons and when a decree that they are to be presumed dead may be passed, but that the best known is that this may be done when the person concerned would have reached the age of ninety. But seeing that adherence to this opinion today causes much difficulty and frequently involves loss of rights by those entitled thereto, and since the true meaning of someone becoming " missing " is seldom realised in modern life (on account of the means of communication available to the public and the ease with which his relatives can trace him, or he inform them of his whereabouts, through the post), it has been decided that the opinion most appropriate for adoption is the one which leaves this matter to the discretion of the Qāḍī, who may make such a decree when he sees this to be beneficial. . . . And this preamble is followed by detailed instructions as to the enquiries to be made by Courts concerned with the administration of the estates of missing persons, or with estates to which missing persons would be heirs, and the data which they must forward to the Grand Qāḍī to enable him properly to exercise this discretion, on the basis of which the Court concerned is empowered to make the appropriate decree.

Again, Circular No. 26, of 3rd February, 1925, provides that the spouse relict should be entitled to the whole estate of the deceased spouse who leaves no other heirs; and this entitlement to the excess over his or her legal share is preferred to that of the " universal legatee ", although postponed to that of any other heir whatsoever. This reform (which is contrary to all four schools and represents a compromise between the majority view and that of certain Companions, who maintained that the spouse relict should be on a par with the other " Sharers "

[1] Defined as treatment not to be borne by persons of that station in life.
[2] Law No. 25, sects. 6-11.

in this respect) was not introduced in Egypt until 1943; but the spouse's right was then preferred even to that of the " acknowledged kinsman ".

Circular No. 28, of 16th February, 1927, on the other hand, largely—but not exclusively—follows similar reforms already promulgated in Egypt. Section 1 has already been noted[1]: but sections 2 and 4 permit a wife to claim the judicial dissolution of her marriage if her husband is afflicted, either at the time of marriage or later, with some grave disease or defect which she did not know of at the time of marriage nor agree to endure if it developed subsequently. This, which is substantially the view of Muḥammad al-Shaybānī and of the three non-Ḥanafī Imāms, was adopted almost *verbatim* from sections 9-11 of the Egyptian legislation of 1920. Sections 5 and 6 concern claims for a wife's maintenance on the grounds of the continuation of her *'idda* period, and represent less an adoption of the Egyptian reforms of 1920 than a partial anticipation of sections 17-18 of the Egyptian Law of 1929, although they do not go so far in the case of nursing mothers (a reservation which is presumably a relic of the influence of the Mālikī view, as enacted in Egypt in section 3 of the Law of 1920 but subsequently abandoned in favour of modern medical opinion). The Sudanese provisions here read as follows: " No claim of maintenance, in respect of a woman observing her *'idda* who is not suckling an infant, shall be entertained for more than one year from the date of her divorce; while if she is giving suck, and alleges that she has had no menstrual periods on that account, her claim shall not be entertained for more than three months after she weans her child. Similarly no judgments given prior to this Circular for maintenance during an *'idda* shall be executed in respect of periods in excess of one year after divorce, in the case of women who are not suckling infants, or in respect of periods in excess of two years and three months after delivery, in the case of those who are."[2] Section 7, on the contrary, provides another instance of a provision to which the Egyptian legislation has no parallel, for it enacts that " In a divorce in consideration of property, or of the abandonment of a claim to property, nothing not specifically mentioned as the consideration for the divorce shall be involved "—which represents the variant Ḥanafī view of Muḥammad al-Shaybānī.

Again, sections 8, 16 and 17 taken together go a long way towards making arrears in a wife's maintenance always actionable before the courts. It is apparent, however, that some Ḥanafī influence still lingers in section 8, which is not so absolute in its terms as section 1 of the Egyptian Law of 1920, for arrears of maintenance still lapse in the Sudan on the death of either party, unless judicial leave to raise such maintenance on credit has been given; on the wife becoming " disobedient ", except where arrears of maintenance have already become due as a result either of a judicial decree or of mutual agreement; and also, but with the same exceptions, if the husband was destitute throughout the period concerned. And it may be added that the Sudan has also followed Egypt in subsequently limiting the period of past maintenance for which the Courts might entertain claims to a maximum of three years (Circular No. 45, of 1936, section 1: cp. section 99 of the Egyptian Regulations of 1931).

Sections 12 and 13 of this very heterogeneous Circular concern matters of procedure, for section 12 provides that witnesses are to be put on oath at the request of the opposite party and, if they refuse this oath, their testimony is to be rejected; while section 13 provides that in administrative enquiries in regard to inheritance no claims to a legacy or to a gift of some item of an

---

[1] See p. 313 above.

[2] This reform, in both Egypt and the Sudan, rests fundamentally on the view now taken of the maximum period of gestation and may be regarded as virtually a modern exercise of the right of *ijtihād* (although some authority in its favour can also be quoted). But the authors of these reforms commonly quote such authority and deny *ijtihād*.

estate shall be entertained without suitable documentary evidence. Neither of these provisions goes so far as the relevant Egyptian Regulations, which provide that witnesses must be put on oath in all cases and that suitable documentary evidence of bequests is essential, after the death of the testator, even in formal litigation before the courts. And section 15, which enacts that a minor's financial competence shall not be established before he or she reaches twenty-one, although his ability is to be tested by allowing him to undertake certain financial responsibilities from the age of eighteen, again follows Egyptian precedents.

Circular No. 34, of 12th December, 1932, provides a connecting link between legislation in which the Sudan has followed the lead of Egypt and that in which she has struck out on a line of her own. In the principle of giving the Court the right to extend the maximum age of *ḥaḍāna* (the right of the mother, grandmother, etc., to the care and custody of children) beyond the age of seven for a boy and nine for a girl, the Sudan Circular followed the lead of section 20 of the Egyptian Law of 1929: but the actual provision in the Sudan goes much further than that in Egypt, and instead of raising the maximum age by only two years (according to a variant Ḥanafī opinion) section 1 has adopted the Mālikī rule of puberty for a boy and removal to her husband's house for a girl. Section 2, moreover, has only adhered to Mālikī principles in providing that where the Court exercises this discretion the divorced mother, or other *ḥāḍina,* shall have no right to claim wages from the father for her care of his children during this extra period, since the Mālikīs never allow wages for *ḥaḍāna* in any circumstances whatsoever.

Circular No. 35, of 22nd March, 1933, on the other hand, is another instance of a change in the law to which the Egyptian reforms provide no parallel: on the contrary, it may well be regarded as the solitary instance where these judicial Circulars have been used for a purpose more retrogressive than liberal, for it was designed to substitute the Mālikī for the Ḥanafī rules regarding marriage guardianship. Thus section 1 provides that a marriage is always invalid unless the contract is concluded by the bride's guardian or his representative on her behalf. Similarly, section 3 decrees that a father who is *rashīd* (fully competent) may marry without her consent not only a minor daughter but also a virgin daughter up to the age of thirty-three to any husband he may choose, provided he is not impotent, insane, or leprous, etc.; while section 4 states that even a feckless father (*safīh*) has the same right provided he is neither insane nor irreligious. Section 6 excepts from such compulsory marriage the virgin daughter whom the father has expressly released from tutelage; but section 7 provides that even a non-virgin daughter of full age may be compulsorily married by her father if she is of loose morals and her guardian cannot adequately protect her. Guardians other than the father should bring the matter before the Courts in such cases: but if, instead, they marry the girl off, the marriage will stand. Sections 8-9 concern the more limited right of the guardian (*waṣī*) appointed by the father's will to marry his wards without their consent. Section 12 enumerates the only circumstances in which a guardian who has no right of compulsion may give in marriage a minor girl, while section 13 provides that a marriage contrary to the terms of section 12 becomes valid by the passage of time, etc. Section 22 lays down that when a guardian with the right of compulsion is within ten days' journey, the marriage of his ward by any other guardian without his prior consent is absolutely void provided he is still supporting her, that her morals are not in jeopardy, and that communications are safe: otherwise, the Court will act, not the next-entitled guardian. If, however, the "compulsory" guardian is far distant the Court will act for him with the girl's consent; while if her morals are in jeopardy, the Court may marry her even by compulsion (section 23). The remaining sections give further details about the essential qualifications of a marriage guardian, and what happens if he becomes ineligible, etc.; while appendices make exceptions to section 22 in cases where delay would mean the loss of a suitable match.

These rules, all of which are taken from the Mālikī school, are far less liberal than the corresponding Ḥanafī provisions which were formerly applicable. Under the latter marriage by compulsion is limited to minors and the insane: but such contracts may be concluded by any entitled guardian, whether father, grandfather, or other relative. If the contract is concluded by father or grandfather it is binding without option, provided the husband is his wife's equal and the dower is suitable (or in all cases whatever according to Abū Ḥanīfa himself, provided the father or grandfather is not noted for bad judgment, carelessness or impiety); while if it is concluded by any other guardian the contract is void unless both spouse and dower are suitable, and even then is liable to be rescinded by the minor on attaining majority. Major daughters may never be married without their consent and may even marry themselves without their guardians' intervention; but the guardians may demand the annulment of such contracts if the husbands are not the girls' equals (while, according to another report, contracts with such persons are invalid *ab initio* if concluded without the guardians' consent) or if the dower is less than the brides would normally expect. A change of law enabling fathers to marry grown-up daughters of even thirty years of age against their will scarcely seems consistent with the trends of modern thought, and is in fact condemned by enlightened Sudanese opinion.

Circular No. 37, of 14th January, 1934, instructs Sharī'a Courts how to deal with estates in which the application of the Islamic law of inheritance would normally lead to the sub-division of land into plots less than the minimum size which may be registered under the Land Registration Rules, 1925. In such cases the co-owners, or such of them as are present, should be informed that the law will not allow less than the specified area to be registered, so it is for them mutually to agree that those entitled to small shares should abandon their claims, with or without compensation, in favour of one or more of those entitled to shares large enough for registration. If, however, they cannot so agree the Court may itself decree that any such share should be merged in any larger share—and this even though the heirs be absent, should the presence of all or some be impossible—and may compel the co-owner whose share is thereby enlarged to compensate the other party or parties.

The earlier sections of Circular No. 41, of 25th March, 1935, provide an outstanding instance of reforms—some of them daring to a degree from the juristic point of view—in which the Sudan has followed Egypt virtually *verbatim*. Thus sections 1—5 represent an adoption of sections 1—5 of the Egyptian Law of 1929 concerning the nullity of expressions of divorce uttered under intoxication or compulsion, or intended as no more than an oath or threat; concerning the reduction of the effect of formulæ of divorce in the triple form to that of a single, and therefore normally revocable, divorce; concerning the interpretation of ambiguous phrases, which might or might not imply divorce, by exclusive reference to the intention of the husband; and concerning the fact that every divorce except a third divorce, one uttered before consummation of marriage, one for a financial consideration, or one expressly stated by legislation to be final, should be regarded as revocable. With regard to compulsion this reform represents an adoption of the view shared, in the main, by the three non-Ḥanafī schools; with regard to intoxication it represents one report from al-Shāfi'ī, which has strong Ḥanbalī and some Ḥanafī support; with regard to oaths and threats and the triple formula the reform—which runs directly counter to the commonly claimed consensus of orthodox Islam—rests on the alleged opinions of certain very early jurists and the extinct school of the Ẓāhirīs in the first case[1] and on cogent inferences from the Qur'ān, a statement attributed to Ibn 'Abbās about the

[1] Supported, in regard to intoxication, compulsion, oaths or threats, by the Ithnā 'Asharī law also.

practice prior to a certain date in the Caliphate of 'Umar, and the support of Muḥammad ibn Isḥāq, Dā'ūd al-Ẓāhirī, various doctors of Cordova and later jurists such as Ibn Taymīya and Ibn al-Qayyim in the second; with regard to the effect of ambiguous expressions of divorce the innovation rests on both Shāfi'ī and Mālikī authorities; while with regard to the effect of expressions of divorce which imply finality the reform rests on the Shāfi'ī view (shared by some Mālikīs) that no such expression can deprive a husband of his divinely prescribed right to revoke the divorce, during the continuance of his wife's *'idda,* unless it were either triple or for a consideration.

Again, section 6 of this Circular, which decrees that the scale of maintenance to which a wife is entitled shall be reckoned with exclusive reference to her husband's means, represents a *verbatim* adoption of section 16 of the Egyptian Law of 1929, which itself constituted an abandonment of the most authoritative Ḥanafī (and Mālikī) opinion that her scale of maintenance should represent the mean between the financial standing of the two spouses, in favour of the normal Shāfi'ī rule. Similarly, sections 7, 8 and 9 correspond exactly to sections 17, 15 and 23 respectively of the Egyptian Law and decree that no disputed claim of inheritance is to be heard if based on the existence of the marriage tie more than one year after widowhood or divorce; that no disputed claim of paternity is to be heard where non-access of the parents to each other, either from the date of marriage or for a year before the claimant's birth, can be proved; and that the 'year' mentioned in these two sections is to be solar. These provisions, which adopt the indirect method of reform which does not attempt to amend the substantive law as such but merely denies judicial relief to claims which do not fall within certain limits, were based on a virtual abandonment of the old views concerning the maximum period of gestation (two years among the Ḥanafīs, four among the Shāfi'īs and five in the most widely accepted of several Mālikī rules) in favour of one advocated by modern medical opinion and, incidentally, supported by Muḥammad 'Abd al-Ḥakam and one Ithnā 'Asharī view[1] (combined, in regard to non-access, with Mālikī, Shāfi'ī and Ithnā 'Asharī[2] principles). And section 10 similarly rests on an Egyptian model (section 19 of the Law of 1929) when it provides that where a married couple dispute regarding the amount of dower which was stipulated the burden of proof must fall on the wife; while if she cannot prove her case the husband's statement will be accepted on oath unless he names a sum which could not be considered a customary dower for a woman of her standing, when "proper" dower will constitute the criterion: and that the same will also be true if the dispute arises between one spouse and the heirs of the other, or between their respective heirs. This rule represents the view of Abū Yūsuf as against that of Abū Ḥanīfa and Muḥammad al-Shaybānī, when the dispute occurs between the spouses, and that of Abū Yūsuf (this time partially supported by al-Shaybānī) as against the "authoritative" Ḥanafī opinion, in regard to their heirs.

The remaining sections of this Circular,[3] sections 11—15, represent material peculiar to the Sudan, since they concern the subject of gifts—which, as we have seen, in Egypt no longer fall within the competence of the Sharī'a Courts. Thus section 11 states that ownership passes on the donee taking possession of the thing given, whether he does so with or without the donor's permission. If, however, possession is not obtained until after the donor's property is sunk in debts incurred subsequent to the date of the gift (section 12), or until after the donor has been smitten with madness or some other disease which only ends

[1] Except that he and they advocated a lunar, not a solar, year.

[2] In the case of the Mālikīs and Shāfi'īs, only in regard to non-access from the date of the contract; but the Ithnā 'Asharīs include non-access at any time and for any reason.

[3] Except for section 16, which concerns the application of the Circular.

with his death (section 13), the gift becomes void: but if the donor recovers and possession is then taken, ownership passes (section 13). A gift by one spouse to another, or by a mother to a young child, of a piece of furniture, etc., standing in the house they both occupy is valid, if witnesses are called to the gift, without any such "lifting of the donor's hand" (i.e., abandonment of control of the property) as would normally be necessary (section 14). Jewelry with which a boy or girl, major or minor, is decked by father or mother, or fine clothes in which their parent dresses them, or mounts he buys for them to ride, books for study, or weapons for self-defence or show, are all to be regarded as gifts to which the other heirs of that parent have no claim, unless witnesses have been called to the fact that only the grant of their use was intended (section 15). These provisions are all of Māliki origin.

Circular No. 46, of 25th April, 1936, concerns certain repercussions and present effects of the now officially extinct status of slavery.[1] Thus section 1 provides that certificates of freedom given by the Administration to persons previously of slave status shall have no effect on a prior marriage, although a woman to whom such a certificate is given is to be regarded as thenceforth free, with all that this involves, by the Sharī'a Courts; section 2 that neither Courts nor *ma'dhūns* are to register a marriage contracted on behalf of a woman by anyone in the capacity of her owner unless she is herself present, willing and a party to the contract; and section 3 that the Courts shall not entertain any plea of the marriage of an ex-slave woman to her former master, to his children, grandchildren, or former slaves, even if they do not live with him, or to any other relative of his who does in fact live with him, unless the marriage is proved by an official certificate, etc., and the woman concerned was present, willing and a participant in the contract. And in just the same way the Courts shall not entertain any plea of marriage contracted by a man on behalf of a woman in the capacity of her owner except as provided in section 2 above. Similarly, section 5 decrees that the Courts must not entertain any claim of inheritance on the grounds of ownership, but that any such claim lies in the exclusive competence of the Governor[2]; section 7 that if any dispute arises regarding slavery the Sharī'a Court is to refer it to the competent authority, namely the District Commissioner, and then decide the case according to the Sharī'a on the basis of his decision; section 8 that the Sharī'a Courts shall apply the rules applicable to freemen, exclusively, in every case concerning the following matters—dower and *jihāz*; restitution of conjugal rights; custody of children and a mother's right to take her child from one town to another; *khul'* and *mubāra'a*; wages for custody, suckling and maintenance; proof of divorce; judicial divorce for failure of maintenance, fear of adultery, cruelty or disease; appointment of an executor; legacies and gifts; requests for decrees of putative death; inheritance; etc.: while section 9 enacts that where the subject of a suit is anything other than the above and one of the parties was formerly a slave the Court must refer the matter to the Grand Qāḍī before it gives its decision. All these provisions represent safeguards against any exploitation of persons formerly of slave status.

Circular No. 48, of 10th July, 1937, forbids fathers of minor children to sell their real property without the consent of Court, on the grounds that the Sharī'a allows a father to deal with such property belonging to his minor child in some circumstances but not in others, and that only the Qāḍī knows the appropriate rules. It also lays down the considerations which must guide the Courts in giving or withholding such consent. In Egypt such matters fall within the competence of the Ḥisbīya Courts and are all covered by detailed safeguards.

Circulars No. 49, of 24th May, 1939, and No. 51, of 20th October, 1943, con-

[1] The first three sections largely reproduce sections 9-11 of Circular No. 28, two of which sections are thereby expressly declared to be repealed.

[2] i.e., of the Province concerned.

cern the law of intestate succession, and their brief provisions provide the only Sudanese parallel to the comprehensive Law of Inheritance promulgated in Egypt in 1943. Thus section 1 of Circular No. 49 follows the Shāfi'īs and Mālikīs in allowing full brothers and sisters to participate in the special share of the estate reserved for uterine brothers and sisters in the circumstances (known as the problem of the "*Mushtaraka*") where under Ḥanafī law they would get nothing; while section 2 of the same Circular provides that full or consanguine brothers or sisters should no longer be excluded from rights of inheritance by the father's father. These reforms antedate the Egyptian Law by four years. It is noteworthy, however, that section two of this Circular introduced the view of the Two Companions (which is also that of Mālik and al-Shāfi'ī and is derived from Zayd ibn Thābit) with regard to the respective shares of full and consanguine brothers or sisters in competition with the paternal grandfather, while the Egyptian Law adopted a compromise between the views held respectively by Zayd ibn Thābit and 'Alī ibn abī Ṭālib which can, perhaps, fairly be described as an instance of *talfīq*[1] which leads to a thoroughly logical and consistent principle: and this was subsequently introduced into the Sudan by Circular No. 51, of 20th October, 1943, which rescinded the previous provision.

Finally, Circular No. 53, of 3rd October, 1945, again anticipated the relevant Egyptian legislation—the comprehensive Law of Testamentary Dispositions of 1946—in introducing one of the most controversial of the provisions then under discussion, and ultimately promulgated, in Egypt. Thus, section 1 provides that a bequest which does not exceed the "bequeathable third" of the testator's estate is valid and effective, whether to an heir or non-heir, without regard for anyone's consent; while one in excess of the third is valid but not effective unless the heirs, being competent to make a gratuitous disposition of property and knowing what they do, consent thereto. Similarly, section 2 declares valid a testamentary distribution of the items of an estate between the testator's heirs, provided that any excess over his proper share thus allotted to any individual should be regarded as a bequest (and governed by the appropriate rules). This was a startling innovation, for Sunnī Muslims have been agreed for centuries that no legacy at all may be left to an heir, at least unless the other heirs consent; while the Ḥanafī jurists forbid even a testamentary distribution of the items of the testator's estate, however strictly this conforms to the value of property due to each under the law of inheritance, lest a certain tinge of favouritism intrude. This Sunnī view was based on the belief that the "Verse of Legacies" (Sūra 2: 179) was abrogated or at least limited by the "Verses of Inheritance" (Sūra 4: 11, 12, etc.) and on the acceptance of a tradition which alleges the Prophet to have said "There is no legacy to an heir". True, this tradition is weakly attested: but once it had become generally accepted it was regarded as confirmed by consensus (*ijmā'*). The Sudanese Circular and the Egyptian Law, however, have completely reversed the unanimous Sunnī practice of centuries and given a testator the right to make bequests to heirs or non-heirs within the "bequeathable third" of his property—in accordance with the view of the Ithnā 'Asharī and some of the Zaydī sub-sects of the Shī'īs, who have never accepted the Sunnī view in this matter. The authors of this startling innovation have justified their action by an appeal to the Verse of Legacies and to the interpretation put thereon by certain Sunnī commentators (whose comments appear in fact to have been largely limited to maintaining that the verse was still applicable—either within the limits of the Verses of Inheritance, or to such of a man's relatives as were not in fact entitled heirs, or perhaps to such heirs as were more needy than others); to the views of certain "other doctors" (unnamed), i.e. the Shī'īs; and, more particularly, to the "needs of society".

It is clear, then, that the simple expedient of legislation providing that the

[1] See Glossary.

Sharī'a Courts must follow the dominant Ḥanafī opinion except where the Grand Qāḍī, with the agreement of the Governor-General (as expressed by the Legal Secretary), has issued some judicial Circular directing that the opinion of some other reputable jurist is to be preferred, has been used to great effect in the Sudan. Similar directions that the dominant Shāfi'ī opinion is to be abandoned in favour of some other dictum have, as we have seen, been issued in the Qu'ayṭī Sultanate of Mukallā and Shiḥr and also in Laḥej[1]—and it seems clear that the procedure could beneficially be used in other territories also.[2] Where the head of State is a Muslim the directions should, of course, go out in his name and authority; where there is any jurist whose position corresponds to that of the Grand Qāḍī in Khartoum the directions might well go out in his name, under suitable legislative authority; while elsewhere appropriate legislation might enforce a recommendation agreed by the leading Muslim jurists available. And in the case of the Waqf Commissioners Ordinance issued in Kenya in 1900, moreover, this principle of selecting the most suitable dicta of different jurists and applying them to all schools indiscriminately was used in a British Colony, at a very early date, without, it seems, any elaborate preparations or any adverse reactions.[3]

It may be added that the reports of a Qāḍī detailed to inspect the work of the Native Courts in the Sudan, particularly, but not exclusively, in regard to their "Sharī'a" jurisdiction,[4] reveal many points of interest. The following are, perhaps, worthy of brief mention in this context:

(1) It seems that a widespread custom exists, especially among the cattle-owning tribes, for a husband to insist on his wife promising to return all or most of her dower before he will grant her a divorce (even, it seems, when it is really he who desires the divorce, for he will then begin to treat her in such a way as to make her demand it). The wife herself is commonly unable to provide this; so her former husband waits until she remarries and then sues her new husband for the amount. In such circumstances, it seems, the Native Courts normally force the new husband to pay the previous husband a reasonable sum, but not necessarily the exact amount promised by the wife. In some areas, moreover, the Courts apparently authorise a woman in such circumstances to marry a man who cannot afford to pay as her dower the full sum which she owes her former husband, and then force the latter to accept whatever amount the new husband can afford to pay. This is, of course, quite contrary to the Sharī'a, under which judgment should be given against the woman alone for whatever she named (unless the husband exerted pressure, when she should properly be absolved from any payment whatever): but it is enforced by the Native Courts, chiefly on the basis of local customary law, but partly, perhaps, as a sort of abbreviation of the more orthodox procedure.

(2) Where a girl has been promised to one man, who has thereafter provided her with clothing and oil at each successive festival, and then been given in marriage to another, the Native Courts compel her parents to repay her fiancé's expenses. This is, of course, in accordance with normal African usage elsewhere.

(3) The Inspector always instructs Native Courts that sums charged by Muslim "holy men" for charms to aid in the recovery of lost stock, etc., should not be enforced "for want of any true consideration," and as usually obtained by lying claims.

---

[1] See pp. 16 ff. and 32 f.

[2] For a full treatment of the fascinating reforms which have been introduced on these principles in various Arab countries, see a series of articles entitled "Recent Developments in Sharī'a Law" contributed to successive numbers of *The Muslim World* from October, 1950, till October, 1952, by the author of this Survey.

[3] It is noteworthy, however, that legislative innovations in regard to matrimonial causes or matters of inheritance are more jealously regarded by the Muslim than similar action concerning the administration of waqf property, etc.

[4] See above, p. 309.

(4) In some parts of Kordofan Province and among certain nomad tribes[1] a woman's property passes to her brothers on her marriage (and they, not the husband, remain responsible for her torts, etc.). But in any case referred to the Sharī'a Courts this custom would allegedly not be recognised.

(5) The Magdumate Court was found to have refused to hear evidence from non-Muslims. It was informed that such evidence must be admitted in the Sudan.

(6) A Nubian husband offered his wife to any man who would repay his expenses. He was sentenced to six months' imprisonment for what was held to amount to slave-dealing.

(7) Where a husband divorced his wife on condition that she paid him £2 if she did not marry a certain person, but £10 if she did, a certain Native Court enforced this. But it was told that she must only pay £2 in either case, since the second stipulation was illegal as " in restraint of marriage ". And the same argument was held to vitiate the judgment of a Native Court inflicting a punishment on a man who had sworn that he would not marry another man's wife even if she were divorced, and then had subsequently married her.

(8) In parts of Darfur professing Muslims frequently have more than four wives, and all are commonly regarded as " legal ". This shocked the Inspector.

(9) In many Native Courts an attempt is made to deal with questions of divorce by conciliation. This is admirable on social grounds, and corresponds with African custom over wide areas: but where the formula of divorce has once been uttered, this procedure is, of course, utterly at variance with the Sharī'a and was sternly discouraged.

(10) It seems common in many parts for Sheikhs to hear " Sharī'a " cases when sitting without the assistance of an *'ālim* and without the specific consent of both parties to such jurisdiction. This is contrary to the law, although especially common in cases involving absent husbands.

(11) The Native Courts are continually found to have acted on the local interpretation of Mālikī principles, in complete disregard of the Regulations for Sharī'a Courts and the judicial Circulars described above. One instance of this is their attempt to insist on the evidence of four women, where the Ḥanafī law applicable in the Sharī'a Courts would accept that of one only; while another is provided by the grant of divorce to wives whose husbands have sworn by the triple divorce to provide them with clothing within a fixed period but failed to do so (although such a divorce is, of course, contrary to the terms of Circular No. 41, section 2[2]). The Inspector always tries to induce uniformity of practice in such cases, but it seems doubtful how far this is, strictly speaking, required by law.

[1] e.g., the Kabābīsh.

[2] p. 316 above.

APPENDIX B

THE IMMIGRANT MUSLIM COMMUNITIES

The immigrant Muslim communities of East Africa include Indians, Baluchis, Persians and Arabs from all parts of Arabia,[1] while the much smaller number of immigrant[2] Muslims on the West Coast are mostly made up of Lebanese, Syrians, "Arabs" from North Africa and a few Indians. In matters of law the Indians of East Africa are divided into Sunnīs and Shī'īs, the former almost exclusively Ḥanafīs (including some Cutchi Memons and, for practical purposes, the Aḥmadīs also), while the latter are sub-divided first into Ithnā 'Asharīs and Ismā'īlīs, and then further, in the latter case, into the Eastern and Western[3] Ismā'īlīs respectively: but it is to be noted that most of the Indian Ithnā 'Asharīs in East Africa are Khojas who have abandoned Ismā'īlī for Ithnā 'Asharī allegiance and tenets. The Baluchis and Persians, on the other hand, are almost exclusively Ḥanafīs and Ithnā 'Asharīs respectively; while the Arabs are mostly Shāfi'īs, but include certain Ibāḍīs, from 'Umān, and Shī'īs of both the Zaydī and Western Ismā'īlī sects, from the Yemen. The Lebanese and Syrian Muslims of West Africa, again, are chiefly Ḥanafīs or Ithnā 'Asharīs ("Mutawālīs"); while the Indians are mixed, but chiefly, perhaps, of the Aḥmadī persuasion.

In matters of litigation these very diverse elements cause singularly little trouble, at least in so far as family law is concerned. In Kenya Baluchis, Arabs, Somalis, etc., are subject to the jurisdiction of the Qāḍīs; in Tanganyika they may submit to the jurisdiction of the Liwalis by mutual consent; while in Somaliland even the Indians commonly litigate in matters of personal status, if at all, before the Qāḍīs[4]: and the only point which needs emphasis here is that neither Ḥanafī Baluchis nor non-Shāfi'ī Arabs can expect the application of anything other than the Shāfi'ī personal law, as locally understood and enforced, in any such courts. In Zanzibar, of course, both Shāfi'ī and Ibāḍī Qāḍīs are available, in courts subordinate to both the "British" and the "Zanzibar" Courts. For the rest, however, immigrant Muslims in East Africa are subject to the jurisdiction of the British courts, in matters of personal status, either under Bombay Regulation 4 or within the terms of some local Ordinance[5]: but in practice extremely few such cases ever reach the courts. In so far as the Ismā'īlīs, whether of the Nizārī or Musta'lī sub-sects, are concerned, this will be adequately explained below: but even among the Ḥanafīs and Ithnā 'Asharīs, who have less reason to avoid the ordinary courts, matters of personal status are nearly all settled either by mutual agreement or by the intervention of the community councils.[6] And the same is true of the Syrians and Lebanese of West Africa, who seem to settle matters of personal status either by mutual agreement or by reference to their own courts when they visit their home countries.

Little need be said in this Survey regarding the law applicable to Indian Ḥanafīs, since British courts in East Africa naturally avail themselves of the

[1] Besides, of course, Malagasies, Comoro Islanders, etc.

[2] Excluding, that is, those from other parts of West Africa.

[3] i.e., the Nizārīs and the Musta'līs: or the Khojas and the Bohoras, according to the usual nomenclature.

[4] As also, in theory, in the Aden Protectorate (see the Introduction to this Survey). But it is doubtful how far this is legally justified in Somaliland.

[5] Except in Nyasaland, where there is no court competent to hear the matrimonial causes, etc., of immigrant Muslims under Islamic law.

[6] Partly, at least, because they do not appreciate the thought of a non-Muslim attempting to apply the Sharī'a.

numerous text books of Anglo-Muhammadan law[1] available, together with the relevant cases in the Indian Law Reports. The latter, of course, are not binding authorities in East Africa, but exercise a strongly persuasive influence; while the vexed question of whether the former decisions of the Privy Council on appeal from India constitute precedents binding on British courts in East Africa has now received an authoritative and affirmative answer in *Fatuma binti Mohamed bin Salim* v. *Mohamed bin Salim*.[2] But it is noteworthy that no legislation comparable to the Dissolution of Muslim Marriages Act, passed by the Indian Legislature in 1939, has appeared in any of the territories covered by this Survey.

It is, however, relevant in this connection to observe that the leading case of *Abdurahim Haji Ismail Nathu* v. *Halimabai* (1915), 6 E.A.L.R. 113, established that the Memons settled in East Africa must be regarded as governed by the Islamic (Ḥanafī) law of succession rather than the Hindu law by which their community in India was still governed at that date. This decision was reached on the grounds that when a family of Cutchi Memons (a community of ex-Hindus who had accepted Islam but for long retained Hindu law and custom regarding inheritance) emigrate from India and settle among Muslims elsewhere the presumption arises, if their actions are such as to raise the inference that they have cut themselves off from their old environment, that they have accepted the law of the people whom they have joined; that on the facts proved in this case such an inference in fact arose in regard to the law of succession to intestate estates among Memons domiciled in Mombasa; but that this was subject to the custom whereby ornaments given to a wife in her husband's lifetime remain with the widow only during her life or until her re-marriage. Now, however, the law applicable to Cutchi Memons has changed in India also, for first the Cutchi Memon Act, 1920, allowed a Cutchi Memon to declare that he wished to subject himself in all respects to the Muhammadan law of inheritance; then the Shariat Act, 1937, made the community automatically subject to that law in so far as intestate succession was concerned, but preserved their customary right to dispose of the whole of their property by will unless they declared under section 3 that they wished to be governed by Muhammadan law in this respect also; and finally the Cutchi Memons Act of 1938 took away even this option and subjected them to the Ḥanafī law in all particulars.[3]

The Ithnā 'Asharīs in East Africa are mostly Indians—although there are a few Persians, and here and there traces of early "Shirāzī" influence remain. Most, again, are Khojas who have repudiated the Imāmate of the Agha Khān for one reason or another, and embraced Ithnā 'Asharī tenets. The Khojas as a whole were originally, like the Memons, Hindus of the trading caste, hailing from Sind and Cutch, who were converted to their brand of Islam chiefly through the efforts of Pīr Ṣadr al-Dīn,[4] a missionary said to have been sent to Sind in the fifteenth century by Shāh Islām, one of the ancestors of the Agha Khān: and the history of their community was summarised by Mr. Justice Arnould in the "Agha Khan Case" (*Advocate-General* v. *Muhammad Husen Huseni* (1866), 12 Bom. H.C.R. 323-63), where it was held that they were not Sunnīs; while it

[1] e.g., Wilson's Anglo-Muhammadan Law, Ameer Ali's Mahommedan Law, FitzGerald's Muhammadan Law, Mulla's Principles of Mahomedan Law, Tyabji's Muhammadan Law and Fyzee's Outlines of Muhammadan Law.

[2] Privy Council Appeal No. 47 of 1950. See Appendix D.

[3] An even more recent enactment concerning Cutchi Memons is Act XXV of 1942. But this only removed from the Statute Book a section of the Act of 1938 which was spent and redundant.

[4] Reputed to have been the author of the Das-Avatār, a book in which the incarnations of Vishnu are described as leading to Islam (the first nine incarnations being treated in Hindu fashion, and the tenth as having materialised in the Imām of the Ismā'īlīs). See article on "Khôdja" in Encyclopaedia of Islam.

was also judicially established that they were not Ithnā 'Asharīs in *Haji Bibi* v. *H.H. Sir Sultan Mahomed Shah* (1908), 11 Bom. L.R. 409. To the main body of the Khoja community in East Africa reference will be made below: but it is noteworthy here that it has been held in one Zanzibar and one Tanganyika case (*Shumbana binti Juma* v. *The Administrator-General* (1927), 3 Z.L.R. 51, and *In re Hasanali Jadavji deceased* (1947), 5 T.T.L.R. 211) that the considerable proportion of these Khojas who have embraced Ithnā 'Asharī tenets have given up the custom whereby they were governed by Hindu law in matters of inheritance and succession and have adopted that of the Ithnā 'Asharīs. For the rest, the Ithnā 'Asharī law as applied by the courts in India is covered in the same text books as those enumerated above in regard to the Ḥanafīs, while relevant decisions of the Indian courts are also available: and any litigation concerning matters of personal status between Persian Ithnā 'Asharīs in East Africa would no doubt be decided by British courts on the same principles.[1] In certain matters of detail, however, the Ithnā 'Asharī law is less definite than the Ḥanafī, for among the former the right of *ijtihād* (independent deduction from the sacred sources) is still regarded as in part extant: and, e.g., in certain petitions for dissolution of marriage by misused wives, regarding which no express rule of law has become established in their school, only a *mujtahid*[2] or someone to whom such *mujtahid* has given his authority may dissolve the marriage—acting, as it were, in the name and authority of the Hidden Imām.[2]

But the best organised and most progressive "Muslim" community in East Africa is that of those Khojas who are still Ismā'īlīs. These believe that in the person of their Imām, the Agha Khān (the forty-eighth Imām in their order of succession), they have an impeccable and infallible Successor to the Prophet and to 'Alī—the former an incarnation of Universal Reason, the latter of Universal Soul. Thus although in theory they profess great reverence for the Qur'ān, they believe that its injunctions have been frequently and widely superseded by the continuing Divine Voice in their Imāms. As a consequence, the law of personal status governing the Ismā'īlī Khojas of East Africa is chiefly to be found in the "Constitution, Rules and Regulations of His Highness the Agakhan Ismailia Councils of Africa". This provides, in Chapter 5, for all cases of this nature, and even commercial cases between members of the community, to be brought before the local Provincial Council, which may decide them *ex parte* if the defendant fails to appear to answer the plaint (section 17) and which gives its decision by a simple majority of votes (section 28)—but subject, in all cases, to an appeal to the Supreme Council and thence to His Highness the Agha Khān in person.[3]

Again, it is interesting to note that the rules concerning marriage preclude betrothal until a boy reaches eighteen and a girl sixteen[4]; while the betrothal form must be signed by both parties in person,[5] and anyone "guilty of child marriage or a party to giving the bride for monetary consideration shall be punished".[6] If either party changes his or her religion after their betrothal and before their marriage the betrothal is considered null and void: and where it is the bridegroom who changes he cannot demand the return of any gifts he has given to his bride, while if it is the bride such gifts are all forfeit.[7] Where,

---

[1] But in Zanzibar such would come within the jurisdiction of the Zanzibar Court; while it is most unlikely that Anglo-Muhammadan law would in all cases satisfy Persian litigants.

[2] See Glossary.

[3] See detailed rules regarding procedure, arbitration, fees, fines, the execution of judgments, punishments, etc., in Chap. 5.

[4] Ibid, Chap. 9, sect. 3.

[5] Sect. 5(*a*).

[6] Sect. 5(*e*).

[7] Sect. 6. But this is a case where the bridegroom might well appeal to the courts.

however, a betrothal is broken off for other reasons the Council may make what order regarding such gifts it sees fit.[1] The *mahr* (here spelt "*mohor*") must never be less than Shs. 1,000 and should, in the case of a well-to-do bridegroom, be much more.[2]. When, moreover, a non-Ismā'īlī couple,[3] or a non-Ismā'īlī who is married to an Ismā'īlī, joins the Ismā'īlī faith there is now no need for their re-marriage.[4] An Ismā'īlī may never marry a second wife without the permission of the Council, which will only be given "for reasons of serious illness, insanity, cruelty or non-bearing of children of his first wife"; and such petition may in no case be made less than three years after the marriage in cases of illness, insanity or cruelty and six years in cases of childlessness, and must always be accompanied by a medical certificate.[5] Such applicant must, moreover, if his petition be granted, deposit with the Council not less than Shs. 10,000, as fixed by the Council, the income from which shall be paid to the husband only so long as his first wife continues to live with him; while a monthly allowance shall be allotted to the wife whenever she ceases to live with him,[6] except in case of divorce. A wife may apply for a divorce on the grounds of her husband's "serious illness, insanity, cruelty, or non-bearing of children", subject to the same delays as in the case of a husband's petition to marry a second wife on similar grounds.[7] Where a husband is given permission to marry a second wife, moreover, the first wife may claim a divorce; but in such cases she will have no right to the sum deposited by the husband, although she may retain her clothes and ornaments.[8] A divorced woman may not remarry until the expiration of four months from the date of such divorce.[9] If either a husband or wife (or both) desire a divorce the Council will appoint two persons to persuade them against it, and divorce will only be granted where the Council considers this unavoidable.[10] Where the applicant for such divorce is the husband he shall be made to pay his wife a sum to be fixed by the Council; while where the applicant is the wife she must forfeit "her allowance in respect of *mahr* or otherwise".[11] On divorce the Council "may give the minor children, if any, to the wife until they attain the age of seven years", while the cost of maintenance shall be borne by the husband[12]: but in no case of divorce shall the decision of the Council be enforced until any appeal has been decided.[13] If either party changes his or her religion after their marriage the other shall be entitled to a divorce: and if it be the husband who changes the bride may keep all clothing and ornaments, etc.; while these are forfeit if it be she who leaves the community.[14] Where, moreover, a widow wishes to remarry the Council must see that any minor children of the previous marriage receive such property of the deceased father, in the way of ornaments, etc., as are in her possession.[15]

Unlike the position in India today as a result of the Shariat Act of 1937 (under which the intestate succession of Ismā'īlī Khojas is now governed by

---

[1] Sect. 7.
[2] Sect. 11.
[3] Here, of course, "Ismā'īlī" means an Eastern Ismā'īlī only.
[4] Sect. 18.
[5] Sect. 19(*a*).
[6] Sect. 19(*b*).
[7] Sect. 19(*e*).
[8] Sect. 21.
[9] Sect. 22.
[10] Sect. 23.
[11] Sect. 23.
[12] Sect. 24.
[13] Sect. 26.
[14] Sect. 8. But again this is a case in which the aggrieved party might well appeal to the ordinary courts.
[15] Sect. 27.

Muhammadan law, while they still retain the right to make unlimited bequests), the Ismā'īlī Khojas of East Africa still follow Hindu law in regard to both testate and intestate succession. This has received judicial recognition in *In re Kassum Premji deceased* (1924), 1 T.T.L.R. 53, and *Fatmabhai d/o Jaffer Dhalla* v. *Mahomed Ladha* (1928), 1 T.T.L.R. 55, where it was held that the Ismā'īlī Khojas, unlike the Memons of Mombasa, had established a distinctive political and social organisation for themselves, and had never been absorbed in the general body of Muslims: so their " customary law ", which they had done nothing to change in East Africa, still prevails in this matter. It seems, however, that the members of this community in East Africa almost always make wills, so intestate succession is extremely rare; and that although advice is freely given, a testator's liberty of disposal is virtually absolute. In addition, adoption is allowed,[1] and an adopted child is entitled to inherit from his adoptive father. There are also detailed rules regarding both excommunication and voluntary secession from the community: and the reason why so few cases concerning Ismā'īlī Khojas ever reach the courts is that the decision of the Agha Khān is regarded as the voice of God, disobedience to which would probably entail immediate excommunication from his community.[2] It should, moreover, be added that the Agha Khān spends much of the money paid to him so lavishly by the members of his community on schools, clinics, hospitals, libraries, etc., and that he has stood out strongly for the emancipation of women.

The other branch of the Ismā'īlīs, the Musta'līs, is also found in East Africa. This branch is itself subdivided into the Dā'ūdīs, the Sulaymānīs and some smaller sects; but only the Dā'ūdīs seem to be represented in East Africa. All the Bohoras, as the Indian Musta'līs are usually called, recognise a sequence of twenty-one Imāms up to and including al-Ṭayyib ibn al-Āmir, who is believed to have become *mastūr* or hidden —since when the real power has been in the hands of the Imām's assistant, the Dā'ī'l-Mutlaq[3]: and where the sub-sects differ between themselves is regarding the person of this representative of the hidden Imām. Thus the Dā'ūdīs accept the Mullaji Ṣāḥib of Bombay, His Holiness Sayyid Ṭāhir ibn Muḥammad Sayf al-Dīn. Technically, of course, he is not regarded by the Bohoras, as Dā'ī, as of quite the standing accorded by the simpler Ismā'īlī Khojas, at least, to the Agha Khān, who is their infallible Imām in person: but in the absence of the infallible Imām the Dā'ī, as his representative, is regarded as virtually infallible (" *ka ma'ṣūm* "); so his decision is final and authoritative on all points of law or dogma, and any disobedience would cause the miscreant concerned to be expelled from his community. It is for this reason, again, that so few cases of personal status between Bohoras ever reach the British courts, for where one of their community is unwilling to accept the decision of the local 'Āmil, or religious head, reference is made by post to the Dā'ī himself.

The legal text regarded as authoritative by the Musta'lī section of the Ismā'īlīs is the Da'ā'im al-Islām, by the Fatimid Qāḍī Nu'mān, now in course of publication by A.A.A. Fyzee (himself a Bohora). But from conversations with the 'Āmils in Dar es Salaam and Zanzibar the following points emerged. There is ordinarily no provision for a wife to obtain a judicial divorce for cruelty or failure of maintenance in their community: but where a Bohora woman complains that her husband fails to support her he will be warned to do so, and if after three months' grace no maintenance were forthcoming she *might*[4] be granted

[1] By contrast, of course, with the Sharī'a.

[2] It is chiefly, therefore, where parties have been prepared to go to this length, or where a member of another community has been involved, that such cases have reached the ordinary courts.

[3] The community believes that al-Ṭayyib ibn al-Āmir has been succeeded by a succession of " hidden " Imāms, one of whom must always be in existence; but no one knows how many there have been or can establish contact with them.

[4] In theory rather than normal practice, it seems.

a divorce on the authority of the Dāʿī; while where she complains of cruelty the husband will allegedly be forced, by pressure of public opinion or, in the last resort, by the authority of the Dāʿī, either to mend his ways or to grant her a divorce. Dissolution of marriage is, however, regularly granted in cases where one of the spouses is seriously diseased and conceals this fact from the other party[1] at the time of the contract. The custody of the children of divorced parents is granted to the mother, under the usual rules, up till the age of two only in the case of boys and seven in the case of girls. Intestate succession follows much the same rules as among the Ithnā ʿAsharīs, attributed by both sects to Jaʿfar al-Ṣādiq: but among the Bohoras no bequest is allowed to an heir.[2]

In the absence of any special legislation in West Africa regarding immigrant Muslims it seems that in Nigeria there is no court which is competent to decide any question of family law or personal status in respect of such litigants under the Sharīʿa[3]; while in the Gold Coast, the Gambia and Sierra Leone the courts would be competent only within the terms of the Marriage of Muhammadans Ordinance, the Muhammadan Marriage and Divorce Ordinance and the Muhammadan Marriage Ordinance respectively. The very few foreign Muslims in Nigeria comprise a handful of Indian Aḥmadīs, a much larger but heterogeneous colony of Lebanese and Syrians (which includes Sunnī, Shīʿī and Christian elements) and a number of Arabs from North Africa. The Lebanese Consul in Lagos confirmed that no litigation on matters of personal status from his community ever reaches the British courts: instead, matters of marriage are always arranged among themselves; divorces are registered before the Consul and reported to Lebanon, while there is no provision whatever for judicial dissolution of marriage or for litigation regarding the custody of children; and matters of inheritance are arranged by mutual consent, but mostly according to Islamic law (whether Sunnī or Shīʿī)—while any serious problem is referred to the Lebanese courts when the parties return to that country. Many Lebanese (who all regularly call the Africans *ʿabīd* or "slaves") take African women as consorts, but they always regard these as "slave concubines" and never refer to them as wives (except, it seems, in the case of certain half-caste women in the Kano area); and such women are not themselves accorded any right of inheritance, it appears, although their children are regarded as legitimate. For the rest, it is to be noted that the law applicable to Lebanese and Syrian Ḥanafīs in their home countries is not the pure Ḥanafī law but that law as considerably modified, chiefly by borrowings from other schools, under the Ottoman Law of Family Rights, 1917, as now applied in Lebanon and Syria respectively.[4]

It is, of course, possible that certain Lebanese, or, indeed, some of the Tripolitanian Arabs who visit Kano and elsewhere, sometimes refer matters of personal status to the Alkalai; as also that non-native Muslims in the Gambia may occasionally have recourse to the Qāḍīs' courts in that territory. If they do, however, this can only be regarded, strictly speaking, as a form of arbitration; while the litigants can, of course, expect nothing but the Mālikī system to be applied. In the Gold Coast, the Gambia and Sierra Leone, on the other hand, British courts have a very limited competence in such cases, as we have seen, and would always, presumably, attempt to obtain expert testimony regarding the personal law of the litigants concerned: but the Gold Coast case of *Mohammed Wahib Huzaifeh* v. *Hussein Saba and Maria Elina Sabeh* (1939), 5 W.A.C.A.

---

[1] As in all the schools of law today except that of the Ḥanafīs.

[2] By contrast, of course, with the Ithnā ʿAsharīs.

[3] Since Islamic law is there applied exclusively as "native law and custom".

[4] For details of this interesting legislation, see "Recent Developments in Sharīʿa Law" (cp. p. 320, note (2), above).

181, illustrates how difficult this might be.[1] And it may be added in this context that the Zanzibar case of *Hamed bin Suleman el Mandri* v. *Sadha binti Suleman, etc.* (1912), 1 Z.L.R. 398, established the fact that, so far as British courts are concerned, a Muslim female belonging to any of the four Sunnī schools may, after she has reached puberty, elect to belong to whichever of these she pleases, and her subsequent acts will be governed accordingly; nor can there be much doubt that British courts would extend this principle to cover the right of any adult Muslim to transfer his or her allegiance even between the Sunnī schools and the " heterodox " schools of the Ibāḍīs on the one hand and the several Shī'ī sects on the other—while the right to change from the Ismā'īlī to the Ithnā 'Asharī branches of the Shī'a has already, as we have seen, been judicially recognised in several East African cases.

It should be added that the chief legal problem liable to arise regarding the Aḥmadīs is whether the adoption of Aḥmadī tenets by a non-Aḥmadī husband constitutes such apostasy from Islam as to cause a dissolution of his marriage to a non-Aḥmadī wife. British courts have decided to the contrary, on the grounds that Aḥmadīs not only call themselves Muslims but say the Muslim creed, etc.: but the indigenous courts are apt to take the contrary view, that the Qādiānī sect have cut themselves off from the true community of Islam by recognising their " Promised Messiah " as a Prophet.[2] For the rest, however, the Indian Aḥmadīs follow Ḥanafī law except where it has been varied in certain particulars by the pronouncements of the " Promised Messiah " and his Successors: but in the unlikely event of any litigation on matters of personal status being referred to British courts[3] the ordinary Ḥanafī law would almost certainly be applied.

It may be useful to append a summary of the position of immigrant Muslims in these territories in so far as litigation is concerned.

A. Matters of Marriage and Divorce.

1. The following legislation confers jurisdiction on British Courts to entertain matrimonial suits between immigrant Muslim litigants under Islamic law:

KENYA. The *Muhammadan Marriage, Divorce and Succession Ordinance,* 1920.

TANGANYIKA. The Asiatics (*Marriage, Divorce and Succession*) (*Amendment*) *Ordinance,* 1947—introduced to fill the gap revealed by *Fatuma Bachoo* v. *Majothi Kara* (1946), 13. E.A.C.A. 50.

UGANDA. The *Marriage and Divorce of Muhammadans Ordinance,* 1906.

THE GAMBIA. The *Muhammadan Marriage and Divorce Ordinance,* 1941.

Note. All of these except the second also apply to indigenous Muslims.

---

[1] See p. 251 above.

[2] Orthodox Islam maintains, of course, that Muḥammad was the " seal " and last of the Prophets. The Aḥmadīs accept him as the seal of the Prophets, but maintain that their Founder was indeed a Prophet but one who came in the spirit of Muḥammad and within the revelation of Islam (see Glossary). All the same, the caution of orthodox Muslims appears justified in the light of the extravagant language used, it seems, by the Promised Messiah about his " Promised Son ", the present Khalīfa—which may be illustrated by a quotation from *The Knowledge,* Jan., 1950, p. 5: " He is the Word of God because Grace and Jealousy of God has sent him with his Word of Glory . . . Beloved son, honoured and respected, Manifestation of the First and the Last. Manifestation of the Truth and the Height as if God has alighted from the Heavens. His advent will be very blessed and manifestation of Divine Majesty. He is the light whom God has anointed with the perfume of His pleasure . . ." When it is remembered that the Promised Messiah himself is accorded an even higher place than the " Promised Reformer ", as the present Khalīfa is often termed, it is difficult to take the assertion of the Qādiānīs' orthodoxy seriously. But the same clearly applies, *mutatis mutandis,* to such sects as the Ismā'īlīs.

[3] For practice in Pakistan, see the Gold Coast section of this Survey, p. 284.

2. The following legislation empowers British Courts to recognise a Muslim marriage or divorce which is valid in Islamic law, but not to entertain matrimonial causes thereunder.

NYASALAND. *Asiatics (Marriage, Divorce and Succession) Ordinance*, 1929.

THE GOLD COAST. *Marriage of Muhammadans Ordinance*, 1907. But the marriage or divorce concerned must be registered thereunder.

SIERRA LEONE. *Muhammadan*[1] *Marriage Ordinance*, 1905.

Note. The last two Ordinances apply to all Muslims, indigenous or immigrant.

3. In ZANZIBAR, SOMALILAND and ADEN the jurisdiction of British Courts is founded on *Bombay Regulation No. 4* of 1827 (see *Rana Ramji* v. *Radabai Natha* (1937), 5 Z.L.R. 91, the legislation on which it was based, and similar legislation in Somaliland and Aden). In ADEN this is reinforced by the *Interpretation and General Clauses Ordinance*, 1937, section 41, while the *Child Marriage Restraint Ordinance*, 1939, is also applicable.

B. Matters of Inheritance.

1. The following legislation provides for the estate of a deceased immigrant Muslim to be distributed according to Islamic law.

ADEN. The *Interpretation and General Clauses Ordinance*, 1937, section 41. *Note.* This provision expressly authorises the application of the "rules or customs" of the community concerned. The *Succession Ordinance*, 1938, moreover, exempts Muslims from those provisions which run counter to the Sharīʿa in any important respect (see sections 3, 19, 28, 58, etc.).

ZANZIBAR. The *Succession Decree*, 1917, section 7. *Note.* This provision expressly authorises the application of the personal law to which the deceased was subject. Section 5(1) also exempts Muslims from the provisions relevant to the execution of wills.

KENYA. *Muhammadan Marriage, Divorce and Succession Ordinance*, 1920, section 4 [Provided the deceased was the child of a Muslim marriage or had himself contracted such a marriage]. *Note.* This provision expressly authorises the application of the law of the sect of the deceased.

THE GOLD COAST. *Marriage of Muhammadans Ordinance*, 1907, section 10. [Provided the marriage of the deceased had been duly registered thereunder.] *Note.* This provision simply authorises the application of Muhammadan law; but presumably the differences between the sects and schools would be recognised.

SIERRA LEONE. *Muhammadan Marriage Ordinance*, 1905, section 9(1). [Provided the deceased was either unmarried, or a party to a Muslim marriage, at the time of his death.] *Note.* This provision, again, simply authorises the application of Muhammadan law; but presumably the differences between the sects and schools would be recognised.

2. The following legislation makes the same provision, but with the proviso that so much of the law as deprives any person of a right of succession to property by reason of having renounced or been excluded from the communion of any religion shall not be in force.

TANGANYIKA. *Marriage, Divorce, and Succession (Non-Christian Asiatics) Ordinance*, 1923, section 6(1). *Note.* This provision simply authorises the application of the "law of the religion" professed by the deceased at his death; but presumably differences of sect or school would be recognised.

[1] Usually spelt "Mohammedan" (etc.): but see the Introduction to this Survey regarding the liberty I have taken in re-spelling Arabic words, to avoid confusion, even in the titles of Ordinances.

NYASALAND. *Asiatics (Marriage, Divorce and Succession) Ordinance,* 1923, section 6(1). *Note.* This provision, again, simply authorises the application of the " law of the religion " professed by the deceased at his death; but presumably any difference of sect or school would be recognised.

3. In UGANDA the estates of Muslims have been exempted from the provisions of Part V of the *Succession Ordinance,* 1906 (concerning the distribution of an estate on intestacy), while section 50 of the Ordinance declares the will of a Muslim to be valid if made according to Islamic law. No provision exists, however, actually authorising the application of the Islamic law of intestacy, and in *Re. Mahomed Habash deceased* (1920), 3 U.L.R. 26, it was held that, as far as non-native Muslims were concerned, there was no room for the application of Islamic law to land and that such succession was regulated by English law—presumably, though the judgment does not say so, by reason of Article 15(2) of the Uganda Order in Council, 1902.

4. In SOMALILAND the personal law of the deceased would, presumably, be applied under *Bombay Regulation No. 4* of 1827.

C. Matters Concerning Waqf.

ADEN. The *Muhammadan Waqf*[1] *Ordinance,* 1939, combines the main provisions of the Indian *Mussulman Waqf*[1] *Validating Act,* 1913, with provisions for the better management and control of waqf property, and applies to all communities.

ZANZIBAR. Under the *Waqf*[1] *Validating (Amendment) Decree,* 1951, section 2 (which replaces section 5 of the Decree of 1946), Muslims who are neither Arabs nor Africans are empowered to create waqfs in accordance with the law of the school to which they belong, provided such waqfs would be recognised as valid under the Indian *Mussulman Waqf Validating Act,* 1913.

KENYA. The *Waqf*[1] *Commissioners Ordinance,* 1951, deals only with waqfs created by Arabs, members of the Twelve (Swahili) Tribes, Baluchis, Somalis, Comoro Islanders, Malagasies and natives of Africa (cf. definition of "Muslim" in section 2). But section 3 provides that any other person professing Islam may appoint the Waqf Commissioners as trustees of any property which he has made waqf, in which case " the property shall be administered in accordance with this Ordinance ". This section, moreover, clearly implies that immigrant Muslims other than those named can make valid waqfs (in which connection cp. argument at the beginning of the Kenya section of this Survey about the application of Islamic law in Kenya, particularly in the Protectorate—where the law of Zanzibar was formerly applicable and seems never, in this respect, to have been abrogated or replaced); while in *Daud Abdulla and another* v. *Ahmed Suleman and others* (1945), 13 E.A.C.A. 1, litigation concerning a waqf was decided under the relevant English law.

SOMALILAND. Presumably litigation concerning a waqf created by an immigrant Muslim could be taken under Islamic law under *Bombay Regulation No. 4* of 1827.

ELSEWHERE there is no authority for the application of the law of waqf as such, and in so far as mosques and religious endowments are concerned the law to be applied is the general law relating to religious and charitable endowments—while private waqfs would be governed by the law of trusts, etc. But in *Omar Fakirmohamed and another* v. *Remtulla Talab and another* (1927),

[1] Here spelt " wakf ": but see note (1), page 329 above.

I.T.T.L.R. 38, a case which concerned the management of a mosque built by Indian Muslims in Dar es Salaam, the High Court of Tanganyika followed the decision of the Privy Council in *Mohamed Ishmael Ariff* v. *Ahmed Moola Dawood* (1916), I.L.R. 43 Cal. 1085, and quoted therefrom a summary of the relevant provisions of Muhammadan law. And it seems probable that a similar attitude would be adopted in suitable circumstances in other territories also.

D. Matters of Pre-emption.

In ADEN the law of pre-emption, presumably as applied in the Bombay Presidency, is applicable under the *Interpretation and General Clauses Ordinance*, section 41.

In ZANZIBAR it has been judicially held in *Saleh Lalji* v. *Muhomed bin Ahmed and another* (1913), 1 Z.L.R. 423, that the principle of pre-emption by right of vicinage has no application in Zanzibar,[1] as it is not applicable in the Shāfi'ī or (on the " better view ") the Ibāḍī law locally applied. Thus, unlike Aden, where the law of pre-emption is regarded as a purely personal right, in East Africa the " local law " apparently prevails in this matter (for in regard to land tenure in general the *lex loci* has been accepted as the criterion by British Courts: see *Secretary of State* v. *Charlesworth, Pilling & Co.* (1901), 1 Z.L.R. 105), and the acquisition of land by an alien Muslim will not stamp that land with the character it would have had in his own country (cp. *Joosab Jacob and others* v. *Administrator-General* (1946), 13 E.A.C.A. 38.

It seems, moreover, that no right of pre-emption whatever is in practice recognised throughout East or West Africa.

[1] Although it is noteworthy that this judgment betrays a hopeless confusion between the relevant rules of the Ḥanafī, Shī'ī and other schools of law.

APPENDIX C

BRIEF NOTES ON CERTAIN POINTS OF LAW

Space forbids any adequate treatment here of the vast majority of the points of law covered in this Survey.[1] A very general summary of a few technical terms may, however, be found in the Glossary, while passing reference to isolated points has been made, from time to time, in the text and footnotes. This Appendix must be limited, therefore, to a very few particulars which seem to demand separate treatment.

JABR. (MARRIAGE BY COMPULSION).

The dominant Shāfi'ī view on this matter, together with the considerably more liberal view advocated by some Shāfi'ī authorities, may be conveniently summarised in the following extracts from *al-Tuḥfa* (since Ibn Ḥajar is regarded as the arbiter of orthodoxy throughout a large part of East Africa and Southern Arabia). Commenting on the phrase " The father may give his virgin daughter in marriage without her consent ", Ibn Ḥajar continues:

" The conditions essential to the validity of such action are the fact that the bridegroom is her equal; that he is able to provide her proper dower, in the generally accepted view; that there is no hostility between bride and groom; and that there is no manifest hostility—i.e. such as is not hidden from the people of the neighbourhood—between the bride and her father. The assertion that the non-fulfilment of this last condition affects the permissibility[2] rather than the legal validity of the marriage is not correct . . . In the case of an agent (*wakīl*) empowered to conclude a marriage, on the other hand, no condition exists regarding the manifest nature of any hostility, because of the obvious difference between father and agent: for the compassion which a father feels for his daughter should make him consider her interests even where hidden hostility exists between them, while this does not apply with regard to a (mere) agent . . . To insist that the bride must not suffer from such a marriage, e.g. by being married to a very old or blind husband, or the marriage will be dissolved, and that she must not be under a duty to go on pilgrimage, or her consent to the marriage must be obtained (lest her husband should prevent her), represent two weakly-supported views, while the latter is an anomalous (*shādhdh*) opinion". (*al-Tuḥfa,* vii, pp. 243, 4).

It is, however, clear from this last statement that even Ibn Ḥajar does not regard the condition that the bride must not " suffer " from a marriage by compulsion as an " anomalous " opinion, although he regards it as contrary to the dominant view of the school: and I am informed that his Yemenī contemporary, Ibn Ziyād, insisted that such a marriage must be of benefit (*maṣlaḥa*) to the bride. And this view could, of course, be made the basis of a legislative enactment.[3]

In this respect the Mālikīs are considerably less liberal than even the stricter Shāfi'ī view. A short extract from al-Dasūqī's commentary on *Mukhtaṣar Khalīl* will illustrate this: —

" Then the father who is of discretion—or otherwise his own guardian—may give (his virgin daughter) in compulsory marriage even to a blind man, or one

[1] Any such treatment must await a Handbook which I have been asked to write.

[2] i.e., Ibn Ḥajar rejects the view that this is a condition of *iqdām* (or *mubāshara*) rather than *ṣiḥḥa* (see Glossary). On the view which he advocates the conditions of *iqdām* (over and above those of *ṣiḥḥa*) are that the proper dower should in fact be paid, and paid promptly, in the currency of the country concerned (unless there is a local custom to the contrary).

[3] cp. the judicial Circulars issued, under legislative authority, in the Sudan (pp. 311 ff.): and cp. also pp. 16 ff., etc.

inferior to her in social position or in wealth, or one repulsive in appearance, or for a dower of only a quarter of a *dīnār*[1]—even though her proper dower would be very large. But this is not allowed to any other guardian, such as a *waṣī*.[2] For a *waṣī* who has been instructed to give a girl in compulsory marriage, whether to a particular suitor or not, may do this provided the latter pays proper dower: but he is not on a par with the father in all respects . . . A virgin may be given in marriage even if an " old-maid "[3] of sixty years of age, or more, except to a man who is physically defective."[4] (*Ḥāshiyat al-Dasūqī,* ii, p. 251).

It should, however, be noted that where a virgin daughter has been expressly emancipated from tutelage by her father she may no longer be given in compulsory marriage, but is like a previously married woman in this respect; while some Mālikī authorities extend this to all women who have reached a specified (but more or less advanced)[5] age of spinsterhood.

It is also noteworthy in this context that the Ḥanafīs: —

(1) Limit marriage by compulsion (of the sane) to those under puberty.

(2) Allow such marriages to be concluded by the nearest guardian, agnate or cognate, and not only by father and father's father (c.p. the Shāfi'īs) or father and *waṣī* (c.p. the Mālikīs).

(3) Allow an " option of puberty " (i.e. to repudiate the marriage on reaching puberty) to a minor so married by any guardian other than father or grandfather, while such a contract is invalid *ab initio* if the groom is not the bride's " equal " or if (on one view) the dower is less than " proper ".

(4) Regard such a marriage as valid and binding, when contracted by a father or father's father not known for bad judgment[6] or immorality,[7] even where the groom is not his bride's equal and the dower less than her proper dower.[8]

(5) Regard such a marriage as valid and binding when concluded by a father or father's father known for bad judgment or immorality provided only that the groom is his bride's equal and the dower not less than her proper dower, but consider such a marriage, where either of these conditions are wanting, invalid *ab initio.*

It is also noteworthy that three early jurists—Ibn Shubruma, 'Uthmān al-Battī and Abū Bakr al-Aṣamm—denied the validity of any guardianship in marriage over those who have not reached puberty, on the grounds that the basis of guardianship is the benefit of the ward and that there is no benefit in marriage before puberty. And this view—contrary though it is to the general view of all four schools—has been made the basis of major reforms which are in force today in Egypt, Lebanon, Syria and Jordan.[9]

THE PRIORITY OF MARRIAGE GUARDIANS

The attitude of the Mālikīs in this matter may be illustrated by an extract from al-Dasūqī's commentary on *Mukhtaṣar Khalīl*: —

---

[1] This represents the " minimum " dower of Mālikī law: cp. p. 231, note (4).

[2] i.e., the executor of a deceased father (in this context).

[3] *Ānis.*

[4] e.g., an eunuch, leper or madman—i.e., one afflicted with some disease or defect of the sort which justifies dissolution of marriage.

[5] Several different ages have been suggested by different jurists.

[6] *Sū' al-ikhtiyār.*

[7] *Fisq.*

[8] This view is attributed to Abū Ḥanīfa himself, while his Two Companions are said to have insisted on both equality and proper dower in such cases.

[9] See my articles " Recent Developments in Sharī'a Law " III and VIII, in *The Muslim World,* April, 1951, and July, 1952, respectively.

"And where marriage guardians of different degrees of priority co-exist, a marriage contracted by a more remote guardian, in place of the one with a prior claim, is valid provided that the latter had no right of *jabr* . . . But it is for the Ruler, and not for any other guardian, to give in marriage a daughter who is subject to *jabr* of a father who is absent, if there is no hope of the latter's speedy return . . . while if there is reason to fear her moral condition, then the Ruler may even marry her by *jabr,* in the generally accepted view . . . Similarly, when the prior guardian who has no right of *jabr* is more than three days' journey distant, the Ruler should give the ward in marriage, not her more distant guardian . . . But where the prior guardian, with or without the right of *jabr,* is imprisoned or missing, then the more distant guardian, and not the Ruler, should give her in marriage." (*Ḥāshiyat al-Dasūqī,* ii, pp. 256 ff.)

In this respect the Shāfi'īs are more rigid than the Mālikīs, for in normal circumstances they regard a marriage concluded by a more distant guardian, in place of one with a prior claim, as null and void. They hold, however, that where the prior guardian is disqualified by minority, madness, immorality, or difference of religion, etc., the next entitled guardian should act in his place, but that where the prior guardian is more than forty-eight miles[1] distant, the Ruler must assume responsibility.

The Ḥanafīs, again, insist that only the prior guardian may act if he is present; but where he is at such a distance that an opportunity for a suitable match might be lost by awaiting his return, or by sending to consult him, the Ḥanafīs (unlike both the Mālikīs and Shāfi'īs) hold that the next entitled guardian, and not the Ruler, should give the girl in marriage.

All three schools, however, agree that if the prior guardian refuses, without adequate reason, to give his ward in marriage, application may be made to the Ruler (or Qāḍī), who will investigate the matter and then either order the guardian to conclude the marriage or, in default, do so himself.[2]

It is also noteworthy in this connection that it is on the basis of the right of the Ruler to give in marriage a bride whose prior guardian is more than forty-eight miles distant that the Shāfi'īs allow the procedure of *taḥkīm* and *tawlīya*[3] where there is no official Qāḍī to represent the Ruler—on the grounds that any suitably qualified Muslim may in these circumstances be given the right of an arbitrator (*ḥakam*) or the duties of a guardian (*walī*). There seems to be no equivalent to this among the Mālikīs, except for the concession that a woman who is *danī'a* (i.e. not *sharīfa*) may, in default of either father or *waṣī,* ask any suitable Muslim to give her in marriage—and the term *sharīfa* is defined in this context as a woman of either wealth or beauty.

DISSOLUTION OF MARRIAGE FOR CRUELTY, NEGLECT, ETC.

Only the Mālikīs allow a woman to claim a judicial divorce for proved cruelty, while both Mālikīs and Ḥanbalīs allow divorce or dissolution of marriage to a wife whose husband goes away and deprives her of both companionship and marital relations. The Mālikī view in this matter may be illustrated by a short extract from al-Dasūqī: —

"And the Ruler shall be free to use his discretion, and not be bound by the period prescribed for *īlā',*[4] in cases of . . . deprivation of sexual intercourse with the intention of injuring a wife, and shall divorce her after such period as

[1] *Masāfat al-qaṣr* (a journey long enough to justify the shortening of prayers).

[2] al-Dasūqī states, in this connection, that a woman may thus force her marriage to the man of her choice, where her guardian can show no lawful objection; "while if she wishes to marry one suitable suitor and her guardian to give her in marriage to another, her choice shall be preferred".

[3] See Glossary.

[4] See Glossary.

he sees fit—even where the husband is absent. Indeed, where she has suffered injury from deprivation of intercourse she shall be divorced even if her husband did not intend to injure her. But in the case of an absent husband his absence must have lasted for at least one year, and a letter must have been sent to him" (*Ḥāshiyat al-Dasūqī,* ii, p. 488).

The Qur'anic prescription for all cases of marital discord, whatever their cause, is, of course, that two arbitrators (one—preferably—from each family) should be appointed and charged with a full investigation of the facts and an attempt to reconcile the parties. Where, however, such reconciliation seems impossible, the dominant view of the Ḥanafī and Shāfi'ī schools is that the powers of the arbitrators cease, and that they may arrange a divorce or *khul'* only where they have been specifically empowered to do so, as authorised agents, by the husband in the first case and by both spouses in the second. In the dominant view of the Mālikī school, on the other hand, the arbitrators have the right to decide that nothing but divorce or *khul'* (according as the husband or wife is primarily at fault, or the blame must be apportioned between them) will meet the case, and this decision will be upheld and enforced by the Court. It is interesting to note, therefore, that this is also a minority Shāfi'ī opinion, as the following extracts from al-Sharbīnī, and even Ibn Ḥajar, show: —

" In one view they (the two arbitrators) are two judges (*ḥākimān*) appointed by the Ruler (or by the Judge: i.e. *ḥākim*). This view has been preferred by many on the ground that the Qur'ān has named them " arbitrators " (*ḥakamān*), and an agent is not an arbitrator . . . So the consent of the two parties is not a condition of their appointment, and they may give what judgment they consider beneficial, whether it be that the marriage should be continued or dissolved" (*al-Mughnī,* iii, p. 344).

" And they are two agents who may act only by consent of the parties. But on another view they are two judges (*ḥākimān*) appointed by the Ruler " (*al-Tuḥfa,* iii, p. 126).

It is clear, then, that this view, which is dominant in the Mālikī school and represents " another view ", which is " preferred by many ", among the Shāfi'īs, could be made the basis of legislative reforms.

DISSOLUTION OF MARRIAGE FOR FAILURE OF SUPPORT

In this regard the dominant Mālikī opinion is again more favourable to ill-used wives than is the dominant Shāfi'ī view, although a minority view exists in the Shāfi'ī school which is at least equally liberal. But here the Ḥanafīs are more rigid than even the dominant Shāfi'ī opinion.

The Mālikī view may be summarised as follows: —

(1) Where the husband is present, is able to support his wife[1], but refuses to do so, a judicial divorce may be granted without delay; while where he is unable to do so he will be granted a period of respite, in order to allow him to improve his position, determined at the discretion of the Court (e.g. one month)[2].

(2) Where the husband is absent the wife will similarly be granted a judicial divorce in all cases, but not until the husband has been warned, if this is feasible, and given a suitable period of respite (with or without notice, according to whether, or not, he can be contacted without too long delay).

The dominant Shāfi'ī view, on the other hand, may best be summarised under five headings, as follows: —

[1] But none of his property is such as can be taken in execution of a maintenance order.
[2] But the wife who married with a knowledge of his destitution has no such claim.

(a) *Where the husband is present, but unable to support his wife.*

In such cases the wife is entitled to a judicial dissolution of her marriage. This is agreed by all, but the "better" view prescribes that a respite of three days should first be granted. It is noteworthy, however, that Ibn Ḥajar remarks that "such dissolution is not allowed on the ground that the husband cannot pay for past maintenance,[1] or for a servant; and the matter must first be referred to, and the husband's inability to support his wife be proved before, a Qāḍī or an arbitrator, who shall either himself dissolve the marriage or give her permission to do so". (*al-Tuḥfa*, viii, p. 335.)

(b) *Where the husband is present and could support her but refuses or fails to do so.*

Here the dominant Shāfi'ī view utterly refuses any dissolution of marriage, since the husband is not "destitute" and the wife is held to be able to obtain her rights by reference to the Courts. See (d) below.

(c) *Where the husband is present but all his property is at a distance.*

Here the dominant view differentiates as to whether his property is more or less than forty-eight miles[2] distant. Where it is nearer than this no dissolution of marriage is allowed, but he will be ordered to collect it without delay; while where it is more distant even Ibn Ḥajar decrees: —

"If the husband be present and his property at a distance and he does not support her on credit, then if his property is more than forty-eight miles distant she has a right to the dissolution of her marriage, on grounds of hardship (*ḍarar*)". (*al-Tuḥfa*, viii, p. 337.)

(d) *Where the husband is absent, but of known whereabouts and able to be contacted.*

In such circumstances the dominant view is much the same as if he were present—i.e. dissolution is allowed, after three days' respite, if he can be shown to be destitute, but no dissolution is permitted if he is in a position to support her. Thus Ibn Ḥajar asserts: —

"And the more correct view is that no dissolution of marriage is allowable where a husband who is well-off or of medium means fails to maintain (his wife), whether he be present or absent, since she is in a position to obtain her maintenance from him, even if he is elsewhere. *al-Mughnī* says that this is because she may obtain her rights either by means of the Courts or by helping herself, where this is possible . . . ; while *al-Nihāya* says that this is because the quality of destitution, which (alone) justifies dissolution of marriage, is lacking and because she could obtain her rights. . . ." (*al-Tuḥfa*, viii, p. 341.)

Other authorities, however, have severely criticised this view, as will be shown below. But it must in any case be observed that while the fact that an absent husband was destitute when he went away is not accepted as itself constituting proof of his present destitution (even by the doctrine of *istiṣḥāb*[3]), yet testimony to the fact of his present destitution is regarded as admissible even where that testimony is in reality based only on a knowledge of his past destitution and an extension of this to his present condition by means of this same doctrine.

(e) *Where the husband is missing or cannot be contacted.*

Here, again, the rigid doctrine of Ibn Ḥajar refuses dissolution of marriage. He says: "There can be no dissolution of marriage where the husband has means, even if no news can be obtained of him and no maintenance procured from his

[1] This is true of the Mālikī view also.
[2] *Masāfat al-qaṣr.*
[3] See Glossary.

property. This is stated in *al-Umm*[1] and has been accepted by the school. True, our Sheikh[2] in his *Minhāj* asserts that dissolution of marriage is allowable in the case of one of whom no news can be obtained and who has no property available for maintenance; but this assertion is contrary to the tradition of the school". (*al-Tuḥfa*, viii, p. 337.)

On this point, however, there is a strong body of opinion in the Shāfi'ī school contrary to this doctrine (e.g., according to *Bughyat al-Mustarshidīn*,[3] al-Ramlī,[4] Zakariyā' al-Anṣārī, Ibn Ziyād and many others).

It is noteworthy, moreover, that some Shāfi'ī jurists go further than this very limited concession of al-Nawawī and others. Thus it is stated in *Bughyat al-Mustarshidīn* that "Many have preferred the view, and Ibn 'Ujayl, Ibn Kubunn, Ibn al-Ṣabbāgh and al-Rūyānī have given *fatwās* accordingly, that where a wife can obtain no maintenance from her husband for a period of three days she is entitled to dissolution of marriage, whether her husband be present or absent. Ibn al-Ṣalāḥ has supported this view, which is regarded as the stronger view by Ibn Ziyād, al-Ṭanbidāwī, al-Muzjid, the authors of *al-Muhadhdhab* and *al-Kāfī* and others, where a husband goes away and no maintenance can be obtained from him, even, e.g., by means of a complaint. Ibn Qāsim, moreover, said that such circumstances represent a stronger case (for dissolution of marriage) than that of one whose property, only, is absent, yet the latter is regarded as justifying dissolution of marriage". (p. 287.)

This last argument seems extremely strong. The fact that dissolution of marriage is allowable where the husband is present but his property absent shows that the criterion must be his relative, rather than absolute, destitution: and from this it has been argued that the term "*mūsir*" (affluent) in *al-Umm* must be interpreted as meaning one with adequate means *available*. It is certainly difficult to defend the logic of the view that dissolution is allowable where the husband is himself present but his means absent, and precluded where both husband and means are equally distant. This more liberal view, therefore, might well be made the basis of any such reform as may appear necessary in this matter.

It should be added that the Ḥanafīs refuse dissolution of marriage for failure of maintenance in all cases—i.e. whether the failure is wilful or involuntary, whether the husband is absent or present, and whether his whereabouts are known or unknown. But many later Ḥanafīs have said that *fatwās* may be given according to the Mālikī school, in case of hardship, in such circumstances.[5]

MAINTENANCE ORDERS AGAINST ABSENT HUSBANDS

Where, on the other hand, the wife of an absent husband demands maintenance rather than dissolution of marriage, the following points are relevant:—

(a) Where the husband is of known whereabouts, the Qāḍī should first write to the Qāḍī of his locality asking the latter to tell him either to return to his wife, to send her maintenance, or to empower an agent to support her. If, after a suitable respite, he has failed to do any of these things, the Qāḍī of the wife's locality should make a maintenance order appropriate to the husband's means and order its execution out of any available property—after the wife has proved her marriage, etc., and taken the oath of *istiẓhār*.[6]

---

[1] i.e., by al-Shāfi'ī himself.
[2] al-Nawawī.
[3] p. 287. This book is often called *Fatāwā Mashhūr*, and is much esteemed in South Arabia.
[4] In *al-Nihāya*.
[5] cp., for instance, the preamble to the Indian Dissolution of Muslim Marriages Act, 1939: see Appendix E.
[6] See Glossary.

(b) Where the husband is of unknown whereabouts, the Qāḍī should first write to the localities to which it seems most likely that he has gone. If no result is forthcoming he should then, after proof and oath as above, make a maintenance order at the rate applicable to the very poor (unless the husband can be shown, by suitable testimony,[1] to be more affluent than this).

(c) Where no property belonging to the absent husband is available for the execution of a maintenance order, the Qāḍī should give the wife permission to obtain her maintenance on her husband's credit.

It is noteworthy, however, that Ibn Ḥajar remarks that where a husband is for any reason *unable* either to return to his wife, send her supplies or appoint an agent to act on his behalf, no maintenance order should be made, since this is only allowable where the husband has fallen short in his duty! (*al-Tuḥfa*, viii, pp. 321 ff.)

It is clear, moreover, that in default of movable property even immovable property may be sold in execution of a maintenance order.

" TRIBAL " MARRIAGES

In addition to the remarks in the Tanganyika section of this Survey regarding the vexed question of " tribal " marriages it may be observed: —

(a) That the Ḥaḍramī jurist Ibn 'Ubaydillāh (see pp. 23, 26, etc., above) argued for their full validity, on the grounds that, just as marriages of non-Muslims who subsequently accept Islam are to be regarded as valid, whatever their form, unless between parties precluded from inter-marriage under Islamic law, so the contracts of the ignorant are to be considered valid provided they are based on genuine consent. He told me that 'Abd al-Raḥmān Sulaymān al-Ahdal, the " Muftī of Zabīd ", had written a treatise in support of this view.

(b) That Ibn 'Ubaydillāh asserted that both Dā'ūd al-Ẓāhirī and 'Aṭā'[2] maintained that neither the presence of the woman's guardian nor of witnesses was essential to a marriage, but that where a woman gave herself in marriage to a suitable husband this was a valid contract; and that al-Ramlī, but not Ibn Ḥajar, regarded this view as raising a sufficient *shubha*[3] in such cases to avert the punishment for *zinā* and to secure the legitimacy of any children. But this scarcely covers the case of " tribal " marriages, where the defect does not concern either guardian or witnesses but rather the lack of any formal declaration and acceptance of marriage (i.e. the *ṣīgha*, or form of the contract).

(c) That Sharaf al-Dīn al-Muqrī has given what appears to be strong support to the contention under (*a*) above, by asserting that wording which conforms to the custom (*'urf*) of the locality is binding, where its purport is intelligible, even when used by one who knows the correct usage: and this is quoted, apparently with approval, even by Ibn Ḥajar. (*al-Tuḥfa*, vii, p. 220.)

(d) That Ibn 'Ubaydillāh maintained that, should a wife acknowledge (*tuqirr*) that she was married to A by her guardian B in the presence of C and D as witnesses, and should A confirm this, then even the categorical denial of both guardian and witnesses would not disprove the marriage—although the latter would only be established from the date of such acknowledgment.

DOCUMENTARY EVIDENCE

Here the dominant Shāfi'ī view is much stricter than the Mālikī doctrine. This may be illustrated by an extract from *Bughyat al-Mustarshidīn* (p. 327): —

" An acknowledgment (*iqrār*) may not be established by means of a written document, even if it be granted that the hand-writing is that of the acknowledgor or of a trustworthy Qāḍī, in the more generally accepted view of the school.

[1] Including, presumably, testimony based on *istiṣḥāb* (see above).
[2] cp. p. 137 above.
[3] See Glossary.

And if a Qāḍī were to give judgment on such evidence in, e.g., a matter of debt, his judgment should be quashed, since it is an anomalous opinion that reliance may be placed on hand-writing."

Suffice it to say, however, that here even the Kathīrī Courts have abandoned the stricter view, as a matter of necessity, in favour of a more reasonable attitude.[1]

ARE THE COURTS BOUND BY THE DOMINANT VIEW OF THEIR SCHOOL?

There is a considerable cleavage of opinion among the Shāfi'īs on this subject. Thus Ibn Ḥajar himself, in his *al-Fatāwā'l-Kubrā*,[2] attributes to both al-Rāfi'ī and al-Nawawī, who themselves got it from al-Ghazzālī, the view that, should a *muqallid*[3] be made a Qāḍī, *faute de mieux*, and should he give judgment according to the view of someone other than his own Imām, his judgment is not to be quashed—since it is a rule that a *muqallid* may follow whom he wishes.

Similarly, Ibn Ḥajar quotes al-Subkī as saying that where a Qāḍī gives judgment according to a minority (but not wholly anomalous) view in his school this is valid provided he is capable of weighing the arguments and is convinced that the view concerned is best supported.[4]

In other texts, on the other hand, Shāfi'ī jurists maintain that, while such choice between variant views may be allowable, within limits, in a *muqallid's* private life, yet a Qāḍī or Muftī is bound, in his official capacity, always to follow the dominant view of his school; and that a judgment to the contrary should be quashed.

This, moreover, appears to be the dominant view of the Mālikī school. Thus al-Dardīr asserts: —

" (A *muqallid*) must give judgment according to the view of the one whose opinion he follows, i.e. the dominant view of the school of his Imām, not the view of another school or a weak view in his own school. And if he gives judgment according to a weak view, his judgment should be quashed." (*Aqrab al-Masālik*, vi, p. 147.)

It seems, however, that among the Shāfi'īs, at least, the basic principle of most modern reforms of the Sharī'a (namely, that where the Ruler orders his Courts to apply some view other than the dominant opinion of their school, this order may—or must—properly be obeyed, provided the view he enjoins coincides with that of some authoritative Muslim jurist) is fully accepted, for the Ḥaḍramīs attribute to Ibn Ḥajar the view that: —

" If the Sultan orders something which conforms to some reputable opinion held by some recognised Muslim Imām we shall apply this and are not permitted to quash a judgment given accordingly . . . ."[5]

I found, moreover, that this principle was accepted as authoritative even by those Kathīrī jurists who were most anxious to prevent its application. (See p. 23 above).

[1] In this connection reference should be made to a most illuminating monograph by Emile Tyan, *Le Notariat* (Lyon, 1945).

[2] ii, p. 212.

[3] See Glossary, under *mujtahid*.

[4] Ibid. And in *Bughyat al-Mustarshidīn* it is stated that if a Shāfi'ī gives a decree of dissolution of marriage where a wife can get no maintenance from an absent husband " because he considers this view preferable, if he is adequately qualified, or because he sees the hardship caused to the wife, this decree must stand . . . and not be quashed, for it is permissible to give *fatwās*, or to act, on this view in case of need, since hardship requires relief and this is no instance of seeking the easiest judgments " (p. 287).

[5] But I cannot trace this. Again, the author of *Bughyat al-Mustarshidīn* attributes to Ibn Ḥajar the statement that " If the Ruler gives orders that any particular school is to be followed, this is obligatory and may not be quashed " (p. 243).

APPENDIX D

FATUMA'S CASE

(Fatuma binti Mohamed bin Salim v. Mohamed bin Salim [1952] A.C.1.)

Brief reference has been made in certain footnotes (c.p. pp. 84, 93, 97, etc.) to this latest decision of the Privy Council regarding the validity of waqfs which may be said to represent family perpetuities, as also to the previous decision in *Abul Fata* v. *Russomoy,* 22 I.A. 76, on which it was based. *Fatuma's case* had not yet been decided by the Privy Council when I visited East Africa, and the comments on that case in the text of the Kenya section of this Survey were written in terms of its decision by the Court of Appeal for Eastern Africa with no knowledge that it had even been referred to the Judicial Committee: so it was only subsequently that brief footnotes regarding the Privy Council decision were added. In view, therefore, of the fact that this decision runs directly counter to more than one thesis put forward in this Survey, it may be in place to mention, with great respect, the points to which their Lordships' attention seems to have been inadequately directed or which appear to have been given insufficient weight. These may conveniently, perhaps, be summarised as follows: —

(1) The judgment not only omits all reference to the important juristic distinction between the Colony and Protectorate of Kenya (c.p. pp. 81 ff and 107 of this Survey), but their Lordships remarked that " It was, however, in the Colony of Kenya that the waqfs now in question were created " (c.p. p. 13 of the judgment), in spite of the fact that the " Province of Seyidie " in which the land concerned is situate (see p. 2) is not in fact in the Colony, but in the Protectorate. According to the view taken in this Survey[1] this fact is of no great significance in this particular instance, since the law applicable thereto would in either case appear to be the Shāfi'ī law as locally accepted and applied (see pp. 81-4 of this Survey): but the fact that the term " Colony " was used in regard to a case which in fact concerned the Protectorate—even with the intention, no doubt, of making a distinction between the whole of Kenya and certain other Colonies or Protectorates, rather than with reference to any internal distinction—serves to emphasise the extent to which the difference between the Colony and Protectorate has fallen into oblivion (c.p. p. 107 above).

(2) It is significant, in view of the thesis put forward in this Survey, that in spite of this fact their Lordships did " not doubt that the learned Judge was correct in saying that the rights of the parties are governed by Muhammadan law " (p. 14). When, however, they immediately go on to remark that " it would not appear that this, now at least, rests in any way upon the Native Courts Regulations ", it remains a matter for speculation—and of extreme interest—on what foundation their Lordships did consider the relevance of Muhammadan law to rest; for it seems to the present writer that it is precisely to these same Regulations that its applicability must even now be traced (see pp. 82-4 above).

(3) Turning, next, to the major point at issue, it was, no doubt, natural that both the learned trial Judge and the Court of Appeal for Eastern Africa should feel bound by the decision of the Privy Council in *Abul Fata's case* unless they could distinguish it from the case before them, whatever may be said in general terms regarding the question whether Privy Council decisions on appeal from one Colony or Dominion of the Commonwealth are to be regarded as binding authorities elsewhere (c.p. Mr. G. W. Bartholomew's argument referred to at

[1] But on another view regarding the basis on which Muhammadan law is applied throughout Kenya, this point might well be fundamental. See pp. 81-5.

p. 97 above). Similarly, it was, perhaps, almost equally natural that their Lordships themselves should feel extreme reluctance to respond to learned counsel's pressure that they should review *Abul Fata's case* and declare it to have been wrongly decided (c.p. p. 12), even though it be true in theory that the Privy Council is not bound by its own previous decisions. There is, moreover, much cogency in the argument which they advanced in support of that unfortunate decision (and of several similar ones, such as *Bikani Mia's case*, 20 Cal. 116) that "whatever views might have been entertained in the 18th and earlier centuries, by the end of the 19th the trend of judicial opinion was firmly set in favour of the view that such waqfs were invalid, and . . . the conclusions to which the High Court of Calcutta and this Board came were inevitable"[1]—provided, only, that this is understood to refer to India alone. But when their Lordships remark, in the next paragraph: "Nor does it avail the appellant that in parts of the world outside India where Muhammadan law obtains, whether in Africa or in Asia, such waqfs as these are considered to be valid. Their Lordships are not satisfied of the general truth of this proposition; but, even if it were so, that would not be such fresh light as would justify the Board in reversing its previous decision . . .", it becomes, with all respect, extremely difficult to conceive (*a*) what evidence (in addition to the general consensus of the authoritative texts of all schools of Islamic law, the decisions of the Courts in those independent Muslim countries where the law of waqf is still applied[2] and the series of Validating Acts, Ordinances and Decrees which the contrary decisions of Courts under British influence have provoked in India, Aden, Zanzibar and Kenya) would suffice to "satisfy their Lordships of the general truth of this proposition"; and (*b*) what "fresh light" would in fact "justify the Board in reversing its previous decision" if the truth of this proposition, even if accepted, would be regarded as inadequate.

(4) It seems, however, that it would have been eminently possible both for the Courts in East Africa and for their Lordships themselves to have distinguished, rather than reversed, *Abul Fata's case*. This could, it is suggested, have been adequately based on the bare fact that the former case concerned Ḥanafīs, while the present case arose between Shāfi'ī litigants. It is, of course, true that there is no difference between the two schools in so far as both recognise family perpetuities as perfectly valid and enforceable, but the important distinction remains that whereas the Ḥanafīs insist that such a waqf, to be valid, must end in a gift[3] to some philanthropic or religious interest of a permanent character, the Shāfi'īs make no such stipulation whatever. Instead, a Shāfi'ī waqf may be created for the benefit of any number, definite or indefinite, of generations of beneficiaries, without any ultimate dedication to charity at all.[4] Since, therefore, so much stress was laid, in the Indian cases, on the fact that in waqfs which primarily constitute family perpetuities the ultimate gift to the poor, etc., is inadequate and "illusory", it would seem eminently reasonable to distinguish therefrom a case to be decided under a law which makes no condition regarding any gift whatever to the poor, whether immediate or ultimate, real or illusory. This consideration, however, appears never to have been brought to their Lordships' attention.

[1] p. 12.

[2] Unless under some legislative reform, such as that enacted in Egypt in 1946 or in Lebanon in 1949: see my articles on "The Religious Element in Waqf Endowments", in the *Journal of the Royal Central Asian Society,* October, 1951, and "Recent Developments in Sharī'a Law IX", in *The Muslim World,* October, 1952.

[3] Whether express, in the view of Muḥammad al-Shaybānī, or implied, in the view of Abū Yūsuf; for this is still a matter of dispute in the school.

[4] And after the extinction of all such beneficiaries, in a waqf of this character, the Shāfi'īs devote the income to the then "heirs of the founder". See "The Religious Element in Waqf Endowments," pp. 293 and 4.

(5) But it would also seem that the cases could well have been distinguished on more general grounds—i.e. on the essential difference (in several respects, and in the point at issue in particular) between the Muhammadan law as now administered in India and that law as applicable, e.g., in East Africa. In refuting this very argument, admirably expressed by Hamilton J.[1] in the early Kenya case of *Talibu bin Mwijaka* v. *Executors of Siwa Haji* (2.E.A.L.R. 33), their Lordships remarked: —

" On the contrary, it has not been suggested that, apart from the differences existing among the Shāfi'ī, Ḥanafī and other sects . . , Muhammadan law is not the same in East Africa as in India. The appellants have themselves relied on its universality and invoke the text of the Qur'ān and the writings of learned commentators who expounded the law not of East Africa or any part of it but of the whole Muslim world." (p. 14).

But this statement of fact emphasises in the strongest terms the universality of the Islamic law of the schools and the classical texts, a law solidly contrary to the decision which their Lordships ultimately reached: it makes no reference whatever to any differences of local custom or application contrary to those texts or, in particular, to the fact that the law now applied among Muslims in India is customarily (and appropriately) referred to as " Anglo-Muhammadan law " precisely in order to emphasise the vital influence which English legal concepts and English rules of evidence and procedure—to say nothing of plain misinterpretations of the ancient texts—have exercised over its development. This was aptly expressed, in terms of the immediate problem, by Hamilton J. in the words: —" the law of waqf as originally understood by the Commentators and Muhammadan jurists has in India since the commencement of the latter half of last century been profoundly modified by the decisions of the Privy Council. A study of the question shows that while the Muhammadan law, uninfluenced from outside sources, permitted perpetuities and the erection of waqfs for family aggrandizement solely, the influence of English Judges and of the Privy Council has gradually encroached on this position . . ."[2] Just so: but the law so developed, however reasonable and beneficial it may be, can scarcely lay any claim to " universality "; and it seems unnecessary, as well as unfortunate, that it should be held applicable in the Protectorate of Kenya, where it is not only contrary to the classical Shāfi'ī doctrine regarded as binding in this and other respects in the dominions of the Sultan of Zanzibar[3] (c.p. the Zanzibar Waqf Validating Decree, 1946, which purports to declare the law of waqf as it has always obtained in the Sultanate), but also to local custom and practice.

(6) It may, perhaps, be added that it seems regrettable that a Committee consisting of three English Law Lords and one ex-Chief Justice of Madras, whose experience of Islamic law was entirely confined to India, was chosen to consider such an important point of principle for Muslim territories as a whole.

[1] But strangely overlooked by the appellants in their original pleadings: although those pleadings were accurate enough *per se*.

[2] These words were quoted by their Lordships shortly before the preceding extract from their judgment.

[3] And it must be remembered that the present case arose within those dominions, although in a part administered today by the Government of Kenya—in which Zanzibar legislation is not, of course, now applicable as such.

APPENDIX E

THE DISSOLUTION OF MUSLIM MARRIAGES ACT

(passed by the Indian Legislature in 1939)

In the "Statement of Objects and Reasons" it is emphasised that:

"There is no provision in the Ḥanafī Code of Muslim Law enabling a married Muslim woman to obtain a decree from the Courts dissolving her marriage in case the husband neglects to maintain her, makes her life miserable by deserting or persistently maltreating her or absconds leaving her unprovided for and under certain other circumstances. The absence of such a provision has entailed unspeakable misery to innumerable Muslim women in British India. The Ḥanafī Jurists, however, have clearly laid down that in cases in which the application of Ḥanafī Law causes hardship, it is permissible to apply the provisions of the "Mālikī, Shāfi'ī or Ḥanbalī Law".[1] Acting on this principle the *'Ulamā'*[2] have issued *fatwās* to the effect that in cases enumerated in clause 3, Part A of this Bill [now see section 2 of the Act], a married Muslim woman may obtain a decree dissolving her marriage. A lucid exposition of this principle can be found in the book called *al-Ḥīlat al-Nājiza*[3] published by Maulana Ashraf Ali Sahib who has made an exhaustive study of the provisions of Mālikī Law which under the circumstances prevailing in India may be applied to such cases. This has been approved by a large number of *'Ulamā'* who have put their seals of approval on the book.

"As the Courts are sure to hesitate to apply the Mālikī Law to the case of a Muslim woman, legislation recognising and enforcing the above-mentioned principle is called for in order to relieve the sufferings of countless Muslim women." (Gazette of India, 1936, Part V, p. 154).

The text of the Act—India Act No. VIII of 1939—is as follows: —

An Act to consolidate and clarify the provisions of Muslim law relating to suits for dissolution of marriage by women married under Muslim law and to remove doubts as to the effect of the renunciation of Islam by a married Muslim woman on her marriage tie.

WHEREAS it is expedient to consolidate and clarify the provisions of Muslim law relating to suits for dissolution of marriage by women married under Muslim law and to remove doubts as to the effect of the renunciation of Islam by a married Muslim woman on her marriage tie; It is hereby enacted as follows: —

1. (1) This Act may be called the Dissolution of Muslim Marriages Act, 1939.
   (2) It extends to the whole of British India.

2. A woman married under Muslim law shall be entitled to obtain a decree for the dissolution of her marriage on any one or more of the following grounds, namely: —
   - (i) that the whereabouts of the husband have not been known for a period of four years;
   - (ii) that the husband has neglected or has failed to provide for her maintenance for a period of two years;
   - (iii) that the husband has been sentenced to imprisonment for a period of seven years or upwards;
   - (iv) that the husband has failed to perform, without reasonable cause, his marital obligations for a period of three years;
   - (v) that the husband was impotent at the time of the marriage and continues to be so;

[1] Here spelt "Hambali" [sic.].
[2] Here spelt "Ulemas".
[3] Here spelt "Heelat un Najeza".

(vi) that the husband has been insane for a period of two years or is suffering from leprosy or a virulent venereal disease;

(vii) that she, having been given in marriage by her father or other guardian before she attained the age of fifteen years, repudiated the marriage before attaining the age of eighteen years:

Provided that the marriage has not been consummated;

(viii) that the husband treats her with cruelty, that is to say—

(*a*) habitually assaults her or makes her life miserable by cruelty of conduct even if such conduct does not amount to physical ill-treatment, or

(*b*) associates with women of evil repute or leads an infamous life, or

(*c*) attempts to force her to lead an immoral life, or

(*d*) disposes of her property or prevents her exercising her legal rights over it, or

(*e*) obstructs her in the observance of her religious profession or practice, or

(*f*) if he has more wives than one, does not treat her equitably in accordance with the injunctions of the Qur'ān;

(ix) on any other ground which is recognised as valid for the dissolution of marriages under Muslim law:

Provided that—

(*a*) no decree shall be passed on ground (iii) until the sentence has become final;

(*b*) a decree passed on ground (i) shall not take effect for a period of six months from the date of such decree, and if the husband appears either in person or through an authorised agent within that period and satisfies the Court that he is prepared to perform his conjugal duties, the Court shall set aside the said decree; and

(c) before passing a decree on ground (v) the Court shall, on application by the husband, make an order requiring the husband to satisfy the Court within a period of one year from the date of such order that he has ceased to be impotent, and if the husband so satisfies the Court within such period, no decree shall be passed on the said ground.

3. In a suit to which clause (i) of section 2 applies—

(*a*) the names and addresses of the persons who would have been the heirs of the husband under Muslim law if he had died on the date of the filing of the plaint shall be stated in the plaint,

(*b*) notice of the suit shall be served on such persons, and

(*c*) such persons shall have the right to be heard in the suit:

Provided that paternal uncle and brother of the husband, if any, shall be cited as party even if he or they are not heirs.

4. The renunciation of Islam by a married Muslim woman or her conversion to a faith other than Islam shall not by itself operate to dissolve her marriage:

Provided that after such renunciation, or conversion, the woman shall be entitled to obtain a decree for the dissolution of her marriage on any of the grounds mentioned in section 2:

Provided further that the provisions of this section shall not apply to a woman converted to Islam from some other faith who re-embraces her former faith.

5. Nothing contained in this Act shall affect any right which a married woman may have under Muslim law to her dower or any part thereof on the dissolution of her marriage.

APPENDIX F

SOMALILAND ADDENDA

Since my visit to Somaliland there have been a number of interesting developments which could not be included in the text of this Survey, which was already in print, but which may be briefly recorded here: —

(1) By the time when this Survey is published the Bombay Civil Courts Act, 1869, will have been repealed in its application to Somaliland (c.p. pp. 40-1). This means, of course, that Bombay Regulation 4 will, in all probability, no longer be applicable, with all that this involves (c.p. pp. 41 and 44).

(2) It is no longer true that " No non-Sharī'a native courts of appeal have yet been set up " (p. 43), since the Subordinate Court of Civil Appeal was established by warrant in August, 1952.

(3) A Chief Qāḍī has now been appointed (c.p. my remarks at p. 56), his court has replaced the Sharī'a Court of Appeal, and appeals thereto are no longer subject to the permission of the High Court (c.p. p. 43 and remarks regarding the Sharī'a Court of Appeal at p.55).

(4) The remarks about the revision of the judgments, etc., of subordinate courts at p. 43 require modification in view of the fact that such review by the High Court is now limited to criminal cases only (c.p. Ordinance No. 22 of 1951, as amended by Ordinance No. 6 of 1952).

(5) The Akils' court at Hargeisa has now been replaced by a subordinate court of the more modern type (pp. 43, 44, 47, 49 and 50 refer). Such subordinate courts have also been established at Elayu/Boran, Ainabo and Zeila.

(6) The Conferences of Qāḍīs suggested at p. 56 have now been instituted, and are, it seems, not only much appreciated by the Qāḍīs themselves but are also regarded as beneficial by the Government.

APPENDIX G

Table of Ordinances, Decrees, etc.

(Giving the references of all such legislation mentioned in this Survey in the latest Revised Editions of the Laws)

For spelling of Arabic terms, see Introduction

ADEN

(Caps as in the Revised Edition of 1945)

Child Marriage Restraint Ordinance, 1939 (pp. 35, 329) ...	Cap 19.
Cutchi Memons Ordinance, 1939 (p. 34)	Cap 35.
Divorce Ordinance, 1938 (p. 35)	Cap 40.
Evidence Ordinance, 1939 (pp. 34, 36)	Cap 49.
Guardians and Wards Ordinance, 1937 (p. 34)	Cap 59.
Interpretation and General Clauses Ordinance, 1937 (pp. 2, 33, 329, 331)	Cap 74.
Majority Ordinance, 1937 (p. 34)	Cap 81.
Marriage (Christian) Ordinance, 1940 (p. 35)	Cap 82.
Muhammadan Waqf Ordinance, 1939 (pp. 34, 93, 330) ...	Cap 90.
Oaths Ordinance, 1938 (p. 34)	Cap 95.
Qāḍī Ordinance, 1943 (p. 35)	Cap 118.
Succession Ordinance, 1938 (p. 34)	Cap 126.

SOMALILAND

(Caps as in the Revised Edition of 1950)

Abolition of Slavery Ordinance, 1930 (p. 48)	Cap 29.
Cultivation and Use of Land Ordinance, 1930 (p. 55)	Cap 119.
Marriage Ordinance, 1902 (p. 44)	Cap 116.
Natives' Betrothal and Marriage Ordinance, 1923 (p. 46) ...	Cap 117.
Subordinate Courts Ordinance, 1944 (pp. 2, 8, 41–43, 51) ...	Cap 4.

ZANZIBAR

(Caps as in the Revised Edition of 1934)

Administrator-General's Decree, 1925 (p. 63)	Cap 12.
Arab and African Guardianship Decree, 1927 (p. 63)	Cap 17.
Civil Procedure Decree, 1917 (pp. 61, 74)	Cap 4.
Contract Decree, 1917 (p. 61)	Cap 80.
Courts (Amendment) Decree, 1947 (p. 67)	No. 22 of 1947.
Courts Decree, 1923 (pp. 58, 59, 60, 67)...	Cap 3.
Criminal Procedure Decree, 1934 (p. 59)	Cap 8.
District Administration and Rural Local Government Decree, 1947 (p. 67)	No. 14 of 1947.
Evidence Decree, 1917 (pp. 59, 60, 66, 69, 70, 75)	Cap 10.
Fugitive Offenders' Decree, 1923 (p. 58)	Cap 24.
Ground Rent Restriction Decree, 1940 (pp. 65, 67)	No. 14 of 1940.
Imperial Enactments (Application) Decree, 1939 (p. 59) ...	No. 8 of 1939.
Insolvency Decree, 1917 (p. 58) ... Quoted as Cap 63 (but this is in fact the Leprosy Decree).	
Interpretation and General Clauses Decree, 1917 (p. 59 ...	Cap 1.
Jurisdiction Decree, 1934 (pp. 58, 59)	Cap 2.
Juvenile Offenders Decree, 1935 (pp. 63, 75)	No. 22 of 1935.
Land Acquisition Decree, 1909 (p. 64)	Cap 105.
Land Alienation Decree, 1939 (pp. 65, 66)	No. 9 of 1939.

Land Protection (Debts Settlement) Decree, 1938 (p. 66)	No. 2 of 1938.
Limitation Decree, 1917 (p. 60)	Cap 11.
Majority Decree, 1917 (p. 63)	Cap 18.
Marriage and Divorce (Muhammadan) Registration Decree, 1935 and 1936 (p. 62)	No. 8 of 1935 and No. 4 of 1936.
Marriage (Solemnisation and Registration) Decree, 1915 (p. 61)	Cap 69.
Native Christian Divorce Decree, 1925 (p. 62)	Cap 70.
Oaths Decree, 1917 (pp. 60, 61, 70)	Cap 7.
Penal Decree, 1934 (pp. 59, 62)	Cap 9.
Public Land Decree, 1921 (p. 65)	Cap 106.
Registration of Documents Decree, 1919 (p. 65)	Cap 111.
Slavery Decree, 1909 (pp. 63, 76)	Cap 53.
Succession Decree, 1917 (pp. 3, 60, 62, 63, 68, 75, 329)	Cap 13.
Trade Marks Decree, 1930 (p. 58)	Cap 89.
Transfer of Property Decree, 1917 (pp. 61, 65, 66)	Cap 82.
Waqf Property Decree, 1916 (pp. 63, 64, 95)	Cap 34.
Waqf Validating (Amendment) Decree, 1951 (pp. 64, 330)	No. 6 of 1951.
Waqf Validating Decree, 1946 (pp. 34, 64, 77, 78, 93, 94, 330)	No. 5 of 1946.

KENYA

(Caps as in the Revised Edition of 1948)

Abolition of the Legal Status of Slavery Ordinance, 1907 (pp. 90, 118)	Cap 94.
Adoption of Children Ordinance, 1933 (p. 92)	Cap 21.
African Christian Marriage and Divorce Ordinance, 1931 (pp. 87, 88)	Cap 99.
African Property Preservation Ordinance, 1916 (p. 91)	Cap 102.
Age of Majority Ordinance, 1933 (pp. 87, 88, 92)	Cap 10.
Civil Procedure Ordinance, 1924 (pp. 90, 99)	Cap 5.
Courts Ordinance, 1931 (pp. 83, 84, 88–90, 99, 105, 107, 119, 120)	Cap 3.
Credit to Africans (Control) Ordinance, 1948 (p. 92)	Cap 104.
Criminal Procedure Code, 1930 (pp. 99, 107)	Cap 27.
Crown Lands Ordinance, 1915 (pp. 90, 91)	Cap 15.
Custody of Children Ordinance, 1926 (p. 106)	Omitted.
Employment of Women, Young People and Children Ordinance, 1948 (p. 92)	Cap 111.
Indian Acts (Amendments) Ordinance, 1907 (p. 102)	Cap 2.
Interpretation and General Clauses Ordinance (pp. 92, 93)	Cap 1.
Juveniles Ordinance, 1934 (p. 92)	Omitted.
Land (Perpetual Succession) Ordinance, 1923 (pp. 91, 92)	Cap 163.
Land Titles Ordinance, 1908 (pp. 91, 109)	Cap 159.
Marriage Ordinance, 1902 (pp. 87–88, 104–105)	Cap 144.
Matrimonial Causes Ordinance, 1941 (pp. 87, 88)	Cap 145.
Muhammadan Marriage and Divorce Registration Ordinance, 1906 (p. 85)	Cap 147.
Muhammadan Marriage, Divorce and Succession Ordinance, 1920 (pp. 3, 7, 9, 84, 86–88, 101, 105, 106, 107, 112–118, 120, 149, 328, 329)	Cap 148.
Penal Code, 1930 (pp. 87, 88, 107)	Cap 24.
Public Trustee Ordinance, 1925 (p. 110)	Cap 37.
Registration of Documents Ordinance, 1901 (pp. 91, 109)	Cap 162.
Registration of Titles Ordinance, 1919 (pp. 98, 109)	Cap 160.

Revised Edition of the Laws Ordinance, 1948 (pp. 92, 107) ...	No. 87 of 1948
Subordinate Courts (Separation and Maintenance) Ordinance, 1928 (p. 88)	Cap 6.
Trusts of Land Ordinance, 1941 (pp. 91, 92, 98)	Cap 151.
Waqf Commissioners Ordinance, 1951 (pp. 85, 93–96, 330) ...	No. 30 of 1951.

TANGANYIKA

(Caps as in Revised Edition of 1947, with Additions, 1947–49)

Administration (Small Estates) (Amendment) Ordinance, 1947 (pp. 3, 115, 116, 124, 126, 127, 128, 131, 132, 144, 145, 146, 163, 170, 248, 302)	Cap 30.
Adoption of Infants Ordinance, 1942 (pp. 129, 130)	Cap 14.
Affiliation Ordinance, 1949 (p. 130)	Cap 278.
Animals (Native Livestock) Ordinance, 1928 (p. 132)	Cap 157.
Asiatics (Marriage, Divorce and Succession) (Amendment) Ordinance, 1947 (Renamed as amendment to Cap 112 and incorporated therein) No. 44 of 1947.	(now Cap 112.)
Births and Deaths Registration Ordinance, 1920 (p. 132) ...	Cap 108.
Credit to Natives (Restriction) Ordinance, 1931 (pp. 130, 132)	Cap 75.
Crops (Increased Production) Ordinance, 1944 (p. 132) ...	Cap 151.
Destitute Persons Ordinance, 1923 (p. 132)	Cap 41.
District Courts (Separation and Maintenance) Ordinance, 1949 (p. 129)	Cap 274.
Divorce Ordinance, 1929 (pp. 128, 129, 132)	Cap 110.
Interpretation and General Clauses Ordinance, 1928 (pp. 128, 132)	Cap 1.
Intoxicating Liquors Ordinance, 1923 (p. 132)	Cap 198.
Land Acquisition Ordinance, 1926 (p. 133)	Cap 118.
Land (Amendment) Ordinance, 1947–49 (p. 131)	Cap 113.
Land (Law of Property and Conveyancing) Ordinance, 1923 (pp. 124, 131, 132)	Cap 114.
Land Ordinance, 1923 (pp. 130, 131, 132)	Cap 113.
Land (Perpetual Succession) Ordinance, 1927 (p. 130) ...	Cap 119.
Land Registry Ordinance, 1923 (pp. 132, 133, 135)	Cap 116.
Local Courts Ordinance, 1951 (pp. 123, 124, 128, 129, 133, 134, 135, 136)	No. 14 of 1951.
Marriage, Divorce and Succession (Non-Christian Asiatics) Ordinance, 1923 (pp. 7, 124, 125, 126, 162, 163, 248, 300, 302, 328, 329)	Cap 112.
Marriage Ordinance, 1921 (pp. 125, 128, 129, 132)	Cap 109.
Master and Native Servants Ordinance, 1923 (p. 132)	Cap 78.
Muhammadan Estates (Benevolent Payments) Ordinance, 1918 (pp. 3, 123, 124, 128)	Cap 29.
Native Authority Ordinance, 1927 (pp. 132, 134, 135)	Cap 72.
Native Food Stuffs Ordinance, 1924 (p. 132)	Cap 76.
Native Liquor Ordinance, 1924 (p. 132)	Cap 77.
Non-Native Education Tax Ordinance, 1949 (p. 132)	Cap 265.
Penal Code, 1945 (pp. 62, 129)	Cap 16.
Porters (Restriction of Employment) Ordinance, 1928 (p. 132)	Cap 171.
Registration of Documents Ordinance, 1924 (p. 133)	Cap 117.
Religious and Charitable Societies (Disposal of Land) Ordinance, 1929 (p. 130)	Cap 120.
Somalis (Miscellaneous Provisions) Ordinance, 1949 (pp. 127, 128, 132)	Cap 277.

UGANDA

(Caps as in the Revised Edition of 1951)

NYASALAND

(Caps as in Revised Edition of 1946)

NIGERIA

(Caps as in the Revised Edition of 1948)

THE GAMBIA

(Caps as in Revised Edition of 1942)

THE GOLD COAST

(Caps as in Revised Edition of 1936)

Native Courts (Colony) Ordinance, 1944 (pp. 4, 252, 253, 254, 255, 258, 270, 273, 282, 284)	No. 22 of 1944.
Native Courts (Northern Territories) Ordinance, 1935 (pp. 252, 253, 254, 255, 261, 270, 273)...	Cap 85.
Native Courts (Southern Section of Togoland) Ordinance, 1949 (pp. 252, 253, 254, 255, 270, 273, 284)	No. 8 of 1949.
Native Law and Custom (Ashanti Confederacy Council) Ordinance, 1940 (p. 285)	No. 4 of 1940.
Public Lands (Leasehold) Ordinance, 1950 (p. 257)	No. 55 of 1950.
Public Lands Ordinance (Colony and Ashanti), 1876 (p. 256) ...	Cap 113.
Reaffirmation of the Abolition of Slavery Ordinance, 1930 (p. 276)	Cap 91.
Slaves' Emancipation Ordinance, 1874 (p. 276)	Cap 92.
Survey Ordinance, 1922 (p. 256)	Cap 111.

SIERRA LEONE

(Caps as in Revised Edition of 1946)

Administration of Estates Ordinance, 1945 (pp. 288, 297) ...	Cap 2.
Children's Ordinance, 1926 (p. 289)	Cap 31.
Christian Marriage Ordinance, 1906 (pp. 289, 296)	Cap 32.
Civil Marriage Ordinance, 1910 (p. 289)	Cap 35.
Courts Ordinance, 1945 (pp. 288, 289, 295)	Cap 50.
District Councils Ordinance, 1950 (pp. 289, 290)	No. 17 of 1950.
Interpretation Ordinance, 1945 (p. 287)	Cap 1.
Married Women's Maintenance Ordinance, 1888 (p. 295) ...	Cap 138.
Muhammadan Marriage Ordinance, 1905 (pp. 3, 9, 287, 288, 289, 290, 295, 296, 300, 327, 329)	Cap 145.
Native Courts Ordinance, 1933 (p. 288)	Cap 149.
Oaths and Affirmations Ordinance, 1930 (p. 290)	Cap 154.
Protectorate Ordinance, 1933 (pp. 287, 290)	Cap 185.
Tribal Administration (Colony) Ordinance, 1932 (p. 295) ...	Cap 244.
Young Persons and Children Ordinance, 1945 (p. 289) ...	Cap 270.

THE ANGLO-EGYPTIAN SUDAN

Civil Justice Ordinance, 1929 (pp. 307, 308) ...	Title XXI,	Sub-title 2.
Land Registration Rules, 1925 (p. 316)	Title XII,	Sub-title 2.
Ma'dhuns Regulations, 1912 (pp. 302, 303) ...	Title XXI,	Sub-title 3.
Native Courts Ordinance, 1932 (pp. 308, 309) ...	Title XXI,	Sub-title 4.
Non-Muhammadan Marriage Ordinance, 1926 (pp. 309, 310)	Title XVIII,	Sub-title 1.
Official Administrator Ordinance, 1928 (p. 310) ...	Title XVIII,	Sub-title 4.
Penal Code, 1925 (p. 309)	Title XX,	Sub-title 1.
Pre-emption Ordinance, 1928 (p. 311)	Title XII,	Sub-title 6.
Public Trustee Ordinance, 1937 (pp. 310, 311) ...	Title XVIII,	Sub-title 5.
Sudan Muhammadan Law Courts Fees Regulations, 1935 (p. 307)	Title XXI,	Sub-title 3.
Sudan Muhammadan Law Courts Ordinance, 1902 (pp. 301, 302, 303, 308, 311)	Title XXI,	Sub-title 3.
Sudan Muhammadan Law Courts Organisation and Procedure Regulations, 1915 (pp. 303–307, 311)	Title XXI,	Sub-title 3.
Wills and Administration Ordinance, 1928 (p. 310)	Title XVIII,	Sub-title 3.

APPENDIX H

Table of Cases Cited

A. REPORTED CASES

1. Abdi Nuri *v.* B.E.A. Corporation and Rukiya (1909) 3 E.A.L.R. 12 (p. 101).
2. Abdullah b. Athman *v.* Abdulla b. Masood (1910) 3 E.A.L.R. 76 (p. 103).
3. Abdulrahim Haji Ismail Nathu *v.* Halimbai (1915) 6 E.A.L.R. 113, 1 Z.L.R. 669 (pp. 60, 323).
4. Abdulrahim *v.* Hatiji (1905) 1 E.A.L.R. 86 (p. 103).
5. Abdureman b. Khamis and Aisha bti. Safi *v.* Khamis b. Malim (1918) 7 E.A.L.R. 110 (p. 105)
6. Abul Fata *v.* Russumoy (1894) 22 I.A. 76 (pp. 78, 96, 97, 98, 146, 340, 341).
7. Adamji Abdulali *v.* Admin-General and Sherifali Mohamedali (1918) 7 E.A.L.R. 206 (p. 106).
8. Advocate-General *v.* Muhammad Husen Huseni (1866) 12 Bom H.C.R. 323 (p. 323).
9. Ahmed b. Abdulla *v.* Administrator of Native Estates (1925) 10 K.L.R. 136 (pp. 90, 118).
10. Aisha bti. Vali and Nyanya bti. Hamis *v.* Fatuma bti. Shaabek (1902) 1 E.A.L.R. 44 (p. 105).
11. Aley b. Saleh Abdisalami *v.* Mohamed b. Saleh Abdisalami (1929) 4 Z.L.R. 63 (p. 70).
12. Ali b. Amor *v.* Mwana Nziga bti. Ngwali (1919) 2 Z.L.R. 2 (p. 74).
13. Ali Buzu *v.* Suli Shardow, etc. (1929) F. Ct 1926–29, 357 (p. 251).
14. Ali Ganyuma *v.* Ali Mohamed (1927) 11 K.L.R. 30 (pp. 112, 113).
15. Ali b. Nassor b. Khalad *v.* Zwena bti. Hamood (1911) 1 Z.L.R. 365 (p. 77).
16. Athman b. Mahomed *v.* Ahamed b. Ali (1911) 4 E.A.L.R. 30 (p. 103).
17. Athman b. Mohammed *v.* Ali b. Salim and another (1915) 6 E.A.L.R. 91 (pp. 71, 100).
18. Atiya bti. Maaruf *v.* Khamis b. Abein el-Maaghi el-Hadhrami (1941) 6 Z.L.R. 37 (p. 75).
19. Babayi of Wandie *v.* Bornu Native Administration (1936) 13 N.L.R. 18 (p. 202).
20. Baraka bti. Said Bahmishi *v.* Salim b. Abed Busawadi (1939) 20 K.L.R. Pt. I, 34 (pp. 99, 100, 123).
21. Bikani Mia *v.* Shuk Lal Poddar and another I.L.R. 20 Cal. 116 (p. 341).
22. British Resident *v.* Hafiz b. Mahomed b. Hamed el Busaidi (1917) 1 Z.L.R. 526 (p. 66).
23. Campbell *v.* Hall (1774) 1 Cowp. 204 (pp. 2, 123).
24. Daud Abdulla and another *v.* Ahmed Suleman and others (1945) 13 E.A.C.A. 1 (p. 330).
25. Dr. Francis Charlesworth *v.* Naranji Rawji and others (1906) 1 Z.L.R. 186 (p. 76).
26. Edward Powys Cobb *v.* Rashid b. Salim (1909) 3 E.A.L.R. 35 (p. 102).
27. Eshugbayi Eleko *v.* Nigerian Government and another [1931] A.C. 662 (p. 4).
28. Ex-Officio Agent (etc.) of Sadati b. Sanawiya *v.* Shahasi bti. Sheikh Terro (1930) 12 K.L.R. 129 (p. 105).
29. Fatmabhai d/o Jaffer Dhalla *v.* Mahomed Ladha (1928) 1 T.T.L.R. 55 (pp. 117, 326).
30. Fatma bti. Hafidh *v.* Admin-General. P.C. Appeal No. 81 of 1947 (p. 76).
31. Fatuma Bachoo *v.* Majothi Kara Juma Bolia (1946) 5 T.T.L.R. 163 (pp. 125, 163, 328) 13 E.A.C.A. 50.
32. Fatuma bti. Mohamed b. Salim Bakhshuwen and another *v.* Mohamed b. Salim Bakhshuwen [1952] A.C.I. (pp. 84, 85, 93, 97, 323, 340 ff).

33. Fatuma bti. Mzee *v.* Ali Hirji (1921) 9 K.L.R. Pt. 1, 49 (p. 104).
34. Fazalan Bibi *v.* Tehran Bibi and Mahomed Din Kashmiri (1921) 8 K.L.R. 200 (p. 105).
35. Fazaldin Satardin *v.* Din Mahomed and Hajra Begum (1928) 11 K.L.R. 41 (p. 153).
36. Fundi b. Hamadi Saburi *v.* Mpunga bti. Abubakar Mzee (1941) 20 K.L.R. Pt. 1, 44 (p. 106).
37. Gbadamosi Apatira and another *v.* Raliatu Akanke and others (1944) 17 N.L.R. 149 (p. 216).
38. Gulam Mohamed *v.* Hadayat Bibi (1922) 9 K.L.R. Pt. 1, 76 (p. 105).
39. Haji Bibi *v.* H.H. Sir Sultan Mahomed Shah (1908) 11 Bom. L.R. 409 (p. 324).
40. Hakim Khalil Ahmad *v.* Malik Israfi (1917) 2 Pat. L.J. 108 (p. 134).
41. Hamed b. Suleman el Mandri *v.* Sadha bti. Suleman b. Mahomed and others (1912) 1 Z.L.R. 398 (p. 328).
42. Hamisi b. Ali *v.* Mariamu bti. Ali (1929) 12 K.L.R. 51 (p. 106).
43. Hussein b. M'Nasar *v.* Abdulla b. Ahmed (1936) 17 K.L.R. Pt. 2, 95 (p. 99).
44. In re Hasanali Jadavji, deceased (1947) 5 T.T.L.R. 211 (p. 324).
45. In re Kassum Premji, deceased (1924) 1 T.T.L.R. 53 (pp. 117, 326).
46. In re Mwana Mkame (1909) 3 E.A.L.R. 48 (p. 102).
47. In the Matter of Zenebah Mustapha, etc. (1936) Sierra Leone Law Recorder III, 19 (p. 289).
48. Ismailji Mohamedali *v.* Hasan (1936) 5 Z.L.R. 87 (p. 61).
49. Joha bti. Rashid *v.* Mwana Iki bti. Salim (1911) 4 E.A.L.R. 27 (p. 104).
50. Joosab Jacob and others *v.* Admin-General of Zanzibar (1946) 13 E.A.C.A. 38 (p. 331).
51. Katsina Native Authority *v.* Abdullahi Kogo and others (1930) 14 N.L.R. 49 (pp. 193, 202, 203).
52. Khamis b. Ahmed *v.* Ahmed b. Ali b. Abdurehman and others (1934) 1 E.A.C.A. 130 (p. 3).
53. L. Matthews, Binti Masood and Vussonji Haridas *v.* Mancherji Pestonji and others (1887) 1 Z.L.R. 26 (p. 76).
54. Marko Kajubi *v.* Kulanima Kabali (1944) 11 E.A.C.A. 34 (pp. 4, 156).
55. Masood b. Said and Hafsa bti. Said *v.* Said b. Salim b. Mohamed Ghulam (1946) 14 E.A.C.A. 32 (p. 101).
56. Mbaruk b. Diwansap *v.* Hamsini b. Jumbe Kimemeta (1927) 11 K.L.R. 56 (p. 106).
57. Mbwana *v.* District Commissioner, Pemba (1938) 5 Z.L.R. 20 (pp. 69, 71).
58. Mensah *v.* Wiaboe (1925) D. Ct. 1921–25, 170 (p. 4).
59. Mirza Amir Beg *v.* Saadat Begum and Mohamed Bashir (1946) 22 K.L.R. 12 (p. 105).
60. Mohamed *v.* Abdulla (1938) 5 Z.L.R. 26 (p. 69).
61. Mohamed b. Abdulla *v.* Mwana Mkuu bti. Hussein (1903) 1 E.A.L.R. 55 (p. 104).
62. Mohamed Hassan *v.* Nana bti. Mzee (1943) 11 E.A.C.A. 4 (p. 106).
63. Mohamed Ishmael Ariff *v.* Ahmed Moola Dawood (1916) I.L.R. 43 Cal. 1085 (p. 331).
64. Mohammed Wahib Huzaifeh *v.* Hussein Saba and Maria Elina Sabeh (1939) 5 W.A.C.A. 181 (pp. 251, 327).
65. Muluwa Gwanombi and others representing the Jibana tribe *v.* Abdulrasool Alidina Visram (1914) 5 E.A.L.R. 141 (pp. 101, 102, 110, 131).
66. Mwana Arafah bti. Jambeni and others *v.* Tambaki bti. Mshamu b. Kombo el-Butavi (1930) 14 K.L.R. 69 (p. 104).
67. Nana bti. Mzee *v.* Mohamed Hassan (1932) 20 K.L.R. Pt. 1, 3 (p. 106).
68. Narantakath *v.* Parakkal (1922) 45 Mad. 986 (p. 134).

69. Omar Fakirmohamed and Gulam Mohamed etc. *v.* Remtulla Talab and another (1927) 1 T.T.L.R. 38 (pp. 130, 330, 331).
70. Parenti *v.* Barclay and the Crown Advocate (1911) 4 E.A.L.R. 80 (pp. 102, 131).
71. Rana Ramji *v.* Radhabai Natha (1937) 5 Z.L.R. 91 (pp. 40, 60, 85, 329).
72. Raschid Nanji *v.* Salem b. Issa (1918) 1 Z.L.R. 614 (p. 66).
73. Re Mahomed Habash, deceased. Vasila *v.* Worsta Sophia (1920) 3 U.L.R. 26 (pp. 150, 330).
74. Russell *v.* Russell (1924) A.C. 687 (p. 70).
75. Said b. Awad *v.* Mahfuz b. Ahmed (1906) 1 Z.L.R. 189 (p. 66).
76. Said b. Mohamed b. Kassim el Riami and others *v.* Wakf Commissioners, Zanzibar (1946) 13 E.A.C.A. 32 (pp. 77, 78, 96).
77. Said b. Seif *v.* Shariff Mohamed Shatry (1938) 19 K.L.R. Pt. 1, 9 (p. 101).
78. Salah *v.* Admin-General (1938) 5 Z.L.R. 8 (p. 77).
79. Saleh Lalji *v.* Muhomed b. Ahmed b. Hemid and another (1913) 1 Z.L.R. 423 (p. 331).
80. Salim Mustapha *v.* Lola Mustapha (1938) Sierra Leone Law Recorder III, 20 (p. 288).
81. Secretary of State *v.* Charlesworth, Pilling and Co. (1901) 1 Z.L.R. 105; 28 I.A. 121 (pp. 60, 101, 102, 331).
82. Shawana bti. Seif *v.* Ali b. Said (1922) 3 Z.L.R. 6 (pp. 68, 77).
83. Sheikh Burhan b. Abdulaziz el-Amawi *v.* Khalfan b. Salim el-Barwani and another (1929) 4 Z.L.R. 90 (p. 109).
84. Sheriff Abdulla b. Mohamed Shatri *v.* Bwana Nasibu and Mzee etc. (1910) 3 E.A.L.R. 90 (p. 103).
85. Sheriff Abdulla b. Mohamed *v.* Zuena bti. Abedi (1912) 4 E.A.L.R. 86 (pp. 101, 105, 106).
86. Sheriff Jaffer and Co. *v.* Bwana Mzee (1912) 4 E.A.L.R. 94 (p. 103).
87. Shumbana bti. Juma *v.* Admin-General (1927) 3 Z.L.R. 51 (p. 324).
88. Soud *v.* Jokha (1936) 5 Z.L.R. 16 (p. 74).
89. Sulia Ayoola and others *v.* Muritale Folawiya and others (1942) 8 W.A.C.A. 39 (p. 4).
90. Talibu b. Mwijaka *v.* Executors of Siwa Haji (1907) 2 E.A.L.R. 33 (pp. 97, 104, 342).
91. The Jibana case. See Muluwa Gwanombi, etc., above.
92. Wakf Commissioners *v.* Saada (1937) 5 Z.L.R. 6 (p. 77).

B. UNREPORTED CASES

93. Abdulla Juma *v.* Kaluli Kashaga. Tanganyika. A Tabora case (p. 143).
94. Adamawa Native Authority *v.* Koji of Cike. Nigeria. 1950. Kaduna file No. 11454/S/176. (p. 200).
95. Admin-General *v.* Saada bti. Said and others. Zanzibar. H.C. case No. 18 of 1941 (p. 77).
96. Alpha Suliman *v.* M'Balley. Sierra Leone. Reference 199/43 (p. 295).
97. Baraka Mjanakhiri *v.* Khamis Nahoda. Zanzibar. C.A. No. 9 of 1945 (p. 70).
98. Bornu Native Authority *v.* Abatcha Magudama. Nigeria. W.A.C.A. case dated 11th January, 1946. (pp. 198, 202, 203).
99. Bornu Native Authority *v.* Abba Gaha of Mastaram in Geidam district. Nigeria. (p. 202).
100. Bornu Native Authority *v.* Yusus and Dauna of Marte. Nigeria. Kaduna file No. 11454/S/178 (p. 199).
101. Brown *v.* Jelaelay. Sierra Leone. Reference 362/45. (p. 295).
102. Enzi bti. Mohamed *v.* Saidi Larusai. Tanganyika. Secretariat file No. 13879/158. (p. 139).

103. Fatuma bti. Mohamed b. Salim and another *v.* Mohamed b. Salim. Kenya. C.A. No. 33 of 1948 (pp. 93, 96).
104. Hamisi Kallaghe *v.* Nemkondo bti. Ali. Tanganyika. Secretariat file No. 13879/268. (p. 139).
105. In re succession to Sepiriya Bingo Kadumukasa, deceased. Uganda. Miscellaneous Appeal No. 13 of 1949. (p. 156).
106. Isa *v.* Okoye. Nigeria. Kano case K/18A/1943. (p. 192).
107. Jackson *v.* Weeks. Sierra Leone. Reference 363/45. (p. 295).
108. Juma Shamte *v.* Mohamed Safr. Tanganyika. Dar es Salaam Appeal No. 1 of 1942. (p. 138).
109. Kano Native Authority *v.* Gwandai Bembem and Ahmadu Shokana. Nigeria. 1950. Kaduna file No. 11454/S/178. (p. 199).
110. Katsina Native Authority *v.* Gambo of Katantu in Kantara district. Nigeria. Katsina file No. 3341. (p. 201).
111. Katsina Native Authority *v.* Gaude and Ramatu of Mayona in Kogo district. Nigeria. Katsina file No. 3341. (p. 196).
112. Katsina Native Authority *v.* Yakudi of Hadaba and Danboko of Rimage. Nigeria. Katsina file No. 3341. (p. 200).
113. Khadija bti. Masood *v.* Masood b. Seif and Abdulla b. Seif. Zanzibar. C.A. No. 27 of 1946. (p. 78).
114. Mallam Abba *v.* Mary T. Baikie. Nigeria. 1943. Kano case K/20A/1943. (p. 216).
115. Matar Ismail *v.* Asha bti. Ukashi. Tanganyika. Secretariat file No. 13879/71. (p. 139).
116. Mohamed Ahmad *v.* Baraza Nampunga. Tanganyika. Lindi case No. 1/336. (p. 139).
117. Mohamed Atiki *v.* Mohamed Salim Mohamedi. Tanganyika. Lindi case No. 1/356. (p. 144).
118. Mohamed b. Issa *v.* Njanja b. Hamisi. Tanganyika. Lindi case No. 1/283. (p. 144).
119. Mohamed b. Juma Mzaramo *v.* Mtumwa bti. Mohamed Mzaramo. Tanganyika. Secretariat file No. 13879/111. (p. 139).
120. Mohamed Selemani *v.* Mohamed Saidi Allay. Tanganyika. Lindi case No. 1/355. (p. 141).
121. Mohammad b. Juma and four others *v.* Sufiah bti. Nassor. Zanzibar. Application to appeal No. 4 of 1944. (p. 72).
122. Mwajuma bti. Fundi Mgindo *v.* Mariam bti. Abeid and others. Zanzibar. Application to appeal No. 4 of 1945. (p 77).
123. Nasor *v.* Mohamed. Zanzibar. C.A. No. 2 of 1935. (p. 76).
124. Native Authority *v.* Nlebe Konkomba. Gold Coast. 1949. Yendi case dated 18th August, 1949. (p. 263).
125. Omar b. Mihombo *v.* Abdulla Ali. Tanganyika. Secretariat file No. 13879/82. (p. 143).
126. Ramadhani Simba *v.* Fatuma bti. Ali. Tanganyika. P.C. Dar es Salaam Appeal No. 3 of 1949. (p. 139).
127. Rex *v.* M'fa Nonko and others. Sierra Leone. Supreme Court case dated 1st July, 1927. (p. 290).
128. Rex *v.* Salla Silla. Sierra Leone. Supreme Court case dated 1st July, 1927. (p. 290).
129. Rex *v.* Usman Acida. Nigeria. 1949. Kano case K/381/49. (p. 182).
130. Rhematbai bti. Hirji *v.* Sonaru Ismail Mohamed and Co. etc. Zanzibar. Civil case No. 20 of 1942. (p. 78).
131. Said b. Abdulla Shikely and Sabuhu bti. Ali b. Khamis *v.* The Waqf Commissioners and the Registrar of Titles, Mombasa. Kenya. Civil case No. 40 of 1949. (pp. 98, 99).

132. Said b. Salim *v.* Masood b. Said and Hafsa bti. Said. Kenya. C.A. No. 15 of 1945. (p. 99).
133. Saumu bti. Uleidi *v.* Khamis b. Sorigoro. Zanzibar. Pemba C.A. No. 7 of 1944. (p. 76).
134. Seif b. Mahomed El-Mauli *v.* Admin-General. Zanzibar. C.A. No. 21 of 1947. (p. 71).
135. Seleman b. Sudi *v.* Hassan b. Ali. Tanganyika. Secretariat file No. 13879/246. (p. 137).
136. Tsofo Guba *v.* Gwandu Native Authority. W.A.C.A. case dated 5th May, 1947. (pp. 181, 198).
137. Wakf Commissioners *v.* Abdulla Hemraj. Zanzibar. H.C. case No. 15 of 1942. (pp. 77, 78).

C. CLASSIFICATION OF CASES

CASES CONCERNING CONTRACT AND QUASI-CONTRACT (INCLUDING NADHR, ETC.).
Nos. 2, 4, 22, 26, 33, 46, 49, 60, 61, 65, 66, 72, 75, 77, 79, 81, 83, 84, 91, 113, 130.

CASES CONCERNING GUARDIANSHIP.
Nos. 7, 17, 18, 36, 42, 56, 57, 62, 67.

CASES CONCERNING HOMICIDE.
Nos. 19, 51, 94, 98, 99, 100, 109, 110, 111, 112, 129, 136.

CASES CONCERNING THE LAW APPLICABLE TO THE PERSONS OR CIRCUMSTANCES.
Nos. 3, 8, 13, 14, 17, 23, 27, 28, 29, 39, 41, 44, 45, 50, 52, 54, 56, 57, 58, 60, 65, 70, 71, 73, 81, 82, 87, 89, 91, 93, 97, 98, 104, 108, 114, 115, 116, 127, 128, 129, 130, 131, 132, 134, 135, 136.

CASES CONCERNING MARRIAGE, DIVORCE, ETC.
Nos. 12, 17, 20, 31, 34, 35, 38, 47, 57, 59, 64, 68, 80, 88, 96, 101, 102, 104, 107, 108, 115, 116, 119, 120, 121, 124, 126.

CASES CONCERNING PATERNITY.
Nos. 5, 10, 74, 85, 93, 117, 125, 134, 135.

CASES CONCERNING PROCEDURE AND EVIDENCE.
Nos. 1, 11, 17, 19, 20, 22, 43, 48, 51, 55, 72, 75, 77, 85, 97, 98, 99, 106, 111, 125, 132, 134.

CASES CONCERNING SECTS AND SCHOOLS OF LAW.
Nos. 3, 8, 29, 39, 40, 41, 44, 45, 82, 87.

CASES CONCERNING SLAVERY (AND PATRONAGE).
Nos. 9, 30, 117, 118, 127, 128.

CASES CONCERNING SUCCESSION.
Nos. 3, 9, 14, 29, 37, 44, 45, 54, 73, 87, 105, 113, 114, 117, 118, 133, 135.

CASES CONCERNING TORT.
Nos. 16, 25, 53, 86, 123.

CASES CONCERNING "USURY" OR INTEREST.
Nos. 4, 22, 60, 72, 75, 83, 84.

CASES CONCERNING WAQF.
Nos. 6, 15, 21, 24, 32, 45, 63, 69, 76, 78, 90, 92, 95, 103, 122, 137.

GLOSSARY

A

'adl (pl. *'udūl*). A competent witness—i.e., one fulfilling all the requirements of the Islamic law. As such he must be a major, sane, free Muslim who faithfully performs his religious duties, leads a moral life, and has no personal interest in the case (although fidelity in ritual and morals is seldom in practice called in question in African territories today). Not only in criminal cases but in all matters other than financial, moreover, the Mālikīs and Shāfi'is insist on the witnesses being males—except in certain particulars which, from their nature, would be known only to women.

The term for a witness' competence is *'adāla,* and for the establishment of such competence *ta'dīl* (q.v.); while the more competent of two witnesses or groups of witnesses is sometimes referred to as the *a'dal.*

aḥad al-ajalayn. Literally, one of the two fixed terms, i.e., death or divorce. The term is used in connection with deferred dower (*mahr or ṣadāq mu'ajjal*), when this is payable on death or divorce.

aḥbās. See under *waqf.*

ahl al-qarāba. Those who base their system of priority between the uterine heirs (i.e., those heirs who are neither agnates nor "sharers") on the principle of which is most closely related to the deceased, according (*a*) to their "order" [descendants, ascendants, collaterals through the parents and collaterals through grandparents, etc.], (*b*) to their degree and (*c*) to the strength of the blood-tie.

ahl al-tanzīl. Those who base their system of inheritance of uterine heirs (see above) on the principle of regarding all such as stepping into the shoes of the primary heir, whether agnate or sharer, through whom they are related to the deceased.

Aḥmadīya (sect). This sect was founded by Mīrzā Ghulām Aḥmad Khān, who was born in Qādiān in the Panjab in 1839 (circ.). In 1889 he announced a divine revelation giving him the right to accept *bay'a* (fealty), and in 1891 he announced that he was both the *Mahdī* (the "rightly-guided one") whom Muslims expect and the promised Messiah. Thenceforth he was involved in bitter controversy with Muslims, Christians and others. A *fatwā* bearing the seals of many well-known Indian *mullas* was issued declaring him to be an apostate and the destruction of his followers to be lawful; while he on his part indulged in denunciations of his enemies. From 1892 an English monthly magazine, the *Review of Religions,* has been published; and most of the distinctive teaching of the movement can be found therein. But the claims of Aḥmad can best be understood, perhaps, in the words of Dr. Griswold, for in a conversation with him Aḥmad apparently made the astounding statement that "as Moses is to Christ, so Muḥammad is to Ghulām Aḥmad; or again, as Muḥammad is to Moses, so the Mīrzā Ṣāḥib is to Jesus Christ. In a word, as Moses is a type of Muḥammad, so Jesus of Nazareth is a type of Aḥmad of Qādiān".[1] He also claimed for himself numerous Messianic prophecies in the Old Testament, the Qur'anic references to Aḥmad, and that he was an *avatār* of Krishna; while he is acknowledged by his followers as a Prophet—a claim plainly at variance with the dogma of orthodox Islam that Muḥammad was the last and seal of the Prophets (although the Aḥmadīs are careful to add that the Promised Messiah came in

[1] *Mīrzā Ghulām Aḥmad, the Mehdi Messiah of Qādiān,* p. 21 (quoted at p. 27 of *The Aḥmadīya Movement,* by H. A. Walters. Cp. the latter throughout this note).

the spirit and within the religion revealed by Muḥammad, and to interpret the term " seal " in a manner consistent with this claim).

Aḥmad died in 1908, and was succeeded in the leadership of the sect by his " first Khalīfa " (Successor), Ḥākim Nūr al-Dīn. On the latter's death a split occurred, for the Mīrzā Bashīr al-Dīn Maḥmūd Aḥmad, the eldest son of the founder by his second wife, was elected his second Khalīfa, but an opposition party seceded and maintained that there should be no Khalīfa, but that the Chief Aḥmadīya Society (Anjuman-i-Aḥmadīya) should control the affairs of the community. Thenceforth the secession group, known as the Lahore party, has tended to approximate more and more to orthodox Islam, while the Qādiān party has continued what seems to be the authentic Aḥmadī teachings under the " Promised Son of the Promised Messiah ", or the " Promised Reformer ", some of whose stupendous claims have been quoted at p. 328 note (2) above. It is the Qādiān party which is represented in Africa: and the logic of their teachings, however much they claim to be true Muslims, is that any one who rejects the claims of the Promised Messiah is in error (even an " unbeliever "); while orthodox Muslims take an equally strong attitude towards them.

It may be added that the Lahore party have a mosque in Woking, and the Qādiānīs in Putney; that the Promised Messiah claimed that the *jihād* should be waged by propaganda, not the sword, and abjured political activities; and that the Aḥmadīs are distinguished from orthodox Muslims *inter alia* by their adoption of the theory of Venturini that Christ was in fact crucified but taken down from the Cross while still alive, and by the fantastic claim that he ultimately died and was buried in Srinagar.

Aḥmadīya (Ṣūfī brotherhood). This is the name given in Somaliland to the followers of the mystic rule of Aḥmad b. Idrīs, who died in 'Asīr in the first half of the nineteenth century. It is therefore, presumably, synonymous with what is elsewhere termed the Idrīsīya, and is an Order derived from the Khāḍirīya or Khiḍrīya and closely related to the Mirghanīya of the Sudan, Egypt and Eritrea and the Sanūsīya of North Africa, etc. The Ṣāliḥīya, also found in Somaliland, broke off from the Aḥmadīya under the leadership of Muḥammad Ṣāliḥ, who lived in Mecca and was previously a disciple of the Sudanese mystic Ibrāhīm al-Rashīdī, the disciple of Aḥmad b. Idrīs. The so-called " Mad Mulla " started by proclaiming himself a true follower of Muḥammad Ṣāliḥ, with whom he had become personally acquainted when he performed the pilgrimage in 1895: later, however, his increasing popularity led him to assume a more ambitious role than that of an agent of the Ṣāliḥīya; but it was undoubtedly a severe blow when Muḥammad Ṣāliḥ repudiated him, for he had already provoked the hostility of the Qādirīya. The other branch of the Aḥmadīya is sometimes termed Andarāwīya in Somaliland.

'ālim (pl. *'ulamā'*). A learned man; particularly a man learned in the Muslim sciences of the traditions and the sacred law.

'amd. Intention, e.g., in homicide, where the broad division is into intentional homicide (*qatl al-'amd*) on the one hand and accidental homicide (*qatl al-khaṭa'*) on the other. Abū Ḥanīfa confined the first category to homicides committed by means of some weapon which cuts or pierces (possibly extended to fire or any instrument of iron); his Two Companions limited it to some direct act likely to kill on the spot; while al-Shāfi'ī and Aḥmad ibn Ḥanbal defined it as a homicide by means of any behaviour intrinsically likely to kill. The followers of all these jurists, moreover, postulate an intermediate category of quasi-intentional homicide (*shabah 'amd*) in which they put homicides in which the killer meant to injure but not to kill (or rather, not to do an act of the sort which they regard as manifesting an intention to kill). The normal Mālikī view, on the other hand, excludes this intermediate category, and extends *'amd* to include (*a*) homicides by any means whatever as a result of a hostile and unjustified assault, and (*b*) homicide in the course of play or legitimate chastisement by means of some act intrinsically likely to kill.

'āqila. i.e., a man's male relatives, who are collectively responsible for the *'aql* or *dīya* (q.v.) in respect of any unintentional homicide which he may commit. The Ḥanafīs and some Mālikīs say that the man who did the deed should himself contribute, while others exclude him. Again, the Ḥanafīs regard the *'āqila* as extended, in this respect, to include co-members of a guild, neighbours, etc., on the grounds that the Caliph 'Umar made Muslim soldiers whose names appeared on the same lists (*dīwāns*) mutually responsible for each other's blood-wit. See Encyclopaedia of Islam.

'Aqīqa. This is the name of a ceremony, frequently held on the seventh day after an infant's birth, which is regarded as "commendable" (*sunna*) by the religious law. The usual procedure is to name the child, shave off its hair, and kill a victim; while it is also normal to weigh the hair and give not less than its equivalent in gold or silver as alms. The ceremony is a survival of pre-Islamic custom, alleged to have been sanctioned, and thus islamicised, by Muḥammad: but local variations in its performance reveal the survival of animistic practices in connection with this ceremony until today. See Encyclopaedia of Islam.

arsh. Compensation, e.g. for a wound for which no fixed porportion of the full *dīya* (q.v.) has been laid down.

'aṣaba. Agnatic relatives, i.e., relations whose relationship is traced through males. They were (*inter alia*) the principal heirs of pre-Islamic Arabia, and have retained a special position in the law of inheritance according to all the Sunnī schools, although extended by Muḥammad to include certain females (the *'aṣaba bi ghayrihinna* and *ma'a ghayrihinna*) and with the special heirs (the *aṣḥāb al-farā'iḍ*) superimposed.

aṣḥāb al-farā'iḍ (or *al-furūḍ*). The "sharers" or quota-heirs of the Islamic system of inheritance. Such, in the Sunnī system, are the mother, "true" grandmother, daughter (when not agnatised by a son), son's daughter (when not agnatised by a corresponding, or sometimes more remote, son's son), germane or consanguine sister (when not agnatised by a corresponding brother or with a daughter or son's daughter), uterine brothers and sisters, and the husband or wife; while the father and "true" grandfather also inherit on this principle when excluded from inheriting as nearest agnate by a son or son's son, and both in this capacity and also that of nearest agnate when in competition with a daughter or son's daughter. Of these sharers nine were expressly alloted their respective shares or quotas in the Qur'ān, while three (the true grandfather, true grandmother and son's daughter) were added on analogy by the Sunnīs, but are not accepted as such by the Shī'īs.

awqāf. Plural of *waqf* (q.v.)

B

bay' al-khiyār. This, like the *bay' al-iqāla, bay' al-wafā'* and the *'uhda*, is a form of conditional or redeemable sale. These contracts are used in different parts of the Muslim world largely as a device, somewhat similar to the mortgage, by which an advance of money may be obtained not only on the security of land or house but by the provision of what virtually amounts to interest out of its produce or rental. As such all these contracts are regarded as illicit by the purists; but all have been accepted as legitimate devices, largely on grounds of necessity, by others. The *'uhda* is very common in South Arabia; the *bay' al-khiyār* was previously widespread in Zanzibar and the Kenya Protectorate, etc.; the *bay' al-iqāla* is favoured in Somaliland; while the *bay' al-wafā'* was common in the Ottoman Empire (e.g., Egypt). In Zanzibar, for instance, the usual practice was for the vendor (or mortgagor) to retain the property on lease from the vendee, the rent representing the interest on the loan, and it was judicially declared (4 Z.L.R. 90) that the Qāḍīs had repeatedly upheld this transaction "to enable persons needing money to obtain credit without incurring the possible guilt of dealing in transactions by way of interest".

bay' al-iqāla. See *bay' al-khiyār* above.

bayt al-māl. This is the Muslim treasury, into which the land tax (*kharāj*), the poll-tax (*jizya*), the legal alms (*zakāt*—including the *'ushr* on land), the fifth part (*khums*) of booty, of the produce of mines and of treasure-trove, and the estates of all Muslims who die without agnatic heirs (and without sharers whose shares exhaust the estate) should properly be paid. There were, however, strict rules as to the ends to which some of these receipts must be devoted: but Muslim rulers have seldom, if ever, followed these rules meticulously. Where there is no *bayt al-māl*, or where it is regarded as improperly organised, most schools of Islamic law allow sharers (other than the spouse relict) whose prescribed shares do not exhaust the estate to take the residue by the doctrine of the return (*radd*); and in default of such sharers they also allow uterine heirs to inherit.

bulūgh. Puberty.

D

daf'. Literally "payment", is the name given in S. Arabia to the chief marriage payment.

ḍamān. May mean suretyship, responsibility, accountability, or the restoration of some article or its value. In the case of a legacy expressed as "*'an ḍamān*", it implies that this legacy is either the payment of a debt or the discharge of some other obligation. As such it is a common device among the Ibāḍīs to avoid the ordinary rules of testate and intestate succession.

ḍarar. Injury, damage. Used of cruelty or ill-treatment in marriage, and in a multitude of other senses.

dhikr. Literally rememberance or mentioning, it is used as a technical term for the Ṣūfī practice of repeating over and over again certain names of God, or other pious phrases, either aloud or in the mind, with special control of the breath and physical movements (which may or may not be accompanied by music, etc.). Each Ṣūfī brotherhood has its own formula: and this is used on some occasions, but not all, in order to induce a state of ecstasy.

dīya (or *'aql*). Blood-wit, payable in respect either of homicide or certain wounds. Where a free, male Muslim has been unintentionally killed one hundred camels are payable (made up of twenty she-camels of one year old, twenty males and twenty females of two years old, twenty she-camels of three years old and twenty she-camels of four years old); while in the case of quasi-deliberate homicide all the hundred must be she-camels (twenty-five of one, two, three and four years old respectively). The money equivalent was fixed at 1,000 *dīnārs* or 12,000 *dirhams*. As for wounds, many of these were computed as representing some definite fraction, or even the full equivalent, of the *dīya* payable for homicide. The *dīya* for a woman is normally half that for a man, but in the Mālikī system this only applies where the *dīya* exceeds one-third of the full amount; while for a Christian or Jew half that due for a Muslim is payable according to most jurists, but only one-third in the Shāfiʿī system. Mālikī authority exists for rating the Zoroastrian (or even, perhaps, the apostate) at one-fifteenth that of a male Muslim; and this is applied in some of the Emirates of Northern Nigeria in the case of a pagan.

In cases of quasi-deliberate homicide (or deliberate, where *dīya* rather than talion is exacted) the offender alone is responsible, but in cases of accidental homicide the *ʿāqila* (q.v.) is collectively responsible and must pay the sum within three years. Hence the term " *dīya*-paying group ".

F

faskh. Annulment or rescission of a contract. In regard to marriage the word sometimes means annulment of the contract *ab initio* and sometimes dissolution of the contract as from some particular date; and while in some circumstances this is regarded as occuring *ipso facto*, in others a decree of court is required. A judicial dissolution of marriage at the request of the wife is normally termed *taṭlīq* (divorce) by the Mālikīs, but *faskh* by the other schools.

fatwā. A formal legal opinion, given by an official or unofficial *muftī*, i.e., person appointed, or at least competent, to give such opinions. The request for such an opinion may be made by a Qāḍī, by the State, or by a private individual: and on the basis thereof the Qāḍī may decide a case or the individual order his behaviour. For *mujtahid bi'l-fatwā*, see under *mujtahid*. The plural is *fatāwā*.

fiqh. Literally intelligence or knowledge, it is the technical term for the science of the law. The *uṣūl al-fiqh* (sources of the law) is the term for jurisprudence, and the *furūʿ al-fiqh* (branches of the law) for the substantive law. It covers every aspect of a man's life. If the Sharīʿa (literally, the way to a watering place, then in a technical sense the totality of Allāh's commandments) is the divine law regarded from the point of view of its origin and authority, *fiqh* is the same law regarded from the point of view of the science of its deduction and arrangement.

G

ghaṣb. Taking another's property wrongfully and by force, trespassing on his land, etc. It differs from *sariqa* not only by being of wider application but also in that the latter must be by stealth.

ghīla. An aggravated form of homicide. This is often limited to homicides committed in order to facilitate a further offence, e.g., theft or adultery, but is sometimes extended to a homicide where the killer persuades his victim to accompany him to some suitable spot, etc. See pp. 198, 199 above.

H

ḥaḍāna. The care and custody of young children. Where a marriage has been broken up by death or divorce this belongs to the mother rather than the father, unless she is married again to someone outside the prohibited degrees of relationship to her child or shows herself unfit for the office. In default of the mother the right to custody passes, according to most schools, to the mother's mother, and then to a series of relatives of whom it may be postulated in general that females are preferred to males and the mother's side to that of the father. But this only lasts until seven in the case of a boy and nine in the case of a girl in the usual Ḥanafī view; the age of discernment (e.g., seven) for both a boy and girl, followed by an option, in the usual

Shāfi'ī doctrine; puberty in the case of a boy and removal to her husband's house in the case of a girl in the dominant Mālikī view; and weaning (or two years) in the case of a boy and seven in the case of a girl in the normal Ithnā 'Asharī opinion. These rules, however, are often subject to local variations.

There are, moreover, further complications. Thus a father is normally allowed to claim his child at any age if he is going to some other locality in order to settle there, while a mother is not usually allowed to take the child further from the father's place of residence than would allow him to visit his child and return home in the same day. Again, the father is responsible for the child's maintenance, and also for paying his divorced wife wages for suckling and care (in most schools): but where, e.g., someone else offers to do this free, the child's mother is frequently given the choice between doing the same or forfeiting her claim; while the father retains certain rights of guardianship throughout. After the age of *ḥaḍāna* ends the Mālikīs and Shāfi'īs properly give the child an option which parent he will live with, but the father in any case retains the right to supervise his education and put him to work, etc. The one who exercises the right of custody is termed the *ḥāḍina* or *ḥāḍin*; and no male is allowed to do this in respect of a female child outside the prohibited degrees of marriage.

ḥadd (pl. *ḥudūd*). Literally boundary, limit, etc., then the limits or bounds laid down in the law (cp. Sūra 2: 183). In the criminal law *ḥadd* means an unalterable punishment prescribed by God for certain specific offences, e.g., stoning or scourging for illicit intercourse (*zinā*), cutting off of hand or foot for theft (*sariqa*) or worse for brigandage, and scourging for slander of a chaste Muslim's continence (*qadhf*) or for drinking wine (*shurb*). Such (except for *qadhf* in the Shāfi'ī system) are regarded as primarily the right of God (*ḥaqq Allāh*), so they are not commutable by the victim or anyone else: but the punishment may be imposed only after the offence has been proved by the testimony of the requisite number of competent witnesses or a sustained confession by the offender (for most jurists allow a confession once made to be retracted in such cases at any time before punishment has been inflicted).

Ḥanafīs. The followers of the largest of the four schools of law which mutually recognise each other as orthodox. The Ḥanafīya represents the ancient school of Iraq, and derives its name from Abū Ḥanīfa, one of its leading jurists. But Abū Ḥanīfa's "Two Companions", Abū Yūsuf and Muḥammad al-Shaybānī, were scarcely less influential; while another very early jurist, Zufar, is also often quoted. The Ḥanafīya is far the most wide-spread and numerous of all the schools of law: it was adopted by the Ottomān Turks as their official school and thus represents that of the courts, if not always of the population, in Egypt, the Sudan, Palestine, Syria, Iraq, etc.; while it is also the dominant school of Central Asia and India.

Ḥanbalīs. The followers of the smallest of the four orthodox schools of law, they are largely limited today to the Wahhābīs of Arabia. Strictly speaking, however, the Wahhābīs are regarded as having put themselves outside the confines of orthodox Islam, for they have repudiated the authoritative Ḥanbalī tenets on a number of points. Instead, they are enthusiastic supporters of the teachings of the two Ḥanbalī reformers, Ibn Taymīya and Ibn al-Qayyim.

ḥaqq (pl. *ḥuqūq*). In legal parlance, a right. Thus *ḥuqūq* is used of the Islamic law of obligations in general; *ḥuqūq Allāh* of "rights of God" or crimes against the community; and *ḥuqūq 'ibād* (or *ādamīya*) of what we should call torts, contractual rights, etc.

ḥarām. Forbidden by law. It is used in many different senses, but is especially relevant to this Survey in regard to divorce. Where a husband tells his wife, by one of several possible phrases, that she is henceforth *ḥarām* to him, most jurists regard this as equivalent to a divorce by the triple formula—since only by means of a triple (or third) divorce is a woman who is not within the prohibited degrees of relationship, etc., made "unlawful" to him in the sense that even a new contract of marriage would not make her lawful (without, that is, an intervening marriage).

ḥarīm. Literally, "forbidden". It is the term used by Arabs of the quarters where their women-folk live, and also of these women-folk themselves.

hiba. The ordinary gift of Islamic law, by contrast with *ṣadaqa*, which is a gift made to obtain a heavenly reward. In the case of all gifts, by contrast with legacies, ownership only passes on delivery, whether real or constructive: it is only by means of a vow (*nadhr*) that a promise of a gift can be made legally binding according to most schools, although the Mālikīs allow the enforcement of delivery of articles given and accepted by *hiba* (except in certain circumstances). But even after delivery the Ḥanafīs allow a *hiba* to be retracted except between certain relatives or where it has been alienated, destroyed or changed in nature, etc.; while the other schools in general allow revocation only between certain close relatives or where a return was stipulated but not given. A *ṣadaqa* cannot be revoked.

ḥirāba. Highway robbery. A homicide committed in the course of this is regarded as a crime rather than a tort, is more severely punished, and may not be pardoned or compounded by the heirs of blood.

ḥukm (pl. *aḥkam*). A judgment given by a court, or a rule of substantive law.

I

Ibāḍīs. A sect of Muslims regarded by the ("orthodox") Sunnīs as heterodox, and themselves regarding the Sunnīs as in error. The only surviving representatives of the Khārijī seceders of early Islam, the differences between them and the Sunnīs are today comparatively trivial. In North Africa they represent a Berber community which probably accepted Ibāḍī teachings largely in order to keep themselves aloof from the Arab invaders; in 'Umān they early established an Ibāḍī Imāmate, whence they crossed to Zanzibar and parts of the mainland of East Africa; while the two communities seem today to be drawing closer together in those minor points of law on which their opinions tended previously to differ.

'idda. The period during which a divorced or widowed woman may not remarry. In the case of widowhood this lasts four (lunar) months and ten days, or until delivery if the widow is pregnant: but in the case of divorce it properly lasts three periods of legal purity, in the Mālikī and Shāfi'ī view, or three menses, in the Ḥanafī opinion—or until delivery, by agreement, where the woman is pregnant; while a woman who has reached her menopause must observe an *'idda* of three lunar months. In the case of a slave wife these periods are halved (i.e. two months and five days, one and a half months, or two periods of purity, etc.). But there are several further complications, such as the fact that where a woman who has not reached her menopause ceases to menstruate during her *'idda* this may be protracted, in the Ḥanafī and Shāfi'ī view, until three months after she has reached the "age of despair"—while the Mālikīs regard the *'idda* as ending, in such cases, as soon as she has passed one lunar year without menses. But even where a woman avers that her *'idda* has ended any child born to her within four years of her widowhood or divorce, in the Shāfi'ī view, or within five years, in the most generally accepted Mālikī view, is regarded as the legitimate child of her former husband, unless she has already been remarried for at least six months.

Where the divorce was revocable the husband may, at any time during the *'idda*, retract it and resume marital relations, without the wife's consent and without any new dower or contract (although the payment known as *raḍwa* is customary in some localities). Where, however, the divorce was irrevocable a new contract and dower are essential, and the wife must consent thereto: but the new contract may be concluded during the *'idda*, unless the divorce were of the triple variety—in which case the remarriage of the spouses is forbidden unless the woman has previously been validly married to some other man. A revocable divorce becomes irrevocable at the end of the *'idda*.

A husband is responsible for his wife's lodging and maintenance in all cases during the *'idda* of revocable divorce (unless the wife is *nāshiza*, or disobedient) and even during the *'idda* of final divorce where she is pregnant: but the widow, by agreement, and the finally divorced wife who is not pregnant, in the Mālikī and Shāfi'ī as opposed to the Ḥanafī view, is only entitled to lodging. During the *'idda* of widowhood the wife should observe strict mourning, while during that of divorce she must also comport herself properly; and not only may she not remarry, but no direct proposal of marriage should be made to her (although indirect allusions are permitted). A marriage, during the *'idda*, to another man is invalid; and in the Mālikī view the consummation of such a marriage bars the couple concerned from ever marrying each other.

The *'idda* was one of the major reforms introduced by Muḥammad, designed partly to remove doubts about the paternity of children and partly to give the husband the opportunity to think better of a hasty divorce. But the rules of the four Sunnī schools, which enforce the triple divorce in a single formula, even when the wife is not in a state of legal purity, have largely defeated the second of these intentions: and this is why recent reforms in Egypt, the Sudan and Jordan have followed Ibn Taymīya and Ibn al-Qayyim in opposing this—in company, it may be observed, with the Ibāḍīs and Ithnā 'Asharīs (although the latter go further still in this matter).

ījāb. Declaration. This is one of the essentials in any contract, e.g. in marriage. It must normally be expressed, in Arabic, in the tense of completed action: which is why the term "declaration" is preferred to "offer". The subsequent acceptance (*qabūl*) must correspond thereto, and must follow at the same *majlis* (i.e. on the same occasion); while both must be uttered by persons competent to make a contract of that kind, and either by the principals themselves or by those entitled, whether by " nature " or by power of attorney, to act on their behalf.

ijmā'. Consensus or agreement. The orthodox view is that this constitutes a valid source of law, for although an individual jurist may err in his deductions from the sacred texts (*nuṣūṣ*), the community as a whole is infallible. Much difference of opinion has prevailed, however, as to what in fact constitutes *ijmā'*. Some limit it to the agreement of the Companions of the Prophet; some to the consensus of the whole Muslim people: but most regard it as adequately fulfilled if the leading jurists of any age are in express or implied (presumed) agreement. There are many other points of dispute; but suffice it to say that in practice this principle has habitually been invoked by conservatives to discredit all reforms, so it is only natural that it is attacked by all would-be reformers, and largely discredited among modernists today.

It may be added that the principle is used not only as an independent source of law but to validate some particular application of the Qur'ān or the authenticity of some particular Tradition. Again, it is confined, in its usual form, to the four Sunnī schools: but the Ibāḍīs recognise the *ijmā'* of their own *mujtahids*, and so to some extent do the Uṣūlīs among the Ithnā 'Asharīya.

ijtihād. See under *mujtahid,* and contrast *muqallid* and *taqlīd*.

ikhtilās. This word is often used of an act which amounts to theft but does not come within the technical definition of *sariqa*—often because the act is not done clandestinely, but by force; or for some other reason.

īlā'. A vow of continence. If a husband takes such a vow regarding his wife for a period exceeding four months (or two, some say, in the case of a slave-wife), this constitutes *īlā'*—as does also a vow of continence for an indefinite period when this in fact extends to more than four months. At the expiration of this period the marriage is automatically ended, in the Ḥanafī view, by a single, final divorce, while the Mālikīs, Shāfi'īs and Ithnā 'Asharīs allow the wife to apply to the court, which will give the husband the choice between resuming marriage relations (with expiation of his vow, where this is necessary) or divorce. The *mūlī* (one who pronounces *īlā'*) must be adult and sane, and in the Ithnā 'Asharī view fully intend what he is doing; while the *mūlā* (one concerning whom it is pronounced) must be a validly married wife or one undergoing her *'idda.*

Imām. Leader. It is used of a prayer-leader by all Muslims, and also of the founders and leading jurists of the different schools. In addition it is used by some, and especially the Shī'īs, for the leader of the whole Muslim community, whom the Shī'īs insist must have been divinely designated and whom they regard as impeccable and infallible. In details their attitude varies from sect to sect: the Zaydīs are the most moderate, although even they consider their Imāms to be rightly-guided leaders; the Ithnā 'Asharīs regard their Twelve Imāms as possessed of a divine light-substance, the "sole and permanent channel of sanctifying prerogatives and illuminative inspirations", to obey whom is a primary religious duty; while the Ismā'īlīs go even further. The leader of the Ibāḍī community in inland 'Umān is also named Imām, but purely in the sense of the ruler of the community and the upholder of the religious law.

iqdām. This term is relevant to this Survey only in regard to marriage by compulsion (*jabr*), wherein some jurists distinguish those circumstances which justify the guardian in concluding the contract (*shurūṭ al-iqdām*), and the absence of which makes the act sinful although legally valid, from those circumstances which make the contract liable to annulment even if concluded (*shurūṭ al-ṣiḥḥa*).

iqrār. Admission or confession. In Islamic law an admission made in court, or even out of court if two competent witnesses testify thereto, is final and irrevocable in all cases in which human rights predominate (*ḥuqūq ādamīya*), and judgment may immediately be given accordingly, even in homicide cases. In regard to those offences in which the right of God preponderates (*ḥuqūq Allāh*), however, a confession may be retracted, according to most jurists, at any time before the penalty is complete. An acknowledgment of paternity has the effect of establishing legitimate paternity for all purposes, provided it is physically possible (i.e. the parties differ in age by at least twelve and a half years), and cannot be disproved: but this is regarded not as a means of legitimating the illegitimate, or adopting a child of unknown origin, but rather of establishing a legitimacy which cannot otherwise be proved.

irtidād. Apostasy from Islam, for which the proper punishment is death. The Ḥanafīs hold that a female apostate should not be executed but kept in prison until she repents or dies; while most schools grant an apostate three days' respite in which to save his (or her) life by returning to Islam.

Ismā'īlīs. See under Shī'īs.

istibrā'. The "inquiry whether the uterus of a slave woman is empty". The law prescribes a period for this purpose which ends with the first menses (or delivery if pregnant), during which a Muslim who acquires a slave girl may not co-habit with her. The term is also used by most jurists for the waiting period which a woman who has had illicit intercourse is required to observe.

istiṣḥāb. Literally "seeking a link", it is used as a technical term for the principle whereby a state of affairs known to have once existed is regarded as having persisted unless the contrary can be shown. It has found its major application among the Shāfi'īs, who apply it even to the acquisition of new rights; whereas the Ḥanafīs and Mālikīs apply it only to the retention of existing rights.

istiṣnā'. One of the distinctive contracts of Islamic law, it constitutes a clear exception to the usual principles regarding the sale of goods not yet existent. The contract consists in giving a craftsman an order to make a specified article, with an agreement to pay a specified price for the article when complete. The relevant rules are precisely defined in the law books.

istiẓhār. See under *yamīn*.

Ithnā 'Asharīs. See under Shī'īs.

'iwaḍ. Consideration, whether for an ordinary contract or for a divorce of the *khul'* variety, etc.

J

jabr. Compulsion, relevant to this Survey as the act of the *walī mujbir*, the guardian who has a right to give his ward compulsorily in marriage. This is confined by the Ḥanafīs and Ithnā 'Asharīs to the insane and those under puberty, while the Mālikīs and Shāfi'īs extend it also to adult virgins (but according to some Mālikīs only up to various ages, or if not emancipated). The father is a *walī mujbir* according to all schools, and so is the father's father in the Ḥanafī, Shāfi'ī and Ithnā 'Asharī view; while the Mālikīs prefer the father's executor (*waṣī*). In default, the Ḥanafīs allow the nearest guardian, whoever he or even she may be, to act in this way, subject to the ward's "option of puberty"—i.e. option to repudiate the contract on reaching puberty: but the other schools exclude such action unless—among the Mālikīs—the agnatic guardian considers his ward to be in moral peril. There are further differences between jurists as to whether this right is unfettered, or what the limits may be. Some say that the husband must be his wife's equal, and the dower must conform to custom for a bride of her standing; while others do not insist on this in the case of a father or grandfather. Again, most say that manifest hostility between the girl and her guardian will invalidate this act; some say that any hostility between her and her groom will have the same effect, or at least make the conclusion of the contract sinful—i.e. the absence of such hostility is a condition either of the validity (*ṣiḥḥa*) of the contract or of its conclusion (*iqdām*) by the guardian; while some also admit that where the groom is senile or blind, or even where the bride can prove some other factor which shows that she has been injured by the marriage, the contract can be annulled by the Qāḍī.

jihād. Holy war, i.e. war to extend the bounds of Islam. In the case of pagans they were to be given the choice between Islam or the sword, while the "people of a Book" were to be given the further alternative of submission, tribute and protection. Booty was to be divided, while land taken by force must be divided among the army (Shāfi'īs), constitute a waqf in favour of the Muslim state (Mālikīs) or be disposed of at the discretion of the Imām (Ḥanafīs).

jihāz (or *tajhīz*). A wife's "trousseau", commonly consisting of certain garments, jewelry and household furniture. According to the Ḥanafīs and Shāfi'īs her husband cannot insist on this being supplied out of her dower (*mahr*, *ṣadāq*), for the latter is her own property, which she may use as she likes. Among the Mālikīs, however, a husband who has paid his dower in advance may insist on the scale of *jihāz* locally customary in such circumstances. It is common, moreover, to find some relation between the size of the dower and the scale of the *jihāz*: but there are wide differences from locality to locality as to whether the one exceeds the other, or vice versa.

jum'a means week, *yawm al-jum'a* means Friday, and *ṣalāt al-jum'a* the congregational prayer in the mosque on Fridays.

K

kafā'a. Marriage equality, for in Islamic law a woman may not marry or be given in marriage to one who is not her equal (*kuf' laha*) unless both she and, in most schools, her guardian consent (while the 'Alawīs of Ḥaḍramaut, for instance, carry this principle still further). But there are many differences between the leading jurists as to the constituents of such equality. In one Mālikī view only freedom from physical defects and piety count: but in the opinion of the Ḥanafīs, Shāfi'īs and other Mālikīs considerations of blood, profession or trade, and wealth (at least to the extent that the husband must be able to produce the prompt dower and enough for his wife's support) are all relevant. The Ḥanafīs also differ among themselves as to whether a contract concluded by an adult woman with one who is not her equal is invalid *ab initio,* suspended on her guardian's consent, or merely voidable on that guardian's motion, etc.

Khalīfa. Caliph or Successor. This term was used by Sunnīs of the head of the Muslim community until the abolition of the Ottoman Caliphate. In the orthodox view, however, the *Khalīfa* must be of Qurayshī blood, and possessed of a number of other attributes: but he was the upholder, not the interpreter, of the law; the ruler, not the pontiff, of the community. The term is also used, however, of the Successors to the " Promised Messiah " among the Aḥmadīs and of the successors to the headship of many of the Ṣūfī brotherhoods.

kharāj. The land tax which was originally exacted from non-Muslims only, but was subsequently often exacted from Muslims also if they purchased or developed land subject thereto. But practice in this respect differed widely from age to age and locality to locality.

khiṭba. A demand for a woman in marriage, or an " engagement " (if accepted). This is not binding in Islamic law.

khul'. Divestiture, or redemption of herself by a wife. Based on Sūra 2: 229, a *khul'* is a dissolution of the bonds of marriage (*a*) by use of this word or its derivatives, etc., and (*b*) for a consideration which the wife pays or promises to pay. The husband must be competent to divorce his wife; the " wife " must be a woman in regard to whom divorce would be applicable; and she must also be competent to enter into a contract for consideration. But there are differences between the schools as to whether a *khul'* counts as a divorce should the parties subsequently remarry, and whether or not all outstanding financial claims arising from the marriage relationship must be regarded as lapsing thereon, in addition to any other consideration specifically named. Again, some jurists regard *mubāra'a* (mutual release of the spouses, whereby the marriage is dissolved by mutual consent and, in the majority view, all financial claims arising therefrom are released) as a mere variety of *khul',* while others regard it as a distinct and different form of dissolution of marriage. Both may be included in the term " *ṭalāq 'alā māl* " (divorce for property), which may also include a similar arrangement couched in other terms.

khuṭba. Sermon, speech or exhortation, particularly that commonly given at the Friday congregational prayer. In colloquial speech *khiṭba* and *khuṭba* are frequently pronounced in the same way.

L

lawth. A form of proof or evidence which falls short of the standard required to establish a homicide of itself but is regarded as sufficient to justify the *qasāma* procedure (q.v.). Different schools and jurists give different lists of the various forms of *lawth* which justify this. Thus both the Shāfiʿīs and Mālikīs include the accused being found near a corpse holding a weapon, or with signs of blood upon him; or one eligible witness (or several ineligible ones) to the deed: but the Shāfiʿīs include obvious hostility between the accused and the deceased, and the Mālikīs an accusation by the deceased after he was wounded but before he died. And there are other varieties.

liʿān. The term used for a procedure by which a husband who has accused his wife of unchastity may avoid the punishment for slander to which he would otherwise be liable, in default of adequate proof, by swearing a five-fold oath in support of his accusation; while the wife on her part may avoid the punishment for adultery by taking a similar oath to her innocence. This procedure has the effect of dissolving the marriage and bastardising any child concerned. There are, however, points of difference between the schools as to whether the oaths of the husband or of the wife respectively, or the decree of the court, is the factor which actually dissolves the marriage. The re-marriage of two parties who have ended their marriage by this procedure is impossible—unless, in the Ḥanafī view, the husband retracts his accusation (and thus makes himself liable to the punishment for *qadhf*). The procedure is based on Sūra 24: 6 ff.—and some jurists insist on the husband having either caught his wife *in flagrante delicto* or having the evidence of a pregnancy which he did not cause; while others admit the procedure in any case of suspicion.

M

maʾdhūn. An official authorised to register contracts of marriage and different forms of divorce. He is commonly required to have some knowledge of the law regarding these matters.

mafqūd. A missing person, i.e. one who disappears and about whom no further news is obtainable. Among the Ḥanafīs no decree of putative death may be given until all his contemporaries have died, which some put at 120 years after his birth, others at 90, and others at 70. The Mālikīs, again, do not allow such a decree for the purpose of any claim to inheritance until 70 years after his birth, but they allow his wife to keep the *ʿidda* of widowhood, and then remarry, after a waiting period of four years in normal circumstances, if all attempts to get news of him fail. The Hanbalīs, again, allow a decree of putative death after four years where his death seems probable, and after such longer period as the Qāḍī sees fit in other circumstances, in respect of both wife and property.

Again, all schools regard the missing person as entitled to retain the ownership of his own property until death or decree of putative death. While, however, the Ḥanafīs and Mālikīs put on one side for him, meanwhile, any share in another's estate to which he would have been entitled, they do not regard this as actually accruing to him unless it can be proved that he was alive when the other died: but the Shāfiʿīs regard it as passing to him unless it can be shown that he died previously. This difference is due to the variant attitudes which they adopt towards the doctrine of *istiṣḥāb* (q.v.).

al-Mahdī. The "rightly-guided one", an eschatological figure whom almost all Muslims expect. To the Sunnīs the coming of the *Mahdī* is much confused with the return of Jesus (*ʿĪsā*), for one or other of them is to kill *al-Dajjāl* (the Deceiver) and restore the pre-eminence of the pure Sharīʿa. Among the Shī'īs, on the other hand, the concept is bound up with that of the hidden *Imām*, now in retirement, who will subsequently re-appear. To the Ithnā 'Asharīs, therefore, the *Mahdī* is the Twelfth Imām, to the Sunnīs he is the last *Khalīfa* of the Prophet; and to the Aḥmadīs he appeared in the person of their Founder.

mahr (or *ṣadāq*). This is the dower of Islamic law. In theory it is the absolute property of the wife, but in practice is often taken by her father (in Africa, at least). It is often divided into *mu'ajjal* and *mu'ajjal*, i.e. prompt and deferred, the former being payable before the marriage is consummated (and the woman may refuse consummation until she receives it, although she may agree to defer this too if she likes), and the latter either after a specified number of years or on widowhood or divorce—and it is a common device in some countries for the bride's father to insist on a large dower, much of which is so deferred, in order that this may act as a deterrent to frivolous divorce or as a more adequate provision for his daughter's widowhood than the meagre share in her husband's estate to which she would normally be entitled under the law of inheritance. Where no dower, or dower which is not legal property, is specified (*mu'ayyan*), the Ḥanafīs and Shāfi'īs regard the marriage as valid and the wife as entitled to "proper" dower (*mithlī*), i.e. what a woman of her family, beauty, education, etc., would normally receive: but the Mālikīs regard such a contract as invalid unless or until the marriage is consummated, when they too prescribe "proper" dower. The Ḥanafīs also prescribe ten *dirhams* as "minimum" dower, and a woman who marries for less can claim the completion of this sum; while the Mālikīs substitute three (¼ *dinār*) and the Shāfi'īs and Ḥanbalīs have no minimum.

A woman is entitled to full dower as soon as the marriage is consummated or if she or her husband dies before this: but she is entitled to half dower only if she is divorced, and to nothing if the marriage is annulled on her motion, before such consummation. The Ḥanafīs regard "valid retirement" (*khalwa ṣaḥīḥa*) as equivalent to actual consummation in this respect, and the Mālikīs so regard a year's residence in the husband's house. Where a woman who has married without stipulating how much dower she is to receive is divorced before the marriage is consummated, she is entitled only to the present known as *mut'at al-ṭalāq*. A woman is also entitled to dower even where a contract of marriage which is itself invalid—or even non-existent—is consummated, except where the act of intercourse constitutes the offence of *zinā*. The Mālikīs prescribe stipulated dower in such cases, the Shāfi'īs "proper" dower, and the Ḥanafīs whichever is less.

māl ẓāhir. Visible or available property (which often, today, means registered property). In Islamic law *māl* means any legal property: so the *māl ẓāhir* of a husband is any legal property on which the court is able to lay hands (e.g. in execution of a maintenance order, etc.).

Mālikīs. The followers of the school of law which grew up in the Hijaz and subsequently adopted Mālik ibn Anas as their nominal founder. One of those four schools which mutually recognise each other's orthodoxy, the Mālikī school preponderates in the Sudan, Upper Egypt and throughout North Africa, while in West Africa it is virtually unrivalled.

mawāt. Waste land, outside village boundaries. This may be brought into private ownership by *iḥyā'*, bringing to life—i.e. by enclosure and cultivation.

mu'allim. Teacher. Used of a learned man in many parts of the world: e.g., in Swahili, in the form of *mwalimu* and, in Hausa, in the form of *mallam*.

mubāra'a. See *khul'* above.

muḥtasib. The *muḥtasib* is one who performs the duty of *ḥisba*, e.g. to encourage virtue and discourage, or if possible prevent, vice. This is a duty on the whole Muslim people, but one which is adequately discharged if some do it (*farḍ 'alā'l-kifāya*). In fact, however, the *muḥtasib* has frequently appeared as the holder of a specific appointment. His was the duty of supervising the market and its weights and measures; of guarding public morals; of enforcing some of the observances of religion; and of acting as a summary magistrate where an offence against any of the above was committed in circumstances which—technically at least—did not require formal methods of proof.

mujtahid. One qualified to exercise the function of *ijtihād*, i.e. independent deduction of some rule of law from the recognised sources. Among the Sunnīs the door of *ijtihād* was until recently regarded as having become progressively closed during the third century of the *Hijra*, since when all jurists were regarded as mere *muqallids*, i.e. as bound to accept the rulings of their predecessors as authoritative without independent examination. *Mujtahids* have been classified as "absolute" (*muṭlaq*), as "within the school" (*fī'l-madhhab*) as "with the right to decide disputed points" (*bi'l-masā'il*), or "with the right to give *fatwās*" (*bi'l fatwā*) etc., in a descending scale. The duty of a *muqallid* is *taqlīd*.

The modernists of Sunnī Islam claim that the door of *ijtihād* was never really closed and that the faculty may be exercised by any jurist who is adequately qualified today. The Ithnā 'Asharīs (of the Uṣūlī persuasion), the Zaydīs and the Ibāḍīs, on the other hand, have always had jurists who claimed the right of *ijtihād*, although in fact they only exercise this faculty to a comparatively limited degree.

murābiṭ. Often spelt "marabout" in English, this term originally signified one who lived in a *ribāṭ* (a sort of monastery) or acted as a guardian of the frontiers, but has come to mean a "holy man", an ascetic, or one possessed of supernatural powers—especially in North Africa. Colloquial, *marbūṭ*.

mut'a. A form of temporary marriage, which only the Ithnā 'Asharīs permit today. It often amounts to little more than prostitution, yet is hotly defended by Ja' farī (Ithnā 'Asharī) jurists.

mut'at al-ṭalāq. A present to which, alone, a wife is entitled if she is divorced before consummation of marriage after a contract in which no legal dower was stipulated. It varies according to locality and custom, but frequently amounts to three articles (or sets) of clothing.

Mutawālīs. The name given to the Ithnā 'Asharīs in Syria and Lebanon.

mutawalli. The *mutawalli* or *nāẓir* is the administrator of a *waqf*.

musāqāt. A contract similar to *muzāra'a* (q.v.) but regarding the irrigation and cultivation of palm trees, etc.

muzāra'a. One of the distinctive agricultural contracts of Islamic law, by which an owner of land enters into a sort of partnership with a cultivator on the basis of a division of the crop.

N

nadhr. A vow. It may be used in Islamic law as a means of incurring an obligation which cannot be revoked, such as a fast, gift or any undertaking which may be regarded as a *qurba*, or means of approach to God. The Mālikīs never enforce this in court; but among the Shāfi'īs it is used to make promised gifts enforceable or executory (and even as a device to evade the rules of inheritance).

nafaqa. Maintenance—of wife, child, parents or relatives. It consists of food, clothing and accommodation, and while the texts commonly include toilet requisites, etc., most do not include medicine or medical fees. *Nafaqa* is incumbent on a husband whether rich or poor, and regardless of his wife's means, either as soon as the contract has been concluded and the wife is old enough for married life, in the Ḥanafī view; from the time of *tamkīn* (q.v.), in the Shāfiʿī opinion; or from the time when she goes to live in her husband's house, in the Mālikī law. Again, the proper scale of such maintenance is calculated by exclusive reference to the husband's means, in the Shāfiʿī view, but represents the mean between the circumstances of the spouses, in the authoritative Ḥanafī and Mālikī opinion. The wife's entitlement lapses on *nushūz* (q.v.), by agreement: but there is a major difference between the schools regarding arrears of maintenance. In the Mālikī and Shāfiʿī law maintenance is a debt, may be claimed from the time when the husband failed to provide it, and does not lapse except by release: but the Ḥanafīs deny that it is an actionable debt at all unless or until some specified sum is mutually agreed or decreed by court, and even then maintain that arrears lapse on the death of either party, on the wife's *nushūz,* or even (as some maintain) on divorce—unless the necessary funds have actually been obtained on the husband's credit by leave of court. Where a husband who is present refuses to support his wife all agree that he should be made to do so, but only the Mālikīs allow his wife a judicial divorce; while where he is unable to support her the Shāfiʿīs and Mālikīs allow the marriage to be ended, but the Ḥanafīs do not. Where the husband who fails to support her is absent, moreover, there are further differences, for the Ḥanafīs never allow dissolution of marriage, some Shāfiʿīs allow dissolution only where it can be proved that he is unable to support her, while the Mālikīs and Ḥanbalīs regularly allow it, after various periods of respite.

In the case of children, on the other hand, maintenance is only incumbent on their parents if they have no property of their own. In such circumstances a father becomes responsible for the maintenance of his minor, disabled or (in suitable circumstances) student sons and unmarried, widowed, or divorced daughters. Children, again, are responsible for the support of their destitute parents. In default of ascendants and descendants, moreover, the Ḥanafīs and Ḥanbalīs accept the responsibility of collaterals (within the prohibited degrees of marriage, in the Ḥanafī view, or any heirs, in the Ḥanbalī opinion) to support destitute relations; but the Mālikīs and Shāfiʿīs do not regard this as legally enforceable. There are, however, many complications.

nāshiza. Used of a disobedient wife. See under *ṭāʿa* below. It is also used of a husband who fails to do his duty by his wife.

nushūz. Wifely disobedience (see under *nāshiza* above). But it may also be used of a husband who fails in his marital duties.

Q

qabūl. Acceptance. See *ījāb* above.

qaḍāʾ. Sentence, or judgment.

qadhf. The offence of imputing unchastity to a free Muslim, male or female, who cannot be shown to be unchaste. For this a *ḥadd* punishment of eighty lashes is prescribed. According to the Shāfiʿīs this is primarily a *ḥaqq ādamī,* while the other Sunnī schools regard the *ḥaqq Allāh* as preponderant therein: see under *ḥaqq* above.

Qāḍī. The judge of the Sharīʿa law. Sometimes also called Ḥākim (e.g. in Iraq). The Qāḍī is regarded as strictly bound by the Sharīʿa in both procedure and substantive law: which is partly why criminal and commercial law were seldom, if ever, left exclusively to him. The books lay down elaborate, but divergent, rules as to the qualifications which a Qāḍī must possess. In theory he may be either a *mujtahid* or a *muqallid*, although the Sunnīs regard all present-day Qāḍīs as the latter. Some jurists allow him to give judgment according to his own knowledge of the facts of a case, while others compel him to judge only by the evidence of witnesses or the confession of the defendant—although some add that such judgment must never be contrary to his knowledge of the true facts: and it is only in the screening of witnesses that almost all accord him a considerable discretion (See *tazkīya*).

The Qāḍī must normally follow in every particular the most authoritative view of his school, and this is sometimes stated in his terms of appointment (e.g. the requirement in parts of the Aden Protectorate that the Qāḍī should follow the views of Ibn Ḥajar). Even so, however, there are nearly always some points in which the courts adopt some variant view (e.g. the matter of *'uhda* in the Aden Protectorate), while in some localities the Qāḍī has a considerable discretion as between variant views within his school (e.g., in Zanzibar, between the different commentaries on the *Minhāj*). Many jurists, moreover, regard the command of the Sulṭān as so strengthening an otherwise "weaker" view in the Qāḍi's own school, or even the opinion of some other school, as to make it dominant and binding on the courts: and this is the basis for most of the modern reforms in Sharī'a law, as applied in different Muslim countries. For this some Ḥanafi and some Shāfi'ī authority can be quoted.

Qādirīya. A Ṣūfī brotherhood, named after 'Abd al-Qādir al-Jīlānī, the principal of a school of Ḥanbāli law and also of a *ribāṭ* (a sort of monastery) in Baghdad, who died in A.D. 1166. The Order is very widespread in North, East and West Africa; it is loosely organised, with considerable local variations; and in parts its tenets amount to little short of the worship of the saint, while elsewhere it is far less extreme.

qarīna. Context, indication, circumstantial evidence.

qasāma. A system of compurgation which forms a third mode of proof (in addition to the testimony of two competent witnesses or the confession of the accused) in cases of homicide. But differences between the schools, and even individual jurists, abound. Thus the Ḥanafīs allow the procedure where, e.g., a corpse is found in some locality with signs of violence upon it and the heirs of the deceased accuse the local inhabitants: the latter must then either prove who did the deed or else up to fifty of the original inhabitants of the place, chosen by the accusers, must take an oath repudiating the charge (the fifty oaths being divided up among them if they are less than fifty in number). Even so, however, they are liable to pay blood-money; while if they decline the oaths they should be imprisoned until they make up their minds either to confess, to swear, or to prove someone else guilty.

In the Mālikī, Shāfi'ī and Ḥanbalī view, on the other hand, it is the heirs who normally take these oaths, not the accused. The Mālikīs, in cases of *'amd*, confine this to males and insist on at least two such; while the Shāfi'īs allow women also to participate, dividing the fifty oaths in proportion to their rights of inheritance. This is only allowed, however, where there is adequate *lawth* (see above); and the heirs must specifically allege intention (*'amd*) if they believe the homicide to have been intentional. In such cases the Mālikīs moreover even allow *qiṣāṣ* (*qawad*, i.e. talion), but against one only of several accused persons: but while the older Shāfi'ī view allowed talion against several participants in an allegedly deliberate homicide even on the basis of *qasāma*, al-Shāfi'ī's later view precluded talion altogether on this basis, except where the oaths had been put to the accused and refused, or returned to the heirs, by them.

qatl. Homicide. see under *'amd* above.

qiṣāṣ. Talion, whether in the form of a life for a life or a limb for a limb. In the Sharī'a talion is allowed only in cases of deliberate homicide, when its infliction depends upon the demand of the heirs of blood, or of deliberate wounding, when infliction depends upon the demand of the wounded man. But differences abound between the schools and between individual jurists in regard to points of detail. Thus the Mālikīs and Shāfi'īs normally allow the heirs of blood to inflict *qiṣāṣ* in the way in which the original homicide was committed, while the Ḥanafīs prescribe decapitation in all cases; the Shāfi'īs always allow the heirs to insist on *dīya* instead, the Ḥanafīs deny their right to this in cases of deliberate homicide but allow them to accept financial compensation if offered, while among the Mālikīs both views are found; the Shāfi'īs deny the right of the heirs to inflict talion until an absent, minor or insane heir has returned, matured or recovered, while the Mālikīs allow any sane major heirs who are present to take action. Further differences concern accomplices, etc. Again, only the Ḥanafīs normally allow a Muslim to be put to death for the homicide of a non-Muslim, or a free man for a slave. In cases of wounding, moreover, talion may only be claimed in cases where exact reciprocity can be achieved. See Encyclopaedia of Islam.

qiyās. Analogical deduction. This consists in the extension of the *ḥukm* or rule contained in one text (*naṣṣ*), or even consensus, to somewhat different facts conceived to be covered by the same *'illa*, or efficient cause of the *ḥukm*. The validity of *qiyās* is acknowledged by all Sunnīs today, while the Ithnā 'Asharī Uṣūlīs and the Ibāḍīs use the terms *'aql* and *ra'y* for much the same principle: but jurists differ considerably as to how the *'illa* is to be determined, and thus in the degree to which they confine or extend the application of *qiyās*.

R

raḍwa. A gift by a husband to his wife when he revokes a revocable divorce or when he marries a second wife. It is commended, but not enjoined, by the Sharī'a.

Rifā'īya. A brotherhood named after Aḥmad ibn 'Alī Abī 'l-'Abbās, who died in A.D. 1183.

rahn. Pledge, security. The one who gives it is termed the *rāhin*, and the one who takes it the *murtahin*. According to the strict law the *rāhin* is responsible for its maintenance, while only the Shāfi'īs allow him its use: again, all except the Ḥanbalīs refuse to allow the *murtahin* to use it, although all except the Shāfi'īs insist on the latter keeping it in his possession. It is partly because of the strictness of these rules that devices such as the *bay' al-khiyār* and *'uhda* have been introduced, to cover a sort of usufructary mortage (see above).

Ramaḍān. The fast month of the Islamic year, during which the Muslim must not eat, drink, smoke nor have sexual intercourse, between first light and sunset. Exceptions are, however, made in the case of young children, pregnant or nursing mothers, travellers and the sick.

rashīd. One who has reached *rushd*, or maturity of mind, i.e., ability to manage his own affairs. In Islamic law a boy (or girl) is normally entitled to take control of his property from the hand of his guardian when he reaches both *bulūgh* (puberty) and *rushd*—although there are the usual differences in points of detail. Thereafter he can be deprived of this control only if placed under interdiction (*ḥajr*) because he is *safīh* or *dhū ghafla*, i.e. deficient in judgment, whether prodigal or an easy prey to a deceiver.

ra'y. Opinion, i.e. the speculative judgment of a *mujtahid* as to a certain rule of law. Originally *ra'y* was virtually synonymous with *ijtihād*. The influence of the traditionists restricted this faculty more and more, until it became limited to formal *qiyās* and certain survivals such as *istiḥsān* (the Ḥanafī principle of thinking some other rule better than the one reached by the more obvious form of analogy); *istiṣlāḥ* (the Mālikī principle of preferring something deemed more beneficial); and *istiṣḥāb* (the principle, most extensively used by the Shāfi'is, of deeming a state of affairs to persist until the opposite can be proved). The term *ra'y* is still used among the Ibāḍīs for the deductions of their *mujtahids*.

rushd. See under *rashīd*.

S

ṣadāq. See *mahr* above.

ṣadaqa. See *hiba* above.

salam (or *salaf*). Another contract of sale of future goods, limited in this case to things which can be replaced (e.g., so many bushels of wheat) and must be accurately described, as also the place and (except among the Shāfi'is) the time of delivery; while the price must be paid down. Like *istiṣnā'* this provides an exception to the usual rule that goods may only be bought and sold if capable of immediate delivery. It is often used as a device to evade the prohibition on usury; for the immediate payment of a small price will be accepted, by one in urgent need of cash, for the future delivery of a considerably more valuable quantity of wheat, etc.

Ṣāliḥīya. See under *Aḥmadīya* above.

sariqa. The theft of Islamic law, for which amputation of the hand (or, subsequently, foot) is the *ḥadd* punishment, while for the more serious form of *sariqa* (highway robbery or brigandage) the punishment is even more severe. But the theft which is punishable by mutilation is carefully defined: it is only the clandestine removal, from the safe-keeping of another (*ḥirz*), of legally recognised property (*māl*) which is of not less than a specified minimum value (*niṣāb*), and to which the thief has no right or claim of ownership—while the thief must also have reached puberty, be sane, have the intention of stealing and not be acting under compulsion. The offence must also be proved by the testimony of two eligible male witnesses to the very act, or by the sustained confession of the thief: but even a retracted confession, or the testimony of one male and two female witnesses (etc.), will suffice to enable the aggrieved person to recover the stolen article or its value.

sayyid. An alleged descendant of the Prophet. So, too, *sharīf*.

Shāfi'īs. Those who adhere to the school founded by al-Shāfi'ī. Like the Ḥanafis, Mālikis and Ḥanbalis, the Shāfi'is represent one of the four "orthodox" schools of law. It is predominant in Lower Egypt, East Africa, much of Arabia, the Red Sea Littoral, and throughout South East Asia.

Shādhilīya. A Ṣūfī brotherhood named after Abū 'l-Ḥasan 'Alī ibn 'Abd Allāh al-Shādhilī, whom some assert to have been born in A.D. 1197. He seems to have been of Moroccan origin, although his disciples trace his lineage back to the Prophet through al-Ḥasan. The Order is very wide-spread, especially in French North Africa, and has given rise to a large number of more recent Orders.

shahāda. The Muslim creed: "There is no God but God, and Muḥammad is the Prophet of God". Many of the Shī'is add "And 'Alī is the saint of God". For practical purposes the recitation of the creed is normally regarded as enough to make a convert a Muslim. *Shahāda* also means testimony in litigation.

Sharī'a. See under *fiqh* above.

shaykh (pl. *shuyūkh*). Commonly spelt "sheikh" in English, this term has a variety of meanings, ranging from old man, head of an Arab tribe, or ruler of a small state, to student of al-Azhar University (or of some other institution of the traditional type), etc.

Shi'is. Originally used of the "*Shi'at 'Ali*" or sect of 'Alī, the term now covers a number of different sects all of which are regarded by the four Sunnī ("orthodox") schools as heterodox and all of which similarly regard the Sunnīs as in error. In reality, however, the subsects of the Shī'a are of very different degrees of "heterodoxy", as is well recognised by Sunnīs today. Closest to Sunnī doctrines stand the Zaydīs (who are chiefly found in the Yemen). These recognise any descendant of Fāṭima as Imām, provided he is adequately learned and can establish himself as such: and when so established they regard him as rightly-guided by God. The Ismā'īlīs, on the other hand, represent the opposite wing of the major Shī'ī sects (although certain smaller sects, and communities which now scarcely claim the name of Muslim,' are equally, or even more, extreme). They are split into two main divisions, the Eastern Ismā'īlīs, or Nizārīs, who regard the Agha Khān as their forty-eighth Imām, and the Western Ismā'īlīs, or Musta'līs, who hold that the twenty-first Imām went into hiding and has been succeeded by an unknown number of hidden Imāms (represented by Dā'īs who are the virtual heads of further subsects of the community). To all the Imām is infallible and impeccable, a partial manifestation of the Diety. But the central, and far the largest, Shī'ī sect is that of the Ithnā 'Asharīs, or Ja'farīs. These believe in Twelve Imāms, also impeccable and infallible, the last of whom is regarded as having gone into hiding but never to have died: instead, he will one day reappear in triumph. Meanwhile their *mujtahids* (q.v.) expound his teachings. This is the dominant sect of Iran, is very strong in Iraq, and is well represented in India, Syria, etc.

shubha. Confusedness or dubiousness (Lane), whether objectively in a contract or circumstances, or subjectively in the mind of a person—i.e. a "semblance" or a "doubt". Any *shubha* regarding the ownership of the property concerned prevents the infliction of the *ḥadd* punishment for *sariqa,* and any *shubha* with regard to a man's right to sexual intercourse with a woman prevents the punishment for *zinā* (and may prevent the act from being regarded as *zinā* at all). *Shubha* has been variously defined as what resembles something firm (*thābit*) although in fact it is not firm; as what falls between what is forbidden and what is allowed; and as what causes a man to be in doubt about something. Again, it has been subdivided, as regards the law of *zinā,* into *shubha fī'l maḥall* (or *ḥill*), *shubha fī'l fi'l* (or *shubhat ishtibāh*) and *shubha fī'l-'aqd.*

shuf'a. Commonly, but inaccurately, translated "pre-emption", this term represents the right of a co-owner compulsorily to take over a third party's purchase of another co-owner's share in jointly owned land. The Ḥanafīs extend it to include, *inter alia,* the right of a neighbour to take over a stranger's purchase of neighbouring land.

shuhra. General repute, or hearsay evidence.

shurb. The offence of drinking wine, for which the *ḥadd* punishment is eighty lashes for a free, adult, sane Muslim or forty for a slave, according to the Ḥanafīs, Mālikīs and Ḥanbalīs, while the Shāfi'īs regard it as forty and twenty respectively. There are further differences about grape syrup which is normally unfermented (*ṭilā'*) and spirits prepared from dates or raisins (*nabīdh*)—which latter the Ḥanafīs, alone, allow in strict moderation. The offence must be proved by a sustained confession or two eligible male witnesses to the act of drinking, among the Shāfi'īs; while the Ḥanafīs and Mālikīs regard adequate testimony to the odour of intoxicants or to the signs of drunkenness as enough. The offence is not committed by one who acts under compulsion, in ignorance of the nature of the drink, in minority or insanity, etc., nor by one who is dying of thirst and can find nothing else to drink.

ṣiḥḥa. Validity (of a contract). A marriage which is not *ṣaḥīḥ* (valid) must either be validated, in the Ḥanafī view, or the parties must be separated. Many Ḥanafīs, however, make a distinction between marriages which are *fāsid* (irregular) and those which are void (*bāṭil*), as regards their legal effects if consummated: but the other schools, and some Ḥanafīs, assert that there is no real distinction between *fasād* and *buṭlān* in marriage. The Mālikīs, however, distinguish cases where the "marriage" is to be annulled before consummation, but not after; or before pregnancy, or child-birth, but not after. See also under *iqdām* above.

siyāsa. Policy, or politics. A *siyāsa* punishment is one imposed by the Ruler in the interests of law and order, where none, or some lesser penalty, is prescribed in the Sharī'a. A punishment may similarly be omitted or reduced in special circumstances. See also under *ta'zīr* below.

ṣubḥīya. A gift customarily given, in many localities, by a bridegroom to his bride on the morning after the consummation of their marriage.

Ṣūfī. Literally "woollen", it is a term used of the mystics of Islam, because of the woollen garments they were accustomed to wear. The Ṣūfī path is similarly termed *taṣawwuf.* Today almost all "mystics" belong to one or other of the great Ṣūfī Orders or brotherhoods.

T

ṭā'a. Obedience, used particularly of the obedience which a wife owes her husband in everything prescribed by law, particularly in not leaving his house, if he so demands (except for those purposes and at those times which the law specifies), and in matters of sex, when there is no legal impediment. Where a wife leaves her husband's house without legal justification she becomes *nāshiza,* or disobedient, and is no longer entitled to maintenance (*nafaqa*). The husband's remedy is then to bring an action for *ṭā'a,* or restitution of conjugal rights. A wife who lives with her husband in her own house becomes *nāshiza* if she forbids him entrance without first demanding that he provide the usual marriage home and allowing him a certain time to prepare one; but thereafter she may lawfully shut him out. Similarly a wife may refuse to consummate her marriage until her prompt dower has been paid, without thereby becoming *nāshiza* or forfeiting her right to maintenance; while in certain circumstances a maltreated wife may offer her husband *ṭā'a* among her own people, but refuse to leave them for a distant locality.

ta'dīl. To declare a witness *'adl* (q.v.). See also under *tazkīya* below.

tafwīḍ. See under *ṭalāq* below.

taḥkīm is the term used when a man and woman who wish to marry in the absence of both her guardian and of any regular Qāḍī (or Ḥākim) agree to empower someone with an adequate knowledge of the law to act for the latter in marrying them; while *tawlīya* is the term used when a woman who wishes to marry in the absence both of her guardian and of any regular Qāḍī authorises anyone eligible as a witness to act in the place of the former (i.e. her guardian, or *walī*).

taḥlīl. The making of something or someone lawful. It is particularly used of a marriage which serves to make a triply-divorced woman lawful once more to her former husband, the man who so marries her being termed the *muḥallil.* Abū Ḥanīfa and Zufar regarded such a device as lawful even if the purpose of the intervening marriage were expressly mentioned in the contract; some Mālikīs and Ḥanbalīs regard a marriage as void if concluded with even the unexpressed intention of *taḥlīl*; while the majority of jurists allow the device provided the intention is not expressed (and, where it is, Abū Yūsuf, for instance, regarded the intervening marriage as irregular in itself, while al-Shaybānī regarded it as valid *per se* but not as making the woman lawful to her former husband). But all insist that the intervening marriage must be consummated, and that the woman must observe first the *'idda* of divorce following her first marriage, and then that following the second, before being married once more to her former husband.

tajhīz. See *jihāz* above.

tajrīḥ (or *ṭa'n*). The discrediting of a witness by an attack on his *'adāla* (q.v.). There must normally be two competent witnesses to some deficiency therein: and if these are forthcoming the testimony of the witness concerned must, in the view of the majority of jurists, be utterly excluded, however convinced the court may be of its reliability in the particular circumstances. It is a tempting device, therefore, in some localities to discredit witnesses on grounds of slackness in their religious observances, etc.: although some jurists have said that in degenerate days the court must be content with the best witnesses obtainable, lest the rights of many litigants be lost.

ṭalāq. Repudiation, or divorce. This is allowed among all Muslims at the unilateral decision of the husband, although it is commonly regarded as sinful to divorce one's wife without good cause. When done only once or twice the divorce is revocable (except, according to some, when expressed in terms which imply finality) during the *'idda* period, while when this ends it becomes decisive. If, however, the divorce is for the third time (or, in the view of the great majority, in the triple form, etc.) it is not only immediately final but the parties are also precluded from remarriage unless or until the wife has undergone an intervening marriage. A divorce may also be suspended, or made conditional on some future event or contingency (this is called *ta'līq al-ṭalāq*); while a husband may delegate his power to divorce his wife, either absolutely or in certain circumstances, to someone else—even the wife herself—by an irrevocable delegation (this is termed *tafwīḍ al-ṭalāq*). Both these last-named devices are used, in different or even the same localities, as a protection for a wife against ill-usage, desertion, etc.

Among the Shī'īs, on the other hand, a divorce must always be immediately effective, must be pronounced when the wife is in a state of legal purity, must be expressed in the correct words, must be fully intended, and must be witnessed by two witnesses. By contrast, some Sunnīs recognise a divorce even if uttered under the influence of drink or by compulsion; while almost all regard it as valid if pronounced in jest, as an oath or threat, or in contravention of many of the details of the Prophetic precedent (*sunna*).

talawwum. Delay. It is used for the period of respite granted by a court, e.g. to a husband who has failed to support his wife, before the court proceeds to dissolve the marriage.

talfīq. Literally patching together, this is a term used of the combination of the views of two different schools or jurists in a single whole. Some use it of a Code of law compiled on this eclectic principle; others deny its applicability unless the combination concerns some particular *ḥukm* or rule of law, or even some particular detail therein; while yet others repudiate its use unless the resultant rule is such that none of the jurists concerned would have recognised.

ta'līq. Suspension. See under *ṭalāq* above.

tamkīn. To make possible. The term is used, *inter alia*, of a wife putting her husband in a position to consummate their marriage, or offering to do so.

ṭa'n. Calumniation. It is used of discrediting a witness. See under *tajrīḥ* above.

taqlīd. The acceptance of a rule of law on the authority of another.

taṭlīq. Judicial divorce among the Mālikīs. The other schools prefer the term *faskh,* or annulment or dissolution of marriage. In the Mālikī view the Qāḍī acts in the place of the husband, even against the latter's will, in divorcing his wife.

tawlīya. The commissioning of someone to act as *walī* in giving a woman in marriage. See under *taḥkīm* and *walāya.*

ta'zīr. A discretionary punishment imposed by the court for an offence which does not fall within the definition of one of those offences for which a particular penalty (*ḥadd*) is prescribed. The difference between *ta'zīr* and a *siyāsa* punishment is that the former lies within the ordinary powers of the courts, whereas the latter rests on the right of the Ruler to take exceptional measures when the public interest requires.

tazkīya. The examination of a witness's eligibility. See also under *'adl*.

Tijānīya. A Ṣūfī brotherhood founded by Abū'l-'Abbās Aḥmad al-Tijānī, who died in A.D. 1815 in Fez. He was admitted to the Qādirīya, Ṭaybīya and Khalwatīya Orders, and his own Order is regarded as a branch of the last. Its adherents, however, are strictly forbidden to join any other Order; while they are enjoined to be loyal to the established government. It is chiefly found in North and West Africa, where it has made notable advances at the expense of the Qādirīya. See Encyclopaedia of Islam.

U

'uhda. See under *bay' al-khiyār* above.

'ulamā'. See under *'ālim* above.

'urf. Custom (as also *'āda*). This is not a formal source of law under the Sharī'a, although in reality a great part of the latter is derived therefrom. In theory *'urf* must always give way to a *naṣṣ* or text; but in practice local customs often survive and are applied by the courts. In the stricter localities these are usually brought into superficial reconciliation, at least, with the Sharī'a by some form of legal device (*ḥīla*): but often this is omitted, even, e.g., in the strictest parts of Northern Nigeria. The pioneer in this latter subject is Dr. J. Schacht.

'ushr. The correct term for the Islamic land tax levied on land owned by Muslims, except where the latter took over *kharāj* land and continued to pay the latter tax, or developed land watered by *kharāj* water (etc.). It is part of the *zakāt,* or legal alms, in the general view. See *kharāj* and *zakāt*.

W

walā'. Patronage—i.e. by ex-master or mistress to ex-slave. *Inter alia* it includes the right to inherit the property, or residue of the estate, of the ex-slave if the latter dies without either agnatic heirs or sharers whose quota-shares exhaust his estate. When the primary patron dies his right passes to his own agnates in their own right, and this applies also with regard to the children, etc., of the ex-slave. But there are complications, and certain minor differences between the schools, in points of detail.

walāya. Guardianship, chiefly relevant to this Survey in the sense of marriage guardianship (*walāyat al-nikāḥ*). This is sub-divided into those guardians who have the right of compulsion (*jabr*: q.v.) and those who have not. But even when there is no question of compulsion the Mālikīs and Shāfi'īs insist that no woman may be married without a male guardian acting on her behalf, or at least someone acting in place of such guardian; whereas the Ḥanafīs and Shī'īs allow an adult to act on her own behalf in such cases. There are also detailed rules among the Mālikīs and Shāfi'īs as to the proper procedure in the absence of the guardian with the prior right, and in the Ḥanafī school as to the position if an adult woman marries herself to a man who is not her equal, or for less than her proper dower, without her guardian's consent.

walī. A guardian (*inter alia*). See above.

waqf. (Plural *awqāf*). Used in Islamic law to cover religious endowments, family trusts, etc.; while in North Africa, in particular, the term *ḥubs* (*aḥbās*) or *ḥabīs* (*ḥubus*) is more commonly used.

The differences of opinion between Muslim jurists with regard to *waqf* are greater than those regarding any other point. Thus Abū Ḥanīfa probably disallowed *awqāf* altogether, but is represented as regarding them as valid but not binding; Abū Yūsuf probably allowed temporary *awqāf*, but is represented as insisting on their perpetuity but regarding the use of the word *waqf* as sufficient indication of an ultimate dedication to some charity which cannot fail; al-Shaybānī insisted that a *waqf* was invalid unless its deed expressly provided for some such ultimate dedication; Mālik allowed temporary *awqāf*; al-Shāfi'ī, it seems, regarded them as perpetual but made no condition about the specification of their ultimate disposal; while the Ithnā 'Asharīs and Ibāḍīs each have their own views. Somewhat similiar differences concern the type of property which may be dedicated as *waqf*, the person and powers of the administrator, and the concept of where the ownership of the property concerned must be held to lie. The subject is further complicated by the attempts of British Courts in India, and the Privy Council itself, to apply English legal principles to this essentially different concept—and the consequent demand that the Islamic principles should be re-imposed by the Legislature in India, Aden, Zanzibar, Kenya, etc.

waṣī. Executor. In Mālikī law he is accorded much the same power as the deceased father to give virgin daughters in compulsory marriage; while in all schools he is frequently empowered to act as guardian of the property of minor children, as well as administering an estate.

waṣīya. Bequest or will. This need not be written—in fact the basic form, particularly in the Ḥanafī and Shāfi'ī law, is an oral declaration before two witnesses—but must never, in the Sunnī view, be in favour of an heir (at least unless the other heirs consent thereto, after the testator's death).

wird. (pl. *wurūd*). Special prayers enjoined by different Ṣūfī Orders to be added by their adherents to the set prayers prescribed for all Muslims.

Y

yamīn al-istiẓhār. Literally, the oath of revealing. This oath must be taken by, e.g., the wife of an absent husband who is claiming maintenance, or in some cases divorce, to the effect that the husband did not leave her, and has not sent her, any maintenance; that she is not *nāshiza* and so disentitled thereto; and that she is not, to her knowledge, divorced, etc. Only after proof of marriage and the taking of this oath will the court give judgment in such a case *ex parte*. See below.

yamīn al-qaḍā'. Literally, the oath of judgment. This is another name for the *yamīn al-istiẓhār* (or *istibrā'*). It is regarded as incumbent in many different circumstances: e.g. where a man produces two witnesses that some article in another's possession is his, he must take this oath that he did not sell it nor give it, etc., to its present possessor. It is also used in almost all claims against a deceased man's estate, or *ex parte*.

yamīn al-tuhma. The oath of suspicion. This is the oath which one accused of some offence without adequate evidence must take to clear himself. Some jurists insist that he must first be shown to be the sort of person on whom such suspicion might reasonably fall. This oath may not be returned by the accused to the accuser, since the latter does not claim certain knowledge.

Z

zākat. The legal alms obligatory on all Muslims. Detailed rules are laid down in the texts as to the property on which these alms are to be levied (and there are certain differences in this between the schools), the percentage payable, etc.; and also regarding the purposes to which the proceeds are to be dedicated. In some Muslim lands these alms are collected, and disbursed, by the Government, while in others they are left to the conscience of the individual (and in Sa'udi Arabia today half are collected by the Government and half left for private charity). The *'ushr* on land represents one part of the *zakāt*. But much that is not really Islamic has been given an Islamic nomenclature, in this as in other points, in certain African territories.

ẓihār. This is an ancient Arabian formula whereby a husband likens his wife to the back, or some other part of the anatomy, of his mother or other close female relative. In the developed Islamic law the use of such a formula means that the husband must perform some specific expiation before he resumes marital relations with the wife concerned; while some jurists allow her to demand a compulsory or even judicial divorce if he persistently refuses either to divorce her or resume normal relations—at least if this exceeds the period prescribed for *īlā'* (q.v.). But the formula is often used in conjunction with some express formula of divorce.

Zaydīs. See under Shī'īs.

zinā. Illicit sexual intercourse. This is elaborately defined in the books, as also the punishment for other but similar forms of wrong-doing. But in *zinā* proper there is a prescribed (*ḥadd*) punishment of stoning in the case of the free offender who has ever enjoyed valid married life, and one hundred lashes in the case of one who has never had this experience (i.e. the *muḥṣan*, and the *ghayr muḥṣan*, respectively); while half the latter penalty is alone applicable in the case of slaves. The offence must, however, be proved either by a sustained confession by the guilty party or by the testimony of four competent male witnesses to the very act—except that the Mālikīs regard it as sufficiently proved, in the case of an unmarried woman, by the fact of pregnancy without proof of innocence, while the Ḥanafīs and Shāfi'īs disagree. As a consequence the infliction of the penalty of stoning has always been extremely rare. There are, of course, the usual differences between the schools on points of detail, e.g. what penalty is applicable if one of the guilty parties is *muḥṣan* and the other not, or if one is insane or minor and the other adult and sane, etc.

Any accusation of *zinā* which cannot be proved as above makes the accuser liable to the punishment for *qadhf* (q.v.) unless, in the case of the husband, he resorts to the procedure of *li'ān* (q.v.). In some parts even a defence to a charge of murder to the effect that the husband caught the deceased *in flagrante delicto* with his wife is subjected to the same standard of proof.

INDEX